Business in Context

Business in Context Series

Editors:

David Needle
Head of Postgraduate and Corporate Programs, East London Business School,
University of East London

Professor Eugene McKenna
Chartered Psychologist and Emeritus Professor, University of London

Accounting in a Business Context (3rd Edition)
Aidan Berry and Robin Jarvis
ISBN 1 86152 090 5

Behaviour in a Business Context
Richard Turton
ISBN 0 412 37530 3

Business in Context (3rd edition)
David Needle
ISBN 1 86152 358 0

Economics in a Business Context (3rd edition)
Colin Haslam, Alan Neale and Sukhdev Johal
ISBN 1 85152 400 5

Human Resource Management in a Business Context
Alan Price
ISBN 1 86152 182 0

Law in a Business Context
Bill Cole, Peter Shears and Jillinda Tiley
ISBN 0 412 37520 6

Books in the series are available on free inspection for lecturers considering the texts for course adoption. Details of these, and any other Thomson Learning titles, are available by writing to the publishers (Berkshire House, 168–173 High Holborn, London WC1V 7AA).

Business in Context

An introduction to business and its environment

THIRD EDITION

David Needle

Business Press
Thomson Learning™

Australia • Canada • Denmark • Japan • Mexico • New Zealand • Philippines
Puerto Rico • Singapore • South Africa • Spain • United Kingdom • United States

Business in Context: 3rd Edition

Copyright © 2000 Thomson Learning

Business Press is a division of Thomson Learning. The Thomson Learning logo is a registered trademark used herin under licence.

For more information, contact Business Press, Berkshire House. 168–173 High Holborn, London, WC1V 7AA or visit us on the World Wide Web at: http://www.thomsonlearning.com.

Britsh Library Cataloguing-in-Publication Data
A catalogue record for this book is available from the British Library

ISBN 1-86152-358-0

This edition published 2000 by Thomson Learning

First edition published 1989
Second edition published 1994 by Chapman & Hall

Typeset by Saxon Graphics, Derby
Printed in Italy by G. Canale & C. S.p.A.
Cover design by Ian Youngs
Text design by Ian Foulis Design Associates

Contents

List of cases

Chapter 6

Chapter 7

Chapter 8

List of key concepts

Series foreword

This book is part of the 'Business in Context' series. The books in this series are written by lecturers all with several years' experience of teaching on undergraduate business studies programmes. When the series first appeared, the original rationale was to place the various disciplines found in the business studies curriculum firmly in a business context. This is still our aim. Business studies has continued to attract an ever-growing band of students, with every sign that its popularity is increasing. There are clear indications that its appeal has broadened, and business studies, as well as a specialism in its own right, is now taken with a range of other subjects, particularly as many universities embrace modular degree structures. We feel that the books in this series provide an important focus for the student seeking some meaning in the range of subjects currently offered under the umbrella of business studies.

With the exception of the text *Business in Context*, which takes the series title as its theme, all the original texts in our series took the approach of a particular discipline traditionally associated with business studies and taught widely on business studies and related programmes. These first books in our series examined business from the perspectives of economics, behavioural science, law, mathematics and accounting. To these was added human resource management. The popularity of the series across a range of courses has meant that the third and fourth editions of many of the original texts have been or are soon to be published.

Whereas in traditional texts it is the subject itself that is the focus, our texts make business the focus. All the texts are based upon the same specific model of business illustrated in Figure 1. We have called our model 'Business in Context' and the text of the same name is an expansion and explanation of that model.

The model comprises four distinct levels. At the core are found the activities that make up what we know as business and include innovation, operations, marketing, human resource management and finance and accounting. We see these activities operating irrespective of the type of business involved and they are found in both the manufacturing and service industry as well as in the public and private sectors. The second level of our model is concerned with strategy and management decision-making. It is here that decisions that influence the direction of the business activities at our core are made. The third level of our model is concerned with organizational factors within which business activities and management decisions take place. The organizational issues we examine are structure, size, goals and organizational politics, patterns of ownership, and organizational culture. Clear links can be

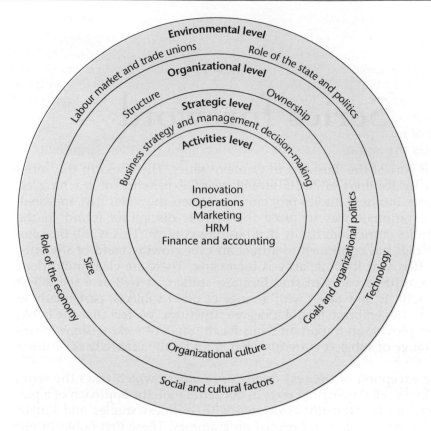

The Business in Context model.

forged between this and other levels of our model, especially between structure and strategy, goals and management decision-making, and how all aspects both contribute to and are influenced by the organizational culture. The fourth level concerns itself with the environment in which businesses operate. The issues here involve social and cultural factors, the role of the state and politics, the role of the economy, and issues relating to both technology and labour. An important feature of this fourth level of our model is that such elements not only operate as opportunities and constraints for business, but also that they are shaped by the three other levels of our model.

This brief description of the 'Business in Context' model illustrates the key features of our series. We see business as dynamic. It is constantly being shaped by and in turn shaping those managerial, organizational and environmental contexts within which it operates. Influences go backwards and forwards across the various levels. Moreover, the aspects identified within each level are in constant interaction with one another. Thus the role of the economy cannot be understood without reference to the role of the state; size and structure are inextricably linked; innovation is inseparable from issues of operations, marketing and finance. The understanding of how this model works is what business studies is all about and forms the basis for our series.

In proposing this model we are proposing a framework for analysis and we hope that it will encourage readers to add to and refine the model and so broaden our understanding of business. Each writer in this series has been encouraged to present a personal interpretation of the model. In this way we hope to build up a more complete picture of business. Models are now often used as the frameworks of texts. We believe our model has stood the test of time in that it has the virtue of dealing with a rapidly changing business world and of incorporating key contemporary issues.

The issues the authors deal with may be complex but their treatments are not. Each book in this series is built around the 'Business in Context' model, and each displays a number of common features that mark out this series. First, we aim to present our ideas in a way that students will find easy to understand and we relate those ideas wherever possible to real business situations. Second, we hope to stimulate further study both by referencing our material and pointing students towards further reading at the end of each chapter. Third, we use the notion of 'key concepts' to highlight the most significant aspects of the subject presented in each chapter. Fourth, we use case studies to illustrate our material and stimulate further discussion. Fifth, we present at the end of each chapter a series of questions, exercises and discussion topics. To sum up, we feel it most important that each book will stimulate thought and further study and assist the student in developing powers of analysis, a critical awareness and ultimately a point of view about business issues.

We have already indicated that the series has been devised with the undergraduate business studies student uppermost in our minds. We also maintain that these books are of value wherever there is a need to understand business issues, and their adoption across a range of undergraduate, postgraduate and professional courses in the UK and elsewhere is a testimony to that.

David Needle and Eugene McKenna
January 2000

Preface to the third edition

The origins for this book lie in a course I developed and taught at the University of East London and at Queen Mary and Westfield College. An important theme of the course was the interrelated nature both of business activities themselves and their relationships with the strategic, organizational and environmental contexts in which they operated. A second important theme was the identification of what were considered at the time to be key issues in business. These two themes remain the basis of *Business in Context* as it goes into its third edition.

As we state in the Series foreword, business is treated throughout the series in its widest possible context, and this book is no exception, including as it does illustrations drawn from a variety of contexts. Indeed, over the past 20 years we have witnessed a convergence of all types of organization, including hospitals, universities and charities, on a business model. The book follows closely the model introduced in the foreword and explained in more detail in Chapter 1.

While the book is aimed specifically at first- and second-year undergraduates studying business and management, the book is useful wherever there is a need for an overview of business or a treatment of business and the environment. As a result, previous editions of this text have been adopted on MBA programmes and on some professional courses.

A number of key themes appear throughout the book. Businesses are perceived as operating through a complex network of interrelationships and our model is a simplification of this complexity. While business activities are undoubtedly influenced by their strategic, organizational and environmental contexts, those same business activities help shape those very same contexts. In all aspects of business life we need to remind ourselves that decisions are made by people. An understanding of behavioural and political issues is therefore important, as is the need to view issues from a number of different perspectives to gain a more complete understanding. Very rarely can we view business activities in isolation, as decisions made in one area inevitably have significant consequences, not only for other parts of the same business but for other businesses and even the wider community. Many of the new ideas, issues and techniques that have emerged over the years are undoubtedly products of influences that were operating at the time. While some have stood the test of time, others have become passing fashions and fads.

One development that is both permanent (insofar as anything in business can be permanent) and far-reaching is globalization and this edition acknowledges its impact on aspects of business. As we enter a new millennium, the business world is as dynamic as ever. Japan has moved from a dynamic leader to an also-ran (albeit still a powerful one) and the 'Asian Tigers' are still reeling from the events of 1997. The optimism that accompanied the free market 'experiment' in the former Soviet Union at the start of the decade has turned to pessimism in the face of economic collapse in many former Soviet countries. Around the world there is a loss of confidence in financial institutions, with the collapse of Barings and the problems of Japanese banks. Against this there are exciting new business opportunities offered by globalization, by the Internet and other developments in IT, and, in Europe, we even have a new currency with which to do business. Many believe the dynamism that is a key feature of business life in Asia will lead to a resurgence in that region.

In this edition I will reflect most of the above changes and many more. There are enlarged and, in some cases, highly modified treatments of strategy, marketing and operations. Some cases have disappeared and new ones have been added, including 'The European car industry', 'Disneyland Paris', 'Renault and Volvo', 'Grand Metropolitan and Guinness', 'Eberspächer and Mercedes Benz', 'Telemarketing' and a review of the rise and decline of the 'Asian Tigers'. Almost all the retained cases have been brought up to date.

The first chapter offers an explanation of the 'Business in Context' model and illustrates this with reference to the Europen car industry and the UK-based News International. The next three chapters offer a detailed look at the contexts within which business operates, focusing respectively on the environment, the organization and management strategy. The next five chapters each focus on a specific business activity and cover innovation, operations, marketing, human resource management and finance and accounting. Aspects of all these activities are clearly defined and, in addition, they are placed within their environmental, organizational and strategic contexts. The book therefore offers both general and specific views of business.

The core elements of previous editions are retained. Each chapter highlights key concepts and illustrates key issues by using cases. Furthermore, each chapter is supported by a summary, a list of discussion questions and suggestions for further reading. This edition will be supported by a website, accessed through http://www.thomsonlearning.co.uk. The website will contain links to general business sites and links to the homepages of each of the case study companies. To assist those lecturers who adopt the text, there will be general advice on how the book may be used as part of a planned series of lectures, PowerPoint presentations will be avialable to accompany each chapter and there will be suggested answers to the discussion questions.

In my preface to the first edition in 1989, I stated that with any book that takes the broad sweep that this one does there is bound to be a great deal of selectivity. This is as true today as it was then, as is the main criteria for their inclusion, that they interested me. Many of the ideas are attributed to their rightful source, but many are the product of years discussing business issues with students, friends and colleagues. I acknowledge all those sources here, with the rider that the misinterpretations are all my own.

David Needle
January 2000

Acknowledgements

There are many who deserve my thanks for helping me write this book. The students and staff at the University of East London assisted me in developing many of the ideas, which resulted in the first edition. For this edition, I thank, at UEL, Keith Brouthers and Peter Taylor for reviewing the chapters on strategy and marketing respectively, Marisa Ker and Tracy King for assisting with the data collection on some of the cases and the administrative staff in Corporate Programmes for keeping the system going as well as unblocking the photocopier every time I used it. Philip Cahill at Portsmouth Business School provided excellent advice on the Finance and Accounting chapter. Although Anna Faherty at Thomson came to the project quite late, I have found her an unfailingly helpful and encouraging editor.

This book and those that preceded it could not have been completed without the help and support of my wife Jacquie. Apart from forcing me to go to Lanzarote to write part of the book she has been an excellent source of information and a superb sounding board.

CHAPTER 1

The concept of Business in Context

The major theme of this book, and of the series of which it forms a part, is that businesses are complex. They cannot be understood by reference to their activities alone. These activities which include innovation, operations and production, marketing, personnel/human resource management, finance and accounting and so on take place in a series of contexts. It is our contention that they can only be understood fully when those contexts within which they operate are also understood. In this first chapter we will explain what we mean by business and identify the relevant contexts. It is also our contention that the relationship between business activities and these contexts is dynamic. In the foreword we introduced a model of business around which this and other books in the series are based. We present the model once again in Figure 1.1 and use it to illustrate the elements of this dynamic relationship. The workings of the model are explained by two case studies. The first concerns the European car industry and focuses upon strategies used by companies in a static and highly competitive market. The second case focuses more specifically on a single organization, News International, and the events surrounding a major dispute with its workforce in 1985. The cases demonstrate that the model can be applied to the analysis of a major industrial sector as well as to events at a single firm. We introduce briefly two theoretical approaches to the analysis of business organizations: the systems and contingency approaches. These are often used as the starting point for our analysis throughout this book and reference will be made to them in other chapters. We will conclude this first chapter by outlining the layout of this book.

Businesses and their contexts

The popular image of a typical business firm is invariably that of a manufacturing industry, and probably large-scale mass production at that. Such an image is somewhat misleading, as the service industries, and particularly financial services, assume the greater part of a nation's economic activities in many countries. In this text we hope to present a broad view of business. Businesses operate in all kinds of areas, including manufacturing industry, but also embracing such activities as retailing, banking and other financial services, transport and so on. The publishers of this book are engaged in a business activity, involving the production, marketing and selling of books to

> # KEY CONCEPT 1.1
> *Business*
>
> A business is the organized effort of individuals to produce and provide goods and services to meet the needs of society. We view business as a broad concept, incorporating profit-making concerns such as manufacturing firms and banks, and non-profit-making concerns such as schools and hospitals.

generate income both to make profits and to finance future operations. Businesses also vary considerably in terms of size. Indeed, in recent years, the focus has shifted away from large-scale operations and small businesses have become popular with governments and academics alike and, accordingly, will be acknowledged in this text.

The image that businesses are exclusively profit oriented will also be challenged. Business systems and methods operate in all kinds of organization. Many institutions of higher education operate with budgets in excess of £75 million, and represent fairly complex organizations in which all the activities normally associated with business may be identified. For example, there are few colleges that do not market their courses, or have to operate in highly dynamic and competitive markets. Hospitals too are large complex organizations experiencing the type of management problems found in businesses anywhere. In recent years this has been acknowledged by the creation of new hospital top management posts, many of which have been filled by candidates from the private business world. In any case, the distinction between profit and non-profit organizations has become increasingly blurred. All universities and colleges must rely increasingly on generating their own income owing to changes that have taken place in public funding. The growth of medical provision outside the National Health Service has seen the growth of profit-oriented private hospitals which compete in the market place for customers and advertise their services internationally as well as nationally.

As we can see from Figure 1.1, we have identified a number of business activities. In this book we deal with them under five main groups. These are innovation, operations, marketing, human resource management and accounting. Each of these groups is sufficiently broad to cover a number of related functions. For instance it is acknowledged that supply chain management is an important business activity, but it is dealt with under the heading of operations for the purposes of this text. The operations function itself is present in all forms of business organization and not confined to the production function of manufacturing. Operations is a key function in the service sector, as it is in manufacturing.

When examining business activities there are two points to consider. First, the activities interact with one another, so that operations decisions influencing the quantity and quality of the goods produced and the services provided will have significant implications for the other functional areas. Second, as we have already indicated, these activities do not exist in a

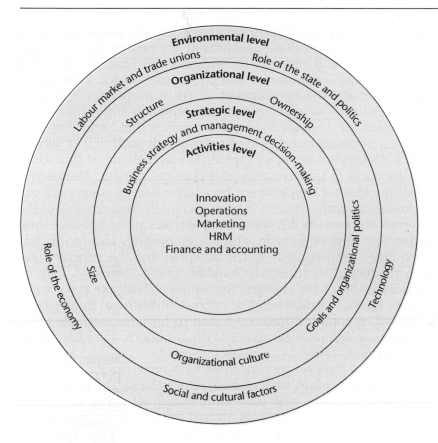

Figure **1.1** The Business in Context model.

vacuum, but are shaped by and in turn shape the contexts within which they operate.

In our Business in Context model we have identified three types of context: strategic, organizational and environmental. We will deal briefly with each of these in turn.

At the strategic level we are concerned with those management decisions, and the influences on those decisions, that determine the direction of business activities. Strategic decisions will influence such factors as the range of

---

KEY CONCEPT 1.2
Strategy

A strategy comprises a set of objectives and methods of achieving those objectives. A strategy is usually formulated by top management and is based on a mixture of careful analysis of the environment and the organization, the personal preferences of the managers involved, and a process of negotiation with various other stakeholders.

products and services, the amount spent on advertising, the nature and use of the labour force and so on. Strategic decisions in the case of joint ventures will determine the shape and nature of the organization. Strategies are often a question of reconciling opportunities and constraints, which exist within both the organization and the environment in which it operates. The managing director of a small firm with a potentially profitable innovation often faces a strategic dilemma. Its organizational size means that expanding production capacity is impossible and its credit standing is such that it may be unable to raise sufficient development capital. The availability of finance is, in any case, a function of the economic and political climate. Alternatives might be to sell the idea for development by a larger firm or simply sell out to a larger organization, both of which may be personally unacceptable to the owner of the small business. In this way, strategic issues are inseparable from the organization and environment in which they operate, and can in fact alter those two other contexts. It is widely accepted that the structure of a firm is often a product of its strategy (Chandler, 1962). Economic, cultural and political globalization have changed the nature of business and created globally complex business structures. The overseas investment strategies of large multinational corporations have been seen to have considerable influence on the economic and political affairs of other nations, especially those in the Third World.

At the organizational level we are concerned with such issues as size, ownership, goals and structure. Many such issues are interrelated. The public ownership of business firms may well mean the pursuit of social as well as business goals, and publicly owned firms invariably have bureaucratic structures. This is partly a function of organizational culture, and partly a function of the large scale of most public sector operations. All firms as they increase in size tend to adopt more formalized structures. Such organizational factors can place limitations on the nature of business activities. Formalized structures can inhibit certain types of product and process development and the existing size can be a restriction on expansion, as we saw in our illustration of strategic issues. In more general terms these organizational factors combine with management strategy to create distinctive organizational cultures.

We have identified five factors that operate at the environmental level. These are the economy, the state, labour, technology and culture. Some of these factors are deliberately broad. The state includes discussion of government, legal and political issues; labour takes into account both the workings

---

KEY CONCEPT 1.3
Organization

An organization refers to the way in which people are grouped and the way in which they operate to carry out the activities of the business. We define the key elements of the organization as the goals of the business and the way they are formulated, ownership and control, size, structure and organizational culture (Chapter 3).

of the labour market and the activity of trade unions; culture includes social factors related to business as well as those issues that differentiate businesses in different countries. As with the other factors in our model there is considerable interaction between these various environmental factors. The membership and power of trade unions are a function of the level of economic activity and the restrictions imposed by the law, which in turn reflects the policy of governments. The composition of the labour market reflects changes in technology, and the mobility of labour within different countries varies with the social and cultural traditions of those countries. Technological innovations are often motivated both by declining economic fortunes and by direct state intervention. Similarly we can cite illustrations of the interaction between the environment and our other contexts. The technological complexity of the product market in which the firm operates will largely determine the extent of its research and development activity, and hence its strategies and structure. In traditional manufacturing industry, a strong trade union presence will determine the size, shape, policies and activities of the HR department. Goals, size, structure and activities all tend to change as the economic environment changes.

The interplay that typifies the relationship between business activities and the contexts in which they operate will be a constant theme in this book. We will attempt to show that many of the relationships are two-way. The economic environment referred to above not only shapes businesses, but is in turn a product of business activity. Changes in technology are products of innovation activity at the level of the firm. We are thus able to build up a model of business as a constant interplay of interactions and influences.

We are able to illustrate the workings of the model by reference to two cases, the first concerning the European car industry and the second focusing on a single, albeit large firm in the newspaper industry. In both cases we will explain the events and central issues, following this with an analysis of each case using our Business in Context model as a framework.

The European car industry

This case study examines aspects of the European car industry in the late 1990s. It focuses upon the major problems facing the industry and examines some of the strategies management have used to tackle those problems.

For many years now the car market in Europe has been cyclical. In more recent years it has been static as revealed in Tables 1.1 and 1.2. These show the total passenger car use and total new car sales in Europe 1990–6, highlighting the four largest markets of Germany, France, Italy and the UK. Where there are small upward trends, these are probably attributable to the unification of Germany and the changes following the dismantling of the Soviet bloc in Eastern Europe. The figures, particularly those for new car sales, reveal a market that has essentially reached its limits.

The industry was hit by the oil shocks of the 1970s and was plunged into deep recession in the early 1980s. The growth in the late 1980s was short-lived and recession hit the industry once again in the early 1990s. Although

Table **1.1** Passenger cars in use in Europe 1991–5 (in millions)

	1990	1991	1992	1993	1994	1995
France	23.5	23.8	24.0	24.8	24.9	24.9
Germany	34.6	35.3	38.4	39.3	40.2	41.4
Italy	27.4	28.5	29.5	30.1	31.3	32.3
UK	19.7	20.1	19.9	20.1	20.0	19.9
Europe total	145.5	149.2	154.3	158.0	160.7	164.0

Source: Consumer Europe 1996

Table **1.2** New registrations of passenger cars 1991–5 (in millions)

	1990	1991	1992	1993	1994	1995
France	2.3	2.0	2.1	1.7	1.9	2.0
Germany	3.0	3.4	3.9	3.1	3.2	3.4
Italy	2.3	2.3	2.4	1.9	2.1	2.2
UK	1.9	1.5	1.5	1.7	1.8	1.9
Europe total	13.2	12.7	13.5	11.5	12.3	12.8

Source: Consumer Europe 1996

sales in the UK rose to record levels in 1997, an 8.3 per cent increase on the previous year, output fell by 6 per cent. This growth of sales in the UK was in stark contrast to France where falls in sales were a major cause of concern. Despite the optimism of periodic surges in sales, the inescapable fact remains that the European car market is essentially stagnant. It is an industry that relies mainly on replacement purchases, and, as such, is referred to as a mature cyclical market. In times of recession when money is tight and jobs become less secure, the replacement purchase is delayed. Market opportunities have arisen in the emerging economies of Eastern Europe, but these have attracted players from outside Europe, and the cheaper cars from lower-cost countries such as Korea would seem to have more appeal in the lower-wage economies of the former Eastern bloc.

The European car industry faces problems of over-capacity and oversupply. The market is both fragmented and highly competitive. There are a large number of national players, many of whom, in the past, have been supported directly and indirectly by their national governments. As a result, many of these firms are small, almost certainly too small to be effective on a global scale in an industry where size matters. The smaller European manufacturers face the highly organized competition of much larger firms operating with much larger economies of scale. In addition, the cost of relatively high wages and related social benefits places much of the industry at a disadvantage in comparison to the emerging economies of Korea and Malaysia. The currency crisis in South East Asia in 1997–8 has made such imports even more competitive and the relative weakness of the yen has increased Japanese competitiveness as well.

Across Europe, car manufacturers are engaged in a series of strategies to remain in business. It is important that such strategies are successful, not just for the firms themselves, but for their national economy. The car industry is the world's largest single manufacturing industry and embraces not only car production, but also a vast parts industry, retail network and used car market. It does not end there. Many car firms now earn as much from selling finance to enable customers to buy their product as they do from manufacture. In addition, large financial services, insurance and repair industries depend on the car industry, as does an entire fuel supply industry.

We will examine some of the major strategies employed by firms in Europe to search for new products and new markets, to seek economies of scale through joint ventures and acquisitions and to cut costs through a variety of measures. Such strategies have extended beyond the production companies themselves, to embrace the supply industry as well. There have been significant job losses and inevitable closures. As in the past household names such as Riley, Hillman and Austin have disappeared, many more are expected to follow in the next few years.

Before dealing with the strategies in more detail, we will first take a closer look at the extent of over-capacity and competition.

Over-capacity and competition

At the beginning of 1998, Alex Trotman, the then CEO of Ford Motor Company, estimated world over-capacity at 40 per cent. The cheaper products available from Japan, Korea and Malaysia, as a result of the Asian currency crisis, added to over-capacity by oversupply. The analysts Charterhouse Tilney measured European capacity at 16.3 million vehicles, while European output was measured at 12.8 million. On this basis, Europe could easily lose a capacity of around 3.5 million vehicles and still meet market demand for local vehicles. As several have commented, this gap is about the size of the German car industry. A 1998 survey by Pricewaterhouse Coopers was even more pessimistic, putting European over-capacity at 7 million vehicles.

Over-capacity is undoubtedly the product of an industry that is ever optimistic, fed by the belief amongst senior management that the next cyclical upturn is just around the corner and that their new model will take market share from their competitors. In the past this has been encouraged by governments wishing their national company to be a world player in an economically important industry. Given the size of most car plants and their contribution to local economies, most governments are reluctant to sanction plant closures, thereby adding to the problems of over-capacity.

Such optimism is faced by the reality of a largely static market with too many competitors. In terms of market share, local manufacturers still come out on top in national markets, but the position is less clear cut than before. European manufacturers still face considerable competition from the Japanese. The slow growth of Japanese imports in the early 1990s was a product of the high value of the yen, EU import restrictions and voluntary restraint on behalf of the Japanese themselves. The high yen against the US dollar meant that European producers enjoyed considerable export success in the US market. By the late 1990s, that position had changed; the yen had weakened significantly and import restrictions were due to end in 1999. The issue of quotas is still one of fierce debate. Without them, European manufacturers fear that the Japanese may swamp the market, yet the Japanese argue that quotas have been always been much higher than actual imports. The key issue here is the role played by Japanese transplants, Japanese manufacturing plants operating overseas, which have grown during the decade with plans for considerable expansion into the twenty-first century.

Competition also comes from the Koreans. Daewoo began selling in the UK in 1995 and achieved the fastest-growing car sales of any manufacturer. By the end of the 1990s the future competitiveness of Korean manufacturers is difficult to predict. The industry grew rapidly on the strength of relatively low wages and long working hours and considerable investment in plant. That same investment led to every major company over-stretching itself and the inevitable economic crisis, with the near collapse of Daewoo at the end of the decade. This has led to a slowing down of production, which is partly offset by a cheap product, owing to rapid devaluation of the currency, and an expansion in Eastern Europe, tapping a relatively new market.

Problems of over-capacity and competition have been tackled by the various European producers utilizing a number of different strategies. It is to these we now turn.

Product strategies

Amongst the European producers there has been a tendency for the consolidation of components across a wide range of models, utilizing just-in-time methods based on closer ties with a smaller number of suppliers. In 1994, Volkswagen announced a radical restructuring of its vehicle manufacture, reducing the number of chassis types from 16 to 4 across its entire range of Volkswagen, Audi, Skoda and Seat cars. The process had already begun with the VW Passat and the Audi 4 through shared engines and tracking systems. Other companies, like Ford, saw the ultimate consolidation for a global company in the form of a world car, and launched the Mondeo. However, there are undoubted cultural barriers to the world car concept, with car buyers expressing different national preferences. The stereotypical British buyer opts for performance, in France it is styling, in Sweden safety, in Germany engineering sophistication and so on.

Some manufacturers such as Mercedes decided to extend their product range, launching a competitively priced small sports coupé in 1996, which proved so successful that demand outstripped supply with a resulting two-year waiting list. A multi-purpose vehicle is being developed, as is a two-seater micro city car in an unusual joint venture with SMH, the company that launched the Swatch watch. Such developments have given Mercedes a high profile. Not all their ventures were successful. The launch of the 'A' Class, a small family saloon, achieved notoriety when it overturned in manoeuvres for its Swedish press launch. The subsequent correction cost amounted to DM50 million, the resulting bad publicity caused many orders to be cancelled and the company share price fell.

The attempt by Mercedes to broaden its product range was a strategy pursued by other manufacturers, the majority preferring the acquisition route. Ford moved out of the mass market and into the luxury market to acquire Jaguar and Aston Martin, while BMW, in acquiring Rover, entered the small family car sector as well as the four-wheel drive market via Land Rover. Volkswagen purchased the Rolls Royce factory, but obtained the right to manufacture only the Bentley car. The right to manufacture the Rolls Royce was held, not by the factory, but by another company, Rolls Royce Aero-engines, who opted to sell this right to BMW. This illustrates the rather complex nature of acquisitions.

Despite the consolidation and the development of new models, the Europeans still spend less on R&D than their US or Japanese counterparts.

New market opportunities

In 1994, 80 per cent of the world's population lived outside the three major car producing areas of the USA, Europe and Japan, yet accounted for only 8 per cent of the total market. The attention of the car manufacturers has turned to such emerging markets as a solution to the problems of stagnant home markets. Opportunities clearly exist. New car sales in China were 78 000 in 1990, rising to 430 000 in 1993, and with 1 million forecast for 1999. In Eastern Europe sales are predicted at least to double from 1996 to 2006. With such potential, it is hardly surprising that the industry has swarmed around the emerging markets like bees around a honey pot. General Motors has used its European company, Opel, to gain advantage in India, Indonesia and Thailand, while its US counterpart has led the initiatives in China. Amongst the Japanese, Toyota has established strongholds in Thailand, Indonesia and the Philippines, and Mitsubishi dominates in Vietnam, as does Suzuki in India. In China, the market is led currently by Volkswagen and PSA (Peugeot-Citroen). The major European players see Eastern Europe as a natural extension of their current market, but here they face strong competition from the Koreans, and more especially Daewoo, with plants either opened or planned in the Czech Republic, Poland, Romania and Uzbekistan. The prospect of an already cheap Korean product being manufactured in great numbers by cheap Eastern European labour may leave little opportunity for the rest. Already there are fears of over-capacity in the emerging market of Eastern Europe.

Excessive competition is only one of the problems faced by firms entering emerging markets. Many such markets have weak infrastructures, with poor road systems creating major problems of congestion. While prospects of higher income levels are good in parts of Eastern Europe, along with a growing credit industry, the very low income levels in China and Indonesia should not be a cause of great optimism. In many of these countries there is a shortage of hard currency. In China, as with other emerging markets, entry is a highly political process at both local and national levels. Entry costs are high and where, as in China, strict emphasis is placed on the localization of parts, there are problems of supply, both in quantity and quality, resulting from skills shortages in the local population.

Restructuring strategies

All the European firms have made significant attempts to cut costs in the 1990s. Some of that cost cutting has been associated with investment in new technology and new methods of manufacture both to achieve economies of scale through automation and in an attempt to achieve the efficiencies of some of their Japanese rivals. The attempts by US and European firms to copy Japanese methods, especially those associated with Toyota, have been dubbed lean production. (A fuller debate of this can be found in Chapter 6.) However, there are limits to productivity and efficiency gains through automation and methods alone. Some commentators believe that, for the better plants in Europe, those limits are about to be reached. If this is the case then further cost cutting can only be made by plant closure and by downsizing and delayering, the 1990s euphemisms for shedding labour.

Ford Motor Company made a budget cut of US$3 million in 1997 and planned a further reduction of US$1.7 million for 1998. These cuts follow a massive worldwide restructuring exercise to create a global matrix organization based on five vehicle centres, four in the USA and one in Europe. The aim was to break down barriers in the organization and bring together functional expertise wherever it is located. This was accompanied by a significant delayering exercise with many job losses, and the creation of cross-national teams. The aim of such major restructuring was to make the company more responsive to a rapidly changing global environment through the creation of a more appropriate structure to speed the decision-making process, facilitate the exchange of ideas and change the cultural mindset of the employees. (Further discussion of this and matrix organizations in general is to be found in Chapter 3).

In both Sweden and France, plants were closed following the failure of Volvo and Renault to agree to a merger. In Germany the workforce was reduced from 788 000 in 1991 to 588 000 in 1994, together with an increase in outsourcing and the introduction of short-term contracts and flexible working. In 1993 the unions at Volkswagen agreed to a cut in pay and a reduced working week in an attempt to preserve 30 000 jobs. However, in 1996 further attempts at cuts were resisted by the same union, which was supported by the State Government of Lower Saxony (a 20 per cent shareholder in Volkswagen). The State's involvement was motivated by the fear of rising unemployment as a result of increased outsourcing, particularly to the cheaper labour markets of the former East Germany. The Lower Saxony government also attempted to block European grants to the East for the same reason.

The above illustrates the highly political nature of the industry, hardly surprising given its contribution to GDP and employment. Lower Saxony has not been alone in attempting to protect the local car industry.

Almost all European governments have, at one time or another, given support to their national car industry, either through part ownership in the case of British Leyland (UK), Renault (France) or Volkswagen (Germany), or through trade barriers and general assistance programmes. The Italians and the French have at one time or another erected significant trade barriers to protect local industry. The same two countries have, along with Spain, set up special programmes of tax incentives or rebates to encourage the scrapping of old cars and the purchase of new ones. This policy has also been pursued in non-manufacturing nations such as Denmark and Ireland, partly to aid local supply industries, but mainly to encourage the replacement of older, air-polluting models with their environmentally friendly modern versions. However, such measures do not always have the desired effect. The 5,000 franc incentive to buyers of new cars launched by the French government in 1994 led to the purchase of as many foreign as home cars and had the effect of putting more cars on the road, thus displeasing the environmental lobby.

Such measures have been notably absent in the UK, owing largely to the free market policies pursued by successive Conservative governments from 1979–97, and, some would argue, beyond. Opinions are divided on the impact of this on the UK car industry. Critics have claimed that it has hastened the demise of UK companies both through acquisition by foreign competitors and through the encouragement of Japanese transplants. Supporters have claimed that it actually protected local industry by aligning it with more powerful companies and that the growth of transplants has been a boost to the local supply industry. Certainly there is no evidence to suggest that job losses in the UK are any greater than under the more protectionist regimes of France and Italy.

Mergers and acquisitions

In 1960 there were 47 major car companies in Europe. By 1998 there were just 17, with predictions of further consolidation. Many of the reasons for such rationalization have already been mentioned and include the need to achieve economies of scale, to share the high costs of research and development and to confront the problems of over-capacity, stagnant prices and severe competition. In general, cars firms have merged to survive in a global industry requiring global companies. Table 1.3 gives an indication of who owns whom in the world car industry as in 1999. Undoubtedly that picture will change in the next few years. This section will examine two such mergers: the successful acquisition of Rover (UK) by BMW (Germany) and the failed merger of Volvo (Sweden) and Renault (France).

In 1994 BMW paid £800 million for 80 per cent of Rover and took over debts of some £1 billion. Some years earlier Rover had been privatized and sold to British Aerospace for £150 million and the company had benefited from a joint venture with Honda. The complexities of the relationship with Honda, not least Honda's supply of engines, has meant that ties with the

Table **1.3** Who owns whom in the European car industry in 1999

General Motors (USA)	General Motors, Vauxhall, Opel, Saab (50%), Isuzu (37%), Suzuki (3%)
Ford (USA)	Ford, Jaguar, Aston Martin, Volvo Cars, Mazda (33%), Kia (9%)
Toyota (Japan)	Toyota, Lexus, Daihatsu (25%)
Volkswagen (Germany)	Volkswagen, Audi, Seat, Skoda, Rolls Royce
Fiat (Italy)	Fiat, Ferrari, Alpha Romeo, Lancia, Maserati, Iveco
PSA (France)	Peugeot, Citroen
Daimler Benz (Germany)	Mercedes, Chrysler
BMW (Germany)	BMW, Rover, Land Rover
Proton (Malaysia)	Proton, Lotus
Renault (France)	Nissan (37%)

Japanese company have not been cut entirely despite their displeasure at the BMW takeover. The attraction of Rover to BMW was undoubtedly access to the smaller family saloon market and the acquisition of Land Rover, still a prestigious marque. Rover's gain was the link with a highly popular, luxury car manufacturer and access to a much wider market. In 1998 Rover announced 1500 redundancies from its 39 000 workforce and proposals for much greater labour flexibility incorporating the move to a four-day working week. The reasons for the cutbacks were cited by BMW as strong sterling, which contributed to operating losses of £98 million in 1997, despite investments totalling £2.5 billion since the acquisition in 1994. Those investments included rebuilding the Cowley plant at Oxford and the Land Rover plant at Solihull.

By 1999 there was considerable uncertainty surrounding BMW's UK operations. Losses at Rover were announced at around £650 million for 1998. The losses were attributed to rising costs, model changes, an over-strong pound, falling sales and the cost of restructuring the company. A further factor involved Rover's policy of using predominantly UK suppliers, when, owing to the strong pound, parts could have been sourced more cheaply overseas. The damaging impact of the losses on the overall profits of the parent company led the German press to refer to Rover as 'the English Patient' (using the title of a successful book and film). At the same time, BMW had plans for a rebuild of the Longbridge plant at a cost of £1.5 billion. They had expected the UK government to provide at least £300 million in grant aid, but viewed their original offer as 'derisory'. In any case such government support met with fierce opposition from other European manufacturers. BMW announced that further cost cuts were inevitable and at least a further 1000 job losses were predicted. The failure of the UK government to dance to the BMW tune was accompanied by suggestions that Rover production could be moved to Hungary. The problems facing Rover led to resignations at board level and a rapid turnover of senior management, all moved into Rover from Germany, but none able to stem the tide. Rumours were rife that the Quandt family, who own 46 per cent of BMW, were disturbed by the events at Rover and that the problems made the company vulnerable to acquisition.

The proposed merger between Renault and Volvo in 1993 seemed a natural extension of existing joint ventures and partial ownership arrangements, both companies holding a proportion of shares in the other. The merger was seen as the means to turn around the fortunes of two established but ailing companies by achieving economies of scale, by reducing R&D costs and forming a stronger alliance to face Japanese competition. After a protracted negotiation, plans for the merger came to naught. There would appear to have been several reasons. Renault, through management statements and reports in the French media, clearly saw the merger as a takeover, with the French as the dominant partner, reinforced by a proposed 65–35 stakeholding favouring the French, and the appointment of a French CEO for the new company. The French government had a major stake in Renault, but with plans for privatization. The fear amongst Swedish shareholders was that the shares would be floated below market value to ensure that the privatization was a success, thereby forcing down the share price of the merged company. Middle management in Volvo were concerned that the merger would, at worst, lead to job losses, with the Swedes bearing the brunt. At best it was feared that there would be a conflict of managerial styles, the Swedes being more open, with greater delegation, while the French were more hierarchical. Culturally the Swedes are more international and outward-looking than the French. The merger was supported by the Swedish government, but consistently opposed by the workforce and Swedish public opinion. There were clear cultural and political reasons for their unease. There were also economic factors. The cost of employing workers in Sweden was much higher than that in France. Sweden has both higher rates of taxation and health and social security payments. It was feared that a combined Renault–Volvo company would mean significant job losses in Sweden (a more detailed version of the Renault–Volvo case can be found in Chapter 4). Volvo Cars was eventually acquired by Ford in 1999 and in the same year Volvo Trucks was bought by Mitsubishi. Renault turned its attention to Japan and acquired a 37 per cent stake in Nissan and managerial control through the secondment of Carlos Ghosn as the CEO of the Japanese company.

Restructuring in the supply industry

A similar pattern to that found amongst the car manufacturers themselves may be observed in the supply industry. In 1995–6 there were 157 mergers of car components firms in Europe, 79 involving cross-border deals and 39 involving non-European companies. The largest consolidation has taken place in brakes and seating. Seating is now dominated by two US companies, Johnson Controls and Lear Seating. Between them they control 50 per cent of the total market and 70 per cent of the outsourcing market.

For car manufacturers themselves, outsourcing is yet another means of cutting costs. Components suppliers, feeding a number of firms, can achieve economies of scale and, through specialization, are able to maintain product innovation. Wages are lower in the components industry than in the car firms themselves, so it is hardly surprising that outsourcing has increased dramatically. In recent years the trend for the major manufacturers has been to focus on a small number of dedicated suppliers with whom they forge a special relationship, as between Mercedes and the tyre manufacturer, Continental. Such close relationships invariably include joint development of new products, joint training of staff and, in some instances, part ownership. Hand in hand with this development is the increasing use of components supplies from low-cost countries, including some in Europe such as Poland and the Czech Republic.

Merger and acquisition activity in the global car industry has had its impact on the supply chain. For example, the part acquisition by Renault of Nissan and the poor financial performance of the Japanese company led to a more focused strategy as far as suppliers were concerned. Plans were drawn up to reduce the number of suppliers from 1145 to 600 and suppliers wishing to win contracts must operate globally, cut costs and work together with Nissan/Renault engineers. Such policy changes will have an impact on those UK firms supplying the Nissan factory in Sunderland.

The increasing use of outsourcing has not met with universal approval. There have been industrial relations problems in plants where jobs have been lost as a result of outsourcing strategies and, as we have seen with Lower Saxony, there can be political pressures to resist the shift to lower-cost areas.

Changes in the supply industry have not been matched at the distribution end of the supply chain. There has been some move towards rationalization amongst dealerships, but, compared to the USA, European dealerships are small, fragmented and have limited turnovers. The car industry in Europe is still protective of dealerships that specialize in one brand and has been granted exemption from EU competition policy. Even though they are the same company, Rover and BMW products will rarely be seen in the same showroom.

Concluding remarks

The pattern that emerges at the end of the 1990s is complex. It is clear that there are too many manufacturers chasing a limited number of European customers. Hopes that a rapidly expanding Eastern European market would benefit home producers have receded in the face of intense competition and cheap imports. The big five producers, General Motors, Ford, Volkswagen, Daimler-Chrysler and Toyota, would seem to be secure, but several European producers are vulnerable, notably Peugeot-Citroen, Renault and Fiat. Some of these companies have been kept alive through government support based on its perception of their contribution to the national economy and to national identity.

Elsewhere we see an end of nationalism in car manufacture, as global operations can mean that a US company such as Ford can produce cars in Spain for the UK market, using Japanese parts made in the Philippines. There has been an increase in cross-border acquisitions involving producers outside Europe. The major acquisition has been that of Chrysler by Daimler, but we should not forget the purchase of Lotus, the specialist UK company, by Proton from Malaysia. Consolidations in chassis type, body shells, engines and a whole range of parts mean that the era of the world car is upon us. Despite the trend to conformity, the picture is still very mixed. Acquisitions have resulted in much greater product variety within the same company resulting, in such as Fiat, in a product range that embraces both the Fiat Uno and the Ferrari Testarossa. Despite such ranges, producers continue to spend huge advertising budgets to ensure brand differentiation.

The European car industry in a business context

Environmental factors

The case demonstrates the important role of the car industry in the **economy** of the major European producers. It is the region's largest single manufacturing industry with a large number of related industries and jobs. However, it is also an industry where supply is greater than demand, which makes it vulnerable to recession and external forces, such as dramatic increases in the price of oil, as occurred in the 1970s. The market is essentially static, cyclical and highly competitive. Competition occurs not just amongst European firms, but from Japan and, more recently, South Korea. The global nature of the industry has meant that many firms have taken advantage of economic differences and moved or outsourced some of their operations to low-wage areas. Some of those areas with growing economies, including parts of Eastern Europe, are seen as important emerging markets. Here as at home there is intense competition and the economic problems of the less prosperous emerging markets such as India and China present barriers to entry. The industry is especially sensitive to economic changes, including currency movements, in other parts of the world. For many years, the strength of the Japanese yen against European currencies was a constraint on Japanese imports. The problems of the Japanese and many other South East Asian economies in the late 1990s, with the subsequent weakening of their currencies, have meant that imports are more competitively priced.

The economic importance of the industry has led to the involvement of **the state**. Over-capacity within the industry is viewed by some as a direct result of government protection of uneconomic plants. In many of the countries for many years, the state has been a whole or part owner of such firms as Renault, Volkswagen and British Leyland. In general, national firms are still supported by national governments although much of the industry has undergone privatization. Variations in government intervention exist between countries such as the UK, where a free market ideology has resulted in less protective policies, and those such as France, with more directive, protectionist policies. Such policies have included investment, trade barriers and incentives to the public to buy new cars. The political importance of the industry can be seen, as in Lower Saxony, by attempts to prevent closure, downsizing or movement of jobs to other areas. Politics also plays a part in gaining entry to emerging markets, most notably in China.

The oversupply and over-capacity in the industry has had a significant impact on **labour** and employment through plant closure, downsizing and delayering. Throughout firms in Europe there have been major reductions in the workforce. The response of governments and unions has been mixed. As we have seen, state protectionism does exist and in a strongly unionized industry, unions have fought hard to prevent the growth in outsourcing. In other cases, they have agreed to reductions in pay and the working week and to greater flexibility in order to save jobs.

In terms of **technology**, the industry has made significant investment to improve both products and processes. While not in the same league as the pharmaceutical firms, the industry is still a major investor in R&D. The changes in process technology have been exclusively focused on cost reduction with the widespread introduction of automation and methods associated with lean production, such as just-in-time manufacture. Many of these technological changes have been carried out in close relationship with major suppliers.

The case also demonstrates differences in **culture**. Despite the trend towards the concept of the world car we can still see variations in national preference. Cultural differences also played a part in the failure of Renault and Volvo to negotiate a successful merger, both in terms of management and organizational style and in arrangements for aspects of pensions and insurance.

Organizational aspects

Size is a significant issue in the car industry. We have seen that several of the European firms are too small to be effective on a global scale and more mergers are predicted as a route to survival. The investment needed for firms to be successful calls for economies of scale and access to global markets and global suppliers.

In terms of **structure**, there have been significant changes in the past decade. Mergers between firms like BMW and Rover have had inevitable implications for the management and the structures, particularly of Rover as the weaker partner. The closer links between some manufacturers and major suppliers, with the creation of dedicated supply systems, have had implications for structural arrangements in both manufacturer and supplier. We have seen that in order to face global challenges, some firms such as Ford have undergone major restructuring, creating a global matrix organization.

As far as **ownership** is concerned, acquisitions and mergers have been rife in an industry that must grow to stay in business. There are examples of majority ownership as with BMW's 80 per cent stake in Rover, and of minority interest as with Ford's 33 per cent stake in Mazda. The growing trend is for ownership patterns to cross not just national borders but continental boundaries as well. The picture is highly complex, none more so than the case of Volkswagen, who purchased the Rolls Royce car factory, but not the right to manufacture Rolls Royce cars. That right was sold separately to BMW. In BMW itself, board decisions are influenced considerably by a single family owning 46 per cent of shares. Changes in ownership patterns have affected the supply industry as well, with an even greater extent of consolidation through merger and acquisition, but with an increasing share of ownership in the supply chain by the major manufacturers. Whatever the patterns of ownership, the expressed **goals** of the manufacturers invariably reflect an optimism for expansion, either through new markets or new models, that is not always matched by the realities of the market place.

Issues of **organizational culture** come to the forefront with mergers and acquisitions as new alliances struggle to adapt to different cultures at the level of the firm. When these are compounded by national differences, as in the case of Renault and Volvo, they can threaten the success of the alliance.

Strategic aspects

The case illustrates a number of key generic strategies. Product strategies are exemplified by the regularity of model renewal by the manufacturers, although the frequency of that renewal is tempered by economic conditions. A favoured route to new products is through acquisition. Through its purchase of Rover, BMW gained an entirely new range of cars, including the specialist Land Rover models. Rather than develop its own range, Ford entered the luxury car market by acquiring both Jaguar and Aston Martin and strengthened its position in the big car market through its acquisition of Volvo. Other companies such as Mercedes chose to develop their own products, in their case to enter the non-luxury market through the 'A' Class and the micro car. The static nature of home markets has led producers to go further afield and the emerging markets of Asia, Latin America and Eastern Europe have been pursued vigorously. All companies have engaged in a series of strategies focusing on cost reduction, including automation, plant closure, introducing more efficient production methods, reducing the labour force and seeking economies of scale through merger and other forms of consolidation.

Functional aspects

Innovation The case contains several examples of innovation in terms of new product and process development. Other forms of innovation are present in terms new global structures, as with Ford, or new forms of relationship with suppliers, as with Mercedes.

Operations A major production issue in the European industry is overcapacity, with the inevitably of future plant closures unless new markets can be found. Changes in production methods have resulted in considerable efficiency gains, although further gains are unlikely in some of the better plants. A major trend has been the consolidation of production through the sharing of parts across model ranges, including body shells, chassis and engines, as well as a whole range of smaller components. The Japanese have extended their influence in Europe through the expansion of transplants. The Europeans for their part have relocated some of their production, particularly the supply industry, where labour is cheaper, including parts of Eastern Europe.

Marketing Most of the companies have been active in the search for new markets either by development or acquisition. While competition in the emerging markets is fierce, the real potential of some, like China, is unknown. Through mergers and acquisitions there has been a growth in differentiated markets within the same company. Luxury producers have moved down-market, while mass producers have acquired luxury and specialist marques. Despite this, and despite the sharing of body shells by different model ranges, marketing specialists within the companies have made considerable investments to ensure brand differentiation. This is reinforced by systems of dealership across Europe that protect brand specialization, irrespective of patterns of ownership.

Human resource management Twenty years ago the key issues were undoubtedly dealing with unions to negotiate wages and conditions and to resolve conflict. With a changing economic climate and the weakening of trade unions in countries such as the UK, the focus has shifted. The key issues are undoubtedly the creation of more flexible patterns of work, in terms of time and function, the holding down of wages and the shedding of labour through schemes for early retirement and redundancy.

Accounting and finance Cost management has been a major consideration for all manufacturers and has occurred across the whole range of their activities, including the manufacturing process, component supply and labour. Cost reduction has been at the heart of most strategies. The producers themselves have expanded their activities to establish finance companies, which adds to their range of products. Customers are now sold not just a car, but a financial package as well. For some producers this has been their major source of profit and has part-subsidized less profitable manufacturing operations.

News International and Wapping

For almost a year, every Saturday evening the residents of a fashionable warehouse conversion on the edges of London's docklands were denied free access to their property. The residents' access was blocked by mass picketing resulting from an industrial dispute between News International and its former Fleet Street employees over the printing of newspapers at the company's newly commissioned Wapping plant. In this case we will examine the background to the dispute and focus on events from December 1985 to February 1987. A postscript has been added to deal briefly with events after 1987.

Although what has become known as the Wapping dispute focuses on the events of that period, the seeds of that dispute were laid much earlier. As with the car industry, we will see how this case illustrates our model of business.

News International is a company controlled by Rupert Murdoch, Australian by birth but with American citizenship, and with considerable newspaper and other media holdings in Australia and the USA. The British company controls two daily newspapers, *The Times* and the *Sun*, and two Sunday newspapers, the *Sunday Times* and the *News of the World*. The *Sun*, the *Sunday Times* and the *News of the World* are the best-selling newspapers of their type in Britain and *The Times* is arguably the nation's most famous daily paper. A third daily paper, *Today*, was held briefly by News International until its demise.

In 1978 land was purchased in Wapping with a view to building a large printing works using the latest technology in newspaper production, and construction began within two years. At that time News International owned just the *Sun* and the *News of the World* and the plant was part of a plan to increase both the output and the size of both newspapers. In 1981, the company purchased both *The Times* and the *Sunday Times*, in the face of accusations that News International would be operating a monopoly against the public interest. Once again there was a desire to increase both the production runs and the size of both newly acquired newspapers. In all cases the size of the newspapers and the quantity of production were restricted by the size of the existing plants around the Fleet Street area of central London and what management saw as uneconomic manning levels imposed by the trade unions. The issues of new technology and trade union control over work practices lay at the heart of most major national newspaper disputes. No national paper was immune and in 1985 alone 95.6 million copies were lost to industrial disputes of one type or another.

A little background

The major technological innovations were direct input and photocomposition. This means that the printing operation could in effect be carried out by journalists or typists, eliminating the need for traditional print working through a method referred to as 'cold-type' printing. Computer keyboards and VDUs are used to input material to be stored on a central computer which also contains programs for page composition. The computer prints off its stories and advertisements on photographic paper, which are then pasted up to form the eventual pages of the newspaper. These are photographed and a negative is produced. The negative is converted into a flexible polymer plate to be clipped to the existing presses for the printing to commence.

Under this method around 3000 lines a minute could be typeset compared with seven lines per minute using the conventional technique, with the added advantage that stories and whole pages could be changed and mistakes corrected quickly and cheaply. Such methods had been used by American newspapers since the early 1960s. In Britain, however, the introduction of new technology had been slow. There was a strong adherence to the traditional process of using linotype, a method involving the creation of the type from molten lead, sometimes known as the 'hot metal' process. This method is labour intensive and is often performed by compositors using equipment some 50 years old. The new generation of printing presses are much cheaper and can therefore be scrapped when further technical improvements are made. Even where photocomposition had been introduced the process was not used to its full potential as, under management–union agreements, keyboard operations were still being performed by print workers and not journalists or typists.

The printing industry is one of the most traditional of the craft industries and has a long history. The print unions have been vigilant in maintaining control over the apprenticeship system, entry to the profession, and over the way the job is done. These are traditional craft controls aided by the rigid enforcement of a union closed shop. Such controls were greatest in Fleet Street where job entry was reserved only for existing members of a recognized trade union (a pre-entry closed shop). The two major unions are the National Graphical Association (NGA), covering the printers themselves, and the Society of Graphical and Allied Trades (SOGAT 182), covering despatch, distribution and clerical workers.

In this way the union controlled work allocation and above all, manning levels for each job. Frequent management complaints concerned overmanning and the inability to implement changes that would invariably be accompanied by uneconomic staffing requirements. There was considerable resistance to the introduction of new technology, as this would effectively reduce the craft control of the job and make it accessible to those not trained as printers.

Despite management's frequent complaints, the situation was largely of their own making. Concessions to trade union control of manning levels had been made owing to the highly competitive nature of the national newspaper industry, the highly perishable nature of the product, and the need for maximum flexibility, especially when dealing with late changes in news items. Competition was not just for readers, but for advertisers. Lost production could never be regained and lost distribution could not be sold at a later date. These factors also gave the trade unions considerable strength in wage negotiation and Fleet Street workers were able to achieve higher rates than those earned by other print workers.

It was partly competition that led to Fleet Street management adopting a new approach to the introduction of new technology. The relative cheapness of cold type over hot metal reduced one of the major barriers to entry to newspaper production. The initial challenges came in the provinces with the growth of the 'free newspaper' industry. These are essentially cheaply produced local papers where advertising takes precedence over news items. The income from advertising is such that the newspapers can be distributed free to all householders in a given area. This sharpened competition in the local paper market. The response among some existing local papers was to force through the introduction of new technology. The *Nottingham Evening Post* in the face of union opposition from the NGA simply replaced the print workers.

The real focus was in 1983 with the case of the Messenger group of free local newspapers in south Lancashire and its proprietor Eddie Shah. In expanding his distribution and introducing direct input printing he overcame bitter opposition from the NGA. He was backed in his quest by new laws redefining industrial disputes and imposing greater restrictions on picketing, drawn up by a government intent on curbing the power of the unions. The NGA were fined by the courts and Shah achieved all his objectives. He built upon his success with the local newspaper industry and launched a new national daily paper, *Today*, using new technology and non-traditional workers in a labour force one-tenth the normal size for such a newspaper. At the same time plans were announced for the launch of other new daily and Sunday national papers. Although Shah's ownership of *Today* was brief and unprofitable (he sold the paper to Lonrho, who in turn sold it to News International), the relationship between Fleet Street management and the print unions had changed irrevocably. At the same time Express newspapers announced plans to reduce its workforce by 30 per cent.

Competition came not just from within the industry but through the coverage and the expansion of the television news services. The advent of breakfast television posed an even greater threat to an already declining total newspaper readership. The newspaper industry needed new technology to provide a better quality product with clearer newsprint and sharper pictures and an ability to respond quickly to changing news stories.

Events at Wapping

Before Murdoch's acquisition *The Times* had attempted to force the new technology issue, but an 11-month shutdown in 1978 altered very little and the NGA retained exclusive control over typesetting operations. The completion of the plant at Wapping and the expense involved in interest payments alone gave new urgency to some form of agreement with the print unions. However, negotiations to move the production of the *Sun* and *News of the World* broke down in early 1984. The unions had refused to give way on the issue of staffing levels and demarcation. Murdoch was clearly frustrated by the failure to reach agreement and, undoubtedly spurred by Shah's action against the NGA, ensured that Wapping was protected against the action of pickets. During the dispute the building was popularly known as 'Fortress Wapping'. Plans were laid to treat Wapping as a greenfield site for the production of a new London evening paper staffed with non-Fleet Street people. At the time the unions saw this as a diversion to mask the true intention of transferring production of all four newspapers to Wapping.

Whatever the intention, Murdoch was determined to introduce total management control over staffing levels and achieve total labour flexibility. News International terminated all its existing collective agreements with the unions with the aim of replacing them with a legally binding contract and a no-strike clause, the elimination of the closed shop, and binding arbitration in the case of a dispute. The penalty for breaking the agreement would be instant dismissal for individuals and the right to sue the union for unlimited amounts. Such a strategy was calculated to confront the unions on the issue of job control and, not suprisingly, was rejected by NGA and SOGAT '82. The two unions insisted that any move to Wapping should be accompanied by no redundancies and the maintenance of existing work practices. As a result Murdoch declared that negotiations were over and gave his print workers six months' notice and no option of jobs at Wapping.

One union, the Electrical, Electronic, Telecommunication and Plumbing Union (EETPU), was prepared to negotiate on the basis of the new proposals, much against the advice of the trade union movement's central body, the TUC. For some time the electricians' union had been keen to expand its membership in new areas and viewed its members as key workers in all work-places increasingly operating under the demands of new technology. One of those areas was printing, and the union had even gone so far as to provide training for its members in newspaper production.

Electricians were recruited by News International initially to commission the new presses. However, by the end of January 1986 the Wapping plant was producing the four newspaper titles amid much secrecy, using electricians recruited from outside London and transported daily by an organized bus net-work. This led to considerable recriminations within the trade union move-ment and calls to expel the EETPU from the TUC. They were eventually expelled at the 1988 TUC Conference, not for activities at News International, but for 'poaching' members from other unions in South Wales. The move had also affected the journalists on all papers. Many moved to Wapping for increased salaries but several refused to work under the new arrangements. For their part, the print unions held a secret ballot, which showed that most were in favour of strike action. Picket lines were set up outside Wapping and SOGAT attempted to prevent the distribution of the newspapers with the help of the transport workers union (TGWU). Both unions were countered by the law. In the case of the TGWU the threat was sufficient, but SOGAT was fined £25,000 and had its assets sequestrated by the High Court for persistent attempts to prevent newspaper distribution.

By the following month News International agreed to the involvement of ACAS. The main issue that emerged was that of redundancy payments for those on strike. The company had always maintained that those choosing this course of action forfeited their right to severance pay and had effectively dismissed themselves. The company did offer the unions the old *Sunday Times* printing plant so that they could set up their own newspaper staffed by the displaced workforce. The offer was rejected by the unions, who insisted on the maximum number of workers being taken on at Wapping and generous redundancy payments for the rest. Increasingly, however, the union position was being undermined by events elsewhere. New technology agreements were being reached with unions at the Express and Mirror newspapers and several national newspapers announced their own plans to move to Docklands. In all cases the owners saw the move as an opportunity both to expand and negotiate fresh deals with the trade unions.

By May 1986 the company made what they claimed was a final offer in a bid to end the picketing at Wapping. This comprised a redundancy payment deal totalling £50 million, an opportunity for all workers to apply for vacan-cies at Wapping as and when they arose, a withdrawal of all legal actions against the unions, and a promise to review the issue of union recognition after a year. The offer was rejected. Picketing was intensified, accompanied by a significant involvement of the police and further legal proceedings to prevent the picketing taking place. As a result of these proceedings SOGAT estimated its losses at £1.5 million. The estimated costs of policing the dispute up to June 1986 were £1 million.

In September News International made a revised offer of redundancy payments to the dismissed workers, again rejected by the NGA and SOGAT '82. The mounting costs of the dispute forced SOGAT to appeal for funds among its membership nationwide. The appeal was rejected.

The first anniversary of the strike in January 1987 was accompanied by the largest mass picket to date and extremely violent clashes between the police and the pickets. Part of the violence was undoubtedly attributed to a growing frustration among the workers and a realization that the unions could no longer afford to continue. The cost of legal proceedings, the general cost of running the dispute and an impending contempt of court action was too much for the NGA and SOGAT to bear and would have resulted in the elimination of all their assets. By February 1987 both unions, along with the journalists' union, accepted a redundancy package for the dismissed employees and the dispute ended.

Postscript

At the time of the Wapping dispute, the UK newspaper industry employed over 30 000 people. By 1990, that number had fallen to less than 15 000. At the same time, newspapers had increased considerably the size of each edition and had introduced colour printing as a standard feature in almost all newspapers. Colour printing had a significant impact on advertising. In 1990 the Wapping plant benefited from a £500 million investment in state-of-the-art printing presses.

By the mid-1990s News International at Wapping was part of a large global network of companies. The network embraced around 50 national newspapers in six countries, 80 regional papers in Australia, over 30 magazines around the world and the major book publisher, Harper Collins. A large number of acquisitions were made in broadcasting. News International had a controlling interest in major cable and satellite companies in the UK, USA, Germany, Latin America, Australia and Asia. It owned 20th Century Fox Films and the TV company, Fox Broadcasting, as well as control of 12 US TV stations. In Australia it owned Network 7. Amongst the company's many other interests could be numbered the transport firm TNT and the Australian airline, Ansett. The global network of companies comprises a highly complex organizational structure making full use of variations in national tax laws through a system of effective financial management. In 1995 the company made profits of £793 million, yet had to pay less than 10 per cent in tax, when the average for most firms is 20–40 per cent.

Table 1.4 shows 1999 newspaper sales for the best-selling titles in four categories. News International claimed top spot in three out of the four with the *Sun*, *News of the World* and *Sunday Times*, while *The Times* was second behind the *Daily Telegraph*. The mid-1990s was notable for a number of price wars

Table **1.4** Best-selling newspaper titles by category, March 1999

Tabloid daily	
Sun	3 813 381 copies sold
Daily Mail	2 362 184
Daily Mirror	2 303 510
Broadsheet daily	
Daily Telegraph	1 045 336
The Times	746 403
Guardian	402 494
Tabloid Sunday	
News of the World	4 313 502
Mail on Sunday	2 319 272
Sunday Mirror	1 993 074
Broadsheet Sunday	
Sunday Times	1 366 464
Sunday Telegraph	808 826
Observer	401 403
Source: Guardian	

amongst the daily titles, inevitably involving News International and its major rival in each category. *The Times* and *Daily Telegraph* competed on price and special offers, as did the *Sun* and the *Mirror*. In all cases profits were sacrificed for market share. However, the biggest gains made during the 1990s have been by the Daily Mail Group.

In terms of trade union activity, the EETPU soon lost its favoured status and was de-recognized by the company. Despite the decline in trade union membership and influence in the UK, News International would still appear to be sensitive to the events of the 1980s. Proposals by the New Labour government of 1999 to give employees the right to join trade unions have led to News International discussing plans to establish an Employee Consultative Council as a non-traditional company union in an attempt to avoid having to deal with an independent trade union.

The News International case in a business context

The case illustrates all aspects of our Business in Context model.

Environmental aspects

Economic factors are represented by the highly competitive nature of the newspaper industry. The high potential profit from a national title led to fierce competition for circulation and advertising. Traditionally this resulted in a fierce rivalry and lack of cooperation between the owners. The availability of new technology combined with external competition from television and radio meant that technological changes were sought to reduce costs and maintain profit levels. Furthermore, the relative cheapness of that new technology lowered a significant barrier to entry, thereby increasing competition. This has broken the oligopoly of Fleet Street and led to new national titles as well as major changes in regional newspapers resulting from the growth of the free newspaper industry. In a much broader sense, a high level of unemployment may have increased the resolve of the electricians' union to expand its field of activity and influenced the lack of wider support for the print workers in their dispute.

The **state** had a considerable influence on events at Wapping both directly and indirectly. There was a direct involvement through the policing of the dispute with extensive costs over a period of a year. The Employment Acts of 1980 and 1982 and the Trade Union Act of 1984 brought about changes in the legal definition of a dispute, and placed restrictions on both picketing and the formation of a closed shop. The unions were challenged on the legality of their dispute and were found wanting. The subsequent clashes between the unions and the courts led to substantial fines being imposed, which eventually brought an end to the dispute. Prior to the events at Wapping, the government of the day had, in 1981, become embroiled in a monopolies issue when News International negotiated to buy *The Times* and *Sunday Times* when it already owned the biggest-selling national and Sunday papers. The deal was allowed to go through on the undertaking of editorial freedom for the newly acquired titles. More sceptical observers, like Harold Evans (successively the editor of the *Sunday Times* and *The Times*), saw the acquisition as a reward for News International's editorial support for the government in the previous general election (Evans, 1983). Whatever the situation, this aspect of the case raises the important issue of the relationship between politics and the press. Fear of new legislation in 1999 to give employees rights of trade union membership brought a swift reaction from the company in the proposal of alternative structures.

Technology, or more specifically the introduction of new technology, was a central issue in this case. Changes in the technology of newspaper production brought about the possibility of changes in work allocation. The elimination of traditional printing work through the substitution of direct input and photocomposition challenged the job control of the print workers and ultimately the bargaining position of their trade union. Printing operations could now be performed by journalists and typists, considerably reducing operating costs and presenting much greater scope for editorial changes, allowing newspapers to be much more responsive to changes in the news and hence the needs of the market place. Traditional craft unions like the NGA do not yield their historical controls willingly, hence the intensity and at times the bitterness of the dispute. New technology also gave management a new strategic weapon in dealing with the trade unions and was doubtless seen by some as a means of gaining greater control over costs and workplace practices, especially manning levels. After the dispute continuing technological change made possible the introduction of colour printing and even further reduced staffing levels.

Labour issues, as we can see, are inseparable from those relating to technology. New methods not only mean changes in work allocation, but also an ultimate reduction in the number of jobs. The bargaining position of the trade unions was being challenged on the issue of job control at a time when their response was further weakened by high levels of unemployment. The case is not simply a matter of management versus the unions, but illustrates the complexity of the dispute on the union side. The Fleet Street workers had, for a very long time, considered themselves to be the 'aristocrats of labour', positioned at the very top of the printing hierarchy (Bassett, 1986). This had often rankled with print workers outside London, and may have explained their reluctance in giving full support to their Fleet Street colleagues. The *Independent* newspaper, launched in 1986, was printed at regional sites away from London, and its management had little difficulty in gaining the agreement of NGA and SOGAT '82 on the use of the new technology. Quite apart from the differences amongst the print workers themselves, their position was further challenged by the willingness of the electricians to be trained in newspaper operations. This forms part of a much broader debate within the trade union movement, as individual unions, mindful of a declining membership, seek to insure their own future by offering the kind of stoppage-free deals sought by management. In the case of Wapping the EETPU were more than happy to replace the print workers and on a broader front to see themselves ideally placed to become the key trade union of the future in workplaces increasingly controlled by computers. Changes in the trade union movement are thus reflecting wider occupational changes. Weakened print industry unions will need to widen their appeal to attract new members. This would further dilute the traditional power base of the craft union in printing.

The aspect of **culture** is relevant to this case in at least two ways. First, we have the issue of the distinctive culture of Fleet Street, brought about by the competitive nature of the industry and the job control of the craft unions. Work practices, manning levels and wage rates have marked off Fleet Street from the rest of the British newspaper industry. The distinctive Fleet Street culture has been especially resistant to change and thus a major factor in the dispute. Second, comparative studies of the newspaper industry reveal marked differences between Britain and other countries, notably the USA. The newspaper industry in the USA has embraced new technology with little union opposition. Moreover, in Britain there is much greater evidence of cooperation and solidarity between print workers, ancillary staff and journalists than exist in most other countries.

Organizational aspects

While the case clearly shows the interaction and influence of the environmental aspects of our model, there are significant organizational influences at work too.

In terms of **size**, News International's British operation was already large. Yet part of the motivation behind the move to Wapping lay in the desire to expand. At its previous locations around Fleet Street the opportunities for expansion were denied both by available space, limiting production capacity and distribution, and by manning agreements limiting the size of each edition.

The change to Wapping and the adoption of new printing technology had clear implications for organizational **structure**. A much more flexible structure has emerged for the newspaper industry. The role of the journalist has potentially broadened to assume responsibility for typesetting as well as content. The electricians have emerged as a fast-growing occupational group within the industry. Such changes in work allocation have implications also for management control.

Changes in the newspaper industry have been related to major changes in the **ownership** of national titles. The acquisition strategies of News International led to the grouping of five major titles under a single ownership. More significantly, the ownership style was one that had developed in Australia and the USA, where new technology in the newspaper industry was well established. Ownership changes away from Fleet Street were also having an impact. We have already made reference to the catalytic effect of Eddie Shah, but ownership changes in some local newspapers like the *Notts Evening Post* led to a much more aggressive style by management, especially towards trade unions and the introduction of new technology.

Changes in ownership often went hand in hand with changes in goals. Historically newspapers have often been regarded as a special kind of product under the control of individual press barons, such as Lord Beaverbrook at the *Daily Express*. As such, profit goals have co-existed with the less common business goals of political, social or moral reform. Increasingly major titles have come under the control of business groups in which newspapers represent just one of a highly diversified stable of products. An extreme case here would be the holding company Lonrho's acquisition of the *Observer* Sunday newspaper. It is unlikely that such changes have taken place without a corresponding elevation of purely business goals. The case illustrates goal conflict in various ways. At its most obvious this is represented by the unions' need to retain job control in the face of a management desire to reap the cost savings of new technology. The NGA and SOGAT's goal of union solidarity is sharply contrasted with the EETPU's goal of expansion. From an industrial relations perspective the case is interesting in revealing how goals shift as disputes develop; in this case from issues of job control to the negotiation of an acceptable redundancy package.

Strategic aspects

We have seen that changes at News International and in Fleet Street generally have been part of a pattern of interrelated environmental and organizational factors. These changes have resulted in changed culture within national newspaper organizations. A significant contribution to that changing culture has been the changes that have taken place in management strategy. In general terms Fleet Street management appears to have shifted from a reactive, crisis-induced strategy to one typified by long-term, planned technological and organizational change. A combination of a technological imperative and market and economic conditions has led management to adopt a more confident and, as some would term it, aggressive approach in dealing with the trade unions. A widely voiced speculation concerning the strategic implications of News International's move to Wapping was that it represented a deliberate confrontation with the trade unions as a prelude to changing work practices once and for all. The unions certainly believed that Wapping was never intended for a new evening paper and that all along it was designed as the operating centre for the company's major titles. Certainly the initial management proposals, effectively removing the union's traditional control of work practices, were ones to which the union were never likely to agree.

Aside from management, the case is an interesting illustration of strategy from a trade union perspective. Trade unions are faced with the problem of declining membership in an unfavourable economic and political climate. Like businesses in a declining market they have to be very careful about their choice of strategic option. In such a situation the case of new technology presents an interesting dilemma; its acceptance by unions would inevitably entail job losses, yet a refusal to negotiate may have far more serious consequences for the future bargaining position of the union. Just as some businesses find declining markets favourable for growth, some trade unions can take advantage of seemingly disadvantageous conditions by proposing deals acceptable to management. In this way the EETPU has embarked upon a fairly vigorous growth strategy, not only securing recognition rights, but in doing so creating work for electricians.

On a broader front, the case illustrates the increasingly global nature of business strategies. News International has always been far more than Wapping, but, since the dispute, News International has grown into a vast complex global network of companies with more recent acquisitions focusing on film and television, and most growth taking place in the USA. The complexity of this global structure and the variations in national tax laws have been used by the company to its advantage.

Functional aspects

At the heart of management strategy in this case are the implications for the functional operations of business. All our functional areas are implicated by News International's move to Wapping.

Innovation

Changes in News International's operations have obviously been made possible through process innovations in the newspaper industry. Other types of innovation are illustrated by this case, more especially the entrepreneurial activity of industry newcomers like Shah, attempting to break the traditional Fleet Street monopoly on national newspaper titles.

Operations

The new site operating under the latest technology offers management a speedier and more flexible operation with a capability of increased capacity. The new location offers all the benefits of a greenfield site, with particular improvements in the supply of raw materials and the distribution of the finished product.

Marketing

In marketing terms, the case illustrates how the need for change has arisen through increased competition and reduced barriers to entry for would-be competitors. The new printing processes offer the reader and the advertiser the potential for a much improved product. In the 1990s, major newspapers used product size and price as major competitive weapons. During one period of intense competition, profits were secondary to increased market share.

Accounting

Major motivations behind changes in the newspaper industry have been declining readership and reduced profits. The cost of setting up a new operating plant and its commissioning with state-of-the-art technology represents a considerable short-term investment with a potential for long-term cost saving. It is, however, important from a management perspective that operations commence at the new plant as soon as possible. The globalization of News International's operations meant that opportunities for enhanced profit were available through the management and movement of finances across national boundaries.

Human resources

The case focuses around the industrial relations aspects of the transfer to Wapping and the introduction of new technology. The marketing and accounting factors identified above put pressure on the need for a speedy agreement with the unions. On the other hand the setting up of a greenfield site has presented management with an ideal opportunity to introduce a completely new set of personnel and industrial relations policies.

The systems and contingency approaches

We have stressed both in the editor's foreword and elsewhere in this introductory chapter that the various elements of our model interact with one another and influences go backwards and forwards across the various levels (see Figure 1.1). We are presenting an interaction–influence model. The idea of such a model for businesses is not new but forms the basis of the systems and contingency approaches, which have been developed as part of organization theory. It is not our intention to present either a comprehensive review or a critique of these two approaches. Instead we present a brief summary of their main ideas. Their importance as far as we are concerned is that they offer the student of business an important framework for analysis.

KEY CONCEPT 1.4
The systems approach

The systems approach is a view of business involving two related concepts. First, businesses are made up of a series of interactions, involving the various business activities, the various aspects of the organization, and aspects of the environment. What we identify as a business is the sum total of all these influences and interactions. Second, the systems approach views business as a series of inputs from the environment, internal processes and eventual outputs.

The systems approach assumes that all organizations are made up of interdependent parts which can only be understood by reference to the whole. As such, organizations may be analysed in terms of inputs, processes and outputs, as we illustrate in Figure 1.2. We can see from this that there are many similarities with our own model.

The development of systems thinking from an organizational perspective starts with the analogy of the firm as a living organism. To be effective, the firm, like the organism, must adapt to its environment in order to survive. The inputs, processes and outputs must be balanced so that the firm can

Figure **1.2** The systems approach.

obtain equilibrium, especially with its environment. The application of the systems approach in organizational analysis first gained prominence through the utilization of a socio-technical systems perspective. This is based on the assumption that the social system of the firm and its technical system inter-act in a complex way. The approach was popularized in the work of the Tavistock Institute and its associated researchers throughout the world using the same framework of analysis in different cultural settings (see for example Trist and Bamforth, 1951; Rice, 1958; Emery and Thorsrud, 1976). Unless the social system and the technical system work in harmony, a firm will be inefficient.

KEY CONCEPT 1.5
The contingency approach

The contingency approach focuses on the relationship between the organization and its environment. It embraces the notion that business activities and the way they are organized are products of the environment in which they operate. The most successful businesses are therefore those that are organized to take advantage of the prevailing environmental influences.

The contingency approach can be traced through the work of Woodward (1965) and Burns and Stalker (1966), although the term itself was popularized in the work of Lawrence and Lorsch who wrote,

> Organizational variables are in a complex interrelationship with one another and with conditions in the environment. If an organization's internal states and processes are consistent with external demands ... it will be effective in dealing with the environment.

> (Lawrence and Lorsch, 1967, p. 157)

The contingency approach starts with an analysis of the key environmental variables, which shape the organization. It then proceeds with the assumption that the successful firms are those that adapt to the key influences and achieve some kind of best fit with their environment. This approach has been very influential in the area of corporate strategy. The strategist attempts to match the environmental opportunities and threats with the organization's own strengths and weaknesses to develop an optimum strategy for the firm in question.

Both the systems and contingency approaches are based on the concept of an organization interacting with several key elements in its environment and adapting to them. Some writers (e.g., Burrell and Morgan, 1979, pp. 164–81) regard the contingency approach as an extension of the systems analysis of organizations. Both approaches have been criticized for focusing on a limited range of environmental variables, for being deterministic, and for ignoring both the influence of the organization on its environment and the values and behaviour of management and the workforce. It is our view that such criticisms place unnecessary limits on the use and value of both approaches. In developing our model of business we wish to use systems and contingency thinking to present a broad analytical framework, enabling us to gain a greater insight into the way businesses operate. We are concerned to show, however, that businesses, while influenced by their environments, are not wholly determined by them. Business strategies can and do influence environmental contingencies.

The layout of this book

The chapters which follow will analyse each of the various elements of our Business in Context model. After examining these elements students are recommended to return to the European car industry and News International cases presented in this opening chapter.

Chapters 2 to 4 will look at the environmental, organizational and strategic contexts respectively. The variables identified in Figure 1.1 will be examined in turn. In our discussion of these variables certain issues emerge which call for more detailed consideration. One such issue is globalization. In our treatment of culture as an environmental variable we deal at some length with the phenomenon known as 'Japanese management', and in viewing size as an organizational variable raise the topic of small businesses. Such issues are chosen both for their interest to the student of business and, more significantly, because they illustrate further the workings of our Business in Context model by drawing together the various activities and their contexts.

Chapters 5 to 9 will focus on the functional areas of business we have chosen to examine: innovation, operations, marketing, human resource management and finance and accounting. Once again we will emphasize their relationship with each other and with our three levels of interaction and influence. The final chapter of the book will attempt to draw together the key interactions and influences involving businesses in recent years.

Summary

In this introductory chapter we have outlined the workings of our Business in Context model and in so doing mapped out the rest of this book. In the model we identify a number of key variables which interact with business. We have arranged these variables in a series of levels, which we have termed environmental, organizational and strategic. We believe that our understanding of the way businesses and their key activities operate is enhanced by placing them in this contextual framework.

The workings of the model can be seen by reference to two cases. The first deals with the European car industry and in particular the strategies employed by management in the face of oversupply and high levels of competition in a static home market. The second case looks at a single company, News International, and focuses on the events surrounding relocation, technical change and a major labour dispute in 1985. The theoretical underpinnings of the model are discussed with reference to the systems and contingency approaches to organizational analysis.

Discussion

1. We have identified five environmental and five organizational variables in our model. By necessity these represent broad categories. What are the possible elements that might be considered under the various headings used in our model of business?

2. Using the way we have analysed the two cases as your guide, take in turn an industry, a firm and a specific issue, and analyse each using the Business in Context model.

3. What is the value of the systems and contingency approaches to an understanding of business?

CHAPTER 2

The environment and business

In Chapter 1 we introduced the model which forms the basis of our analysis of business. In this chapter we focus on a major element of that model, namely the environment. We define the environment as comprising all factors that exist outside the business enterprise, but that interact with it. As we pointed out in the last chapter, all firms are to a greater or lesser extent constrained by the environment within which they operate, but the activities of businesses themselves also change that same environment. This two-way process is an important theme throughout the book.

In devoting just one chapter to the business environment, the material is necessarily highly selective. Five key areas have been identified, namely the economy, the role of the state, technology, labour and culture. We devote a section to each of these topics and identify issues that illustrate the interaction between the firm and its environment. Each of the areas selected also interacts with the others, as the matrix presented in Figure 2.1 shows.

For the business manager, the environment therefore comprises a number of key variables, which interact with the business either singly or jointly. The complexity does not end there. These interactions may occur on a number of different levels, as shown in Figure 2.2. First, a firm interacts with a local environment, in which expansion plans may need approval from the local council, and where its marketing and personnel strategies will be significantly influenced by firms operating in the same local market. Second, interaction occurs in a national environment, influenced by such matters as government laws, bank interest rates, the rate of inflation, and national employment policies. Third, we have the international environment in which the firm may be affected by international money exchange rates, competition from cheap labour economies, and the regulations of supranational bodies such as the World Trade Organization and the European Union. In recent years the international environment has become increasingly significant for businesses through the process of globalization. As a general rule, the ability of managers to influence their environment diminishes as they move further away from the local environment. As with all such rules there are exceptions, since the ability to influence the environment tends to increase with the size of the firm. We shall see in our discussion of globalization and multinationals in the next section that the management of larger conglomerates can exert influences that extend beyond national boundaries to change international economics and politics, with a significant impact on local economies and labour markets.

		Technology	State	Economy
State				The extent and direction of state intervention in the economy. The power of the multinationals in influencing policy
Technology			State support of innovation and technical change and the specific impact on certain industries, e.g. defence	The impact of innovation on economic growth.
Labour		The impact of technical change on skills and trade union policy towards such changes.	Government policies to direct the supply of labour. Legislation to regulate trade union activities.	The impact of the economy on the type and levels of employment.
Culture	Cultural influences on human resource strategies.	The impact of changes in technology on society. Cultural attitudes towards technology	Cultural explanations for the differences between nations regarding state intervention.	The nature of the economy shaping family life, e.g. agricultural vs industrial societies. The influence of cultural values on the directions of economic development and specialization.

Figure **2.1** The interaction of environmental factors: some illustrations.

We will deal with each of our five variables in turn. As we stressed in Chapter 1, each of them represents broad categories; for example, the role of the state will deal with issues pertaining to the general political environment. The chapter closes with a treatment of 'Japanese management', despite the relative decline of the Japanese economy in the 1990s. The issues of Japan and 'Japanese management' remain highly relevant for a number of reasons. Japanese methods have had a considerable influence in many areas of business, most notably in operations management. The issue of the rise of the post-war Japanese economy provides us with insights into the relative significance of cultural, economic and political variables. Moreover, Japan represents a fascinating case study of a business community being shaped by and shaping its environment.

Figure **2.2** Levels of the environment.

The economy and business

With many aspects of our environment we are faced with the immediate problem of deciding where the environment ends and business begins and vice versa. In looking at the relationship between business and the economy this becomes particularly acute since much of what we label as the economy is the product of business activity. By the same token, business enterprises are influenced significantly by economic developments. Figure 2.3 is an attempt to illustrate this relationship in the form of a simple model. In this section we will examine the model by focusing on the experience of Britain in the post-war period, although, inevitably, comparisons will be drawn from other countries. Britain along with most capitalist countries is an example of a mixed economy, where free enterprise is mixed with state involvement through public ownership, legal regulation, and various forms of planning and direction. In the 1980s attempts were made through government policy to change the balance of that relationship to favour the workings of the free market. For this reason there is considerable overlap between the economy and the role of the state, dealt with in the next section. We will examine the impact of the post-1980 policies as we enter the twenty-first century. Obviously a much fuller account of the relationship between business and the economy can be found in the economics text in this series (see Neale *et al.*, 2000).

The economy interacts with businesses at all three levels depicted in Figure 2.2. At the local level, immediate competitive issues related to firms operating in the same product market are the most significant. If the Virgin record store in London's Oxford Street reduces the price of all its compact discs by £1.00 or more then the management of the large HMV store just down the road must determine their most appropriate strategic response. This may involve adopting the same price strategy or it may involve a more selective strategy offering larger discounts on big-selling items. In the 1960s labour shortages meant that firms actively competed for labour and often increased pay and bonus rates to attract labour from their competitors. Such conditions re-emerged in the market for IT specialists in the late 1990s. Such competition

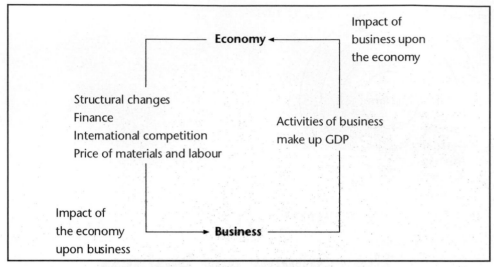

Figure **2.3** Business and the economy.

can reach particularly fierce proportions and many firms prefer to cooperate rather than compete on issues like price or wage rates. In this way some businesses form themselves into cartels which may be an effective way of controlling the immediate competitive environment, and perhaps the wider environment too, as in influencing government policy. There are several examples of groups of local grocers being formed to buy in bulk from suppliers in an attempt keep prices down and combat the threat posed by large supermarkets. The supermarkets themselves, while not behaving as a cartel, employ staff to keep a watch on the prices displayed by their competitors and respond accordingly. We deal with the competitive environment in more detail in Chapter 4 and students are referred to Porter's model illustrated in Figure 4.3. For the rest of this section we will illustrate the relationship between the firm and the economy by focusing on issues mainly, but not exclusively, at the national and international levels.

The impact of business on the economy

All businesses produce goods and services and provide employment. In doing so they contribute to a nation's income, its capital assets, and its economic growth. Economies are often compared on the basis of their gross domestic product (GDP), the sum total of the net outputs of each sector of the economy. In Table 2.1 we show actual levels of GDP and the GDP per head of population (GDP per capita), both expressed in US dollars. There are some omissions but nearly all the leading countries in their various regions are included. Tables 2.2 and 2.3 take the top 10 countries by GDP per head and total GDP respectively.

The data reveals a number of interesting points. There is an obvious gap between the rich and poor nations of the world. The gap is actually greater than shown, given that the poorest countries are not included in the tables.

Table **2.1** GDP per head estimates for 1999 in rank order by region

Country	Total GDP $bn	GDP per head $
Europe		
Switzerland	273.2	37 891
Norway	165.3	37 339
Denmark	186.4	35 073
Sweden	251.3	28 312
Germany	2 431.4	27 418
Austria	222.2	27 347
Belgium	259.8	25 445
France	1 622.7	25 425
Finland	131.2	25 364
Netherlands	396.7	25 159
United Kingdom	1 450.6	23 478
Ireland	83.2	22 537
Italy	1 294.3	21 685
Spain	592.1	15 032
Portugal	117.6	11 846
Greece	124.0	11 739
Czech Republic	56.6	5 538
Hungary	51.9	5 134
Estonia	4.8	4 275
Poland	160.7	4 149
Romania	43.5	4 149
Slovakia	19.5	3 613
Turkey	207.5	3 159
Ukraine	45.6	3 158
Russia	239.7	2 466
Bulgaria	13.0	1 585
Asia Pacific		
Singapore	87.6	27 181
Japan	3 190.0	25 129
Hong Kong	159.6	23 474
Australia	368.6	19 462
New Zealand	52.4	13 502
Taiwan	264.7	12 074
South Korea	287.0	6 135
Malaysia	63.0	2 772
Thailand	131.7	2 135
Philippines	69.0	899
China	978.3	779
Indonesia	122.9	590
Pakistan	61.4	405
India	376.8	382
Vietnam	25.7	324

*Table **2.1** continued*

The Americas		
USA	8 848.4	32 616
Canada	622.2	20 250
Argentina	223.9	6 177
Chile	82.6	5 497
Brazil	789.4	4 820
Venezuela	111.0	4 606
Mexico	452.4	4 559
Colombia	102.6	2 466
Middle East and Africa		
Israel	97.6	16 138
Saudi Arabia	149.2	7 126
Lebanon	18.6	4 389
South Africa	105.1	2 616
Algeria	51.3	1 657
Jordan	8.6	1 439
Egypt	89.5	1 386
Iran	85.7	1 352
Kenya	9.0	295
Nigeria	30.6	276
Iraq	5.7	247

Source: Economist Intelligence Unit, 1999.

Table **2.2** GDP per head estimates for 1999 for top 10 countries

Country	Total GDP $bm	GDP per head $
Switzerland	273.2	37 891
Norway	165.3	37 339
Denmark	186.4	35 073
USA	8 848.4	32 616
Sweden	251.3	28 312
Germany	2 431.4	27 418
Austria	222.2	27 347
Singapore	87.6	27 181
Belgium	259.8	25 445
France	1 622.7	25 425

Source: Economist Intelligence Unit, 1999.

Table **2.3** Total GDP estimates for 1999 for top 10 countries

Country	Total GDP $bn	GDP per head $
USA	8 848.4	32 616
Japan	3 190.0	25 129
Germany	2 431.4	27 418
France	1 622.7	25 425
United Kingdom	1 450.6	23 478
Italy	1 294.3	21 685
China	978.3	779
Brazil	789.4	4 820
Canada	622.2	20 250
Spain	592.1	15 032

Source: Economist Intelligence Unit, 1999.

The relative gap also shows between the countries of West and East Europe and reveals the especially poor position of Russia, given its large population. The large populations of China and India also account for the very low GDP per head compared with the total GDP. In total GDP terms, China appears as the seventh largest economy in the world, yet the GDP per head is only US$779 per year. The figures for many of the Asian economies reflect the crash of 1997 and the the troubled 1990s for Japan means that the world's second largest economy does not feature in the top 10 economies when measured in terms of GDP per head. Japan has lost its top spot in the region on GDP per capita to Singapore. (Further aspects of these economic changes can be found in Cases 2.4 and 2.5.) The UK features as the world's fifth largest economy but in terms of GDP per head it ranks only 11th in Europe and 14th in world terms.

Key issues for business managers are also key economic issues. These may be identified as products, productivity, markets, profits and the supply of labour. These themes re-emerge when we discuss the role of the economy in the chapters on the various activities of business. For example, in Chapter 5 we examine the view that economic growth is dependent upon product and process innovation.

The impact of the economy on business

There are a variety of ways in which economic changes have affected businesses in this country. We will illustrate these changes through the changing nature of world economies, including structural changes, the supply and price of raw materials, increased international competition and the emergence of globalization as a dominant influence. Central to the development of globalization is the impact of multinational firms. These illustrate the difficulty of isolating business and environmental influences. Many businesses in this country have undoubtedly been influenced by a world economy increasingly dominated by multinational corporations. These same multinationals are themselves businesses with the ability to influence national and international economies.

Changes in the world economy have, for a country like Britain, led to major structural changes involving the decline of the manufacturing sector (de-industrialization) and the growth of the service sector, especially the financial sector. In turn these changes have had a significant impact on levels of employment, causing high levels of unemployment in those areas formerly dominated by traditional manufacturing industry, while creating many new jobs in the emerging financial services industry. We deal with these issues in more detail at the end of this section on the economy.

The availability of key resources can not only have a significant influence on the fortunes of individual firms, but can also lead to structural changes. In 1973 OPEC, representing the oil-producing countries, decided to restrict the supply of oil, with a subsequent dramatic increase in price. Similar price rises occurred in 1979. The impact on businesses in this country were several. Increased costs were passed on in the form of increased prices, or resulted in reduced profits, with some firms unable to compete. Some industries sought substitute products with corresponding increases in demand for products of the coal and gas industries. Rising petrol prices meant increased costs of transport and led to major product changes in the car industry. These changes were even more significant in the USA, with a dramatic reduction in car size and the imposition of a national speed limit on all roads, the legacy of which remains today. When Britain became a major oil producer, changes in the price of oil had an effect upon the exchange value of sterling. An exchange rate strengthened by an oil economy meant that British exports became more expensive and particularly damaging for those businesses that depended for a large proportion of their revenue on exported goods. The whole issue of the exchange value of sterling is presented in more detail in Case 2.1, which charts the fall of the pound against other major currencies in 1992 and the impact this had for certain types of business.

Changes in the car industry, as we saw in Chapter 1, and the problems brought about by shifting exchange rates identified above are linked to a marked increase in the international dimension of most types of business. This has taken the form of a dramatic growth in international competition, initially from Japan, but more recently from other South East Asian economies such as Taiwan and Singapore. (Cases 2.4 and 2.5 examine the link between economics, politics and business in the Asian Tigers.) The decline in competitiveness of many of Britain's industries, such as shipbuilding, motorcycles, domestic electrical products and cars, has been attributed to the rise of cheap labour economies, especially those in the Far East, or the product superiority of manufacturers in countries such as Japan and Germany. However, our perspective of international competition must be revised constantly, so dynamic are the forces at work. While de-industrialization in many 'advanced

Case 2.1: Black Wednesday and the collapse of the pound

In the four months leading up to September 1992 the British government under Prime Minister John Major was optimistic that their economic policies would bring about a long-awaited recovery. The government was re-elected in the previous April when many predicted a clear defeat. Both inflation and interest rates had fallen, and Germany with the strongest economy and strongest currency in Europe was experiencing economic problems following reunification. The prime minister himself had begun a six-month presidency of the European Community and to the UK media he had expressed a prediction that sterling would once again emerge as the leading European currency.

Britain was a member of the European Monetary System (EMS) within which 11 EC members operated fixed exchange rates within agreed margins of fluctuation. This was known as the Exchange Rate Mechanism (ERM). The German Deutsche Mark, as the strongest currency, was the benchmark against which all other currencies were measured. By Wednesday 17 September, the pound had reached its ERM floor level of DM2.77 on the foreign exchange market. The Chancellor of the Exchequer, Norman Lamont, attempted to support the falling pound by using UK foreign currency reserves to buy sterling. Estimates ranged from £10 billion to £15 billion as to the money spent. Interest rates were immediately raised from 10 to 12 per cent with a further 3 per cent increase promised the following day. This had no impact on the downward trend of the pound and it fell to DM2.68 almost immediately. By the end of the next day it had reached DM2.62 and closed the week at DM2.61. The pound also fell against the US dollar, from US$1.92 at its highest point in the week to US$1.74 by the close. The EC Monetary Committee met during the week and Britain requested a lowering of German interest rates to save the falling pound. This was not forthcoming and Britain, along with Italy, temporarily left the ERM, while Spain devalued by 5 per cent.

There are several reasons for the fall in sterling and the decision to withdraw, albeit temporarily, from the ERM. One of the major factors was a problem in the German economy. The cost of unification with the former East Germany was considerable, not least of which was the government's support of the old East German currency, assimilated into the German system on a par with the Deutsche Mark. The subsequent increase of cash in the German economy had led to an increase in the demand for goods which supply could not meet. This in turn led to price increases and the German economy was faced with an inflation rate of 4.8 per cent. While not large by world standards, it was for the Germans, who possess a fear of inflation linked to the problems of the 1930s. In order to combat inflation, the German government raised interest rates to 9.75 per cent. The strength and stability of the Deutsche Mark has always seen it as the favoured currency for investors. As a result of the rise in the German interest rate, other countries were forced to do likewise to prevent their currencies being sold to buy Deutshe Marks. The USA was one country that did not raise its interest rates. Economic policy in the USA saw low interest rates as a means of stimulating an economy in recession. With low interest rates firms might be encouraged to borrow money to invest in new products and processes or to expand existing businesses. Interest rates in the USA had fallen to 3 per cent and US investors, seeing the rise in German interest rates, bought marks. As a result the Deutsche Mark became even stronger.

Three other events occurred around 17 September that added fuel to the sterling crisis. The Italian lira was also in trouble in the ERM and the currency was devalued by 7 per cent. Experts were quick to point to other currencies in trouble, with the pound as the prime candidate. There was also considerable speculation about a forthcoming French referendum on the Maastricht Treaty, an important plank in the EC move towards greater unity. The referendum was an attempt by the French government to strengthen its own position by gaining popular support for its policies on EC unity and the move towards a single European currency. However, the polls were predicting a close vote. This in turn caused further speculation on the money markets with the growing weakness of lira and sterling. At the same time there was a leak of an interview that Deutschebundesbank President Helmut Schlesinger had allegedly given to *Handelsblatt*, the German business paper, and to the *Wall Street Journal*. While the precise details of the text were disputed, the message given by the media was that he believed that sterling should be devalued along with the lira.

▶

Continued

The factors identified above were cited as the prime reasons for speculation and foreign exchange activity leading to the fall in the value of the pound. However, some saw these events as triggers which exposed Britain's fundamental problem, its weak economy. Many dealers and economic experts considered the pound to be overvalued at DM2.77, particularly since imports were greater than exports despite a fall in UK spending. A UK interest rate of 10 per cent was also viewed by many as an obstacle to economic recovery. The two-year membership of the ERM had, for some, masked the problem of an overvalued currency, which events of the week of 14 September had simply exposed.

Contributory factors were undoubtedly the structure of the UK financial market and the increased sophistication of information technology. A previous Conservative government under Mrs Thatcher, as part of its commitment to free markets, had deregulated the financial markets and abolished exchange controls. This had made it easier for investors to buy and sell not only shares but currencies as well and had led to a dramatic increase in both financial services firms and the number of dealings. Most of these firms had access to the latest information technology. This has made possible electronic international money transfers and provides instant information on such deals and anything else that might affect the market. The slightest change in patterns of buying and selling currency is known instantly around the world, as are the actions of governments and even rumours. In this way a slight shift in the value of the pound can turn easily into a major movement. The actions of Chancellor Lamont to stem the fall of the pound were known at once around the world, and probably interpreted as a sign of panic, resulting in further sales of sterling.

The immediate impact of the pound's fall and the UK government's decision to leave the ERM was profit for the dealers and a loss to the UK economy of between £750 million and £1 billion on its own dealing to protect sterling. Share trading increased, as did fears amongst the business community of higher inflation and even higher interest rates that both would hinder economic recovery. However, not all were threatened. Firms such as Shell, BP, British Aerospace, Rolls Royce Aero-engines and British Airways conducted their businesses to a greater or lesser extent in US dollars, and thus the sterling value of their dealings would rise. Some firms with a large US market, like Jaguar, anticipated increased sales. Overall, however, the UK imported £17.3 billion and exported £14.6 billion worth of goods to Germany and imported £13.7 billion worth of US goods as opposed to exporting £11.3 billion. Unless the balance in the volume of goods were to change, the impact of a lower pound would be a widening of the trade deficit.

In the UK much party political capital was made of the government's failed economic policies of stable exchange rates and lowering interest rates. In Europe there was much bickering. John Major blamed the Germans for maintaining high interest rates and there was an intensification of the debate on Maastricht, the ERM and even the whole issue of European unity.

Ultimately it would appear that market forces, so beloved of John Major's predecessor, had operated against government policy. Sterling had probably entered the ERM at too high a rate. Almost certainly this affected UK competitiveness and had prevented interest rates coming down below 10 per cent. As Ruth Lea, the Chief Economist for Mitsubishi Bank, stated, 'the ironic thing is that we may get an economic recovery because the Government's policy failed.' (*The Independent*, 18 September 1992).

Almost a year later, in August 1993, the pound was valued at DM2.54 and US$1.48, and the UK interest rate was 6 per cent. High German interest rates persisted and the French franc was under pressure to devalue along with the Spanish pesata, the Portuguese escudo and the Danish krone. Speculation was rife as to the future of the ERM, with a number of countries threatening to leave.■

(*Sources*: *Financial Times*, *Independent*, *Independent on Sunday*, *Observer* 17–20 September 1992, 1–3 August 1993)

economies' was linked to a switch of manufacturing to those aforementioned cheap labour economies, such economies are becoming less cheap and, far from lagging behind, they began to take the lead in certain areas of manufacturing technology and product development. The dynamic forces continue to work, as we see in Case 2.4, leading to an economic downturn amongst the former rising stars of South East Asia.

Globalization

We have already referred to globalization as the dominant force operating in business today. If globalization is the force, then it is carried by the battalions of multinational corporations to impact on every corner of the globe. In this section we offer an overview of globalization and then focus on the multinational corporation.

Globalization has been defined as,

> A social process in which the constraints of geography on social and cultural arrangements recede and in which people become increasingly aware they are receding.
>
> (Walters, 1995, p.3)

KEY CONCEPT 2.1
Globalization

Globalization is a process in which the world appears to be converging economically, politically and culturally. It is considered by many to be the dominant force in modern business. In economic terms, many firms are producing goods and services for global markets, using labour in various locations in the world and using global sources for raw materials and components. In the past 20 years there has been an acceleration of cultural exchange across the globe, helped, in part, by advances in travel and communications. Business and cultural globalization have been accompanied by political globalization through the activities of supranational bodies such as the United Nations, World Trade Organization and the European Union. There are strong links between globalization and the multinational corporation (Key Concept 2.2).

Walters offers a predominantly sociological approach, but a broad-based definition, where geographic and national boundaries become increasingly irrelevant economically, politically and culturally. A UK citizen buying a Ford car is buying the product of an American multinational corporation, which could well have been made in Germany by *Gastarbeiters* from Turkey and Italy, fitting spark plugs from the Nippondenso corporation in Japan but spark plugs made in the Philippines. The internationalization of production and supply has been accompanied by the internationalization of finance. This in turn has been accompanied by the internationalization of telecommunications, which has facilitated global transactions in production and finance and greatly increased the diffusion of technology, ideas and information. As a result, both markets and societies have become extremely sensitive to changes happening in other parts of the world. In Case 2.1 we examine the volatility of currency markets and in Case 2.4 we look at the 1997 crisis in South East Asia, both of which demonstrate this sensitivity. Economic globalization is connected with cultural globalization as new product markets are created by the global expansion of certain brands like Coca Cola, Nike or McDonald's, as well as films and

45

television programmes such as the *The Simpsons*. Such developments say as much about culture change as they do about economic change, a point we return to in our discussion of convergence and culture later in this chapter. Economic and cultural globalization are accompanied by political globalization and the increasing importance of supranational bodies, a point we return to in our section on the state and business.

Predictions of the growth of globalization can be traced back to the end of the eighteenth and beginning of the nineteenth century in the writings of such as Marx, Lenin, Weber and Durkheim. The former two saw globalization as the inevitable consequence of capitalism and the need for expanding markets, while the latter writers saw a growing similarity in many societies as a result of the processes of industrialization. The ideas of Weber and Durkheim re-emerged in the 1950s as part of the 'convergence hypothesis' (Kerr *et al.*, 1973). Kerr and his colleagues maintained that societies were becoming more alike as a result of the diffusion of productive technology. This meant that manufacture the world over was based on similar principles, using similar machine tools. This led to similar forms of occupational differentiation requiring similar forms of training and hence a convergence of educational systems the world over. Developments in productive technology led to mass production, which in turn led to the need for mass markets and global products. The changes taking place in training and education, together with the spread of global products, resulted in a change of values and hence culture change. The ideas of convergence through manufacture developed into ideas of convergence through the micro-electronics and telecommunications revolution and the creation of the so-called post-industrial society (Bell, 1973). As a result of this, UK holiday-makers to Spain can obtain their favourite tabloid newspaper on the morning of issue. As we see in Case 2.1, money market and stock market changes in London are instantly visible in Frankfurt, New York, Tokyo and anywhere else in the world with the technological capability. Further implications of developments in electronics and telecommunications are presented in the section on technology later in this chapter.

As we shall see in the next section, developments in globalization are closely linked to the growth of the multinational corporation. For some writers, notably Reich (1993), there has been a change over the past 25 years in which multinationals have moved from being seen as representatives of their country of origin to be, in effect, independent global players. Under this system, exports are superseded by inward investment as measures of a nation's economic success. The key driver of this change has been the need for firms to find markets large enough to match the scale and cost of their technological investments. In some cases this has been accompanied by the growth of cross-border strategic alliances between firms and in all cases facilitated by the relative ease of travel and electronic communication. As we shall see in the next chapter, some firms such as Ford have changed their organization structure to match a borderless, global operation. However, not all writers see a reduced role for the nation state. Porter (1990), while acknowledging the general principles of globalization, argues that in the development of national economies, growth is a function of a set of competitive conditions which result in clusters of successful firms operating in the same industry and reinforced by the growth of associated industries as suppliers to the major firms. He cites the car industry in the USA, the chemical industry in Germany and the electronics industry in Japan as examples. It is undoubtedly true that economic development in a particular country is accompanied by a concentration of like firms in a particular area, such as the car industry around Detroit, Michigan and the computer industry around 'Silicon Valley' in California.

The multinational corporation

We have already noted that an important aspect of globalization has been the market dominance of the multinational corporation. Trade and finance have always been international and there are many interesting examples of early multinationals. Kikkoman, the Japanese company manufacturing soy sauce, established a factory in Denver in the USA in the 1890s to supply the Chinese workers on the expanding US rail network. The British American Tobacco Corporation had established itself in China by 1914 and employed 25 000 Chinese workers by 1920. The company invested in cinemas and the film industry in China in the 1920s, not only to sell cigarettes and tobacco at cinema outlets, but also to feature cigarette smoking in all their films to promote sales (Jones, 1996). It was not until the post-war period that the large American conglomerate with its divisionalized structure was attracted to expanding European markets. While Europe initially provided an open door to American investment, later protectionist policies set up by the then European Economic Community accelerated the growth of American subsidiaries in Europe. Japanese firms have also invested in both Europe and the USA for the same reasons.

The multinational has had a significant impact on national economies in a variety of ways. Multinational companies tend to be very large. Table 2.4 shows that if we equate GDP with sales, then 20 of the world's 60 largest economic entities are companies. If the list included measures of market capitalization, then Microsoft would feature at $200 billion. Such tables raise a number of issues about the relative power of corporations and nation states

---

KEY CONCEPT 2.2
The multinational corporation

A multinational firm is one that operates from bases in a number of different countries. While small firms can and do operate multinationally, most multinationals are large corporations with diverse interests coordinated by a centrally planned global strategy. Many multinationals tend to compete in oligopolistic markets. Multinational growth was originally associated with firms from the USA and Europe, although there has been a significant growth in multinational activity from firms in Asia, notably from Japan. The growth of the global economy has resulted in many multinationals becoming truly international businesses with weakening ties with their original country of origin. Some writers have referred to such firms as transnational corporations.

Table **2.4** The world's top 40 economic entities in 1995. Countries listed by GDP. Companies listed by sales value

		US$ bn
1.	USA	7100
2.	Japan	4964
3.	Germany	2252
4.	France	1451
5.	United Kingdom	1095
6.	Italy	1088
7.	China	745
8.	Brazil	580
9.	Canada	574
10.	Spain	534
11.	South Korea	435
12.	Netherlands	371
13.	Australia	338
14.	Russia	332
15.	India	320
16.	Mexico	305
17.	Switzerland	286
18.	Argentina	278
19.	Taiwan	260
20.	Belgium	251
21.	Austria	217
22.	Sweden	210
23.	Indonesia	190
24.	Mitsubishi (Japan)	184
25.	Mitsui (Japan)	181
26.	Itochu (Japan)	169
27.	Turkey	169
28.	General Motors (USA)	169
29.	Sumitomo (Japan)	168
30.	Marubeni (Japan)	161
31.	Thailand	160
32.	Denmark	156
33.	Hong Kong	142
34.	Ford Motor (USA)	137
35.	Norway	136
36.	Saudi Arabia	134
37.	South Africa	131
38.	Toyota (Japan)	111
39.	Exxon (USA)	110
40.	Royal Dutch/Shell (Netherlands/UK)	110

Source: Observer, 8 March 1998.

and the impact that the former can have on the latter. Some commentators have noted that while, in most cases, governments are accountable to their electorate, multinationals are accountable, if at all, only to their most powerful global shareholders.

While they tend to be highly diversified, the multinational tends to concentrate in oligopolistic industries, those dominated by a few large companies, where the general pattern of competition is through expensive product development and expensive promotional strategies. The multinational corporation is able to draw upon a worldwide pool of skilled labour and exploit the advantages of centralized control and a centralized research and development function. Business empires are thus based around a centrally planned global strategy. Such a process has been formalized through the planning process of companies like 3M (Case 4.2). As a result of the economic and political dominance of multinationals they have been viewed as a key device in the diffusion of management ideas and methods.

A number of changes have been charted in the development of multinationals. The USA is still dominant in terms of the number of firms but has been joined by the expansion of the Japanese and European multinational. As Table 2.4 shows, the large Japanese conglomerates dominate in terms of value of sales. The focus for the location has also shifted, from Europe, then to Canada and Latin America, and most recently to South East Asia. With successive shifts in location there have been successive changes in rationale. The traditional motivation for multinational growth was associated with accessing both the supply of raw materials and new markets. The growing investments in process and product technologies meant that home markets were too small and overseas expansion was imperative to exploit economies of scale. Concern then shifted to reducing costs and locations were sought that gave access not only to low-cost materials, but also low-cost labour, low-cost rents and low rates of corporate taxation.

Bartlett and Ghoshal (1995) see these developments in terms of a number of stages, which they term international, multinational, global and transnational, as indicated below.

Stage 1: **International** This is typified by a focus on a home base and the growth of exports.

Stage 2: **Multinational** Export markets continue to grow and the firm establishes operations outside the home country.

Stage 3: **Global** With increased competition, costs become the major consideration and operations are switched to locations offering cost advantages, e.g. low-cost labour markets.

Stage 4: **Transnational** International operation is a function of survival as high volume sales become essential to recover investment costs, particularly those associated with shorter product life cycles.

Associated features of the transnational corporation are the growth of alliances and the development of more complex strategies. We deal with alliances much more in Chapter 4; however, from the perspective of multi-national expansion, they offer such advantages as a sharing of R&D costs and access to new technologies, new products and new markets. The strategies move away from the focus on a single issue of market, supply or cost to embrace a mixture of strategies. Low-cost operation in cheap labour economies may be pursued for mass-market goods, whereas accessing skill and know-how may be more significant with more complex, high value-added products. LG, the Korean electronics firm, uses South East Asian locations for its mass-market products, such as televisions and video recorders. The same firm uses its US operations, and the experience of its subsidiaries such as Zenith, to develop more advanced products. High-cost start-up operations in such countries as China can be offset by more profitable ventures elsewhere.

Some writers (Adam, 1975; Harrison, 1981) see this shift in production as following a set pattern occurring in traditional declining labour-intensive industries with a reasonably long product life cycle or in the labour-intensive aspects of the more technologically based industries as with electronics or car manufacture. Both the shift in location and the emphasis on reduced costs have had a considerable impact upon the ability of non-multinationals to compete in manufacturing industry and upon levels of employment in the West, and especially Britain.

Much has been written about the impact of the multinational corporation on the economy of Third World countries (for example Harrison, 1981). While involvement in the Third World is done with the cooperation of host governments, leads to an inflow of capital, provides local employment and improves the balance of payments, there are considerable problems involved. These include the exploitation of natural resources, allegations of bribery and corruption, the expatriation of profits, price speculation, the tendency of multinationals to move both capital and financial assets to gain the most favourable tax and exchange rate advantages, and so on. In general, Third World economies become dominated by companies whose primary aim is the maximization of profit, when those countries might benefit more from a planned, local approach to development. Such issues relate to the accountability of multinational firms.

Multinationals continue to play a significant part in the UK economy. With the single exception of the USA, Britain invests more overseas than any other country. As for inward investment, Britain's attraction to foreign investors is bettered only by the USA and Canada. Apart from the obvious contribution foreign multinationals have made to UK employment, Britain's active role in multinational activity appears to have done little to enhance its economic position. The investment activities of UK firms overseas is focused on portfolio investment and, where manufacturing is concerned, the focus has been on low-tech goods for local markets. In both cases the contribution to GDP and balance of payments has been negligible. While the attraction of foreign manufacturers to the UK is encouraging, the marked trend is towards highly specialized aspects of a particular industry. This could result in a highly fragmented manufacturing base, an inappropriate base for sustained manufacturing growth. It is to this aspect that we now turn.

The impact of a changing economy on British business

> If you want to buy a small business, buy a large one and wait.
>
> (New English proverb)

The major changes in the UK economy since 1970 have been the decline of manufacturing and the growth of the service sector, the growth in numbers of long-term unemployed, the weakening of trade unions, and the shift from public to private ownership. We will deal with the last two aspects elsewhere in this chapter and here focus on the shift away from manufacturing to the service sector, and on rising unemployment. In the next section we argue that such changes are political and ideological as well as economic.

The decline of manufacturing industry in the UK has been well documented. Since the 1950s UK industry has lost market share to overseas competitors. In shipbuilding the UK was the world's leading exporter in 1950, yet in six years its market share fell from 38 per cent to 14 per cent. In 1955 the UK produced 70 per cent of the world's motorcycles, but was unable to meet the challenge first from the Italians and then from the Japanese. UK manufacturers retreated up-market only to be pursued and overtaken by the Japanese in every market segment. Case 2.2, Norton-Villiers-Triumph, explores the political dimension of the decline in motorcycle manufacture but an interesting dimension is the link between R&D and market share, an aspect explored in more detail in Chapter 5. In the late 1970s Norton-Villiers-Triumph employed 100 staff in R&D, while its Japanese competitors, Honda and Suzuki, employed 1000 each (Bowen, 1992).

While market share has declined, the domestic consumption of manufactured goods has increased. From 1973 to 1988 domestic expenditure on manufactured goods increased by 30 per cent while domestic output remained about the same (Wells, 1989). The impact of this has been a rise in imported goods and a worsening of the balance of payments deficit.

Apart from market share, the numbers employed in manufacturing are a good indication of the relative health of the manufacturing sector. Table 2.5 shows the decline of numbers employed in manufacturing 1971–91 relative to those employed in the USA, Germany and Japan. While other countries maintained their employment base in manufacturing, the UK lost 40 per cent of its manufacturing workforce. The decline in manufacturing employment was most severe during the recession of 1980–2. Optimistic commentators point to the impact such changes have had in clearing out ineffective and inefficient firms and how some firms and even entire industries are now more efficient and competitive. While this may be true, there is a real danger that manufacturing capacity has been lost to such an extent that it will be difficult to recover. As Wells (1989) states,

Table **2.5** Employment in manufacturing 1971–91

	UK	USA	Germany	Japan
1971	100	100	100	100
1972	97	103	98	99
1973	98	108	98	100
1974	98	108	96	99
1975	93	98	89	94
1976	90	102	87	91
1977	91	106	86	90
1978	91	110	86	89
1979	90	113	86	88
1980	85	109	87	89
1981	78	108	85	90
1982	73	101	82	91
1983	69	99	78	91
1984	67	104	78	92
1985	67	103	79	94
1986	65	102	80	94
1987	64	102	80	93
1988	65	104	80	94
1989	65	104	82	96
1990	64	103	84	97
1991	60	99	85	100

Source: Datastream International.

> UK manufacturing production which remains at the end of the Thatcher decade may well be leaner, fitter, have a higher level of labour productivity and be more profitable than before – but it is totally inadequate in terms of the volume of its internationally competitive capacity.
>
> (Wells, 1989, p.58)

The decline in manufacturing has often been linked solely with the policies of the Thatcher administration in the 1980s. With hindsight, political policies were part of a process that saw the shift of much of manufacturing to lower-cost countries as a result of globalization. However, as Table 2.5 shows, the speed of the process, assisted by policies of monetarism and non-intervention, undoubtedly meant that more companies failed to survive into the 1990s than would otherwise have been the case. The growth of manufacturing in electrical and computer-related industry in the UK of some 60 per cent may be encouraging signs of manufacturing recovery, but many of the new firms are foreign owned. The UK ends the twentieth century as the world's fifth largest economy, behind the USA, Japan, Germany and France, and its manufacturing firms are coping with the problems of a strong currency. With a strong currency, exports become more expensive, with the effect that selling prices must fall faster than costs for firms to compete globally. The 1997 fall of the Asian economies has made their products even cheaper and intensified that competition. Moreover, the growth of foreign ownership in UK manufacturing has threatened the UK supply industry with a switch from traditional sources to lower-cost alternatives elsewhere.

The decline of manufacturing in the UK has been contrasted with the rise in the service sector of the economy. For example, while all employment fell by 6.2 per cent between 1979 and 1986, employment in the service sector rose by 6.6 per cent. In some sectors such as financial services the increase in employment has been quite dramatic accompanying the deregulation by the government of financial markets. The growth of the service sector of the economy undoubtedly has its roots in the historical development of the British economy. The City has always been a focus of attention owing to early British dominance in world trade and the international role played by sterling. Later in the chapter we also explore the view that the core cultural values of the British have favoured the development of the service economy at the expense of manufacturing.

High levels of unemployment are, however, a fairly recent phenomenon. Between 1948 and 1966 the average rate in Britain was 1.7 per cent with only 1.1 per cent in 1966. Along with other industrial countries, levels of unemployment have risen sharply since then, with an official figure of 3.25 million people being out of work in 1982, representing 13 per cent of the working population. Since 1982, the extent of unemployment has fluctuated. At the end of the 1990s, unemployment in the UK is lower than that in Italy and Germany and significantly lower than Spain. This masks two social problems. There has been a steady increase in the numbers of long-term unemployed and levels of unemployment vary between regions. Highest levels inevitably occur in regions that were typified by traditional heavy manufacturing and extractive industries. Various policies have been initiated to deal with these problems, including government training schemes, regional aid, increasing public investment and direct state intervention to support ailing firms. Some of these aspects are dealt with in the next section.

Over the past 20 years the impact of the above economic changes alongside globalization on a major UK employer, such as Ford Motor Company, has been considerable. No one single factor has dominated as most of the influences have operated interactively. Along with the rest of UK manufacturing, capacity at Ford Motor Company has been reduced. This in turn has led to a reduction in the range of models produced and in the labour force. The decline of manufacturing throughout the UK has meant that the company has gone further afield for the sourcing of its components and hastened the trend towards the internationalization of manufacturing. The decline of the UK manufacturing base has also meant a decline in the numbers being trained in up-to-date manufacturing skills. Despite the large pool of unemployed labour there is a reduced pool of labour in certain manufacturing skills. The growth in financial services has not gone unnoticed by manufacturing concerns themselves and Ford has joined the growing trend by expanding its activities in this area. Along with other employers Ford has experienced fewer industrial relations problems. Weaker trade unions, unemployment and growing international competition have contributed towards a more cooperative industrial relations climate and management has been able to introduce changes in areas such as flexible labour practices that would hitherto have been impossible. Wage settlements too have been lower. As we shall see in the next chapter, the company has restructured along global dimensions. In functions such as logistics and buying, it is not unusual for UK employees to report to German and US managers and vice versa with the creation of international teams operating in different locations, linked by regular meetings, but dependent on electronic systems for daily communication.

Does manufacturing matter?

To some the growth in the services sector of the UK economy is seen as compensation for the decline in the manufacturing base and simply part of the process of evolutionary economic change. However, several arguments are put forward for the importance of manufacturing in a healthy economy. Only manufacturing can add value to raw materials, and in doing so can provide jobs in numbers that can never be matched by the service sector. While most if not all of manufacturing output can be traded as exports, this is not the case for services. Some estimates put the extent of tradeable services as low as 20 per cent of the total. As Bowen (1992) writes, 'you cannot pay for Japanese cars with British hairdressing'. In many other countries, the health of the service sector depends ultimately on the health of manufacturing industry. In Germany some 50 per cent of the demand for services comes from the manufacturing sector itself (Hahn, 1993).

It is for reasons such as these that successive British governments have been urged to lend greater support to manufacturing industry. It is to this and other aspects of the state's involvement with business that we now turn.

The state and business

Taking his lead from Max Weber, John Scott (1979) defines the state as that body which has a monopoly over taxation, the money supply, and the legitimate use of violence. The state is normally thought of as comprising the executive, parliament, the civil service, the judiciary, the armed forces and the police. It would be wrong to perceive the state as a united body. Tensions can and do occur, as between parliament and the civil service or between parliament and the judiciary. Variations in policy often result from differences in political ideology.

KEY CONCEPT 2.3
The state

The state comprises parliament, the judiciary, the civil service, police and armed forces and so on. Traditionally there have been tensions between the state's need to direct the economy and regulate business and the wishes of the business community to pursue their interests with a minimum of state intervention. Nevertheless, state intervention is a feature of business life and is inevitable in a country such as the United Kingdom where the state is a major employer. Intervention occurs through the legal regulation of market transactions, inventions and employment contracts and through the state's attempt to influence demand both as a consumer and via government economic policy. The business community in turn attempts to influence the state by adopting the various tactics associated with pressure groups. Increasingly, business comes under the influence of the policies of supranational bodies, such as the EU.

The World Bank has identified five core responsibilities of the state in any modern society (World Bank, 1997):

● establishing a legal framework;
● developing economic policies;
● building basic services and infrastructure;
● protecting the vulnerable;
● protecting the environment.

All these responsibilities have an impact on business in some way. We have already noted that the state interacts with business through its management of the economy. The state's influence can also operate in a highly localized and immediate way as the following example shows. In the 1960s the Ministry of Transport had a policy of employing independent firms to act as consultants in the testing of government construction projects such as roads and bridges. The policy coincided with a massive expansion in motorway construction. This resulted in a business boom period for a number of civil engineering firms. Testing contracts were usually given to a small proportion of the larger firms in the industry and, for some firms, this government work accounted for 75 per cent of annual turnover. In 1986 the government, as part of its policy to encourage greater competition, decided to invite bids for such consultancy work from any civil engineering contractor. The firms that had previously relied on such work as a major part of their income were faced with the prospect of either losing out to new competitors or accepting reduced profit margins through having to lower their consultancy fees. In either case, management were forced to rethink their strategies significantly.

In this section we will deal with aspects of the state's activity at both national and local levels in terms of the state's attempt to intervene in business and the attempts made by business managers to influence the workings of the state. Throughout this book we illustrate the interaction of the state and business by examining the relationship through its impact on the various business activities in Chapters 5 to 9. We extend the concept of state intervention at the end of this section by examining briefly the role of two supranational bodies, the World Trade Organization (WTO) and the European Union.

Before we examine more closely the relationship between the state and business it is important to consider the broad ideological underpinnings that have informed state involvement in business in the UK in the twentieth century. The dominant ideology has been that of liberal pluralism.

For liberals, the state is concerned with the maintenance of order and with providing conditions so that business can prosper. The state is seen as a neutral umpire in a pluralist society dominated by voluntary cooperation and exchange, where differences are never fundamental. Under a liberal view of the state, intervention is necessary for the following reasons:

● to protect the workings of the free market against forces that might otherwise disrupt it, such as excessive monopoly power of either business or trade unions;
● to provide and/or control goods and services to individuals such as defence and education, where provision by other means would be impossible or inappropriate;
● to take a longer-term view of economic, social and environmental change than individual businesses are capable of doing.

The liberal perspective allows wide variation, from a highly directive economy to one in which the free market is encouraged to operate unfettered by government controls.

Those criticizing this perspective argue that the state tends to operate to preserve the status quo, that groups in society rarely have equal power to support voluntary cooperation and exchange, and that ultimately the state is not neutral. Marxists take this view a stage further and argue that the state is the instrument of the ruling class in an essentially exploitative society, where massive inequalities exist. Under a Marxist view of the state, intervention is necessary to maintain the status quo in favour of the dominant class. The state will therefore intervene to protect investments or prevent strikes.

Whichever perspective is adopted, it is clear that the twentieth century has seen an increase of state intervention in Britain, much of it aimed specifically at business.

State intervention and business

An examination of UK state intervention in business in the twentieth century, reveals a progression through four stages. Winkler (1977) describes the first three of these as facilitative, supportive and directive. The fourth stage exhibits a radical departure from its predecessor both ideologically and economically and was ushered in with the election of Margaret Thatcher in 1979. We deal with each stage in turn.

The facilitative phase involved minimum intervention, largely through law and order, taxation and currency protection. The primary concern was for the smooth operation of the market. Three factors emerged to challenge this policy: an increase in industrial concentration resulting in large firms being able to override market competition, increasing economic crises of the 1920s and 30s with sharp rises in the level of unemployment, and, ultimately, the Second World War.

Economic crises in particular led to the state adopting a much more supportive role towards business. State policies followed the Keynesian belief that the free market was unable to solve the problems of unemployment and that increasing state intervention was required to redistribute wealth and create employment. The policy was ultimately challenged by a progressively weaker industrial base and the rise of international competition. The state therefore took it upon itself to pursue a more directive line.

Increased direction in the 1960s gained broad support, even from groups not normally associated with such a policy, like the Federation of British Industry (a predecessor of the CBI), and the Conservative government in its setting up of the National Economic Development Council in 1962. Directive policies included attempts to restructure business, the promotion of mergers to encourage both economies of scale and innovation, and incomes policies.

Such state direction in business has been labelled as corporatism. This is essentially an attempt by the government to achieve stability by integration, involving representatives of business and trade unions in the economic decision-making process. Corporatist states tend to favour central planning and the use of extra-parliamentary bodies such as 'quangos' to make decisions. Crouch (1978) has suggested that most countries in Western Europe have set up corporatist machinery at some time in the post-war period, with perhaps Holland and Germany experiencing most success. In Britain, integration has traditionally been resisted by both business and trade unions and attempts at corporatism have failed either through the refusal of one or other of the groups to participate or a lack of consensus. One of the more recent attempts at integration occurred when the Labour government of 1974–9 launched its 'social contract', a device to control the economy with the cooperation of the trade unions through wage restraint. The plan ultimately failed (and the government along with it) with rising inflation being met by ever-increasing wage demands. Some writers are pessimistic about the role of the state in corporatist societies, feeling that a failure of consensus may result in an increasingly directive state and the hastening decline of parliamentary democracy.

The lack of consensus highlights one of the major difficulties of state intervention in business. Jessop writes of the British government's attempts to influence the direction of business to solve the economic crises of the 1960s and 70s,

> far from industrial policy being a consensual panacea for solving the British crisis, it is a major focus of economic, political and ideological struggle.

> (Jessop, 1980, pp. 47–8)

Case 2.2: Norton-Villiers-Triumph

In 1972 the Conservative government, worried about the collapse of the BSA/Triumph motorcycle manufacturers, decided to aid the entire industry by assisting the formation of a merger between BSA/Triumph and Norton Villiers. The new company, known as Norton-Villiers-Triumph (NVT), was launched in 1973, backed by £4.8 million from the government and £3.4 million from the Norton Villiers parent company. The new firm employed 1750 people in three plants, two ex-BSA/Triumph (Meriden and Small Heath) and the other ex-Norton (Wolverhampton).

Faced with intense Japanese competition for the mass bike market NVT's strategy was to concentrate on larger 'super bikes', mainly for the American market. The company would stress its craftsmanship image. To assist its policy, the decision was made to close the largest production plant at Meriden. The reasons behind this decision were the high cost of overheads, representing 50 per cent of BSA/Triumph's losses, low productivity, a high incidence of industrial unrest, and a lack of space for expansion. The aim was to be in profit within three years and to expand on two sites within six years.

The new company was formed during the July shut-down at Meriden and faced an immediate strike there over holiday pay. Announcement of the closure was delayed until the strike was settled, when the government pledged its help with shut-down arrangements. The union at Meriden refused to accept the proposals and initiated a work-in, blockading not only their own management but parts and drawings for other factories, in particular affecting operations at Small Heath.

Workers at Meriden wanted to set up a cooperative and in October 1973 offered £1 million in exchange for NVT guaranteeing a market for Meriden bikes. The offer was rejected and redundancy notices were served on the employees in November. The redundancy notices were accepted but the blockade continued amid considerable media attention. The government intervened, resisting NVT's management's request for an eviction order. The Department of Trade and Industry (DTI) acted as facilitator in talks between NVT management and union leaders and despite much management scepticism, the cooperative were given until the following April to acquire the plant.

The agreement took eight weeks to draft, both sides blaming the other for the delay, by which time NVT and the proposed cooperative faced a number of problems. The affair had drained NVT's working capital, especially as the country was faced with a three-day working week resulting from petrol shortages and a miners' strike. Workers' redundancy money to be used to buy the company was largely spent on living expenses, the company was unable to supply working capital and the government was unwilling to underwrite the exercise. The plan was saved during the General Election campaign of February 1974 when the cooperative agreed to lift the blockade in return for first option on Meriden's assets.

The election of a new Labour government resulted in the reorganization of the DTI. A newly created Department of Industry, headed by Labour left-wingers Benn and Heffer, resulted in increased sympathy for Meriden, backed by an ideology that opposed closures on financial grounds only. Benn proposed further public funding of the cooperative. Meanwhile the blockade continued and NVT obtained a court injunction. The union refused to take action until the government funded the enterprise. However, Benn used his personal influence over the workers, the blockade was lifted and the injunction was not served.

The cooperative appeared to be launched with government financial backing and the appointment of a politically sympathetic manager. The scene now shifted to Small Heath whose workers opposed the plan, demanding that Meriden's products be sold by NVT, and that jobs be secured with government funding at their plant. Such opposition was grounded in the growth of Meriden at the expense of Small Heath when both were owned by BSA, the lack of solidarity shown by Meriden workers when job losses occured at Small Heath, and the fact that the recent blockade had seriously affected operations at Small Heath. The Small Heath workers threatened their own work-in and blockade.

The government asked NVT to prepare a three-factory plan, but at the same time launched the cooperative with a grant of £5 million. The new NVT plan estimated the need for additional government financial backing to the tune of £12–15 million. The Small Heath workers refused to agree unless job guarantees were made and the investments were made in their plant.

In December 1974, the Meriden cooperative reinstated its blockade and NVT continued to lose money. The managing director of NVT blamed goverment intervention, and in particular the conflict between economic and ideological motives, for preventing him taking action to solve what he saw as a domestic industrial dispute.

By 1983 the company had ceased to trade owing to a combination of Japanese competition and lack of investment. However, John Bloor, who had made his money in property, bought the rights to the Triumph name a year later and was confident that there would still be a market for such an historic marque. The revitalized company launched six completely new models in 1990, producing 2000 bikes in 1991, which were sold in the UK, France and Germany. Interest in the Triumph name persisted and production rapidly expanded to meet demand. By 1994 the new company was producing 12 different types of bike and had established offices in the USA, the largest market for motorcycles. From 1991 to 1994 the company grew from 70 to 300 employees. ■

(*Sources*: Sandberg, 1984; Duke, 1994)

Thatcherism and the New Right

Whatever consensus existed in post-war Britain, it was threatened by a series of economic problems that emerged in the 1960s and continued through the 1970s. The problems included rising levels of inflation, wage claims and unemployment; low productivity; and a worsening balance of payments deficit. The Labour government of the 1970s was embarrassed first by the intervention of the International Monetary Fund in the conduct of its economic affairs and second by a series of strikes, especially in the public sector, during the winter of 1978–9. The latter, in particular, saw a weakening of the traditional alliance between the Labour Party and the trade unions, challenged the 'social contract' referred to above, and did much to bring about a change of government.

The first government of Margaret Thatcher introduced an economic doctrine that owed much to the free market ideas of Hayek and Friedman. State involvement with business was seen as being incompatible with efficiency and freedom and measures were taken to 'get the state off our backs' and to control those elements that were likely to interfere with the freedom of both markets and individuals. A number of policy measures were introduced to achieve the government's goals and included the following:

● Monetarist policies were used to tackle inflation, comprising the gradual reduction of money supply and the cutting of public expenditure to reduce the excess of expenditure over taxation and hence the public sector borrowing requirement (PSBR).
● A number of supply-side measures were taken with the primary objective of stimulating economic growth. Taxation was cut between 1979 and 1988 with the base rate falling from 33 to 25 per cent and the top rate moving from 83 to 40 per cent. The tax cuts were intended as an incentive for those out of work to return to the job market on the assumption that the extra funds available would be invested in business growth. The work incentive was further strengthened by a series of welfare benefit cuts. In addition to these measures, steps were taken to reduce the power of the trades unions, to deregulate and privatize a number of industries and to

encourage entrepreneurialism through the growth of the small business sector. The changes in trade union power are dealt with later in this chapter and in Chapter 8. Privatization and small businesses are covered in Chapter 3.

The economic doctrine pursued has been labelled the 'New Right' or neo-liberalism, championing as it does market and individual freedoms and the abstention of the state. The UK was not alone in taking this line. Similar policies were being pursued by the Reagan administration in the USA and by the Kohl government in Germany.

In a number of areas the policies achieved their stated objectives. Inflation fell from 18 per cent in 1980 to around 2 per cent in the first quarter of 1993 and has remained at around 3 per cent ever since. Policies on trades union reform, privatization and deregulation were carried out as planned. However, any assessment of government policy is difficult. To ask whether policies have been successful begs a number of questions. We must ask successful for whom, by what criteria, and at what price? The policies have attracted their critics, who feel that they have done little to enhance UK competitiveness. The critics further claim that the policies contributed directly to the demise of UK manufacturing industry and to a rise in unemployment, although these were in part, the product of globalization and the rise of cheap labour economies. However, there is sufficient evidence to claim that while some have gained, the lower-income groups have experienced a worsening of their standard of living.

Thatcherism to New Labour

The neo-liberal policies established under the governments of Margaret Thatcher were continued under her successor, John Major. In 1997, 18 years of Conservative government came to an end with the election to power of the Labour Party. The party relaunched itself in order to attract a wider group of voters and rebranded itself as 'New Labour'. It was a conscious attempt to broaden its appeal and move away from its traditional working class and trade union base.

Some of its more traditional supporters, hoping for a return to the social democratic traditions of the redistribution of wealth and power, have argued that its policies are little different from those of the previous government. For them, New Labour has simply continued the agenda of market deregulation, privatization, low levels of personal taxation, new managerialism in the public sector and support for the values of self-sufficiency and entrepreneurialism (Hall, 1998). The key factor is undoubtedly globalization. The growth of the global economy has reduced the power of individual governments to set their own economic agendas, as was once the case. They are now concerned to provide a stable framework, which includes low inflation and low labour costs to attract inward investment. The UK government has been criticized for being too reactive.

> New labour deals with globalization as if it is a self-regulating, implacable Force of Nature, like the weather.
>
> (Hall, 1998, p. 11)

Moreover, its policies in education and training have been viewed, not as instruments of social democracy, but as a means to the creation of a flexible labour force for multinational corporations (Hall, 1998). Others take a less pessimistic view. Held (1998) argues that, while the global economy places constraints on policy, governments are far from powerless, and policies such as privatization were policies of the state and not necessarily the product of globalization. He further maintains that the role of the state throughout the world is being transformed through the development of regional and global policies and the growth of supranational organizations and inter-government agencies, as in the cases of the WTO and the EU, which we discuss later in this section.

Whichever view is taken of New Labour and its government at the end of the 1990s, the decade has seen considerable debate about the relationship between the state and business. The changes imposed by globalization have led some writers to consider alternative responses from those of the neo-liberals or even the social democrats. Hutton (1994) criticized the free market global economy and, in particular, the workings of the stock market. The resulting instability created a society where the majority was excluded from decision-making and from the benefits of the global economy. His vision was of a 'stakeholder society' where the market was reformed by governments to the benefit of all, and where individuals had greater representation, both in government and at the workplace. The debate was continued by Giddens (1998), with his notion of the 'Third Way', an updating of social democratic policies to meet the global economy of 2000.

Difficulties with state intervention

The impact of government policy upon business activity is often difficult to measure and direct relationships can be difficult to prove owing to the large number of other variables, which can and do affect the situation. There are other difficulties. While the governments since 1979 have been relatively consistent in their policies, this has not always been the case. Differences both between and within political parties have resulted in different approaches to intervention, as can be seen in Norton-Villiers-Triumph, Case 2.2 and with INMOS, Case 5.2. The business community may oppose attempts by governments to control it. The majority of owners and managers of business have an ideological attachment to *laissez-faire*. In addition, as we saw in the previous section, multinationals tend to have a greater allegiance to their own corporate goals than those of any single nation state.

In the preceding section we have attempted to chart the attempts by the UK government to influence business activities in a number of different ways. We shall now attempt to classify the main types of state intervention.

Types of state intervention

Collective provision

The most obvious form of state intervention is through the provision of those goods and services that would otherwise be too expensive, or too dangerous, or just ineffective if left to private control. Such aspects would include defence, the police, health, welfare and housing. The extent and nature of such collective provision is a matter of political and ideological debate. The British government since 1979 has pursued a policy of reducing its collective provision, as we will see when we discuss privatization in Chapter 3.

The state as employer

The proportion of the working population employed by the state rose from 2.4 per cent in 1851 to 24.3 per cent in 1975. Policies of privatization since 1983 have led to reductions in those directly employed by the state, but it remains a major employer with a profound effect on the labour market. For example, successive governments have attempted to hold down wages in the public sector as part of the policy of reducing public expenditure. In the past, this has resulted in major confrontations with such groups as the miners, nurses, and teachers.

The state as consumer

The case of the civil engineering contracts cited in the introduction to this section is a clear illustration of the state operating as a consumer of business services. As a major employer, the state is also a major purchaser of office equipment and many businesses rely on government contracts as a major source of revenue. The state through its involvement in defence, health and education has a significant influence on the direction of innovation (Chapter 5 has a more comprehensive review of this aspect).

Legal regulation

The legal regulation of business is extensive and complex. The law of contract is used to regulate the market place. Company law deals with such issues as the protection of consumers through the regulation of monopoly power, rules governing the provision of company information and so on. Labour law deals with both the protection of the individual worker and the regulation of collective bargaining. Patent law exists to encourage innovation by granting monopoly rights to patent holders. Illustrations of such legal provisions may be found in the chapters dealing with specific business activities. Some laws operate as constraints while others exist specifically to aid industrial development. With privatization new forms of regulation have been added to protect the consumer and regulatory bodies have been set up for all those public utilities now under private control.

Demand management

All governments attempt to influence and control economic growth, the balance of payments, wage and price stability and the level of unemployment. A variety of measures are used, including fiscal measures such as taxation, monetary measures such as the control of credit, and direct measures such as import controls and assistance to specific firms. We have seen already how the 1979 UK government attempted to stimulate economic growth through monetarist and supply-side policies.

Through taxation and monetary policies the government is able to raise revenue to finance its activities and also to achieve specific objectives, as through the lower rates of taxation levied on food as opposed to tobacco. Successive governments have given aid either for specific purposes, such as innovation (Chapter 5 contains a full discussion of this), or to assist a particular firm or an entire industry. In the 1960s, the Labour government targeted the nuclear, motor vehicles, and electrical industries for special assistance, while the 1970 Conservative government targeted the machine tool industry and woollen textiles. During that period specific firms were given substantial state aid under what was popularly known as the 'lame duck policy'. These firms included Rolls Royce, British Leyland, British Steel, Upper Clyde Shipbuilders, and Chrysler. Such support for individual firms is ideologically incompatible with the 'New Right' economic policies outlined above, which reject the kind of direct intervention seen in the 1960s and early 70s. Despite this, recent governments have targeted the smaller firm for special attention, as part of their commitment to the growth of entrepreneurialism. The small firms policy will be discussed more fully in Chapter 3.

Assistance to individual firms is both facilitated and constrained by policies of the European Union. Whether it wishes to or not, the UK government is forbidden under EU competition law to favour UK firms over those in the rest of Europe. However, funds are available within the EU through its Social and Regional Development Funds to stimulate growth of firms in designated deprived regions and to retrain the workforce.

Training

Government concern about skills shortages and the lack of adequate training in the UK has been a recurrent theme since 1852 and a number of more recent studies have pointed to the greater attention devoted to training by our competitors (for example, Handy, 1987 and Steedman and Wagner, 1987). Successive governments have attempted to redress this balance by such measures as the Education Act 1944, the Industrial Training Act 1964, the creation of a series of Youth Training schemes, and, more recently, the introduction of the National Curriculum in schools and the move towards a national system for the accreditation of vocational skills (NVQs). We deal with these issues in the section on labour in this chapter.

Protection

Governments have to varying degrees attempted to protect their industries against what is viewed as unfair competition from overseas firms and indeed other governments. One direct measure is the use of import tariffs and controls such as quota restrictions. Government representatives will also attempt to influence the policies of supranational institutions such as the EU or WTO to ensure a level playing field for the conduct of international trade.

Marketing

Most governments actively support their own businesses in exporting goods and services. Diplomatic services will inevitably involve a trade function and embassies will act as host to trade delegations as well as influencing foreign governments and businesses through a range of diplomatic connections.

Advisory services

In addition to its policies of regulation and assistance, the state offers various types of advice to business people. Such advice ranges from overseas trade, as identified above, to dealing with industrial relations problems.

The business community as a pressure group

So far this section has concentrated on the way the state attempts to influence business. We now turn our attention to the ways in which the state can be influenced by the business community acting as a pressure group, or more correctly, as a series of pressure groups.

We have already noted that businesses in this country are traditionally resistant to state control and are generally committed to a *laissez-faire* economy, and that as a pressure group, businesses tend to be fragmented with no powerful central body to coordinate policy. Indeed some evidence suggests that British industry is a singularly unsuccessful pressure group because of this fragmentation, and tends to exert pressure only in response to crises (Grant and Marsh, 1977).

However, as with all pressure group activity there is a difficulty both in observing it and in measuring its effect. We can only make deductions based upon open, formally reported attempts to influence. The business community tends to be secretive and many attempts to influence government policy are undoubtedly covert and informal. Nonetheless the business community represents an important source of revenue via taxation and borrowing to enable the state to fund its activities, and for this alone constitutes an important political lobby.

We have suggested that, for the most part, managers tend to be reactive rather than proactive as far as the state is concerned and seem more concerned to predict changes in the political environment than to initiate those changes for themselves. In this way the tobacco manufacturers predicted increased government regulation of their industry and took measures both to diversify and to transfer attention to growing Third World markets. The same companies reacted successfully to further restrictions on tobacco advertising by expanding their interests in sport sponsorship to maintain a high public profile. Some companies, of course, are more successful than others in resisting state intervention. Multinationals can use their protected status as members of another sovereign state to limit the extent of intervention in those countries in which they operate, and by transferring funds from country to country can minimize tax liabilities. The Swiss pharmaceutical company Hoffman-La Roche successfully defended itself against the probing of the

British Monopolies Commission in 1971 on the grounds that the British government had no legal right of access to information belonging to a Swiss company. The case was considerably hampered by a lack of vital financial information. (For a fuller account of this case see Stopford *et al.*, 1980.)

Political risk assessment is a technique or series of techniques used by some firms operating in an international environment, particularly where there is considerable investment planned, as in the establishment of a new manufacturing plant. Risk assessments would be built into the strategic plan and would assess the stability of the country as well as the chances and likely impact of a change in regime. At a more detailed level risk assessment will attempt to predict policy changes and their impact upon operations. There have been a number of well-documented cases where a change of government has resulted in the expropriation or nationalization of assets, as has occurred in such countries as Chile, Egypt, Iran, Iraq and Nigeria. Other risks can incorporate such diverse events as civil war, the kidnapping of key personnel and associated ransom demands, restrictions on borrowing, trades union activities, and policy changes concerning the hiring of local staff. Such assessment is far from easy. Governments can change without any fundamental shift in economic policy and the nationalistic rhetoric of some politicians may threaten foreign investment in the run-up to an election, but be entirely supportive once power has been achieved.

Once genuine risks are forecast, management will wish to take some measures to prevent them. Real pressure group activity exists where the business deliberately attempts to control the political environment in which it operates. In the UK there are a number of groups who attempt to influence government policy. These include professional groups such as the British Medical Association and employers' associations such as the Engineering Employers' Federation. The Confederation of British Industry (CBI) addresses a range of economic and business issues, although its impact as a national body is often weakened by the rather fragmented demands of its constituent industrial groups.

Such groups operate by lobbying government bodies to secure some kind of advantage or to protect themselves from what they see as unfair competition. Thus the fishing industry in both Britain and the rest of Europe is persistently lobbying for increased protection through the extension of territorial waters. As well as lobbying, some firms seek political influence through their donations to political parties. In the UK, these have tended to favour the Conservative Party and, in the 1990s, there were well-publicized donations from such firms as United Biscuits, Glaxo, British Airways, Rolls Royce, Hanson and Forte. An element in the repackaging of 'New Labour' has been to broaden its appeal to business and to increase the proportion of funding obtained from corporate sources.

Not all attempts to influence the state are the products of group pressure. We have already seen the influence of the multinational corporation and the major firms in any country will make some attempt at influencing government policy and may even be consulted. Individuals too represent an important channel of influence. Many references are made to the 'old boy network' that operates in government and business circles and several firms take more direct action by enlisting the services of a member of parliament on its board of directors.

British Airways prior to privatization set up a powerful lobby to protect its own position. The Civil Aviation Authority had published a report recommending that British Airways should give up some of its routes to its competitors, particularly local routes to provincial airlines and international routes to its main competitor, British Caledonian. The report also recommended that British Airways should move some of its services from Heathrow to Gatwick Airport and allow its competitors to move into Heathrow. The lobby was successful and a government White Paper on airline competition policy favoured British Airways. Some sources indicated the active role played by the then BA chairman, Lord King, who was a personal friend of the then prime minister. The government decision effectively prevented British Caledonian from expanding and did much to prepare for its eventual takeover by BA following privatization.

In recent years a number of firms that operate as professional lobbying consultants have emerged. Clients include not just private sector organizations, but local authorities who wish to influence government policy on such issues as the dumping of nuclear waste and are resisting proposals to create nuclear waste sites in their area.

We can see that businesses attempt to influence the state in a variety of ways: through personal influence, by gaining media coverage for their views, by taking out expensive advertisements, by hiring consultants, and by submitting letters to the press, often enlisting the support of other interested parties. The timing of such attempts to influence can be crucial. In 1987 two studies emerged with the expressed intention of influencing government policy on the training of managers. The publication of both reports coincided with a general election campaign, with a substantial loss of impact.

So far in this section we have focused on the way the state exerts its influence over the business community and vice versa. The WTO and the European Union operate as supranational organizations, whose activities increase the complexity of the interaction between the state and business. We deal first with the WTO and then proceed to examine the EU.

The World Trade Organization

The World Trade Organization (WTO) began its life as GATT, the General Agreement on Tariffs and Trade. It was founded as a supranational body shortly after the Second World War. Alongside the World Bank and the International Monetary Fund it was set up as part of the Bretton Woods system for the management of the post-war economy. Although the initial concern was for trade in goods, this was extended to include services. GATT was always seen as a temporary stage in the creation of the WTO, but it was not until the conclusion of the Uruguay Round of GATT talks in 1993 that this became a reality. The WTO, with its headquarters in Geneva, opened for business on the first day of 1995.

GATT was originally founded on the twin assumptions that trade is associated with wealth and that an increase in trade between nations meant a

---

KEY CONCEPT 2.4
World Trade Organization

Emerging from the General Agreement on Tariffs and Trade (GATT), the World Trade Organization (WTO) is a global organization of some 135 nations concerned with the establishment of rules of trade between member states. This it does within the framework of liberalizing world trade and offering assistance to the developing world. The full achievement of its objectives has been thwarted by the continued existence of trade restrictions by many nations and by the activities of some multinationals in moving operations to avoid WTO regulations.

---

reduction in the risk of war. These assumptions were born out of the experience of the 1930s when many nations sought to protect their own economies during depression through the imposition of high import tariffs and through the experiences of global war in the 1940s. With the joining of Estonia in 1999, the WTO comprises 135 members. While most of these are nation states, any region that exists as a separate customs area can be a member. Thus, Hong Kong is a member, but China is not.

Agreements between members are reached through a series of 'rounds' of which there have been eight since 1945. Each round seeks to pursue the basic objectives by furthering the liberalization of trade. In general the WTO operates by:

- establishing rules which govern trading behaviour between nation states;
- attempting to liberalize trade through tariff and quota reduction;
- offering a facility and a legal framework, including a court, for the settlement of disputes;
- monitoring trade agreements and government policies, especially those which may contravene the WTO objective of further liberalization;
- providing technical assistance and training for developing countries.

The WTO offers a more formal structure for the furtherance of trade agreements than existed under GATT. Senior ministers of member states and regions meet once a year and ongoing business is dealt with by the Council of Representatives which meets around nine times in any one year. The Council's work is supported further by a series of standing committees. Members should adhere to rules governing the trading of goods and services and they have a duty to apply these rules and the same tariffs to all other members. Furthermore, members must not discriminate between domestic and imported goods and services. The 135 WTO members embrace well over 90 per cent of world trade. Its supporters point to the dramatic reduction in tariffs and the equally dramatic increase in world trade since the war.

Others are more sceptical, highlighting the emergence of trading blocs as proof of the continued existence of protectionism, the success of countries such as Japan in resisting foreign imports and the growth of informal agreements outside the jurisdiction of the WTO. Such an agreement would include the 'gentleman's agreement' between Britain and Japan and between the USA and Japan to limit unofficially the import of Japanese cars. Such agreements are contrary to the spirit of the WTO. Others have criticized the WTO for taking a weak stance on social and environmental issues. The USA government banned the import of tuna from certain countries, on the grounds that the fishing methods killed large numbers of dolphins and were a threat to the species. The WTO declared the ban illegal in 1991. Many US firms manufacture in Mexico, thus avoiding more stringent US laws on pollution, and there are many cases of multinationals exploiting cheap labour economies and sanctioning the use of child labour. The WTO draws a distinction between the traded goods and services and the methods of production, which critics regard as a flaw in its rules. The only exception is the imposition of trade restrictions on scientifically established health grounds.

The most recent 'round' of talks began in Uruguay in 1986 and took seven years to reach its conclusion at the end of 1993. This particular round concerned itself with the usual tariff issues, but also tackled foreign investment, patents and copyright, trade issues concerning service industries and agriculture. It is this last issue, amongst others, that resulted in the Uruguay talks taking so long to reach a conclusion. Throughout the world agriculture is the most highly subsidized of all industries and any proposal to reduce subsidies and hence liberalize trade have met with stern opposition and ultimately deadlock, resulting in the talks exceeding their deadline date. Even though the Uruguay round was completed at the very end of 1993, it was done amid much last-minute compromise. After talks, agreements must then be ratified by the respective governments, a process that can take years. This lengthy process and the difficulties in reaching an agreement has led many to question the ability of the WTO to regulate international business and trade effectively.

The European Union

The current European Union (EU) embraces 15 nation states. In Table 2.6 we identify the stages in the growth of the European Union since the 1950s. The EU was formed out of post-war idealism as a means of putting an end to war between European nations and to assist in the post-war political, social and economic reconstruction of Europe. Politically the EU saw itself originally as a third major power bloc alongside the USA and the USSR. With the break-up of the Soviet Union, its political position has almost certainly been enhanced. Economically there was a desire to capitalize on the largest market in the advanced industrial world. Protectionism was sought both against a buoyant Japanese export trade and in response to increasing protectionism on the part of the USA. By 1999, the EU comprised 380 million people, compared to 270 million in the USA and 125 million in Japan. From a UK perspective the incentive to join lay in the potential of a growing European market to compensate for declining Commonwealth markets.

While the initial impetus for the creation of the EU was economic (it was originally known as the European **Economic** Community), the EU has formally embraced social and legal issues as well. Social issues pertaining to the workplace have been grouped together under the collective banner of the

---

KEY CONCEPT 2.5
The European Union

The European Union (EU), which began life in 1952 as the European Coal and Steel Community, now embraces 15 member states, with others, notably from Eastern Europe, wishing to join. The key objective of the EU is the maximization of advantages associated with the free movement of goods, finance and people and to capitalize on a large internal European market. In achieving these objectives it is intended to bring the peoples of Europe closer together and operate a single market using a single currency. Key landmarks have been the Treaty of Rome (1957), the Single European Act (1987), the Treaty on European Unity (1992), the Treaty of Amsterdam (1997) and the introduction of the 'Euro' in 1999. There are still serious concerns by some member states, notably the UK, about the timing of the introduction of a single currency and its impact on sovereignty and there still remain considerable differences in wage rates and standards of living between member states.

Social Charter, to which the UK was unable to subscribe in full, the only EU member so to do. However, the Labour government of 1997 pledged to accept those clauses rejected by the previous government.

The political changes that took place at the end of the 1980s and into the early 1990s are likely to change the face of European business, and with the

Table **2.6** Stages in the development of the European Union

1952	The European Coal and Steel Community formed by Belgium, France, West Germany, Italy, Luxembourg and the Netherlands
1957	The above six countries sign the Treaty of Rome and establish the European Economic Community. The UK is invited to join but withdraws from talks at an early stage.
1958	The European Economic Community comes into being.
1973	The initial six members are joined by Denmark, Ireland and the United Kingdom.
1981	Greece joins.
1986	Spain and Portugal join.
1987	The Single European Act is passed to create a single market by 1992.
1992	The Treaty on European Unity, also known as the Maastricht Treaty.
1995	Austria, Finland and Sweden join.
1996	Treaty of Amsterdam
1999	Introduction of the Euro

reunification of Germany, a former communist state has been brought into the EU. In 1999 outstanding applications for membership included those from Cyprus, the Czech Republic, Estonia, Hungary, Poland and Slovenia. There remains much uncertainty about their membership. The moral argument for their inclusion is accepted, provided they embrace existing EU laws. The debate surrounds the financial status of the aspiring members. The future of many of the former communist states, particularly those in the old USSR, is as yet unclear, new business opportunities have been hyped, and the existing members of the EU have found agreement difficult on currency and employment issues.

Discussions which took place in the Dutch town of Maastricht in 1992 to produce the Treaty on European Union and the Treaty of Amsterdam in 1997 both set out to strengthen the EU provisions to achieve even greater unity. The Maastricht Treaty dealt with the workings of the EU institutions, with economic and monetary union, with social policy and with foreign and security policy. The Treaty of Amsterdam was concerned also with making EU institutions more effective and efficient, and, in addition, addressed issues relating to citizens' rights, employment and the role of the EU in world politics.

In this section on the EU we will examine its objectives, the mechanisms through which those objectives are achieved and focus on specific key issues. We will touch briefly on competition issues and deal in more depth with monetary union and employment issues.

EU objectives and instruments

The key objectives of the EU include:

- the maximization of the advantages accruing from the free movement of goods, finance and people;
- the increase of competition and demand;
- the maintenance of stable prices and high levels of employment;
- the coordination of the policies of individual governments and their central banks.

Such objectives rest on a number of assumptions. First, it is assumed that the reduction in trade barriers will lead to increased competition, which will drive more efficient methods of production and result in better quality products at cheaper prices. This in turn will lead to an increase in demand. Second, it is assumed that a united Europe will offer considerable economies of scale and eliminate the waste associated with nation states operating independently. (A full account of these debates may be found in Cecchini, 1988.)

The main instruments through which these objectives are to be achieved are contained within the Treaty of Rome 1957, the Single European Act 1987, the Social Charter and the Treaty of Maastricht, the Treaty on European Unity 1992 and the Treaty of Amsterdam 1997. In general terms, the instruments comprise 'directives', which are binding but give member states flexibility in operation, and 'regulations', which are binding and directly applicable.

A primary objective of the EU is the removal of obstacles to free trade, and hence there are proposals to eliminate frontier controls and work permits and to harmonize both taxation policies and technical standards. The creation of a single European technical standard for car manufacture would, for example, eliminate the need to produce different types of headlamps for the same model of car to meet the various legal requirements in different European countries. The elimination of such differentiation would reduce costs and likely lead to increased demand.

The degree to which such instruments have been introduced has varied according to the nature of the proposed change and between member nations. Not all countries have embraced the proposals as readily as others. The UK has failed to agree to the provisions of the Social Charter and opted out of the Social Chapter of the Maastricht agreement (although as we have seen, subsequently agreed to opt in). A particularly contentious issue is that of monetary union and, as we saw in Case 2.1, this seems increasingly difficult to achieve in the short term. It is to this and other issues we now turn.

EU issues

Businesses have been influenced by a certain harmonization that has taken place in company law, employment law, accounting practice, taxation, and the role of financial institutions. There has been significant cooperation over policies concerning industrial development, regional aid and environmental protection. In the same way that business interests lobby national governments, attempts are made to influence EU policy. Nonetheless there would appear to be two major problems for businesses in dealing with the EU. The first concerns the bureaucracy and somewhat protracted decision-making mechanisms of EU institutions while the second concerns the conflict of interests between constituent nation states. At the root of this conflict is the key issue of sovereignty. The EU will assume powers that formerly belonged only to democratically elected governments of individual nation states. A third kind of problem relates to the differences that exist within the EU. Between countries there are considerable differences in geographical size, population, resources, living standards and a whole range of economic variables that present difficulties in the move to a level playing field. Nonetheless, such convergence is a prerequisite of monetary union.

We will illustrate some of the difficulties by focusing on competition policy, monetary union and workplace issues.

The competition policy of the EU has the avowed aims of preventing cartels, of controlling monopolies, especially state-controlled monopolies, and of restricting state aid to certain industries thereby creating unfair competition. Despite such aims there are many cases of protectionism and unfair competition within the EU. One reason for the demise of the British coal industry lay in the availability of cheaper coal elsewhere and the subsidies offered to coal producers in Germany.

Monetary union had as its initial instrument the European Exchange Rate Mechanism (ERM). This was an attempt to keep the exchange rates of currency between member countries within fixed limits. The problems associated with the ERM have been documented in Case 2.1. While the ERM had its detractors, the major objections are usually reserved for the proposals associated with European Monetary Union (EMU) and the creation of a single European currency. Those in favour of EMU see advantages in terms of increased competition and trade, the reduction of transaction costs, increased certainty in planning, the reduction of inflation and the necessity for greater political cooperation. Detractors have pointed to the problems of maintaining comparable interest rates, as seen within the ERM in 1992 and 1993, and say that there would be unequal costs and benefits. In particular the fear is that EMU would strengthen considerably an already strong German economy and its central position in the European economy. For the British government EMU is seen a loss of sovereignty and hence political control and democratic accountability. For this reason Britain has acted as the chief opponent to full-scale monetary union.

A form of single European currency, the 'ecu', has been used for some time, but mostly only as a paper transaction between member states. In 1999, the new single currency, the 'euro', was introduced by 11 participants. Denmark, Greece, Sweden and the UK have opted out for various reasons, although all see themselves as potential future members. At present the euro is confined to paper transactions, with coins and notes planned for circulation in 2002. The plans to introduce the euro were made at a time of some economic confidence within the EU. Its actual launch, however, coincided with a decline in the economic fortunes of most of its participants, with a resulting fall in the value of the euro against the dollar and sterling.

The development of the EU has been a major reason why trade between member countries has grown much faster than trade with other nations. Its supporters see the euro as a key instrument in strengthening unity between member states and a means to enhance the role of the EU on a world stage.

The claimed advantages of the euro are seen in terms of the following:

- For the consumer it will be easier to shop, as differences in the prices of goods between EU members will become transparent. There is a view that prices will eventually converge. This may be good news for the UK car buyer, given that prices are 40 per cent more expensive than in the rest of the EU, but this could have an impact on UK jobs. Since taking over Rover, BMW has decided to buy parts from other EU countries rather than from UK suppliers on the basis of price.
- Currency exchange, with its expensive transaction costs and the uncertainty owing to fluctuations in the exchange rate, will become a thing of the past. This will benefit trade between firms within the EU as well as obviating the need for travellers to change money.
- The inevitable strength of the euro and the conditions of membership within the single currency will create greater economic stability and end volatile inflation and interest rates. This will enable the EU to withstand severe fluctuations in the global economy, as with the recent Asian crisis.

The introduction of the euro is seen as part of a package of measures, which include the reduction in the social security element of wages. This has the intention of bringing down labour costs and enhancing labour flexibility.

The claimed disadvantages of the euro are seen in terms of the following:

- Opponents of a single currency view it not so much as an economic measure, but as a political one; a major step on the route to a federal Europe. This appears to be less of a problem for some members than others, the UK being the major speaker for the opposition.
- A single currency is incompatible with the management of a large economy. It reduces the freedom of individual governments to respond to economic changes that may have a greater impact on their economy than that of other EU states. For instance, governments will be unable to use devaluation as a means of increasing competitiveness.

The arguments given by the UK government for initial non-participation are based around the notion that the currency will only work given the necessary convergence of economies across Europe in terms of economic structures, business cycles and interest rates. The government claimed that, by 1999, the UK economy had not met the necessary tests of convergence. Supporters of the euro have argued that, at the time of introduction, the UK economy was closer than ever before to the other major economies of Europe, but take heart in their belief that, in the long run, the single currency will be impossible to avoid. The UK public has responded with an apparent lack of interest. Only 27 per cent of the UK electorate voted in the 1999 elections for European members of parliament. This was the lowest turn-out in the entire EU and compared with 50 per cent in Germany and 75 per cent in Greece.

Employment issues were central to the Social Chapter of the Treaty on European Unity, which built on the 1989 Social Charter and dealt with issues relating to wages and workplace conditions. There was an attempt to harmonize practices, not only on wages and conditions, but also on equal opportunities and mechanisms for consultation between management and labour. The UK alone opted out of this element of the Treaty, an act which has provoked much criticism. The problems of unequal wages and conditions were highlighted by the decision of Hoover in 1993 to move 450 jobs from its factory in Dijon in France to Cambuslang in Scotland. This was done on the basis that wages and, in particular, associated benefits are up to 30 per cent cheaper in the UK than in parts of the EU. Around the same period, Philips moved 150 jobs from Holland to the UK at Blackburn. Such transfer of labour for cost advantages has been dubbed 'social dumping' and threatens to undermine one of the key elements of European harmony.

At the time of the Hoover move to Scotland, there was a belief, not least amongst the government, that the UK environment of low labour costs and relaxed labour laws made it a more attractive investment for foreign firms than its EU counterparts. That view has been challenged by Barrell and Pain (1997). They argue that foreign investment is a product of the growing importance of a knowledge-based economy and the opportunities offered by a free trade region. In the case of the knowledge-based economy, they maintain that the competitive edge of innovations and the importance of reputation have meant that firms now prefer to control operations directly than license their intellectual property to another firm. The free trade zone is more important as an incentive for inward investment than cheap labour. Barrell and Pain concede that lower labour costs in the UK were an attraction to Japanese inward investment, but nowhere nearly so significant as UK membership of the EU and hence access to the European market. They support this conclusion by examining outward investment from the UK into Europe, where the majority of investment has gone to France and not the cheaper labour markets of Eastern Europe, nor even those of the EU, such as Greece or Spain. The authors suggest that France was favoured because of its strong commitment to European integration and offer this to the debate on the UK's continuing reluctance to embrace the single currency.

Focus on the initial opt-out of the Social Chapter and cases such as Hoover tend to divert attention from the impact of EU directives and regulations on UK employment practices. In many cases the EU has ruled that UK legislation does not go far enough and, as a consequence, several UK labour laws have been amended. Through EU intervention, UK employees now have greater protection in terms of equal pay for equal work and in terms of continuous employment when firms change ownership. An issue of continuous employment that EU intervention helped resolve concerns the contracting out of public sector services in the UK. Case law has determined that public sector employees who lose their job when the service is contracted out, and are then hired by the contractor, must be treated as if the employment is continuous. The EU has also had an impact via the Working Time Directive, which restricts the working week to a maximum of 48 hours, and through the establishment of European works councils.

Employment issues, particularly those concerned with global competitiveness and unemployment, were central to the agenda of the Treaty of Amsterdam, 1997. Ministers subscribed to what they defined as the 'four pillars of employment'. These are employability, entrepreneurship, adaptability and equality of opportunity. Issues of flexibility and entrepreneurship are dealt with in the next chapter.

Technology

Technology is probably one of the most widely used and least precisely defined terms in business. It is, however, something that affects business in all its forms and activities. We hope to shed some light on what technology represents and where it stands in relationship to the firm in its environment.

The concept is popularly used to imply some form of process, invariably machinery based, so we think of lathes, assembly lines, computers and cash dispensers. In this way technology represents the application of science and engineering for use in business. However, technology not only refers to the artefacts themselves, but also to the way they are used and the theories governing their application. Human knowledge is therefore an essential ingredient of technology. We often distinguish between manufacturing firms according to the nature of the product, especially its constituent materials and its level of sophistication. We can therefore speak of material and product

---

KEY CONCEPT 2.6
Technology

Technology is a broad concept referring to the application of available knowledge and skills to create and use materials, processes and products. Technology is often accorded a dominant role in business and is often viewed as determining products, processes, organization structure and the individual's attitude to work. While there are situations where the prevailing technology is undoubtedly influential, it is the product of human endeavour and many managers do have a choice.

New technology refers to the application through computers of miniaturized electronic circuitry to process information thereby giving managers greater potential flexibility in and control over work operations.

Information technology links new technology with telecommunications to enhance the quantity, quality and speed of transmission.

---

technology. On a much broader scale we distinguish between societies according to their sum total of knowledge and skills and the application of these for the benefit of that society. This too is known as technology. From a business perspective we can therefore speak of technology as the application of available knowledge and skills to create and use materials, processes and products.

Technology is closely associated with operations systems, representing both an input and a transformation device. It is also central to the process of innovation. These concepts are developed further in Chapters 5 and 6. In this section we look at more general issues in the way technology and business interact, and focus on issues associated with 'new technology' and 'information technology'.

Technology: determinant or choice?

A classic view of technology is that it exists as an environmental constraint, which becomes the dominant feature of all businesses. Firms operate within certain technological imperatives, which shape not only the products and the processes they use, but the structure of the organization, relations between people, and individual job satisfaction. Such a view can be found in the work of Joan Woodward (1965) and in Robert Blauner's classic but flawed sociological study of alienation (1964). Galbraith (1972) also painted a picture of markets being dominated by technological considerations rather than consumer choice.

Woodward in particular has been very influential. Her classification of small batch, mass, and process production has featured in most textbooks on management and organization since the 1960s and this book is no exception (Chapter 6 also refers to her work). To Woodward, technology not only determined organization structure, but the relationship between individual departments and the focus of each business. In small batch firms, product development and technical sales were the key issues; in mass production organizations, fragmentation led to tensions between departments, a source of potential conflict; in process organizations, once the system had been created, high volume sales became the key issue. The relationship between technology and structure was, according to Woodward, crucial to the success of a business. In her study of manufacturing firms in South-east Essex she found that the most successful firms financially were the ones that conformed to the organizational type most appropriate for their technology.

Joan Woodward viewed technology as a determinant of both organization structure and the range of possible strategy alternatives. Woodward has been labelled a contingency theorist. However, as we saw in Chapter 1, the contingency approach puts forward a view of business whereby activities at the level of the firm result from the interrelationship of a number of variables such as technology, the behaviour of competitors, the role of the state and so on. The end result is supposedly strategic choice for the individual manager following from an analysis of relevant variables. Woodward's view of technology would appear to give the manager no choice at all. Technology is dominant and managers fail to adapt to it at their peril.

We offer two challenges to this view of technology. First, we look briefly at its relationship with organizational size and second, we view technology as an element of strategic choice.

The first challenge to the notion of an all-pervasive technology is offered by those who champion size as a more influential variable than technology (for example Hickson *et al.*, 1969). Studies such as these conclude that technology may well be an important determinant of the structure and work patterns in smaller plants, but as firms increase in size, it is size itself that becomes the more dominant influence. We examine the variable of size more fully in the next chapter.

Technology is believed by some to determine the structure and processes of business, just as the climate and weather determine agriculture. The knowledge, skills, artefacts and processes that make up technology are, unlike the weather, products of the kind of people who operate technological systems. The assembly line is not a technological imperative, but a device created to satisfy the pressures of mass markets and a product of the foresight of entrepreneurs like Ford and the skill of designers who made the process work. Viewed in this way, technology is not a determinant of business, rather a product of the way managers respond to other environmental influences. Furthermore, the kind of technology employed by businesses may be a matter of strategic choice. The application of socio-technical systems analysis offers managers the possibility of changing the prevailing technology to suit the needs of their own particular workforce and the prevailing social situation in which they operate. Increasingly technology and, more especially, information technology are used as strategies for competitive advantage. We see this to good effect in Case 2.3, Thomson Holidays, where an online computerized booking system was established linking individual travel agents to the central booking facility, thereby giving Thomson the edge in the market place over its rivals. Developments in electronic commerce supposedly offer opportunities for new business and hence competitive advantage. We discuss electronic commerce later in this section.

While we cannot afford the space for a full academic debate on the role of technology and offer a complete critique of contingency and socio-technical systems theory, we may conclude that the relationship between technology and business is highly complex. It involves the interrelationship of other variables such as size and management choice, and cannot be reduced to a simple notion of determinism. A good illustration of this complexity is provided in Chapter 5. Using Rothwell's illustration of the development of railways, we conclude that innovation is neither technology-led nor market-led, but a complex interrelationship of those and other variables, such as the availability of finance and cheap labour (Rothwell and Zegveld, 1981).

An analysis of the role of technology in many organizations offers us insights into a highly dynamic process. A rival tour operator to Thomson Holidays may well feel it necessary to develop its own online reservation system to maintain competitiveness. In this case, the rival management is confronted by the twin forces of technology availability and competition. Management must then evaluate the costs of introducing the new reservation system against the costs of not introducing it, the kind of system to buy and precisely how it will be used in their organization. Thus far technological and competitive determinism have interacted with management decision-making and choice. Once a decision is reached, the new technology assumes a new dynamic, that of reshaping the organization and offering possibilities of new ways of working. At this stage the new technology must interact with the prevailing organization culture and organization politics. This explains why, in some organizations, groups may resist technological change, as in the case of the Fleet Street newspaper industry.

New technology and information technology

New technology is sufficiently old as a concept that 'new' could be considered redundant. However, given that the term still has currency in the literature, we will deal with it here. In this book we define new technology as the application through computers of miniaturized electronic circuitry to process information. We therefore find 'new technology' in a variety of business and non-business settings. In banking and finance, it has enabled money markets all over the world to be linked, with instant access to information and especially market changes. The speed of information flow, the accessibility of that information around the world and the subsequent speed of response were major factors in money and stock market falls in all major markets during the latter part of 1987. The same conditions applied to the fall of sterling and associated ERM crisis in 1992 (Case 2.1 offers more details) and the Asian crisis of 1997 (Case 2.4). In retailing, electronic point-of-sale systems (EPOS) provide instant information on sales trends, cash flows and stock levels. In manufacturing, computer-controlled machines, robotics, and entire computerized flexible manufacturing systems have greatly enhanced a firm's response to changing market demands and improved product quality. In the office, the introduction of word-processing systems can greatly speed up typing operations, especially where large numbers of standard letters are involved, and e-mail systems can reduce the amount of paperwork in circulation. As we see later, electronic commerce has potential to change the way we all do business.

The concept of new technology is often linked to that of information technology. The above illustrations from banking, investment and finance show how miniaturized electronic circuitry has been combined with developments in telecommunications to broaden the information-processing capacities of a single computer system.

Child (1984) and Earl (1989) give us some clues to the popularity of new technology and information technology for businesses, in that they offer the following:

- the opportunity of gaining competitive advantage by offering a product or a service that no one else is able to provide;
- improvement in productivity and performance;
- improved quality of both system operation and system outputs;
- increased efficiency through reduced operating costs and reduced staffing levels;
- improved information and diagnostic systems, leading to improvements in management control;
- the opportunity to develop new ways of managing and organizing.

The kind of advantages outlined above offer, to management, cost reduction and increased profitability; to the workforce, increased job satisfaction; and to the customer, better quality goods and services at competitive prices. Such opportunities were sought and largely gained by Thomson Holidays in Case 2.3.

There are, however, a number of problems which may be created by the introduction of new technology. While desktop computers and

Case 2.3: Thomson Holidays

This case deals with the introduction of the Thomson Open-line Programme, a computerized reservation system giving travel agents instant and direct access to the company. In this way, customers are able to book their holiday through their local travel agent and obtain immediate confirmation. Such systems were not new. Computerized reservation had been used by airline companies for some 15 years before Thomson's decision to adopt the technology. Thomson were not even the first tour operator, as a similar system was already operated by Olympic Holidays. However, Thomson were the first major holiday company to introduce a direct access computerized booking system that was adopted by a large number of travel agents, and which became the industry standard.

Thomson Holidays is part of the International Thomson Organization. The company, with interests in newspapers, publishing and oil, did not enter the travel business until 1965 with the acquisition of Universal Skytours and Britannia Airways. After a shaky start and several managerial changes, the company emerged as one of the United Kingdom's largest operators, largely as a result of a vigorous price-cutting campaign in the early 1970s, backed by attention to customer feedback and quality improvement. With the collapse of Clarksons, its major rival, Thomson Holidays become the top company in 1974 and now commands a market share in excess of 33 per cent, far ahead of its closest rival, the International Leisure Group. As well as being a tour operator, the company has developed in all aspects of the travel industry. In Britannia Airlines it controls the largest holiday charter company in the country. Portland Holidays is one of the largest companies selling holidays direct to the public and, in Lunn

Poly, the company owns one of the largest multiples of travel agents.

Prior to the introduction of a computerized system, holiday booking was done either by telephone or entirely on the basis of a booking form. This information was handled centrally and all booking data was kept on card index. The first technological change came in 1976 with the introduction of the Thomson Reservation and Administrative Control System (TRACS). TRACS established a computer network linking head office with 10 regional centres, through which bookings were made by travel agents. The company bought existing software used by the airline KLM but had underestimated the degree of customization required and the software was almost completely rewritten.

TRACS was viewed by management as a success and was seen as a major factor in the company keeping ahead of its rivals in the turbulent environment of rising oil prices in the 1970s and the subsequent impact on the cost of air travel. Errors in bookings and administration were reduced, credit control was improved, and the system was popular with travel agents. Central booking staff were reduced by approximately two-thirds and those remaining in post had their jobs enhanced as they now operated as a direct interface between the company and travel agents. The person heading the introduction of TRACS was promoted to Systems Director, recognition by the company of the strategic importance of IT.

When TRACS was introduced in the mid-1970s, networking technology was relatively unsophisticated. By the end of the decade, the Post Office had launched Prestel, a nation-wide online processing system with low-cost terminals. This effectively paved the way for a considerable growth in national computer networks. Thomson extended TRACS to a large number of travel agents through the Thomson Open-line Programme (TOP). The relatively low cost of the online system did not limit its use to just the larger multiples in the travel agency business. The accessibility to the small independent travel agency of its computer booking system was an important strategic objective for Thomson.

The company hoped to build upon the efficiency and effectiveness of TRACS, not least the cost savings. TOP became a corporate priority receiving direct top management support and a project team was set up drawing upon staff from all parts of the organization as well as recruiting staff with specific expertise from outside. This was vital given the decision to develop the company's own network, based largely on its experience with TRACS. Travel agents were closely involved throughout the development stage and all participating agents received comprehensive training. TOP was widely publicized by Thomson and the company received a great deal of favourable press coverage. The intended image was created of a company that was not only a leader in the holiday business but also a leader where technology was concerned.

TOP was introduced in 1982 with 2200 participating travel agents. Within a year 3584 agents were involved covering 61 per cent of all bookings. Telephone bookings were withdrawn altogether in 1986 and by 1988, 95 per cent of all bookings were made through the online system. The overall cost of introducing TRACS and TOP has been estimated at a little over £20 million. Between 1978 and 1987 there was a 400 per cent increase in business and Thomson's market share rose from 18 per cent to 29 per cent, with a further rise to 33 per cent by 1990. Throughout this period staffing had remained fairly constant at around 800 and Thomson estimated that savings directly attributable to the new system were of the order of £28 million.

By 1998, Thomson were ready to enter a new phase in their use of information technology. They had introduced BACWAY for Windows, a new computerized system for collecting direct debit payments from travel agents and were planning to use the recent development of interactive digital television to sell holidays. Interactive television bookings had been pioneered in the USA by such as the travel channel. Thomson decided, with British Airways, to become the two launch partners for Microsoft's interactive holiday booking service, Expedia. As well as its work with Microsoft, Thomson have developed their own innovation team under an 'Innovation Manager' to plan and oversee new applications of information technology, e-commerce and digital interactive television. ■

(*Sources*: Peltu and Land, 1987; Daniels, 1991; *Marketing*, September 1998; *New Media Markets*, October 1998).

word-processors can be relatively cheap labour-saving devices for the office, the introduction of entire manufacturing systems based on new technology can be prohibitively expensive. In general terms, the introduction of new technology in the office incurs much lower costs than in manufacturing. The availability of a wide variety of software has reduced considerably the cost of establishing computerized systems. However, the costs of adapting the software to meet local specifications can add greatly to the cost of implementation. Considerable costs were borne by Thomson Holidays in adapting existing software already being used by airline companies. We have made reference to the use of computer control, robotics and flexible manufacturing systems in Chapter 6. Likewise the problems of skills training and industrial relations are dealt with in Chapter 8. Students seeking information on these aspects are advised to refer to the relevant parts of these chapters. Before leaving the topic of technology, we focus on two areas. Considerable claims are made for electronic commerce or 'e-commerce' and its current and future impact on business, and there is some controversy about the relationship between new technology and jobs. We deal with each in turn.

Electronic commerce

> Today's business interests sit on a fault line of the greatest seismic shift since the invention of the printing press … e-business. We are embarking on a journey of such magnitude that it has the capacity to change the course of our entire social order.
>
> (Pricewaterhouse Coopers, 1999, p.5)

Such statements as the above reflect the hype that surrounds developments in electronic commerce, also known as e-commerce and e-business. Commentators such as those at Pricewaterhouse Coopers believe that the way we do business will be revolutionized and that it will level the playing field between large and small firms. In this section we will explore the concept of electronic commerce, its impact on business and the issues it raises.

For many companies electronic commerce is little more than the creation of a website to provide information to customers, while to others it is a means of selling goods and services on an international scale. Essentially electronic commerce is a transaction involving goods, services and information in which the parties to the transaction do not meet, but interact electronically. Much of that interaction is carried out using the Internet. This has led to the growth of Internet companies such as Amazon.com, one of the pioneers of electronic retailing. Amazon offers a large catalogue of books, which are offered over the Internet, often at much cheaper rates than in retail outlets. An order can be made and paid for by credit card electronically and the book is sent by post. In addition to retailing, information can be accessed using the Internet. Much of the information is free to anyone with the means of access, as with versions of many local, national and international newspapers. Some databases, such as collections of academic journal articles, require a subscription fee, and can be accessed by means of a password.

KEY CONCEPT 2.7
E-commerce and e-business

Such approaches connect suppliers and buyers directly through computer-based systems. E-commerce generally relates to trading activity involving information, goods and services. The initial point of contact is electronic although, in the case of goods and services, delivery is made using more conventional systems. E-business generally refers to a much broader range of activities, incorporating all business activities. It enables the various elements of global firms to work more closely together and can form the basis of much business to business activity. The growth of e-commerce and e-business is directly associated with the development of the Internet and company-wide intranet systems. Doing business electronically reduces the supply chain and hence increases convenience, reduces costs and improves speed of delivery. It is predicted that it will revolutionize business although at present take-up rates are quite low, costs of entry are high and there are still some unresolved issues related to privacy and security.

In both the above cases both the supplier and buyer gain through reduced transaction costs. Retailers are able to shorten the supply chain to the customer, thereby reducing costs, as well as gaining access to a global market. Consumers benefit through reduced prices and access to a range of products globally. In the late 1990s book buyers were the favourable recipients of a price war as Barnes and Noble and Borders attempted to gain market share from the market leader, Amazon. Those seeking information have access to a much wider range than hitherto, all of which can be accessed from the home or the office.

A large range of goods, from CDs to cars, can be bought in this way. E-commerce has enabled home access to personal bank accounts and, with some banks like Barclays and First Direct, a full range of banking services. The Internet has made possible ticketless air travel, a system used by many US airlines for internal flights. An airline seat can be purchased electronically and the customer simply produces identification at the check-in desk to pick up a boarding card. Applications for some university courses can be made over the Internet. Supermarket shopping orders can be placed via the Internet with guaranteed delivery times. It is not only shoppers who benefit from enhanced services. Some supermarkets, such as Tesco, use e-commerce as the basis of their sales ordering system with suppliers. As with most supermarkets, items scanned at the check-out provide vital information for stock reordering levels. In the case of Tesco, the information is transferred automatically to a central computer system, which automatically raises orders to suppliers, which are then despatched to the appropriate store. This version of retailing just-in-time eliminates the necessity for Tesco to hold stock in central warehouses, thereby reducing costs. We saw in Chapter 2 how Ford Motor Company moved to a global organization, creating cross-national teams in management and the key functions. In support of this the company has developed its own intranet system incorporating databases and e-mail and linked to a video conferencing system. In this way, design teams working from different country bases can collaborate on complex design issues.

Companies such as Ford Motor Company are part of a group of pioneers in the use of e-commerce and e-business. According to a recent *Economist* survey, others include Cisco Systems, Dell, General Electric and Visa (*Economist*, 26 June–2 July, 1999). While the media focus is on the impact for the general public, the size and value of business to business transactions far exceeds the use of e-commerce by the ordinary consumer. Businesses have shown themselves much more willing to use the Internet for transactions than the general public, even in the USA, which has the highest proportion of Internet users per head of population in the world. Firms such as those listed above regularly use e-business to deal with both suppliers and customers. The rate of take-up of such methods by businesses would appear to be linked to the level of competition and whether Internet trading is done by major competitors. It is a system that has enabled some companies to come from nowhere to be leading players in their field, as in the case of Dell Computers.

There are, however, a number of barriers to overcome before the seismic shift of Pricewaterhouse Coopers' claim can occur. A major constraint is one of access to the Internet. In this respect Europe lags behind the USA. Fewer than 9 per cent of Western Europeans have access to the Net compared to 37 per cent of Americans (source: Jupiter Communications, 1999). Even with access, many in the USA as well as Europe are reluctant to make purchases over the Internet using a credit card. Evidence suggests that fraud is a problem operating against both the seller and the buyer. Even when the system works there are frequent complaints of delays in accessing the Internet and in the processing of orders. In order to circumvent a clogged Internet system, many firms in the USA have resorted to sending information through the post in the form of a CD-ROM, thereby adding to the cost of the transaction. A frequent complaint in business to business transactions in the USA is the proliferation of 'junk' CD-ROM mail.

The costs of setting up an effective e-commerce system are considerable, which poses particular problems for SMEs. This has led to transnational initiatives to encourage the use of e-commerce by smaller firms. For example the G7 countries have launched such an initiative, which they call 'A Global Marketplace for SMES'.

In the case of information, privacy and security become key issues and banking services are at the forefront of developing secure systems. As well as developments in security systems, e-commerce has led to the creation of new laws to protect electronic transactions. Such legal rulings become particularly important where the transactions occur across national borders and hence, across different legal systems. Electronic transactions pose particular problems where there are differences in contract law, consumer protection, sales tax and customs duty. In 1999 the EU was developing laws to clarify such issues and which country's law would apply in the case of cross-border purchase.

As with many well-publicized developments in business we find that the reality is neither as extensive nor as simple as the image. We may stand on the threshold of a revolution, but the threshold would appear to have a larger entrance than e-commerce supporters envisaged. Undoubtedly there is potential for growth, underlining the developments in globalization that are a part of modern business. Consumers have the potential to access a much wider range of goods and services from a much wider range of suppliers. Given that the use of electronic exchange is more prevalent in business than amongst the general public, business organizations are bound to experience change in their structures and functions. There will also be repercussions for the labour market, to which we now turn.

New technology, jobs and labour

There would appear to be three perspectives on the impact of new technology on jobs and labour. First, we have the kind of view associated with such writers as Braverman (1974). New technology is seen as a deskilling agent reducing the amount of discretion an individual has over his or her job, at the same time increasing management control over both work process and worker. The thesis associates new technology with job cuts and rising unemployment and the greatest impact of both deskilling and job losses is felt by skilled craft workers. The second perspective offers an optimistic scenario. New technology is seen as creating new opportunities for the workforce in the form of new and different types of labour with opportunities for existing workers to learn new skills. The third perspective is also optimistic, viewing new technology as a liberating device, eliminating the need for human labour in repetitive, dangerous or unpleasant tasks, and, in some cases, freeing people to engage in socially beneficial work. The evidence supporting these three perspectives is mixed. We will view the effect on the numbers employed, on the types of jobs involved, and on the content of those jobs.

The impact of new technology on job numbers received much attention in the 1980s. A comprehensive survey in the UK by Daniel (1987) revealed that job losses had occurred in manufacturing, but that it was difficult to isolate the impact of new technology from other changes, notably declining markets. He also found that actual dismissals were very rare and that reductions were generally met by redeployment, early retirement and (in some cases highly attractive) voluntary redundancy schemes. In terms of the service sector, Daniel found job gains associated with the introduction of word processors and computers. The introduction of new technology has been used to increase productivity and provide an improved service through retaining existing employment levels. In Case 2.3, Thomson's computerized booking system resulted in staff reductions when it was first introduced. However, over time the increase in the volume of bookings meant that staffing was restored to its former level, with the staff handling a far greater volume of work than previously.

Similar findings were made in an extensive study across the (then) 12 member states of the EU (Gill *et al.*, 1992). In a study of mechanical engineering, electronics, banks, insurance and retail, they found that new technology had created jobs. However, they acknowledged that job losses could well be felt in those firms not employing new technology and thus losing competitive edge and market share. Woodall (1996) points to the case of the

USA and Japan. Both are countries that have invested more than most in computerized manufacturing, yet, compared to their counterparts in Europe, they have not suffered the same levels of unemployment.

The impact of new technology has been shown to vary according to the type of job. In general, the demand for unskilled labour has fallen while that for skilled labour has risen. Far from causing mass unemployment this has led to job shortages in some areas, notably computing and information technology. While jobs have disappeared, new jobs, particularly in IT and financial services, have emerged. This uneven impact has in some cases led to a transfer of skills from one group of workers to another. Wilkinson (1986) found that the introduction of the computer control of manufacturing equipment shifted work from the craft jobs on the shop floor to computer programmers and analysts. In many firms this represents a shift in the location of power within the organization and a subsequent impact on organization structure. In her study of changes brought about by the 'information age' Stanworth (1998) concluded that the impact of new technology on structure was far more significant than its impact on jobs.

More pessimistic views on the impact of new technology on employment levels emerged in the mid-1990s. Some estimates in the USA suggest that 2 million jobs are being lost annually, and, where replacement is taking place, it is in the form of part-time or temporary work (Rifkin, 1995). The same author sees job losses in manufacturing and service sectors alike. In the latter, banking has experienced numerous branch closures and considerable staff reductions in the face of automatic teller machines, telephone banking and electronic commerce. Unlike previous types of technological change, information technology in particular affects all kinds of jobs and places fewer restrictions on location. Using the advantages offered by information technology, such as global networks and the capacity to re-route telephone calls, the same job can be done equally well in Mumbai as Manchester. In this respect, both British Airways and Swissair have centralized their ticket accounting function in India, taking advantage of cheap labour. RCI, the world's largest company dealing in time-share holiday exchanges, have established their European operations centre in Cork, closing down smaller offices in other countries. Where the job involves telephone sales or telephone information, it matters little where the jobs are located. These operations are known as 'call centres', and in 1997 it was estimated that there were 3500 in the UK alone, employing 163 000 people (Davis, 1999). US hotel chains have operated such centralized systems for years and many other businesses have followed suit. In Europe, Cork has established itself as the leading 'call centre' with firms taking advantage of Irish government grants and the language skills of the local population. British Airways have centralized their flight information service in Newcastle, where office rentals and labour are cheaper than in London.

However, as Daniel had found a decade earlier, it is difficult to isolate the impact of new technology from that of other influences. In the 1990s there were considerable changes related to the impact of economic globalization, including increased competition and the transfer of jobs to lower cost labour markets. Under such competitive conditions, new technology could have been introduced to reduce operating costs and thus preserve jobs in the face of such competition. Such a position is compatible with our view of business as a set of complex interactions.

The debate about job numbers is matched by that concerning job content. We may conclude from the findings of the 1980s research in the UK that on balance new technology enriched the jobs of those affected in both manual and office settings, with greater possibilities being afforded the latter group. In deference to Braverman, the surveys do make the distinction between enhanced satisfaction in terms of job content and reduced autonomy through the centralization of management control. Research in the 1990s confirms these earlier findings. New technology would seem to be replacing 'mass labour' with 'elite labour' (Rifkin, 1995), emphasizing more creative knowledge-based work. In manufacturing, automation has greatly enhanced the work environment of jobs such as paint spraying. In the office the use of word processors has reduced the drudgery of typing numerous addresses. Nevertheless the benefits derived through the introduction of such advanced systems can be offset by the cost in manufacturing, and by the time taken to encode information in the office, before such benefits can accrue.

The main point to be taken from all the studies is that new technology should not be viewed deterministically. Its impact is based on a number of different factors, including the nature of the product and service, the type of organization involved and the competitive environment in which it operates, the management strategy employed, and the attitude of trade unions and employees. The majority of studies in the 1980s and 1990s are all fairly inconclusive on the impact of new technology on jobs. We may conclude that the job losses arising directly from the introduction of new technology are less than originally envisaged and must be viewed in the context of job losses resulting from other causes, such as global competition. However, three notes of caution have been sounded:

- While there was an initial transfer of jobs from the manufacturing to the service sector, some areas of the service sector, notably banks, suffered significant job losses in the 1990s.
- New technology is generally associated with growth industries. Rather than focus on job losses, perhaps we should be more concerned about the lack of job gains (Daniel, 1987).
- In terms of job losses, the hardest-hit group has been the low skilled workers. Since female labour is over-represented in such jobs, the introduction of new technology may have a significant impact on unemployment levels among women workers (Williams, 1984).

Despite such problems the failure to adopt new technology could have far more damaging consequences. Williams (1984) writes as follows.

> ... if the United Kingdom introduces new technology more slowly than other industrialised nations, there will be a real danger of job losses through declining competitiveness without the wider benefits which new technology can bring.

> (Williams, 1984, p. 210)

This point, in a more global context, is reinforced a decade later, but with a significant rider on the unequal impact of IT and globalization:

> The worst thing governments can do is to try to slow down the process of adjustment through regulation, subsidies or protectionism. They may save a few people from pain but they will depress living standards and employment growth for the country as a whole … Both information technology and globalization favour the highly skilled. For the unskilled the future could be bleak.
>
> (Woodall, 1996, p.23)

Labour

Labour interacts with business through the workings of the labour market and through the activities of trade unions. Aspects to consider are the changes in both the level and nature of employment and the role played by trade unions in the operation of business. We have already noted in this chapter how the forces of globalization, technological change and changes in both the ideologies and actions of the state have had an impact upon labour markets and trade unions. In the next section we will see how both types of employment and employee relations can be influenced by cultural factors. Managers influence the workings of the labour market through various strategies of recruitment, training and payment. Variations in management strategy also account for the way different companies handle issues of employee relations. In this section we will look at three aspects of labour. These are employment trends, links between education and training and the power of trade unions in influencing management decisions. A more detailed discussion of human resource and employee relations strategies may be found in Chapter 8.

Employment trends

We have seen elsewhere in this chapter that changes in the economy have significant effects on both the type and levels of employment. The changes affecting Britain, and indeed many other industrialized nations, may be summarized as follows:

● In the 1960s and 1970s considerable job losses were experienced in the primary sector (mining, agriculture, fishing etc.). During that period the primary sector workforce was cut by one half, although, largely through mechanization, its share of total output was increased. In the 1990s further employment losses were incurred by the primary sector through an extensive programme of pit closures in the coal-mining industry; 440 000 jobs have been lost in mining alone since 1981 (Labour Market Trends, 1998).

● The process of de-industrialization has led to considerable job losses in the manufacturing sector. Table 2.3 shows how manufacturing industry in the

UK shed 40 per cent of its labour between 1971 and 1991. We have noted that this was partly as a result of government policy, but mainly the effects of global competition. A fuller discussion of the de-industrialization process is offered in the first section of this chapter.

- Job gains have been experienced in the tertiary sector of the economy, particularly in the financial sector, catering, the professions and professional services. Since 1981 the greatest gains have been in computing and IT with 916 000 extra jobs and social work with 450 000 extra jobs (Labour Market Trends, 1998).

- Many changes in the nature of employment are attributable to changes in technology. References to this are made throughout this book and aspects of new technology have been dealt with earlier in this section.

- There is some evidence that firms in this country and elsewhere are following the Japanese practice of establishing a dual labour market comprising a trained core of employees supported by workers on a less permanent basis. A fuller discussion on flexibility is presented in the following chapter. Over the past decade there has been a marked increase in the numbers of part-time workers and several firms already express a clear preference for part-time employees.

- Related to the increase in part-time workers and the rise in long-term unemployment amongst males, there has been an increase in women workers from 33 per cent of the work force in 1951 to 48 per cent in 1990 (Edwards et al., 1992). By 1998 the proportion had risen to over 50 per cent, but the findings of a recent survey confirm the continued existence of well-documented trends. Women are still over-represented in certain types of employment, notably health, education and local government, and they are significantly under-represented in management in all sectors of employment. Indeed the proportion of women managers is about the same in both the private and the public sectors, despite the much higher proportion of women working in the latter (Cully et al., 1998).

- Dore (1997) noted changes in job allocation associated with the growth of 'graduate calibre' jobs and the raising of the educational entry requirements for jobs across the board. His prediction is that this will lead to a polarization within society. There will be those with good education and scarce skills who will obtain challenging jobs, although the impact of global competition and technological change will end the concept of a job for life. However, an increasing proportion of the population will be faced with either poor jobs or unemployment, with little chance of acquiring the necessary skills to move into more challenging work.

Education and training

One way of changing the composition of the labour market and thus addressing some of Dore's concern is through education and training. We offer a brief summary of the history of the UK concern for its relatively poor performance in training and education against that of its major competitors and we examine the approach to vocational training in Germany.

> The British entered the twentieth century and the age of modern science and technology as a spectacularly ill-educated people.
>
> (Hobsbawm, 1968, p. 169)

Hobsbawm's view reflects that of many commentators in the final half of the nineteenth century. The Samuelson Commission of 1884 accused the UK government and industry of falling behind its major competitors in the adaptation to economic and technical change. The Commission singled out education and training as the key drivers of change. From 1850 to the present day there have been a number of studies and reports, each drawing similar conclusions. Government policy reacts to these findings from time to time in response to falling competitiveness and technology lag.

In the 1980s there was considerable work carried out by the National Institute for Economic and Social Research (NIESR), focusing largely on comparative studies of education and training between the UK and Germany. The reports concluded that the UK workforce was poorly trained, which resulted in the production of poor quality goods and services with an adverse effect on the nation's economic performance. Such findings were confirmed by Handy (1987) in a major study of managerial training across five countries. In general, our competitors such as France, Germany, Japan and the USA have a much greater proportion of the population educated to a higher level, more finish training with recognized qualifications and there is greater integration between education in schools and the training system. In addition, the Handy Report points to the poor quality of much of UK management training.

A number of reasons have been given for the shortcomings of vocational education and training in the UK. These can be summarized as follows:

● Many have commented on the apparent divorce between education and training, compared to the integration found in such countries as Germany and France. The UK education system has been heavily influenced by the traditional public schools and their historical emphasis on non-vocational education. A continuing debate amongst educationalists is that of education of the whole person versus more job-related education. This has re-emerged in the current Labour government's emphasis on skills and employability.

● Traditionally the government in the UK has tended to see training as the responsibility of individual companies. Despite this there have been a large number of initiatives over the past 25 years to tackle specific problems such as youth unemployment and falling competitiveness. Such initiatives, however, have tended to be isolated responses without the framework of an overall long-term strategy.

● Many managers in the UK regard training as a cost, which, given the short-term orientation of many strategies, results in the reduction of training budgets at the first signs of financial reversal. This lack of a long-term approach is one reason for the continued decline in apprenticeships in the UK, despite several attempts to reform the system.

Collin and Holden (1997) suggest the emergence of an overall strategy in the

1990s. This involved a philosophy based on the notion of competencies and a structure around the National Council for Vocational Qualifications (NCVQ). To facilitate more training, regional Training and Education Councils (TECs) were established to provide finance and resources and to link up with companies in their area. Finally an award was developed, 'Investor in People' (IIP), to reward those companies that conformed to high standards of training and development. The new strategic directions do not appear to be very popular. Several managers remain ignorant of the various measures, while others have been critical of the bureaucracy associated with them. It would seem that UK managers prefer to go it alone or not at all. Amongst those firms with a reputation for investment in training there is an apparent preference for training to support the need of internal labour markets for multi-skilling and flexibility. This may, in part, explain the reluctance to embrace yet another set of government initiatives.

Germany: a training ethos

We have already noted the findings of the NIESR and the Handy Report, which compare the Uk unfavourably with Germany. Handy (1987) found that approximately 80 per cent of German managers were graduates, while Britain boasted fewer than 50 per cent. In Germany the degrees are vocationally oriented with engineering and other technical subjects predominating. In Germany it is normal for the better educationally qualified managers to hold the more senior positions in the hierarchy and to have risen through the ranks rather than by switching companies as is the norm in the UK and USA (Lawrence, 1980; Child *et al.*, 1983). It is not uncommon to find German managers with a degree and a technical apprenticeship.

Germany lays great store by its system of youth training referred to as the 'dual apprenticeship system'. A very high proportion (around 85 per cent) of all school leavers who do not go on to higher education enter a three-year apprenticeship across a range of occupations (Casey, 1986). The apprenticeship involves training in a mixture of job-specific and general work skills with one day a week spent in a specialist vocational college. The scheme has been successful in supplying the labour market with skilled workers that are easy to retrain because of the presence of general work skills and the emphasis on attitude training. The scheme is highly regulated by the state and is administered by national and local government, employers and the trade unions. The scheme is also supported by the broader education system. Support also comes from the trainees themselves, whose acceptance of low wages in the first few years helps fund the scheme. For example, a 16-year-old trainee in Germany can expect to receive only 25 per cent of the adult wage for the job, compared to 50 per cent in Britain (Casey, 1986). It is this social acceptance of training costs against likely future benefits that does much to underpin the system. No such ethos exists in Britain, and attempts at introducing youth training schemes have met with a consequent unenthusiastic response. The result has been that Germany boasts three times the number of skilled workers as can be found in the UK.

Such differences between Germany and the UK have been used by some studies to explain the differences in strategies, export performance and profitability of German and British industries. Training and skills were particularly significant in explaining such differences in the German and UK kitchen industries (Steedman and Wagner, 1987). However, more recent reports from such as the German Federal Labour Authority indicate problems arising from the mismatch between the qualifications of apprentices and the skills needs of employees. There are also indications of rising unemployment upon the completion of the apprenticeship. This is due partly to a marked rise in general levels of unemployment in Germany, but also to a growing preference for employers to prefer graduates from the higher education system. It is too early to assess the impact of such developments on the system as a whole.

Trade unions

KEY CONCEPT 2.8
A trade union

A trade union is a group of employees who formally come together to achieve mutual goals. Such goals normally include job protection, improving pay and conditions and attempting to influence management decision-making. In the United Kingdom, trade-union membership cuts across individual firms and entire industries, although different patterns exist in other countries, notably industrial unions in Germany and company unions in Japan. There is considerable ideological debate concerning the influence of trade unions in business decisions.

Trade unions are formally organized groups of employees with the aims, among others, of job protection, the improvement of pay and conditions, and the widening of industrial democracy. Such aims often bring unions into conflict with their employers, a conflict normally resolved by a process known as collective bargaining. We will examine first the changing nature of trade union membership before assessing the power unions can use to influence business decisions.

Trade union membership has both grown and declined considerably in the twentieth century, as we see in Table 2.7. A number of key changes indicated by the table are summarized as follows:

● We find marked variations in union membership in different types of employment. A high union density has traditionally been found in such industries as coal mining, which consistently achieved membership levels of over 90 per cent. High densities are also associated with local government and the engineering industry. Low levels of membership are found in retailing, and in hotel and catering. The changing pattern of union membership is illustrated in Table 2.8. The table shows that not only has membership declined in even the strongest unions, but that traditional

Table **2.7** Trade union density as a percentage of the working population 1913 to1992

Year	Density (%)
1913	23
1920	45
1933	22
1945	38
1964	44
1974	50
1979	55
1983	50
1985	46
1988	42
1992	36

Sources: Price and Bain (1983); *The Employment Gazette.*

strongholds of unionism such as the miners do not appear in the figures for 1996. This is a clear reflection of the changing patterns of UK industries and employment.

● The number of unions has declined from 1323 in 1900 to 393 in 1983 and to 275 at the end of 1991. This change is attributable to a mixture of amalgamation and structural changes in the economy. De-industrialization has accounted for the loss of a number of specialist unions in manufacturing. The amalgamation process has meant that the growth of the firm was, for a time, matched by the growth of the large trade union. At the peak of membership in the late 1970s, the biggest union, the Transport and General Workers Union, almost topped 2 million members. Table 2.8 shows the top 10 trade unions affiliated to the TUC in terms of membership. Currently the largest union is UNISON, formed through the amalgamation of three unions in the public sector, the National Association of Local Government Officers (NALGO), the National Union of Public Employees (NUPE) and the Confederation of Health Service Employees (COHSE). Almost all the unions in Table 2.8 have been formed by merger, the majority of which have occurred in the past 20 years.

● Taking a broad historical perspective, unions in older established industries such as coal mining and the railways have suffered large membership losses as employment has declined, while union growth has been most marked in the white-collar sector and among public employees. More recent membership increases are to be found among part-time workers and female employees of all types. Between 1990 and 1991, a time of general membership decline, female trade union membership rose by 20 000. Despite these growth trends there is clear evidence that trade unions are failing to secure members in many new areas of employment (Edwards *et al.*, 1992).

Table **2.8** Top 10 unions affiliated to the TUC by membership 1996

	1996	1991 comparison
	000's	000's
UNISON	1355	1526*
Transport and General Workers Union	897	1127
GMB	740	863
Amalgamated Engineering and Electrical Union	726	980**
Manufacturing Science and Finance Union	446	604
Union of Shop Distributive and Allied Workers	282	341
Communication Workers Union	275	N/A
Graphical Paper and Media Union	217	282
National Union of Teachers	175	N/A
National Association of Schoolmasters/ Union of Women Teachers	157	N/A

Source: Kessler and Bayliss (1998).
*In 1991 this figure represented the combined membership of NALGO, NUPE and COHSE.
**In 1991 this figure represented the combined memberships of EETPU and AEU.

- The major change since 1980 has been the overall marked decline in membership. Between 1979 and 1991, trade unions lost 3.7 million members, some 25 per cent of the total (Bird *et al.*, 1993). In each year during that period and since there has been a consecutive fall in total membership. Table 2.8 shows the changes in membership of the largest unions from 1991–6. In all cases unions have lost members, including the public sector and white-collar unions. Indeed the most dramatic decline over this period is in the white-collar union MSF, losing almost 30 per cent of its membership. This has been attributed to the loss of white-collar jobs in manufacturing and to the introduction of the check-off as a legal requirement. Under this requirement members must periodically re-register their membership and it is assumed that many have simply failed to do so.
- Along with the decline in membership there is evidence that collective bargaining has also declined (Millward *et al.*, 1992). This is the traditional mechanism used by unions to negotiate wages and conditions with management and many firms are clearly seeking alternative ways of wage determination.
- The Labour Force Survey of 1998 reported the first increase in union membership for 19 years, with a 4000 increase on the previous year. The largest increases have occurred amongst women, part-time workers and those of Asian origin. There remained a marked difference between the public and private sectors, the former reporting 60 per cent membership and the latter 19 per cent. Membership in manufacturing continued to fall. There was

considerable regional variation, with the highest membership being in Wales at 41 per cent of the working population and the lowest in South-east England at 22 per cent. The survey reported some optimism associated with the proposed measures of the Labour government to create a legal right to join a union.

Union growth and decline have mirrored economic, political and social changes. Increasing levels of unemployment have not only led to a reduction in trade union membership, but undoubtedly weakened their bargaining power. Two other developments may be noted. First, the influence of unions has been further weakened by the dismantling of many tripartite forums, associated with the Labour governments of the 1960s and 70s, and hence the removal of unions from the political arena and the development of economic policy. Second, following the pattern set by American and Japanese multinationals, it is not unusual to find firms with no trade union representing the workforce, or where a union does exist, it operates under single union, no-strike agreements. These strategies are analysed in Chapter 8. Despite this weakening of trade union power there is still a concern that unions often operate against the interests of private property and the public at large. This has been a key theme in the government's policies since 1979. It is to this issue of trade union power we now turn.

Trade union power

At an obvious level, trade unions do have influence. For example, wage rates in general are higher in unionized firms than in non-unionized firms in the same industry, and certain groups such as the Fleet Street print workers were able to resist technical change in their industry for many years. The union supporter would doubtless claim that the trade union acts as an important check and balance in management decision-making, preventing management from acting unreasonably and improving the quality of the decisions made.

Some, however, regard trade unions as being too powerful. This is a particular view of the 'New Right'. Their belief is that unions disrupt the mechanisms of the free market, particularly by pricing jobs according to bargaining strength rather than demand. This favours only a minority, pricing jobs out of the market and adding to the problems of unemployment. In addition, individual freedoms are challenged by strikes affecting the supply of goods and essential services. This was the view of the Conservative governments from 1979–97, resulting in a series of laws to restrict union action and, ultimately, to weaken their position. (Hayek, 1984 offers the ideological perspective behind this position.)

There is a view that argues that unions have never been particularly powerful and have been concerned only with marginal improvements in pay and conditions, without ever seriously challenging management control. By contrast, management are seen to wield considerable power, which is actually strengthened by the formal procedures used in dealing with unions. (A further analysis of this position may be found in Hyman, 1972 and Goldthorpe, 1977).

Many of the above arguments have their roots in different values and party politics. This influences not only the position taken, but the way facts are selected and interpreted. As with all influences on the management decision-making process there are insuperable problems of measurement. Even then we have to be content with observing the formal procedures when so much influence is undoubtedly the product of informal communication.

Whichever view is taken it is clear that, since the early 1980s, management's hand against the unions has been strengthened by rising levels of unemployment and changes in labour law. In addition, an increasingly competitive product market has led firms to seek greater flexibility both in the labour force itself and in working practices. Unions, weakened by membership losses and fearing job losses, have agreed to many such changes. Some view this state of affairs as permanent, while others see reasons for the decline of unions as a temporary phenomenon, linked to specific factors that will change over time. One such change was the election of a Labour government in 1997 with a considerable majority. However, despite the reported optimism of the 1998 Labour Force Survey, Kessler and Bayliss urge caution:

> The return of a Labour Government in 1997 marked a turning point. There is no longer an inherent enmity to trade unions. There will be interchange and the union's voice will be heard. But there will be no return to corporatism, there will be no major change in the balance of power, and there will be no major change in Conservative legislation.
>
> (Kessler and Bayliss, 1998, pp. 268–9)

Cultural influences and business

Culture may be defined as that part of human action that is socially as opposed to genetically transmitted. It comprises ideas through which we perceive and interpret the world, symbols we use to communicate these ideas, and institutions, which enable individuals to become socialized and satisfy their needs. Trompenaars (1993) recognizes that culture operates in three layers. At its most visible it represents those artefacts and goods that most readily distinguish one culture from another, such as architecture, food, ceremonies and language. At a deeper level it comprises our notions of 'right' and 'wrong', our norms, and our notions about what is 'good' and 'bad', our values. Many problems associated with the relationships between people of different cultures stem from variations in norms and values. At its deepest level, however, culture comprises a set of basic assumptions that operate automatically to enable groups of people to solve the problems of daily life without thinking about them. In this way, culture is that which causes one group of people to act collectively in a way that is different from another group of people.

Culture is a highly complex subject and interacts with business in three different ways:

- Our socialization, the influences which shape our behaviour in a particular social setting, will determine our individual orientations to work.
- We tend to see organizations as societies in microcosm with their own specific cultures and ways of transmitting these cultures to their members. In some companies, like Hewlett-Packard, the creation of a corporate culture is seen as a priority and a great deal of time, effort and expenditure is given to induction and training (Case 3.5).
- We use culture as an analytical device to distinguish one society from another.

KEY CONCEPT 2.9
Culture

Culture represents all human activity that is socially, as opposed to genetically, transmitted. It includes norms, values and beliefs that manifest themselves in behaviour, practices and institutions. Culture pervades all areas of business life. A particular interest is the extent to which we can learn from the business experiences of other cultures and transplant ideas developed by one culture and use them in a different cultural setting.

We deal with the concept of corporate and organizational culture in the next chapter and focus here on the third meaning of the term, viewing the wider cultural environment as one of the influences that shape business. Culture is of course the most pervasive of our five environmental factors in the model, having an impact on the other four. Factors such as the role of the state, the application of technology, and the orientations of the labour force to their work can all be viewed as being culturally determined. As with the other elements of the model the relationship with business is not just one-way. The way businesses conduct their affairs affects and often changes the particular culture in which they operate, the operation of the multinational corporation in the Third World being a case in point.

Interest in cross-cultural research blossomed in the 1960s following the popularity of the convergence thesis, a claim that the imperatives of industrialization would eventually cause all industrialized liberal democracies to become more like one another. The contending views of convergence versus cultural diversity are often referred to as the 'culture free' versus the 'culture specific' debate. In the following sections we examine briefly the main points in that debate and attempt to draw some conclusions.

The 'culture-free' hypothesis

A visitor to the Ford car plant at Dagenham in the UK will find many features in common with a General Motors car plant in the USA, a Renault factory in France, a Volkswagen operation in Germany, a Toyota plant in Japan, and the Proton factory in Malaysia. Such features include a common technology, similar types of organization structure, individuals with similar skills and job titles and work being carried out in much the same way. The culture-free hypothesis argues that businesses in the same sector in all countries are converging on similar types of technology, strategies, products and forms of business organization. Moreover, some believe that the speed of this convergence is increasing as a result of the growth of global travel and global communications. We have already examined many of these arguments in our discussion of globalization earlier in this chapter.

For the manager the key advantages of convergence are twofold. First, it enables manufacturing to take place on a global scale through the creation of global technologies and global products. This creates economies of scale to reduce costs and makes possible globally integrated supply chains and manufacturing. Second, ideas and techniques developed in one cultural or national setting may be transferred to another and used effectively. Furthermore, developing nations are able to learn from those more advanced countries and thus benefit from the mistakes of others. Such thinking is clearly behind the adoption by British and American firms of Japanese techniques such as quality circles and just-in-time and the focus on American theories of motivation by British management trainers. Belief in the transferability of techniques has led management to turn elsewhere for solutions to problems.

In the late 1980s, management at the Ford plant in Dagenham wished to reduce the average time for resetting the presses and turned to international comparisons for assistance in tackling the problem. The time taken to change the set-up of metal presses at the beginning of the production process is a key element in the overall efficiency of that process. Such changeovers are frequently necessary given the large number and variety of metal parts in a modern motor car and delays at this stage have an impact on the entire process. It was found that Ford workers at the Genk factory in Belgium could, with similar technology, effect the changeover in approximately half the time of the Dagenham workers. As a result a massive training exercise was undertaken and every member of the line-setting teams (those responsible for setting the presses) at Dagenham was sent to observe the Belgian operation. Lessons were learnt and the time was improved in the UK. However, the improvements did not match the time taken by the Belgian workers, which suggested that there were less tangible cultural factors accounting for the difference in the set-up times in the two countries.

The underlying theory behind all the above is that convergence on a particular type of technology and business organization is more significant than the cultural features of a particular society. The key elements in the convergence process are technology, the growth of big business and professional management and the impact of multinationals. The arguments were first developed by Kerr *et al.* (1973) and Harbison and Myers (1959). The main imperative of all nations was seen as efficient production and the key elements were developments in science and technology that were available to all. Businesses in all nations, faced with the same problems, adopted the same solutions. These included increasing size, increasing specialization and formalization, the development of similar systems of authority, occupational types and structures and adopting similar systems of education and training.

To Kerr *et al.* the ultimate development was that of industrialism which would transcend differences formerly ascribed to culture and political economy.

Support for the convergence hypothesis may be found in the universality of similar forms of productive technology, in the growth of big business, the multinational and professional management. The assumption is widely held that the theories and approaches to management and organization are universal, and that the same recipes (usually American) could be applied irrespective of the cultural context.

KEY CONCEPT 2.10
Culture-free versus culture-specific

This lies at the heart of the debate about transferring business practices and ideas from country to country. A culture-free perspective suggests that culture has less influence over business practices and ideas than, for example, technology and economics. Culture-free advocates argue that practices and ideas across the world are converging and that businesses can borrow ideas from their counterparts in other nations. A culture-specific perspective suggests that business practices and ideas are rooted in specific cultures and that transference is only possible between nations displaying similar cultural characteristics. This is not an either/or debate and elements of both perspectives can be found in business.

The 'culture-specific' hypothesis

Hofstede (1980a, 1980b) believes that there are significant national differences in the way people approach work and organizations. Hofstede's major work was based around a survey carried out between 1967 and 1973 of 116 000 employees of IBM across 40 different countries. The survey was an attempt to measure a number of cultural variables and hence determine the extent to which business activities were culturally defined. IBM is noted for its distinctive corporate culture and the deliberate strategy of developing that culture irrespective of national boundaries. Hofstede was dealing with an organization that had the same technology in all locations, the same organization structure and jobs and pursued the same strategies. The conditions were ripe for convergence. However, Hofstede found differences, which could be explained by reference initially to four variables. Further work in South East Asia with a colleague led to the development of a fifth variable, which explained more fully differences found between operations in the West and in Asia.

- **Power distance** This is the extent to which members of a society accept that power is distributed unequally in organizations. In all societies there is inequality between people, be it based upon physical, economic, intellectual or social characteristics. Hofstede found societies like France, Mexico and Hong Kong where the power distance was large and formed the basis of social relations. In societies such as Germany, Sweden and the USA, the power distance was small and such societies were noted for their attempts to reduce inequality.

- **Individualism versus collectivism** Individualistic societies such as the USA and the UK are depicted by a preference for looking after yourself or your immediate family group, a belief in freedom and a tendency towards a calculative involvement with work organizations. Collectivistic societies such as India, Singapore and Mexico show concern for a much wider group and emphasize belongingness which can extend to organizations.

- **Uncertainty avoidance** This is the extent to which members of a society feel uncomfortable with uncertainty. Members of societies displaying strong uncertainty avoidance, as in Argentina, Switzerland and Japan, tend to be anxious about the future and have an inability to tolerate deviant ideas. Weak uncertainty avoidance as displayed in Hong Kong, USA and Thailand is associated with a willingness to accept new ideas and take risks.

- **Masculinity versus femininity** Masculine societies such as Japan, the USA and Germany tend to display a preference for achievement, assertiveness and material success and display a strong belief in gender roles. Feminine societies like Sweden and Holland place more emphasis on the quality of life, care for others and equality, more especially between the sexes.

- **Long- versus short-term orientation** Hofstede and Bond (1988) identified a fifth variable through their work with firms in South East Asia. They found that some societies, particularly those influenced by Confucian philosophy, were much more future oriented, valued perseverance and thrift and were much more adaptable than many societies, especially those in the West. They also called their variable 'Confucian dynamism'. It explains the difference between the long-term orientation of managers in Japan, Singapore, South Korea and Hong Kong as opposed to the more short-term strategies of the UK, the USA and Canada. A long-term orientation was also found in Brazil and a short-term orientation in Pakistan and Nigeria.

These variables shape the values and hence the behaviour of people operating in work organizations and enable us to explain differences in the way different countries conduct their business affairs. They may also explain why work systems developed in one country will not work in another. For example, Hofstede reported that American car workers from Detroit working at the Saab-Scania plant in Sweden disliked the work system, which placed a great deal of emphasis on group work. The Americans, with the exception of one woman, were much happier with a system that stressed individual achievement. Hofstede noted that many management theories originated in the USA. The USA is typified by ratings that are below average for power distance and uncertainty avoidance, above average for masculinity, and has the highest rating on measures of individualism than any other country in Hofstede's survey. American motivation theory has been particularly influential and, in particular, the approaches of Herzberg, McClelland and Vroom reflect typi-cally American features. These are the need for individual achievement and performance (high individualism and masculinity) and involve the accept-ance of risk (weak uncertainty avoidance). The implication is that such theo-ries will not work so well in societies that are more collectivistic and feminine and whose people are risk avoiders.

The 'culture-specific' hypothesis claims that cultural influences in different societies will result in different styles of organization behaviour and different patterns of organization structure, as well as variations of influence in the business environment, such as the role of the state or trade unions. As a result, the policies of multinational corporations may well need to vary in dif-ferent countries and managers operating out of their home environment need specific training in cultural differences. This latter theme has been taken up by Fons Trompenaars (1993).

Trompenaars, like Hofstede before him, believes that much of management behaviour is culturally determined and that the key to successful interna-tional management lies in the understanding of these cultural differences. Trompenaars uses an anthropological approach and attempts to examine cul-tural differences in the way we relate to others, in our attitudes to time and in our attitudes to the environment. The few examples presented below offer a flavour of this type of approach.

In terms of how we relate to others, Trompenaars focuses upon five vari-ables relating to how we use rules, individualism, how public and private we are, the extent to which we show emotion and the extent to which we are achievement oriented. For example, in countries such as the USA, Switzerland and Germany, the prevailing culture is much more universalistic and rules are applied irrespective of the situation. On the other hand, cultures such as Malaysia and Indonesia tend to apply rules in a much more particularistic fashion and personal relationships can be more important in some situations than the rules governing conduct. In such universalistic cultures greater use is made in business of lawyers and contracts, and in multinational operations the head office plays a more directive role. Cultures also differ in the way they display emotion. Neutral cultures such as those in Northern Europe and Japan tend to keep feelings hidden and debate and argument are seldom personal-ized. On the other hand emotional cultures such as those found in Italy or Latin America show their feelings and find it difficult to distinguish between issues and personalities. In some societies such as Japan much more empha-sis is placed upon age, seniority, status and professional qualifications whereas in others, like the USA, respect tends to be earned on the basis of job performance. There may also be very different approaches to policies of pay and promotion. Such differences, as illustrated above, can have a significant influence on doing business with people from a different culture, and on the operation of multinational corporations.

The implications of a culture-specific approach are twofold. First, we must be extremely cautious in the way we borrow business and management ideas from other cultures. A management technique developed in one country may only work in that country because it is based upon a particular set of cultural values. The failure in the UK and the USA of many attempts to introduce

Japanese-style quality circles was due, in the main, to an incomplete under-standing on the part of the adopters of the particular cultural values under-pinning such an approach. The technique could be transposed but the conditions necessary for healthy growth could not. Second, in our dealings with people from other cultures we must recognize that differences do exist and be prepared to adjust behaviour and expectations accordingly. This is the theme of many recent initiatives in training for international management.

Towards a mixed approach

While convergence as an idea represents a somewhat superficial analysis, we have seen that its practical implications are that because industrialized soci-eties are moving in the same direction, we may therefore learn from the mis-takes of others further along the route. We have seen also that the supporters of the 'culture-specific' hypothesis believe that specific aspects of business are especially susceptible to cultural and national influences. As well as the work of Hofstede and Trompenaars, studies have identified the most likely as atti-tudes to work, management behaviour, organization structure, industrial rela-tions, recruitment and training (see for example Brossard and Maurice, 1976; Child and Kieser, 1979; Sorge and Warner, 1980). If we accept the culture-specific hypothesis then we need to be cautious in our approach to manage-rial panaceas. Useful ideas and methods may be transplanted but care must be taken to see that they have been adapted to the new cultural setting and that there is an understanding of the supporting conditions needed for their devel-opment.

Reality of course never fits neat conceptual explanations. Both our models may be used to explain the rapid emergence of Japan as an industrial nation. Elements of its business organization, management techniques and state machinery have been imported from other cultures, while other elements are clearly products of its own cultural past. Its late start to industrialization enabled businesses to learn from the mistakes made in more advanced coun-tries such as Britain, the USA and Germany. The specific elements of the Japanese culture undoubtedly gave these ideas a fresh impetus, so much so that the West has in the 1980s become fascinated by Japanese business meth-ods. This is the reason that books on business and management have, since the 1970s, paid homage to the phenomenon we call 'Japanese management'. This topic has assumed great importance in academic, business and political circles and we devote much of our review to it. For this we make no excuses, because a study of Japanese business and management practices is truly a study of 'business in context', for nowhere is the interrelationship between business activities, management strategies, organizational culture and envi-ronmental factors more clearly illustrated.

This mixed view is taken by Dore (1973) in his comparison of a British and a Japanese factory in the electronics field. He found similarities in the tech-nology and in the complex nature of work organization. In the case of Japan, he noted the impact of late development and that ideas had been borrowed from the UK, Germany and the USA. However, significant differences were found in motivation, recruitment, training and supervision. Dore noted that late developers can overtake their mentors, when they in turn become the focus of attention for would-be copiers. This is clearly the case with Japan.

Such a mixed approach may also be found in Case 2.4, where the development of Singapore owes much to both the traditional cultural values associated with Confucianism and the impact of foreign multinationals. The approach may also explain that while quality circles were less than successful when introduced into UK and US firms, just-in-time methods of manufacture have transferred quite successfully. A fuller discussion of JIT can be found in Chapter 6.

In illustrating the relationship between culture and business we examine specific aspects of Britain and offer a cautionary note on the dangers of cross-cultural comparison. We end the chapter with our analysis of Japanese business and management.

Case 2.4: The Asian Tigers

As we move towards the year 2000, Asia will become the dominant region of the world: economically, politically and culturally. We are on the threshold of an Asian renaissance.

(Naisbitt, 1996, p. viii)

Two years later, commentators were reporting the collapse of the major Asian economies.

'Tiger economies' is the name given to the second wave of Asian economies, which emerged after the post-war rise of Japan. There is general agreement that the four main 'tigers' are Hong Kong, Singapore, South Korea and Taiwan. These first-tier 'tigers' have been followed by second- and even third-tier 'tigers' in the form of Malaysia, Thailand, Indonesia, Philippines, China and Vietnam. This case will examine, in general terms, the rise and fall of the so-called 'tiger' economies of Eastern Asia. The next case study will focus specifically on Singapore, perhaps the most successful 'tiger' of all.

As the following table shows, the growth of the 'tiger' economies has been significant.

Percentage increase 1980–90

	GNP per capita	Earnings
South Korea	121.8	115.8
Taiwan	80.0	102.7
Singapore	77.5	79.8
Hong Kong	64.2	60.0

Source: World Bank

Over the same period the average annual growth rate for all first- and second-tier 'tigers' was 7.3 per cent. Such growth has rarely been seen anywhere else in the world, particularly in a region that had suffered years of disruption as a result of wars and political change. The economic success of the region has had a significant impact on standards of living for the majority, and, as some commentators have noted, has been accompanied by a **fall** in income inequality. This is in marked contrast to the West, where economic growth has usually been accompanied by **increases** in such inequality.

Several explanations have been offered for this economic growth. These include culture, the operation of external forces, the impact of market forces and the role of the state.

Cultural explanations have focused on the concept of Asian values and, in particular, their link to Confucianism. Hofstede and Bond (1988) have labelled such Asian values as 'Confucian dynamism' and the key features include a future, long-term orientation, perseverance in the face of adversity, thrift, a recognition of the importance of education and adaptability and dynamism. Hampden-Turner and Trompenaars (1997), based on a survey of 38 000 managers, argue that Eastern managers differ from those in the West in terms of their preference for collectivism over individualism, for consensus over conflict, for relationships over contracts and for their belief in virtue for its own sake. Eastern managers, they found, also differ in their attitude to time and the environment.

It is such cultural values that have often been

▶

Continued

heralded as the source of competitive advantage, not just for the 'tigers', but for Japan as well. However, such explanations have their limitations. The exact nature of precisely how culture impacts upon economic performance is difficult to show and measurable links are notable by their absence. If Asian values are so significant in their explanation of economic growth then we must question why such growth has not occurred until comparatively recent times. Equally, if culture is accountable for the growth, can it also be used to explain the decline? If culture is part of the answer then other factors are at work as well. It is to these we now turn.

A popular explanation for the rise of new industrial economies is that of the late development effect. As we have seen elsewhere in this chapter, this is part of convergence theory and suggests that those countries industrializing later have an advantage in terms of being able to learn from the mistakes of the early industrializers, through technology transfer and by operating from greenfield sites. This was used to explain the rise of Japan at the end of the nineteenth century, a country that, in turn, has had a significant impact on the development of the 'tigers'.

One factor that marks out Asian economies from the rest of the world is the proportion of the economy that is given over to savings. In East Asia savings account for 35 per cent of GDP, while the equivalent figures for the USA and Europe are 18 per cent and 12 per cent respectively. While the inclination to thrift is Confucian in origin, its current manifestation has much to do with the role of the state. A combination of low taxes, low inflation, high interest rates and controls over the direction of saving and the saving institutions themselves have all contributed to high levels of saving. This, in turn, has led to a large pool of investable income to be channelled into economic development. A further contributory factor is the relative lack of provision for social welfare and the historical reliance the people have placed on savings for family support during, for instance, sickness and old age.

The labour forces of most 'tiger' economies are relatively young and highly active. Furthermore, most East Asian countries have invested heavily in education, more especially at the primary and secondary levels. The nations are typified by intensive schooling regimes and high levels of literacy and numeracy. In the early stages of development in all countries people generally worked for long hours and low wages, factors which only changed in more recent times.

The governments of 'tiger' economies have clearly played a major role, although in their operation we can see a number of paradoxes. The governments tend to be more interventionist than those of the Western economies, yet spend less as a proportion of GDP. They are both more authoritarian and paternalist than those of the West, yet families are expected to be more self-sufficient. Their economic policies have tended to favour the operation of the free market, but with considerable assistance to the foreign multinationals, especially those representing export-led products. Governments are actively pro-business and there are many instances of intervention in labour markets to ensure their flexibility or to eliminate potential disruption.

The explanation of the rise of the 'tiger economies' is almost certainly a combination of all or most of the above factors. However, it is misleading to regard all first- and second-tier 'tigers' as the same. There are differences in economic structures, prosperity and cultures. There are significant differences in prosperity between first-tier countries, as with Singapore and South Korea, and cultural differences operate within as well as between countries as illustrated by both Singapore and Malaysia. By the same token the economic crash that affected the region in 1997 did not affect all countries in the same way as the following table illustrates.

Economic collapse in 1997

	% fall in currency against US dollar	% fall in stock market value
Indonesia	70	53
Thailand	55	59
South Korea	51	42
Malaysia	45	61
Singapore	20	53
Japan	13	29

Source: Guardian

While the changes were variable, they were significant across the whole region and even the established economy of Japan was not immune. A major factor in the collapse was that most of the local currencies were pegged to the US dollar. Over the years the dollar had strengthened, while growth in the local economies had slowed down. For many economists this was a re-run of events in Mexico in 1994/5. Thailand was the first country to devalue its currency, followed by the Philippines, Malaysia, South Korea and Indonesia in that order. This led to a rapid worsening of the position in all these countries and the problems spread to other parts of the region, including the stronger economies of Hong Kong, Singapore and Japan. While the link to the US dollar was the catalyst, a number of contending theories have been put forward to explain the underlying causes. It is to these we now turn.

Some consider that the fate of the 'tigers' is a function of their rapid growth, in that growth was the goal, irrespective of the price to be paid at a later date. The weak underpinnings of the economy, injudicious lending and the workings of the stock market were of particular relevance here.

Most of the 'tigers' had opted for a relatively restricted manufacturing base in terms of product variety. This meant that they were especially vulnerable to global price changes. In South Korea, the three major electronics firms, Hyundai, LG and Samsung, had grown rich through their focus on the manufacture of the 16-megabit DRAM computer chip. South Korea had 30 per cent of the world market and these companies took most of the 30 per cent. The very success of the product led to over-investment, resulting in over-capacity. By the end of 1996, the price for the chip had dropped 80 per cent, resulting in a fall in profits in that year of 93 per cent for Samsung, 92 per cent for Hyundai and 88 per cent for LG.

Considerable borrowing had been allowed to fund investment in firms such as those in South Korea. This left many companies with debts far in excess of their total assets. The debt/equity ratios of the three electronics firms were 437 per cent for Hyundai, 347 per cent for LG and 267 per cent for Samsung. The growth of company debt was a feature throughout the region, particularly in the relatively weaker economies. Problems that have been identified include a lack of scrutiny of many investment projects, some attracting the additional criticisms of nepotism and corruption and too many prestige projects with little hope of pay-back. In some countries, especially Thailand,

bad banking debts mounted as a consequence of poor lending strategies, mostly involving land and property speculators. The problem of bad debt was heightened by short-term borrowing from overseas banks and the ensuing difficulty of repayment, as the currencies destabilized.

The fast growth of the 'tiger' economies in the early 1990s attracted a large number of overseas stock market investors. At the same time there was a growing movement of investment away from manufacturing and into land and property. Many investors were interested only in short-term gains and tended to view the region as an entity. This meant that, at the first signs of trouble, investments were withdrawn across the whole region. Short-term speculation was not confined to the stock market. The artificially high currencies pegged to the dollar attracted considerable inward investment. While this operated as a virtuous circle when the economies were growing, it became a vicious circle as currencies were rapidly sold at the first signs of problems. Some politicians, such as the Malaysian Prime Minister, Dr Mahathir, attributed the economic collapse of 1997 to the activity of currency speculators. While this was a factor, it is only one amongst many, and other commentators have suggested that currency speculation was a symptom rather than an underlying cause.

In countries such as Thailand and South Korea, the economic problems of 1997 led to swift intervention by the IMF, imposing severe restrictions on both borrowing and growth. In Indonesia, the economic problems were followed by political problems and social unrest. Without doubt, the economy of the East Asia region has been destabilized. The pessimists view this as an inevitable consequence of uncontrolled growth and forecast further problems ahead. Those of a more optimistic persuasion see the problems of 1997 as a warning and an opportunity for countries to place their economies on a sounder footing. Whichever view is taken, the imact on individual countries will vary substantially owing to the inherent differences contained in this far from homogeneous region. ∎

(*Sources*: Hofstede and Bond, 1988; World Bank Report, 1993; Naisbitt, 1996; Rohwer, 1995; Hampden-Turner and Trompenaars, 1997; Henderson, 1998; Jomo, 1998; *Financial Times* and *Guardian*)

Case 2.5: Business and management in Singapore

Singapore stands out from the other Asian Tigers in terms of the strength of its economy, particularly its GDP per capita, as shown in the table below, but also in terms of its relative resilience in the face of the 1997 East Asian collapse. The growth of the Singapore economy is associated with a number of interrelated factors, which include geography, culture, the role of the state and the role played by multinational corporations of several countries.

GDP per capita 1996

	$US	1996 ranking	1990 ranking
Switzerland	42 350	1	1
Japan	38 120	2	2
Norway	35 710	3	5
Denmark	34 620	4	6
Singapore	32 878	5	17
Germany	30 300	6	7
USA	29 600	7	9
Hong Kong	27 130	11	8
UK	20 900	17	16
South Korea	11 910	24	25

Source: Hampden-Turner and Trompenaars (1997)

Singapore is a relatively small island of some 2.5 million people linked to the Malaysian Peninsula by road and rail. Its geographical position made it an important staging post for world shipping. Singapore was established as a trading post by the British in 1819 and expanded rapidly in the 1860s, as a result of increasing trade with China and Japan and the opening of the Suez canal. The growth was consolidated by the exploitation of rubber and tin in the surrounding regions, with Singapore operating as a vital export channel. This economic expansion led to considerable immigration to a virtually uninhabited island. The majority of immigrants were Chinese. This is reflected in the current ethnic mix of 76 per cent Chinese, 15 per cent Malay and 7 per cent Indian. A white, largely expatriate population makes up the remainder. In 1959, Singapore achieved self-

government from the British and in 1963 joined the Malaysian Federation. The political alliance with the Malay States was short-lived and Singapore became a fully independent nation state in 1965.

Throughout the 1950s and early 1960s there were a number of key problems to be faced. Britain withdrew its bases and hence their impact on the local economy. Relations with Malaysia became problematic. The country had no natural resources and there were insufficient jobs in trade alone to support the population. Its domestic market was small by international standards and the nation faced increasing competition from the growing economies of the region. Politically, at that time, Singapore was far from stable and its businesses were dogged by labour relations problems.

In the mid-1960s a strong government emerged under Lee Kuan Yew and outside help was enlisted. Following the recommendations of a UN Task Force, Singapore embarked on a policy of labour-intensive manufacturing to establish jobs and to substitute imports. Israel, a relatively new state, surrounded by potentially hostile forces and with few natural resources, was seen as an ideal role model, and several visits were made to Israel by leading Singapore politicians. The Singapore government tackled the then regional problem of communism through job creation and the establishment of a vigorous public housing scheme. Trade unions were brought into the system of state capitalism by giving them the island's taxi service to manage and by enabling them to run a major pension and insurance company. A senior government official is head of the trade union movement. Labour problems disappeared. Considerable investment was made in education, to create a unified system and end the division along racial grounds. Most significantly, the government established the Economic Development Board (EDB) to plan and oversee the nation's economic development.

Following the phase of job creation and import substitution, the EDB launched a campaign to attract overseas investment in the form of export-oriented multinational corporations. At the same time there was considerable investment in the port, which is now one of the largest and most modern in the world and certainly one of the busiest. The policies were so successful in terms of job creation that the problem shifted to one of labour shortages and rising wages. The EDB targeted investment that was high-tech, knowledge based and high value added. The country soon became the world leader in the computer disk drive industry. More recent policies have focused on establishing Singapore as a regional centre with outward investment in neighbouring countries. Singapore is now a major investor in Vietnam.

By any economic measure the policies have been successful. The table above shows recent and comparative GDP data. From 1985 to 1997 the country enjoyed uninterrupted GDP growth averaging at over 8 per cent per year. Unemployment fell to below 2 per cent in 1991 and became steady at less than 3 per cent. Inflation has been kept low at around 3 per cent, falling to less than 2 per cent in 1995. Over the same period wages rose by around 9 per cent per annum. A balance of payments deficit in 1980 of minus 3.3 million Singapore dollars was turned into a surplus of 21.3 million dollars by 1995. Output in manufacturing increased over 10 per cent year on year during the 1990s. The problems facing the region in 1997 meant that manufacturing output fell that year by 0.8 per cent overall and labour cuts were announced by major companies such as Hewlett-Packard, Philips and Motorola. Nonetheless, the strength of the Singapore economy meant that its problems were less severe than those of its near neighbours.

Three major reasons have been given for this remarkable economic growth: cultural explanations, the role of the state and the part played by multinational corporations. Foreign direct investment has played a significant role in the economic development of the island, but its attraction has also been a major government policy.

In our discussion of the 'Asian Tigers', which include Singapore, we defined the core cultural values in terms of the importance of a number of key features. These include the family, education, hard work, thrift, perseverance, adaptability and a long-term orientation. The core values originated from Confucianism, which also emphasizes duty and hierarchy, rule by humanity and moral persuasion, meritocracy and the supremacy of ethical standards. In business and economic life, such values are seen in loyalty to the nation's rulers and the support of officialdom, loyalty to the firm by a hard-working and responsible workforce, the importance of family firms, thrift, adaptable entrepreneurs, and a concern for education and self-improvement.

Undoubtedly in Singapore there is a commitment to the goals of the government that is rare in other countries, although high levels of labour turnover as a result of labour shortages and subsequent spiralling wages suggests that loyalty to the firm can be compromised. The concern for education is evident in a population eager to accumulate qualifications and by a massive state support of schools, polytechnics and universities, as well as training for industry. The people are clearly hard working and thrifty. The Singaporeans save a higher proportion of their income than anyone else, assisted largely by the state-run Central Provident Fund (CPF), which takes around 20 per cent of wages, matched by a further 20 per cent from the employer. The CPF then offers interest on savings, provides finance for home ownership and acts as a retirement pension fund. Withdrawals are also possible to buy blue-chip stock. Family firms play an important part in the economy of Singapore and there are many large and powerful Chinese businesses. Some of these businesses are linked to Chinese clans, to which people belong on the basis of their family origins, traced back to a particular village in China. Amongst the Chinese there is also some evidence that groupings of people who speak the same Chinese dialect are attracted to specific sectors. For example, Hokkien-speaking people tend to dominate in banking, finance and trade. However, there is also evidence to suggest a weakening of such traditional networks and value systems. Many of the new generation have acquired university education, often overseas, and experiences have been broadened beyond traditional values. In several local firms family control is being replaced by professional management.

Undoubtedly the state has played a major role in establishing the conditions for long-term economic growth to take place and for controlling the direction and pace of that growth. Its agency, the EDB, has been particularly influential. The state is viewed as being pro-business, establishing pragmatic policies when needed to support business growth. This has been complemented by a substantial investment in education and training, particularly technical training, and in housing and welfare.

Since independence, Singapore has been effectively a one-party state, with control in the hands of the People's Action Party (PAP). The government is noted for its strong social control. Opposition parties do exist but their parliamentary representation is negligible. State leadership has

▶

Continued

been highly directive and proactive, particularly in defence, education and training and the economy. Many Singaporeans work directly for the state and government employment tends to attract the most talented from the population. Its government ministers are the most highly paid in the world, reinforcing a strong desire for stability and incorruptibility. The economic policies embrace the attraction of foreign direct investment and the establishment of a number of government-linked companies. Some of these, like Singapore Airlines, are highly successful and pursue policies that are both aggressive and progressive. As well as the government-linked companies, the state plays a part in local investment through the Development Bank of Singapore. In more recent years economic policy has involved a closer relationship with Malaysia and Indonesia, to broaden both the product and labour market. Much of Singapore industry's unskilled labour travels daily across the causeway linking Singapore to Malaysia and the government has backed offshore manufacturing in both Malaysia and the nearby islands of Indonesia.

For many years Singapore has been an attractive location for multinational investment and many leading firms from the USA, Japan, Germany and the UK have manufacturing operations on the island. There are now over 3000 foreign firms operating in Singapore, attracted by a number of features. Singapore is viewed as a very safe and relatively attractive posting for expatriate employees. The EDB has been behind several initiatives to improve the social amenities of the city in ways favoured by expatriates. The redevelopment of the areas around the river to provide areas of restaurants, bars and entertainment is one such initiative. There are tax incentives and state provision of factory shells and related infrastructure. The Singaporean

government has been quite selective in its dealings with multinationals, favouring high-tech, capital-intensive firms. Such companies have also been attracted by the political stability of the country and the absence of effective opposition either from political parties or from hostile trade unions. The available local labour force is generally well educated and well trained, although there are labour shortages and competition for highly skilled managerial and technical talent is fierce.

The very success of Singapore and the increasing prosperity of its population have been recognized as a problem. There are fears that the country, like Japan, will become too expensive, with a widening gap between rich and poor. The signs are there in the form of escalating salaries and rents for office and factory space. These have pushed up significantly the cost of operating in Singapore. Increasing affluence has brought with it increasing individualism, which poses a threat to traditional values, and, perhaps, social and political stability. Labour shortages, labour mobility and continuous annual wage rises have both increased workloads and resulted in a workforce with high expectations. For some, Singapore is still too dependent upon foreign investment and foreign managerial talent. Moreover, its very success has acted as a role model for others in the region with the consequence of increased competition, more especially from lower-wage economies.

For many, the strength of the state and the strength of the national systems will overcome such potential problems. For others the 1997 slowdown will act as a catalyst for change.■

Sources: *The Singapore Yearbook* (various years); Chong Chi Loy, 1990; Wong Kwei Chong, 1991; Schein, 1996)

The British and business

A popular topic that emerged in the 1980s, and has continued ever since, is the search for an explanation of Britain's economic decline (Wiener, 1981; Gamble, 1985). Wiener uses cultural variables to explain an economic phenomenon. He believes that the British are no good at business because their hearts are not really in it. The prevailing values in Britain are those espoused by the land-owning gentry and as a consequence, business and especially industry are rejected as being representative of something fairly unpleasant. The consequences of this prevailing attitude are that the pursuit of economic gain is half-hearted and talent is directed away from industry. Government and the professions are favoured as occupational routes, capitalists aspire to be land-owning gentry, and the education system is dominated by a public school ethos which shuns science, technology, business and industry. While university graduation rates are comparable to those in former West Germany, only 0.7 per cent of British students are engineering graduates compared to 19 per cent in Germany (OECD, 1993). Moreover, almost 40 per cent of German managers have an engineering degree. Our half-hearted approach to business is consolidated by leaving management to the sometimes gifted but most times untrained amateur.

While it is not the job of this text to examine contending theories of Britain's economic decline, views such as those expressed by Wiener have a certain appeal. They are easy to understand and focus on easy targets, such as the public school system and the land-owning gentry. However, the hypothesis is highly speculative, difficult to verify and probably represents an exaggerated and idealized view. There is no explanation for the success of British entrepreneurs, the energy that accompanied the industrial revolution, nor the economic growth of the banking and finance industries in the post-war period. While it is true that the best products of our education system tend to be attracted not to industry but to the civil service and the professions, that situation is also true of Japan, a country we tend to hold as our economic role model.

Despite such criticisms, there are cultural elements that seem to have a significant impact on business. The class structure of this country provides us with greater insights into the relationship between management and workers. Certainly we assume that anyone with the 'right' background and a reasonable level of education can assume managerial responsibilities with no professional qualifications or training. Wiener's hypothesis might also explain the popularity of accounting as a profession and the leading role played by many UK financial institutions.

The difficulties involved in using culture as a variable

Culture remains a fascinating concept but a difficult analytical tool. The following points attempt to give some indication of the difficulties involved:

● Many studies that use culture as a central concept tend to define culture in rather broad, generalized terms. In many instances it is a kind of residual variable, a catch-all to explain away differences that cannot be explained by differences in the economy, technology, role of the state, size of the firm and so on.

● Lewis *et al.* (1996) argue that the impact of cultural values on economic performance is only identified with hindsight. Not only do they argue that such analyses are a post hoc rationalization, they suggest that such analyses are highly selective, ignoring evidence that does not fit. In this way, accounts of Japan may be biased, in that they focus on the successful but not the unsuccessful firms.

● Comparisons with other countries are often difficult because of the different rules governing the collection of data. Thus, strike statistics are notoriously difficult to compare because different countries use different yardsticks to define and measure a strike.

● Cultural comparisons tend to be made from the perspective of one culture only. We may make conclusions about another culture based on our own values. A study of the car industry worldwide showed that European and US manufacturers outperformed the Japanese on criteria they deemed most relevant: profitability measured by accounting ratios. The Japanese, however, laid greater store by market penetration and growth, and on these criteria easily outperformed the European and American manufacturers (Bhaskar, 1980).

● In many cases language presents a serious barrier to full understanding. Certain concepts do not translate easily. 'Technik' is a central concept to German manufacturing, yet has no direct translation in English.

● We have seen that we possess preconceived notions about other cultures, often expressed as stereotypes. These can creep into our analysis and become self-fulfilling prophecies; we see what we expect to see. Our ready acceptance of such stereotypes prevents us from digging more deeply. For instance, an analysis of German management will reveal a much greater formality in superior–subordinate relations than exists in Britain or the USA. We may conclude from this that the Germans have less interest in people-management, when all evidence points towards good working relations existing in German firms. Such stereotypes are often deliberately used in training, when preparing managers for cross-cultural management, as we saw in our discussion of the work of Trompenaars. Clearly such approaches need to be used with considerable caution.

● Cultures can and do change over time and our perceptions can become dated. For example, management students in Singapore are keen to challenge Hofstede's classification that classifies Singapore in terms of low uncertainty avoidance, typified by a willingness to take risks. They claim that while that may have been true in the early stages of independence in the late 1960s, the prevailing culture of the 1990s is much more risk-averse and conservative.

Japanese business and management

Management literature since the late 1970s has been preoccupied with Japan. Serious and popular newspapers alike have jumped on the bandwagon and television documentaries have followed the fortunes of British recruits to Japanese multinationals as they exchange Newcastle Brown Ale for sake. Despite such exposure, our knowledge of Japanese management, while much greater, appears to have done little for our real understanding. In many respects Endymion Wilkinson's quote is still valid:

> I examine the European image of Japan and find it composed of an arsenal of stereotypes founded on the shifting sands of

indifference, ignorance, prejudice, and fear, rather than on any effort to seriously understand the Japanese.

(Wilkinson, 1983, p. 17)

The stereotypes to which Wilkinson refers have changed dramatically over the years from a manufacturer of cheap, unreliable products, to a menacing military and then economic imperialist, to a view of Japanese methods as the panacea for the ills of Western capitalism and, currently, to a nation in decline.

Even allowing for the difficulties of comparing the economies of different nations it is clear that Japan has emerged in the post-war period as the world's second largest economy behind the USA. There is a widely held view that this is some kind of post-war miracle in which a modern Japanese economy arose from the ashes of a completely devastated country. A similar view is often proffered for Germany. In both cases, the foundations of a strong economy were laid much earlier. Nevertheless, post-war growth has been significant and in Japan's case, particular advances were made in the decade from 1955. Despite the marked reduction in that growth in recent years, or even because of it, there remains a fascination in the way that the Japanese organize their business affairs. We offer a flavour of the complexity and paradoxes of that area known as Japanese management. We will do this by looking at various explanations that have been offered for Japanese economic growth since 1945 and for the decline of the 1990s. We examine also the investment and experience of Japanese firms in other countries, notably Britain, and the process known as 'Japanization'.

The simple explanation for the growth of the Japanese economy in the 1950s and 1960s is the cost advantage Japanese firms had over major competitors in manufacturing. This enabled Japanese manufacturers to make significant inroads into the markets of key competitors, while import controls enabled the same firms to dominate the home market. The cost advantages were derived initially from a labour force that worked long hours for low wages. Firms became cash rich, which enabled them to invest in new methods

KEY CONCEPT 2.11
Japanization

Japanization refers to the process through which Japanese business practices are incorporated in the businesses of other countries. This occurs directly through Japanese multinationals, where business practices from Japan are transplanted in a host country and have an impact both on the internal workings of organizations and on relationships with suppliers. A more indirect form of Japanization occurs when Japanese methods are adopted by non-Japanese managers and firms. Examples of such adoption include the widespread use of just-in-time methods in manufacturing industry across the world. There are difficulties in operating Japanese methods outside Japan and these are linked to cultural differences.

and new technologies to reduce the build time of their products (Williams *et al.*, 1992a and 1992b). As wages rose and hours of work reduced, competitive advantage was maintained by further investments. Behind these simple economic facts lie a number of interrelated factors, which embrace cultural, political, economic and managerial explanations. It is to these we now turn.

Cultural explanations

According to Ronald Dore, in his excellent book *British Factory–Japanese Factory*, Japan has benefited greatly from the 'late industrialization effect', whereby the diffusion of ideas from advanced industrial societies into totally different settings gives those ideas a new impetus (Dore, 1973). In the case of Japan, Dore believes, the system has developed to permit a culturally conservative society to adjust to rapid technical change.

Below we examine the Japanese in terms of Hofstede's four original values and how these values translate into business practice.

- The Japanese have moderately **high power distance** and consequently attach considerable importance to vertical relationships, which are typified by loyalty, dependence and a sense of duty. This is reflected in lifetime employment, the absence of job-hopping and the seniority principle, all discussed later in this section. The existence of these values, alongside collectivism, explains the Japanese loyalty to the group, be it the country, the family, or their company.
- The Japanese score very **high in terms of uncertainty avoidance**. Their unwillingness to take risks is reflected in many aspects of business life. It explains both the time taken in the planning process and the detailed content of the plans themselves. It may also explain the preference of the Japanese for incremental product development.
- **Collectivism** is a feature of the Japanese and is reflected in the importance placed upon harmony and teamwork in all aspects of working life. Peer group recognition is very important to the Japanese worker. Consultation is a feature of decision-making in Japanese firms and, with uncertainty avoidance, explains the time taken in the decision-making process.
- The Japanese score **very high in terms of masculinity**. This may explain why their alliance partners in other countries often view them as assertive. It may also explain the absence of women in senior positions in Japanese firms, in that a masculine society favours traditional gender roles.

The 'confucian dynamism' or **'long-term orientation'** defined by Hofstede and Bond (1988) echoes both the conservatism and adaptability noted in Dore's earlier work. Both historically and emotionally Japan is a closed society, owing largely to a sense of isolation and a lack of resources. This has resulted in the Japanese placing more emphasis on bank savings than their counterparts in other industrial nations, their willingness to adapt to changing conditions for survival and their preference for seeing things in the longer term. The planning horizons of Japanese firms are much greater than those of their Western counterparts, and it is not unusual for the management of a company to have a 250-year plan.

The role of the state

Historically the state has always had a significant role in the development of the Japanese economy. The big five companies known collectively as the '*Zaibatsu*', which dominated the Japanese economy in pre-war times, developed with the specific assistance of the government. Their legacy today is in the large holding companies known as the '*Keiretsu*' which lie at the heart of the Japanese economy.

For many years Japan has enjoyed a highly stable political framework. The Liberal Democratic Party has been in power since 1954, although in 1993 its majority was reduced to marginal proportions and it has since been forced into coalition governments. The state in Japan represents a network of influence between politics, the civil service and business operating a system of targeted development and trade protection at home, with selective investment overseas. Elites within this system tend to circulate; the civil service recruits top graduates from the best universities, the most successful of whom tend to move at a later stage in their careers to politics or business. Such relationships are ripe for those who favour conspiracy theory, and images have been painted of a mafia-style command economy. However, the images do not bear close examination. Conflict exists, not only between business and the state, but also between companies themselves competing for the same markets. The ruling party, the LDP, is far from a cohesive body, and consists of different factions competing for power. The credibility of the party has been stretched by the banking crisis of the 1990s, which we deal with later. Senior politicians have been linked with accusations of corruption in the financial sector, there has been a rapid turnover in prime ministers and the party suffered a major split in 1996. The LDP remains the largest parliamentary party, but by 1999 the opposition parties were probably stronger than at any time since 1954.

A central feature of the state's influence is the role played by the civil service, in particular the two departments known in the West as MITI (Ministry of International Trade and Industry) and MOF (Ministry of Finance). Traditionally they have helped to coordinate and direct Japan's economic strategy. Specifically, MITI has targeted those industries that are internationally competitive as in the case of cars and micro-electronics. Industries operating in preferred sectors have been offered prime locations, were allowed to expand and received tax relief on modernization programmes. MITI also ensured that such industries received priority in foreign investment. The department has been especially active in encouraging cartels both for purposes of rationalization and for exploiting world trading conditions, both occurring in the case of the shipbuilding industry. In Chapter 5 we examine the role of the state in R&D and the establishment of research cartels amongst major manufacturers in a given sector. The other side to this strategy has been a marked lack of assistance for those businesses operating in non-designated sectors of the economy. Despite this, industries outside the favoured sectors, such as hi-fi, pianos, television manufacture and, above all, motorcycles, have enjoyed considerable success, suggesting that state support may be only one of several factors.

MOF controls the Bank of Japan, which in turn has significant influence over the major commercial banks and hence the direction of investment. It is important to know that in Japan, banks are the major shareholders in industry and commerce, with direct individual investment playing a minor role. This system is actively encouraged by the intervention of MOF. Additionally, with MITI, MOF assists in the process of channelling foreign investment to high priority companies, especially when capital is short, and targets Japanese investment abroad, in particular to those areas rich in the kind of natural resources and business opportunities coveted by Japan.

Japanese banking is not only influential in the investment process, it plays a major part in survival of some firms under threat of closure. In the mid-1970s Toyo Kogyo, the producer of Mazda cars, faced bankruptcy with a 1975 loss of US$ 70 million, resulting largely from increased wage costs at a time of dramatic fall in sales and export orders. The Sumitomo Bank, a major shareholder, stepped in and initiated a major turnaround operation, taking control and installing new management with new strategies (Pascale and Rohlen, 1983). As a result of the bank's intervention, the company not only survived, but it developed a new range of models, which enhanced its export performance and world standing and attracted Ford into a joint venture. A less reputable side of Japanese banking came to the public attention in the 1990s and banks were held by some to be responsible for the continued economic decline of Japan through the 1990s (see later in this section).

Undoubtedly the state has played a major role in the development of the Japanese economy, more especially by accelerating market forces. The big firms have clearly benefited from their influence with MITI and MOF. However, Callon (1995) feels that major companies have now outgrown MITI. He acknowledges the debt the major firms owe to MITI, particularly for protectionist and growth policies during the 1960s and 1970s. He charts the decline of MITI influence by focusing on the failure of MITI-led consortia in computing. Paradoxically he sees MITI's failure as a product of market forces and Japan's economic success. Companies so dependent upon MITI in an earlier time had become self-sufficient and viewed MITI's attempts to establish consortia as unwarranted government interference. The market had become less protected as a result of US pressure and Japanese companies emerged as market leaders, forced to become more innovative in a highly competitive environment. Callon's study exposes the limitations of state intervention when companies are dealing with state-of-the-art research. He also debunks the myth of Japan as a consensus society. His study of the MITI consortia in computing is a study of warring bureaucracies, warring private firms and, ultimately, conflict between the state and business.

Economic organization

Duality is the central theme that dominates Japanese economic life. This duality operates both in the organization of the manufacturing sector and in the labour market. Every large firm in Japan uses a large number of smaller firms as subcontractors and it is not unusual, for a firm employing 1000 workers, to have 160 subcontractors (Armstrong *et al.*, 1991). In this way a hierarchy of manufacture is built up, with larger firms subcontracting to smaller and so on. In every case, the relationship between the firm and its supplier is carefully specified, with deliveries being requested not by the week or even day, but by the hour. This is a central feature of the just-in-time system, discussed in more detail in Chapter 6. Furthermore, it is quite usual for the purchasing company to get involved in work organization and job design in the subcontractor's factory, often in an attempt to reduce costs and hence the price of supplied parts.

Such a system tends to favour the large corporation, and the Japanese economy is indeed dominated by big businesses operating as giant holding companies controlling a number of (often) highly diversified firms. For example, the Sumitomo Group has divisions dealing with mining, cement, chemicals, electrical goods and heavy industries; the Mitsubishi Group deals with chemicals, glass, rayon, paper, automobiles, steel and heavy industries. Additionally, both these groups along with the other large holding companies have banking, insurance and real estate divisions. The role of banks as major shareholders has already been mentioned, but here we have a case of banking operating as yet another division of the holding companies. This not only gives such firms access to sources of investment, but also places them at the centre of a network of information. The relationship with subcontractors is further cemented in that the bigger firms, often through their banks, are major shareholders in the smaller companies. In general the relationship is very close and 'parent' companies tend to be very loyal to their subcontractors. In recession it is not unnatural for subcontractors to be supported and protected by the major company, who will often reduce its own labour force to cut costs rather than sever the link with its supplier. The idea of a close relationship between manufacturer and supplier is now embedded in much of manufacturing strategy throughout the world, a lead undoubtedly given by the Japanese.

In Figures. 2.4 and 2.5 we offer a very specific view of the competitive advantage offered by the traditional system of subcontracting in Japan manufacturing industry. We can see from Figure 2.4 that, compared with the UK, smaller Japanese firms pay less in wages than their UK counterparts. In Figure 2.5 we can see that a much larger percentage of Japanese labour operates in smaller firms. Given that the smaller firm predominates in the Japanese subcontracting network, there are substantial cost benefits derived from lower wage costs.

In terms of the labour market, a great deal of publicity has been given to the Japanese concepts of lifetime employment and seniority payment systems. However, such benefits only apply to the minority of Japan's workforce and a dual labour market operates. The system works as follows. The labour force is divided into 'permanent' and 'temporary' workers. The 'permanent' workers have tenure and receive the pay and welfare benefits normally associated with Japanese firms, while those classed as temporary workers have no such security, have few employment rights and enjoy none of the benefits of their permanent counterparts. The majority of 'temporary'

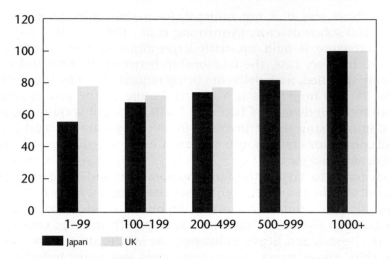

Figure **2.4** Wage gradients by firm size in 1989. *Source*: Williams *et al.* (1992a)

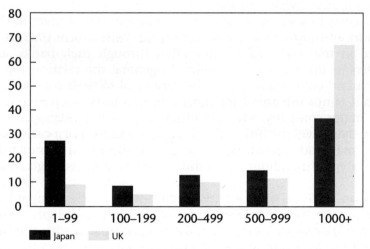

Figure **2.5** Percentage share of employment in 1989 by firm size in the UK and Japan. *Source*: Williams *et al.* (1992a)

workers operate in a largely unregulated small firms' sector. According to such rare accounts as Satoshi Kamata's experience as a temporary worker for Toyota, the lot of the temporary worker is far from idyllic (Kamata, 1983). Precise statistics concerning the proportion of workers in each category are difficult to obtain, but various accounts estimate the 'permanent' group to represent around 35 per cent of the total workforce, although this varies considerably according to the size and nature of the organization. A major firm like Nissan will have 'permanent' employees in the majority, perhaps around 75 per cent, the remainder being made up of workers who are classed as temporary. Nissan's major subcontractors will likewise have a large proportion of 'permanent' staff, but further down the subcontracting hierarchy the proportion of 'temporary' workers rises sharply, many smaller firms having no 'permanent' workers whatsoever. No farm workers and very few women in Japan have 'permanent' status.

We will look at the negative aspects of this dual system later. From the point of view of the country's economy there would appear to be some advantages to this economic organization, not least of which is a built-in elasticity to cope with changing demand. A firm like Nissan will cope with increased demand by taking on more temporary workers and either increasing its number of subcontractors or placing greater demands on its existing suppliers. Reduced demand will be met by lay-offs of temporary workers, as experienced by many such workers in the 1990s. Such is the importance of the relationship with suppliers that it would be rare for subcontractors to be dropped in times of reduced demand, and assistance may even be given to help them out. The system would appear to succeed because of the privileged position and economic strength of the larger companies and the ready supply of temporary workers, a proportion of whom aspire to 'permanent' status, and a proportion who are basically farm workers seeking seasonal work. Such a model of a flexible labour force has found favour with many Western employers and it is an issue we will discuss in the next chapter.

Management and management strategies

Management

Studies such as those by Storey *et al.* (1991) suggest that 95 per cent of Japanese managers are university educated and most do not reach management status until they reach 35–40 years of age. While there is considerable mobility within the same function, fewer than 5 per cent of managers in the survey by Storey and his colleagues had ever worked for another firm. There would seem to be little in the way of structured training, and most of the training that does occur is both on-the-job and instigated by the individuals themselves. There is regular performance appraisal and considerable importance is attached to role models and mentors. Management in Japan is still male dominated despite changes in the law to promote equal opportunities. Apart from cultural values, which stress differentiated gender roles, a major obstacle to more female employment is the dearth of child-care facilities. Employment with a major corporation is for most Japanese, management and worker alike, an important source of social status.

Decision-making

'The process of communication within a Japanese organization is very much akin to the mating dance of penguins'. (Sethi *et al.*, 1984, p. 37.) As this quotation implies, there is considerable ritual and a great deal of consultation. Much attention has been focused on consensus and collective decision-making ('*ringi sei*'), when in practice there would seem to be considerable initiatives and decisions taken by top management alone. However, the consultation process ('*nemewashi*') is very important and large numbers of workers do in fact participate. The consultation process is part of a corporate culture, which is reinforced by the trappings of egalitarian society, including company uniforms for all, compulsory exercises for all at the start of the day, and a sharing of the same canteen facilities.

HR policies

These are often the most publicized aspects of Japanese firms, but as we have seen, they only really apply to about a third of the workforce. They include lifetime employment, pay based on seniority, an attention to employee welfare, and fringe benefits such as company housing and holidays. As Beardwell (1997) points out, lifetime employment should really be termed lifetime commitment, in that employees can be transferred to another company in the group or even to a supplier. Reward linked to seniority is an important strategy in strengthening the ties of the individual to the firm. Recruitment and selection tend to be rigorous even for comparatively low-level employees. As we see in the Nissan case on p. 120, the selection of supervisors is a highly competitive affair, candidates being subjected to a battery of tests and strenuous interviews. The selection process for all workers is followed up by an equally rigorous training programme where employees are expected to master most aspects of a particular process. The emphasis is clearly on flexibility, reinforced, in most cases, by an absence of organization charts and job descriptions.

Industrial relations

All Japanese trade unions are company unions and employees have no choice as to which union they join. The particular system of company unions has its origins in a four-month dispute in 1953 involving workers at the Nissan car factory. The dispute led to a lock-out by management that was backed by the major shareholder, the bank, and the US authorities. The stipulation for a return to work was the acceptance by the workforce of a company union with the motto 'those who truly love their union love their company' (Hetherington, 1986). Other companies took Nissan's lead and set up their own unions. Not surprisingly, plant-level industrial relations are comparatively harmonious and are more akin to joint consultation than collective bargaining. Disputes do occur at national level, but they tend to be highly predictable affairs based on annual pay negotiations (referred to as the 'Spring Offensive') or concerned with the size of the autumn bonus. Since the early 1980s the unions have been increasingly opposed to Japanese investment overseas, on the basis of its impact on jobs in Japan. However, on such issues unions carry little political clout to affect policy.

Manufacturing orientation

For many, the attention paid to the operations function is the key to Japanese manufacturing prowess and export success (for example White and Trevor,

1983; Hayes and Wheelwright, 1984). While attention has been focused on specific techniques such as 'quality circles' and 'just-in-time', the essence is almost certainly a meticulously planned, integrated system, in which attention to quality plays a central role. To this we must add an orientation to product innovation which pays particular attention to the needs of the customer. A pivotal figure in this production system is the first-line supervisor, which perhaps explains the attention paid to his selection. The production orientation is supported by a system that places considerable emphasis on rules, regulations and discipline. Dore's comparison of Hitachi with English Electric noted, in the Japanese case, the emphasis placed on attendance and timekeeping and the willing participation by Japanese employees in the widely found practice of sacrificing holidays in favour of the company (Dore, 1973). British companies dealing with the Japanese for the first time are often astonished at both the time spent in planning and the inordinate level of detail involved in the planning process. A more detailed review of Japanese manufacturing methods can be found in Chapter 6. Despite the emphasis on manufacturing, there has been a considerable growth of the service sector, both in Japan itself and in Japanese operations overseas. By the mid-1990s the service sector rather than manufacturing had emerged as the preferred destination for Japan's university graduates.

An investment in R&D

In Chapter 5 in we show the extent of innovative activity through a series of patent indicators. There is clear evidence to suggest that the Japanese place a higher priority on new product development than any other nation. Furthermore, companies are encouraged to collaborate in joint R&D ventures. These too will be discussed in more detail in the chapter on innovation.

The result of such management strategies has been the creation of the firm as a community and a high level of identification with the company on the part of individual employees. There is, however, an alternative explanation for Japan's economic growth.

Japanese management: an alternative view

The cultural, political, administrative, economic, organizational and strategic factors identified above have all been cited as explanations for Japanese economic superiority over the West. Kamata's view of life as a temporary worker for Toyota, with accounts of production speed-ups, excessive overtime and the oppression of the bachelor dormitory, paints an entirely different view (Kamata, 1983). Other analyses, some of them Marxist in their approach, conclude that Japan's economic success is based on carefully planned exploitation (especially Armstrong *et al.*, 1991).

This exploitation takes several forms. First, the 'temporary worker' is exploited in terms of his or her lack of security and must bear the brunt of any recession; a case could even be made for the exploitation of the 'permanent' employee through an employment system that ties him to a single employer. Second, the larger firms exploit the dependent position of the smaller firms through the system of satellite subcontractors. Third, we have the suppression of independent trade unions, which renders plant-level collective bargaining somewhat meaningless. Finally, it has been argued that the economic system exploits the cultural characteristics of the Japanese people themselves, namely their loyalty, discipline, and commitment to national goals.

It is difficult for someone brought up and operating in a particular culture and value system to draw accurate conclusions about the exploitation that is supposed to occur in an entirely different cultural context. More accounts like Kamata's would be welcome, especially since it dates from the early 1970s. However, the system has resulted in considerable increases in the standard of living for a large number of people. While larger firms can and do exploit the relatively weak position of their suppliers, there are also many examples of cooperation, mutual benefit and support.

Japanization

In recent years the concept of 'Japanization' has emerged, referring to two related phenomena. First, it refers to the process of Japanese foreign direct investment (FDI), by which Japanese firms set up operations overseas. Second, it relates to the process whereby Japanese business and management methods are practised in other countries either as a direct consequence of FDI or through the process of cross-cultural transference as mentioned earlier in this chapter. The former are referred to as 'transplants' and non-Japanese companies pursuing Japanese methods are known as 'adopters' (Elger and Smith, 1994). As far as the UK is concerned (and perhaps other countries as well), the favourable reception given to Japanization in the manufacturing sector by government, employers, employees and, in some cases, trade unions appears to rest on two assumptions. First, it is believed that Japanese manufacture overseas will increase the value added in the host country by stimulating economic growth and employment and by reducing the number of Japanese imports. Second, there is a belief that Japanese manufacturing methods set the kind of examples that the rest should follow. In the case of the latter, it is certainly true that just-in-time methods of production are standard practice amongst manufacturing firms in many countries. (A further discussion of this may be found in Chapter 6.) However, in focusing upon manufacturing we should not forget that the majority of Japanese FDI is in non-manufacturing, particularly in financial services and much, during the 'bubble economy', in land and property speculation. While the adoption of Japanese methods is apparent in manufacturing, it is less so in the service sector.

A relatively early series of studies of Japanese manufacturing plants and financial concerns in the UK concluded that many features associated with Japan, namely a stable, highly committed workforce, complete cooperation in change and low levels of conflict, simply did not exist in the UK (White and Trevor, 1983). Nevertheless the Japanese firms did exhibit higher levels of productivity than their British counterparts. In achieving these levels of productivity, White and Trevor found that typically Japanese employment practices such as the lifetime employment and the seniority principle were not used, but that great attention was paid to selection and training. They found no real difference in levels of employee satisfaction, but the real distinction lay in certain work practices. These were a highly organized approach with an emphasis on fine detail, especially in the planning process, the elevation of quality as the top priority and a much greater sense of discipline throughout the various organizations. They noted a quite exceptional acceptance of management authority, which tended to be more favourable the greater the Japanese presence, almost as if employees were more willing to legitimize the position of Japanese managers than their British counterparts. White and Trevor attributed this to the greater egalitarianism displayed by the Japanese and the greater willingness on the part of the Japanese manager to get involved in the operations. As the authors note:

> The predominant response of employees was one of approval and often some pride at being part of such an exceptional effort.
>
> (White and Trevor, 1983 p. 130)

Although the study was carried out almost 20 years ago and in a different era as far as UK industrial relations are concerned, the conclusion that successful transfer of certain Japanese methods is possible obtains today. The main elements would appear to be a careful attention to detail in the planning process, incremental product design, focus on low costs, focus on quality systems, a greater investment in training and a much more egalitarian approach to management. There may be elements which are too embedded in the cultural values of the Japanese and which will be difficult to transfer. These include the stability of employment, the strong company identification and work ethic and the ability of Japanese managers to employ a management style that is a mix of paternalistic, disciplinarian and egalitarian methods. This may explain why many UK and US firms found difficulty in introducing Japanese-style quality circles.

Such perspectives on the advantages of Japanization are not shared by all. Williams *et al.* (1992b) are particularly sceptical. They produce evidence to show that 70 per cent of Japanese overseas investment is in non-manufacturing areas such as financial services and the purchase of land, activities that do not create jobs. They claim that the influence of Japanese firms has been exaggerated by the media since Japanese firms employ only 0.6 per cent of the UK workforce and only 1.1 per cent in the USA. Moreover, the value of Japanese exports is 40 times that of goods produced by Japanese firms in the UK. Contrary to popular belief they found that Japanese manufacturing in the UK, especially amongst the car companies, was not particularly profitable. In a re-examination of Japanese manufacturing effectiveness in the car industry they claim that, Toyota excepted, some European manufacturers such as BMW perform better than the Japanese in such areas as stock turnover and work in progress, traditional measures of manufacturing effectiveness.

While the expansion of Japanese multinationals in Britain is part of the general process of the internationalization of the Japanese economy, two additional factors stand out. First, the interest Japanese firms have shown in

Britain is seen as a mechanism to circumvent EU trade restrictions on Japanese imports. This has resulted in many joint ventures between British and Japanese firms, as existed between Austin Rover and Honda in the development and manufacture of the Rover 800 series, and the Triumph Acclaim before that. Second, those Japanese firms that have established themselves in Britain have tended to favour development areas where government grants and other advantages are available. Such areas include the North East of England and Scotland, where there are high levels of unemployment. It is undoubtedly much easier to ensure the compliance of a workforce and the cooperation of trade unions, even to somewhat alien work practices, when the alternative is long-term unemployment. There is no doubt that the situation also favours the company in its relationship with its local suppliers. When suppliers are struggling to survive in a harsh economic climate, it is much easier for the purchaser to negotiate contracts that are highly favourable to him in terms of price and delivery.

Case 2.6: Nissan UK

Nissan, the major Japanese car manufacturer, produced its first British-built car at its Sunderland plant in April 1986. The firm was coveted by several county councils seeking to stimulate business and employment in their areas and competition to attract a major company like Nissan was fierce. Tyne and Wear in the North East, an area of de-industrialization and high unemployment, was selected.

The plant uses robots for welding and has a fully automated paintshop, but these are hardly unique features in modern car manufacture. For many the real difference at Nissan lies in its approach to industrial relations and its personnel policies.

Acknowledging the traditional labour relations problems with the car industry in Britain and a strike frequency of over seven times the norm for manufacturing industry, the company on the advice of personnel director, Peter Wickens, opted for the recognition of a single union only. The policy alternatives of either a non-union shop or the recognition of several unions were felt to be recipes for antagonism and chaos respectively. The competition for union recognition among trade unions hungry for members was considerable. Nissan represented a potential of 2700 new members when most trade unions were losing members at an alarming rate. Recognition was eventually achieved by the Amalgamated Union of Engineering Workers (AUEW) and a deal embracing terms and conditions of employment was signed between the union and company representatives before production started in 1985.

The deal was unique both for the car industry and for the AUEW.

The agreement between the union and the company lists certain key principles upon which it is based. These include mutual trust and cooperation; a commitment to quality, productivity, and competitiveness, using modern technology; a need for change and flexibility to maintain the competitive edge; a belief in open and direct communications. Most significantly there is an adherence to the avoidance of any action that interrupts the continuity of production and the union's recognition of management's right to make the final decision in the best interests of the company.

These principles have been reinforced by several mechanisms. First, terms and conditions form part of a two-year agreement, which is binding on both sides and includes a no-strike clause for the duration of the agreement and during any negotiation or arbitration. Second, in exceptional circumstances, when agreement cannot be reached ACAS will be called upon to arbitrate, but a straight choice must be made between the two alternatives in a system of pendulum arbitration. Third, negotiations are made between the company and the Works Council, not the trade union. The Works Council is made up of elected representatives, each representing part of the plant. Although the election is supervised by the union, representation is open to all employees. In fact one estimate has put union membership at only 18 per cent. As well as negotiating salaries and conditions, the Works Council concerns itself with issues of productivity, quality and planned change.

The personnel practices are also new to the car industry. All employees are treated as single status, share the same canteen, wear the Nissan blue uniform, and receive annual salaries paid in equal monthly installments. Employees are not required to clock on and are only asked to clock off when overtime is being worked so that a record may be kept. Workers are paid a guaranteed week of 39 hours. Management has retained the right to review both the clocking-on procedure and the guaranteed week in the light of operating experience, and to lay workers off without notice should production be disrupted by industrial action either at Nissan itself or one of its suppliers.

Competition for jobs at Nissan has been high. In an area of 20 per cent unemployment an estimated 3500 applied for the first 22 supervisory positions. An estimated 11 000 applied for the 240 production jobs. Selection processes were exacting. The potential supervisors were all put through a series of psychological tests, while the production workers were narrowed down through successive hurdles, including pencil and paper aptitude tests and at least two interviews for short-listed candidates. The emphasis was on seeking employees with a strong positive commitment to the goals of the company, thereby reducing future potential conflict. Apart from the management, nearly all recruits were under 40 years old, few had previous experience in the car industry and only a minority was unemployed. By comparison the senior management nearly all had motor industry experience and were recruited from such companies as Ford, Austin Rover and Rolls Royce. In total the company started with three British and four Japanese directors.

Peter Wickens has claimed that Nissan's policies are not peculiarly Japanese, and feels them to be a distillation of American, German and British as well as Japanese methods. Indeed, he operated similar policies in his previous employment with an American company based in North Wales. Whatever the origins, the novelty of Nissan's approach lies in its single union, no-strike deal and in its insistence upon absolute commitment to the goals of productivity, quality and continuity. The approach has formed the basis of its advertising campaign, orchestrated by Saatchi and Saatchi under the slogan, 'They don't half work'.

The Sunderland plant continued its success in the 1990s and was in profit even when Nissan were making overall losses. The annual survey on car industry productivity, produced by the Economist Intelligence Unit, has identified Nissan, Sunderland as the most productive plant in the UK since 1995. In 1998 it became the most productive car plant in Europe and the 10th most productive in the world behind eight Japanese and a single Korean plant. It became the first plant to produce over 100 cars per employee per year, some 25 per cent better than its nearest European rivals, the VW plant at Navarra in Spain and the GM plant at Eisenbach in Germany. Despite this profits have fallen, owing entirely to the strength of the pound.

Nissan management in the UK ascribes the plant's success to three major factors. First, they believe that a major source of success is the willingness of staff to embrace change. Their selection and employment practices have done much to eliminate more traditional 'resistance to change' cultures. Second, each department operates a Kaizen (continuous improvement) system that is both self-funding and involves all employees. Finally, supervisors are given considerable freedom and responsibility, including the hiring of staff. ∎

(*Sources*: Burrows, 1986; Tighe, 1986; *Guardian* and *Financial Times*, 1998, 1999)

However, there is evidence in the North East of England that many of the workers taken on by Japanese firms are neither unemployed nor refugees from the most depressed industries such as mining and shipbuilding (Tighe, 1986). There is also little evidence to suggest that the Japanese are treating English suppliers any differently to those in Japan, where exacting cost, quality and delivery requirements are the norm. Moreover, there is significant evidence that Japanese companies are giving customers what they require, with a growing trend towards the customization of products for local markets.

Further insights into the Japanese in Britain may be found in the Nissan case.

Japan and the problems of the 1990s

> Japan has suffered the characteristic consequences of oppor-
> tunism in the good time. Management has become careless, the
> banking system over-optimistic and both the economic and the
> business structure overly bureaucratic.

> J. K. Galbraith (*Observer*, 21 June 1998)

The Japanese economy, which had begun to slow down in the 1980s, experienced a series of problems throughout the 1990s. A number of factors were
interrelated and included the high value of the yen, the lack of regulation and
confidence in the financial sector, increased competition both in product
markets and from low-wage economies, and bad management decisions.
There were signs of recovery in 1997, which were dashed as Japan was
plunged into the South East Asian crisis in the latter half of that year. The cultural characteristics of the Japanese, particularly the importance attached to
saving face, loyalty to the group, a distrust of outsiders and a preference for
dealing with difficulties internally, have meant that there was a tendency to
hide or even cover up problems. This was apparent in the scandals associated
with the finance companies Daiwa and Yamaichi.

Massive trade surpluses forced up the value of the yen. This in turn led to
the easy credit of the late 1980s, which created in Japan a 'bubble economy',
typified by land and property speculation and profligate investment by major
manufacturing corporations. In terms of the labour market, Japan had moved
from a low- to a high-wage economy. In manufacturing industry efficiency
gains had kept pace with wage rises, but to some, many of the leading firms
had reached the limits of cost reduction (Williams *et al.*, 1992a).

The home market in Japan in the 1990s fell by 20 per cent overall. In 1998
alone, retail sales in department stores fell by 25 per cent and home car production fell from 13 million vehicles in 1991 to 9 million vehicles in 1996.
Owing to the high value of the currency, many firms suffered severe losses in
their overseas operations. During the period 1992–5, most major companies
posted losses, including Toyota, Mitsubishi, Mazda and Nissan. The 1997
crisis caused losses the following year for such as NEC and Mitsubishi, while
Nissan and Toshiba saw a fall in profits from 1997 to 1998 of 97 and 85
per cent respectively (Sources: *Financial Times* and *Guardian*). Across
manufacturing industry there were severe cutbacks in R&D and even plant
closures.

Between 1991 and 1999, Nissan saw a fall in its global market share from
6.6 to 4.9 per cent. In 1999, with its CEO seconded from its partner, Renault,
Nissan announced global job cuts of the order of 21 000, which would
include the closure of three manufacturing plants and two power train plants
in Japan itself.

The problems of the major companies like Nissan had their impact on the
labour market. By 1998 unemployment had reached 4 per cent. While this is
not high by European standards, it was by Japanese and undermined Japanese
confidence in their own system. Overtime was invariably cut and in many
cases eliminated, thereby depriving many workers of an important

component of their wages. Bonuses were also reduced by up to 20 per cent. Many manufacturing firms placed an embargo on the hiring of temporary labour and placed pressure on older workers to take early retirement. In Nissan, new 'non-Japanese' practices were introduced, including merit rather than seniority-based promotion and share options for senior management. Restructuring occurred in most major companies. In some cases this eradicated the over-staffing of many management hierarchies but it also resulted in job losses. The attack on job security and, by implication, lifetime employment has probably done much to undermine the stability of the Japanese employment system. For many years salaried, lifetime employees, referred to as 'salarymen', had enjoyed job security for life and benefits which included anything from subsidized housing to haircuts. Security was further enhanced by labour laws, which made shedding labour difficult. Such systems have been found to be incompatible with the economic crisis of the 1990s.

A key element in the problems of the 1990s is the banking and financial system. We have already commented upon the high levels of personal savings. These are used, through the mechanisms of the financial system, as an important source of investment for business. We have also noted the key role played by the banking system in business survival and growth. The 1990s witnessed a rapid loss of confidence in the Japanese banking system both locally and globally as bad debts mounted and a succession of malpractice scandals emerged. The major features were bad lending and poor investment during the period of the 'bubble economy'. From 1992 bad debts held by the banks rose significantly, when in 1996 they outstripped operating profit. By 1998, total bad debts in the banking system were US$560, approximately the GNP of Canada. Many of the bad debts were associated with loans to buy land and property. The property and land boom of the late 1980s was followed by a price collapse in the 1990s. Commercial land prices in major urban areas increased sixfold between 1979 and 1989 to fall below twice the 1979 figure by 1996 (Source: Bank of Japan). The collateral upon which many of the loans were based had disappeared and banks were left with little hope of recovering their debts.

Alongside and part of the problem of bad debt, several major financial companies were found guilty of illegal trading. Nomura, one of the largest and most successful financial companies in the world, was found guilty in 1991 of dealing with a gangster syndicate and making illegal payments to favoured clients to cover their losses. A similar scandal occurred in the company in 1997. In 1995 the Daiwa Bank in the USA attempted to hide losses illegally and was barred from trading in the USA by the US Treasury. Yamaichi, the 10th largest securities company in the world, was forced into liquidation in 1997 with overall debts of £14 billion. The management was found guilty of illegal deals in which some losses were placed in offshore accounts, while others were shifted from one company to another in an attempt to keep them hidden.

As a direct consequence of problems in the financial sector, the government has created the Economic Planning Agency attached to the office of the Prime Minister and removed the planning role from MOF. This is one of a set of proposals aimed at tackling a declining economy, a banking system perceived as corrupt, rising unemployment and skills shortages in key economies, notably telecommunications. The measures include:

- the reform of the financial system by deregulation, which will effectively remove government protection from the traditional banks and finance houses and expose them to the scrutiny of the market place;
- a review of state bureaucratic procedures to confront the problems of corruption and to lead to more effective and efficient government decision-making;
- a move away from lifetime employment with the same company through the creation of a more flexible labour market;
- A series of tax reforms which will cut personal taxation and therefore increase spending power;
- investment in education, science and technology to address skills shortages and in health to face the problems of an ageing population.

Japanese management: some conclusions

The specific nature of Japanese culture, state intervention, the subcontracting system, the dual labour market, management strategies and practices, company unions, and the exploitation hypothesis have all been used individually or in combination to explain the post-war growth of the Japanese economy. All contain elements that are highly plausible, and in all probability the real explanation is a complex interaction of all factors, with some factors being more important than others at particular times.

Many in the West, including business leaders, politicians and some academics, would like to reject the cultural hypothesis, since this offers us little hope of practical gain, unless we all become Japanese. We have noted already that interest in the UK centres on two phenomena:

- the expansion of Japanese multinationals and the subsequent employment of UK workers (transplants);
- the use of 'Japanese management' practices by management in firms.

Hayes and Wheelwright (1984) have argued that there is nothing peculiarly Japanese about the way they run their businesses. The emphasis on high growth rates, market penetration, low costs, careful planning, long-term as opposed to short-term profits and quality is good business sense in any culture. A number of factors temper this enthusiasm. First, the elements mentioned above may well represent excellent management practice, but their successful application in Japan may be due to a supportive state, a particular form of economic organization, and draw upon specific characteristics of the Japanese people. Second, writers such as Williams *et al.* (1992a, 1992b) have questioned both the contribution of Japanese firms to the UK economy and the effectiveness of their practices.

Most significantly, as we have seen in the previous section, the system would seem to be under threat in Japan itself as management adapt to changing economic circumstances. Many of the proposed changes such as deregulation and flexible labour markets would appear to be moving Japan more towards Western practices. It will be interesting to observe the impact on traditional management practices. There is evidence that, fed on tales of Japanese economic problems and inefficiencies, enthusiasm for things Japanese has waned. Other views are less pessimistic. Dore (1997) argues that despite the longest post-war recession in Japan's history, the system is inherently resilient, many of the key institutional features have survived and lifetime employment is still the norm. His explanation lies in the view of the firm by its members. Firms, he argues, are seen as communities of people and not institutions run by managers to enhance share value.

Summary

In this chapter we have identified five key aspects of the environment, namely the economy, the state, technology, labour and culture. For each of these we have selected issues that highlight the interaction between business enterprises and the environment in which they operate. A key theme in all the sections is that of globalization. Economies are linked globally as never before, assisted by developments in information technology. The impact on economies, governments, labour markets and culture has been significant.

The **economy** is viewed as a product of its constituent business activity as well as exerting considerable influence upon the way businesses operate. These influences work through resource availability and allocation, international competition, especially via multinational enterprises, the extent of state direction and levels of employment. Major changes have taken place since 1979 involving both the structure of the UK economy and the relationship between the economy and the state.

The **state** is examined from the perspective of increasing intervention as an employer, a collective provider, an advisor, a legal regulator, and most significantly for business as a demand manager. Business interests for their part attempt to influence government policy through pressure group activity, with mixed results. Businesses also interact with supranational bodies such as the WTO and EU and are affected by associated changes such as the introduction of a single currency for the EU. The role of the state is illustrated by reference to the UK and the transition from Thatcherism to New Labour.

Technology is viewed as the application of available knowledge and skills to create materials, processes and products. It is viewed both as a constraint and an opportunity as well as a product of innovation by business. New technology is seen as an opportunity for businesses to reduce costs, while increasing the quality of their products and the effectiveness of their service. Evidence concerning its impact on both job content and levels of employment is mixed. With some developments in information technology such as electronic commerce it is perhaps too early to draw firm conclusions.

The relationship between business and **labour** is seen through the workings of the labour market, issues in education and training and the influence of trade unions. Changes in the economy have resulted in changes in the type and availability of jobs. The focus on trade unions is on their changing role in the face of economic and political changes.

Culture is viewed as a pervasive factor shaping the entire environment of business. Dominant cultural aspects of society leave their mark upon businesses operating in that society and lead to certain generalizations about the value different societies place upon business. Interest in culture has been stimulated by the prospect of learning from others and transplanting business methods from one society to another, as with the popular pastime of analysing Japanese business methods. This book joins in that pastime by giving its own account of Japanese business. This is not only illustrative of the cultural debate but also represents an extended case of the way businesses in a particular society interact with key elements of that society.

Further reading

The changing nature of the interaction of business and its environment means that the best sources of current material are inevitably the better newspapers and the more reflective magazines. The references provided below will offer a useful overview and starting point.

The relationship between the economy and business and the role of the state are well treated by P. Armstrong *et al.*, *Capitalism Since 1945* (Basil Blackwell, 1991) and D. Childs, *Britain Since 1945: A Political History* (Routledge, 1992). A view of the state in the wider perspective can be found in World Bank, *The State in a Changing World* (OUP, 1997) and an interesting review on the transition from Thatcherism to New Labour in the UK is presented by several writers in the special edition of *Marxism Today* (Nov–Dec, 1998). A good source for issues relating to Europe is N. Harris, *European Business* 2nd edn (Macmillan, 1999). C. Randlesome, *Business Cultures in Europe* 2nd edn (Butterworth/Heineman, 1993) is an effective bridge between EU issues and the more general issues relating to culture. Although dated, J.Woodward, *Industrial Organization: Theory and Practice* (OUP, 1965) is a good account of the influence of technology on business organization, while illustrations of the impact of new technology can be found in D. Preece, *Organizations and Technical Change: Strategy, Objectives and Involvement* (Routledge, 1995) and for information technology specifically in B. P. Bloomfield *et al.*, *Information Technology and Organizations: Strategies, Networks and Integration* (Oxford University Press, 1997). Good sources for labour and trade union issues are S. Kessler and F. Bayliss, *Contemporary Issues in Industrial Relations* (Macmillan, 1998) and M. Cully *et al.*, *The 1998 Workplace Employee Relations Survey: First Findings* (DTI, 1998). An interesting account of the impact of culture on business in Britain can be found in M.J. Wiener, *English Culture and the Decline of the Industrial Spirit 1850–1980* (CUP, 1981), while excellent sources for culture in general are G. Hofstede, *Cultures and Organizations* (McGraw Hill, 1994) and F. Trompenaars, *Riding the Waves of Culture: Understanding Cultural Diversity in Business* (Economist Books, 1993). A good treatment of Japanese management, dated but still relevant, is R. Dore, *British Factory–Japanese Factory* (University of California Press, 1973). A good review of Japanization can be found in T. Elger and C. Smith, *Global*

Japanization? The Transnational Transformation of the Labour Process (Routledge, 1994).

Discussion

1. In what ways can a business influence its immediate economic environment through its R&D, production, marketing and human resource strategies?

2. Using the illustrations of a) a mass producer of cars, b) a university, and c) a small accountancy practice, examine how a firm interacts with its economic environment at the local, national and international level.

3. Assess the impact of globalization on businesses in your local region. What has been the cause of such changes and how have they affected manufacturing firms in general?

4. To what extent is the state a facilitator and to what extent a constraint in the operation of a business? What does the Norton-Villiers-Triumph case (2.2) tell us about the state's involvement with business?

5. Using the three illustrations offered above in topic 2, identify how management could influence the state and the directions this influence might take.

6. Examine Case 2.1. What are the key issues and what are the implications of such events for businesses in the UK and for the future of the EU?

7. Identify the various types of change that are likely to occur from the introduction of business systems based around information technology. What opportunities and threats exist for management and the workforce? What problems will be created and how may they be overcome?

8. Examine the major changes in the labour market and trade unions in the past 20 years. What impact have such changes had on the operation of business at the level of the individual firm? In the UK, what is the likely impact of the transition from Thatcherism to New Labour?

9. How useful is the concept of culture in explaining the way businesses operate in different countries? To what extent can business ideas and management techniques developed in one cultural and national setting be transferred to another?

10. What is Japanization and how might it be affected by the 1990s recession in Japan? What is the likely impact on Nissan's UK operation (Case 2.6)?

CHAPTER 3

Organizational aspects of business

In the previous chapter we examined aspects of the environment that interact with business. Such aspects constitute the outer level of our model. In this chapter we examine a second level of interaction and influence belonging to the organization itself. We will consider five aspects in our model: goals, structures, size, ownership, and organizational and corporate culture.

As with other aspects of our model there is considerable interaction and overlap between these organizational issues. As well as pointing out the areas of overlap in each individual section, the way that issues relating to goals, ownership, structure and size come together is examined in more detail through the concept of organizational culture. In addition, we highlight three specific issues, ethics and business, the public sector and small businesses, all of which illustrate the complex nature of these organizational relationships. The relationship between ethics and business is highly topical as each decade throws up examples to place ethical considerations at the forefront. In the 1980s there were the well-publicized cases of Chernobyl and the *Exxon Valdes* and the late 1990s has the raging debate on genetically modified crops, which has brought the US company Monsanto to the public's attention. The public sector has been chosen since it is a good illustration of the interaction and tensions within the organizational elements as well as those operating between the organization and its environment. In addition, government policy of privatization, deregulation and the commercialization of the public sector has meant that the distinction between public and private concerns is becoming increasingly blurred, further justifying our focus. The treatment of small businesses raises key economic and political issues as well as highlighting the very specific nature of business problems found in this sector.

Goals

In this section we shall examine the nature of goals, the purposes they serve and how they emerge. We shall also consider the potential problem arising from a number of different goals operating in the same organization. We often speak glibly of organizations like Marks & Spencer, British Rail, or even our own college as having goals. However, we should not ascribe behaviour to abstract entities such as organizations. Goals should always be attributable to some person or group. Case 3.1 illustrates the goals of five organizations. Logica is a fast-growing UK company, specializing in IT consultancy. Mercedes Benz is a German manufacturer of high quality cars and trucks. Nippondenso is Japanese and one of the world's largest car components manufacturers. LG is a Korean conglomerate with interests in electronics, chemicals, machine tools, construction and finance. Sainsbury is a large UK supermarket chain.

Case 3.1: Illustrations of company goals

Logica

Our mission is to help leading organizations worldwide achieve their business objectives through the innovative use of information technology.

Founded in the UK in 1969, Logica plc provides value-added solutions based on IT consultancy, systems integration, products, services and support.

We work for leading blue chip organizations on a global basis on IT assignments, which are critical to their future business success.

Chief Executive's Review

We believe that the company is ideally poised for its next leap forward. The repositioning we have undertaken to focus on value-added, mission-critical work in growth markets and to establish a global network, provides the framework for continuing good organic growth in the years ahead. To supplement this, we have over the last eighteen months begun a programme of selective acquisitions aimed at:

- adding new territories to widen our distribution network
- achieving critical mass for existing units
- increasing our portfolio of repeatable solutions in our chosen market sectors
- broadening our service offering, particularly in consultancy and support services.

(*Source*: Annual Report and Accounts, 1998)

Mercedes Benz

Mercedes Benz stands, within the Daimler Benz group, for vehicles of the highest quality and the complete spectrum of customer services. The wishes of our customers, the interests of society and the success of our company provide the frame of reference for our work. We build on the traditions of Gottfried Daimler and Karl Benz. These inspire us in a rapidly changing world to boldly grasp the global challenge to make passenger and goods transport even more efficient, environmentally compatible and safe.

Corporate Principles

- We must make customers enthusiastic about the three-pointed star. We must always be a committed partner for our customers throughout the world.
- We want to be the best in terms of innovation, quality and profitability. Our goal is to remain the leading supplier of premium cars and expand our position in the commercial vehicle markets.
- We are actively pursuing an open-minded corporate culture. We create a new dynamic working environment where we can assume individual responsibility and trust each other.
- We integrate our business partners. Their input helps us meet and exceed our goals on world markets.
- We assume ecological responsibility.

(*Source*: Annual Report, 1995)

The Nippondenso philosophy

Mission

- Contributing to a better world by creating value together with a vision for the future

130

Management Principles

- Customer satisfaction through quality products and services.
- Global growth through anticipation of change.
- Environmental preservation and harmony with society.
- Corporate vitality and respect for individuality.

Individual Spirit

- To be creative in thought and steady in action.
- To be cooperative and pioneering.
- To be trustworthy by improving ourselves.

(*Source*: Corporate Guide, 1995)

LG

Since LG's foundation, the Group's business activities have been guided by the ideals of research and development, progress and harmony. These principles have been incorporated and redefined in the Group's new management philosophy: creating value for the customer through management based on esteem for human dignity.

In preparation for a rebirth in the 21st century, LG has established an optimal growth strategy and set out the following Group-wide goals.

- Enhancing customer satisfaction.
- Advancing into promising industries
- Becoming an insider in world markets
- Fostering divisional autonomy
- Winning acclaim in industrialized countries

- Supplying technology and economic assistance to developing markets
- Internationalizing and globalizing through joint ventures
- Participating in international finance.

(*Source*: Corporate Report, 1994)

A statement of company objectives by J. Sainsbury plc

To discharge the responsibility as leaders in our trade by acting with complete integrity, by carrying out work to the highest standards, and by contributing to the public good and to the quality of life in the community.

To provide unrivalled value to our customers in the quality of the goods we sell, in the competitiveness of our prices and in the range of choice we offer.

In our stores to achieve the highest standards of cleanliness and hygiene, efficiency of operation, convenience and customer service, and thereby create as attractive and friendly a shopping environment as possible.

To offer our staff outstanding opportunities in terms of personal career development and in remuneration relative to other companies in the same market, practising always a concern for the welfare of every individual.

To generate sufficient profit to finance continual improvement and growth of the business whilst providing our shareholders with an excellent return on their investment. ■

(*Source*: Annual Report and Accounts, 1988)

The renewal of interest in the role played by goals in influencing the behaviour of organization members has been highlighted through the concepts of the 'socially responsible company' and of the 'excellent company'. Companies such the Royal Dutch/Shell, Daimler Benz and Levi Strauss regularly publicize their commitment to socially responsible and ethical business. In companies like IBM, Hewlett-Packard and Boeing you will find clearly articulated goals which are so dominant that they appear to have a life of their own irrespective of the personnel involved. Closer examination will certainly reveal that such goals are carefully formulated by the chief executives of such companies as part of a policy of establishing a set of dominant values, which guide the behaviour of every organization member. Goals are not just a means of giving members a sense of direction and thereby reducing ambiguity and conflict, they are also used as statements of ethical intent as we shall see later in the examples of Daimler Benz and Royal Dutch/Shell.

Managers who use goals in this way make the assumption that the clear formulation of goals will influence performance. In the internal management of organizations, this assumption has been translated into a set of techniques aimed at influencing the behaviour of individual members, known as 'Management-by-Objectives' or MBO (Drucker, 1964). Where MBO is used, the goals for the organization as a whole are generally broken down into individual goals or targets for each manager, forming an entire network of interconnected and internally consistent goals. The most effective MBO schemes tend to be those where there is some measure of negotiation between manager and subordinate over the precise nature of the goals to be achieved by the subordinate. This raises two points: that goal formulation is part of a political process and that goal achievement is undoubtedly related to the extent to which goals are shared by members of the organization.

However, the evidence on the influence of goals on performance is mixed, and even where such a relationship can be shown, it is unclear how it works. The use of goals to determine performance is easiest to understand where jobs are straightforward so that clear targets can be set and performance measured. Many jobs are more complex and performance measurement is difficult to achieve. Furthermore, employees may be expected to achieve a number of different goals which could conflict with one another or with those of other workers. We shall see that for some organizations internal consistency is difficult to achieve in the face of considerable inter-personal and inter-departmental conflict. The extent to which goals can be used to motivate performance is also a function of management behaviour and individual expectations.

Not every company has such clearly identified goals. For many small firms (as well as some larger ones), goals remain the unstated intentions of the owners; they may be thought of only in the vaguest of terms; employees may be completely unaware of them, and may give priority to their own personal goals, sometimes bringing them into conflict with management. A review of most companies' annual reports will reveal that the explicit statement of the goals is usually marked by its absence. Instead the various missions, objectives and strategies must be extracted or at best implied from the various statements by company chairmen and operating reports.

The nature of goals

> We consider goals to be the ultimate, long-run, open-ended attributes or ends a person or organization seeks.
>
> (Hofer and Schendel, 1978, p. 20)

Allowing for the contention that organizations can engage in goal-seeking behaviour, this definition sees goals in terms of the future orientation of the company, but stated in rather loose, broad terms. The examples in our case illustrate this point. A popular notion is that business firms should possess some superordinate goal, namely the maximization of profit. This view has been challenged. Some, like Handy (1993), see profit as a by-product of other goals like survival, market expansion and enhancing reputation. Marris (1964) sees profit as less important than growth. The reality is that the goals vary over time and according to cultural differences. The variation of goals over time is best illustrated by reference to the public sector. Historically viewed as a public service organization, with the emphasis on service, more recent changes have widened the goals to incorporate notions of best value and the term 'new managerialism' is used to describe strategic shifts that have taken place in hospitals and universities. As we see below, the concept of goals is used differently by different writers. Some see goals as a generic concept, while others see them as part of a hierarchy of a generic concept that they define as strategic intentions (Miller and Dess, 1996). In this chapter we use the concept of goals in its broadest context.

KEY CONCEPT 3.1
Organizational goals

The stated goals of an organization exist to give direction to the activities of its members. In many companies, goals comprise both an overall statement of intent, sometimes referred to as a mission statement, and a set of more detailed objectives to guide strategic planning. Since many organizations are made up of different interest groups the formulation of goals can be a highly political process. This can cause conflict but the goals of most businesses are generally accepted as being those of the senior management team. There has been a renewal of interest in the role of goals to shape the culture of an organization. We deal with this aspect in our discussion of organizational culture (Key concept 3.9).

Hofer and Schendel (1978) make the distinction between goals, objectives and strategies. Goals themselves are seen as being unbounded, generalized statements of intent, whereas objectives represent those intentions that can be measured within a certain time frame. Strategies are seen as the processes by which goals are determined through the adoption of certain courses of action and the allocation of resources. We examine strategies more thoroughly in Chapter 4.

Richards (1978) distinguishes between closed- and open-ended goals. Closed-ended goals are those that have clearly defined and measurable targets to be achieved within a stated time period. By contrast open-ended goals are the type that include some broad statement of intent such as the pursuit of excellence. This broader view of goals has sometimes been defined as a firm's 'mission', which would seem to equate with Hofer and Schendel's concept of a goal. Richards sees a mission as a master strategy which has a visionary content and which overrides all other types of goal (Richards, 1978).

Miller and Dess (1996) place concepts such as goals, objectives and mission as different forms of **strategic intentions**, which can be arranged in a hierarchy as follows.

- **Vision**
- **Mission**
- **Goals**
- **Objectives**

Vision relates to the future orientation of the organization and describes the kind of organization it ought to be. Mission is a statement of the key values, which define the purpose of the organization and, perhaps, its distinctive competitiveness. Goals are more specific statements of intent than mission, while objectives are the operationalization of the goals.

Another classification made by Perrow (1961) distinguishes between 'official' and 'operative' goals. 'Official' goals are statements of intent, which occur in official documents and are the type illustrated by our case illustrations. 'Operative' goals on the other hand reflect the behaviour that is actually occurring, and which may in fact conflict with the official intention. To Perrow the development of a package of operative goals was the process of corporate strategy formulation. This process is developed in the following section.

How goals are developed

Our understanding of how goals develop owes much to the work of Cyert and March and their *Behavioural Theory of the Firm* (1963). They see organizations in terms of individuals and groups who combine to pursue mutual interests as coalitions. The interests need not be shared but the coalition is recognized by all participating interest groups as the most effective way of achieving their goals. This view of the firm reappears in the next chapter under our discussion of behavioural approaches to strategy formulation.

An interest group may be an entire department, such as marketing or research and development, or it might be a particular section within that department such as a project team. It may even be a less formal grouping of managers within a department who collectively wish to pursue a specific policy. The creation of such interest groups may be a deliberate structural device. For example, senior management at Procter and Gamble felt that its interests could best be served through the creation of teams based around a single product or groups of products. The aim was the creation of healthy competition between product teams, and a competition and justification of resource allocation which would operate in the best interests of the firm as a whole. A more detailed discussion of the relationship between goals and structure may be found in the next section.

Interest groups can emerge owing to the complexity of the organization's task and/or its environment, requiring a degree of internal specialization, to deal with specific problems, such as product development, or external bodies such as banks. Interest groups may also develop informally, cutting across formal structures.

Each interest group will determine its goals by reference to the information it collects. Such information generally includes comparative data on other organizations on such issues as price, product design, and criteria for success.

Many interest groups for example establish their goals in relation to competing groups in the same organization. The important point made by Cyert and March is that groups deliberately limit strategic choice by selecting information from the range available and, having decided upon a course of action, often fail to consider alternative strategies. This is perfectly understandable given the range of information and the time available to make decisions. Such a process is sometimes referred to as bounded rationality.

Interest groups combine to form coalitions and in any one organization there will be a number of such coalitions. They are created by a process of influence, negotiation and bargaining between different interest groups. It is out of this process that the goals that guide the behaviour of organization members emerge. However, in any one organization there is usually a group that may be identified as a dominant coalition. Once established, the dominant coalition will set up procedures to ensure that their goals are pursued by the organization as a whole. Such criteria will normally include establishing the procedures for staff selection, promotion and reward as well as laying down the rules of operation. The dominant coalition usually comprises, therefore, the senior management of an enterprise. However, certain groups align themselves with top management to ensure their goals are well represented. Even in those organizations where decision-making proceeds along more democratic lines, as in institutions of higher education, the various coalitions will compete for membership of key committees at which decisions about such issues as resources are taken.

In short, the ability of groups to pursue their goals depends upon the power they wield in the organization, which may depend on a number of variables. These may include their position in the hierarchy, the skills of group members, the resources they command and whether or not their role is seen as legitimate by the rest of the organization members.

It is inevitable that different coalitions will pursue different interests and that some will compete. The process of influence, negotiation and bargaining may be termed organizational politics. Such a concept tends to be viewed pejoratively and political activity in business firms is often seen as a problem. Yet if we subscribe to the views of Cyert and March the process is an inevitable prelude to goal setting. Nonetheless, the potential problem of goal conflict will now be explored through the examination of multiple goals.

Multiple goals

In any organization made up of different interest groups some conflict over goals is inevitable. This has been illustrated by many writers. Marris (1964) speaks of the goal conflict emerging from the separation of ownership and control. He found that while shareholders were concerned primarily about profitability, the professional managers acting as the directors of companies were more concerned with growth. In this instance profitability is a by-product, for it is growth that expands the director's sphere of influence and hence his or her personal power and reward. Despite such potential conflict between director and shareholder goals, some compromise is usually made by directors to protect their own position. Handy (1993) presents several examples of goal conflict, including that between the sales and production departments. The goals of the sales department are normally measured by volume turnover, while those of the production department are measured by cost-efficiency. We return to this particular problem in Chapter 6, when we depict the classic dilemma of the production department as that of satisfying the twin demands of customer satisfaction and operating efficiency.

In some cases such conflict can be seen to operate against the best interests of the organization. A study by Selznick (1949) of the Tennessee Valley Authority is viewed as a classic of its kind. An emerging organization, formed to solve the problems of irrigating and redeveloping a vast area in the Tennessee Valley, tackled its job through delegation and specialization. In this case, each specialist division within the organization (Selznick refers to these as sub-units) developed a greater commitment to its own sub-unit goals than those of the organization as a whole. This fragmented the total effort and resulted in groups devoting a great deal of their time to legitimizing their activities and competing for resources. This set up conflicts with other groups which further strengthened the resolve of each sub-unit to pursue its own goals. Selznick referred to this process as the 'bifurcation of interests'. Burns and Stalker (1966) noted how a similar conflict developed between the production and research and development departments in certain Scottish electronics firms, with the subsequent decline in their competitive standing. In Pettigrew's (1973) study computer programmers saw their status threatened by an emerging group of systems analysts. In response they attempted to control information to preserve their exclusive position and prevent their work being downgraded.

In such cases, activities move away from dealing with customers or even coping with external changes in the market to focus on the resolution of internal tensions and management becomes the management of internal coalitions. Case 3.2 illustrates issues of goal conflict in London Zoo that were brought to the surface at the time of financial crisis in the early 1990s. In many organizations conflict often remains hidden, emerging only when problems get out of hand. In most situations conflict can be contained and managed. A similar situation occurred within the BBC during the summer of 1993. Viewing figures revealed that BBC1 was achieving only 29 per cent of the television audience against ITV's 41 per cent. This created a much-publicized debate about the future direction of BBC programming and there was a belief amongst senior managers at BBC1 that it was catering for an elite upper-income, middle-class audience and needed to widen its appeal. This debate led to further allegations of autocratic management and a stifling of creativity, which led to conflict between different factions within the organization.

We can see that it is quite normal for multiple goals to exist in most organizations. Conflict does occur as can be seen in Case 3.2 and the illustrations above. However, not all conflict of this kind is necessarily a problem. It would appear to be limited by four factors:

● Most groups in an organization will agree to those goals formulated by senior management as a means of achieving their own goals. This is the result of the bargaining and negotiating process between interest groups.

- Most organization members would appear to accept the goals of top management with little question. This would seem to be an implied element of the employment contract.

- The dominant coalition normally sets up a series of controls to ensure compliance to their goals. Such controls have been alluded to earlier and include selection procedures, induction and training to ensure that rules are followed. In addition, management can use technological controls in the form of work design and job allocation, and financial controls in the form of budgets and reward systems. In such ways as these, the management of organizations ensure at least a minimum level of compliance with their chosen goals.

- In many firms senior management acknowledge that different groups may have their own goals which need to be satisfied. This is illustrated in Case 3.1.

Case 3.2: London Zoo

In 1991 London Zoo faced a financial crisis and closure was imminent. The surrounding debate between the owners, the managers and employees was a good illustration of goal conflict within a complex organization faced with considerable external problems.

London Zoo and its sister zoo, Whipsnade, are the property and responsibility of the Zoological Society of London, a body made up of fellows elected on the basis of some special interest and expert knowledge in zoology and its related fields. The zoos had experienced financial problems for a number of years and in 1988 the Society commissioned a consultancy report. It recommended that the two zoos be run on a much more commercial basis and following the publication of the report, the zoos were put under the control of a separate organization, Zoo Operations Ltd. A process of commercialization began which included a reduction in the number of animals, a marketing campaign to attract more visitors, the introduction of a more business-oriented approach and a number of organizational changes. Amongst these were wholesale changes in the terms and conditions of employees. Zoo staff were put on a consolidated pay scale and for the first time were faced with appraisal and performance-related pay. At the same time the problems facing the zoo were cushioned somewhat by a government backing of £10 million.

Despite the changes, the recession in 1991 caused a decline in paying visitors and news of closure was leaked to the press. Paradoxically this led to a sharp increase in visitors to the zoo, perhaps sensing their last chance to see the animals. An appeal was launched and the management embarked on a number of fund-raising and cost-cutting exercises. A panda was borrowed from China in an attempt, amid much publicity, to mate London's own panda and a version of the popular TV programme *Blind Date* was used to gain maximum coverage. It became particularly important to focus on specific attractions since parts of the zoo had been closed as they were unsafe and policies to reduce the number of animals kept were well advanced. Almost each day saw more animals leave the zoo for other destinations or to be destroyed. This was a harrowing experience for most of the keepers who had built up a close relationship with their charges. At the same time staffing levels were being cut and employees were reduced by one-third. This necessitated jobs being combined, and keepers who were used to specializing in a particular area were asked to take on a range of tasks with different types of animals.

These changes highlighted a number of differences between various groups associated with the zoo. Goal conflict has never been far from the surface. As with any zoo there is a basic tension between those who see the zoo as a focus and means of academic research into zoological matters and those who see it primarily as a form of entertainment for the public. Some of the cruder attempts at commercialization were

▶

Continued

anathema to the former group. In general the shift to a business management approach brought a number of tensions to the surface and several factions emerged. The members of the Zoological Society were one group, the management of the zoo another, and a third comprised those keepers and researchers who made up the majority of the zoo's employees. Within these groups there were differences. Some fellows saw commercialization as the only means of survival. Others, however, banded together as a 'Reform Group' opposed to blatant commercialism and questioned the policies of the zoo's management. There was a general debate about the role of zoos in society and the role governments might play. The £10 million grant was unusual for a UK government intent on creating a non-subsidized free market society. Despite this financial gesture many of the fellows were openly critical of the government and cited a much greater financial backing given to zoos in other countries. There was a strong belief that no longer could zoos support themselves. The Reform Group formed a coalition with a group of employees who had established themselves as a 'Survival Group', and who were a useful source of information to the fellows on the daily events at the zoo. Within the employees, a number of different issues emerged. The primary concern of one group focused on changes in their terms of employment. Another group expressed the greatest concern for the loss of animals and the difficulties of providing adequate care for those remaining. Some researchers saw the crisis as an ideal opportunity to further their claim that greater attention should be paid to academic research and the furtherance of zoological knowledge.

The financial appeal and various marketing ploys were partially successful but the impact was essentially short term and when, in 1992, the zoo made further losses and failed to achieve its targets for the number of visitors, closure seemed inevitable once again. The zoo was saved by a donation from the Emir of Kuwait as a gesture of gratitude to the British people for their part in the Gulf War. The publicity surrounding this donation and the plight of the zoo led to still further donations. The basic divisions persisted. There were still those who wanted the zoo to become a profit-making theme park, with animals placed in realistic sets to mirror their natural habitat, with a later addition of a state-of-the-art aquarium. On the other hand there were those who saw that the zoo's only chance for public support, and hence survival, lay in the preservation and breeding of endangered species. This battle for the ideological heart of London Zoo was dubbed by the media as the 'suits' versus the 'beards'.

In the event, the theme park and aquarium concept, at a joint estimated cost of £95 million, were deemed too expensive. The zoo focused instead on conservation work and launched an extensive marketing campaign around the concept of 'Conservation in Action'. Part of the campaign was the introduction of an animal adoption programme, in which members of the public and organizations could sponsor particular animals. The campaign attracted a great deal of media attention through the support of national celebrities and through a BBC programme, *Zoowatch*. In addition the zoo attracted a sponsor, who donated £1 million a year specifically for marketing purposes.

In 1997 the zoo announced an operating surplus of over £1 million. ∎

(*Sources*: *Personnel Management Plus*, July 1993; *Management Today*, July 1993; *Marketing*, April 1994; *Financial Times*, 1995–8.

In this section we have depicted the formation of goals as a complex process involving the resolution of external influences and internal politics. As such, the system is highly dynamic and changes in the goals will occur with changes in the external environment, such as market demand, technology and government policy, as well as changes that take place between interest groups within the organization. A change in ownership or top management may lead to a shift in emphasis of the firm's operations. The acquisition of the department store chain Debenhams by the Burton Group led to a change in operation as well as image. More franchises were awarded to established retailers to operate within each Debenhams store and there was considerable investment on internal refurbishment in all locations. In the late 1990s, Ford Motor Company used a revised statement of goals as a means of re-orienting staff in the face of decline in traditional markets and increased global competition. The process was dubbed 'Ford 2000' and seven goals were set out to add value to the firm, as can be seen in Figure 3.1.

Figure **3.1** Ford 2000 strategies. *Source*: Ford Motor Company.

Goals are not formalized, meaningless statements but the products of a highly interactive and dynamic process. The changing of goals in the face of external and even internal changes is seen to be a prerequisite for the survival of the organization. Those managers who cling to inappropriate goals would appear to place their companies at risk. However, the assumption that the existence of explicit statements of intent, such as goals, is linked to superior company performance has not been widely researched and when it has been, the findings tend to be inconclusive. Bart and Baetz (1999) in their study of links between mission statements and performance amongst large Canadian firms concluded that there was no automatic connection between mission and performance. However, there was evidence of superior performance where a firm had a mission statement to which management subscribed and also where the mission statement had been produced as a result of some form of employee involvement. There would appear to be clear links here to issues of commitment and corporate culture, issues we deal with later in the chapter.

One area where goals have become significant in many companies over the years has been through the explicit recognition that they must be socially responsive. It is to such issues we now turn.

Business and ethics

Some companies have acknowledged that there is enhanced corporate reputation to be gained through recognizing that capitalism will be most successful when it cares for its customers, its producers, the environment and the communities in which it operates.

(McIntosh, 1998, p. 3)

The quote by McIntosh represents a growing concern by commentators from inside and outside business that the goals and activities of business should reflect aspects of social responsibility and concern for the environment. Such concerns, especially when aimed at the environment, are sometimes referred to as the 'greening of business'. Ethical business covers macro issues such as pollution reduction and the responsible exploitation of raw materials and micro issues such as fair pay, sexual harassment and cheating on expenses. Issues cover every business activity. In terms of product development and operations the emphasis has been on safe, non-polluting products and working environments. The Ford Pinto was withdrawn from production in the USA after several accidents involving the explosion of the petrol tank. Exhaust emissions from car engines have been the subject of legislation, leading to the development of new technologies. In marketing, many countries have banned or restricted tobacco advertising and set up commissions to monitor advertising and sales promotions to ensure honest representation. HR policies have been designed to improve working conditions and enhance the involvement of employees in the decision-making process. In finance and accounting, standards have been established about public accountability and, for multinationals, their contribution to the local communities in which they operate.

KEY CONCEPT 3.2
Ethical business

Ethical business is concerned with the social responsibility of business and incorporates such issues as 'green business'. Essentially it is business carried out with concern for the major stakeholders and the environment. The stakeholders could include suppliers, customers, employees, shareholders and the community at large. There is a growing belief that ethical business is linked to enhanced performance, although the link is difficult to prove by hard evidence.

Ethical approaches to business can be traced back to the early paternalism of such employers as Cadbury and Rowntree, although the focus was mainly on the treatment of employees. Pirie (2000) sees the development of interest in ethical issues as a reflection of political and economic trends. Earlier in the twentieth century concerns arose out the growth of big business and the need to curb the power of the large corporation, as with the anti-trust legislation in the USA and as a reaction to the depression of the 1920s and 30s. Lobbying for improved terms and conditions at work arose from the growth of the trade union movement. In the post-war era interest in ethical business was related to the 1960s reaction to materialism, the activities of some multinationals in the Third World and increasing concern and publicity about pollution. Further developments were undoubtedly a backlash to the events of the Thatcher and Reagan era with its emphasis on deregulation, privatization and the enterprise culture. In the UK and elsewhere there was growing public disquiet about such scandals associated with BCCI, Guinness and the Maxwell empire. We can add to this the Chernobyl nuclear reactor disaster in the Ukraine, the massive oil spillage from the *Exxon Valdes* in Alaska, the current concern over genetically modified crops, and the financial scandals in Japan and in such old-established firms as Barings. It is hardly surprising that the backlash called for businesses to put their house in order and begin by behaving ethically.

Such a view is not shared by all. In a famous article Carr (1968) compared business to a card game and even a Wild West shoot-out, where ethics mattered less than winning. He felt that managers could separate business and private life in terms of behaving ethically. Around the same time, Friedman (1970) argued that the social responsibility of business was to increase profits and that ethics would be taken care of by market forces. Both perspectives are the products of a traditional American view of the sanctity of the free market and the role of law to police the transgressors.

The ethical approach to business was once the province of a small number of firms, like the Body Shop, famous for its sourcing of environmentally friendly products from non-exploited labour and establishing its own 'ethical' manufacturing operations. The same company expanded its social responsibility role by backing the *Big Issue*, a magazine produced and sold by the homeless throughout the world. However, there is considerable evidence of a shift in expectations, even in the USA, led by such firms as Levi Strauss. In Europe many companies now publish, as well as an annual company report, an annual environmental report. Here companies set out their goals. For example from Daimler-Benz,

> Even in economically difficult times, a responsible attitude towards the natural foundations of life remains a long-term corporate commitment for Daimler-Benz ... we would also like to establish an open forum – for an external and internal public alike – where environmental questions may be discussed in a critical but constructive manner by representatives from society, politics and science. In short we are always looking for new impulses towards improving environmental protection within the framework of the economically feasible.
>
> (Daimler Benz, 'Environmental Report', 1996, p. 2)

In their 1998 report, 'Profit and Principles – does there have to be a choice?', an appropriate theme in a debate about business ethics, Royal Dutch/Shell explain,

> This report is about values. It describes how we, the people, companies and businesses that make up the Royal/Dutch Shell Group, are striving to live up to our responsibilities – financial, social and environmental ... It is a matter of pride and reassurance to us that

throughout the years these core values have endured. They represent an unshakeable foundation on which to build at a time when society has rising expectations of business.

(Royal Dutch/Shell, Profits and Principles – does there have to be a choice?, 1998, p. 2)

Shell identifies seven principles, which address a number of financial, economic and social goals within an ethical framework. The company regards that it has a responsibility to shareholders, customers, employees, those with whom they do business and society at large.

It is interesting to note that in both these examples, the firms concerned stress that they are concerned with both ethical and socially responsible behaviour and profit-seeking behaviour. There are a number of points that support the view that 'ethical business is good business':

- The branding of goods as 'ethical' or 'socially responsible' is good public relations and can lead to greater awareness and increased sales. Increased sales can mean increased profits, although the problems here are those of measurement and correlation.
- The costs of not behaving responsibly can be considerable. It is claimed that 22 per cent of the total operating costs of Amoco are attributable to environmental costs (Thomas and Eyres, 1998). Companies can attract bad publicity and become the target of action groups such as Greenpeace. Shell suffered a particularly bad press over its attempt to dispose of Brent Spar, a North Sea oil platform, in deep water in the North Sea. The company admitted that whatever the rights and wrongs of the issue, it could have been better handled by them.
- There are increasing government pressures on firms to confirm to national and international standards on social and environmental matters. The UK government launched an 'Ethical Trading Initiative', and an international standard, SA 8000, covers such areas as working hours and the use of child labour. In some cases the pressures are backed by legislation.
- In order to do business with some companies, such as Toys 'R' US, Timberland and Levi Strauss, suppliers must comply with a code of ethical conduct.

There are also a number of problems and issues:

- While awareness and acceptance are widespread amongst large firms like Daimler-Benz and Shell, there are still many traditional managers who still believe there to be a basic conflict between ethical business and profitable business. This is particularly true amongst small businesses.
- In some cases the greening of products has been a marketing ploy and consumers are deliberately misled into thinking they are buying a 'green' product, when this is not the case. Some commentators refer to this as 'greenwash'. In the section on corporate culture later in this chapter we illustrate how some firms use values, not as a means of involving employees, but as a way of controlling them. The fast-food chain McDonalds has been at the centre of criticisms on both counts.

- In some cases the costs of environmentally friendly business can be expensive, resulting in unacceptably high prices. There may also be contradictions. For example, in car manufacture, the switch from solvent-based to water-based paint is indisputably better in terms of the environment, yet it increases drying time and, with it, energy consumption that both pushes up the cost and is environmentally unfriendly.
- Different standards, both legal and cultural, apply in different parts of the world. Firms that operate in a number of markets may have the increased cost of ensuring their products fulfil the requirements of each country. Products that can be legally sold in one market may be illegal in another, as with hand-guns, legal in the USA but not the UK.
- Different stakeholders may have different requirements. In the Brent Spar case, the dumping of the oil platform was acceptable to the UK government, but opposed by some other European countries such as Germany and environmental groups such as Greenpeace.

Such problems as the above create dilemmas for management in their attempts to pursue an ethical business strategy. Survival of the most ethical of companies depends upon achieving financial targets. In 1999, many believed that the Body Shop stood at the crossroads. Its business performance left much to be desired and the company underwent restructure. This involved bringing in fresh blood, but also making people redundant, including the closure of its manufacturing operations. Optimists believed the company's ethical stance would emerge yet stronger and its reliance on a wider group of suppliers would see its value spread to other companies. Pessimists feared that the company would become just another company, undifferentiated from its competitors in its unique ethical stance.

In much of our discussion of goals there are clear implications for organization structure and it is to this we now turn.

Structure

A dominant theme in our discussion of goals was that organizations are made up of different interest groups formed as coalitions. One of the factors that may facilitate or inhibit the way these groups pursue their goals and whether such goals may be achieved is the structure of the organization. In this section we will examine how structures develop, the variations that occur in structural type, and their impact on performance. You should note, however, that any discussion of structure is biased towards the large firm, and most of the studies in this area are of large corporations. This is inevitable in that structural problems tend to be associated with size and complexity. The balance is redressed later in this chapter when we devote an entire section to issues in small businesses.

A structure is concerned with the grouping of activities in the most suitable manner to achieve the goals of the dominant coalition. It is concerned with the organization of work around roles, the grouping of these roles to form teams or departments, and the allocation of differential amounts of power and authority to the various roles. It is associated with job descriptions, mechanisms for coordination and control, and management information systems.

In much of the writing there is an implicit assumption that senior management seek a structural elegance for their organizations to enhance performance. This in turn assumes that managers have a choice and that structures can be deliberately created to affect overall performance. We will now examine those factors that can influence a firm's structure to determine the extent to which structures can be manipulated by management.

KEY CONCEPT 3.3
Organization structure

An organization structure is a grouping of activities and people to achieve the goals of the organization. Considerable variation is possible in the type of structure employed and the influences at work include technology, size, the nature of the environment, management strategy, the behaviour of interest groups, the firm's history and wider cultural factors. In general terms a particular structure emerges to maximize the opportunities and solve the problems created by these various influences. In practice, however, the evidence concerning the influence of structure and performance is very patchy indeed.

The factors that influence structure

There are a number of factors that may influence the structure of an organization. We have identified them under six main headings, placed in no particular order of importance.

Technology

For some, technology is the most important, if not the sole, determinant of a firm's structure. This is part of the concept known as 'technological determinism'. Much of the work in this area is indebted to Joan Woodward's (1965) work on the impact of technology on a hundred manufacturing firms in south-east Essex (also mentioned in Chapters 2 and 6). She and her research team found that differences in manufacturing, from small batch to mass production to process technology, resulted in corresponding differences in a number of factors. These included the size and shape of the management hierarchy, the proportion of management to other employees, the proportion of direct to indirect labour, and the number of subordinates controlled by any one manager (the span of control).

Size

Other researchers find size to be a more significant variable in influencing structure than is technology. This was a particular theme of a group of academics at Aston University in the 1960s and 70s (see for example Pugh *et al.*,

1969). As firms increase in size, additional problems are created in terms of coordination and control, often necessitating structural changes. For example, as the business expands, the owner of a small business often faces increasing pressures on his or her time. No longer is he or she able to maintain a close control of operations and act as the focal point for customers, as well as managing administration and wages. In such cases some formalization and delegation is inevitable and a stage is reached when small businesses take their first steps towards bureaucratization. Such changes in structure with increasing size can be viewed in large as well as in small firms. We can see with Dow Corning in Case 3.3 that significant structural changes were made as the company expanded its product range and its markets. The way firms respond to size may vary, resulting in different types of structure, which we identify in the next section. While there are obvious connections between size and structure, the complexity of an organization's operations may have a more significant impact on its structure than sheer size.

Changes in the environment

In the last chapter we saw how the contingency approach saw organizations as needing to adapt to their environment in order to survive. An important feature of that adaptation is structural. Burns and Stalker (1966) noted that technological and market changes in the post-war electronics industry were best served by a less bureaucratic, more flexible kind of organization. Such organic structures were an essential element in the firms' ability to cope with a highly changing environment, and firms that retained their traditional bureaucratic or mechanistic structures were much less successful. The IBM case at the end of this section illustrates the relationship between structure and a rapidly changing product market.

This theme of the structure fitting the dominant aspects of the firm's environment is the major plank in the work of Lawrence and Lorsch (1967). They believe that different tasks in the organization are confronted by different environmental problems and demands. These differences should be reflected in the structures of the departments carrying out those tasks. In their study of the plastics industry they found a highly uncertain technological environment which called for a flexible R&D function, while the demands imposed on the production department were more predictable, enabling a more traditional, bureaucratic structure to operate. The structural implications of Lawrence and Lorsch's analysis do not end with what they term the 'differentiation' of functions. In order to operate effectively all organizations so differentiated must establish integrative devices, which might include a committee structure or designing special coordinating roles.

Strategy

The influence of strategy on structure is related to the way management perceive their environment. A firm wishing to be a product leader in a technologically sophisticated product market will have a correspondingly large R&D

department in terms of both investment and employees. A firm that places a great deal of emphasis on cost controls may have a larger than average accounting department.

The relationship of strategy to organizational structure owes much to the work of Alfred Chandler (1962, 1977). He based his first work around an in-depth case study of the development of four companies, DuPont, General Motors, Standard Oil and Sears Roebuck. His work, however, had a much broader perspective, that of charting the development of American capitalism and especially the role played by the professional manager. One of the major conclusions of his work is that structure is a product of managerial strategies. The relationship between the two is more complex than many summaries of Chandler acknowledge. He found that structure did not automatically follow strategy and that managements often needed a crisis before they would agree to structural change. This point emerges in Case 3.4 with IBM.

As might be expected of an economic historian, Chandler viewed the rela-tionship between strategy and structure as dynamic and evolutionary. He identified several stages in the development of American capitalism. These were cycles of growth and consolidation, each with its own implications for the organizational structures of the emerging large corporations in his study. The growth of mass markets and the development of the techniques of mass production were accompanied by vertical integration to ensure the supply of materials and secure distribution channels, and by horizontal integration through takeovers to maintain growth. Expansion brought its own problems of coordination and control and subsequent inefficiency. These were solved by the growth of professional management and the development of organi-zations structured around specialist functions, such as marketing and finance. As existing markets became saturated and the benefits accruing from organi-zational restructuring slowed down, new markets and products were vigorously pursued by overseas expansion and R&D respectively. Once again these developments brought their own problems of coordination and control. This time a new form of structure emerged. All four firms in Chandler's study had adopted a multi-divisional structure by 1929, with DuPont and General Motors leading the way. The essential qualities of this structure will be iden-tified in the following section.

Similar cycles of expansion and consolidation through structural change can be found in studies of British companies (see for example Channon, 1973). While such works offer strong evidence for the influence of strategy over structure, we have already noted the complex nature of the relationship. Chandler noted that the motivation for structural change emerged not only from changes in strategy but that it needed the catalyst of an organizational crisis. We can see cases where structural change may be unnecessary or at least delayed by the sheer market power of the firm, as in the case of IBM. There may even be a case for arguing that structure can determine strategy. For example, once a company has adopted a multi-divisional structure, this could well give divisional managers the incentive, confidence and resources for even greater expansion. This interplay of strategy and structure reappears in Chapter 4 and is illustrated by changes in the US multinational 3M depicted in Case 4.2.

Culture

The influence of culture on structure should not be underestimated. There is evidence that different structural forms are favoured in different countries. For example, American firms developed initially through the adoption of divisional structures, while in Britain we favoured the holding company (Channon, 1973). Firms in different countries often reflect different emphases. For example American firms tend to stress the legal, finance and marketing functions, while those in Germany tend to feature operations. Studies on such aspects as the shape and extent of the management hierarchy have also noted differences between countries (Brossard and Maurice, 1976; Trompenaars, 1993). For example the hierarchies in French firms tend to be steeper than in the UK, and much steeper than in Germany. Structure may also reflect specific organizational cultures; for example, those firms favouring the involvement of employees in decision-making may set up participative forums to facilitate this.

Interest groups

Although Chandler noted the resistance on the part of some managers to structural change, the whole issue of interest groups and organizational politics was largely overlooked. The preferences of the dominant coalition can exert considerable influence on the structure, as can the demands of major stakeholders. Those firms where the owners play a major role in management tend to be highly centralized. In the public sector the pressure for accountability often results in elaborate financial control mechanisms and bureaucratic procedures. In some manufacturing firms, the pressure from banks on lending may in times of recession lead to reductions in development activities, with a corresponding impact on the size of the R&D function.

Cases 3.3, 3.4 and 4.2 all show structural changes following management changes. While size, market and other environmental influences inevitably played a major role in Dow Corning, IBM and 3M, the catalyst for new structures in all cases would seem to be changes at the top.

Two important points emerge from our consideration of the six influences above. First, there is considerable overlap between the various factors. For example, the structural changes of firms like Dupont and General Motors link technology, size and strategy; the different structural routes taken by firms in different countries are a function of both cultural differences and variations in environmental factors. In short, the structure of an organization can only be explained by reference to a number of interrelated factors. Once again this is amply illustrated in both the Dow Corning and IBM cases. Second, our analysis raises the issue of the extent of choice senior management have in determining the structure of their organization. Are structures creative innovations to implement changing strategies or are they the inevitable consequences of adaptation to prevailing influences? Such issues are raised in the shipping industry case in Chapter 5; structural changes were an important factor in the implementation of strategic change in a highly competitive environment, but they were also determined by technical innovations in such areas as cargo handling and telecommunications. In short, the structure of the shipping companies would appear to be the result of both prevailing economic and technological conditions and management choice.

Case 3.3: Dow Corning

Dow Corning was formed in 1942 from Dow Chemical and Corning Glass. The original focus of the firm was R&D, and the firm was highly centralized around technology and products. At this stage of its development the products were closely related and the firm operated under a traditional functional management structure.

By 1962, several changes had taken place. The company had grown, largely through product diversity, and central control of product development was no longer appropriate. In addition, there had been a change in top management and the new chief executive established five product divisions as profit centres, each with its own functional structures. The new structure was seen as successful in integrating the functions, and a contributory factor in the firm's continued growth and increased profitability.

Within a short time further international expansion brought its own problems. There was conflict between the demands of the home and foreign markets. Conflict also arose over the central supply of raw materials and the mechanisms for transfer pricing. The impact of an economic recession meant that profit levels fell. These problems were met by a further change in management along with a major structural change to a matrix organization.

The ensuing matrix comprised two major elements: specialist functions and ten business profit centres, newly created from the existing five divisions. Employees reported to a business centre manager and a functional vice-president. Each business centre comprised different product boards. Each product board was led by a particular functional manager and leadership tended to change with the product life cycle, from R&D at the early stages to marketing as the product moved through each stage of the cycle.

Structures and processes were developed within the matrix to enhance coordination and deal with conflict. A great deal of attention was focused on modifying individual behaviour by such techniques as MBO and group goal setting and the firm was assisted in its search for goal congruence by having a management structure dominated by chemical engineers. As the

businesses developed it became clear that the firm needed to rethink the basic components of its matrix structure. In addition to organization by function and by business product, there was also organization by geography, to satisfy the increasing international dimension of Dow's business. In part the focus on area management was made to solve a major problem attributed to the original matrix, that of building too many new plants and failing to capitalize upon economies of scale.

Problems with the matrix persisted. Area managers were seen to have too much power within the organization and were accused of empire-building, employees complained of too many bosses and the matrix created a cumbersome bureaucracy with a great deal of time consumed in meetings. Dow, unlike many other organizations, did not retreat from the matrix in the face of these problems. An expansion into the pharmaceuticals sector through a number of acquisitions meant that some form of flexible, semi-autonomous structure was required. Senior management decided to refocus the evolved matrix structure. A small team of senior executives were given the task of supervising all operations. They also had the responsibility of ensuring that only one of the three elements of function, business and geography took the lead in any venture, thus avoiding conflict and duplication of effort. In addition considerable attention was paid to employee communication, with the result that the matrix was viewed as a more open, less secretive form of organization structure.

By the end of the 1980s the company operated in 32 different countries and was responsible for the manufacture of 1800 different products. The success of its flexible organization structure, particularly the growing interchange of ideas and practices across regions, gave management the confidence to seek out more areas for expansion. More business unit teams were created and were given autonomy to develop new products and encouraged to innovate.

One of the profitable growth markets had been in silicone breast implants. These were found to have caused serious health problems for large numbers of women and the company was sued in the US courts. The damages and potential future damages were so great that the company filed for Chapter 11 bankruptcy in the USA. Under Chapter 11 a company may retain its assets but must develop a payment plan to the satisfaction of its creditors. In other words the firm is pledging future cash flows against its debts. By 1999 new claims were still being made by those injured as a result of breast implants some years earlier.

Dow Corning were also hit by the financial crisis in Asia, which had a particular impact on its core silicone business. Despite this the company had begun to move out of Chapter 11 bankruptcy. It had closed plants in Asia, Europe and the USA and had begun to reorganize around product groups rather than geographical areas, and had set out plans for a consolidation of its global supply chain. ■

(Sources: Galbraith and Nathanson, 1978; *The Economist*, August 1988, pp. 61–2; *Financial Times*, 1998–9)

Case 3.4: IBM

In 1988 the senior management at IBM implemented significant structural changes, following the appointment of a new chairman in 1985. These changes were seen as a product of several interrelated factors, not least of which was an unacceptable fall in profits since 1984.

Before 1988 the organization structure reflected a high degree of specialization between the various functional departments (known somewhat confusingly for our purposes as divisions). Clear distinctions were drawn between the technical division, with responsibility for design, the manufacturing division, with responsibility for making the computers, and the marketing division, responsible for sales. In addition, IBM had no separate department concerned with software development. As a result of this type of structure, management concluded that counter-productive internal conflicts were set up, new designs were delayed by as much as two years, and new models when they were introduced lacked supporting software, enabling competitors to increase their market share in key areas.

In a way IBM had been lulled by its dominant market position and early technical leadership in the field. The company firmly established its leading position throughout the 1960s and 70s. Current management thinking suggests that the company became complacent, highly bureaucratic, ultra-conservative and missed the essential entrepreneurial spirit associated with its early days.

While IBM still dominated the mainframe market, helped significantly by its US government contracts and supplies to many major companies throughout the world, it had not responded to important changes in other markets. The computer market had become technically very diverse and there had been many aggressive new entrants. Such new entrants were not held back by a large bureaucracy; they operated with flexible organization structures that enabled them to respond more effectively to technological change and be sensitive to the needs of the customer. The resulting market became highly fragmented and price competitive. IBM mini systems lost out to Digital and the personal computer market was swamped by IBM compatibles like Amstrad, selling at considerably cheaper prices and offering a more comprehensive range of software.

The structural response of IBM was divisionalization and decentralization. Five divisions were created: mainframes, minicomputers, personal computers, telecommunications, and new technology. Each division became an autonomous unit, and was responsible for its own product design, manufacture, sales, and ultimately profits. By the end of 1991 the company had restructured yet again, creating 14 areas of business, ten concerned with product lines and four with marketing.

In 1998, the trend towards semi-autonomous units, in the UK at least, was reversed. Increased competition, especially from new entrants in the PC market, meant that a consolidated response was needed. The various UK units were brought together under one banner of a Personal Systems Group bringing together the PC division, the network computing division and the consumer division. ■

(Sources: John Cassidy and David Holmes, 'IBM spreads workload for quicker pace', *Sunday Times*, 14 February 1988; *Business Week*, Dec. 1992; *Marketing*, Jan. 1998)

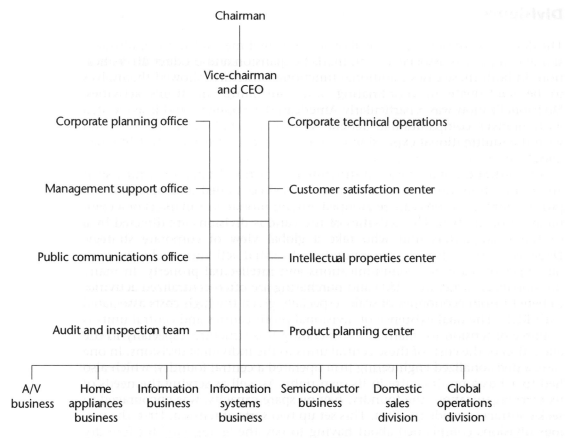

Figure **3.3** A divisional company: Samsung Electronics Corporation. *Source*: Company brochure (1995).

The holding company

This form of organization is associated with the growth of the firm by acquisitions and a high degree of product diversification. It may comprise a group of independent companies controlled by a coordinating group usually made up of the chief executives of the constituent companies. At its extreme form, as exemplified by a company such as Lonhro, this structural type represents as much a form of ownership and investment as it does a kind of organization. Hanson Trust is one such company that has been subjected to considerable criticism for pursuing policies of short-term financial gain at the expense of company development through its selective policies of corporate acquisition and sales. Hanson's attempt to buy ICI in 1991 generated considerable speculation concerning major job losses and future investment in ICI. Amid growing opposition the takeover was eventually thwarted by the ICI board (a fuller account of this debate may be found in Adcroft *et al.*, 1991). Figure 3.4 offers us a different form of holding company, which is made up of constituent companies all bearing the name of the group, in this case the Korean giant, Hyundai. Large Korean firms, like those in Japan, usually comprise a grouping of highly diversified businesses. In the case of Hyundai they are placed in industrial groupings.

Holding companies can be highly diversified, as in the case of Trafalgar House, or built around loosely related products as with the TI Group. Ultramar on the other hand represents a holding company of highly related activities in oil and gas exploration and the production, shipping and refining of crude oil and petroleum products.

As we saw in the previous chapter, the holding company is the prevalent structural form for large Japanese companies. It has also been described as the peculiarly British route to divisionalization (Channon, 1973). There are similarities between divisionalization and the holding company, although in the UK the holding company arrangement is, in many cases, a function of stock

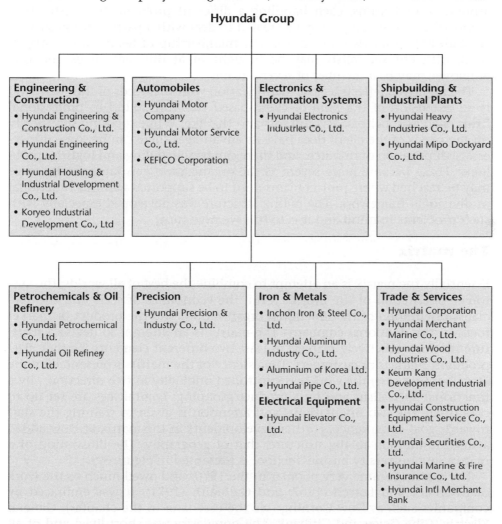

Figure **3.4** Holding company: Hyundai Group 1995. *Source*: Company brochure

market behaviour and the high number of mergers and acquisitions. The holding company is a looser arrangement than the divisional company and may lack the focus.

The project team

These comprise units specially created to cope with a highly unstable environment. In essence they are temporary structures formed around a particular task or problem and reflect technical expertise rather than any notion of management hierarchy. Such structures are commonly found in high-technology firms and some types of service organizations, especially consultancies. In advertising agencies, teams are usually created to deal with specific client accounts. In R&D departments the research work may be organized around several teams, each handling a different problem. In construction companies project teams may be created to deal with a particular job such as the building of a new office block. The membership of teams can be highly fluid; different specialists may be brought in at different times and one employee may be a member of several teams.

The approach reflects a close identification with the needs of the client and is an extension of the kind of client-based structure found in professional firms such as solicitors, accountants and the like. While focusing specifically on the needs of the client does have its advantages there can be some unnecessary duplication of resources and there can be scheduling and logistics problems. These become more severe as the organization gets larger and a stage may be reached where project teams need to be supported within a functional or divisional framework. The matrix structure was developed especially with such problems in mind and it is to this we now turn.

The matrix

Essentially the matrix is an attempt to combine the best of all worlds; the customer orientation of the project team, the economies of scale and the specialist orientation of the functional organization, and the product or market focus of the divisional company. The matrix is an attempt to devise a structure that can effectively manage at least two different elements, be they size, products, markets or customers. The essence of the matrix is presented by the Dow Corning case; the work was controlled originally in two directions, by a functional specialism and by a product grouping, committees are set up to coordinate the two orientations, and attention is given to training the staff towards goal congruence. Further developments in the matrix at Dow added a third dimension to the structure, that of geography. The illustration of a matrix in a university business school is presented in Figure 3.5.

The matrix became very popular in the 1970s and owed much to the work of Lawrence and Lorsch (1967) and Galbraith (1971). It was embraced by companies such as Dow Corning (see the case later in the chapter), General Electric, Ciba Geigy and Citibank. The popularity was short-lived and of all the structural types the matrix has attracted most criticism. In a later work Paul Lawrence referred to the matrix as an 'unnecessary complexity', which

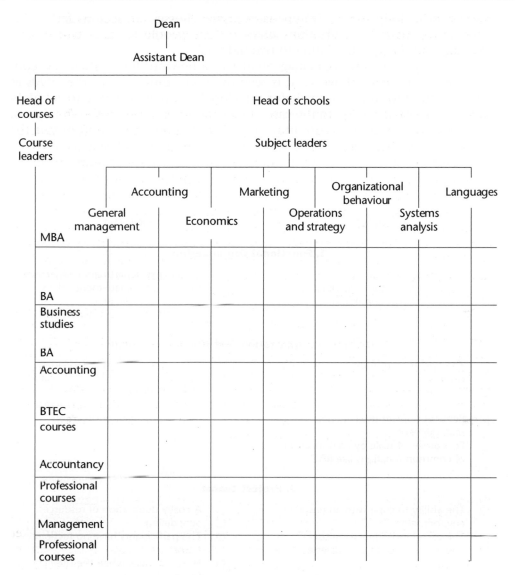

Figure 3.5 Matrix structure: a university business school.

was only justified in certain situations (Davis and Lawrence, 1977, p. 21): first, if two or more of a firm's dimensions, like products and markets, were especially critical to its performance; second, if employees needed to carry out highly complex, interdependent tasks in an uncertain environment; third, if economies of scale were needed, especially in the use of scarce or expensive resources. Unless such conditions are present, the matrix can cause more problems than it solves. Some of those problems are depicted in Case 3.3, as well as the organizational developments introduced by Dow to counteract such problems. Trompenaars (1993) has argued that the effectiveness of the matrix may be limited to specific cultures. Matrix organizations are not successful in Italy where, Trompenaars argues, bosses are seen as father figures. Since matrix organizations often require people to have two bosses, Italians find it difficult relating to two 'fathers'.

For many years, matrix management was a by-word for inefficiency, conflict, delay and cost. However, it is seen by some companies in the 1990s as the structural form that is made for the global company wishing to act globally and transnationally. In the case of Ford Motor Company, the creation of a matrix organization was an integral part of the Ford 2000 strategy (see the previous section on goals). The structure was based around five vehicle centres, four in the USA and one in Europe. These vehicle centres are served by cross-national teams in most of the functional areas. In this way a buyer at

ADVANTAGES	PROBLEMS

1. Functional Organization

☐ Specialization.	☐ Conflicting departmental objectives.
☐ The logic of custom and practice.	☐ Conflicting management values.
☐ A clear chain of command.	☐ A lack of coordination.
	☐ A lack of consumer orientation.

2. Divisional Organization and Holding company

☐ The operation of businesses as profit centres.	☐ Cooperation and interdependence.
☐ The encouragement of entrepreneurship.	☐ Accounting procedures, especially transfer pricing.
☐ Reduces upward dependency on top management.	☐ Increasing diversity of operations.
☐ Economies of scale by centralization of common functions like R&D.	☐ Overall management control.

3. Project teams

☐ The ability to cope with an unstable environment.	☐ A costly duplication of resources.
☐ The use of individual expertise.	☐ Scheduling.
☐ The ability to cope with diverse problems.	☐ The participants have no fuctional home.
☐ Deal directly with the customer.	☐ What happens when the project is finished?

4. Matrix organization

☐ Emphasizes the strengths of the functional and project types.	☐ Coordination and control.
☐ Flexibility of labour.	☐ A proliferation of committees and meetings.
☐ The ability to transfer expertise where it is most needed.	☐ Too many bosses.
☐ Dual control via function and project	☐ Conflicting loyalties for staff.
☐ Closeness to the customer.	☐ Can be slow to adapt.

Figure **3.6** A summary of advantages and problems associated with different types of organization structure

the European supply headquarters in Basildon in the UK could report to a manager in the USA and be part of a team embracing buyers in Germany and Spain. The system is supported by the company's extensive video-conferencing facilities and its own airline company, which facilitates regular meetings between team members. The new structure was introduced by senior management, mindful of the problems of matrix organizations in other companies. Considerable attention was paid to setting clear objectives, having clear definitions of roles, appointing and promoting those people who could operate transnationally and investing heavily in PR and training. The advantages of matrix management were stressed. The then CEO, Alex Trotman, saw its advantage in breaking down the 'chimneys' of the functional structure, which act as barriers, and opening up people to new ideas. Trotman defines the new structure as 'more like jazz than a structured orchestra' (quoted in Lorenz, 1994).

Students should always remember that the structural types identified above represent fairly broad categories. In reality a firm may display a mixture of structures. We have already seen how many divisionalized companies have functional specialisms within each division. In a functional organization we may find that different departments are organized along different lines; the operations department may well extend the functional structure, while the R&D staff may well be organized as project teams. New structural forms are emerging all the time, adapting the traditional approaches to suit their own needs.

Alternative forms of organization structure

A currently popular concept is that of networking. This type of structure has been made possible by developments in computer technology whereby computer systems can interact. Such a system enables people to operate from home and has been heralded as the organization structure of the future. Networking has attracted considerable publicity in both academic journals and the popular press. This attention, however, tends to exaggerate the real extent of networking. Even in pioneer networkers such as Rank Xerox, those employees operating under this system are but a very small percentage of the total employed. Of course, a form of networking has been around for some time in certain types of manufacturing industry in the form of home-working. In this case, individuals or even families engage in simple assembly work (as with electrical components) or in such activities as dressmaking and alteration. Home-working has become a way of life in some countries such as Japan and is a particularly low-cost form of labour.

While the publicity surrounding networking outstrips the reality, this is not the case for franchising, an emerging form of organizational structure akin to the holding company. Under a franchise agreement a parent company will assist in the start-up of a new business enterprise. The terms of that agreement usually involve an initial investment on the part of the franchisee and an undertaking to deal exclusively with the franchisor in the marketing of his or her products. The purchase of the franchisor's products invariably involves the payment of a mark-up in return for the advertising and promotional support of a larger company. A good illustration of franchising is presented by the fast-food industry, such as Kentucky Fried Chicken, although there are more than 300 different franchise operations in Britain, including such diverse operations as the British School of Motoring, drain clearance and wedding dress hire. A recent growth in franchise operations has taken place in the financial service sector, as in the case of insurance broking. In this case the franchisee, instead of buying goods from the franchisor, buys access to a computer database. The main advantage to both parties in a franchise agreement is the spread of risk. As such it has become a popular form of small business venture.

The two illustrations of networking and franchising focus on criteria of flexibility and cost. These are two major considerations in the debate about the concept of the 'flexible firm' and about the relationship between structure and performance. We end this section on structure by examining these two issues.

The flexible firm

The concept of the flexible firm emerged from work carried out by the Institute of Manpower Studies and associated largely with the writing of John Atkinson (his 1984 article offers an excellent summary). The main assumptions behind Atkinson's model are that new forms of organization are required as a strategic response to the combined effects of market stagnation, job losses, technical change, increased uncertainty and reductions in the working week. In the 1990s the focus shifted to emphasize flexibility as the key strategic response to globalization. Murton (2000) argues that in the global economy a premium is placed on responsiveness and adaptability, with the manipulation of labour costs as the easy option. The 1990s has also seen the growth of critical literature surrounding flexible labour market trends, with many of the critics focusing on issues of insecurity and exploitation.

Atkinson's original model identified three types of flexibility:

- **Numerical flexibility** is achieved through management's ability to make rapid alterations to the headcount of the firm to meet changes in demand. A growth in part-time work, temporary contracts and subcontracting were the expected consequences of numerical flexibility.
- **Functional flexibility** is achieved when employees are able to perform a range of jobs and can move between them as the need arises. In many organizations this will see an end to demarcation between trades and result in multi-skilling. Historically, especially in the UK, demarcation has often been viewed as the cause of inefficiencies as well as industrial relations disputes.
- **Financial flexibility** is required to reflect changes in the supply and demand of labour and to enhance the operation of functional and numerical flexibility. This can be achieved through the creation of differential rates of pay for full- and part-time workers, introducing the link between effort and reward for a greater number of workers and the use of incentives to encourage workers to become multi-skilled.

Sparrow and Marchington (1998) argue that there are not three but seven types of flexibility observable in modern organizations and that these flexibilities are both discrete and parallel. In addition to the three defined by Atkinson, they recognize **temporal, geographical, organizational** and **cognitive** flexibility. Temporal flexibility is concerned with changing the time patterns of work, as with the introduction of shift work. Geographical flexibility involves the increased mobility of groups of workers as in the introduction of transnational teams. Organizational flexibility relates to structural and systems changes and cognitive flexibility to the changing mindset of the workforce. Beatson (1995) draws the distinction between micro-flexibility, which occurs at the level of the firm, and macro-flexibility, which deals with changes at the level of the labour market in general.

KEY CONCEPT 3. 5
The flexible firm

Flexibility within organizations occurs in a number of different ways. These include the employment of part-time workers, those on short-term contracts and the use of out-sourced contract work. It also involves getting employees to do a range of different jobs, introducing variations in pay and times of attendance and increasing the geographical mobility of labour. Such changes are seen to be on the increase as a result of globalization, higher levels of competition and the need for most firms to reduce costs. There is clear evidence that all forms of flexibility are on the increase. While the impact is often viewed positively from the perspective of the organization, certain negative outcomes have been noted for the individual worker.

In all its forms the 'flexible firm' will break up traditional organization structures. For Atkinson, the key outcome will be the establishment of two groups of employees, core and peripheral. Core employees are those on permanent or long-term contracts and who hold key skills and positions within the organization. Accordingly, core workers are well rewarded and often have the security of lifetime employment. Peripheral workers comprise two groups. It is envisaged that there will be a group of full-time workers, who will be less skilled and not enjoy the security of the core worker. The second group will comprise part-time and contract workers hired in direct proportion to the demand or to deal with non-core business such as cleaning and catering. The distinction between core and peripheral workers has long been a feature of the Japanese labour market and is referred to in Chapter 2.

There has been a great deal of research into the impact of the flexible firm on organizations in the UK and the rest of Europe and good summaries can be found in Legge (1998) and Murton (2000). The main points are:

● Part-time work has increased in all sectors. In the UK between 1984 and 1996 it increased 31 per cent and it is estimated that approximately 25 per cent of the UK labour force are part-timers. The highest proportion of part-time workers are still found in the service industries and amongst female employees, although more recent trends suggest that part-time employment for males is growing at a faster rate than that for females.

- The use of temporary contracts has also increased by over 30 per cent since 1984, with the largest increase occurring since 1992 and in the public sector. The popularity of temporary contracts in the public sector is as a management response to variations in the budget. For example, the use of such contracts has grown in the university sector where budgets are tied to student numbers, which may be unpredictable.
- There is clear evidence of the increasing use of subcontractors across a range of public and private organizations. Historically a classic feature of the construction industry, this is now used by many local authorities, largely as a direct result of government regulations insisting on competitive tendering for services such as rubbish removal. In the private sector there is increasing use of subcontracting in the production of parts in manufacturing, owing to both globalization and the development of modular manufacturing processes. Many large firms use subcontracting not only for cleaning and catering, but also for key HR functions such as recruitment, training and payrolling and in marketing for promotional and advertising activities.
- Multi-skilling has occurred but the weight of evidence suggests that much of this is as a result of job enlargement and the intensification of work as opposed to a focus on job enrichment for the individual.
- In terms of temporal flexibility, there has been a spread of shiftworking to the banking sector and the growth of call centres and e-commerce will probably lead to further increases. Part of the growth is around the concept of 'customer care', particularly in the service industries, where firms have increased their times of operation to meet customer need, as with the Sunday opening of shops or, in some cases, the 24-hour opening of supermarkets.

Pollert (1987), in an early critique of Atkinson's work, accuses the Institute of Manpower Studies of offering vague concepts and of producing a model that is not supported by current evidence. She argues that elements of the flexible firm model can be seen in many organizations, but they have been introduced as cost-cutting exercises rather than a strategic response to a changing market environment. This is particular true of local authorities and other public sector organizations. She goes on to claim that many of the elements are far from new, citing multi-skilling as a feature of 1960s productivity bargaining initiatives. In some industries, notably fast food, she cites core workers as anything but the skilled, highly paid elite of Atkinson's flexible firm. Finally, she fears that the adoption of the flexible model could lead to more problems than it solves. Such problems as the growth of part-time employment have certainly attracted the interest of trade unions, where it is viewed as a part of the process of decreasing job security.

These themes reoccur in work throughout the 1990s. Dore (1997) sees flexibility in terms of a not necessarily appropriate response to increased shareholder pressures. Legge (1998) questions whether an increase in labour flexibility is a sound strategy and offers a clue as to her position in the title of her work, 'Flexibility: the gift-wrapping of employee degradation?'. She argues that within Western culture we tend to associate flexibility with positive images, yet for the core worker the outcome is often work intensification and stress and for the part-time or temporary worker it means insecurity. However, she does accept that there are advantages for employers in terms of cost reduction and the regulation of industrial relations. For some employees there are advantages. In the case of parents, part-time work provides the opportunity of combining work and child-care and for some it has been an important route of re-entry into the labour market.

There are other issues. The distinction between core and peripheral workers forms part of the debate about inclusion and exclusion in society. The very term peripheral suggests a group on the edge of society and the overall growth of part-time and contract work may lead to a lessening of importance of the firm as a source of identity in society. Hakim (1996) contends that the workforce has polarized into a primary labour market dominated by males and a secondary market typified by part-time jobs and high rates of labour turnover, dominated by females. His research suggests that the female secondary workforce accounts for as much as 40 per cent of the total labour market in the UK.

Ultimately the links between the introduction of the different forms of flexibility and economic success at either the micro or macro levels is still unproven. We end this discussion of structure by extending this theme with a brief look at the relationship between structure and performance.

Structure and performance

We can see from Figure 3.5 and our discussion of the various structural types that some structures are more suited to some situations than others. Conversely a firm that adheres stubbornly to a structure that is totally inappropriate to the contingencies that it faces may be creating problems for itself. However, the evidence on these matters is far from convincing. The major difficulties in establishing a correlation between structure and performance would appear to be first, identifying appropriate measures of performance and second, proving causality. We can make some general points:

● Whatever the relationship between structure and performance, once a structure has been installed it is often very difficult to change it. Equally, frequent structural changes could be damaging in terms of the disruption that takes place and the requirement on the part of staff to learn new systems.

● It is extremely doubtful whether structure alone can lead to improvements in performance. However sound the structure may be, it is unlikely that it can totally overcome problems created by staff incompetence or even divisive internal politics. In some cases a high degree of specialization or divisionalization can lead to a worsening of relationships. We might even speculate that there is more evidence for suggesting that structure can affect performance in a negative way than there is for its having a positive impact. There is some evidence that structure in harness with other variables can lead to improvements in performance (Child 1972). This point

161

was taken up by Galbraith and Nathanson (1978), who argue that effective financial performance is obtained by achieving some kind of congruence between strategy, structure, processes, rewards and people.

● We have noted elsewhere in this book that performance can influence structure and systems (see the discussion on 'organizational culture' later in the chapter). More successful companies are likely to be less bureaucratic, while less successful firms tend to have more controls, particularly cost controls. This fits in with the one of the key assumptions of our Business in Context model: that influences operate in more than one direction, and while organizational factors such as structure can affect the outcome of a firm's activities, that outcome in turn affects the organization.

Ownership

We might assume quite logically that ownership is an important variable in that the owners of a business will wish to determine the goals and the way that business operates. In support of our assumption we could cite illustrations of influential founders such as Henry Ford, Thomas J. Watson of IBM, and the Sainsbury family of supermarket fame. We could also refer to numerous cases of small firms where the owner, often single-handedly, controls the destiny of the business. In the case of the small firm the owners can be clearly defined and their impact easily assessed. Discovering who actually owns and controls businesses becomes much more difficult with large corporations like the major oil companies, or even an organization like British Airways, where privatization has been accompanied by widespread share issue at least in the first instance. It would appear that the greater the size of the organization and the greater the dispersal of share ownership, the more we can question our original assumptions and need to examine the relationship between the ownership and the control of businesses.

The degree of private and public ownership is another issue that holds significant interest for students of business in this country. Organizations that are wholly or partly state owned, like the National Coal Board, the Post Office or the local hospital, raise important issues of management control and public accountability.

In this section we will focus on these two aspects of ownership and examine the implications for business operation. We deal first with the traditional debate surrounding ownership and control. Secondly we examine the issue of the public ownership of organizations and the trend of privatization. The two elements were brought much closer together in the latter half of the 1980s in Britain. Traditional public sector concerns such as hospitals and local authorities have been urged to take a more commercial approach. Since 1983, many organizations like British Telecom, Jaguar, British Aerospace and utilities such as gas, electricity and water have passed from public to private ownership or to a mixture of public and private ownership. This has been accompanied by a massive increase in the proportion of the population owning shares and, in the initial phases at least, a highly dispersed ownership pattern for those concerns. It is this dispersal that is at the heart of the ownership and control debate.

Ownership and control

The issue of ownership and control is one of continuing interest for academics, more especially among economists and sociologists. It is also a debate that raises significant questions for businesses in practice. How committed to the future of an enterprise are managers who have no stake in its ownership, or shareholders who have no interest beyond a return on investment? Are the resulting strategies in the best interests of all concerned: owners, managers, employees, the state, the public at large? How much freedom do managers have in developing business strategies?

KEY CONCEPT 3.6
Ownership versus control

The ownership versus control debate is concerned with potential conflict of interests between the owners of business organizations and those who manage them on a day-to-day basis. The issue is a product of the creation of the joint stock company and the emergence of the professional manager to replace the owner-manager. The key issue is the extent to which company goals are pursued in the best interests of all stakeholders or that of a group of shareholders with no direct involvement with the firm. This issue becomes especially significant in volatile share markets with a large proportion of institutional investors, where high levels of share trading can lead to large numbers of mergers and acquisitions. There is a fear that pressure from shareholders for dividend leads to short-term management decisions that may not be in the long-term best interests of the firm.

The debate around these issues originates from the separation of ownership and control through the creation of the joint stock company and the subsequent dispersal of share ownership. With increased investment businesses grew in size and complexity and control by professional managers became a necessity. The complexity of such growing businesses led to a specialization within the management group and the separation of the firm into different specialist functions and activities. Bureaucratic rules and procedures were developed to coordinate and control such activities. Both the specialization and the bureaucratization reinforced the control of the management group with a supposed weakening in the power of the owner to influence decisions. The owner's main source of control was through the possession of capital stock.

This phenomenon was highlighted in the seminal study of Berle and Means (1932) and developed in later work by Berle (1954). Berle and Means in a study of the 200 largest non-financial corporations in the USA classified the firms by their mode of control. They concluded that 44 per cent of the

attention paid to efficiency and control can cure. According to Heald, the privatization enthusiast's case rests upon two major assumptions. First, public sector organizations are seen as less effective instruments of public policy than those of the private sector and second, the political objectives of public ownership are seen as less valid than the market criteria of private enterprise. The public sector was seen by the New Right Tories as a group of organizations with confused goals and inefficient operations dogged by industrial relations problems. The service they provided was considered poor, leaving its customers dissatisfied and creating a burden for the taxpayer.

The alternative, privatization, offered a number of advantages to different groups. It was envisaged that competition would be stimulated with an accompanying increase in efficiency and effectiveness. For the general public it was an opportunity to widen share ownership and to benefit from an improved service with a greater responsiveness to customer needs. For the newly privatized organizations there would be greatly increased opportunity for raising revenue which could be reinvested in the operation. It was assumed this would stimulate innovation to the benefit of all. For the government, public spending would be reduced and the sales would raise much-needed revenue. Furthermore, the policy was seen by some Conservatives as a further erosion of the power of trade unions and an ideological victory over the Labour Party opposition.

It is clear that share ownership has been broadened and the over-subscription of some issues indicates public support, and some firms, notably British Aerospace and the National Freight Corporation, showed a marked increase in profits. Critics argue that the privatization of vast concerns such as British Telecommunications and British Gas seems not to have influenced the market place at all, but merely changed the ownership status of a monopoly. Further criticisms have been levelled against the pricing policies of newly privatized companies, the inadequate provision for regulating large monopolies and the short-term strategy of 'selling off the public silver'. More cynical critics have pointed to job losses and the large pay awards to those former heads of public corporations.

Even 20 years after the beginning of the privatization boom in the UK it is still difficult to assess the impact. First, the impact has varied across the different organizations. Second, many have changed the nature of their operations to such an extent that it is difficult to make before and after comparisons, particularly where there have been acquisition and changes in ownership since privatization. Finally, there is considerable difficulty in disentangling the ideological, political and economic aspects of the argument. Apart from the social issues at stake there is at the moment mixed evidence to suggest that the private sector is any more or less efficient or effective than the public sector. The following examines some of the available evidence.

● After the original dispersal of the share issue, most of the individual shareholders sold their shares to make a quick profit. Ownership patterns have consolidated and concentrated, with most shares held by institutions. A mixture of a low initial share price and radical cost-cutting following privatization meant, for most companies, a rise in share value. As maturity sets in that share value has stabilized and in the 1990s there were criticisms against such as British Telecom (BT) that its share price had underperformed.

- Consumers benefited from price reductions in some cases. Gas prices fell 20 per cent from 1986 to 1993 and telephone prices fell 29 per cent from 1984 to 1995. Against this the cost of water has risen at twice the rate of inflation since privatization.
- The restructuring and cost-cutting exercises that accompanied privatization, in almost every case, have resulted in significant job losses and a delayering of management. BT moved from 245 000 employees in 1990 to 137 000 in 1995.
- Service levels in terms of response to customer problems and complaints have been recorded for BT, which has also increased its range of services and installed many more call boxes. In some cases, notably the water companies, complaints have increased and in others services have been cut as part of restructuring. The withdrawal of the facility to pay gas bills at gas showrooms has been one such change. For the utilities, privatization has brought new priorities, notably a focus on achieving greater efficiencies. The knock-on effect has been a reduction in R&D expenditure. In British Gas this was reduced by 32 per cent between 1993 and 1997. In 1989 the Central Electricity Generating Board (CEGB) spent £200 million on R&D, but only £178 million in 1997, explained in part by a reduced emphasis on nuclear power.
- After a number of years as private companies, the former public sector organizations have become the target for acquisition by other companies, including those from overseas. The French and the Americans have been particularly active in this respect, to the extent that, by 1999, seven of the 12 electricity companies in England and Wales were owned by US businesses. British Steel has moved in with the Dutch steel firm, Hoogovens. Privatized companies have pursued acquisition strategies themselves, notably BT. Key drivers for this have undoubtedly been globalization, developments in communications technology and the need to pursue growth in the face of a stagnant home market in the early 1990s. For example, BT acquired MCI, the second largest long-distance telephone company in the USA. While it is understandable that privatized companies should pursue business growth in this way, there are concerns that secondary trading of shares could operate against the public interest by attracting the predatory holding companies such as Hanson and Trafalgar House, whose main concerns are financial engineering and the share price, rather than public service.
- Public criticism of privatized businesses has tended to focus on the utilities and particularly the impact on household bills, how the utilities are regulated and the dramatic salary rises of senior management.

In conclusion, it would appear that privatization is an irreversible trend. The new Labour government in the UK would appear to have relinquished most of the ties with its ideological past and has published plans to expand privatization to the Air Traffic Control Service and to British Nuclear Fuels.

The trend is not confined to the UK. Government sell-offs are a feature of virtually every region in the world. In the case of utilities this has been driven by the need for capital investment in the face of restraint on public spending or the inability of some governments, notably those in Latin America and Eastern Europe, to foot the bill. In the case of telecommunications, it is driven by the need for global expansion in a rapidly changing industry. In 1998, over 50 per cent of revenue from privatization across the world was derived from telecommunication sales.

Size

The influence of size as an organizational variable interacts across all levels of our Business in Context model. Many of the issues relating to size are dealt with elsewhere in this book and in this section we simply present a summary of those issues. We do however develop the concept further by examining the issues relating to small businesses.

We have already seen earlier in this chapter how size is an important determinant of structure. Hickson *et al.* (1969) noted that with increasing size the technological imperative gives way to the size imperative. Increasing formalization and bureaucratization are inevitable consequences of the growing firm and the organization structure and management procedures are shaped by the need to coordinate and control large numbers of people. In our earlier discussion we saw how the growth of firms, especially through diversification, was an important element in companies such as General Motors adopting a divisional structure.

With size comes the development of specialist activities. In Chapter 8 we see how the development of personnel management as a specialist function is closely related to the increasing size of organizations. The employment of large numbers of people invariably calls for specialist expertise in the areas of recruitment, training, job evaluation, payment systems and industrial relations. In Chapter 5 we see a relationship between size and the R&D function. In this case it is not simply a matter of the numbers employed, but also a function of the need to maintain a powerful market position through investment in both product and process development and, of course, the ability to attract that investment.

Size is also related to dominance in the market place, as illustrated by the brewing industry in Britain. The industry is dominated by a handful of very large firms who maintain their market position not just by their ability to invest in product and process development, but also by the amount they are able to spend on nation-wide advertising campaigns. Their position is further strengthened by their strategy of acquiring smaller independent breweries, which find themselves unable to compete. The growth of lager sales at the expense of the traditional bitter beers has attracted the attention of the international brewing industry who are investing heavily in the British market. Most of the big brewing firms have grown by merger and acquisition, creating trans-European conglomerates such as Allied-Domecq, Grand

Metropolitan-Guinness (see Case 4.5) and Carlsberg-Tetley. A similar pattern can be found in the music industry. By 1993, the industry was dominated by four companies controlling over 70 per cent of the market. These were Warner, Thorn EMI, Sony and PolyGram. A key element in concentration in the music industry has been the growth in sales of compact discs. Not only do these require considerable investment in technology for their manufacture, favouring the big firm, but the public demand for reissues of old vinyl records in CD format has led to the larger firms buying up smaller independent producers to acquire their catalogues.

The big four CD producers dominate the sector, not just in terms of market share. There is a clear correlation in this industry between size and profitability. The biggest companies announce the biggest profit margins. There is a view that, in some industries, as with the illustration of the CD market, size is important. There is a considerable fear that the decline of the UK manufacturing industry in the 1980s has resulted in a lack of critical mass that is unable to compete in world terms. We have already discussed this issue in Chapter 2.

The ability of the large firm to dominate the market place is only part of its relationship with its environment. The size of a firm may be an important buffer in dealing with the demands imposed by its environment. We saw in Chapter 2 how the multinational corporation is able to dominate its environment, including influencing and in some cases overriding the policies of nation states. Size has also been a factor in attracting government support, not only in terms of R&D investment; the numbers employed by such firms as British Leyland have necessitated government rescue attempts during financial crises for political and social reasons as much for economic ones. In the 1970s in particular, size was often a vital protection against enforced closure.

An important rider to this discussion is the influence of technology. Developments in technology, and more specifically information technology, have meant that, in some industries, size is less significant. The growth of e-commerce and the proliferation of call centres has meant that business activities can be concentrated in smaller units (see Chapter 2 for a fuller account).

Size, structure and market position are themselves important variables in the determination of organization culture, which we deal with in the next section. At the micro-level there has been a great deal written about the impact of organizational size on the individual by focusing on the concepts of bureaucracy and alienation. Large organizations can undoubtedly present behavioural problems in terms of both management control and individual motivation. Such problems have been tackled by a range of devices, including the creation of autonomous work groups in an attempt to break up the organization into more easily managed units. Despite such behavioural problems it should not be forgotten that, at the management level at least, many employees actively seek out large firms for the career opportunities they offer.

While there is considerable evidence supporting the dominant position of the large firm, the problem of control in particular questions whether large firms actually make the best use of their resources. The relationship between size and performance has been challenged by the small firms' lobby, elevated from a 'small is beautiful' campaign in the early 1970s to a near political crusade for the future of Western capitalism in the 1980s. We now deal with the issues and arguments surrounding small firms.

Small businesses

The small firm has played a key role in the development of the business enterprise, particularly in the nineteenth century when economic growth owed much to the activities of individual entrepreneurs. The role of the small firm was overtaken by the development of mass production, mass markets, and above all the creation of the joint stock company which created investment and effectively removed a major constraint to the growth of businesses. Throughout the twentieth century the focus has been on the increasing size of businesses and the market domination by big business and the multinationals in particular.

The watershed came in 1971 with the publication of the Report of the Committee of Inquiry on Small Firms, generally referred to as the Bolton Report, after the Committee's chairman. The Committee's investigation was born out of a concern that the small firms' sector was being neglected, but also out of a disillusionment and fear of the economic and social consequences of domination by big business. The conclusion of Bolton and his colleagues was that the small firms' sector in Britain was in decline, in terms of both its size and its contribution to the nation's economy, and that the decline was more marked in the United Kingdom than in its major economic rivals. The report concluded that despite the decline the small firms' sector 'remains one of substantial importance to the United Kingdom economy' and that 'the contribution of small businessmen to the vitality of society is inestimable' (Report of the Committee of Inquiry on Small Firms, 1971, p. 342). The Report's importance lay not just in its conclusions, but as the first serious and subsequently influential attempt to define the small firm and in its stimulus to later research, much of which takes Bolton as its base point. The stimulus of the 1970s became the academic growth area of the 1980s, with many

---

KEY CONCEPT 3.8
The small firm

The small firm came to prominence in the UK in the early 1970s. The interest was based on the concern that a successful small firms' sector was vital to the economic health of a nation and that the UK lagged behind its major competitors in the size and contribution of its small firms' sector. There followed a series of public policies aimed at generating growth in the small firms' sector, which soon extended to include small and medium-sized enterprises up to 250 employees. There are problems associated with measuring the size of the sector and the evidence is mixed in terms of the contribution of the small firm to the economy, its benefits to the individual and as a provider of jobs.

business schools setting up special small firms' units, both for the purposes of academic research and to provide support for the regeneration of the small firms' sector. The stimulus was fuelled in the 1980s by a government increasingly determined to publicize the small business as the key element in the nation's economic revival. A report published in 1983 by a group of Conservative MPs and researchers stated,

> A high small firms ratio is consistent with high levels of growth and output. The malaise of our small business sector is a symptom and a cause of our comparative decline as an industrial nation.

> (Bright *et al.*, 1983, p. 15)

Such statements were reinforced by a host of measures aimed at supporting small businesses, including special loans for business start-ups and special extension of welfare benefits to stimulate self-employment. In addition changes were made in the stock market through the creation of the Unlisted Securities Market whereby small firms could raise investment capital. The entrepreneur became the hero figure for the 1980s and people such as Alan Sugar and Richard Branson became household names. The rationale for government support was more than a belief in the economic importance of the small firm. At a time of high unemployment the small business start-up offered a practical, and to some, a highly attractive solution. Moreover, it was a solution that was ideologically compatible with the government's views on economic management, welfare and self-help. It would be wrong of us to view the support of the small firm as the sole prerogative of the 'New Right' in British politics. Support for the small firms' sector has come from all sides of the political spectrum and it is one area where the Conservative government of the 1980s met with agreement in many Labour-controlled urban areas (with a notable exception of the now defunct Greater London Council, of which more later). There is no doubt that the government's promotion of the 'enterprise culture' in the 1980s resulted in the dramatic growth of small business start-ups. There were other related factors. Increasing unemployment and reductions in welfare benefits pushed many into self-employment. At the same time, developments in information technology made small firms in some sectors more viable, such as specialist travel agents.

In this section we will look at the extent and nature of the small businesses in this country and assess their value, focusing particularly on the economic arguments for continued state support. Many of the points are illustrated by Case 3.5, which summarizes a study of several small firms in the Nottingham area.

The extent of the small firms' sector

At the end of the 1990s it was estimated that small firms make up around 95 per cent of all businesses throughout the European Union. However, the small firms' sector is notable by its lack of accurate data. Any student of small businesses is immediately confronted with two problems. First, there are serious difficulties in defining a small business. The Bolton Report's working definition included those firms employing fewer than 200 people. The Committee identified three primary characteristics of a small firm; these were having a small market share, being owner-managed and being independent of any larger concern. The Committee, while acknowledging the difficulties, recognized the need for a numerical definition of a small business, but also recognized that the criterion used for manufacturing (numbers employed) would be inappropriate for construction, where much smaller firms were the norm, and for retailing, where the totally different criterion of turnover was seen as more appropriate. Some kind of quantitative definition is essential to the effective administration of government support and the law, small firms being exempt from certain aspects of employment law. The criteria used by Bolton are shown in Table 3.1. Storey (1994) argues that the criteria used by Bolton no longer have relevance, particularly definitions based on output, which are affected by technological change. He prefers the EU classification of:

Small and medium-sized enterprise (SME) fewer than 250 employees
Small business fewer than 100 employees
Micro business fewer than 10 employees

While this offers a simple definition, there are still problems. What may be a small firm in one type of business may be a relatively large firm in another.

Second, a difficulty arises in estimating the size of the small business sector. Official statistics are incomplete as far as small firms are concerned. For example, the Census of Production excludes firms of less than 20 employees and has only limited data on those of less than 100 employees. In addition there is a marked preference on the part of some small businessmen to remain outside official statistics for the purposes of tax avoidance. It has been noted that this area of small business development, known as the 'Black Economy', has increased quite dramatically during the 1980s, with estimates of its contribution to the GDP as anything from 3 per cent to almost 15 per cent (Curran, 1986).

Table **3.1** The Bolton Report definition of the small firm

Industry	Statistical definition of small firms
Manufacturing	200 employees or less
Retailing	Turnover £50,000 p.a. or less
Wholesale trades	Turnover £200,000 p.a. or less
Construction	25 employees or less
Mining/Quarrying	25 employees or less
Motor trades	Turnover £100,000 or less
Miscellaneous services	Turnover £50,000 or less
Road transport	5 vehicles or less
Catering	All excluding multiples and brewery managed houses

Source: Bolton Report 1.9, p. 3.

Because of these problems the estimates of the extent of small business activity and the contribution to the economy can vary considerably. Nevertheless, a recent attempt to summarize the current position, as a review of the Bolton findings 15 years on, paints a much more optimistic picture than the original report. By 1986 it was estimated that 10 per cent of the population worked for themselves and there was an increase in the number of small firms in all sectors, with the exception of retailing, where small businesses have declined. In addition, new types of small firm have emerged, such as producer cooperatives and franchise operations (Curran, 1986). Small businesses still predominate in the distribution, hotel and catering, repair, and construction sectors, but between 1963 and 1980 there was a 25 per cent increase in the numbers of small manufacturing concerns (Source: Department of Employment, quoted in *New Society*, March 1986). The same source points to an increase in the numbers of ethnic minorities setting up small firms. The significant growth in the 1980s came in the service sector with a 20 per cent increase of small businesses over the decade (Daly, 1991).

In addition to the increase in the number of firms, the survival chances of small firms appear to have improved. Although the problems of data accuracy are as acute here as elsewhere, estimates of the failure rate of business start-ups in the 1970s ranged from 50 to 75 per cent within the first two years (Bannock, 1981). More recent and perhaps more reliable data suggest a figure of around 50 per cent for the first two years, but that the chances of survival over 10 years are 40–45 per cent (Ganguly and Bannock, 1985). Daly (1987) based his analysis on VAT de-registrations and found that while the annual failure rate was around 20 per cent in the second and third years of existence, the chances of survival increased over time, falling to around 10 per cent when businesses are better established. There would therefore appear to be a clear correlation between failure rate and the age of the concern. One study found that the death rate of small firms actually slowed down during one of the worst periods of the recession in the early 1980s. However, it was felt that business owners carried on only in the absence of other opportunities (Stewart and Gallagher, 1985 have a fuller explanation). Other studies, however, remain more sceptical of the survival rates of small firms (Binks and Jennings, 1986, summarized in the Case 3.5). The main reasons for failure would appear to be finance, including cash-flow problems, poor products and inadequate marketing and market research. However, small business owners are not always the best people to offer an objective analysis of the failure of their own business.

International figures confirm the view that the small business start-up is a risky venture. A survey of small firms across the world from 1980 to 1990 revealed that, on average, 50–60 per cent of start-ups fail within the first five years. The same report highlighted that in some countries, notably Singapore, the failure rate was as high as 70 per cent (El-Namiki, 1993).

However incomplete the database on small firms may be, there is considerable evidence that the United Kingdom has fewer self-employed than many other comparable industrial nations, and it has fewer small firms making far less of a contribution to the economy. The small firms' sector here is smaller than that in the United States and Germany, and significantly smaller than that in Japan, where small firms play a significant role in the manufacturing economy. (Chapter 2 has a fuller discussion.)

The value of small businesses

The value of small businesses may be viewed in terms of the benefits to the owners, their impact on economic growth, the number of jobs they provide, and their service to the consumer. We will deal with each of these aspects in turn.

In terms of the **individual**, the small firm offers a number of assumed advantages. A Gallup Poll finding in 1986 cited the desire to 'be your own boss' as the main motivation behind small business start-ups, and more significant than unemployment (*New Society*, March 1986). Certainly self-employment offers the individual far greater opportunities for control, and perhaps greater satisfaction through direct involvement, than working for someone else. The small business has for many been the pathway to real wealth, social mobility, and perhaps political power in the local community. Some owners doubtless see their own business as a source of security for their family and as a kind of immortality via family succession. Against such values is the very real risk of failure and serious financial loss for the owner and his or her family, and romantic tales of individualism, wealth and job satisfaction should be set alongside the long working week, the frustration and the stress that many small business owners inevitably experience. The reality for many is that self-employment is less lucrative than working for someone else, and those that are successful either become prime candidates for a takeover bid by a larger firm or fear a loss of control that inevitably comes with growth.

In terms of **the contribution to economic growth**, evidence is patchy. The 1996 Pulse Survey (an Arthur Andersen/London Business School collaboration) concluded that small firms were less likely to grow than larger firms, but when they did, it was at a faster rate. We have already noted that the Conservative government of the 1980s saw the small firm as an essential ingredient of a healthy economy. The most obvious role for the small firm in this respect is to act as a 'seedbed' for future big business and in so doing secure the future of the economy. In addition, the small firm is seen as filling gaps in the market place by offering specialist products that would be uneconomic for the large firm to offer. More significantly the small firm is seen as a force for change by being inherently more flexible and innovative than the larger business. This image of the small firm was strengthened in the 1980s by the publicity given to the success and growth of certain small firms in the computer industry, although the majority of small businesses are decidedly 'low' rather than 'high' tech. In particular the small firm is seen as a useful vehicle in a recession; small firms are seen as price-takers and therefore offer no threat to inflation rates, and are able to plug the gaps left after larger firms have rationalized their operations. The rationalization of bus routes by the major companies together with the government deregulation of bus services paved the way for a number of smaller companies to enter the market, especially in rural areas and on the larger housing estates. These bus companies were able to operate routes that were uneconomic for the larger companies.

Many writers (for example Scase and Goffee, 1980; Rainnie, 1985) are more sceptical of the economic contribution of the small firms' sector, feeling that the small firm is exploited by big business and the main economic advantages of a small business presence accrue to the larger company. Certainly large manufacturing concerns could not survive without the components supplied by a host of smaller companies, and the extension of subcontracting in manufacturing has been a factor in the growth of the small business sector. The relationship may not be exploitative, although, as we saw in our examination of Japanese methods in the last chapter, the purchasing power of the large firm can have a significant impact on the profit margins of smaller companies. Certainly there is evidence of larger firms taking over markets created by smaller companies when those markets prove successful, the activity of IBM in the personal computer market being a case in point.

There is an assumption that small firms are first to the market place because they are inherently more innovative. Supporters of this view cite inventions such as air-conditioning and cellophane, which originated from individual entrepreneurs, and that small businesses often emerge from ideas for new products or clever adaptations of existing products. Big business on the other hand is often accused of channelling R&D along predictable lines and being less cost-effective in its use of R&D expenditure. Apart from the difficulties of measuring such things, the evidence for these claims is very mixed. More recent research suggests that even if small firms are inventive they often lack the development capital for successful innovation. (The distinction between invention and innovation is drawn more fully in Chapter 5.) Moreover, there is evidence to suggest that a high proportion of small business start-ups do not involve new products but involve the owner in replicating his or her previous employment (Binks and Jennings, 1986). This trend becomes especially critical where buy-outs are concerned and may be a primary cause of small business failure among buy-outs. In this case an ailing firm either sells out or divests part of its operation to a group of existing employees, usually management. Their experience and skills give them the optimism to continue operations in the same product market, perhaps ignoring the lack of demand or excessive competition operating in that same market, and they merely repeat the failure of the original firm.

There are obvious benefits of a thriving small firms' sector for the labour market, as **a provider of employment**. As we see in Case 3.4, redundancy and unemployment are big push factors towards self-employment. Small firms have been started and operate successfully in growth areas of the economy such as computer software and consultancy and the service sector in general. Moreover, self-employment is a valuable source of work for those groups such as ethnic minorities who are discriminated against in the labour market. In certain communities an over-dependence on a few large firms for employment can have serious consequences when those firms close, as with many mining communities following the pit closures of the 1980s and 90s. Under such circumstances a healthy small business presence may provide employment diversity and help counter the worst effects of mass redundancy. This view was taken by the government when faced with mass redundancies at the pre-privatized British Steel Corporation in the Sheffield area. The company took advantage of tax advantages by providing venture capital to business start-ups in the area.

However, there are decidedly mixed views on the small firm as a provider of jobs. Storey (1994) maintains that small firms create jobs more consistently and at a faster rate than larger firms and that job creation is a particular feature of the fastest growing small firms. Storey does acknowledge that such firms represent a very small proportion of the sector. Others paint a different picture. A study of the high-tech industry, one of the flagships of the small-firms lobby, in the Cambridge area from 1971 to 1981 concluded that only 800 new jobs had been created during the entire period (Gould and Keeble, 1984). Rainnie (1985) points out that whatever new jobs are created, they can easily be overshadowed by job losses in a large organization, and cites a report of 10 000 redundancies at Britain's largest computer firm, ICL, in 1984. Moreover, we have already seen from the high proportion of start-up failures that small firms are a source of job losses too.

Whatever the arguments for the quantity of employment provided by small firms, there have been several critical accounts concerning the quality of such jobs. Before it was disbanded, the Greater London Council was especially critical of the small firm as an employer, citing exploitation through low wages, long hours and an absence of trade union recognition as the main reason for their lack of support for small business development in the area (GLC, 1983). Obviously, not every small firm exploits its workforce, and many employees prefer the informal and often harmonious working environment that the small firm can provide.

We have already seen in our example of the deregulation of the bus industry how the small firm can **benefit the consumer** by filling the gaps left by the larger company. There is also the argument that the smaller firm is also closer to its customers and can provide them with a more personalized, responsive and specialized service. There are certain highly specialized product markets, such as precision scientific instrumentation, which tend to favour the smaller concern. Whether the smaller firm offers a 'better' service to the consumer is impossible to generalize or even judge. When buying expensive wine for keeping several years, a small specialist firm may be the most appropriate consumer choice, while a supermarket chain may offer the best value on less expensive purchases. The situation becomes particularly blurred when you consider that a number of larger firms of all types pay particular attention to customer sales and after-sales service. At a broader level a small firms' sector may be of considerable benefit to the consumer in challenging the power of monopolies.

The small firm as a case for government support

We believe that the health of the economy requires the birth of new enterprises in substantial number and the growth of some to a position from which they are able to challenge and supplant the existing leaders of industry ... We cannot assume that the ordinary working of market forces will necessarily preserve a small

Case 3.5: Small firms in the Nottingham area

A survey was carried out of 100 small firms in the Nottingham area. The firms were all wholly new businesses that had come into existence since 1977 and were independent, owner-managed and engaged predominantly in manufacturing. The main findings concerned the motivation behind setting up, the choice of product, the advice sought by small businessmen, and the labour costs involved.

The attraction of setting up in business was seen in terms of both pull and push factors, often operating together. The main push factors in order of significance were: redundancy; job insecurity and unemployment; disagreement at a previous firm; and the closure of a previous venture. The main pull factors in order of significance were: the desire for independence; the possession of specialist knowledge; the development of a product idea; and the incentive of financial reward.

The product chosen by the new company was invariably derived from the owner's previous experience, hobby or working skill. Seventy-eight per cent set up in businesses that were the same or similar to a previous employment and only 4 per cent were classed as having innovated a new product or process. The advice available to small business concerns was seen to be not particularly helpful or attractive to the potential entrepreneur. Over 40 per cent took no advice at all prior to starting up, and only 4 per cent attended any type of training course. Labour costs were typified by the owners working long hours for little remuneration, especially in the first two years, and the relatively low wages accepted by employees. The labour cost policy was related to a competitive pricing policy for market penetration.

The researchers conclude that such small-firm growth in manufacturing is a response to economic recession and occurs in established industries with little contribution to product or process innovation, and as such is unlikely to contribute towards economic recovery and growth. Moreover, the pricing and wages policies of the new entrants is likely to have a depressing effect on the local economy by threatening the livelihood of established enterprises. As such, government policies aimed at increasing the number of small firms 'may simply be increasing the throughput of firms rather than the stock'. ■

(*Source*: Binks and Jennings, 1986)

firm sector large enough to perform this function in the future.

(Bolton, 1971, 8.5, p. 85)

Bolton and his committee were clear that government support was necessary to secure the future of the small firm and hence the economy. In spite of its commitment to market forces the Conservative government of the 1980s revealed its support of the small business by a large number of different measures. Despite this apparent attention, many critics still see a gap between government rhetoric and effective action. There would appear to be a need for an effective overall government strategy for the SME and small firms' sector, justified on both economic and social grounds, as in the case of inner city regeneration. As Storey argues,

> The small firm sector in the United Kingdom has now reached a size and importance in which public policy towards it cannot be left entirely to those with a vested interest in the smaller firm.

(Storey, 1994, p. 303)

One of the intentions in our analysis of small businesses was to look behind the current popular support for the small firms' sector and attempt to challenge the view that the encouragement of small business development is a valid strategy for economic recovery and growth. It is indeed difficult to draw any firm conclusions at all, for despite the growth of research data and the space devoted to small businesses in the serious as well as the popular press, many difficulties remain.

Confusion still reigns over an agreed definition of what actually constitutes a small business and the evidence that we do possess is highly contradictory in its findings. A major problem involves politics and ideology, which were as much a part of the Conservative government's support as the GLC's condemnation.

What we do find is that the small firm provides some jobs, offers some hope for the unemployed and meets the subcontracting needs of big business. However, there is very little evidence that a policy of support for the encouragement of small firms will either solve the problems of long-term unemployment or result in substantial economic growth. Behind the rhetoric of politicians there is considerable criticism aimed at those very measures designed to support the small firm. The sheer number and complexity of such measures and the different sources of advice have been shown to be as confusing as they are helpful. Moreover, the cost of government measures such as the Loans Guarantee Scheme has proven much too expensive for many small firms. Outside the government schemes the banks appear keen to provide services for the small firm, but even here the picture must be seen in perspective. German banks on average lend twice as much for longer periods and at lower interest rates than their British counterparts (Bannock, 1981). The relationship with banks is seen as a perennial problem by most commentators on the small firms' sector. The closer relationship enjoyed between banks and small firms in France and, particularly, in Germany may account for the larger small business and SME sectors in those countries.

Bannock's vision of a healthy economic future involves small and large businesses in a kind of optimal balance, with small firms as the 'motivators of growth' and large firms as the 'consolidators and accelerators'. In this way the small firm may play a significant role in the recovery from recession. Others are less optimistic:

> ... the fashionable concern with the contribution of small enterprise to economic restructuring should not be allowed to obscure the dominating presence of the large enterprise.

(Curran, 1986, p. 46)

Concern for the small firm may well be, like the interest in Japanese management, a fashion born out of recession, although it has persisted longer than most. Certainly small business development is important in the future of any economy, but current political interest owes as much to ideology as it does to sound economic argument. For our purposes the case of the small firm is again an excellent illustration of the interplay between the various elements of our Business in Context model.

Organizational culture

We have already encountered the concept of culture in our treatment of the environmental context of business in Chapter 2. There we focused on broad cultural distinctions between different groups of people, particularly in the comparisons of businesses in different countries. In this section we focus upon culture in a more localized setting, that of the organization itself. The goals, structure, patterns of ownership and size of an organization both reflect and are reflected in its culture. Other influences on the culture of an organization include its history and all those aspects we have identified as belonging to the environmental level of our Business in Context model. The importance of the organizational culture is that it sets the scene for the determination of strategy and hence the operational aspects of organizational life. The concept assumes therefore a central position in our model of business.

Interest in organizational culture can be traced back to the early sociological works of Durkheim through Elton Mayo and the Human Relations Movement to 'organizational development' and HRM. Interest was heightened in the USA during the 1970s as American companies, searching for a solution to the problems of the economic recession, looked to the role models of Japanese firms and the more successful firms within their own country. In turn, academic research in business shifted its focus away from individual management techniques to examining the business as a complete entity and viewing the way people responded to their own organization. This was reinforced by the changes in political economy that were taking place in the UK and the USA at the time and by developments in HRM, which focused on culture change at the level of the firm (see Needle, 2000 for a more detailed review of the historical development of organizational culture).

The terms 'organizational culture' and 'corporate culture' are used interchangeably in the literature. In our review we draw a distinction between them in much the same way Smircich (1983) differentiated between 'analytical' and 'managerial' perspectives on culture. In this section we will define

---

KEY CONCEPT 3.9
Organizational and corporate culture

These two terms are often used interchangeably, but in this book they are defined differently. Organizational culture represents the collective values, beliefs and practices of organizational members and is a product of such factors as history, product market, technology, strategy, type of employees, management style, national cultures and so on. Corporate culture on the other hand refers to those cultures deliberately created by management to achieve specific strategic ends. The concept came to prominence in the 1980s with interest in so-called excellent companies and the idea that specific types of corporate culture were a template for success. Such views have been challenged by much of the evidence, although certain cultures can make a significant contribution to coordination and control and levels of employee satisfaction.

culture at the level of the firm and examine further our concepts of organizational and corporate culture. We examine the concept of a strong culture and its relationship to notions of the 'excellent company'. We assess its value as a business tool and offer a critique. We will illustrate these points by reference to Hewlett-Packard, the American computer and electronic instrument firm, presented as Case 3.6.

The terms defined

Culture at the level of the firm has been defined as:

> The way we do things around here.
>
> (Deal and Kennedy, 1982, p. 4)

> The pattern of beliefs, values and learned ways of coping with experience that have developed during the course of an organization's history and which tend to be manifested in its material arrangements and in the behaviour of its members.
>
> (Brown, 1998, p. 9)

> a) A pattern of basic assumptions, b) invented, discovered or developed by a particular group c) as it learns to cope with problems of external adaptation and internal integration, d) that has worked well enough to be considered valid, and e) is to be taught to new members as the f) correct way to perceive, think and feel in relation to those problems.
>
> (Schein, 1990, p. 111)

The quote from Deal and Kennedy is frequently used in both managerial and academic treatments of the subject. It is in fact not the authors' own, but a quote from Marvin Bower, the then managing director of McKinsey, for whom Deal and Kennedy were consultants. Their definition is typical of the language used in many of the managerial texts and is sufficiently broad to add little to our understanding of the concept. Brown and Schein attempt to detail the key elements. These would appear to be beliefs and values that are developed in an organization over time, are learned by its members, are used to guide their behaviour and solve their problems, and are manifested in the language used and in every aspect of organization life.

Organizational culture sees organizations in terms of a unique combination of variables. These include history, technology, product market, type of employees, type of ownership, leadership and strategy. Other influences include the broader culture of the country or region, the prevailing political economy and the behaviour of the stakeholders. Many attempts have been made to simplify this range of variables through the use of models attempting to draw distinctions between generic types of organization. An early and highly simplistic attempt was made by Harrison (1972) who classified the character or ideology of organizations under four categories: power, role, task and person. This same classification was popularized by Handy (1993), who referred specifically to these categories as cultures.

Corporate culture focuses on the use of culture as a control device to enhance performance through the development of greater commitment and the integration of all employees at all levels in the organization. It is this perspective on culture at the level of the firm that attracts the greatest critical attention. Some writers, notably Willmott (1993), view the manipulation of culture in this way as highly questionable, referring to it as the 'dark side of the force' and likening it to an Orwell's 1984. Others, such as Thompson and McHugh (1990), while offering similar criticisms, also see some benefits to employees through the more paternalistic strategies of employers. The idea of a management-led corporate culture lies at the heart of the notions of a 'strong culture' and 'the excellent company', to which we now turn.

Strong cultures and the excellent company

Strong cultures are associated with those organizations where the guiding values of top management are clear and consistent and are widely shared by the employees. Such cultures are typified by a set of strong values passed down by senior management. The values are strengthened by rituals, which emphasize and reward appropriate behaviour, and a cultural network, comprising a system of communication to spread the values and create corporate heroes. A feature of strong cultures is their association with hero figures, who exemplify the key values. Ray Kroc of McDonald's, Bill Hewlett and Dave Packard of Hewlett-Packard and Anita Roddick of the Body Shop are examples of such corporate heroes.

The processes of creating such a 'positive' organizational culture would appear to operate as follows. The senior management of a company set goals and issue guidelines, which promote strongly held shared values; common emphases are enthusiasm, diligence, loyalty, quality and customer care. To ensure that such guidelines are passed on to all employees there is usually a high investment in the procedures of communication and integration. A number of techniques are commonly used to create and maintain a specific corporate culture. Some firms pay particular attention to the physical environment, and some like Hewlett-Packard attempt to create a corporate style that is recognizable wherever they operate. In their case the focus is the facilitation of communication. In IBM a layout that facilitates communication is equally important, as is the use of a corporate colour, blue. The goals of the company are invariably written down, explicit, communicated to all employees and tend to stress the contribution that employees can make to the firm. Heroes and myths play an important role in communicating the core values as illustrated by the 'Bill and Dave stories' in Case 3.6. The same importance is ascribed to rituals, which take the form of team meetings or out-of-work social activities, where participation is the norm. The organization structure strengthens the culture by a common focus upon autonomous units to enhance group identity and loyalty. Recruitment and selection methods tend to be rigorous to screen out unsuitable candidates and ensure a fit between the recruit and the prevailing culture. Considerable emphasis is placed on induction and training as primary vehicles for cultural socialization. All these processes and procedures can be found in firms such as IBM and Hewlett-Packard. A study of three electronics firms in South Korea, Hyundai, Samsung and LG, revealed considerable investment in induction and training as a means of transmitting corporate values (Needle, 2000). All three companies had a separate training centre, where new employees spent up to four weeks focusing exclusively on corporate values. More intensive education around corporate values followed promotion and every employee spent a few days each year at the centre for purposes of reinforcement.

Such strong cultures are a central feature of the so-called **'excellent company'**. Peters and Waterman (1982) may not be the only writers to attempt to identify the features of the excellent company (Ouchi attempted much the same a year earlier), but their attempt proved to be the most successful by far with their book *In Search of Excellence*. Several million copies have been sold since its publication in 1982 and the book arguably ranks alongside Taylor's *Scientific Management* as one of the most influential management texts of all time. Peters and Waterman carried out an investigation of 62 top-performing American companies. Six measures of long-term productivity were devised and only those firms that ranked in the top 20 of their industry on four out of the six criteria were included in their in-depth study. Their final sample numbered 43 firms, including IBM, Hewlett-Packard, Boeing, Digital, Caterpillar, Eastman Kodak, Walt Disney and 3M. The sample was not intended to be representative of all types of firm and banks are notable by their exclusion.

In all, eight attributes of excellence were identified. These were, using Peters and Waterman's own terminology, as follows:

- **'Bias for action'**, being typified by clear objectives and a marked absence of committee procedures.
- **'Closeness to the customer'**, typified by processes and procedures aimed at identifying and serving the customers needs.
- **'Autonomy and entrepreneurship'**, which are best achieved through the creation of small cohesive teams.
- **'Productivity through people'**, with workforce involvement at all times.
- **'Hands on; value driven'**, involving the fostering of a strong corporate culture by top management who are seen to be in touch with all employees.
- **'Stick to the knitting'**, which involves limiting activities to what the firm does best and avoiding diversification into unknown territory.
- **'Simple form, lean staff'**, avoiding complex hierarchies and large administration sections.
- **'Simultaneous loose–tight properties'**, which means that organization structure should display a combination of strong central direction with work group autonomy.

Throughout their work Peters and Waterman stressed the importance of socializing and integrating individuals into a clearly defined corporate culture. The firm becomes much more than a place of work, by offering meaning as well as money, the excellent companies give their employees a mission as well as a sense of feeling great.'

(Peters and Waterman, 1982, p. 323)

At its most influential the corporate culture is seen as having replaced organized religion and the family as the most important focus in a person's life (Ray, 1986).

Case 3.6: Hewlett-Packard

Hewlett-Packard is an American multinational operating in most major countries of the world. It was founded in the late 1930s in Palo Alto, California by Bill Hewlett and Dave Packard, both of whom still have considerable influence on company philosophy. Traditionally the firm has operated in four main divisions each representing different product groupings. These divisions are: the Computer Systems Group, the Measurement Systems Group the Medical Products group and the Analytical Instrumentation group. The company now employs over 120 000 people in more than 110 countries worldwide and has manufacturing and R&D in 52 of them. Its philosophy as a global company is based around a unified corporate culture irrespective of location.

By the end of the 1990s the management had become aware that as a company they needed to change their focus. They recognized that most of their clients were operating in a rapidly changing world. They wanted more than the purchase of hardware systems. Rather, they needed someone to guide them through a period of rapid and confusing change, of which e-commerce was but one element. HP decided to offer a complete service to customers, which they called 'HP Consulting'. This required a change in approach not just for HP employees, but for their customers as well. The methods they used in effecting these changes were based on a central element in all their activities they had used since the beginning. This central element became known as the 'HP Way'.

The 'HP Way', a set of beliefs, objectives and guiding principles, is described by Bill Hewlett as follows:

'... the policies and actions that flow from the belief that men and women want to do a good job, a creative job, and that if they are provided with the proper environment they will do so. It is the tradition of treating every individual with respect and recognising personal achievements ... You can't describe it in numbers or statistics. In the last analysis it is a spirit, a point of view. There is a feeling that everyone is part of a team and that team is HP. As I said at the beginning it is an idea that is based on the individual. It exists because people have seen that it works, and they believe that this feeling makes HP what it is'.

(Quoted in Peters and Waterman, 1982, p. 244)

The HP Way is probably best illustrated from a number of words and concepts extracted from Hewlett-Packard's own publications. These are love of the product, love of the customer, innovation, quality, open communication, commitment to people, trust, confidence, informality, teamwork, sharing, openness, autonomy, responsibility.

It is not just the communication of such sentiments that appears to be important in Hewlett-Packard but that such sentiments appear to be shared by a majority of employees and felt with a certain intensity.

The sentiments are reinforced by a series of processes and procedures which we identify below:

● Communication is the key underlying theme behind all activities in Hewlett-Packard and is an important ingredient of the company's attitude towards innovation and quality. Informal communication is encouraged between all employees of different levels and functions. The physical layout of the offices and work stations has been deliberately created to encourage ad hoc meetings and brainstorming. The use of first names is almost obligatory and is the norm even in the German operations, where employees are used to a much greater degree of formality in personal relationships. Management assists the informal processes by engaging in what Hewlett-Packard term MBWA ('management by wandering around'). At a more formal level there are frequent announcements to the workforce on such

▶

Continued

matters as company performance and all employees are given a written statement of the company goals, stressing as they do the contribution that individuals can make. Regular team meetings are obligatory for groups within the organization and once a week all employees meet for a briefing session by senior management. Less formal channels of communication are still guided by the company, in that employees are encouraged to participate in coffee breaks signalled by a bell. The communication policy is assisted by the company's commitment to decentralization.

An important aspect of communication in Hewlett-Packard is the various stories and myths that are a continual feature of management training, retirement parties, company speeches and in-house journals. These stories generally tell of key moments in the company's history, or recount the exploits of the corporate heroes, usually Bill Hewlett and Dave Packard. These stories serve an important purpose of stressing a collective identity and underlining the goals of the founders.

● Quality, according to Peters and Waterman, is pursued with zealotry. The company certainly sees its prime objective as a commitment to the design, manufacture and marketing of high-quality goods. Commitment to quality is viewed as ongoing with continual product improvement as a major goal. All employees are involved in the definition and monitoring of quality, a process reinforced by procedures such as MBWA and ceremonies to recognize, reward and publicize good work. The company has a stated policy and associated methodologies of continuous improvement.

● Innovation, like quality, is regarded as the responsibility of all employees. Following the espousal to 'stick to the knitting' there is a clear commitment to products related to electrical engineering and the company's existing product portfolio. Openness is encouraged and prototypes are often left for other employees to test and criticize. Employees are free to take company equipment home with them. In relations with their customers the company is guided by yet another principle and mnemonic, that of LACE ('laboratory awareness of customer environment'). A central strategy in R&D is the design of products to customer specifications and the LACE programme gives customers the opportunity to make presentations to the company. Such procedures

stress the strong emphasis on customer service. The 'HP Consulting' initiative is a further attempt to link new developments with the needs of customers. It is also an attempt to assist customers to deal with innovations occurring in their business environment, such as e-commerce.

● Personnel policies are carefully designed to reinforce the HP Way as well as ensuring that it works. Most HP employees have no requirement for clocking-on and many operate on flexible working hours. All employees attend a detailed induction programme with communication of the HP Way as a key ingredient. In terms of selection care is taken to select only those who meet the criteria of being high calibre and possessing flair, adaptability and openness. Most recruits are young. As we have seen, considerable attention is paid to the environment and the general well-being of employees is a major consideration. Employee commitment is reinforced by a highly structured system of objective setting. Objectives are mutually set at all levels and are cascaded down throughout the organization. Salaries are reviewed every three months for each employee through an evaluation based on the achievement of objectives.

● There is a somewhat traditional and conservative approach to finance and accounting. There is an emphasis on careful management of assets, self-financing investment, and minimal long-term borrowing.

The overall impression is often that Hewlett-Packard is too good to be true.

> 'We tried to remain sober, not to become fans. But it proved impossible'. (Peters and Waterman, 1982, p. 246)

Certainly on most measures of performance and employee satisfaction, Hewlett-Packard emerges as a highly successful company. The net profit has never been less than 3 per cent of net turnover and R&D expenditure never less than 10 per cent of turnover. More than 50 per cent of the turnover is generally attributed to products developed in the previous two years. A measure of the employees' commitment occurred in 1970 when in the middle of a recession and bad time for the company financially, a 10 per cent pay cut was agreed rather than lay people off. ■

(*Sources*: Peters and Waterman, 1982; Beer *et al.*, 1984; Needle, 1984; Feurer *et al.*, 1995; Greenly, 1999)

Culture and performance

Those who subscribe to this kind of vision of organizations argue that companies displaying such characteristics are invariably more successful than those that do not (Peters and Waterman, 1982; Deal and Kennedy, 1982). We examine this claim by reference to a number of studies that have been carried out examining the impact of culture on strategy and on performance.

Brown (1998) sees the link between culture and strategy as inevitable. He argues that the culture of an organization will determine key strategic elements, including how the environment is perceived and interpreted, how information is analysed, and how the main players react. This echoes the earlier work of Miles and Snow (1978). They identify three types of organization: defenders, prospectors and analysers. Each of these is culturally different and each pursues different strategies.

The notion of a culture–strategy fit also underpins many studies on culture change, where culture is manipulated to achieve the desired strategic ends. At best, this represents an understanding by management that successful implementation of a strategy requires consideration of behavioural and culture change and a corresponding investment in training and other processes. The case of British Airways is a good illustration of this kind of change process (see Case 8.2). At worst however, it represents a vague hope on the part of management that simple exhortations to culture change will bring about the desired strategic change.

British Airways is often cited as an example of how culture, or more specifically culture change, can lead to improved performance. Goodstein and Burke (1991) attempted to provide links between culture change and the conversion of a $900 million loss into a $435 million profit. Even more measured accounts, such as those of Höpfl et al. (1992), point to some success factors and argue that the 'new' culture at British Airways enabled it to withstand subsequent pressures on business such as those associated with the Gulf War and the deregulation of transatlantic routes. Links between culture and performance were also postulated by Gordan and Ditomaso (1992), who found some correlation between the strength of a widely shared culture and short-term financial performance. In Whipp et al. (1989) an analysis was made of Jaguar, a blue-chip car producer with a sought-after product and strong export market. The placing of Jaguar under BL management in the 1970s resulted in a performance decline, explained as a clash of cultures between Jaguar employees and BL management. It was a case of a specialist versus volume car manufacturer, where energies were diverted as Jaguar management engaged in political battles to retain a distinctive corporate identity. Performance at Jaguar improved dramatically in the 1980s when, free from the restrictions of BL, a new management team attempted to re-create the values of the company's most successful era through a focus on costs, quality and incremental quality improvements.

Yet the studies by Gordan and Ditomaso and by Whipp et al. also point out the dangers of linking culture and performance too directly. Both acknowledge the likely interference factor of a whole range of variables. In the case of Jaguar, the performance of the company, especially in its main export market, the USA, was aided significantly by a favourable sterling–dollar exchange rate. Such limitations have led many to question its utility as a concept. It is to these issues we now turn.

How useful is organizational culture as a concept?

The more analytical perspective of organizational culture attempts to view culture as an amalgam of many variables. The problem with such analyses is the isolation and measurement of variables. It is hardly surprising that so many articles and books are dependent upon anecdotes from key participants as the major form of data. There are other elements that contribute to this complexity. The exhortations of corporate literature and of top management can appear markedly different from the realities of organizational life. In this vein, Watson (1994) makes a clear distinction between official and unofficial cultures existing within organizations at the same time. He argues that each has its own particular discourse, in that while the official culture talks about 'empowerment, skills and growth', the unofficial reflects upon 'control, jobs and costs' (Watson, 1994, p. 112)

The major criticisms are reserved for the research carried out in the so-called 'excellent companies' and for the perspective of managerial corporate culture. The problems identified below are aimed almost exclusively at this perspective.

The rigour of much of the research is challenged. For example, Hitt and Ireland (1987) argue that the excellent companies of the Peters and Waterman study performed no better on stock market valuation than other 'non-excellent' companies appearing in the 'Fortune 1000' listing

The use of corporate culture as a management tool is not feasible. A number of limitations in the management use of culture have been identified. Some authors believe that the significance of culture is overstated, and that variables such as product/market, size and monopoly power are more important (Carroll, 1983). The case of IBM frequently crops up in the literature where it is questioned whether their dominance of the market was a function of culture or monopoly power. The excellence guru himself, in a later book, used market changes to explain the fall from grace of some of his original sample (Peters, 1987). Willmott (1993) argues that changing economic conditions have much more impact on a firm's performance than culture. The strong culture of the three Korean electronics companies, previously cited, made little difference in the face of the economic crisis in Asia in 1997 (Needle, 2000). The kind of culture seen in firms such as Hewlett-Packard and IBM may simply not be appropriate in certain types of organization. Dawson (1986) argues that Peters and Waterman have not uncovered a set of universal principles, but strategies that only work under certain conditions.

> Their 'slim, consensual organizations' of the future are probably applicable to firms employing professionals and technicians from the primary labour market in the development and operation of

new technology or highly fashionable products and processes. They may however be less successful in other technological, product or labour market conditions.

(Dawson, 1986, p. 137).

One may conclude from this that certain types of culture, notably that associated with the 'excellent' companies, is incompatible with certain types of company, specific types of work, and, almost certainly, the presence of an active trade union movement. There is clearly conflict here with the concept of the flexible firm. It may be difficult to establish corporate values and gain commitment amongst a growing number of part-time and contract employees. Labour market issues are clearly important here, particularly when combined with employee characteristics related to job mobility. In Singapore job changing is frequent and an accepted route to career and salary enhancement. As a consequence, firms have difficulty sustaining a particular culture.

Even where conditions are 'favourable', cultures may be very difficult to change. Scholz (1987) maintains that culture change can take anything from six to 15 years. This is in stark contrast to those managers who regard instant culture change as the panacea for all that ails their company. Ultimately, as we have already shown, the utility of the concept is brought into question by the continued difficulty in establishing any meaningful links between culture, strategy and performance. Dawson (1986) raises the fundamental question as to whether culture is a cause or a consequence of a firm's success. In other words, is a firm like Hewlett-Packard successful because it has a particular kind of culture, or does it have a particular kind of culture because it is successful? It is much easier to gain employee consensus when profits are healthy, bonuses are good and job security is guaranteed.

The use of corporate culture as a management tool is not desirable. The key issue here is one of ethics. At worst corporate culture is seen as a form of brainwashing or conditioning and at best it sends out conflicting messages to employees. It is true that in companies such as Hewlett-Packard, employees are encouraged to be creative, yet are expected to conform; to be individualistic within a corporate image of a vast collective; to exhibit freedom, yet be subject to considerable expectations as to appropriate behaviour. The whole issue is probably best summed up by Peters and Waterman's notion of 'simultaneous loose–tight properties'. Under such conditions individuals were encouraged to operate as free, creative individuals, within a cloak of tight collective corporate control. For Willmott the contradictions are part of the use of corporate culture as a control mechanism.

A number of writers, notably Silver (1987), are concerned about the exploitative potential of corporate culture. The essence of such criticism is that the emphasis on the moral commitment of the workforce is simply a means of achieving high productivity on the cheap. Silver singles out McDonald's for particularly harsh criticism.

> The lively, people-oriented culture is but a complement to the speeded up, Taylorized assembly line production of food ...

grease burns, irregular hours, autocratic bosses, sexual harassment and low wages all come with the quarter pounder.

(Silver, 1987, pp. 109–10)

Ethical or exploitative, corporate culture may be undesirable simply because it prevents change. In Rank Xerox, middle management were so cast in an identical mould of strong corporate values that they were dubbed 'xeroids'. Their programmed thinking and a successful company, built on the patent protection of the photocopying machine, rendered them impervious to a changing business climate and, ultimately, unable to respond to increased competition (Williams *et al.*, 1989).

Culture as a useful concept. Thus far in the critique we have focused on the problematic aspects of organizational and corporate culture, yet even some of the more critical writers have identified some benefits. Of course, one must always add the rider, benefits for whom and at what cost? For Ray (1986), corporate culture offers management coordination and control via a moral involvement of the workforce. It is also claimed to reduce conflict and uncertainty, particularly through the emphasis on clear guidelines and effective training (Deal and Kennedy, 1982). Peters and Waterman (1982) stress the benefits to employees, notably a sense of belonging and good pay. Culture has also been viewed as a vital link between the rational and the subjective aspects of determining strategy and is seen as the element that turns strategy into a reality (Whipp *et al.*, 1989). The continued success of firms such as Hewlett-Packard is used as evidence that strong cultures are not necessarily as dysfunctional as the critics suggest.

If for nothing else, an analysis of organization culture may assist us in gaining fresh insights into the realities of organizational life and obtaining a richer picture. For example, a focus on culture and, in particular, subcultures, as large public organizations such as universities and hospitals undergo change, may lead to a greater understanding of the underlying issues. In hospitals, there are tensions between the medical staff and budget-conscious administrators. In universities similar tensions exist between academics and senior management. Academics see traditional freedoms being eroded by management initiatives responding to a harsh financial climate and government funding, increasingly tied to performance indicators. Such external pressures are challenging the traditional values that underpin the culture.

Summary

In this chapter we focused our attention on the organizational elements of business which we identified as goals, structure, ownership, size and organizational culture. As befits our model, all elements interact not just with each other but with aspects of the environment, business strategy and operations.

We view **goals** as the products of a highly interactive and dynamic process such that changing goals may well be a prerequisite for business survival. Goals give a sense of direction to a firm's activities and may be presented in a hierarchy involving a mission, objectives and strategies. The formulation of goals is closely related to the way power relations are worked out in organizations, and often involve highly political processes of influence, conflict and compromise between different interest groups. A number of goals may operate at any one time. These may conflict, but in general the goals of a business follow closely those of the dominant coalition. A key issue in the discussion of goals is the extent to which businesses and their members can pursue ethical behaviour at all times.

The factors that influence **structure** are identified as technology, size, environmental changes, strategy, culture, and the behaviour of interest groups. We identify various models of organizational structure, including functional, divisional and matrix, but acknowledge that very few firms confirm to such ideal types. Many firms have mixed structures and new variations are emerging all the time, with recent attention being given to flexible structures and the operation of flexible labour markets. The relationship between structure and performance is of obvious interest to businessmen, but as yet the evidence is inconclusive.

Ownership is important because of its potential impact on the way businesses are managed. We examine this relationship by focusing on the traditional debate of ownership versus control and the freedom of managers to make decisions in the face of the growing influence of institutional shareholders and the power of interlocking directorships. The dilemmas that can arise in the relationship between ownership and control are examined with reference to the public sector, and, in particular, the growing trend in many countries of the privatization of public companies.

We examine the influence of **size** on such factors as structure, market power, relationship with the state, and the impact on the individual. The main focus of this section is the small firm. The case for government support of the small firm is examined in light of the potential contribution of small businesses to the economy and society. We conclude that the current enthusiasm for small firms owes more to ideology than it does to economic analysis.

Organizational culture is viewed as the product of goals, structure, ownership and size, as well as company history, technology, its product-market environment and several other variables as well. The sum total of those influences distinguish organizations from one another. The main argument surrounding organizational culture is that a particular culture can be created by management to enhance performance. We refer to this as **'corporate culture'**. In spite of the enthusiasm for so-called 'excellent' companies, the research is inconclusive. Culture may be less important than technology or the product-market and we question its usefulness in terms of the feasibility and desirability of culture change at the level of the firm.

Further reading

J. Barry *et al.* (eds), *Organization and Management: A Critical Text* (ITBP, 2000) offers useful contributions on many of the issues raised in this chapter, including organizational culture, business ethics and the flexible firm. Those students seeking an historical perspective on structural issues are advised to look at A.D. Chandler, *Strategy and Structure: Chapters in the History of American Capitalism* (MIT Press, 1962). Probably the best summary of the ownership and control debate is offered by J. Child, *The Business Enterprise in Modern Industrial Society* (Collier-Macmillan, 1969). A good summary of recent research and debates about the role of the small firm is found in J. Storey, *Understanding the Small Business Sector* (Routledge, 1994). Although published almost two decades ago, a good account of the problems facing small firms, which is still relevant today, can be found in R. Scase and R. Goffee, *The Real World of the Small Business Owner* (Croom Helm, 1980). No examination of organizational culture would be complete without a look at T.J. Peters and R.J. Waterman, *In Search of Excellence: Lessons from America's Best-run Companies* (Harper and Row, 1982), although a sounder academic treatment is offered by A. Brown, *Organizational Culture* (Financial Times Pitman, 1998).

Discussion

1. Examine the statements of goals for the various companies in Case 3.1. What are the similarities and differences? How might the differences be explained?

2. How are goals formed and what are the major difficulties encountered in goal formulation and implementation? What do events at London Zoo, Case 3.2, tell us about this process?

3. How far is it possible and desirable for the managers of profit-seeking organizations to pursue ethical strategies at all times? What are the key problems and issues?

4. Identify the various strategic, organizational and environmental factors which led to structural changes in Dow Corning and IBM as illustrated by Cases 3.3 and 3.4. What problems will the new organization structures solve, and what new problems may emerge?

5. Whose interests are served by flexible labour markets and the creation of the flexible firm?

6. How significant is the separation of ownership and control to the way businesses operate?

7. Examine the advantages and the prime beneficiaries of privatization in the UK since 1980. To what extent will privatization solve the problems of managing public sector organizations?

8. Examine the rationale behind government support for the small firms' sector. To what extent are small firms economically relevant today?

9. What is the relationship between the type of corporate culture envisaged by Deal and Kennedy and by Peters and Waterman and company performance in terms of profitability and job satisfaction? Can the internal culture of an organization act as a buffer against environmental influences?

10. What are the advantages and disadvantages of the Hewlett-Packard style as illustrated in Case 3.6? What threats could challenge the effectiveness of such a style?

CHAPTER 4

Management strategy

Management strategy as a linking process between environmental and organizational variables is a fundamental aspect of our Business in Context model. We can examine the various business functions, R&D, the production of goods and services, marketing, human resource management and finance and accounting through their relevant management strategies. In our introduction to this book we highlighted the cases of the European car industry and News International, both representative of the exercise of strategic options in the face of external and internal opportunities and constraints in the two industries concerned.

Management strategy contains a number of interrelated elements. First, it involves a consideration of environmental changes which bring about new opportunities and pose new threats. Second, it is concerned with the assessment of the internal strengths and weaknesses of the institution and in particular its ability to respond to those opportunities and threats. Third, management strategy is the product of a decision-making process influenced by the values, preferences and power of interested parties. Finally, management strategy is concerned with generating options and evaluating them. Management strategy is therefore an all-embracing term dealing with goals and objectives, the firm's environment, its resources and structure, the scope and nature of its activities and ultimately the behaviour of its members. Given the large number of variables involved and the considerable subjectivity of the decision-making process, strategy formulation is a highly complex process. The approach used by management texts (including, to a certain extent, this book) is to reduce such complexity to a series of steps. While this is understandable, it can both oversimplify and give the impression that management strategy is a logical process. Whittington notes that in 1993 there were 37 books in print in the UK with 'Strategic Management' in the title. He writes,

> There is a basic implausibility about these books. If the secrets of corporate strategy could be acquired for £25, then we would not pay our top managers so much ...
>
> (Whittington, 1993, p. 1)

In this chapter we deal with the various elements of management strategy and attempt, wherever possible, to draw attention to the more subjective and political aspects. We begin by examining the nature of strategy, through the way strategy is formed. We refer to this as the strategic process. We then look at the different contexts in which strategic decisions are taken, and go on to identify the various environmental and organizational aspects of management strategy. We end the chapter by examining a number of common strategic options, and a brief look at the criteria for strategic choice.

We prefer to use the term 'management strategy' since most strategies in organizations originate from the management group. The concept crops up in many guises and is sometimes referred to as 'business policy', 'corporate strategy', 'corporate planning' and so on. Although attempts have been made to formulate distinctions between such terms, the general interchangeability of their use indicates a similarity in approach.

The strategic process

An examination of how strategy is formed gives us useful insights into the nature of strategy itself. We identify five different approaches, which we have termed rational, flexible, creative, behavioural and incremental, and a sixth which suggests that some managers operate without a conscious strategy. We deal with each in turn.

KEY CONCEPT 4.1
The strategic process

The strategic process refers to the way in which management strategy is formed. In most organizations this involves a mixture of scientific and rational analysis together with more subjective and political considerations.

The rational approach

This is the classical approach to strategy and is typified by the work of Ansoff (1968) and Porter (1980, 1985). Strategy formulation is portrayed as a scientific and highly rational process, assisted by a range of techniques such as technological forecasting, portfolio analysis, environmental impact analysis and sensitivity analysis. The aim of such techniques is generally profit maximization (Whittington, 1993). The rational approach owes much to the development of contingency theory. In Chapter 1 we noted that the contingency approach stressed the importance of a strategic fit between the firm and its environment. Analyses are made of a firm's environment to assess likely opportunities and threats and of its internal resource position to identify strengths and weaknesses. This process is sometimes referred to as SWOT analysis, a mnemonic for strengths, weaknesses, opportunities and threats. An illustration of the kind of analysis that can be made is offered in Figure 4.1. The approach is based upon the assumption that information is readily available to the strategist and an accurate assessment can be made of its likely impact on the firm. As we shall see later, this is not always the case and the process is both subjective and political, attracting the criticism of 'pseudo-science'. Nonetheless it can be useful in that it collects relevant data, it can give direction, it has a certain face validity and, as Whittington (1993) argues, it can serve as a form of group therapy. Despite such criticisms the rational approach to strategy is popular and is the basis of many texts. It can be a useful starting point, provided managements are aware of its limitations.

KEY CONCEPT 4.2
SWOT analysis

SWOT stands for strengths, weaknesses, opportunities and threats. It is normally associated with more rational approaches to strategy formulation but perhaps its greatest contribution lies in providing the management strategist and student of business a broad framework for analysing the position of a firm at a particular moment in time. It can also be useful in the development of a number of strategic options which attempt to tackle opportunities and threats, build on corporate strengths and avoid weaknesses. An important consideration is that for most management there is a choice of strategy.

OPPORTUNITIES	THREATS
Promotion to other divisions. Increased revenue from success in cup competitions. Sale of town-centre site and redevelopment on the outskirts. Development of a membership squash club and fitness centre attached to the ground. Use of ground for other functions, e.g. rock concerts. Development of retailing activities.	Seven other professional clubs operating in a 25-mile radius. Rising costs of wages and transfer fees, bank interest charges, policing, equipment. Local authority refusing planning permission. Best players will leave. Competitions for spectators' time and money from other sources, e.g. cinema, DIY. Increased levels of unemployment in the area.
The club owns its own ground and car-parks in a good town-centre site. Good housekeeping and relatively low wages. A hard core of 2000 loyal supporters. A successful and well established youth development policy. The image of a 'friendly' club with good connections in local history	Large bank overdraft. Ground facilities in poor order, especially seating and toilets. Insufficient funds to invest in higher wages and transfer fees. A relatively small population to support so many clubs in close proximity. Poor image compared to First Division neighbours.
STRENGTHS	WEAKNESSES

Figure **4.1** An analysis of the strengths, weaknesses, opportunities and threats of Swot United, a Third Divsion football club

In the 1960s and 1970s the emergence of an increasingly complex and turbulent business environment called for modifications in the rational approach.

The flexible approach

The complexity and volatility of the environment may mean that a detailed SWOT analysis is both difficult and inappropriate and profit maximization may be an inappropriate strategy. The environment may be changing so rapidly that many of the historical and current data are meaningless. This kind of situation led the oil companies, like Shell, to adopt a different approach to strategy formulation known as 'scenario planning'. The approach recognizes that uncertainty can never be eliminated, but it can be reduced by plotting different scenarios, each responding to alternative visions of the future. Managements are therefore prepared for a number of possible changes that may occur. Writers such as Williamson (1991) argue that, under such conditions, the best that managers can hope for is to maximize the chances of survival by cutting costs to become more efficient (survival of the fittest) and by playing the market. A good example of the latter is offered by Whittington (1993) citing Sony, who, in the 1980s, produced 160 different models of the Walkman for the US market, but retained only about 20 models on the market at any one time (survival of the most popular).

The creative approach

This takes the flexible approach one step further by stressing the importance of imagination in the strategic process. The idea that such an approach to strategy formulation is actually better has been taken up by management writers in the 1980s. Peters and Waterman believe that the more formal approaches to strategy formulation with the emphasis on complex environmental and organizational analysis can lead to 'paralysis through analysis' (Peters and Waterman, 1982, p. 31). The resulting policies are often too conservative, insufficiently adventurous and positive, and ignore the human contribution. Their 'excellent' companies are typified by a strategic planning approach which recognizes the values of the decision-makers as one of the driving forces giving the firm its competitive edge. The more complex and changing the business environment and the more difficult the problems facing managers, the more creative they need to be.

The behavioural approach

There is strong support for the view that strategy formulation is far from being a rational, logical process (Cyert and March, 1963 and Mintzberg and Quinn, 1991). Instead, strategic choice is the product of the organization's dominant coalition, invariably senior management, and is based upon its values, ideologies and personalities, and upon the process of organization power and politics. The process invariably involves some negotiation between senior management and other groups. The most overt of these processes take place at shareholders' meetings and in collective bargaining with trade unions. However, the most significant negotiations generally take place between competing factions within management itself, over such issues as the allocation of scarce resources, and are consequently much more difficult to observe. Behavioural analyses of the strategy formulation see management values and objectives as more than individual inputs to the planning process. They influence the way the environment is perceived and hence, the choice of opportunities and threats and the assessment of strengths and weaknesses. Because of the bargaining processes involved, the outcomes of the behavioural approach to strategy are likely to be satisficing rather than maximizing.

The incremental approach

This approach has much in common with the behavioural approach. Strategy is not a carefully prepared plan with clear goals, but a process by which management in the organization gradually come to terms with the firm's environment. Limited objectives are constantly modified in the light of experience and through the process of negotiation between interested parties. As a consequence, strategies are continually being changed. The incremental approach has been put forward as a more realistic and more effective method of dealing with complex and changing situations. The concept originated from the work of Lindblom (1959) in an article appropriately titled 'The Science of Muddling Through'. Although his work was mainly concerned with large public sector organizations such as hospitals and universities, there are strong parallels with larger private sector firms. Mintzberg (1990) has sympathy with this perspective and sees many strategies emerging as opposed to being consciously planned. This gives rise to notions of strategic learning as management builds up a repertoire of effective strategies on the basis of what has worked in the past.

An absence of strategy?

Finally, we present the view that strategy formulation is not a conscious management activity. Strategy is not an issue when firms appear to be operating to the satisfaction of management. It becomes an issue only in times of crisis when any attempt at strategy formulation may be too little and too late. There may be several reasons for this. Management may be complacent and reluctant to rock the boat or they may have myopic vision and hence a limited view of alternatives (see Levitt, 1960, and a discussion of the concept of 'marketing myopia' in Chapter 7). It may be that managements are too distracted by the daily business of survival and see themselves too weighed down by resource constraints to contemplate strategic options.

The various approaches we have identified reveal a mixture of rational and non-rational approaches to the formulation of management strategy. Nevertheless, strategies are more than management hunches played out in an information vacuum. More likely, managements select that information that is appropriate for their purposes, and this invariably involves consideration of both environmental and organizational variables. Management values and organization politics are important not only in the choice of strategy but in the selection of information upon which that strategy is based. All six of the approaches we have identified may operate together in the same firm. The following illustration reveals this mixed approach to strategic decision-making.

One of the partners in a firm of solicitors is keen to establish a computerized client record and accounts system. He spends several months persuading his fellow partners that this may be a good idea. The process of persuasion is accompanied by a gathering of information to show the growth of the firm over the past few years and illustrations are well chosen to show the advantages of faster information retrieval and better management information on the current status of client accounts. Information is also collected on the type of hardware and software systems currently available and their price. Quotations are sought from a few computer firms with experience in servicing professional firms. The partners agree to go ahead with the project and a more recent convert to the idea, one of the senior partners, uses his influence to promote and eventually engage a firm of computer consultants. This firm has been set up by the brother of a senior partner in another law firm and he has successfully installed a system in that firm.

The above illustration reinforces the notion of strategy as both an intellectual exercise in information gathering and presentation and a political exercise involving values, power and influence. In this case the situation was a relatively straightforward investment decision with implications for office practice. Strategic decisions to enter a new product market or change radically the structure of the organization involve even greater complexities.

Apart from these six approaches, we can identify three broad planning styles: formalized planning, consultation and negotiation, and entrepreneurship (a similar model is offered by Mintzberg, 1973). In Figure 4.2 we show how these different planning styles interact with the first five of the strategic approaches.

The suitability of a particular planning style may depend on the size and nature of the firm. For example, a formal planning system is more likely to be found in a large firm, smaller firms by their very nature will favour an entrepreneurial style, and a high degree of consultation will be found in larger public sector organizations. Moreover, different styles may be appropriate for

Approach	Style		
	Formalized planning	Entrepreneurial	Negotiation and consultation
Rational	X		
Flexible	X	X	
Creative		X	X
Behavioural			X
Incremental			X

Figure **4.2** Approaches and styles of management strategy.

different functions. While formalized planning may be a key feature of operations strategy, an R&D strategy may benefit more from an entrepreneurial approach. Where trade union influence is considerable, management may need to proceed more through consultation.

Both the approaches and styles may change over time. A university which has operated through a mixture of an incremental approach and a consultative style may, when faced with the kind of threats identified in Case 4.3, need to operate in a much more entrepreneurial way. Indeed, at certain stages of their development, all organizations may require such entrepreneurial inputs to survive (Mintzberg, 1973). The role of the entrepreneur is usually associated with discussions of small businesses. It is our contention that entrepreneurial activity is equally important in large firms too, a theme we develop in Chapter 5.

Strategic contexts

We have identified how managers may employ different approaches to the task of strategy formulation. In addition we can identify various contexts in which the strategic process operates.

First, strategy is not the sole preserve of the profit-making organization. All organizations have strategies, formalized to a greater or lesser extent. We can see strategies at work in such diverse organizations as businesses, schools, the police, charities, professional football clubs, and the church. In recent years there has been a focus on management strategies in the public sector. The health service has actively recruited its area managers from industry and commerce in an attempt to introduce a more businesslike approach, including a greater emphasis on strategy formulation. In Case 4.3 we present the case of the new universities. For a number of years they have operated in a changing environment and have needed to formulate a different kind of strategy.

Second, we may differentiate between those strategies pertaining to entire industries, such as shipping or machine tools, strategies employed by firms operating in a number of different business markets, such as Unilever and General Motors, and strategies pertaining to those operating in a single or restricted product market. Cases 4.1 and 4.2 illustrate the strategic process at the level of an entire industry and within a multinational corporation respectively. The distinction is sometimes drawn between a 'corporate' and 'business' strategy. A corporate strategy is employed by those firms operating in a number of different businesses; it focuses on issues relating to the overall business mix and helps identify the type of businesses management could pursue. A business strategy deals with a single business and concentrates on issues relating to successful competition. A multi-divisional firm like General Motors therefore operates both corporate and business strategies.

Third, we may identify strategies operating at different levels of the organization, from broad strategies at the top, moving through a series of successive stages towards strategies for specific functional areas like human resource management and marketing, and finally to individual targets and budgets.

The uses and value of strategy

We can identify several reasons for management to engage in strategy formulation:

- Strategy assists in the formulation of goals and objectives and enables them to be modified in the light of information and experience.
- Strategy is a form of management control. It is a plan that guides behaviour along a predetermined route. At the operational level it results in budgets and targets.
- A clear strategy both assists in the process of allocating resources and may provide a rationale for that allocation so that it is perceived to be fair by organization members.
- It enables management to identify key strategic issues that the firm may face in the future and prepare appropriate action.
- Strategy performs a useful role in guiding the action of the constituent parts of the organization as well as acting as an integrating mechanism ensuring units work together. The integrating power of strategy is a central feature of 'strong' corporate cultures as illustrated by firms such as IBM and Hewlett-Packard.
- Leading on from that, strategy formulation can be an important element in the process of social change. Strategic objectives are achieved by changing the behaviour of employees. This is the essence of organizational development programmes used by such companies as Shell and part of the current vogue for the creation of a strong corporate culture.
- The formulation of strategy is seen as a useful training ground for the development of future managers.

We have already questioned the extent to which formalized strategy is used by firms. An even more important consideration is the extent to which the existence of a formalized strategy contributes to organizational success. Studies suggest that those companies using some form of strategic planning process perform better than those who do not, and where data are available they tend to show that the introduction of strategic planning methods leads to improvements in performance. (A good summary of a number of studies in this area is presented in Hofer and Schendel, 1978). Greenley (1990) in his review of the link between strategy and performance found very few studies showing a positive correlation.

The difficulty with all such studies is the problem of isolating and measuring the effect of strategic planning on performance, be it return on investment, market share or some other criterion. A firm's financial and market performance, even over time, may be influenced by so many variables outside the control of management that causal links between strategy and performance may be difficult to show. Furthermore, the relationship is complicated in that performance may well influence strategy rather than the other way around. A firm that has been highly profitable may well be stimulated into seeking new investment opportunities either through new product development or acquisition. Conversely a firm incurring significant losses may well be limited in its strategic options and have them determined by people external to the firm such as bank managers or liquidators. In this case the firm's performance is the reason for pursuing a divestment strategy, involving the closure or sale of the least profitable parts.

The environmental aspects of strategy

In the last section we suggested that it was often difficult to establish a clear link between strategy and performance because of the great number of influences at work. Much of that complexity may be attributed to the firm's environment.

The firm's environment is of course a key aspect of our Business in Context model. In Chapter 1 we introduced the notion of contingency theory and the belief that a firm's performance was dependent upon it achieving a strategic fit between itself and the environment in which it operates. In Chapter 2 we identified, with the use of selected examples, significant aspects of the business environment. We noted how these aspects influenced and in turn were influenced by businesses. We further suggested that these elements not only interact with business but with each other, resulting, for most firms, in an environment that is highly complex and changing. In this and the previous chapter we have already noted how that complexity is further complicated by the values of decision makers and the internal structures and politics of organizations. The strategist's task of making sense of the environment is therefore a very difficult assignment.

We can identify two aspects of the environment that may influence strategy. First, there are those issues that affect all firms operating in a given business environment. These are many of the issues we raised in Chapter 2 and may include the state of the economy, the nature of the labour force, changing technology, government policy and social and cultural influences. We call this the 'general environment'. Second, there are those factors that have direct bearing on the firm's competitive position, which we will call 'the immediate competitive environment'. An analysis of both these environments will enable management to arrive at some assessment of the major opportunities and threats facing the organization.

The general environment

An analysis of a firm's general environment is sometimes known as environmental scanning, and usually comprises some sort of assessment of the key environmental influences, how they interact with the firm and with each other and how they change over time. There are many difficulties with such an analysis. Some managers tackle the sheer complexity of the environment by generating masses of information, not all of which is relevant and not all of which is accurate. The use of computers has increased the capacity for information handling and in some firms, managers can be submerged in a sea of data, much of which has only marginal relevance to their needs. At the other extreme there are those who either ignore the environment completely or who have a very blinkered perception of the firm's relationship to it. In such a situation key trends can be missed, and the firm either cedes opportunities to its competitors or is unprepared for changes when they occur.

Our analysis of the general environment is based on a model that classifies the environment as simple and static, dynamic, or complex (Johnson and Scholes, 1997). We deal with each in turn.

Simple and static

Firms operating in a relatively simple and static environment can generally rely on management strategies that are based on historical data. Customer needs and hence sales forecasting can generally be predicted from past records. A company producing Christmas cards knows precisely that demand will peak at the end of the calendar year and will have a good idea of the size of that demand. Similarly, fireworks manufacturers in the UK knew that demand would peak before 'bonfire night' in November each year. However, there is a danger that managers become complacent and the survival of the business may be jeopardized by sudden and unexpected changes, as with a change in the law making the sale of certain types of firework illegal. Other changes can creep up on management. The Christmas card market has become highly competitive, with many new entrants, including charities and societies. The fireworks market has changed too, with a movement towards public displays, and the more general use in celebrations all year round. Even simple and static environments may not be so simple or so static.

Dynamic

A dynamic environment changes quickly and frequently. Managers operating in this environment generally need to be sensitive to the environment and predict those changes that are likely to occur. The home computer market has been particularly dynamic. In the UK, Sinclair was first to the market but failed to maintain the required product development and found its market taken by such as Amstrad, which initially was sensitive to, and even helped create, changing consumer needs. In its turn, Amstrad has been replaced by such as Packard Bell, offering attractive all-in packages and forging important alliances with the major computer superstores. In such a dynamic market, household names quickly come and go. Businesses that fail in dynamic environments are generally those where managements have failed to see the changes which are occurring or are either unable or unwilling to take appropriate action.

The case of professional soccer in England and Wales is one where an entire industry lost ground to a variety of competitors for its customers' time and money, and the general trend towards declining attendance and hence revenue seemed irreversible 10 years ago. The football authorities tackled the problem, in part, by the creation of an elite Premier League and by insisting on major ground improvements for the elite clubs, including the creation of all-seater stadiums. A lucrative television deal for the Premier League was struck with a leading satellite television company and the clubs imported a variety of international stars from other countries. The result has been a major turnaround for the leading clubs, with capacity attendances for most matches and a vast increase in profits. This in turn has led to a rise in wages and much greater mobility amongst players. Increased mobility is a function of an EU ruling giving players freedom of movement at the end of a contract, where previously clubs could demand a transfer fee. In the main, clubs have had to make rapid adjustments to rising costs through increased prices and the growth of merchandising club shirts and other products. Some of the larger clubs have shops on the scale of mini department stores. For the other non-elite clubs the position has worsened. Attendances have continued to fall and the importing of overseas talent has reduced potential transfer revenue. With falling revenue, such clubs are unable to make the necessary investments to offer an acceptable product to an increasingly demanding clientele.

Dynamic environments require entrepreneurs who have the vision to spot opportunities and the motivation to pursue them. They are also suited to more creative approaches to strategy. However, there may be a danger that management could respond unnecessarily to changes in a dynamic environment. For example, some firms, when threatened by new entrants offering much cheaper products in the same market, respond by launching a cheaper version of their own product. This not only shows a lack of faith in the quality of the firm's original product, but it will inevitably take sales away from that product and have a potentially damaging effect on the firm's reputation.

Complex

A complex environment is one in which different demands are placed upon different aspects of the firm's operation. A firm producing a range of different products for different markets could be said to be operating in a complex environment. Most firms in such situations reflect this complexity in their organization structures. We saw in the last chapter how the development of the multi-divisional firm was a direct response to the problems faced by emerging multinational corporations like General Motors in the 1920s. The problem facing firms in a complex environment is the extent to which the complexity needs to be accommodated by organizational changes. Some firms attempt to reduce the complexity by restructuring, which may include selling off some of its constituent units. Such action is a common feature of mergers and acquisitions and will be dealt with later in the chapter.

In the case of dynamic and complex environments a firm faces a number of interconnected problems related to the degree of change, the speed of change, the complexity of its environment and the corresponding complexity of the organization. Managers tend to seek to reduce such uncertainty as much as they can by a variety of measures.

First, the uncertainty may be reduced by collecting relevant information. We have already noted the problems associated with collecting accurate information and with information overload. Second, as we saw in Chapter 2, managers will attempt to influence and control the environment. This can be done by a variety of measures such as technological innovation, forming coalitions with other organizations, political lobbying, acquiring raw material suppliers or retail outlets, stockpiling materials and equipment, training staff in rare skills, and so on. Third, new structures and procedures such as planning and forecasting may be set up to cope with uncertainty. There are, however, dangers with setting up new structures. The establishment of specialist units can create its own problems of cooperation and integration. In the early days of computing in business, the creation of specialist groups of programmers and analysts led to tensions and conflict (Pettigrew, 1973). In Chapters 2 and 5, we can see how attempts by the Japanese to set up research consortia for each industry have not been an unqualified success.

The immediate competitive environment

We will attempt to locate a business in its immediate competitive environment using the model devised by Porter (1980), as shown in Figure 4.3. Porter has identified five forces, which have immediate bearing on a firm's competitive position. We explain and illustrate these forces in turn.

Figure **4.3** A model of competitive rivalry. *Source*: Porter (1980).

The threat of potential entrants

The threat of entry is related to the ease with which a new business can establish itself in the same product market. The relative ease with which new restaurants emerge in a large urban area like London suggests that the threat to existing restauranteurs is very real. However, the ease of entry means increased competition and can result in a highly volatile market, to which the death rate of new restaurants will testify.

The threat posed by potential entrants is reduced if there are barriers to entry. These can operate in a number of different ways. Equipment and associated capital requirements place heavy burdens on investment and firms may have to withstand considerable unit cost disadvantages initially. Such difficulties would be presented to firms attempting to enter mass car production or oil refining. It would be difficult for newcomers to achieve sufficient economies of scale to recover their outlay in a reasonable time.

These difficulties can be increased where access to raw materials is an additional problem. In some types of industry, breaking into a market is difficult owing to the considerable customer loyalty to existing products and brands. A soft drinks manufacturer attempting to launch a 'cola'-type product would have considerable difficulty persuading the market to switch from Coca Cola or Pepsi Cola. In the industrial components industry, getting customers to switch may pose the additional difficulties of part compatibility. Such barriers may be further compounded by the difficulty of obtaining access to channels of distribution. Our soft drinks manufacturer may have considerable difficulty persuading the major supermarket chains to stock its products. Patents held by existing manufacturers can pose a significant obstacle to those wishing to enter the market with imitative products. The patents on the drugs librium and valium owned by Hoffman-La-Roche have enabled the firm to establish a monopoly position in the tranquilizer market. Similarly, patents held by Polaroid posed difficulties for firms such as Kodak to enter the instant camera market. In a more general way the operating experience gained by existing firms over a number of years can place the newcomer at a significant disadvantage.

Apart from the threat of new entrants, competitive rivalry can be heightened among existing competitors if the general growth rate of the industry is slow and if there are many firms of similar size with a relatively undifferentiated product range.

We should not forget that there are barriers to exit as well as barriers to entry. A large manufacturing company with considerable operating losses, but with many employees and a significant investment in plant and machinery, will undoubtedly face pressures to stay in business. Such pressures will be related to the extent of the firm's assets, which may not be recoverable if the firm closes. This fear of lost investment may only be one factor. Senior management may be particularly attached to the company, emotionally as well as financially, and place a high value on its survival, despite market and financial evidence to the contrary. Pressures will undoubtedly come from the local community and, in the case of some firms, from the national government, fearing the effect of closure on local and national economies and on levels of unemployment. In the case of some firms such as British Leyland and Rolls Royce in the 1970s, government pressure was accompanied by significant government investment to ensure the survival of these companies. Barriers to exit operate in small firms as well, where there is likely to be an even greater ego involvement on the part of the owner managers and a subsequent reluctance to accept forced closure in the face of market forces.

The threat of substitution

Substitution occurs where a consumer is able to replace your product with a different type of product performing the same service or satisfying similar needs. The cotton textile industry in Britain was not only threatened by new entrants from cheap labour economies but also by the development of substitute products in the form of man-made fibres. We have already identified some of the threats facing the professional football industry. A major threat has been the growth of substitute activities such as sport on television, active rather than passive participation in sport, and the growing popularity of DIY.

Rail travel in the USA declined as airlines opened up local networks and assisted in the establishment of local airports. The size of the country meant that air travel was perceived as a more effective means of covering large distances. Distances are less of a problem in the UK, yet rail companies face competition from bus companies, competing on price and from a growing network of local air traffic, competing on the basis of speed and comparative price.

The bargaining power of buyers

Buyer power increases where there are a large number of firms offering the same or substitute products, especially where there is little or no cost involved for the buyer in switching from one supplier to another. A restaurateur in Central London faces considerable competition from the large number of other restaurants operating in that area, as well as other attractions competing for the potential client's disposable income. In such situations the product/market strategy of the restaurant becomes of utmost importance. Such strategies will include considerations of product differentiation and quality, market segmentation, price and promotion (Chapter 7 has a fuller account of these strategies). In the industrial components industry, particularly where specialist components are involved, the relationship may be different. There may well have been a mutual accommodation of product changes over a number of years and such a strong relationship forged that the cost of switching would be high. Components suppliers often invest time and energy building up such relationships with customers. In such situations a threat still exists if the customer firm's acquisition strategy takes in a similar components supplier.

The buyer-supplier relationship is highly complex and involves most facets of our Business in Context model. The complexity of the technology plays a major part, as does the competitiveness of the market. We saw in our discussion of Japanese management in Chapter 2 that a mix of cultural and economic factors was also significant. As part of their normal business strategy, Japanese industrial firms operating in Britain rely heavily upon subcontractors to supply components, and tend to build up close relationships with these suppliers. With British government backing, Japanese manufacturing companies have tended to locate in areas of low economic activity. This automatically places such firms in a strong bargaining position with respect to the local components industry.

The power of a buyer generally increases the more he or she buys. This power can be exercised in the demand for discounts or the expectation of preferential treatment in the supply of goods. A factor to consider here is the relative size of the two parties. Buyer power normally exists only if the volume purchased forms a high proportion of the selling company's total sales. The larger supermarket chains have considerable buyer power, particularly over such as the smaller food suppliers. Smaller foodstores have attempted to secure greater buyer power by banding together for bulk purchases, as with associations like Spar, Mace and VG.

The bargaining power of suppliers

Our illustration of the bargaining power of buyers in the industrial components industry works equally well for suppliers. In this and other cases supplier power is stronger where the component is highly specialized and few suppliers exist. Supplier power is also strong where the cost to the buyer of switching allegiance would include major product adaptations. A computer manufacturer can gain additional market power where it develops popular software that can only be used on its own machines. A case of supplier power in the computer industry emerged in the late 1990s around the monopoly power of Microsoft, the creator of the Windows operating system for personal computers. The system is sold as the standard operating environment with most PCs and Microsoft has a 90 per cent share of the market. However, Microsoft came under criticism and was eventually taken to court under US anti-trust law. The company was accused of abusing its monopoly power in its attempt to control the market for access to the Internet via its browser system 'Internet Explorer'. Microsoft was accused of putting pressure on its main rival, Netscape, and of attempting to force the manufacturers of PCs such as Compaq to use Microsoft's system alongside the Windows operating system.

Most firms act as both suppliers and buyers and the bargaining power can be a two-edged weapon. A restaurant operating in an affluent area where there are no other restaurants probably does not face strong bargaining power from its customers and therefore maintains a strong competitive position. However, if there are equally few suppliers of meat, fish and other foodstuffs then these firms have supplier power over the restaurant.

Competitive rivalry

Competitive rivalry lies at the heart of Porter's model and is depicted by Porter as firms jockeying for position. Particularly intense rivalry is found in such situations as a large number of competitors of equal size, where the market has slow growth or where exit barriers are especially high. Such situations exist in the European car industry as we saw in our case study in Chapter 1. Intense rivalry can also be found amongst UK supermarkets, particularly those like Sainsburys, Tesco, Safeway and Waitrose, operating in the same general market segment. Such companies employ staff whose sole job is to monitor the competition through regular product and price checks. Intense rivalry in the IT industry often takes the form of poaching key staff.

The strength of a model like Porter's is that it focuses on the immediate operating environment of the business and avoids prescription by enabling management to examine the forces acting upon their firm. The analysis does, however, depend upon a level of knowledge about competitor, which may not be so easy to obtain as with competing supermarkets. Lynch (1997) offers a number of further criticisms of Porter's five-forces model. As we have seen earlier in the chapter, the model portrays a rational approach to strategy, which may not match reality. The model sees customers as one of several factors, when several current approaches elevate the customer a more central role. Porter also views buyer–supplier relationships in terms of power, when, in some industries, the prevailing trend is towards greater partnership and long-term relations.

The use that managements can make of Porter's model is to establish a position for their firms in the market to maximize defences against competitive forces and where possible turn them to best advantage. Porter identifies three generic strategies of particular advantage in this respect. These are product differentiation, market segmentation and seeking to obtain the lowest costs. Discussion of these strategies pervades our analysis of operations and marketing in Chapters 6 and 7 respectively.

Environmental threats and opportunities

An assessment of the general environment and the firm's immediate competitive position should enable management to identify the major threats and opportunities facing the firm. In Table 4.1 we present an illustrative list of the environmental opportunities and threats using the elements of the 'Business in Context' model. This is usually the first stage in selecting appropriate strategic options. For a firm like First Sound and Vision (Case 6.2), producing gramophone records in a declining market, or a restaurateur opening in Central London, the threats and opportunities may be very clear. However, we can identify several complicating factors.

- A threat to one part of an organization may represent an opportunity to another. Thus in the 1970s when the post and telecommunications services in Britain were part of the same organization, a postal workers' strike led to increased revenue through telephone calls. The closure of some courses in a university owing to falling student demand may divert resources to other areas.
- Defending yourself against a threat or capitalizing upon an opportunity is a function of both the firm's standing in its environment and its internal resource position. Survival in a declining market may be easier if you have a large market share to begin with and raising finance to invest in new products is often easier for larger established firms than the small business. Small firms often face the particular dilemma of spotting a market opportunity but lacking the resources to take full advantage. Laker Airways was relatively successful at breaking into the charter airline market by offering cheaper flights than those currently available. As the firm expanded by introducing flights to the USA it faced direct competition with the larger state-financed airlines. Laker was ultimately unable to compete with the larger firms, who adopted price-cutting tactics, and the company over-reached itself financially through the purchase of a large number of new aircraft in anticipation of increased revenue from the new routes.
- Managements differ in their ability to identify opportunities and threats. The management of a firm doing particularly well in a declining market may ignore the longer-term implications of their position. Even when opportunities and threats have been identified, managements may differ as to their relative importance and may develop different perspectives, based perhaps on their attitudes to risk. Careful analyses of market

Table **4.1** Examples of environmental opportunity and constraints using the Business in Context model, as they affect a small manufacturing firm

Aspects of the environment	Opportunity	Constraint
Economy	Growth in the market and demand for the product.	Increased foreign competition with rising interest rates at home and an unfavourable foreign exchange rate.
State	Tax concessions for small manufacturing firms.	New laws on safety and design necessitating a costly product modification.
Technology	Making more effective use of the computer system for administrative and financial control and information.	The high cost of new manufacturing technology to meet increased demand.
Labour	Local supply exceeds demand and there is a regular supply of part-timers and contract workers.	A shortage of workers in certain key skills and the relatively high wage demands of those workers.
Culture	A traditional small-firm community with a tradition for hard work and company loyalty.	An influx of newcomers to the area from declining industries with a long history of management–worker mistrust.

opportunities may come to naught in the face of a preference for inaction rather than entrepreneurial risk-taking. Failure to take action in the light of environmental change is one form of management myopia. Perceiving the environment as presenting more of a constraint than it need is another.

We can therefore see that the perception of an opportunity or threat is a highly subjective process. It is partly for this reason that strategy formulation is as much a behavioural and political process as it is analytical. There is another important point. We have tended to focus on the environment as offering the management decision-maker opportunities or constraints. A major contention in this book is that the manager can influence and shape the environment. It is not simply the analysis of the environment that provides the answer but the ability of managers to see more in that environment than their competitors and in so doing create their own opportunities.

Case 4.1: Strategic options facing the UK machine tool industry in the 1980s

The machine tool industry provides manufacturing firms with the means by which the products are made, including tools for such operations as metal cutting, stamping and drilling. Larger manufacturing companies with highly specialized machining needs, such as a major car producer, will make some of their own tools, but most will buy from specialist machine tool manufacturers for at least some of their requirements. According to Hayes and Wheelwright (1984), a healthy machine tool industry is an essential prerequisite for a successful manufacturing industry. It is only by using custom-designed tools that innovative products can be made, and only through such products can firms gain a competitive advantage.

The machine tool industry in Britain had been in decline for a number of years. Its share of the world market fell by 50 per cent from 1965 to 1982, while imports rose from 26 per cent to 61 per cent over the same period. A number of reasons have been forwarded to explain the decline. These are as follows:

- the general decline in manufacturing industry;
- the competitive threat posed by Japan and Germany;
- a lack of graduate engineers in Britain;
- over-diversification resulting in short production runs;
- a general lack of automation and computer application;
- a vicious circle of decline resulting in a lack of investment;
- poor marketing;
- low-volume production at high cost.

Several strategic options for the industry were identified:

- **Industry extinction** This involves allowing the industry to die a natural death by starving it of investment and relying solely on imported machine tools. Such a strategy may be detrimental to manufacturing for the reasons outlined above.
- **State Intervention** Attempts had already been made at state intervention, including special provisions for the development of state-of-the-art tools in computer-aided design and manufacture and flexible manufacturing systems. Other measures had included attempts to encourage merger amongst smaller

manufacturers to pool development ideas and achieve some economies of scale. The problems of state intervention lie in possible policy changes with shifts in political ideology and a danger of management complacency. The ultimate form of state intervention would be nationalization, a somewhat remote possibility in the political climate of the 1980s. The government could impose some form of import control, but this could be a dangerous strategy in that other countries may retaliate, and despite its declining market share, British industry does depend on its exports. Furthermore, import controls may speed up the process of Japanese machine tool firms operating from British or other European bases.

- **Rationalization** Not surprisingly, this was the most common strategy. The suitability of such a strategy would seem to depend on a number of mergers also taking place. This may achieve some kind of product standardization, longer production runs and subsequent cost reductions. However, in a rapidly declining market, this may lead to short-term survival, but it could be a route to eventual industry extinction.
- **Foreign investment** This had already occurred and British firms had been bought by US and Japanese interests. However, FDI would only be attractive in the case of highly specialized firms with attractive market niches or to get around the kind of import controls suggested in the second option.
- **Licensing** Under this arrangement British firms would manufacture products designed by firms in other countries. The current success of the Japanese machine tool industry, supported by a large manufacturing base, would make the Japanese attractive partners in such joint venturing. It is not clear what the Japanese would gain from the licensing arrangement beyond a fee for British firms manufacturing Japanese patented products. Licensing can be valuable if it generates innovation on the part of the licensee. The Japanese, however, are very restrictive on what they will allow licensees to do, and this would almost certainly preclude innovation.

The UK machine tool industry was unable to stem the tide and continued in sharp decline throughout the 1990s. The industry was still dominated by the Germans and Japanese with some US firms doing especially well in certain niche markets. Taiwan and South Korea posed a threat to the world order through the ability to manufacture with much lower costs. Their progress was halted by the regional economic problems of 1997. The Germans maintained their reputation as the world's leading exporter of machine tools. The reputation had been built on a strong customer focus stressing product quality and reliability, enabling them to maintain premium prices. In the UK there were some acquisitions, particularly by US interests, but the strategies of most of the firms were largely defensive and concerned only with short-term survival. The UK industry continues to decline. In 1998, output in the UK fell by 8 per cent, when that in the rest of Western Europe rose by 7 per cent. In 1999, a downturn of 25 per cent was predicted for the industry. ■

(*Sources*: Eilon, 1985; Lane, 1985; *European Journal of Marketing*, 1994; *Professional Engineering*, 1998–9)

The organizational aspects of strategy

In this section we will explore the relationship between management strategy and the organizational aspects of our model, and focus on particular issues of resource assessment such as core competences, value chains and portfolio analysis. Organizational analysis is traditionally an integral part of strategy formulation and serves a number of related purposes for management.

- Some kind of resource profile is needed to establish whether the various opportunities, threats and management expectations can be met by the organization in its present state. A knowledge of the resources an organization possesses, and what can be done with them, is a prerequisite for determining future plans and establishes whether a gap exists between what management would like to do and what they can do. This is sometimes referred to as 'gap analysis'. For example, the management of a manufacturing firm would need to know if it could accept and meet a new, large order using its existing product range and its existing machine and labour capacity. The gap analysis will identify for management those resource aspects that may be lacking and that will have to be rectified if opportunities are to be realized or threats are to be successfully fought off. The completion of new orders by our manufacturing firm may be dependent upon product modification, the purchasing of new equipment and the hiring of new staff. This in turn may involve the raising of new loans from the bank and setting up programmes for the recruitment and training of staff. Expansion of this nature has further implications for the size of the supervisory and maintenance teams.
- The way resources are used by management and how various resource elements of the organization link together can create competitive advantage. Examples of this include focusing on efficient low-cost internal systems or a niche market producer developing and maintaining good customer relations. Such issues are dealt with later in this section as core competences and value chains.
- An internal analysis will enable management to assess the attractiveness of the organization, its activities and its products in its current markets and

assess their potential for future investment. This is the particular contribution of portfolio analysis.

A rather narrow, traditional view of strategic planning sees strategy as the result of environmental analysis and the organization factors are seen either to facilitate or inhibit the chosen strategy. Such a view runs counter to the major contention of our 'Business in Context' model, which sees all elements as interacting with one another. Organizational changes are brought about by changes in strategy, but strategic changes are also the product of aspects of the organization. We have already noted in Chapter 3 that it is possible for structure to influence strategy. We can also see that expansion plans will undoubtedly build on strengths or core competencies, a case of the firm focusing strategy around a key resource, such as the skills of a particular group. We deal with more general issues of strategy and organization before turning to the more practical questions of resource analysis, core competencies, value chains and portfolio analysis.

The interaction of strategy and organization

All the organizational elements of our model, goals, ownership, structure, size and culture, interact with the process of strategy formulation.

We have already seen how the goals of an enterprise set targets for strategy to follow. We have also emphasized the behavioural nature of this process in that both goal and strategy formulation are the products of management values, and the processes of organizational power and politics, which have a major influence upon management decision-making.

The process of goal setting and strategy formulation is greatly influenced by **ownership** variables. A group of professional accountants in partnership may each have their own views about the growth of the firm, the recruitment and training of new staff and so on. In a partnership these views are generally resolved by discussion or through the dominance of a particular partner. Our discussion of ownership and control in Chapter 3 showed that for larger companies with diffuse share ownership and professional managers, strategy formulation was more complex and often dependent upon the influence of some shareholder groups. There are numerous illustrations where small business owners may deliberately resist growth strategies in order to retain personal control over the firm. However, the reverse is also true in that strategies involving merger and acquisition have a significant impact upon patterns of ownership and control. Managers may actively pursue acquisitions, which give them more power and enhance their own career aspirations.

We noted in the previous chapter that, according to Chandler (1962), **structure** followed strategy, and this was a dominant feature in the expansion of American multinationals and in particular the development of multidivisional structures. We also suggested that strategy may be influenced by structure. For example, a company with a large and active R&D department would almost certainly pursue vigorous strategies of new product development. The 3M case in this chapter shows how top management were concerned that their existing procedures for strategy formulation were inadequate and set about creating a new structure precisely to give the firm a new strategic impetus. At the operational level the organization structure can facilitate or inhibit strategy formulation and implementation. Two aspects appear to be important here: the authority structure of the firm and the procedures for making decisions. Burns and Stalker (1966) studied the post-war electronics industry and saw differences in the strategic responses of firms to changing market conditions. Those firms that had responded most effectively to changing market demand were firms typified by a more flexible, open structure, which they termed organic. The firms that struggled in the changed environment and failed to adapt were by contrast more bureaucratic, with often lengthy and inappropriate procedures for making decisions, and where structural divisions between departments inhibited cooperation. Organizations, particularly those in the public sector, which rely heavily on committees for the formulation of important decisions, may find the process too cumbersome when a quick strategic response is needed. In a similar way participation, which can facilitate employee motivation and commitment, may inhibit decision-making through the inherent slowness of the procedure. We noted in Chapter 2 how this, in part, accounted for the slowness of the decision-making process in some Japanese firms.

The Chandler approach to strategy and structure falls within the classical, rational tradition of strategy formulation. There are two further positions. To some, structural change is so difficult that the disruptive effects may be counterproductive in achieving strategic goals. An alternative approach suggests that strategic change in a highly competitive environment may only be possible by radical organizational change, which could involve replacing the management team or selling off parts of the business.

Such considerations of structure are inevitably linked to **size**. In very large organizations strategy formulation may be cumbersome because of the reasons given above. There is also a danger that strategy can become fragmented through the diverse nature of operations and locations. It was these conditions that led 3M to reconsider its procedure for strategy formulation, as illustrated in Case 4.2. Another handicap of large size involves the control of a strategy once it is formulated. The larger the organization, the more filters there are to interpret and perhaps distort a central strategy.

We have already discovered that an important element in the core management strategies of firms such as IBM and Hewlett-Packard is the creation of an **organizational culture**, with an emphasis upon shared values. We have stressed the importance of management values in both formulating and evaluating strategy. In this case the creation of a value system to embrace the entire organization is seen by some to be more significant than strategy itself. We have already noted how traditional approaches to strategy have been downgraded by such as Peters and Waterman (1982). Nevertheless, the care with which such firms as Hewlett-Packard embark upon staff recruitment, selection and training to develop such shared values (Case 3.6) would indicate the influence of a very distinctive strategy indeed. Feurer *et al.* (1995) noted that a strength of Hewlett-Packard lay in extending strategic ownership to all parts of the organization. Employees at all levels were engaged in strategy formulation and implementation, giving the company a distinctive edge.

Case 4.2: Minnesota Mining and Manufacturing

The Minnesota Mining and Manufacturing Company, better known as 3M, operates in over 50 different countries producing around 50 000 different products using many different technologies. By most definitions it is regarded as a very successful company. It is truly multinational and multi-divisional, although the company was relatively slow to diversify both internationally and in terms of its product range.

The company was founded in 1902 to mine corundum, but quickly switched its attention to the manufacture of sandpaper, its only product for 21 years. In 1923 the company developed masking tape for paintshops in the car industry and this was followed by domestic adhesive tape and other tape products, such as sound recording tape. Tape products account for some 17 per cent of output, but the company also produces office and photographic equipment, pharmaceuticals and chemicals. Only in 1951 did the company set up operations outside the USA, which remains its biggest market.

It fitted Peters and Waterman's model of an excellent company along several dimensions. First, it was a highly innovative company supported by a corporate goal that 25 per cent of annual sales should come from products developed in the past five years, and a senior management dominated by scientists, who encouraged R&D staff to follow through their own ideas. Second, the company was committed to high-quality goods design to fulfil customers' requirements. Third, a considerable emphasis was placed upon communication throughout the company and management processes were dominated by a network of meetings. In Peters and Waterman's terms it was a 'loose, consensual organization'. Finally, 3M was based around a strong central culture based on a traditional US Mid-West work ethic. Wherever they operated, small-town locations were favoured as best embodying the core values and management recruited staff who best fitted the culture.

In best Peters and Waterman tradition the company had no complex planning mechanisms. By 1980 the firm was undergoing change. The firm had grown considerably in a short period, especially in terms of overseas expansion. A new chairman was appointed and there was a belief that the company had become too committed to short-term goals. In particular, the environment in which the firm was operating was changing in a number of different ways, which included an increased variability in interest rates, high rates of inflation in some operating countries, shorter life cycles for some products, scarcer and more expensive resources, and a declining demand in its traditional markets of office products and magnetic tape.

A major discontinuity was occurring involving changed senior personnel and both organizational growth and an increasingly threatening environment. The priorities identified by management were as follows:

● an even greater effort to be expended on product innovation;
● an improved control and coordination of the firm's global resources;
● a greater concern for the future by establishing a more comprehensive approach to long-term planning.

It was decided that new arrangements for strategic planning would accompany a major structural reorganization. This is shown in Figure 4.8.

The main elements of the new system may be identified as follows:

● It is an attempt to build upon the existing loose consensus by emphasizing the exchange of information and ideas, but facilitating this by more formalized systems. A database was set up to generate information about the company. In particular, managers were encouraged to analyse and discuss the strategic options pursued in other parts of the company. This enabled managers to learn from the actions of others as well as being an excellent method for training new managers.
● A new formalized planning system was introduced whereby global strategies were worked out by the SBCs, the SPC and top management and individual business strategies were worked out by each division using the global strategy as a template. The division was able to set realistic performance measures based on detailed knowledge of its own product market.
● The SBCs acted as centres for the generating of ideas by integrating information and ideas from each of the operating divisions. It was hoped that some form of synergy of ideas would take place. The SBCs focused specifically on product development issues. The generation of ideas was supported by an annual event, during which each operating

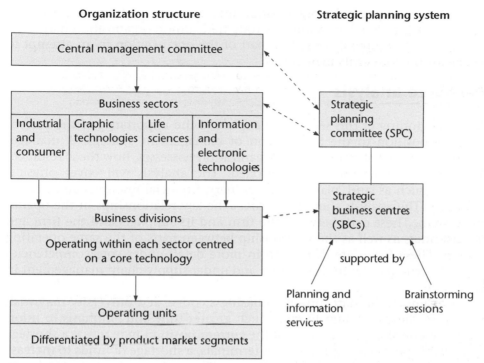

Figure 4.4 Structural arrangements at 3M. *Source*: Kennedy (1988)

unit must submit plans outlining where it will be in 15 years time. This event acted as a forum for creativity outside the normal planning framework and deliberately adventurous ideas were encouraged. In addition to these systems the firm holds regular brainstorming sessions throughout the year. This interactive style of strategic planning became the hallmark of the company.

The new system immediately facilitated greater international activity. In the 1980s, 3M operated in 30 or so countries and by 1995, its activities were across over 50 countries. There was an expansion of R&D work in Japan and Europe through the establishment of new laboratories and joint ventures with universities. Several unproductive businesses were sold and the company attempted to establish a higher international profile through corporate advertising and the sponsorship of the 1988 Olympics. However, the new arrangements also attracted some internal criticism on the basis that while the company had a greater knowledge of and direction over its existing businesses, no significant new ideas had been generated.

By the 1990s, 3M had consolidated the Graphic

Technologies and Information and Electronic Technologies divisions to form the Information, Imaging and Electronics Sector. In 1991, many of the industries supplied by 3M were in deep recession. Nonetheless the company persisted with a strategy of continuous innovation and established 'Challenge 95', a campaign to reduce concept to customer time by a third and reduce costs by 10 per cent. Business growth was boosted by 3M's success in Asia. The company had operated in Japan for almost 40 years (rare for a Western firm), and was the first to establish a wholly owned operation in China. Sales doubled in Asia between 1988 and 1993, attributable to the company's reputation in the region and the tailoring of its products to meet local market needs.

In 1995 3M failed to make its own financial targets for the first time in its history. The company announced job cuts worldwide of 5000, the disposal of all peripheral activities and $650 million worth of businesses in computer diskettes, videotapes and audiotapes. ■

(*Sources*: Peters and Waterman, 1982; Kennedy, 1988; *Economist*, Dec. 1991; *Fortune*, Feb. 1996)

The culture of a particular organization may act as a constraint against strategy implementation. For example, strong trade union organization may resist management's proposals to sell off part of the organization in an attempt to safeguard the jobs of its members.

Resource analysis

At the beginning of this section we explained the importance of the current resource position to the formulation of management strategy. A manager needs to know what resources the organization possesses, how those resources are used and how they are controlled. The analysis will cover physical resources such as land, plant and machinery, financial resources and human resources. The analysis should also cover the key relationships in the operating system. These exist between the firm and its suppliers and the firm and its customers as well as the relationship between parts of the same operating system. These issues are dealt with in more detail under core competencies and value chains later in this section and under supply chain management in Chapter 6.

For example, the staff running a business course at a university may wish to change the curriculum to give much greater time and emphasis to information technology. An analysis of the current position may reveal a shortage of available personal computers and terminals, a shortage of funds to increase the provision, and staff with insufficient skills and experience to teach this subject. Even if funds could be diverted or revenue raised from running extra courses, there may be physical constraints on the establishment of new computer laboratories, in part owing to claims on available space from other departments. In addition, recruitment of appropriate staff may be difficult, so the management may need to seek substitute skills from its existing workforce. It may be possible to use courses offered by the engineering faculty or import engineering staff with spare capacity. However, there may be concern that the approach used by another faculty would be inappropriate to the needs of business students. In other words, the linkages in the system would not be sufficiently strong. In this case an analysis of the resources may reveal that achieving the goal of increased provision by expansion is not possible. Consequently the utilization of the existing provision needs to be examined to reveal where more effective changes could be made and to see what could be achieved using the existing resources. Rather than expand in a different direction, an alternative scenario may be to develop an existing area of competence and build the course around that.

In many firms resource analysis is accompanied by the use of a variety of accounting ratios such as return on capital employed, profitability and so on. Different ratios have more relevance at different stages of the firm's development than at others, so that while profitability may be appropriate for established firms, productivity and sales may be more useful for newly established companies and cash flows may be more significant when firms are in decline.

The value of resource analysis lies not only in assessing the viability of a particular strategic proposal, but also in assessing the ability of the organization to adapt to change. Can the firm deal with changes in demand or can it

Case 4.3: The new British universities

Between 1989 and 1992 the British higher education sector comprising the polytechnics and colleges of higher education experienced a number of significant changes, brought about as the result of government education policy and accompanying legislation. First, all such colleges achieved corporate status, disassociating them from the control of local authorities and causing significant changes in the way they were funded and managed. Second, the government abolished the division between the old university sector and the polytechnics by granting the former, along with some of the colleges of higher education, university status and with it, the power to award degrees. Those polytechnics and colleges achieving university status became known as the 'new universities'. The third change concerned the creation of the Higher Education Funding Council (HEFC), a new body responsible for funding, and the Higher Education Quality Council (HEQC) with responsibility for quality control and enhancement. After 1992, HEQC became the Quality Assurance Agency for Higher Education (QAAHE) and all universities have been subjected to a number of audits, of finance, teaching and research. The Research Assessment Exercise (RAE) and the Teaching Quality Audit (TQA) have resulted in scores being awarded each university, which, in the case of the RAE, has funding attached in line with the score.

The environment in which the colleges operate was also changing. A declining population of school-leavers was predicted to affect traditional patterns of student recruitment. In fact, the effect has been uneven as some courses such as law and business studies continued to grow in popularity, while others such as economics and some engineering courses declined. However, the proposed decline in the numbers of school-leavers was overtaken by the government push to expand student numbers in higher education. The expansion of the sector has been so rapid that the target enrolment for the year 2000 was achieved by 1993. Much of that expansion has occurred in the new universities. At the same time continued government pressure to hold down public sector expenditure has resulted, in some cases, in reductions in staffing and the resourcing of such as libraries, setting up conflict with the increased demand from larger numbers of students. The league table culture that is now a part of the public sector has incorporated the universities.

Frequent publication of university league tables in a variety of national newspapers, all using a variety of criteria, has intensified competition between universities. The older universities have tended to gain higher league table positions than the new universities. This is in part a function of the criteria used and in part due to their greater resource base, in the form of finance, buildings, student accommodation and research-active staff. In addition, a government decision to alter the structure of funding by levying a fee on students themselves has added to the tensions.

Many of the new universities are unsure about their new role. They were established in the 1960s to offer different courses with an emphasis on vocational relevance. Do they continue with a strategy of pursuing different types of courses to the old university sector or do they attempt to compete on similar terms? Do they attempt to compete for research funding, despite the resource advantage enjoyed by the older universities? The research advantage includes staff with fewer teaching hours and more time to engage in research and consultancy.

The new universities therefore face a rapidly changing environment. Many have responded by creating new administrative posts in finance and marketing to meet the new challenges. Most have placed an emphasis on income generation through the winning of research grants, hiring out staff as consultants, and setting up courses to bring in extra fees. For example, the government policy of charging full-cost fees for overseas students has resulted in many universities, old as well as new, seeing such groups as an important source of income and actively searching for new overseas markets. Some colleges have established special units to maximize opportunities in these areas. More attention is being paid to the marketing of courses and the attraction of students from non-traditional sources, especially mature students, to achieve expansion targets and to counteract the impact of falling school rolls. Some see their futures in becoming like the older traditional universities, and have invested in research activity and used this as the single most important criterion in the recruitment of new staff.

The environment continues to change. Competition for overseas students has intensified as the economies and the currency of some Asian countries went into steep decline in 1997. Countries such as Malaysia had traditionally sent

▶

Continued

many students to the UK. New markets were sought in India and South America and franchise operations were established in Malaysia to retain the student market, but at a lower cost for the students. Many of the old universities have been active in the overseas student market and are able to use the league tables as leverage.

While the environment may be similar for all new universities, there is considerable variation in the way each is responding. Colleges differ in their financial position, their resources, their own particular areas of excellence, and their perceived attractiveness to potential students, to businesses and to their central government paymasters. This may cause some to seek greater strength through merger and others to consider their portfolio of courses to build on strengths and eliminate weaknesses. The route that each goes down will inevitably be decided by a mixture of careful analysis, inspirational management, ideology, value judgement, pressure brought by interested parties, and good fortune. ■

withstand increased competition on a global scale? Has it the financial backing to invest in new technology? Do employees possess the necessary skills and is the age profile of its staff sufficiently balanced to ensure succession? Competing through resources is a key theme of both core competencies and the value chain.

Core competences

The idea of core competences is associated with the work of Hamel and Prahalad (1990, 1994) and Kay (1993). Core competences refer to those activities of a firm that make a difference and give the firm a competitive edge. This could be the development of efficient internal operating systems, as with Toyota, whose core competences became a model for other car manufacturers to follow. In certain specialist markets, such as fine wine, a merchant like Lay and Wheeler has built its reputation on good customer relationships and continuing business. A university may develop a reputation in particular subject areas. It can build on that reputation through the attraction of students, bringing increased revenue, and maintain that reputation through the attraction of leading academics in the field.

To Hamel and Prahalad, core competences represented the integration of knowledge, skills and technology to give the customer added value in terms

---

KEY CONCEPT 4.3
Core competence

Core competences refer to those activities of an organization that give it an advantage over its competitors. Such advantages could derive from such as an effective R&D department, an efficient operating system, good internal and external communications, the presence of key individuals, reputation and a loyal customer base. The strategic relevance of core competences is the opportunity they provide management to build upon such specific advantages.

of cost, differentiation from competitors or innovation of new products and processes. Kay identified three areas of core competence. These were:

- **architecture**, referring to relationships both within and around the firm, including those with customers and suppliers; a key component of architecture is information exchange between the various parties;
- **reputation** for quality goods and services and for such as the dependability and speed of delivery;
- **innovative ability** to develop new products and processes to gain competitive advantage through differentiation.

The notion of core competences enables a firm to focus its competitive advantage around its resources rather than focusing exclusively on the market. However, it is important that such core competences are difficult to copy by rival firms, otherwise the basis for competitive advantage is eroded. Toyota maintained a competitive advantage for many years despite numerous attempts by its competitors, both inside and outside Japan, to copy its production system. While some core competences do lend themselves to measurement and analysis, as with stockholding and retention, many others are vague and may only be assessed subjectively.

The value chain

The concept of core competences is closely related to notions of the value chain. We present a brief overview here and return to this topic in Chapter 6. The value chain concept owes much to the work of Porter (1985) and at essence is about the way resources are organized to give value added to the end user. Porter's value chain is illustrated in Figure 4.5. The key element of the value chain is not just the added value that the various resources bring to the whole, but added value that derives from the linkages between them, which to gain competitive advantage should be greater than the sum of the parts.

The value chain thus views the firm as a system and a process. Porter identifies five primary activities, which individually and, more importantly, collectively contribute towards adding value for the customer. The end result for Porter is defined as margin, which is the difference between the cost of

---

KEY CONCEPT 4.4
Value chain

The value chain offers a view of the organization as a cumulative build-up of added value for the customer through the interaction between key operations activities. The end result is greater than the sum of its parts and, for profit-seeking organizations, means increased margins. Porter identifies key elements of the value chain in terms of primary and support activities. Like the Business in Context model, the value chain sees organizations in terms of key interactions between the various parts.

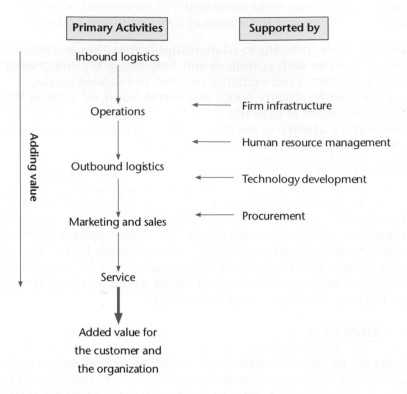

Figure **4.5** Porter's value chain. *Source*: after Porter (1985).

providing the activities and the total value they generate. For the company margin may be translated into profit, while the customer may see it more in terms of value for money.

- **Inbound logistics** refers to those activities concerned with the receiving and handling of goods from suppliers and transporting them within the organization.
- **Operations** transforms these goods into the final product and may comprise a number of different stages and extend across a number of specialist departments.
- **Outbound logistics** deals with storing finished items and distributing them to customers. In the case of services it is concerned with all those processes involved in bringing the service to the customer or the customer to the service.
- **Marketing and sales** help identify customer needs and, through advertising and promotion, make potential customers aware of products and services.
- **Services** cover all those processes involved in before- and after-sales activities such as requirements planning and the provision of customer help lines.

The five primary activities are supported by four other types of activity, referred to by Porter as support activities.

- **Procurement** deals with those activities engaged in the acquisition of the various resource inputs to the primary activities. In manufacturing this can occur at a number of stages. Buyers are responsible for obtaining dependable supplies at high quality and at the best possible price. The transport department is responsible for ensuring the most cost-effective delivery of goods to customers, which may involve subcontracting to another firm, or using the post or rail services.
- **Technology development** occurs in all primary activities. It covers product and process development, which can occur in inbound and outbound logistics as much as in operations. It also involves the development of know-how throughout the organization and the transfer of such know-how via training.
- **Human resource management** is concerned with the recruitment, selection, training and reward systems, which support all activities.
- **Firm infrastructure** relates to the various systems used throughout the organization. It can include materials planning, logistics, operations planning, finance and budget systems as well as the overall strategic plan.

The value chain has drawn criticism for focusing attention on the improvement of existing resources and the linkages between them, when a more radical approach may be required. However, analysis of the value chain can draw attention to major weaknesses in the resource profile and the way the primary activities link together. The concept supports the Business in Context model by viewing the firm's activities as a set of interactions. While the focus is upon internal resource arrangements, the model incorporates elements that exist outside the internal system of the organization, namely suppliers and customers. In doing so it raises the impracticality of defining elements purely in terms of internal or external.

Another approach, which combines internal and external factors, is portfolio analysis. In this case, the elements are products and markets. Portfolio analysis could be dealt with in our discussion of strategic options. We deal with it here as an illustration of the interaction between internal (resource) and external (environmental) factors.

Portfolio analysis

Portfolio analysis is a technique normally associated with those firms operating in a number of different businesses and markets, as is the case with the larger multinational corporations. It may also be applied to those firms who operate in the same market with a number of different products. The technique enables management to assess the attractiveness of their businesses and products in their current markets and assist decisions on the direction of future investment. Through such an analysis the manager may reach conclusions on the particular mix of products and markets, the growth and profit potential of those products and markets and the level of risk involved with

---

KEY CONCEPT 4.5
Portfolio analysis

Portfolio analysis is a technique that can be used by firms operating in a number of different markets and/or with a number of different products. The technique enables management to assess the relative attractiveness of products and markets to assist decision-making on future directions and resource allocation. There are several methods and models available, the most famous of which are probably the Boston Consulting Group Matrix and the General Electric Business Screen.

---

each one. As a result, a clearer idea emerges regarding priorities for corporate effort and resource allocation.

There are several models that may be used in portfolio analysis and two are illustrated in Figure 4.6. The most famous portfolio technique is the matrix developed by the Boston Consulting Group (BCG). This was specifically designed to analyse individual businesses in a company with a range of different business interests. The matrix enables the analyst to plot the position of that business (or product) with reference to the growth of the market and the company's share of that market. We can see from Figure 4.6 that the matrix has been divided into four sectors, each with different product/market characteristics. The products located within these sectors have been labelled 'question marks', 'stars', 'cash cows' and 'dogs' respectively. We will deal with the characteristics of each.

- **'Question marks'** represent products that have a low market share in a market of high growth. The market offers clear potential but the firm invariably needs significant financial and other resource inputs to compete. This may involve product modification, increasing output capacity, increasing promotional activity, recruiting extra staff and raising the level of bank borrowing. Investing in question marks carries a high level of risk, as can be seen through the British government's excursion into microchip development by funding the firm INMOS (Case 5.2). The gains may be significant but the market tends to be highly competitive and the costs of improving market position are invariably high.
- **'Stars'** are those products that have achieved a high share of a still expanding market. A company with a number or even one of such 'stars' is generally envied by its competitors. Nevertheless, the cost of maintaining this position is usually high. A growing market tends to attract a number of competitors and 'stars' usually need continuing investment in product development and promotion. The personal computer market in the past few years has maintained a high growth but the increased competition, particularly in terms of product development and price, has meant that several of its 'stars' have risen and fallen in a relatively short time. Other markets where 'stars' have risen and fallen rapidly include cameras and video cassette recorders.
- **'Cash cows'** are products with a high market share but market growth has

224

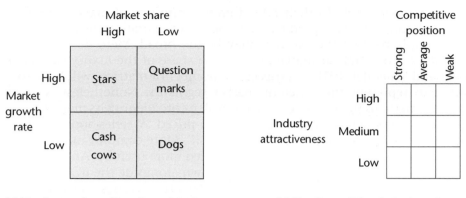

(a) The Boston Consulting Group Matrix   (b) The General Electric Business Screen

Figure **4.6** Illustrations of portfolio analysis. *Source*: Hofer and Schendel (1978).

stabilized. These provide the firm with its greatest return on investment. The market is generally much less competitive and the market position is generally less costly to maintain than with 'stars'. Overall costs are generally lower and economies of scale can be achieved. The surplus funds generated by the 'cash cows' can be used to provide funds for the development of 'question marks' and the maintenance of 'stars'. Zantac, Glaxo's drug for the treatment of ulcers was, for many years, the 'cash cow' that enabled the company to maintain high investments in R&D (see Case 5.1). Such a pattern is typical in the pharmaceutical industry, where development costs are especially high. The pattern has been repeated in other companies such as Hoffman-la-Roche with librium and valium.

● **'Dogs'** are products with the poorest profile on the matrix. Such products tend to be a drain on resources and can be candidates for being dropped altogether or being sold off. This was the reason behind the TI Group's sale of Raleigh Bicycles to Derby International. 'Dogs' are not necessarily worthless. Product ranges and indeed entire companies can be revitalized by perhaps a change of management and some fresh ideas. A 'dog' to one company may experience a new lease of life when sold to another. For example, a highly diversified company may find itself unable to devote sufficient attention to those products that are more peripheral to its central activities, as in the case of a manufacturing firm with a subsidiary whose primary activity is property development. The property business could be enhanced if it were sold to a firm specializing in that area.

The BCG matrix implies that management should seek to establish a balanced portfolio and carries with it a notion of progression. It assumes that 'question marks' should become 'stars' which will eventually turn into 'cash cows' to fund the next generation of developing product/markets. Plotting a firm's products in this way may be a useful guide to acquisition and divestment strategy. These options will be discussed in the next section.

The BCG matrix is not without its critics. Much of the criticism is concerned with the imprecise nature of the four categories. For example, 'stars' can differ considerably in their rate of growth and size of market share and the positioning of some products may be an inaccurate reflection of their value, simply because the category may be too broad. Mercedes-Benz has a low share of the total car market, but a high share of the luxury car market (Hofer and Schendel, 1978). In this case a number of matrices will have to be plotted to represent the different market segments. Nonetheless, such an analysis is perhaps the reason for Mercedes-Benz broadening its market appeal through the production of the smaller, lower-priced 'A' series and the launch of a competively priced sports model, the 'SLK'. More complex matrices have been developed so that products can be plotted more usefully. An illustration of the General Electric Business Screen is shown alongside the BCG matrix in Figure 4.6. In this case the concept of industry attractiveness is used instead of market growth and nine categories have been identified to achieve greater accuracy.

In spite of the problems of plotting and measurement, such methods of portfolio analysis are of use in planning future product/market strategy but also in raising important questions about how business interests are handled. We have already seen that by analysing a 'dog', changes may be possible to improve its position. One company to make use of this type of analysis is 3M. They have developed a matrix to analyse both products and markets, as illustrated in Figure 4.7. The management of 3M is concerned that each of its products and markets are capable of being maintained or improved. It was this method of analysis that led the company to sell off its photocopying equipment business (Kennedy, 1988).

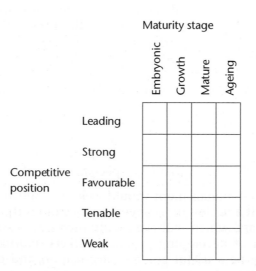

Figure **4.7** 3M product and market portfolio matrix – this matrix is used to analyse both products and markets. *Source*: Kennedy (1988).

Strategic options

So far in this chapter we have discussed the various components of strategic analysis: the environment, resources and dominant values. We have also suggested that strategy may be formulated by a variety of methods, which may involve a highly formalized planning procedure or may simply be no more than the stated preferences of the chief executive. Whatever the process, the outcome is a particular strategic option or range of possible options. In this section we examine a number of strategic options, including diversification joint ventures, strategies to change the competitive position of the firm, deleting operations and consolidation. When there are several options to choose from, some criterion is needed to select the most appropriate strategy and we end this chapter by identifying examples of such criteria. Case 4.1 examines the type of strategic options that may be available to declining industry and should be compared with Case 6.2 which examines the types of strategies employed by a firm in a declining market.

Types of strategic option

There is an assumption in many management texts that the superordinate goal of most businesses is survival and this may only be achieved by pursuing strategies of growth. While it is difficult to argue against the first assumption, it is clear that not all businesses pursue growth strategies, and, for those like the British steel and coal-mining industries, drastic contraction may be the only chance of survival.

Miles and Snow (1978) offer four main types of strategy that competing organizations can adopt within a single industry. They classify firms as defenders, prospectors, analysers and reactors.

- The **defender** organization tends to have a limited product line. By focusing on a niche market the defender can achieve market leadership, although the key focus of most defenders is improved efficiency through low-cost operations. The defender is unlikely to innovate and is best suited to stable environments. Because of the focus on costs, accountants tend to thrive in such organizations.
- The **prospector** organization operates with a wide range of products in a growing and usually fast-moving market. Prospectors tend to focus on innovation and new market opportunities. Such organizations tend to be flexible and decentralized and while efficiency is important, creativity is more important. Prospectors tend to emphasize R&D and marketing as the crucial functions.
- The **analyser** organization will rarely be first to the market, but will follow others after a thorough analysis of the market and competitor behaviour. Analysers can be found in both stable environments where they tend to emphasize cost reduction and in changing environments, where they emphasize product differentiation. The approach to change is usually cautious and the planning function and planning teams play a key role.

● The **reactor** organization tends to have a mismatch between its strategy and the environment in which it operates or it seems to have no strategy at all. Such organizations find it difficult to adapt to new situations and their strategic response is often inappropriate.

While Miles and Snow are concerned with corporate strategies within the same industry, Porter (1985) focuses on **competitive strategies**. These competitive strategies can be applied in any one of Miles and Snow's organization types. Porter presents a relatively straightforward view of competitive options within a single industry. To Porter competitive advantage is a product of positioning within that industry and he identifies two basic types of advantage and hence competitive focus. The first of these is competing on the basis of cost leadership. Firms pursuing this must aim to be the lowest-cost producer, but still be able to compete in terms of product function and quality. The second of Porter's generic competitive strategies is differentiation. Firms pursuing this strategy must aim to produce goods and services that have certain unique dimensions that make them attractive to customers. In aiming at product differentiation, competitive advantage can only be achieved by maintaining cost parity or cost proximity. Porter's approach appeals on the basis of its logic and simplicity. However, business life is never so simple. Furthermore, there are constraints on the effectiveness of such generic strategies. Firms continually strive to reduce their costs and copy each other's methods, as in the case of JIT. In some industries such as car manufacture, there may be limits of cost reduction, which are being approached by the better firms. Differentiation may be short-lived as competitors attempt to emulate each other. British Airways introduced beds as part of their first-class service on long-haul flights. They were soon followed by Singapore Airlines, and Virgin announced plans to offer double beds as an option!

Our classification of strategies depicts different approaches to growth and contraction. These options are not discrete categories and in many cases the distinction between them can be blurred. They also recognize the complex nature of the strategic process and incorporate discussion of both rational and more subjective factors. We examine diversification and joint ventures in some detail before looking briefly at other types of strategy.

Diversification strategies

Diversification is one of the most far-reaching growth strategies open to management, in that it represents a deliberate attempt to change the nature of the business by increasing its portfolio of products and/or markets in a variety of ways. We can identify two types of diversification, related and unrelated. Related diversification can be further classified into backward, forward and horizontal integration.

Related diversification

Related diversification occurs when the new business is related in some way to the old one. Several firms have sought to gain greater control over the source of raw materials or the supply of components by some form of **backward integration**. As we saw in Chapter 2, the larger Japanese manufacturing firms depend on a network of subcontractors for the supply of components. In many cases the larger company has a controlling financial interest in the supplier. In the restaurant business it is becoming more common for some restaurant owners to grow their own herbs and vegetables and bake their own bread, to ensure both the quantity and the quality of the supply. This also provides the restaurant with an additional promotional strategy. **Forward integration** occurs when producers diversify to control the onward processes of delivering their goods to the consumer, as in the case of a manufacturer setting up a transport or retail operation or a group of actors leasing a theatre to stage their own work. British Rail has always been a major source of transport for Post Office letters and parcels. In recent years British Rail has extended its own delivery service, Red Star, which has taken business away from the Post Office by offering a speedier and guaranteed delivery service. An integrated system of backward and forward integration is known as **vertical integration**. **Horizontal integration** occurs most commonly when a firm adds to its portfolio of products by acquisition. Belgo is a successful restaurant in London specializing in traditional Belgian food. Its success led to the opening of a second restaurant in a more central location utilizing the premises of a former restaurant. The group then expanded by purchasing two famous, up-market restaurants and establishing another food theme restaurant, this time featuring food from Alsace. A related strategy to horizontal integration is the move for **economies of scope**. This occurs when the product range is extended to incorporate similar items, as with the case of a firm supplying fitted kitchens diversifying its operation to include fitted bathrooms and bedrooms as well. Laura Ashley began by selling furniture fabrics, moved into dress fabrics and eventually diversified into selling dresses themselves. The economies of scope include shared central functions such as finance. Horizontal integration may be a valuable way of using a firm's spare resources or capacity. The fibreglass operations of Pilkington Glass found that the waste created in cutting standard widths of fibreglass could be put to good use through the setting up of another operation which compressed the material into insulating bricks, thereby creating a different but related product. Case 6.2 shows how a record company has used related diversification into specialized products as a major strategy of survival in a declining market.

Kwikfit presents a good example of a number of kinds of related diversification. The company was formed to offer a speedy, low-cost service to motorists in tyre fitting and exhaust system replacement. The opportunity presented itself as a result of the modular manufacture of cars and the ready availability of standardized parts. The reduction of operations to a series of highly specialized routines meant that low levels of skill were needed and hence labour costs were low. Central buying and computerized stock control were other contributory factors to low costs. As a result of low costs and a while-you-wait service the company became very successful and expanded geographically. The company also expanded its product and service range to include shock absorber and brake replacement. The success of the company

---

KEY CONCEPT 4.6
Diversification strategies

These are strategies that move the organization in different directions involving products or markets or both. Related diversification refers to new activities that are directly related in some way to existing operations, such as a hotel opening another hotel in a different location or acquiring a catering business. Unrelated diversification moves the organization in a totally new direction such as a hotel chain acquiring a newspaper. Highly diversified firms can spread risk across a number of products and/or markets. However, there may be problems associated with coordination and control. Related diversification can lead to benefits of economies of scale and scope.

KEY CONCEPT 4.7
Backward and forward integration

Backward integration is a diversification strategy to gain control of activities and/or firms further back in the supply chain, such as raw material or components suppliers. Forward integration is a strategy to gain control of activities further forward in the supply chain, such as distribution and retailing. Both backward and forward integration can be achieved by acquisition, joint venture or strategic alliance. Both backward and forward integration singly or together are often referred to as vertical integration.

---

in terms of profit and market share made it an attractive acquisition for Ford Motor Company, who thus diversified into after-sales service and parts sales.

Unrelated diversification

Unrelated diversification occurs when management expand their business into a totally different product market. Marks and Spencer have ventured into the selling of financial services, a totally different operation from their core business of clothes and food retailing. Many diversified companies have a mixture of both related and unrelated products. The London Rubber Company's main product range of contraceptives has been augmented by a range of surgical and household rubber gloves, based on the same technology. The company also produces soap and cough medicine. As with many forms of classification, the difference between related and unrelated diversification is often a matter of degree. The 3M case in this chapter is a good illustration of both types. The company switched from the mining of corundum (an abrasive) to the manufacture of sandpaper (using abrasives as a raw material). The company then began producing masking tape, which led to the related products of adhesive tape and all other kinds of tape product. In the 1990s the most profitable arm of Ford Motor Company in the UK was Ford Credit, a company formed to provide finance for car buyers.

The concept often associated with unrelated diversification is synergy. This refers to the collective influence of the various activities of the company producing an overall effect that is greater than the sum of the parts. Synergy is often cited as a major benefit of diversification, although its impact is often difficult to identify and measure.

We have seen how diversification can provide managers with greater control over supplies and distribution and exploit resources. A highly diversified firm may also be one where risks are spread across a range of products and markets. The motives for diversification may be complex and may include the desire of senior management to extend their power and influence as the firm grows larger. In the USA, the diversification of many companies into totally different areas of business was a direct response to anti-trust laws, which put severe restrictions on the creation of monopolies. There are problems with diversification strategies. A highly diversified company often presents special problems of communication and control and resources may be duplicated. It is for this reason that many diversified companies have adopted a structure involving a mixture of autonomous units sharing some central services, such as R&D. (A fuller discussion of structural devices may be found in Chapter 3.) While extra efficiency gains can result from related diversification, unrelated diversification brings extra costs associated with coordination and control.

Joint ventures, mergers and acquisitions

Many of the illustrations of diversification presented above represent activities that have grown out of the firm's existing business. Firms may also add new products and markets through joint ventures and through mergers and acquisitions. This has the advantage of being a much faster method of diversification than internal development. The company is gaining an 'off-the-peg' business with the experience, knowledge, resources and markets already in existence. Much has been written about acquisitions and mergers and such activity presents consistently good copy for financial journalists, particularly when it is accompanied by boardroom battles and accusations of insider dealing on the stock market. Joint ventures include licensing agreements, particular arrangements with suppliers, joint R&D projects and the creation of an entirely new company as an offshoot of two or more independent parent companies. Many mergers, more especially in emerging markets, are political in nature, as in China and India. Until two years ago, in order to operate in India, a company had to establish a joint venture with a local company, with the Indian partner taking a 60 per cent share. Changes such as those in Indian law reflect the growing influence of globalization on joint venture activity and the need for more flexible arrangements. In Figure 4.8 we show the differences between mergers, acquisitions and different forms of joint venture in terms of ownership. These various forms of ownership also reveal possibilities for variations in control.

Evidence in the UK has suggested that acquisitions and mergers tend to occur in cycles (Channon, 1973). Channon's view was supported by the events of the 1980s with another round of mergers taking place, particularly involving firms in retailing and in the food and drink industries. Why such

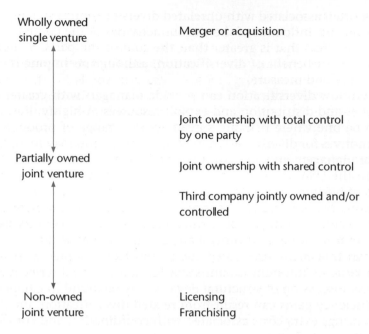

Figure **4.8** Ownership patterns in mergers, acquisitions and joint ventures.

cycles occur has not been fully explained and may represent yet another business fashion. In the UK there are a large number of mergers and acquisitions compared to other countries. This is explained in part by the behaviour of the stock market and the massive turnover in shares (Chapter 9 contains a fuller explanation). Germany has a much more stable stock market, yet mergers and acquisitions are on the increase, particularly with overseas companies. Some of the acquisitions have represented very high stakes indeed, as with the acquisition of the US publishing company Random House by Bertelsmann and of the Westinghouse Corporation by Siemens. The key drivers for German companies include high labour costs, high rates of taxation, a business climate that is highly regulated and shareholder pressure for increased dividend.

The German case is fairly typical of the modern context of joint venture activity around the world. It is clearly on the increase as a product of globalization, increased competition, the attractiveness of emerging markets in developing nations and, for advanced economies, declining growth rates and the increasing cost of home operations, particularly in terms of labour and R&D. The impact of globalization has resulted in some interesting cross-national ownership patterns. The famous US gun-makers Smith and Wesson are owned by Tomkins, a UK company, London Electricity by a company in New Orleans, Northumbrian Water by the French, William Hill, the bookmakers, by Nomura of Japan and Burger King has been in British hands for many years and is currently part of the Diageo stable. Such is the fast-moving nature of global ownership that many of these examples could well be out of date by publication of this book.

The key factor in the success of any joint venture, merger or acquisition is that there is a strategic fit between the parties concerned. The merger between Guinness and Grand Metropolitan (Case 4.5) was made on the basis of a good strategic fit between the two companies. For example, Guinness brought with it a large number of whisky brands and was strong in the Far East, whereas Grand Metropolitan was weak in these areas but strong in vodka and in Eastern Europe, where Guinness was relatively weak. As we see from Case 4.4, the proposed merger between Renault and Volvo, the strengths of each company were complementary. Volvo was strong in large cars, Renault in small; Volvo was strong in North America, while Renault had a larger market share in South America. However, as the failure of the proposed merger between Renault and Volvo shows, strategic fit may not be sufficient to sustain the relationship in the face of other constraints. Medcof (1997) argues that strategic fit must be accompanied by a long-term alliance strategy. What might appear to be a good strategic fit initially may not be sustainable in the longer term. He cites the case of British Airways, who bought a 25 per cent share in US Air, only to switch allegiances to American Airlines on the basis that they were better positioned as a long-term partner.

KEY CONCEPT 4.8
Strategic fit

Strategic fit is an important ingredient of successful mergers, acquisitions and joint ventures. Successful joint activities occur when each party complements the other in terms of their relative strengths and weaknesses. The concept is normally applied to products and markets, but it can apply equally to resources and other forms of core competence. The strategic fit should be compatible with long-term strategic plans, otherwise the partnership may be short-lived or prove to be a costly mistake.

The rationale and claimed advantages for joint ventures and some mergers and acquisitons are several:

● A joint venture will enable partners to pool resources, know-how and capital and use such synergies as might accrue to gain competitive advantage. Such pooling of resources has potential for cost reduction. Facilities can be shared and larger capacity can lead to economies of scale. In the case of global joint ventures, high-volume, low-tech work can be concentrated in low labour cost regions.

● Market considerations could include access for all partners to a bigger market. Access to local markets might also be important as in China and India, but with that access new entrants may be able to build on local knowledge, especially where culturally distinctive products and practices are important.

● Technological considerations include the reduced costs of R&D via pooling resources and access to new technologies. This was one reason for the acquisition of the US television manufacturer Zenith by the Korean electronics giant LG. A key feature of the technologically motivated joint venture is the desire to reduce risk. This is apparent in the proliferation of joint ventures in the 1990s in telecommunications and was the main reason for the Anglo-French collaboration on Concorde.

● Political factors predominate where entry to emerging markets is concerned. We have noted that joint ventures are a legal requirement for access to India. A joint venture in any country can gain advantage from political support, which then facilitates access to channels of influence and scarce resources.

In most joint ventures it is not one factor that predominates but a combination of the above. In the case of Airbus Industrie, a collaboration between the UK, France and Germany, which started in 1970, a number of factors were at work. A joint venture reduced entry costs for the companies involved in a notoriously expensive business. The partners were supported by their respective governments, initially in a move to compete on a global scale with the US firms Boeing and McDonnell Douglas. In addition there was a clear demand from the major European Airlines for a new type of mid-range carrier (Lyons, 1991).

In examining the advantage of joint ventures, there would appear to be at least two major problems. The first is the problem of measuring outcomes. Brouthers *et al.* (1997) argue that this is far from simple, since it depends on the rationale behind the joint venture. For example, financial criteria would be inappropriate if the reason for the joint venture were either technology transfer or expanding market share. They cite the case of the alliance between KLM (Holland) and Northwest Airlines (USA). The alliance would appear to be successful on all financial criteria, yet the two companies and, more especially, the respective managers were unhappy at working together. This supports further the view that we can only assess advantages from a particular perspective. In the above case, while the shareholders may be satisfied, the managers of the two firms were not. The issue of subjectivity lies at the heart of the second problem. Datta (1988) argues that too many joint ventures are assessed only from the perspective of the dominant partner. He feels this is especially apparent in the entry of established firms into emerging markets. In most cases there will be trade-offs. Otis Elevators (USA) established a joint venture in Tianjin, China, to access a large potential market. The Chinese, however, were more concerned with gaining access to elevator technologies and to foreign currency. In all joint ventures, especially transnational ones, any analysis of the advantages and rationale must consider the various stakeholders, which include the managers of the two companies, the shareholders, the suppliers, the employees, the customers and political interests at local and national levels.

The evidence concerning joint ventures is very mixed. Medcof (1997) cites evidence that successful alliances outperform single businesses, but he does point to a high casualty rate amongst joint ventures. Peters and Waterman (1982) present a rather negative view, especially of acquisitions. They cite the case of ITT and the difficulties the firm encountered when it diversified out of telephones by acquiring banking and hotel interests. They claim that synergy rarely happens through acquisition, and the whole exercise takes up a disproportionate amount of management time and effort. As befits two proponents of firms adopting a strong central image and consensus culture, Peters and Waterman see great difficulties in achieving a cultural fit between two different enterprises and advise managers to 'stick to the knitting'. Other research echoes Peters and Waterman's concern and tends to warn against unrestrained diversification. A study of 200 companies in the USA from 1949 to 1969 concluded that the poorest performers were those operating in a number of unrelated businesses and those that had attempted vertical integration. The best performers were those that had diversified only in related areas around a set of core activities and skills (Rumelt, 1974). It is interesting to note that while vertical integration is a complementary extension of a firm's core activities, it often requires totally different skills from that core activity. For example, a successful manufacturer of domestic electric appliances may turn out to be a very poor retailer and provider of repair services.

The difficulties associated with joint ventures, mergers and acquisitions are several, and probably account for the high casualty rate. Medcof (1997) sees the problems connected with capability, compatibility, commitment and control, which he dubs 'the 4 Cs':

- **Capability** is concerned with what each of the parties brings to the joint venture and is about the expectations each has of the other. Medcof cites the case of General Motors and Daewoo in South Korea, where GM managers felt that the alliance was weakened by the lack of capability of the Koreans on quality. Differences in capability were a key issue in the creation of the Beijing Jeep Corporation, a joint venture between Chrysler and the Beijing Auto Works and reported in Aiello (1991). This was a classic case of technology transfer in return for market entry. There were numerous project delays owing to the inability of local suppliers to produce on time and at the required quality. The service and spare parts industry was relatively undeveloped in China. Chrysler officials accused the Chinese of poor labour discipline and low productivity, while Chrysler management, with one exception, were unable to communicate in Chinese.
- Problems of **compatibility** arise in working together and often do not emerge until the implementation phase. Such problems can arise as a result of differences in culture, management style and personality and in administrative and accounting procedures. Datta (1988) found that such social and cultural issues were the ones most often overlooked by managers in establishing joint ventures. A major difficulty in establishing joint ventures between universities, involving the exchange of students, occurs around differences in teaching style, differences in the academic calendar and different requirements for assessment. In the previously mentioned case of KLM and Northwest Airlines, a key problems would seem to arise from the different management styles of the senior executives. A good example of compatibility problems is presented in Case 4.4 involving the failed alliance between Renault and Volvo, although these occurred before

the implementation stage. Difficulties with compatibility were a big issue in the aforementioned Beijing Jeep Corporation. There were problems arising from differences between the US and Chinese accounting systems, and the large pay of the Americans compared to the local managers became a source of resentment for the locals. The biggest problem for Chrysler, however, lay in their frustrations arising from the highly political nature of doing business in China. The political problems involved dealing with a cumbersome bureaucracy, having to accept local suppliers recommended by local government and the increasing involvement of national government in the post-Tianamen Square period.

● **Commitment** is the extent to which the partners are willing to invest resources and effort on a continuing basis, more especially when problems arise either in fulfilling expected objectives or between the partners themselves. Many alliances fail through the lack of staying power.

● Many problems can arise out of issues of **control**. Where one partner is dominant, the weaker partner may have its core competences actually weakened. In a study of Japanese joint ventures with US companies, Lei (1989) found that almost invariably the Japanese company was the dominant partner. Senior management was dominated by the Japanese, and the Japanese firm took over the critical skills of the US partner. One of the reasons for failure in the Renault–Volvo case was the belief amongst the Swedes that French management and French strategies would predominate in the new company. Control becomes even more of an issue when joint ventures involve more than two partners.

Case 4.4: The failed merger between Renault and Volvo

In 1993 merger talks finally broke down between Renault and Volvo. A merger between the two companies had seemed the inevitable consequence of a number of years of collaboration and the plans seemed well set.

Cooperation between the two firms had begun in 1990 when Renault took a 25 per cent share in Volvo cars and a 45 per cent share in their truck division. Volvo for its part took a 20 per cent share in Renault. The early collaboration took the form of an exchange of engines, the joint purchasing of components and joint developments in quality control. The cooperative arrangements between the two companies were a constant source of internal criticism, which focused on the highly bureaucratic procedures that had been established. In this sense a full merger was seen by both parties as the more favourable option.

The strategic fit between Renault and Volvo seemed ripe for merger. Volvo had strengths in the large car market, where Renault had consistently failed to make an impact. Renault's strengths lay in the manufacture of small cars and in diesel technology. In terms of market, Volvo was stronger in Northern Europe and especially North America and Renault had a larger market share in Southern Europe and South America.

Both companies were probably too small to survive in a globally competitive volume-car market. In Europe and the USA merger was a route for survival, particularly in the face of increasing Japanese competition. The major markets had stagnated and both companies had experienced fall in profits. In the early 1990s Volvo was the more vulnerable of the two companies. It had cut almost a quarter of its workforce and had closed manufacturing plants at Kalmar and Udevalla owing to excess capacity. Its focus on high-priced models made its sales variable with the economic cycles. The size of Volvo's export sales, especially to the USA, made it vulnerable to exchange rate fluctuations. Renault too had reduced its labour requirements, but had done so on the back of a 50 per cent improvement in productivity between 1985 and 1991. A merger seemed to make sense in terms of reduced costs, increased economies of scale and the opportunity to share increasingly expensive R&D costs. The costs of developing new products in the car industry had risen dramatically, necessitating high-volume sales to obtain a return on investment and hence the reason behind much of the merger activity in the industry in the 1980s and 1990s. The senior management of the two companies supported the merger, as did the Swedish and French governments. In any case Renault was part-owned by the government and, despite plans to privatize the company, would never have allowed merger talks to begin without their support.

The reasons for the merger not taking place were several, involving economic, social, political and cultural aspects. To the surprise of many in Sweden, the alliance would favour French ownership to the ratio of 65–35. In return for its 65 per cent share of the new company, Renault would pay nothing in cash. The ownership ratio would come about simply on the basis of share redistribution. The CEO of Renault, Louis Schweitzer, was to be the CEO of the new company, which would have its headquarters in Paris. The Swedes were suspicious of this arrangement, especially when French newspapers spoke openly of a Renault takeover and Schweitzer predicted in the press a profound restructuring of Volvo's Swedish operations. In part, the unease of the Swedes could be traced back to their ambivalence about EU membership, which they eventually took in 1995.

Opposition mounted in Sweden amongst several groups of stakeholders. The merger was to take place before the privatization of Renault. The French government had no published timetable for the sale and Swedish shareholders feared either a nationalization by the French of Volvo or a fall in share price. They believed that the share price would be devalued, fearing that the French government would under-price the company to ensure a successful sale. Volvo employees, including many of the less senior managers, became increasingly convinced that a merger would mean a loss of Swedish jobs. Renault had

already demonstrated its ability to make significant productivity improvements and there was a belief that such methods would be transferred to Sweden, resulting in yet more restructuring. This fear was understandable given the difference in labour costs in the two countries. Swedish workers enjoyed the highest wages and lowest working hours of any in the European auto industry. In 1991, hourly labour costs in Sweden were 169 Swedish kronor compared to 96 in France. The inevitable conclusion was that jobs would migrate from Sweden to France, and the Swedish government, even if they wished, would be prevented from giving special assistance to Volvo by EU competition policy, even though Sweden was not a member at the time. Eventually these fears found expression in the Swedish media and public opinion turned against the merger.

While the strategic fit between Renault and Volvo was good, the cultural fit was less so. Significant differences exist between French and Swedish management styles. The French are more hierarchical, less flexible and less open. The Swedes are much more likely to delegate and push responsibility for decisions down the organization. As a consequence Swedish organizations tend to have fairly flat structures, while the French reflect their belief in hierarchies through a greater number of levels. Swedish managers tend to be much more international in their perspective and the French more parochial. Surveys of consumer attitudes reflect a Swedish preference for safety, quality and environmental friendliness in their products, while the French score more highly on design and style. Such cultural differences undoubtedly contributed to the failed merger, as did incompatibility in terms of language.

In the face of such problems, the merger collapsed. Since then both companies have sold their respective shares in each other's company. The French government delayed the full privatization of Renault and moved instead from 75 to 50 per cent ownership. Volvo has cut back yet further and closed more plants. In 1998, the Volvo car division, but not the truck, became part of Ford Motor Company. For its part Renault acquired a 37 per cent share of Nissan. ■

(*Sources*: Williams *et al.*, 1994; Medcof, 1997; Brown, 1998; Hampden-Turner and Trompenaars, 1993)

Case 4.5: Guinness and Grand Metropolitan

In June 1997 a merger was agreed between Guinness and Grand Metropolitan to create the world's largest drinks company. The two companies could claim 24.7 per cent of the world market, with the nearest rival, Allied Domecq, coming in at 10.8 per cent. The 1996 sales of both companies combined amounted to £12.9 billion with profits of £1.6 billion, 60 per cent of which came from the manufacture and sale of spirits. The merger was completed in December 1997 after approval from the UK Government, the EU Commission and the US Federal Trade Commission. The terms of acceptance required the companies to sell Dewars Whisky and Bombay Sapphire Gin and reduce their market power in some smaller European countries. The company surprised everyone by announcing the new company name as Diageo, when the expectation was for the more obvious choice of Grand Metropolitan Guinness.

Ownership was split 52.7 and 47.3 per cent in favour of Grand Metropolitan and four new divisions were created. These were Guinness Brewing Worldwide, Burger King, Pillsbury and United Distillers and Vintners, the last being the largest division by far.

There was a clear strategic fit between the two partners. Guinness brought considerable strength in whiskies, with such brands as Bells, White Horse and the world's best-seller, Johnnie Walker. In addition to whiskies, Guinness possessed household-name brands such as Gordon's Gin, Harp Lager and Kilkenny Beer, as well as its famous dark stout. Its 34 per cent stake in LVMH, the French luxury goods firm, incorporated Hennessy Cognac and Moet Chandon Champagne. Grand Metropolitan's strengths lay in vodka and white spirits generally. It owned the world's best-selling vodka brand in Smirnoff and had led the market in the production and sale of popular spirit combination drinks such as Malibu and Baileys. Whereas Guinness was predominantly a drinks firm, Grand Met owned Pillsbury, the US-based dough and cake makers, Burger King and Häagen Dazs ice cream. Guinness had particular strengths in the Far Eastern markets where Grand Met was weak, and Grand Met was strong in Eastern Europe, where Guinness was weak. Grand Met also brought significant strengths in the US market through its vodka sales and its food interests. The joint venture served both interests in a declining world spirits market and growing competition from supermarket and retail chain own brands. Global sales teams now had more to offer their customers.

Neither party was new to joint ventures. Grand Met has had a fairly volatile history in this respect. The company began life as a hotel chain, which it then sold off. Most of its brands were acquisitions such as Burger King and Pillsbury. The company has owned and subsequently sold Watney Mann Truman, Mecca Bingo Halls and Express Dairies. Guinness for its part acquired the Distillers Company and Cruz Campo and obtained a large share in LVMH (Louis Vuitton Moet Hennessy). The merger was initially opposed by Bernard Arnault, the head of LVMH, whose company owned a 14 per cent share in Guinness. He was a member of the Guinness board and feared losing his place in the new order of things. He preferred a three-way deal, which was rejected by the two heads of Guinness and Grand Met, both of whom were reported in the press as being highly compatible.

The drinks industry has a long history of considerable merger activity and the deals that preceded and followed the creation of Diageo illustrate the highly volatile nature of merger activity in the UK and beyond. When Watney Mann Truman was sold by Grand Met it became part of the Courage group. Courage then merged with Scottish Newcastle Breweries to form Scottish-Courage. A rival company, Carlsberg Tetley, wanted to merge with Guinness. The strategic fit was good in that Carlsberg Tetley brought with it a large number of public houses and strength in bitter and lager beers. However, the company's interest in Guinness came after an unsuccessful attempt to merge with Bass. That proposed merger was blocked by the government as being against the public interest on the forecast of price rises and job losses. This had a knock-on effect for Allied Domecq who saw any merger involving Carlsberg Tetley as a means of extricating itself from an expensive supply agreement with the company. Bass, unsuccessful in its attempts to merge with Carlsberg Tetley, then turned its attentions to the bookmakers William Hill, given that Bass already owned another major betting firm in Corals. In the event, William Hill was bought by the Japanese firm, Nomura. ∎

(*Sources*: *Financial Times, Guardian, Observer*)

Other strategic options

Strategies to change the competitive position of an existing business

Whereas diversification and joint ventures represent fundamental changes in the nature of a firm's business, strategies in this category attempt to improve the market position of the existing range of products and services. There are a number of strategic options available, most of them are discussed more fully in the chapters focusing on the functional areas:

- **new product development** (Chapter 5);
- **improved market penetration** by deploying the various elements of the marketing mix, such as promotion or price strategies (Chapter 7);
- **seeking new markets** by aiming the product at new market segments or by export (Chapter 7);
- **improving the quality** of the product or service (Chapter 6);
- **seeking cost reductions** through an improved utilization of resources such as improvements in productivity (Chapter 6).

Many of these strategies are related. A firm that wishes to move 'up market' and aim its product at a more quality-conscious but less price-sensitive consumer group may need to accompany product changes with an intensive promotion campaign. We pursue this theme in more detail in our discussion of marketing strategies in Chapter 7.

Attempts to change the competitive position of the business can be made through acquisitions which improve the product range and gain access to new markets. Such strategies carry the same advantages and disadvantages outlined above. A growing type of competitive strategy involves franchising ('Structure' in Chapter 3). Through franchising its products or services to individual small businesses, a firm can reach a wider market and, at the same time, spread the risk of that expansion.

All the above options improve the competitive position of the firm by focusing on existing products and services. The strategies can therefore be achieved by internal change strategies. Expansion into new markets may be accompanied by increased promotional and sales activity in that area. However, the more successful change strategies take time and involve more than simply exercising another strategic option. Moves to effect changes in product quality and productivity may involve HRM strategies (Chapter 8) and attempts to change the organizational culture (Chapter 3).

Deleting operations

The decision to cut back and/or sell off part of the operations of a firm is referred to as rationalization or divestment. At its ultimate level this will include liquidation and closure. Such strategies can pose enormous difficulties for the firm involved. The cutting back of activities such as R&D and training to achieve short-term savings may have damaging long-term repercussions. Reducing product lines and services may alienate customers. Cutbacks and closures are generally vigorously opposed by trade unions. The National Coal Board's plans in 1984 to close the Cortonwood Colliery in Yorkshire precipitated one of the longest and most bitter disputes in the history of the industry. On a more general level, rationalization strategies may cause a lowering of employee morale to such a level that existing operations are endangered.

Nevertheless, for some firms, rationalization is the only viable option and may, as successful management buy-outs have shown, offer a new lease of life to part of an organization. In 1981, the shoe manufacturer Norvic was forced to go into liquidation, and one of its subsidiaries, the Mansfield Shoe Company, was faced with closure and most of its workforce were made redundant. The Mansfield subsidiary was saved by a management buy-out which raised extra capital from local industry and from employees exchanging their redundancy payments for shares in the new company. Freed from the financial burden of helping to support an ailing parent company, the newly formed organization found new markets and became reasonably successful, expanding its operations by acquisitions in other parts of the country. However, by the late 1990s, increased competition from lower-cost producers once again placed the company's survival at risk. One of the responses was renewed rationalization through divestment of its previous acquisitions.

Consolidation

A consolidation strategy involves the firm operating in the same product market at existing levels. It is, however, far from a 'do nothing' strategy. Even to stand still firms must keep pace with their competitors. This may involve all the kinds of strategies outlined above, and will certainly involve considerations of product development, quality improvement, marketing and cost reduction.

Stategic choice

Faced with a number of strategic options a manager must make a choice. We have already indicated that the process involves consideration of a number of factors, which we may summarize as follows:

- an analysis of environmental threats and opportunities;
- an analysis of company resources;
- the stated objectives of the company and those of the management team;
- the values and preferences of management decision-makers;
- the realities of organizational politics.

The various options must be tested for their suitability, feasibility and acceptability. The suitability of a strategy would include such considerations as its ability to tackle major problems, improve competitive standing, exploit strengths, and the extent to which it meets corporate objectives. The feasibility of a strategy is the extent to which that strategy can be achieved given the financial, physical and human resource base of the company. Even if a strategy is both suitable and feasible it must still be acceptable to various interested parties, such as management, employees, shareholders and customers. Shareholders may be particularly sensitive to strategies of acquisition. The ultimate acceptance of a particular strategy might depend on the attitude of senior management to risk.

The Strategic Planning Institute in Britain and the USA offers assistance in strategic choice by identifying those strategies most likely to result in increased profit levels. They have set up a scheme known as PIMS (Profit Impact of Market Strategies). In essence PIMS is really a huge database generated by those companies participating in the scheme. A record is kept of strategic options and their links to profit levels. Firms participating in the scheme have access to the data generated by other companies and may therefore learn from their successes and failures. Analysis of the information to date suggests a positive relationship between profitability and market share, but a negative relationship between profitability and the intensity of investment. Surprisingly, the PIMS data have uncovered that investment is not such a safe option as many assume. Intense investment usually occurs in highly competitive businesses and companies tend to engage in damaging price wars or find that excessive investment proves a barrier to exit (Beasley, 1985).

The way a strategic choice is made will depend very much on the power and authority structure of the organization. In some firms the strategy may be highly detailed with little scope for interpretation by functional managers. In other firms a great deal of freedom is given to functional management to develop appropriate strategies within broad guidelines. We deal with specific functional strategies in Chapters 5 to 9. A theme stressed throughout is that R&D, production, marketing, HR and financial strategies should achieve a high level of internal consistency, irrespective of where in the firm the strategy was formulated.

A key factor often overlooked in the choice of strategy is its **sustainability**. This refers to the extent to which the strategy is difficult for others to copy. Such a concept has much in common with core competence, discussed earlier in this chapter. Product and process innovation can lead to a sustainable competitive advantage that persists for many years, especially when protected by patents and trademarks as in the case of Rank Xerox. Toyota achieved sustainable advantage over rival car manufacturers both within and outside Japan through continuous refinements in its system of lean production. Coca Cola's sustainable advantage lay in its secret formula and branding policies. However, the history of strategic initiatives is littered with examples of non-sustainable advantages. An excellent illustration of this may be found in the rivalry between UK supermarkets. Each major supermarket chain rigorously monitors its rivals so that any product and price advantage is quickly countered. All followed one another to introduce petrol stations, cafeterias and loyalty cards and as one announced diversification into financial services, it was followed quickly by the others.

KEY CONCEPT 4.9
Sustainability

Sustainability is the extent to which an organization's strategy is difficult to copy and is therefore the source of competitive advantage over time. This concept is linked to that of core competence (Key Concept 4.3).

Summary

In this chapter we have portrayed the formulation of management strategy as a complex process involving the consideration of environmental and organizational factors as well as management values and organization politics. As a result the process is a mixture of rational techniques and subjective decision-making processes, including a consideration of management values and negotiations between interested parties.

We have identified a range of approaches and styles, which may operate at the same time, although at different stages of the firm's development one type of strategy may be more appropriate than another. The formulated strategy has several functions, not least of which is to anticipate the future by coordinating activities and focusing resources towards chosen objectives. However, we note that the links between strategy and performance are difficult to prove.

An analysis of the general environment and a focus on the immediate competitive environment will enable management to identify significant opportunities and threats, although how these are interpreted is a function of the values and creative ability of management. We identify four kinds of resource: product, physical, financial and people. All are important in enabling management to formulate strategy around the organization's strengths. These strengths may be examined through an analysis of a firm's core competences and its value chain. Portfolio analysis offers both an analysis of resources and an insight into strategic options.

We examine a number of strategic options, including a debate on the advantages and disadvantages of joint ventures, and suggest that each option should be assessed in terms of its suitability, its feasibility and its acceptability. The final criterion stresses a central theme of this chapter: the importance of management values and organization politics in the strategic process.

Further reading

There are three popular texts, all of which have features to commend them. They are G. Johnson and K. Scholes, *Exploring Corporate Strategy: Text and Cases*, 4th edn (Prentice Hall, 1997), R. E. Lynch, *Corporate Strategy* (Pitman Publishing, 1997) and B. de Wit and R. Meyer, *Strategy: Process, Content,*

Context: An International Perspective, 2nd Edn (International Thomson Business Press, 1998). While covering much of the same ground, they approach the subject in slightly different ways. They possess a wealth of illustrations and there are some good cases in all of them. An added feature of De Witt and Meyer is its inclusion of a number of classic journal articles. A different and interesting view of strategy is taken by R. Whittington, *What Is Strategy – And Does It Matter?* (Routledge, 1993). At a more specific level, a good analysis of the competitive environment is offered by M.E. Porter, *Competitive Strategy: Techniques for Analyzing Industries and Competitors* (Free Press, 1980). Some still rate this as his best book.

Discussion

1. Examine the role of the scientific method in the process of strategy formulation. Is there a place for subjectivity and creativity?
2. What is the purpose of strategy and how might a particular strategy be evaluated?
3. Identify the major environmental opportunities and threats faced by a city centre restaurant, a large retail store, a high street bank, a university, and a firm manufacturing television sets.
4. Using Porter's five-forces model, identify the specific competitive forces operating in the five situations defined in the previous question.
5. In what ways can management use resource analysis and portfolio analysis to guide strategy? What are the major strengths and weaknesses of the models for portfolio analysis identified in this chapter?
6. Assess the usefulness of core competences and the value chain in analysing resources and developing strategy.
7. Make a critical analysis of the different approaches to diversification and joint venture.
8. What are the key lessons to be learnt from the two joint ventures described in Cases 4.4 and 4.5?
9. Identify the environmental, organizational and management considerations which led 3M in Case 4.2 to rethink its planning procedure. What further threats might the company have to face?
10. Using Case 4.3 as a starting point, what strategic approaches, styles and options would best fit a new university for the twenty-first century? What problems do you foresee with these approaches, styles and options?

as a new model of car, a new form of insurance policy, or a restaurant offering a new special vegetarian menu. Process innovation is concerned with how the product is made or delivered to the customer. The development of robots in manufacturing industry is a form of process innovation, as is a restaurant opening a self-service section in addition to an existing waiter-service operation. In cases like the Toyota production system, process innovations can offer a firm an enviable competitive advantage.

● We have already noted that innovation may occur in every aspect of the organization's operations. We can therefore classify innovation by **function**. Innovations occur in the selection and use of raw materials, in the way goods and services are produced, in the marketing activities and in the way the organization is structured and managed. For example, the introduction of work-group participation in management decision-making is a form of innovation, as are types of job enrichment to enhance worker motivation.

We can also make a distinction between **basic** and **incremental** innovations. The latter represent innovations that are modifications and improvements on existing products and processes. In fact the great majority of innovations are not major breakthroughs but modifications, often of a very minor nature. This incremental approach to innovation is pursued successfully by many Japanese companies and is the reason why camera producers such as Minolta and Canon bring out a new model at regular intervals.

Illustrations of all these types of innovation are presented in Table 5.1.

Table **5.1** Different types of innovation

Type of innovation	Extent of the innovation	
	Basic	Modification
Raw material	The use of plastic in place of glass in bottles.	Changing the components of the plastic in the bottles to make them tougher.
Product	The use of integrated circuits on microchips to replace transistors.	Employing electronic controls in a washing machine.
Process	Introducing robots to perform the welding operation in a car assembly plant.	Increasing the number of stages in a car painting process to gain a better finish.
Marketing	The opening of a high street shop by a mail order book-club to widen sales.	Using television personalities instead of politicians in a televised political broadcast.
Organizational	Creating a matrix form of organization to replace the traditional arrangement based on specialist functions.	Creating a separate training function within the Personnel department.

In addition to the various types of innovation, we might add a fourth category. This has been termed 'pseudo-innovations' (Mensch, 1979). These are often introduced to revitalize a stagnant market, but in fact no real change has taken place. Such pseudo-innovations are often the product of marketing campaigns to change the fortunes of a flagging product. The product may be relaunched under a different brand name, repackaged to suggest product changes or advertised as containing a 'new improved formula' when no significant change has taken place. A case in this area is that of the washing powder Square Deal Surf. Its forerunner, Surf, was experiencing a declining market share in a market where every new product appeared to come with a new formula for washing whiter. The company aimed the product at a segment of the market that they had identified as 'anti-gimmick'. To emphasize this point they offered the product with a changed name, which suggested to consumers that they were getting a better deal than those offered by competitors. The change and repositioning of the product in the market was highly successful and sales increased. We deal with aspects of market segmentation and positioning in more detail in Chapter 7.

The case of Square Deal Surf illustrates the complexity of innovation. To Mensch it undoubtedly represents a pseudo-innovation in terms of product, yet the marketing strategy employed was highly innovative. Moreover, not all innovations are visible. Where washing powders have radically changed their formula this is not instantly apparent to the consumer and the company relies upon its marketing effort to convey this information, reinforcing the importance of an integrated innovation and marketing strategy.

Research, development and design

We can define research and development as the organization of innovation at the level of the firm. It is that activity of an organization that both seeks to satisfy a market need by developing new products and methods and find uses for scientific and technological inventions. This introduces to the concepts of **demand-pull** innovation (fulfilling a market need) and **technology-push** innovation (applying existing knowledge). R&D is clearly associated with science and technology, although the R&D function can be performed in all types of industry. We have seen that the process of new product development occurs in non-scientific and technical situations. In many organizations there is a group of people whose primary task is the generation of new business ideas, as in the case of television companies, which have a department for new programme development.

In some industries, especially those involved in complex, competitive environments, R&D is a vital part of the business. Firms like IBM and Hewlett-Packard in the computer industry and Roche and Glaxo Wellcome in the pharmaceutical industry have large teams of staff engaged exclusively in R&D work. The importance of R&D to Glaxo Wellcome is shown in Case 5.1. In the case of Hewlett-Packard, innovation is part of the organizational culture and is stressed as a responsibility of all employees (Case 3.6). The institutionalization of R&D can bring its own problems, which are raised when we look at organizational aspects later in the chapter.

KEY CONCEPT 5.2
Research and development

Research and development or R&D is the name give to the organizational function that is usually the focus for innovation within a firm. R&D can refer to an activity or the name of a specific department. Expenditure on R&D and the size of an R&D department have been used as measures of levels of innovative activity, although they are probably best used as indicators rather than exact measures owing to the presence of other variable which can and do influence innovation.

KEY CONCEPT 5.3
Demand pull versus technology push

These refer to the sources of innovation. Demand pull refers to the development of new products and processes as a direct result of market demand. Technology push is the utilization of known technologies to develop innovative products and processes. Many innovations, for example the CD player, are developed as a result of both demand pull and technology push.

The British government, through the Innovation Advisory Board, part of the Department of Trade and Industry, now publishes league tables of R&D spending. The UK R&D Scoreboard, as it is known, uses R&D as a proportion of sales turnover as a measure of R&D intensity. Such information is now available for stock exchange listed companies as a requirement of SSAP 13 (Statement of Standard Accounting Practice). Tables 5.2 and 5.3 show expenditure on R&D by companies in the United Kingdom and worldwide respectively. The highest-spending British company, Glaxo Wellcome, ranks 34th in the world in terms of R&D spending.

R&D is an incremental process. We illustrate this by using as a framework the classification of R&D developed by Burns and Stalker (1966). Although their classification is biased towards technological industries, it gives us further insights into the innovative process.

● **Pure research** is concerned with advancing the state of knowledge in a particular field with little immediate concern for its commercial application. Very few firms engage directly in this kind of research, and on the whole it is generally left to the university sector. Business concerns are involved indirectly in so far as some of them sponsor research activity in some universities.

● In **basic research** firms do get involved since this kind of research is directed at advancing the state of knowledge in a particular applied field with the very real hope that it will prove useful. The managements of these firms hope that such research will lead ultimately to those product and process innovations that will give the business its competitive edge.

Table **5.2** Ranking of top 20 companies in the UK by R&D expenditure 1997

Company	Rank	1997 R&D spend £000	% sales
All companies composite		10 485 417	1.8
Glaxo Wellcome	1	1 148 000	14.4
SmithKline Beecham	2	841 000	10.8
Zeneca	3	653 000	12.6
Unilever	4	546 000	1.8
General Electric	5	458 000	7.0
Shell	6	403 000	0.5
Ford Motor	7	338 000	4.9
Pfizer	8	313 200	99.1
British Aerospace	9	301 000	3.5
BT	10	291 000	1.9
Reuters	11	235 000	8.2
ICI	12	229 000	2.1
Rolls-Royce	13	216 000	5.0
Siebe	14	183 800	6.1
Nortel	15	165 000	13.6
Lucas Varity	16	159 000	3.4
British Petroleum	17	141 000	0.3
Siemans	18	124 700	6.2
Cable and Wireless	19	119 000	2.0
BTR	20	118 000	1.5

(*Source*: DTI scoreboard (1998))

In some firms, like 3M, the active encouragement of staff to develop their own research projects is an important part of company policy, and many ideas generated from the staff's own programmes have been turned to profitable use by the company (Case 4.2). Other companies, like Glaxo Wellcome, have a more organized approach to basic research (Case 5.1). Basic research is increasingly important in industries dealing with such as micro-electronics, biotechnology, genetics and the development of new materials. There has been both an increase in such types of research and an increase in government support in the USA, Japan and Germany. In the United Kingdom, basic research, an area of traditional strength, was by the late 1980s seen to be in relative decline (Freeman, 1989).

● **Industrial research** stands in relation to basic research as innovation does to invention. Industrial research attempts to transform pure and basic research into some form of profitable use.

● **Development** takes research a stage further by translating the outcome

Table **5.3** Ranking of top 40 companies worldwide by R&D expenditure 1997

Company	Rank	1997 R&D spend £000	% sales
All companies composite		131 067 451	4.6
General Motors, USA	1	4 983 591	4.9
Ford Motor, USA	2	3 845 266	4.1
Siemens, Germany	3	2 748 690	7.6
IBM, USA	4	2 617 601	5.5
Hitcahi, Japan	5	2 353 534	5.9
Toyota Motor, Japan	6	2 106 695	3.7
Matsushita Electric Industrial, Japan	7	2 032 720	5.7
Daimler-Benz, Germany	8	1 914 146	4.6
Hewlett-Packard, USA	9	1 870 670	7.2
Ericsson Telefon, Sweden	10	1 856 885	14.5
Lucent Technologies, USA	11	1 837 243	11.5
Motorola, USA	12	1 670 111	9.2
Fujitsu, Japan	13	1 649 168	7.8
NEC, Japan	14	1 629 157	7.0
Asea Brown Boveri, Switzerland	15	1 614 805	8.5
El du Pont de Nemours, USA	16	1 576 516	5.8
Toshiba, Japan	17	1 554 453	6.1
Novartis, Switzerland	18	1 538 814	11.8
NTT, Japan	19	1 535 634	3.7
Volkswagen, Germany	20	1 487 240	3.9
Intel, USA	21	1 426 401	9.4
Hoechst, Germany	22	1 348 656	7.7
Bayer, Germany	23	1 339 868	7.2
Sony, Japan	24	1 320 805	5.2
Northern Telecom, Canada	25	1 304 850	13.9
Johnson & Johnson, USA	26	1 300 596	9.5
Bell Canada Enterprises, Canada	27	1 236 303	8.8
Philips, The Netherlands	28	1 216 273	5.3
Roche, Switzerland	29	1 209 634	15.5
Honda Motor, Japan	30	1 173 841	4.7
Pfizer, USA	31	1 171 752	15.8
Microsoft, USA	32	1 169 928	16.9
Boeing, USA	33	1 169 321	4.2
Glaxo Wellcome, UK	34	1 148 000	14.4
Alcatel Alsthom, France	35	1 112 896	6.8
Robert Bosch. Germany	36	1 100 896	7.0
Chrysler, USA	37	1 033 183	3.0
Merck, USA	38	1 023 277	7.1
Monsanto, USA	39	986 386	21.6
AHP, USA	40	946,903	11.0

(*Source*: DTI Scoreboard (1998)

of research into something more tangible. At this stage in the design of a new product, a prototype or a sample would be produced.

● **Design** is the final stage in the R&D process, which translates the development into the final product for the consumer. The design stage attempts to fuse certain elements, which are referred to as the 'design mix'. These elements are effective operation, safety, easy maintenance, value for money and aesthetic considerations. These are all focused on satisfying customer needs.

The design aspect of research and development is an obvious area of overlap with both the production and marketing processes, to the extent that product design is seen as an essential element in both fields. Design and styling assume particular importance in industries such as car manufacture, where products are often sold as much on their appearance as their inherent product qualities. A firm like Bang and Olufsen produces televisions and hi-fi equipment to high technical specifications, yet its distinctiveness in the market place owes much more to its visual appeal. Making their products look very different from their competitors is a deliberate Bang and Olufsen strategy.

The British government targeted design for special consideration by businesses in 1985. Part of this targeting was an encouragement to schools and colleges to seek ways of incorporating design in the curriculum. A major concern has been the place of design in manufacturing industry. An underlying assumption behind such developments is undoubtedly the view that Britain as a manufacturing nation is falling behind its rivals, notably France, Germany, Japan and the USA, in the perceived quality and desirability of its goods. We discuss the importance of quality in Chapter 6.

It is not only in manufacturing industry that design is important. A good illustration is presented by the clothing retail chain Burton at the beginning of the 1980s. The company had always been fairly successful catering for the needs of a middle-of-the-road male market segment. However, the firm suffered a serious decline of its market share and profitability. The styling of its clothes had not kept pace with the needs of an increasingly fashion-conscious market, particularly those in the younger age group who spend a good proportion of their income on clothes. Moreover, the image of its shops and store layout was decidedly old fashioned and unappealing to the new consumer. As a result of a very detailed research programme to identify and meet the specific design needs of different consumer groups, the management introduced a completely new range of clothes to capture the growing market and invested in a modernization programme to give their stores a new image. This conscious effort in design management was held to be mainly responsible for the profit increase from £16.4 million in 1981 to £80.22 million in 1985.

Entrepreneurship

We noted at the beginning of this chapter that the activities of the entrepreneur were crucial to the process of innovation. Innovation happens because the entrepreneur has initiated it, as illustrated by the work of Ronald Hickman and the 'Workmate' in Case 5.3. The entrepreneur creates new

Case 5.1: Glaxo Wellcome

Glaxo Wellcome was formed by merger in 1995, creating the world's largest pharmaceutical company. Upon merger it was estimated that the new company controlled 35 per cent of the world gastro-intestinal drug market, 25 per cent of the antibiotic market, 25 per cent of the respiratory market and 70 per cent of the anti-viral market. The focus of the company remained the prescribed pharmaceuticals market, despite considerable growth in the over-the-counter non-prescription drugs market. The British company has a presence in over 50 countries, manufacturing in over 30 of them. Glaxo Wellcome operates in a competitive world market where research plays a highly significant role both in terms of expenditure and in terms of the ever-present need to develop innovative products.

Glaxo had risen to prominence with the development and manufacture of the world's best-selling drug, Zantac, a treatment for ulcers. The drug was launched in 1981 and became the world top-seller by 1986. However, the company did not emerge as a leading-edge researcher until the 1960s when the acquisition of a research-based operation led to the development of Ventolin, a successful drug for asthma sufferers. The company had developed in the early part of the twentieth century as a family business selling powdered milk for babies, with a gradual extension into products related to infant nutrition. The real point of entry into the drugs market came with the Second World War when the company began to produce penicillin. Zantac transformed Glaxo from a moderate UK company into a world leader. Wellcome was founded in the late nineteenth century as a UK company, Burroughs Wellcome, by two Americans. The company developed the rubella vaccine, but its best-selling item, Zovirax, a treatment for herpes, was lauched, like Zantac, in 1981. By 1996, Zantac was the world number one and Zovirax the world number six in terms of drug sales. Overall the company had six medicines in the top 40 best-selling pharmaceutical products.

Before the merger, both companies were noted for their commitment to R&D. Between 1987 and 1992 more than 50 per cent of Glaxo's capital spending went towards equipping research laboratories. In 1992 Glaxo built a large new research complex at Stevenage to employ 1700 research scientists. In 1992, the Stevenage research laboratories were the largest investment project in the UK after the Channel Tunnel and

Sizewell B. The laboratories are now the research HQ for Glaxo Wellcome. Following the merger, the company was able to rationalize its R&D operations, saving £600 million a year. At the same time, it became the top listed UK company in terms of R&D expenditure, spending £1.14 billion in 1997. In world terms its R&D expenditure was third amongst all pharmaceutical companies, marginally behind Roche of Switzerland and Pfizer of the USA.

While Glaxo Wellcome has its research HQ in the UK, it has research operations in the USA, Japan, Spain, France, Singapore, Switzerland and Italy. Glaxo Wellcome's R&D strategy is an extension of that pursued by Glaxo. The company operates a fairly ruthless approach to weeding out the potentially successful from the unsuccessful developments at a relative early stage and the marketing of innovative drugs at relatively high prices. There is a strong belief in different approaches to problem-solving and Glaxo Wellcome not only attempts to capitalize upon cultural differences in the approach to research, but moves its researchers around the various locations. The organization of research is invariably flexible with the emphasis upon small teams feeding into project approval committees. There is a strong support of pure research and links with the university sector are seen as crucial. In 1992, Glaxo supported University Chairs and projects to some £7 million. The location of its laboratory in North Carolina is in the 'research triangle' between three of the State's most prestigious universities and the Stevenage development resembles a university campus. Such a commitment to pure research underlines the long-term view of R&D strategy. This is inevitable in an industry where it is not uncommon for the development process to take between 10 and 15 years. An important feature here is the good relationship that the management of the company have deliberately fostered with City financial institutions.

The development of Zantac by Glaxo owed much to initial work carried out by a British scientist, James Black, whose findings were published in 1972. Black was working for the US firm Smithkline French, who were the first to the market place with their anti-ulcer drug Tagamet in 1978. The scientists at Glaxo were convinced that by reworking Black's studies they could develop their own superior product. An intensive research programme and product trial resulted in Zantac being launched in 1981. The research and development period for Zantac was highly concentrated, with a subsequent shortening of product lead-time. Effective use was made of patent protection to differentiate the product from its main rival.

The success of Zantac as a product was invariably linked to its acceptance in the USA. Apart from its being the largest market for drugs there were fewer price controls than elsewhere and hence a greater potential for profits. Zantac was initially marketed in the USA by the Swiss company Hoffman LaRoche, well known in the American market through its own products, Librium and Valium, the world's biggest-selling tranquilizers. Zantac was priced higher than Tagamet and it is widely acknowledged that the marketing campaign was aggressive. Not only were the superior claims of Zantac over Tagamet forcibly made, but Glaxo emphasized the negative side-effects of the rival drug. Subsequent pressure by the US regulatory body, the Food and Drug Administration, has resulted in Glaxo withdrawing some of the claims made concerning the superiority of Zantac. Nonetheless, Zantac took the US market from Tagamet to become the world's best-selling drug. At its peak, sales of Zantac accounted for some 40 per cent of Glaxo's total sales.

However, by the mid-1990s there were a number of serious threats to the market dominance of both Zantac and Zovirax.

- In 1993 a new administration was elected to power in the USA. A key policy of the new administration is the reduction in healthcare costs, which were the highest of any nation. There was considerable pressure to reduce the costs for the elderly, who generally have inadequate insurance and must pay the full cost of treatment. There was also pressure to bring down health insurance premiums and to reduce the cost of state-funded health care. The drug companies, who charged premium prices for their products, became an obvious target. The US government encouraged the purchase of cheaper generic drugs developed in lower-cost labour markets such as Puerto Rico. The threat at the time to both Glaxo and Wellcome was significant given their reliance on the sales performance of Zantac and Zovirax in the American market.
- The above threat was magnified by the expiry of the patents on both Zantac and Zovirax in

1997. This meant that others could enter the market, producing generic versions of the drugs at a much lower price. This in turn forces the originator to lower their prices to remain competitive, with the risk of a substantial fall in profits. Glaxo Wellcome attempted a number of legal manoeuvres to retain their patents, to no avail. The company also attempted to gain some ground on the generic drugs manufacturers by negotiating a deal with the manufacturer, Novopharm, to produce Zantac ahead of the patent expiry date. Nonetheless the initial impact of the expiry of the patent was a 3 per cent fall in total sales for Glaxo Wellcome in 1997.

There were a number of factors that mitigated these threats:

- The merger itself had resulted in both Glaxo and Wellcome reducing their dependence on a narrow range of products, and enabled the new company to have a broader product portfolio.
- As well as saving substantially on R&D costs, the merger resulted in a global reduction of labour costs, with 7500 jobs being lost.
- New opportunities had opened up in emerging markets, which by 1997 accounted for 15 per cent of world sales in pharmaceutical products.
- The management consider that their continued investment in R&D enables them to replace Zantac and Zovirax with other best-selling drugs. Since 1990, Glaxo Wellcome has launched 24 new products, which in 1997 represented 34 per cent of sales. The company has great hopes for Imigran in the treatment of migraine and Epivir in the treatment of Aids. Other developments include drugs to alleviate the side-effects of chemotherapy and considerable investment in the development of gene guns to deliver vaccines and treat cancers.
- In January 2000, the company announced a merger with Smithkline Beecham to create Glaxo SmithKline to take effect by the summer of 2000. The merger would create a company with an R&D budget of around £2.4 billion. Within a month, the deal was called off. ■

(Sources: Fagan, 1991; Connon, 1992; Kay, 1992; Buchan, 1993; *Economist* 25 Jan., 1995; Company Reports 1998, *Medical Marketing and Media*, May 1999)

products, new markets, and new means through which products are made and markets reached, based around new forms of organization and new means of managing people. Entrepreneurs have therefore been key figures in business history.

KEY CONCEPT 5.4
Entrepreneurship

Entrepreneurship is the activity of entrepreneurs, who are responsible for the creation of new products, processes, services and markets. They develop new ways of doing business, create new forms of organization and new way of managing people. Entrepreneurship is the act of making such changes happen through the mobilization of physical, financial, human and information resources. Such resources are often combined in new ways to achieve improved levels of perfomance. Entrepreneurs are usually willing to lead and take responsibility for their actions.

Table **5.4** A definition of entrepreneurship

A desire to own and be accountable for one's performance.
A willingness to engage in a rich and broad network of learning situations and to incorporate learning into one's ongoing activity.
A fundamental motivation to be successful and make a contribution for one's self and/or other groups within society as a whole.
The capability and willingness to move beyond the accepted and orthodox if such methods are failing to achieve sufficient value addedness.
An intellectual and skill-based capability to weigh up the riskiness of innovative courses of action and the ability to manage such risk for the benefit of self and others.
The capacity to focus activity upon the achievement of tangible and recognised outputs.
A willingness to move ahead and innovate without being constrained overly by currently available resources.
Source: 'Entrepreneurial activity and entrepreneurship within higher education', Durham University Business School, DTI Conference, 1998.

A broad definition of entrepreneurship is presented in Table 5.4.

The centrality of entrepreneurs to business development has led researchers to seek out those characteristics that make a successful entrepreneur. The research has shown that entrepreneurs are hard workers, risk takers, outsiders, but, not surprisingly, no distinctive set of personality traits that adequately define entrepreneurs has emerged. Perhaps the most significant finding was that which suggested that successful entrepreneurs had a high need for achievement and a moderate need for power, while the less successful had a low need for achievement and a positively high or low need for power (McClelland, 1961). The message from this research is clear: entrepreneurs are achievers but those seeking entrepreneurial activity only as a means of achieving power over others are likely to fail.

For a time, the role of the entrepreneur in business was understated as the focus turned to the growth and activities of the large corporation. However, the entrepreneur re-emerged in the 1980s as a hero figure, when both government and the media highlighted the success of certain businesses when those around were failing. Success through a general recession made household names of such as Alan Sugar at Amstrad, Anita Roddick at the Body Shop and Richard Branson at Virgin.

The success of certain entrepreneurs to rise above the recession prompted a 1980s UK government, already committed to a free market, to encourage even more entrepreneurial activity in the form of small business development. We deal at length with issues pertaining to small business development in Chapter 3. Suffice it to say here that not every small firm is entrepreneurial, since many merely replicate existing forms of business. Becoming self-employed to run a newsagent's shop has little to do with innovation and entrepreneurship. Nonetheless, people were encouraged to develop 'enterprise' as a route to prosperity both for themselves and the nation. The concept of 'enterprise culture' emerged as important government rhetoric supported by a number of significant policy changes to deregulate markets, reconstruct the public sector along business lines, influence curriculum in schools, and to remove impediments to enterprise. Such impediments were seen as an obstructive trade union movement and a welfare state, which was seen to offer little incentive for people to be self-reliant. The Department of Trade and Industry was given the official slogan 'the Department of Enterprise'. Such policy changes and the ideologies behind them are examined in more detail in Chapters 2 and 3.

However, the focus upon small firms and the view of the entrepreneur as the exclusive province of the small firms' sector has detracted from the importance of entrepreneurship in large businesses. In his study of General Motors, Sears, Dupont and Standard Oil, which we referred to in our discussion of structure in Chapter 3, Chandler stressed the importance for managers to be able to see beyond the daily problems of controlling a large corporation and develop new business ideas for the future. More attention is now being paid to the role of the entrepreneur in large firms. However, the qualities that give rise to a successful entrepreneur are not necessarily those of an 'organization man'. This may make entrepreneurs difficult to manage, an issue we discuss later in the chapter.

It is our view that all firms irrespective of size need the introduction of new ideas to survive. In Chapter 4 we introduced the concept of entrepreneurial decision-making as a type of strategy employed by all organizations at some stage. Whether innovation through entrepreneurship is most successful in a small or a large setting, or how it is best organized, are questions we leave to our discussion of organizational aspects. We turn now to environmental issues in innovation.

The environmental aspects of innovation

Four aspects of our model are particularly significant here. We will look first at the relationship between innovation and the economy, which leads logically to a discussion on the role of the state in encouraging innovation. This in turn leads to the differences in the way nations approach innovation, which we examine by looking at cultural influences. There is a clear relationship between technology and innovation, which we acknowledge in our assessment of the contending influences of technological development and the market place. We will not discuss the relationship between innovation and the labour market here. It is an important relationship as the skills of the workforce and their attitude towards change, more especially changes in technology, are crucial to the successful implementation of innovation. These themes are developed in Chapters 2 and 8 and the relationship is explored in Case 5.5. A core element in all these discussions is the role of the economy, and the belief that innovation stimulates economic growth.

The role of the economy

There have been many attempts to link innovation with economic growth. In general, innovation is perceived as the means through which economic regeneration occurs. As such it has held a particular fascination for those who see government investment in research and development as a positive strategy for tackling the problems of economic decline. More specifically economists have attempted to prove links between innovation and such factors as per capita growth and export competitiveness. In this section we will view briefly the general debate which sees innovation as the key mechanism in long-wave economic cycles and then examine attempts to identify more specific relationships.

Innovation and long-wave cycles

The relationship between innovation and economic activity owes much to the work of the Russian economist Kondratieff. He put forward the view that economic activity exhibits regular long-term cycles of growth and depression, followed by a further period of growth and so on (Kondratieff, 1935). Each cycle is characterized by a particular form of economic activity; thus the period 1785 to 1842 was dominated by iron ore, coke and the cotton industry, whereas the following period to 1897 centred around the development of the railways. If we extend the cycles to the present day, we can see periods of economic activity based around electricity, chemicals and the automobile and more recently focusing upon aerospace, electronics and computers.

The explanation for the operation of these cycles has been taken up by a

> ### KEY CONCEPT 5.5
> #### Long-wave economic cycles
>
> Long waves are used to denote cycles of economic growth and decline spanning over 40 years. The idea gained popularity through the work of Kondratieff who saw upswings in the economy related to the development of particular industries over time and down-swings as a result of saturated and contested markets. Schumpeter argued that movement out of economic depression is the function of bursts of innovation creating new products and processes, which re-stimulate markets. Long-wave supporters argue that such cycles not only repeat themselves, but are regular in shape and length. Critics argue that the whole approach is far too deterministic.

number of economists. For Schumpeter the key was innovation. Each phase of economic recovery can be attributed to clusters of innovations, enabling capitalism to evolve and usher in a new period of prosperity (Schumpeter, 1939). He thought that most innovations occurred when the economic climate appeared more favourable, thus acting as a stimulus for entrepreneurial activity. However, some believe that innovations only occur in the depths of depression, when profits are so low that entrepreneurs are stimulated into risk-taking ventures (Mensch, 1979).

The notion of economic cycles has generated considerable debate among economists and others, who, despite the absence of hard data, have felt more than capable of contributing to the debate as to when the cycles begin, how long they last, and what the key innovations are. The problems with long waves are the task of identifying and dating the major innovations and the highly deterministic nature of cyclical activity, leaving some economists to view the theory as convenient rather than meaningful.

> The belief that mankind is in the grip of mysterious forces which it is powerless to change recurs in periods of stress and difficulty.
>
> (Brittan, 1983)

This may explain the resurgence of interest in long-wave theory in times of recession.

Innovation and specific measures of economic performance

A growing number of studies have been carried out in an attempt to provide hard data linking innovative activity and some measure of economic performance at the level of both national economies and the individual firm. Many of the studies highlight significant differences in measures of innovative activity between nations. We return to this theme when we discuss cultural and national differences later in the chapter. An indication of the types of study carried out is offered below.

KEY CONCEPT 5.6
Innovation and economic growth

There is considerable debate concerning the relationship between innovation and economic growth, both at the level of national economies and that of the individual firm. Several theories have been passed around the assumption that innovation leads to economic growth and has a key role in leading economies of out depression. Despite the plausibility of several of these claims, it is difficult to measure the precise impact of innovation on the economy or establish much in the way of causility. Indeed, as with many aspects of business, the isolation of a single factor such as innovation can present an oversimplified view of the complex nature of most business interactions. Nevertheless, the importance accorded by governments to innovation as the stimulus for economic growth has resulted in considerable state intervention in this area.

- There is evidence to suggest that investments in R&D, particularly those relating to technical change, are the major cause of improvements in productivity and output. Some studies suggest that increasing the quantity of either capital equipment and or labour are by themselves insufficient for economies to grow and remain competitive and as much as a 90 per cent improvement can be attributed to process innovations (Solow, 1957).

- There is evidence to suggest that the development of new products leads to improved market performance (a selection of evidence is presented in Souder and Sherman, 1994). Analysis of the performance of those companies that feature high on the DTI scoreboard (Tables 5.2 and 5.3) reveal that those companies with a high and rising investment in R&D generally perform better than those where R&D expenditure is falling. However, this is not always the case. General Motors was the world's biggest investor in R&D in 1992, spending £3.1 billion, yet, over the same period, made a loss and halved its dividend to shareholders. This illustrates the difficulty of examining R&D in isolation. R&D expenditure by General Motors may well have contributed to product and process improvements, but these could have been negated by other factors such as the stagnant US car market or a lack of management strategy to capitalize upon the investment. Furthermore, the time horizon for the investment may be such that the pay-back will be at some time in the future.

- Tables 5.5–5.8 represent a series of tables and graphs pertaining to patents. As with published expenditure, patents represent an easily measured output of R&D. Table 5.5 examines the number of patent applications per million population filed in the home country by eight manufacturing nations from 1979 to 1989. The same study revealed a correlation between patent applications and GDP and between patent applications and manufacturing output. The clear fact to emerge from the graph is the prolific patent behaviour of the Japanese. In 1989 the Japanese filed 2580 applications per million population, more than the rest put together and five times that of Germany. The dominant market position of Glaxo

Wellcome's drugs Zantac and Zovirax is in part a function of patent protection, and the expiry of the patent resulted in other manufacturers entering the market (Case 5.1).

● A correlation also exists between the number of registered patents and export performance. Between 1937 and 1975 West German patents registered in the USA outnumbered those from any other foreign country. During the same period, the former West Germany was the leading exporter to the USA (Rothwell and Zegveld, 1981). Since 1975, Germany has been replaced by Japan on both counts. In 1987 and 1991, the top three companies receiving patents in the USA were all Japanese (Table 5.6). In fact, eight Japanese companies feature in the top 20 for 1987 and five out of the top nine in 1991. By 1997 the picture had changed. IBM was the leading company in terms of US patent activity, with Motorola and the US government prominent. This may reflect the continuing recession in Japan as well as the increase in investment amongst US firms. It should not be forgotten that, despite the recession, Japanese firms make up seven out of the top 11 companies. Table 5.7 shows the US patents granted to automobile firms between 1986 and 1990. Once more the Japanese dominate despite General Motors showing a 50 per cent increase on the previous four-year period and Chrysler a 100 per cent increase on the same period. Both Volkswagen and BMW show a decline in patenting activity, although Table 5.8 shows the relative dominance of Germany amongst other European countries.

● There is some evidence to suggest that consumers appear willing to pay more for goods of superior technical quality. Once again Germany features, this time in comparison with Britain. Between 1971 and 1975 Germany's share of exports to OECD countries was 22 per cent compared to Britain's 10 per cent, despite the fact that the unit value of German exports was 40 per cent greater (Rothwell and Zegveld, 1981). The assumption here is that investment in improving the quality of goods will pay back in the form of increased sales.

Despite the research findings and the persuasive pleas for investment in R&D, the links between innovation and economic performance remain speculative.

KEY CONCEPT 5.7
Patents

A patent is a legal device that enables the holder to maintain a monopoly in an invention for a stated period, which in Britain stands at 20 years. The state grants this monopoly in return for a full disclosure of the invention. Such a system exists in all industrialized countries. A patent protects the inventor from would-be copiers and enables him or her to exploit the invention for profit and/or the good of society. It is believed that the benefits of such a system will actively encourage invention and innovation. A patent holder may issue manufacturing licences to third parties and thus derive further financial benefit.

Table **5.5** Patent applications filed by residents in the National Patent Office per million population

Year	Australia	Germany	France	Japan	Korea	Spain	UK	US
1979	327	502	211	1300	27	51	348	269
1980	448	466	204	1419	32	50	350	273
1981	425	484	202	1629	34	45	369	271
1982	435	497	196	1780	40	43	364	272
1983	451	515	204	1909	40	39	353	253
1984	461	532	206	2135	49	46	337	261
1985	415	528	218	2270	66	38	347	266
1986	361	527	219	2388	88	43	354	270
1987	400	517	228	2546	117	44	350	280
1988	370	519	222	2518	136	47	360	305
1989	407	503	224	2580	166	54	345	331

Source: Needle and Needle (1991)

Table **5.7** US patents granted to automobile firms, 1986–90

Toyota	1218
Honda	1218
Nissan	1054
General Motors	993
Mazda	568
Ford	399
Mercedes	377
Chrysler	176
Mitsubishi	123
VW	97
BMW	62

Source: Narin (1993)

Table **5.8** US patents granted to European firms by country as a percentage of all European

	1963	1985
Germany	34	42
UK	26	16
France	12	15
The rest	28	27

Source: SPRU Database, quoted in Bowen *et al.* (1992)

Table **5.6** Corporation and organizations receiving US patents by rank order 1987–1997

1987			1991			1997		
Rank	Corporation	No. of patents	Rank	Corporation	No. of patents	Rank	Corporation	No. of patents
1	Canon K. K.	847	1	Toshiba	1114	1	IBM	1724
2	Hitachi Ltd	845	2	Mitsubishi Denki	936	2	Canon	1381
3	Toshiba Corp.	823	3	Hitachi	927	3	NEC Corporation	1095
4	General Electric Corp.	779	4	Eastman Kodak	863	4	Motorola Inc	1058
5	US Philips Corp.	687	5	Canon	823	5	U.S. Government	935
6	Westinghouse Electric Corp.	652	6	General Electric	809	6(tie)	Fijitsu Limited	903
7	IBM Corp.	591	7	Fuji Photo	731	6(tie)	Hitachi	903
8	Siemens A.G.	539	8	US Philips	650	8	Mitsubishi	892
9	Mitsubishi Denki K.K.	518	9	Motorola	613	9	Toshiba Corporation	862
10	RCA Corp.	504				10	Sony	859
11	Fiju Photo Film Co., Ltd	494				11	Eastman Kodak Company	795
12	Dow Chemical Co.	469						
13	E.I. du Pont de Nemours & Co.	419						
14	Motorola, Inc.	414						
15	AT&T Co.	406						
16	Honda Motor Co., Ltd	395						
17	NEC Corp.	375						
	Toyota Jidosha K.K.	375						
19	Bayer A.G.	371						
20	General Motors Corp.	370						

Source: 1987 – Intellectual Property Owners Inc., March 1988; 1991 – *Intellectual Property Newsletter* Volume 16 Issue No. 1. January 1993; 1997 – US Patent and Trademark Office

One difficulty is our inability to measure innovation. Indicators that have been used, such as patents and the amount of money a firm has invested in its R&D activities, can at best be considered a rough guide. For example, a patent may be registered and then never used to produce anything of value; improvements in products and processes can originate as much from individual inventors and equipment users as they can from organized R&D departments.

We have already noted in the case of General Motors that significant expenditure is no guarantee of short-term financial success. More significantly the attempts to isolate innovation may give a false impression. The export success of 'upper range' German cars such as Mercedes Benz and BMW may well be attributed to the technical superiority of the product when compared to other cars in the same range. Such an explanation fits the research findings identified above. There is another explanation. Both firms have been particularly active in carefully targeted advertising campaigns, which not only stress the technical superiority of their product but also attempt to give the product an image of exclusivity and high status. To what extent are their sales attributable to technical innovation and how much to an effective advertising campaign? This illustration confirms the interrelationship of innovation and marketing that we identified earlier. It also emphasizes a key theme in this book: that business activities are interrelated and there are dangers in viewing one activity, such as innovation, in isolation.

Throughout this section we have made reference to the role of state intervention, and it is to this aspect we now turn our attention. We will view the role of governments in general terms and we then explore how governments in different countries operate with respect to the stimulation of innovation, with a specific note on the UK.

The role of the state

In almost every country, the state has a significant involvement in innovation. Table 5.9 shows government-funded R&D as a percentage of GDP in six major countries. Three main reasons may be given as motivation for this involvement:

● Using the kind of economic evidence presented in the last section, there would appear to be a clear belief that innovation and entrepreneurship are major factors in economic expansion and export competitiveness.

● We have already noted that investment in innovation is both long term and high risk. The mechanism of the free market may be inadequate in generating those basic innovations upon which economic expansion is based, hence the need for state subsidy when individual companies are reluctant to invest.

● Intervention is often necessary for political and strategic as well as for social reasons. In Britain and the USA defence spending forms a major part of all expenditure on innovation, as Table 5.9 shows. Many countries have seen space exploration as a goal of national importance and prestige, and the same could be said for the British and French governments'

Table **5.9** Government-funded R&D as a percentage of GDP, 1988

	Total	Defence	Civil
UK	0.96	0.42	0.54
France	1.37	0.51	0.86
Germany	1.05	0.13	0.92
Italy	0.80	0.08	0.72
Japan	0.47	0.02	0.45
USA	1.23	0.83	0.40

Source: OECD Main Science and Technology Indicators, quoted in Bowen *et al.* (1992).

involvement with the development of the supersonic jet airliner, Concorde. Investment in the nuclear fuel industry is viewed by several governments as a desirable energy strategy.

In the UK the state is involved in innovation in a number of different ways. It invests in R&D in individual firms, government research establishments and in universities. It has established the legal protection of inventions through the patent system. Various state departments are actively concerned in the stimulation of innovation; currently the Department of Trade and Industry proudly announces itself as 'The Department for Enterprise'. The state's financial support is clearly biased towards technological innovation in the manufacturing and defence industries but exhortations for innovation and enterprise are usually aimed at all firms in all sectors and we have already noted the state's commitment to the establishment of an 'enterprise culture'. Occasionally such exhortations are transformed into government policies and schemes, such as those aimed at innovation through small business development (Chapter 3).

The activities of the state in subsidizing, protecting and encouraging innovation provide an excellent illustration of the interrelationship between the state and business at a more general level. In this section, we attempt a classification of the types of intervention specifically concerned with innovation and examine the associated problems.

Types of state intervention in innovation

We examine state intervention under six main headings; procurement, subsidies, education and training, patents and licensing, restrictive and enabling laws and, finally, import controls. These types of innovation occur even where the government has expressed its ideological opposition to interference in the workings of the free market.

Procurement

The need of the state for certain products has stimulated research in many areas. UK private industry only funds a half of all R&D activity, but carries out

Case 5.2: INMOS

The Inmos saga ... provides 1980s evidence of Britain's still unbridged 'two cultures' gap, through politicians' ignorance of technology and technologists' naivety about politics.

(*Guardian*, 3 December 1985)

Inmos has been a hostage of political incompetence, City misunderstanding and corporate chaos.

(*Guardian*, 31 March 1987)

In 1978 under a Labour government the National Enterprise Board (NEB), in its role as an industrial holding company, invested £50 million in a newly formed company, INMOS, to develop, manufacture and market semiconductors, popularly known as microchips. The company was formed by a small group of capitalist entrepreneurs, including an Englishman and two Americans, and was based originally in the USA. NEB accepted the proposals of the new company even though it had no product or even design for one at the time. The motivation behind the government's involvement was the desire for Britain to develop its own semiconductor industry, not only because this was seen as a valuable and growing market, but also as part of a wider strategy for the development of the government-backed electronics industry. This included at the time such firms as Ferranti and ICL and the industry was identified as central to the country's economic development through the 1980s. An important factor was the decision to join a race for the development of a new form of microchip, which would perform the functions of several types of semiconductors on a single chip. This creation of a 'minicomputer' on a single chip was seen as the next development in 'Very Large Scale Integration' (VLSI) technology.

At the time, the semiconductor market was dominated by the Americans with Texas Instruments leading the field. The Japanese, however, were launching a collaborative effort by leading companies to develop the next generation of VLSI. By contrast, European firms had a weak position in the market and prospects looked none too good. The management of INMOS decided that its main strategy was to push ahead and be the first company to produce the revolutionary chip, its particular version to be known as the Transputer. In the meantime it was decided to design and manufacture conventional semiconductors and the company set up two

production plants at Colorado Springs in the USA, designated the corporate headquarters, and at Newport in Wales. The British operation was controlled from a research base in Bristol. INMOS saw its success in a highly volatile industry as being based upon, first, the development of an entirely new product acceptable to the majority of users as the best, and second, on high-volume sales to offset the high development costs.

At the outset INMOS faced a number of difficulties. There was scepticism in the City, among the civil servants, from some trade unionists and from potential American customers wary of a state-controlled company. There was opposition from within the ranks of the Labour Party, especially left-wing members who objected to the three founders acquiring such a large stake in the company and in particular to the large amounts of money being paid to the two Americans. More significantly, several experts in the field felt that insufficient investment had been made, given the nature of the company's strategy. Worse problems were to follow with the defeat of the Labour government at the hands of the Conservatives in the 1979 election. The incoming government were less than enthusiastic about INMOS, preferring to give support to those companies like ICL that were already established in their field. Moreover, there were proposals to limit the activities of NEB and an ideological commitment to privatization. This not only placed the future of INMOS in some doubt, but there were delays in necessary funding at a crucial time in the company's development.

In 1984, after investing an estimated £100 million in the company, the government sold its interests to Thorn EMI for £95 million. This followed a well-established pattern in the microchip industry, that of small innovative companies being bought up by large multinational organizations. In Thorn's case it was seen in the City as a hasty acquisition, after the company had been refused in its attempts to merge with British Aerospace. The following year the microchip market suffered a downturn and INMOS was forced to cut back its activities by 20 per cent, with lay-offs in both Britain and America. Later in 1985, Thorn EMI announced that it was looking for a development partner for INMOS, possibly from Japan, and was willing to relinquish up to 49 per cent of its shares.

There can be little doubt that the ideological and political differences, the selling of INMOS at a crucial stage in its development, and the continued uncertainty of its role within the Thorn EMI stable arrested the company's growth. However, the Transputer was developed successfully, it was ahead of its rivals and began to sell well. Thorn EMI did manage to sell INMOS, which became part of SGS-Thomson, now known as STM. In 1992 the company joined forces with QPL International, a Hong Kong based firm, to develop high-tech digital and mixed signal technology to customize the manufacture of microchips. By 1998, competition, especially from South Korea, oversupply and the fall in demand for microchips led to the company calling in the administrators to run its three factories in South Wales. ▪

(*Sources*: Stopford *et al.*, 1980; McClean and Rowlands, 1985; *Guardian*, 1985–87, *Financial Times*, 1998–9)

over two-thirds, the difference being linked to government contracts (Bowen *et al.*, 1992). Defence work offers the clearest illustration with implications not only for the armaments industry itself, but also in electronics, computing and aerospace. Businesses in the USA have seen the armed forces as a very large and very stable market. There is a view that the goals of business and the military have become intertwined and form an important part of the image-building that goes on between ideologically opposed nations in a cold war (Galbraith, 1972). The significant political changes that have occurred in the former Soviet Union and Eastern Europe have certainly altered this position. In Britain the needs of the National Health Service have stimulated developments in the pharmaceutical industry and in most nations the fear of disappearing natural resources has led to government-backed research to find synthetic materials.

Subsidies

Subsidies to individual firms occur in the form of investments, grants and tax concessions. We have seen how special policies exist, such as those to encourage innovation through small firms. Most subsidies aim to support a particular form of research and development. For example, EU funding, particularly through the European Social Fund, is biased towards the use of more innovative business solutions, particularly in IT.

The coordination of the UK policy of selective intervention has been placed in the hands of the British Technology Group. This body was set up in 1981 to incorporate both the National Research and Development Council and the National Enterprise Board. It seems clear that the government wishes to align itself with more progressive industries and establish a more proactive role. The National Enterprise Board was often viewed as reactive and was all too often identified with policies to prop up ailing industries, as in the giving of financial support to British Leyland and Rolls Royce. The development of INMOS presented in Case 5.2 illustrates the role of British governments in subsidizing R&D and the dilemmas which often accompany it.

Education and training

There is an underlying assumption that state investment in education and pure science will have a significant impact in increasing the level of innovation and thus benefit both the economy and society. The relationship between primary research and the knowledge-based activities of higher education institutions is supposedly one of the key features of the modern age. Galbraith observed of educators and scientists that they 'stand in relation to the industrial system much as did the banking and financial community in the early stages of industrial development' (Galbraith, 1972, p. 283)

There are certain well-publicized developments in both Britain and the USA that lend substance to the post-industrial society thesis. Developments in 'Silicon Valley' in California and, in the UK, the growth of the science parks around major universities such as Cambridge show the relationship between industrial research and major universities with a reputation for science. The growth of some American high-technology companies such as Hewlett-Packard in Palo Alto, California is clearly associated with this phenomenon, as is the development of a network of businesses in computing and related fields in the vicinity of Cambridge. We have noted in Case 5.1 that Glaxo chose to locate one of its USA research laboratories in the midst of universities in North Carolina. Such illustrations support the view that competitive endeavour amongst firms in close proximity to each other is a spur to economically successful innovations and that there is synergy to be gained both through such competition and through collaboration with the university sector.

In spite of such developments, British institutions of higher education are often subjected to financial stringencies as part of the government's determination to reduce public expenditure. On the positive side this has, in many cases, pushed industry and universities much closer together. Some universities like Warwick have generated significant funding from industry. The critics of this type of development see a danger of weakening the primary research base and restricting university research to projects related to the very specific requirements of a limited number of companies. This could restrict opportunities for breakthroughs in basic technology considered essential for industrial regeneration. The experience of Warwick would refute such claims. As well as attracting significant external funding it has established itself as a leading research institution as rated by the UK universities 'Research Assessment Exercise'.

The state sometimes intervenes in skills training and comparative research of training in Britain, and Germany ascribes its advantage in product and process innovation to its superior craft training schemes (Steedman and Wagner, 1987). Clearly a skilled workforce is one that can adapt readily to technical changes. Skills shortages in the United Kingdom may have been responsible for the relatively slow adoption of computerized aids to manufacturing, such as CNC machines. This aspect illustrates the interaction between innovation and the labour force in our model. The effectiveness of innovation depends upon it being supported by employees with the requisite skills. The development of new processes may prove even more costly if they remain idle waiting for the skills of the workforce to catch up, as Rolls Royce found to its cost in the early 1970s. The development of the high-performance jet engine, the RB 211, encountered many problems. Although the focus was upon the mounting costs of the project, costs which almost forced the company out of business, a contributory factor was the lack of expertise to overcome the many technical difficulties which arose at the development stage. In the 1970s many firms invested in computer hardware and software in the belief that this would change their business overnight. In some of these companies the systems were under-utilized, as insufficient consideration had been given to training the employees.

Patents and licensing

A patent is a legal device that enables the holder to maintain a monopoly in an invention for a stated period, which in Britain stands at 20 years. In exchange for granting this monopoly, the owner of the invention must make available its details to the general public. The patent system operates in almost every country in the world, including the People's Republic of China. The stated benefits of such a system are, first, that it actively encourages new developments by offering protection to the patent holder against others copying the invention, as illustrated in Case 5.1 with Zantac and Zovirax. Second, by revealing the details of the invention, it encourages further inventions and innovative activity along similar lines. Third, it prevents the duplication of research, and fourth, it ensures that the benefits of research are passed on to society. A real benefit to the patent holder is the opportunity to issue manufacturing licences, as illustrated in Case 5.3 by the licence bought by Black and Decker to manufacture and sell the Workmate.

A firm holding a patent on a particular type of manufacturing process may allow another firm in the same business to use that process upon the payment of an agreed fee. In the case of major inventions this can be an important source of revenue for the patent holder. The revolutionary method for the production of glass, the 'float process', was developed by the St Helens firm of Pilkington Brothers Ltd in the early 1960s, since when licences have been granted to glass manufacturers all over the world enabling them to use the same process. Licensing is clearly a vital source of revenue for some companies. In 1991 Texas Instruments made $415 million from licensing its semiconductor patents, while in the same year its manufacturing activities made a loss of $203 million. In certain cases the law has had to intervene to enforce the issue of licences where it was felt that some companies were operating an unfair monopoly. This occurred in the case of Roche, the Swiss pharmaceutical company. In 1971 the British Patent Comptroller ordered Hoffman-La Roche, as the company was then called, to grant licences to two British firms, Berk Pharmaceuticals and DDSA Ltd, for the manufacture of the tranquilizers librium and valium. Despite frequent requests the Swiss drugs company had repeatedly refused manufacturing licences on the grounds of the safety standards of the finished product. However, the British patent system held that the refusal to grant licences gave the Swiss company an unfair monopoly in the drugs industry (the Hoffman-La Roche case in Stopford et al., 1980 has further details).

Since that time, the law relating to licensing has been amended and compulsory licences may now be issued only in the case of the non-manufacture of the product by the patent holder or in cases where the product is not

Case 5.3: The Workmate

In 1973 a Design Council Award was made to Ronald Hickman, the inventor of the Workmate. This was only the third time such an award had been made for a tool. The Workmate is a combination of a work bench, a sawing horse and a vice, but whose versatility as a tool is much greater than the sum of its parts. It is small, lightweight, and easily stored. The device is bought in great numbers by DIY enthusiasts, but also by professional carpenters and building firms.

Hickman, who had received only a high school education and possessed no technical qualifications, came to Britain in 1955, working first as a bookkeeper in a music store and then with Ford Motor Company in the styling department. By 1958 he had been doing freelance design work for Lotus cars and eventually joined them as a designer. He was entirely responsible for the Lotus Elan, and in five years had become the design director of the company. He reached the stage where the job was taking all his time, and in 1967 he left Lotus to form his own company Mate Tools.

The idea for the company arose during his time at Lotus. He had moved house and had invented a device to assist him in building fitted furniture to his own design. After various modifications the Workmate Mark 1 emerged, which he patented and sold through mail order, advertising in such magazines as *Do-it-yourself*, *Homemaker*, *Radio Times* and newspapers such as the *Daily Mail*. Sales started in 1968 and the product became an instant success. The demand for the product was greater than Mate Tools could satisfy. As a result several imitators appeared and Hickman began to look for a larger firm to take on manufacture and sales.

The patent protection saw off the imitators, sometimes after court action and damages awarded to Hickman. In 1972, Hickman granted Black and Decker an exclusive licence to manufacture the Workmate which was now redesigned as Mark 2.

When the Mark 2 was launched in 1972 the demand was so great that all stocks were immediately exhausted. The Mark 1 had achieved an annual sales growth of 120 per cent and under Black and Decker sales of the Mark 2 were growing at over 138 per cent per year. By 1976 over one million had been sold and by 1983 the product was being manufactured in Britain, France, Italy, Spain, Canada, Japan and Eire. Mate Tools still sold the Workmate itself but bought them ready made from Black and Decker.

(*Source*: Reports of Patent Cases, 1983)

manufactured in this country. The main idea behind such laws in most countries is to stimulate the development and use of the invention in that country and hence assist local businesses.

Restrictive and enabling laws

Most countries possess laws that control manufacturing standards and relate to such aspects as safety and pollution. Not only do these laws ensure that innovations conform to certain standards, but they aim to encourage research into socially desirable end-products such as car engines with low fuel consumption or car exhaust systems that restrict pollution into the atmosphere. The ends are not only socially desirable but can have an effect on business performance as well. A firm that meets government standards of product quality enters the market place with additional competitive edge. As we see in Chapter 6, there is a growing trend in Britain for firms to show that they have met British Standards of quality assurance. There is a strong prediction that firms with strong policies on quality, like Marks & Spencer, will, in the future, only deal with suppliers that have met these standards.

Such regulations can benefit some firms but handicap others. The determination on the part of the 1993 USA administration to reduce the healthcare budget posed a threat to Glaxo Wellcome (Case 5.1), but may lead to the development of cheaper generic drugs. The use of restrictive laws has been greatest in the USA and there is a lobby that sees a danger that excessive government regulation may hold back technological innovation and hence the country's economic growth. However, as with the relationship between innovation and economic growth, there is a difficulty in establishing a direct causal link between such laws and innovative activity at the level of the firm. As an illustration, we can see that increases in the price of oil in 1973 resulted, in both Britain and the USA, in new laws relating to speed limits and exhaust emission. However, the ensuing trend in motor manufacture towards the design and manufacture of smaller cars would almost certainly have occurred in response to increased oil prices irrespective of any legislation.

Import controls

The theory here is that restriction on the imports from other countries will have a beneficial effect in stimulating research in the home country or intensifying the search for a substitute product or process. Import controls enforced by Japanese governments since the Second World War has often been cited as the major impetus to considerable innovations by Japanese businesses. There is, however, a danger that other countries may well retaliate and impose their own restrictions. Concern about the trade imbalance between the USA and Japan, in favour of Japan, has resulted in presidential delegations to Tokyo and agreements on import quotas. The Americans themselves have in the past been fond of using import controls and the development of the synthetic fibre industry in the USA owes much to restrictions on the import of woollen products. The GATT agreements and the creation of the World Trade Association have been part of the process to bring an end to such import controls (see Chapter 2 for more details).

Some problems with state intervention in innovation

We have seen that the main motive for state intervention to encourage and support innovative activity is the desire to improve economic performance. We have also seen the difficulties of showing a direct relationship between investment in innovation and economic growth, whether measured at national or organizational levels. There are other difficulties with the state's involvement and we identify these below.

An over-reliance upon state funding may have serious repercussions at times of reductions in government expenditure. It is noticeable from Table 5.9 that Japan, despite its commitment to innovation, has relatively low levels of government-funded R&D, firms preferring to rely on generating their own investment income.

A major difficulty lies in the ability of government employees to make decisions in highly specialized technical and scientific areas, and decisions that are in the best interests of the business community as a whole. Government support may well be important in stimulating innovation but the critical skills and knowledge reside in the firms themselves or the higher education sector. For intervention to be successful, extensive consultation is required and there needs to be freedom for individuals to pursue their own research goals, otherwise there is a danger that intervention can be misdirected. Several highly publicized government-backed ventures such as Concorde or gas-cooled nuclear reactors have not met with the success predicted for them as a result of these difficulties. In 1985, with much publicity, the US government launched its proposals for the Strategic Defence Initiative, a missile defence system in outer space. The initiative was to give a boost to the USA computer industry and, in Britain, firms and universities looked forward to lucrative research contracts. The project was officially cancelled in 1993, partly as a result of a changing world political scene, but mainly as a result of the impracticality of the project in the first place.

The issue of freedom raises the most fundamental questions of an ideological kind and is especially troubling for those governments committed to *laissez-faire* economic policies. As we saw in the INMOS case, the British government was at the same time pursuing a policy of support through the British Technology Group, while planning to sell the company to the private sector. Such conflict of interests may well be detrimental to innovation since political considerations may come to dominate business development. Underpinning many of the difficulties outlined above is the view that governments have the power to constrain innovation and entrepreneurial activity by bureaucratic interference and restrictive legislation.

The direction of state intervention may raise conflicts within the agencies of the state as well as raising certain ethical issues. Proposals by one department such as the Department of Trade and Industry may be opposed by another, such as the Department of the Environment. For example, new developments in air travel, in particular the increased passenger-carrying capacity of aircraft, have necessitated airport expansion. This can be of benefit to the local economy by stimulating the job market and offering opportunities for local businesses. The same proposals will almost certainly be opposed by local residents and environmentalists. Such debates have surrounded the siting of London's third airport and the expansion of the airport at Heathrow to incorporate a fourth terminal complex. An overemphasis on government defence contracts may result in a loss of competitiveness in civil markets. This is a criticism levelled at GEC and Plessey. In 1988, defence contracts accounted for 33 per cent of GEC's overall turnover and 50 per cent of its turnover in electronics. Despite increases in its own R&D investment GEC spends only one-sixth the amount on R&D spent by one of its main European rivals, Siemens (*Independent*, 9 June 1992).

Issues like these deal with aspects of business ethics and question the purpose, direction and outcomes of innovative activity. Kumar is especially sceptical and he sums up the whole argument most appropriately:

> There are the familiar examples of the atomic bomb, other weapons of the biological and chemical kind, space exploration and large scale capital intensive technology with its propensity to pollute the environment and exhaust the world's supply of fossil fuels. Then there is the ingenious and expensive gadgetry of the

mass consumer industry with its built-in principle of planned obsolescence and marginal technical improvements ... medical research seems equally skewed in the direction of people with power to persuade and pay ... and 99 per cent of the knowledge effort of the industrial societies is devoted to the problems of the developed world.

(Kumar, 1978, p. 230)

Cultural and national differences

So convinced have we become of the dependence of the total social, political and economic order on technical development that national output of scientific discoveries and the rate of technological advance have begun to appear as the ultimate criterion of culture and different political and social systems are compared as facilitators of this kind of achievement.

(Burns and Stalker, 1966, p. 19)

Nearly all governments in the major industrialized countries have attempted to influence the direction of innovation in some way. While there is a danger of creating cultural stereotypes and perpetuating myths, the response of different governments has varied and different areas have been targeted. Not only this, but investment in R&D has been taken as an indicator of a nation's economic health and future prosperity. We will explore both these issues.

Britain has always been typified as placing emphasis on basic research with its application in defence, nuclear energy and space research. The spin-offs have been few and limited to a small range of companies, but making little impact on the manufacture of commercial products. The USA too has been criticized for emphasizing big projects in defence and aerospace, usually with government backing, and consequently with a corresponding reluctance on the part of private companies to invest in their own long-term projects. France on the other hand is typified as giving strong central direction and significant financial support to private industry in a bid to achieve scientific and technological independence, by creating a domestic supplier in every major world industry. The Germans conform to a less directive model but give specific assistance to those areas where market success is guaranteed, a policy particularly successful in the machine tool industry. In addition, we have already noted in Chapter 2 how much emphasis is placed in Germany upon supporting businesses through a national system of training, thus ensuring the workforce possesses the required skills to enable them both to develop and to exploit innovations. These particular views of the UK, USA, France and Germany are reinforced by the data presented in Table 5.9.

The greatest number of myths and stereotypes has probably been aimed at the Japanese (for further details see the section on Japanese management in Chapter 2). Japanese economic success has been linked to the import of key innovations and technologies from other industrialized nations, imperative for such a late industrial starter. The widespread belief soon developed that

Japanese businesses could not innovate. While there is little doubt that Japan has gained from bought-in technology, there is also clear evidence that Japan is now probably the world's most innovative industrial nation (Tables 5.5 and 5.6 support this view). The Japanese have made significant advances in machine tool technology and in particular in developments in automated plant and robotics, and in modifying existing technologies. While products such as the transistor and the video cassette recorder were invented elsewhere, the Japanese have shown considerable innovation in commercializing such products.

Japan has more of its workforce engaged in industrial R&D than Britain, France or Germany (Peck and Goto, 1982). Japanese businesses spend five times the amount on R&D that their British counterparts do (Bowen *et al.*, 1992). In addition to private investment, considerable assistance is offered by the Japanese Ministry of International Trade and Industry (MITI). MITI has been active in monitoring trends, in particular those pertaining to foreign investment. It has negotiated licences for Japanese companies and has acted as a channel through which the diffusion of innovation has occurred. At the same time the internal market has been jealously protected against incursions by foreign suppliers. The government role in R&D is thus far greater than Table 5.9 might suggest.

The two key strategies pursued by the Japanese are incrementalism and collaboration. The large number of patent applications by Japanese firms (Tables 5.5, 5.6 and 5.7) bear testimony to the importance Japanese firms place upon incremental developments. In terms of collaboration, MITI provided both encouragement and facilities to enable Japanese computer firms to engage in big budget research in the 1970s in areas such as VLSI (Very Large Systems Integration). Six of the largest computer companies were organized into two research associations to collaborate on new developments. The early focus of such collaborative ventures was the facilitation of access to existing research rather than the developments of new products. Firms collaborated in reverse engineering exercises to analyse the products of foreign competitors to determine how they were made. As the limits of such technological transfer were reached and as foreign firms became less inclined to license to Japanese firms, the focus of collaboration shifted to the development of entirely new products. While collaboration has been an undoubted feature of the Japanese approach to innovation, some research has suggested that the approach has not been without its problems. Mowery and Rosenberg (1989) suggest that some collaborative ventures between Japanese firms have been typified by a less than full disclosure by the participants and by some firms sending second-rate researchers. Additionally firms are less inclined to participate fully the closer the research is to the frontiers of technology. This view is supported by Callon (1995), whose analysis of collaborative research in computing concluded that the major firms had, to a certain extent, outgrown MITI, and wished to retain a considerable measure of independence to protect market advantage. He cites this as a major factor in the failure of Japanese collaborative research in advanced technologies. Further reference to Callon's study can be found in the section on Japanese management in Chapter 2.

An underlying theme in the comparative analysis of national attitudes to research and development is one developed in our earlier section on economic aspects of innovation: that trends in R&D investment are correlated with national economic growth. Under-investment in R&D has been cited as the main reason for the decline in American competitiveness in the 1970s (Hayes and Wheelwright, 1984). More recent evidence would suggest that leading US firms have heeded Hayes and Wheelwright's warning.

R&D in Britain

Hayes and Wheelwright's criticisms of the USA could easily apply to the UK, except there is considerable evidence to show that R&D expenditure by UK firms has not risen to the same extent as in the USA. In comparison with other major industrial countries, we continue to spend less on R&D as a proportion of GDP and the UK employs fewer research scientists as a proportion of its labour force than its main competitors. Furthermore, numbers of research scientists in the UK have fallen between 1981 and 1989 while numbers have increased in France, Italy and Japan (Freeman, 1989). In 1990, 71 per cent of German companies spent over 5 per cent of their revenue on R&D, while the same could be said of only 28 per cent of British companies (DTI Innovation Advisory Board, 1990). The pattern of innovation amongst private sector British firms is one of great concentration. In 1990, 20 UK companies accounted for 64 per cent of civil R&D and 50 companies accounted for 80 per cent (*Independent on Sunday*, 30 June 1991).

There is evidence that R&D expenditure for UK firms has risen in the late 1990s. In some industries, notably pharmaceuticals, the UK has world-class R&D performers in the likes of Glaxo Wellcome, SmithKline Beecham and Zeneca. In other industries, notably chemicals, UK firms have fallen behind. In 1991 the top-spending UK firm was ICI, ranked 35 in the world on R&D expenditure. By 1998 ICI was ranked 132 in the world and only 12 in the UK. Expenditure increases that did occur were probably a feature of a strong pound and a restoration of R&D cuts in the 1980s. The reality is that UK still lags behind many of its major competitors. The DTI scoreboards for R&D in 1998 and 1999 both reveal that whereas the average expenditure on R&D for the world's top 300 companies was over 5 per cent of sales turnover, the corresponding average for the UK top 100 was just over 2 per cent. These scoreboards show the commanding lead in R&D taken by the USA and Japan. Not only does the UK have far fewer companies amongst the top 300 spenders, but those firms spend less as a proportion of turnover than firms in the USA and Japan, although they are on a par with their European counterparts.

A number of reasons have been put forward for the relatively low investment in R&D by many UK firms. The behaviour of the stock market is frequently cited, more especially the payment of high rates of share dividend linked to short-termism. While share dividend is higher in the UK, short-termism is also a criticism levelled at US managers, yet this does not seem to deter R&D spending to the same degree. The withdrawal of the state from direct support is also given as an explanation. This was particularly apparent under the free market ideologies of successive governments since 1979.

There is a clear line of thinking going back through such writers as Galbraith to Schumpeter, which believes that developments in technology depend upon expensive research programmes of the kind that can only be found in the large corporation. Accordingly, big firms are deemed to be best and monopolies even better. The complexities of modern technologies and the corresponding development costs set up irrevocable pressures towards the growing scale of organizations. Evidence in the 1960s was fairly clear in that large manufacturing firms spent proportionally more on R&D, had a larger share of innovation and were quicker to adopt new techniques of manufacturing (Mansfield, 1963). Findings such as these led to the assumption that R&D could only be economic once a certain size of firm had been reached. Certainly this line of thinking influenced British public policy in the 1960s with its encouragement of merger activity.

There can be little doubt that the large firm is able to invest in projects that carry a higher element of risk. Furthermore, the large firm has greater access to finance both from external sources and from the internal generation of funds. The Convair Division of the General Dynamics Corporation was able to ride a loss of $425 million on its production of jet aircraft because of the highly diversified nature of its operations (Galbraith, 1972). However, there are two pieces of evidence that appear to favour the smaller company.

- Small firms spend more on R&D as a proportion of total sales and employ proportionally more staff in R&D than the larger firms (Child, 1969), though this could be a case of economies of scale operating in favour of the larger firm, rather than any significant differences in their innovative capacities.
- Firms of less than 1000 employees account for more than 20 per cent of innovations in Britain, far greater than their share of R&D investment, but less than their share of employment or net output (Pavitt, 1983).

Those who subscribe to the small-firms lobby would argue that the smaller company is much more adaptable, much closer to the consumer, and hence, the source of far more significant innovations than the big firm. We deal with such arguments in more detail in the section on small businesses in Chapter 3.

Jewkes has consistently championed the cause of the small inventor but found that size is a far less significant factor than the competitive nature of the market in which the firm operates (Jewkes *et al.*, 1970). We may conclude from this that highly innovative firms are more likely to be found in very competitive markets, as illustrated by the previously mentioned case of Canon cameras, and that this occurs irrespective of the size of the firm.

There are, however, important variations according to the nature of the sector in which the firm operates. Most innovations in the electrical, electronic, food, chemical and vehicle industries occur in large companies. In the case of mechanical engineering, instrumentation, leather and footwear, it is the smaller firm that tends to dominate (Pavitt, 1983). There is a danger with such analyses in that they confine innovation to products and processes. Significant innovations in such as retailing and financial services tend to be overlooked.

We may conclude from all this that there is no clear relationship between size and innovation, but we are able to make the following observations. The investment required in some types of innovation, and the need for high volume production for a return on that investment, clearly operates in favour of large companies. A good example here would be the chemical and pharmaceutical industries. An influencing factor would seem to be the sector of operation. Some sectors, like chemicals, tend to be traditionally dominated by large companies, while in others, especially instrumentation, the small firm still plays a significant role. There are cases of breakthroughs being made by small firms in all sectors, but they may have to align themselves with larger companies to obtain the necessary development capital, production capacity, or access to markets, the Workmate, Case 5.3, being a good example. However, where markets are especially volatile, any firm, irrespective of size, may have to keep innovating to maintain market share. It is in such situations that entrepreneurial activity becomes most important.

The main difficulty with analyses of this nature is that they tend to view relationships at one point in time, when in reality the innovative process and the size of firms can be viewed as highly dynamic. Henry Ford produced five different engines in quick succession, prior to the Model T, in a relatively small, jobbing-based organization. No product change then took place for 15 years, as the emphasis shifted to the development of mass-production process technologies and incremental product improvements (Abernathy and Utterback, 1978).

Examinations of business histories show us that the most fundamental product innovations usually take place at a relatively early stage of a firm's development, when it is still relatively small. As the firm develops, more emphasis is placed on process innovations. A stage may well be reached where the growth of mass markets and the need for economies of scale in the production process mean that fundamental change is resisted as being too costly. In other words the goals of the company change over time with changes in size and the nature of the innovations. A longitudinal study of the development of Computer Aided Design (CAD) systems in manufacturing found that from 1969 to 1974 initial innovations took place in small computer software companies. From 1974 to 1980 the main developments were taking place in much larger companies. Either the original firms had expanded, or they had been bought out by firms such as General Electric, wishing to buy into the new technology. In both cases, size was seen as an important factor in the attraction of venture capital. From 1980 onwards, smaller firms once again entered the market, concentrating on the development of highly specialized CAD systems, with a limited field of application (Kaplinsky, 1983).

We have noted in this section the need for some small firms to align themselves to larger companies for access to development capital and markets. There are some larger firms who pursue a deliberate strategy of innovation through acquisition. This can be a useful strategy where the acquired firm operates in the same product market, but, as we saw in the last chapter, difficulties can arise where diversification is totally unrelated.

In recent years the phenomenon of corporate venturing has emerged. This involves a larger established business collaborating with a smaller, less established but entrepreneurial firm to exploit business opportunities. The large firm offers finance, management expertise, access to markets, an established financial control system, and perhaps the benefits of an established reputation. The entrepreneurial firm offers new ideas and perhaps a greater ability to respond to changing markets and technologies. The French-based multinational, Rhône-Poulenc, invested in Calgene, a small American firm operating in the biotechnology market. The market was developing, but Calgene was in serious financial difficulty. Rhône-Poulenc's investment gave it instant access to a new technology and Calgene obtained much needed finance. The firm recovered, went public and provided Rhône-Poulenc with a tenfold return on its original investment (*Sunday Times*, 14 August 1988).

Innovation and organization structure

> When novelty and unfamiliarity in both market situation and technical information become the accepted order of things, a fundamentally different kind of management system becomes appropriate from that which applies to a relatively stable commercial and technical environment.
>
> (Tom Burns, in the preface to the second edition of *The Management of Innovation*, Burns and Stalker, 1966, p.vii)

The starting point is appropriate, since it was Burns and Stalker's study of the post-war electronics industry, and in particular the failure of some of the Scottish firms in their study to set up effective research departments, that has been so influential, not only in the development of organization theory, but as a practical guide to innovative firms on the development of appropriate structures. In this section we will examine why such a 'fundamentally different kind of management system' is necessary, the problems encountered in setting up such a system, and the attempts that have been made to provide solutions to those problems. We illustrate the arguments by focusing on the R&D department in typically science-based industry. The same arguments apply for any group within an organization with the primary responsibility for initiating innovation. For example, in an advertising agency, tensions often arise between staff who manage client accounts, and who have to adopt a business orientation, and those whose primary responsibility is the generation of creative ideas.

The R&D function and those connected with it have various claims for different treatment from the rest of the organization. There is a fundamental belief that the creativity inherent in the function requires its workers to communicate freely both within and outside the organization and to be free of the kind of bureaucratic controls to which other departments are subjected. The very nature of the work demands that there be flexibility as far as the allocation of priorities, patterns of working and normal management control systems are concerned. Specifically there is a demand for the relaxation of hierarchical controls and a need to see investment in R&D as a long-term issue.

Those companies where innovation is a key activity have tended to respond by creating special R&D departments. The kind of problem that tends to arise most frequently is that this sets up a clash of cultures between R&D and the other departments. The need for flexibility as outlined above challenges the existing bureaucratic controls and with it, the existing power base. The old order with its allegiance to the organization and the status quo can be shaken by a group of scientists and technologists with their allegiance to a knowledge base whose source lies outside the organization. In such a situation it is often convenient for top management to isolate the R&D department both politically and sometimes geographically. In this way it presents less of a challenge to the status quo and can be conveniently amputated when costs need to be cut. It is not uncommon in times of economic recession for firms to cut back or close down altogether their R&D function. This sets up an interesting paradox between the need to reduce expenditure and the central role ascribed to innovation in economic recovery.

However, it is often the scientists themselves who support this isolation within the organization. It absolves them of responsibility and gives them the kind of freedom they seek to pursue their own goals. This can involve role-playing to a widely held image of the eccentric scientist. As Burns and Stalker note,

> a reputation for eccentricity may be helpful not only in creating a complaisant attitude in industry towards the transgression of normal rules and towards a claim for privileges but also in furthering a career ... also taken to imply in some degree abdication from claims to leadership in the general management of business concerns.
>
> (Burns and Stalker, 1966 p. 176)

The result for the organization is invariably a lack of coordination between R&D and other activities like production and marketing, a situation which, as Burns and Stalker found, retarded the innovative process and was detrimental to the effective operation of the firm as a whole. A great deal of time can be wasted on internal politics and the situation can lead to a proliferation of committees and intermediaries to operate in a coordinating capacity, creating jobs like methods engineers.

In many ways, the R&D department needs to be different because its goals are different, the time horizon on which it is evaluated is different, and it has different needs with regard to the formality of its operations. An R&D department needs an informal structure because of the uncertain nature of its work and its need for a flexible response to both technological and market changes. Specialists may need to be brought in from outside, possibly on a temporary basis, decision-making and responsibility may have to be decentralized, and there will usually be a very loose specification of jobs and work procedures. Integration may be achieved through the management information system, by creating cross-functional teams, or by using some managers in special integrating roles.

There are dangers with this approach. Catering to the special demands of the R&D function can lead to the kind of isolation we have already discussed and the various attempts at integration can all too often result in paperwork jungles or the creation of supernumerary roles whose sole reason for existence is to act as go-between. In his study of the management of innovation in eight different firms, Parker found that a great deal of attention had been paid to structural considerations, setting up departments, creating special teams, training and coordination. However, he found this to be less important than an effective strategy for innovation, which he found to be lacking in most instances (Parker, 1982). Part of the problem according to Chaharbaghi and Newman (1996) is that innovation is viewed differently by different people in different functions. This often results in a fragmentation of effort.

Communication and coordination would appear to be key issues. Multinationals that can draw effectively upon a worldwide network are generally more innovative than those who operate as separate national entities. Companies such as Glaxo Wellcome and Siemens have established global innovation networks, vital in fast-moving industries such as pharmaceuticals and electronics. As we saw in Chapter 2, many Japanese firms have built up close and effective relationships with their suppliers, which has led to new developments in both products and processes. In all firms a close relationship between R&D and marketing is essential to provide information which reduces uncertainty concerning the acceptability of innovative products.

Firms operating globally would seem to have three options. Innovation can be the prerogative of some centralized unit such as a central R&D division, or it can be a decentralized activity or a combination of both systems. A centralized system offers economies of scale and may offer advantages in the development of totally new technologies. However, where it is important to develop local products for local markets, and particularly where supply chains are involved in the development process, a decentralized system may be more effective. Most global firms, such as Hewlett-Packard and Ford, have R&D operations in most of their main markets. Tidd *et al*. (1997) argue that the key factors involved in centraliztion versus decentralization and global versus local are as follows:

- Where basic research is important, as in the pharmaceutical industry, centralization tends to be the norm, as it does where a period of trial and error is needed after a fundamental breakthrough.
- Firms following long-term strategies tend to have more centralized R&D than those pursuing more short-term, market-led strategies.
- They report a tendency for most global firms to locate the majority of their innovative activity in the home country. In the case of Germany, Japan and the USA, they note that as much as 80 per cent of high-spending R&D is located at home. The main use of foreign R&D would appear to be to adapt products for local markets. Of course, in the case of certain complex products, such as passenger aircraft, even this may be unnecessary. Localized R&D would seem to operate best when there is a need to exploit local conditions, as in the case of working with local raw materials or using specialized local knowledge and skills.

Some believe that effectiveness is achieved through the organization of the firm around its dominant competitive issue. In this way, if innovation were identified as the priority then the firm should locate its centre of power and influence around that activity. Successful innovative firms not only see innovation as a priority but build an entire organization culture based on innovation. In the next section we reinforce this theme. Organization changes, which follow technical innovations, can underline the competitive advantage of the innovation. The impact of containerization and advances in telecommunications offered opportunities to shipping companies, but full advantage was only gained following corresponding changes in jobs and organization structure (see Case 5.5 for more details).

The role of organization culture

In the previous section we dwelt at length on the structural issues pertaining to the operation of an R&D function. We have maintained throughout that innovation is not the sole prerogative of science-based manufacturing industry, nor does it depend on the existence of a formally established R&D department. We have already established that innovation applies to all forms of business, and many firms are entrepreneurial and innovative largely because it is seen as a responsibility of all staff irrespective of their function.

A culture of innovation may be built up in a variety of ways. One way may be to recruit innovative and entrepreneurial staff and, by using training programmes, to develop creative thinking. More significantly, the lead normally comes through the activities and energy of senior management, and their creation of an organization to foster innovation. In the Hewlett-Packard case and in our reference to excellent companies in Chapter 3 there would appear to be some correlation between the existence of a strong corporate culture and innovative activity. Ekvall (1991) reported on a research programme about creativity and found, not surprisingly, that creative organizations were typified by high trust, freedom, idea support, playfulness and risk-taking. Such supportive climates are typical of Peters and Waterman's 'excellent companies'.

Deal and Kennedy's (1982) innovative organization of the future is highly decentralized, in which each member of staff is allowed to be his or her own entrepreneur. They refer to this as the 'atomized organization'. We came across a similar phenomenon when we discussed networking as a structural form in Chapter 3.

Innovation and management strategies

Throughout this chapter we have seen that both management and representatives of governments have operated on the clear assumption that innovation is linked to increased productivity, market share and profitability, as well as being an indication of the state of a nation's economic health. A strong lobby exists for the promotion of an innovation strategy as the key to competitive advantage. Typical of the lobby is the stance taken by Hayes and

Case 5.5: The shipping industry

The shipping industry is concerned with the transport of goods by sea, and is not to be confused with shipbuilding. The information for the case is taken largely from a study of the shipping industry, titled *Innovating to Compete* (Walton, 1987). Walton examines eight countries: Denmark, Holland, Japan, Norway, Sweden, United Kingdom, USA, and the former West Germany. The choice of the eight nations is significant in that they represented the world's traditional merchant fleets and accounted for 74 per cent of the entire world tonnage in shipping prior to the Second World War. Since the war the powerful position of these shipping nations has been challenged by a variety of factors. By 1973 their collective tonnage had fallen to 43 per cent and by 1983 to 26 per cent. The case study identifies those factors and examines the strategic responses of the shipping companies concerned. It should be remembered that while merchant fleets are invariably linked to nation states, shipping is operated as a business and shipping companies are privately owned.

In Walton's study, two phases were identified, the first 1963–73, and the second 1973–83.

Period 1: 1963–73

For the eight nations listed above, this period was one of economic prosperity. The demand for shipping exceeded supply and that demand was increasing throughout this period at a rate of 7 per cent a year. It was also a period in which unemployment was extremely low and the shipping industry faced intense competition for its labour from land-based industries. The lure of seafaring had declined with the prospect of long periods away from home and the increasing development of functional ports in unglamorous locations away from the main centres of urban life. Furthermore, time spent in port had been sacrificed to the fast turnaround of vessels to save cost and maximize operational time. Combined with these factors was a growing resistance to the quasi-military regime of the merchant navy, especially in the face of attractive job opportunities elsewhere. Labour shortages became the norm in the shipping industry of all these nations. Under such conditions the bargaining power of trade unions is substantially strengthened, as was the case in the majority of companies covered by the study. Wage rates were increased to attract and keep labour, with a corresponding increase in costs. Nevertheless,

demand for shipping was still high and the industry remained relatively healthy, with increased costs being borne by the customer through increased freight charges.

Period 2: 1973–83

1973 was a watershed for the shipping industry in the eight nations. The problems caused by the high costs of labour were superseded by very high interest rates and a dramatic increase in the cost of fuel. Unfortunately as far as these developed countries were concerned, price competition within the industry had increased through the activity of two types of new entrant.

First, there had been the fast growth of shipping operating under 'flags of convenience'. Such shipping is associated with such countries as Liberia and Panama, where the cost of registering and insuring ships is much lower than in traditional shipping nations. The advantage to the ship owner is not just in terms of registration and insurance. The regulations covering shipping operations and shipboard practices tend to be far less restrictive, and labour tends to be cheaper too. A country like Liberia has actively marketed this service and sees it as an important source of foreign investment. Under such a mechanism, overheads and labour costs are kept to a minimum, and shipping operating under a 'flag of convenience' is able to enter the market place offering an attractive price to the customer. It is hardly surprising that the eight nations saw a defection of ship owners from their fleets to such 'flags of convenience'. The bulk transport of the world's oil supply quickly became the prerogative of the Liberian tanker fleet, heavily underwritten and supported by the major multinational oil corporations.

Second, certain governments, particularly those of the former Soviet bloc nations and those of developing countries, see their own shipping industry as a means of achieving highly prized international recognition. The industry becomes both metaphorically and literally a flag carrier for its sponsoring nation. Government-backed shipping from such countries has, like the 'flags of convenience', reduced the price and widened the choice for the customer.

The problems facing the eight nations were therefore intensified and by 1983 the entire industry was suffering from problems of over-capacity. This became particularly acute as the decade from 1973, unlike its predecessor, marked a decline in the demand for shipping.

The strategic options of shipping companies in the established nations

We can see that a combination of rising labour costs, rising fuel costs, high interest rates, cheap competition and over-capacity had seriously weakened the competitive position of the eight developed nations in Walton's study. Those firms still operating were faced with a number of options in order to maintain their competitive position. The strategic options and the problems associated with them may be identified as follows:

- Some firms found that the move towards much larger vessels enabled them to achieve economies of scale and compete on price. Such an option was not available to all owing to the very high investment costs needed for this type of strategy.
- Some governments decided to assist their own shipping industry by setting up subsidies and by granting generous tax allowances. Protectionist strategies and trade agreements have been used to safeguard the position of national fleets. Such agreements might include the provision that all coastal traffic should use national carriers, or that the exchange of imports and exports must be accompanied by a corresponding exchange of shipping services. While some governments were committed to such policies, others showed a complete disinterest and, in some cases, ideological opposition to state intervention.
- A popular strategy involved product specialization. Some companies decided that they could not compete with developing nations and 'flags of convenience' in the transport of bulk cargoes or in the oil tanker trade. Instead, they opted for those cargoes requiring specialist facilities and handling, such as liquid gases and other dangerous chemicals; or they chose to operate with highly mixed loads in relatively small batches. However, over-specialization can be threatened by the lack of demand, and the cost of transporting loads in small batches raises its own logistics problems.
- A classic response to the problems of labour shortages and increased labour costs was process innovation. Containerization has been a popular option in many cases; cargoes come ready packed in large containers, reducing the need for dock and shipboard handling. Inevitably containerization was supported by the development of the 'roll on–roll off' process, where the containers are driven directly onto the ship and unloaded by container lorry,

obviating the need for cargo handling at all. Such developments have been matched by the automation of shipboard engineering, control and monitoring processes and changes in telecommunications rendering traditional methods of ship-to-shore communication redundant. In all cases such innovations reduced the need for labour or enabled formerly specialized tasks to be substituted by those with a lower skill requirement. However, such changes carry high investment costs and often meet employee resistance to change, more especially union opposition to both reduced manning levels and more flexible work practices.

- In shipping, as with all industries, technical innovations invariably offer the possibility of organizational changes to underline the advantages of the former. In particular, automation and changes in telecommunications introduced the possibility of flexible manning, and hence even greater labour savings. Some companies went even further and attempted to introduce permanent crews operating as a team and ensuring continuity of labour, a radical innovation in an industry built on a history of casual hiring. The move towards teamwork was a deliberate attempt to improve the quality of working life and was accompanied, in some cases, by the creation of less hierarchical organizational structures. These new structures offered more opportunity for delegated authority and participation. Some companies saw such moves as inevitable to match conditions in shore-based industries and to change the merchant navy's image of authoritarian man-management systems to attract labour. Bringing about such changes is not without its difficulties. The very structures that are identified for change are likely to provide the biggest obstacle. The shipping industry is typified by highly bureaucratic structures and shipboard relations steeped in naval tradition where ship captains are highly resistant to participative forms of management.

The options are not mutually exclusive and some shipping companies had pursued all five options in an attempt to maintain their competitive position. Far from being mutually exclusive, some of the options were dependent upon the support of others for maximum effectiveness. The major point of Walton's study is that competitiveness can only be achieved when technical innovations are accompanied by organizational innovations.

(*Source*: Walton, 1987)

Wheelwright. They maintain that firms must innovate to survive, since strategies that depend on imitation and following market trends will ultimately lead to a saturation of the market. While some firms will survive better than others by clever marketing strategies and introducing the kind of 'pseudo-innovations' we discussed at the beginning of the chapter, real growth is dependent upon the development of new products. An important feature of the Hayes and Wheelwright hypothesis, as far as manufacturing industry is concerned, is the primacy of individual machine tool technology. Only through this will firms be able to manufacture products that are distinct from those of their competitors (Hayes and Wheelwright, 1984). Clearly their hypothesis is biased towards manufacturing but has application for other sectors as well. We will return to this argument in the next chapter and refer you to Case 4.1, which deals with the decline in the British machine tool industry.

In this section we will examine two types of innovation strategy, 'first to the market' and 'follower strategies'. Following our discussion of organization structure and culture we will revisit the concept of integrated strategies before closing the section with an examination of some constraints to innovation.

Types of strategy

'First to the market' strategy

According to Ansoff and Stewart (1967), organizations pursuing this type of strategy see research and development as a central part of their operation. There is a strong commitment to basic research, technical leadership and hence a willingness to take risks with comparatively large investments. Research tends to be close to the state of the art and the organization employs a high proportion of top-rate research scientists. There is considerable coordination between research, production and marketing and planning is usually long-range. The large pharmaceutical companies like Roche and Glaxo Wellcome fit into this category. They use R&D and a 'first to the market' strategy as a deliberate attempt to dominate the market. As we see in Case 5.1, Glaxo employs large numbers of research scientists, has close links with universities in various parts of the world and successfully developed the anti-ulcer drug Zantac before its rivals, achieving a very large and very profitable market share.

Being first to the market gives a firm a number of distinct advantages. First, the firm can use the patent system to create a monopoly position and earn income from licensing activities, as we saw earlier with Texas Instruments. Second, those first to the market can control limited resources. The first development in a new beach resort can occupy the prime site and buy land when prices are relatively cheap. Those following, especially if the resort becomes fashionable and popular, are faced with less desirable locations and higher prices. Third, those that are first can set the industry standards that others must follow, as in the case of computer hardware and software. The battle for market share in the UK satellite TV industry was fought between Sky and BSB, with the two companies operating different systems. In some respects BSB operated a technically superior system, but being first enabled Sky to gain the largest market share. BSB experienced financial difficulties and were eventually taken over by Sky.

However, being first to patent the invention is insufficient in itself. Sony was not the first company to patent the Walkman, but was the first to produce it cheaply and market it effectively. Rank Xerox was first to the market with the photocopying machine and used the patent to create an effective monopoly, but failed to compete effectively for several years with Canon and Toshiba when they entered the market as followers. Being a follower can have advantages and it is to this we now turn.

'Follower' strategies

A variety of follower strategies can be identified. Some firms, such as Philips operating in the domestic electrical market, are highly innovative and take state-of-the-art technical knowledge invented elsewhere and use this to develop their own product range. Other firms in the same market, such as Hotpoint, will follow somewhat cautiously behind the state-of-the-art technology, concentrating more on design modifications. In the two cases above, the companies possess R&D departments and, while not first to the market, are still concerned with innovation. By contrast there are some followers who have no R&D function as such. They exist largely on a strong manufacturing base and have the ability to copy others' products quickly and effectively. Successful firms of this type operate on low costs, have a comparatively low selling price and the ability to deliver on time. They rely on being highly competitive as opposed to innovative. Firms operating in this way do not tend to be household names.

Being a follower has its advantages. Goods can often be introduced more cheaply as high development costs do not have to be recouped. Those coming after can learn from the mistakes of the pioneers. For example, Boeing developed its highly profitable 707 range of aircraft by learning from the metal fatigue problems that dogged the early versions of the British Aircraft Corporation's Comet and, as a result, gained a much larger market share (Bowen *et al.*, 1992). Coming second also means that a market is already established, with support mechanisms such as knowledgable retailers, service and maintenance facilities and complementary products. In the computing area, later arrivals entered a market place where software standards were established and they could develop their products accordingly.

Follower strategies can be pursued in specific circumstances by otherwise highly innovative and well-known companies. We have noted already that when Rank Xerox's patent on the photocopier expired, several companies, including Canon, Toshiba and Gestetner, used the available technology to manufacture their own versions. In many cases those coming second not only have the advantages highlighted above, but can also build upon their reputations in other fields. In the case of Canon and Toshiba they developed photocopiers that were not only cheaper, but more reliable as well. This in turn resulted in Rank Xerox rethinking its own strategy and led to a focus on quality and the development of 'total quality management' techniques in an attempt to recapture its former market position.

Integrated strategies

> Although innovation is a primary source of competitive advantage, it is usually an effective source only if it can be deployed in concert with some other sources of competitive advantage, or if it is at least supported by other strategic weapons.
>
> (Kay, 1992, p. 127)

Our illustrations of the 'first to the market' and 'follower' strategies above suggest that the two are not mutually exclusive and that a firm can pursue different strategies in different product markets. The quote from Kay suggests that whatever strategy is pursued it is insufficient in itself without the support of the rest of the organization. This reinforces the theme raised in our earlier discussion of the relationship to innovation of organizational structure and organizational culture. We may conclude from the works of Kay, other authors and various case histories that the strategic implications for a firm wishing to be innovative are as follows:

- In general there needs to be a risk-taking ethos that is supported by top management. There ought to be a willingness to experiment and therefore a freedom to fail.
- This should be supported by the recruitment of people with creative talents and, where appropriate, with technical and scientific backgrounds.
- Recruitment policies need to be reinforced by training and development programmes which place emphasis on innovation and the acquisition of the required technical knowledge. Promotion strategies should include technical know-how and a commitment to innovation as key criteria.
- The exchange of ideas should be encouraged, not just within the firm, but, especially for those operating in science-based industries, by fostering links with universities and other research establishments.
- Mechanisms that facilitate communication can be set up, such as suggestion schemes and more radical methods of employee participation, but more generally, innovation may be encouraged if the organization is flexible and decentralized. Innovation is about learning and change and is linked to the currently fashionable concept of the learning organization.
- Whether a special R&D department is created or not, attention needs to be paid to integrating the function of innovation with rest of the organization's activities. Kay (1993) goes further and speaks not only of the importance of integration within the firm, between departments, between management and labour but also between the firm and its suppliers and the firm and its customers. The close relationship between many Japanese manufacturing firms and their components suppliers illustrates this, as does the policy of Hewlett-Packard of consulting customers in the innovation of new products (see the section on Japanese management in Chapter 2 and the Hewlett-Packard case in Chapter 3).

Probably the most significant feature to emerge from the points made above is the need to create a particular organization culture or climate that is supportive of innovation. This in turn needs to be supported by an environment where emphasis is placed on developing the skills of the workforce and where innovation is encouraged by banks and by effective political policies instead of rhetoric. The absence of these features presents the innovative firm with considerable constraints.

Constraints to effective innovation strategy

Despite the central role ascribed to innovation, there are constraints, which may significantly limit its effectiveness. For any new idea there is a high probability of failure. If we add this to a tendency on the part of many managers to underestimate the costs involved, then it is easy to see why some companies have found innovation a particularly risky strategy. Lockheed and Rolls Royce in the aerospace industry are good illustrations of this. This is compounded by yet another problem. Managers in many industries, faced with the pressure for career development and pressures from shareholders for a generous dividend, may opt for safer short-term investments, which preclude more radical innovative strategies. Undoubtedly the problems associated with short-termism in general highlight the importance of a supportive financial system for effective innovation. The time lags between development and commercial exploitation can be highly variable, a process taking an estimated 22 years as far as television was concerned. In addition to all these problems, economic, social and political conditions may militate against effective innovation. We have already seen the importance of a skills infrastructure and supportive political policies. Objections by trade unions fearing losses in job security, either real or imagined, can set back the introduction of process innovations, as we have seen in the newspaper industry (Chapter 1). High interest rates offered by banks as a result of high inflation can add to the reluctance on the part of managers to invest in new ventures.

Difficulties of the kind identified above have led to the preference of some firms to seek alternative strategies. A common alternative is the use of the patent and licensing system, identified earlier in this chapter. Instead of developing products and processes itself, a firm will manufacture a product or use a process that has been developed elsewhere, on the payment of a licence fee to the patent holder. This is not only a strategy for the avoidance of R&D costs, but can save a great deal of time in the development process by eliminating duplication of effort. The high cost of development in the electronics industry was considerably reduced for many firms, by using as their starting point the original patent for the transistor owned by the Bell Telephone Corporation. Licensing may not be totally passive and may in fact be a spur to modifications, resulting in a company developing its own innovations.

In addition to licensing, the costs of innovation may be reduced by undertaking joint development with another company, buying in specific research work as needed from a specialist research consultancy firm, or even through acquisition strategy. In this way a firm can add to its stable of new products, processes and patents by purchasing particularly innovative companies, operating in their chosen direction of diversification. In some cases a spin-off company can be established to focus on a specific project, as SmithKline Beecham did with Adprotech.

In discussing innovation strategies, students should always remember that the strategies are never as discrete as textbook models would like them to be. We have already noted that a firm can be first to the market place with some of its product range while following other firms in other types of product. A firm may well have a strong R&D department with a record of successful innovation. At the same time it could license developments from its competitors and even pursue an acquisition strategy of buying up certain highly specialized units.

What does appear to be important is an integrated strategy, a theme that appears central to the innovative process. A good idea may be wasted without corresponding policies in production and marketing, the respective themes of our next two chapters.

Summary

Invention, innovation, research and development, design and entrepreneurship are all related concepts. For businesses it is the process of innovation that is the key concept, turning an invention into something profitable. Innovation can relate to products, processes, marketing and organization, and can range from the most fundamental to the most minor changes. Evidence suggests that the more successful innovations are those that are integrated, with product, process and organizational change occurring together. Integration would appear to be an important theme in innovation.

We view innovation as the key to increased productivity, increased market share, and hence profitability and the firm's continued survival. The theme has been translated to the scale of national economies and we have seen how some regard innovation as the source of economic recovery out of a recession. These relationships are difficult to prove but there can be no denying that without innovation there can be no new products or processes.

The importance of innovation has been recognized by governments all over the world, although there are considerable variations in the extent and direction of intervention. Government support for innovation is seen not only for economic, but for political and social reasons too, although there can be significant ideological and practical difficulties in the state's involvement. All societies need to support innovation by ensuring that the workforce is educated and trained in the required skills.

There are clear links between innovation and technology, although in practice it is difficult to determine whether an innovation is a result of 'technology-push' or 'demand-pull'. Most important innovations in business are the product of a range of different factors. An understanding of the market place is particularly important, and innovation and marketing are interrelated activities.

At the level of the individual firm there is no clear evidence linking the size of a company with its propensity and ability to innovate, although very expensive research tends to be concentrated in large companies. The sector in which the firm operates and the volatility of the market all interact with the size of establishment in a rather complex way. What is fairly clear is that firms with an R&D department have special problems in the integration of R&D with other activities and in particular, production and marketing. The most successfully innovative companies tend to be those that have paid attention to the creation of a particular organization culture and the encouragement to all staff to be creative.

Some firms clearly see themselves as technical and market leaders and invest a high proportion of their income in developing new ideas, products and processes. Other firms are more content to sit behind the field and rely upon minor developments or strategies of copying. There are a range of possible strategies that can be adopted either singly or together.

Further reading

J. Tidd *et al.*, *Managing Innovation: Integrating Technological, Market and Organizational Change* (John Wiley & Sons, 1997) offers a well-researched account which touches upon most aspects of this chapter and is particularly good in its focus on technology, strategy, markets and organizational issues. A good approach to the economics of innovation, state involvement and, in particular, the links between innovation, corporate strategy and marketing can be found in A. Bowen and M. Ricketts (eds) *Stimulating Innovation in Industry: The Challenge for the United Kingdom* (Kogan Page/NEDO, 1992). Although a little dated, a good overview of research into innovation, the role of the state and small firms can be found in R. Rothwell and W. Zegveld's *Industrial Innovation and Public Policy* (Frances Pinter, 1981). A broader-based view of entrepreneurship may be found in most of the books written by Peter Drucker, especially P. Drucker, *Enterprise and Innovation* (Heinemann, 1985). Although the study is 35 years old, there are few better nor more relevant books on the organization of innovation than T. Burns and G.M. Stalker's *The Management of Innovation* (Tavistock, 1966). More strategic issues are the focus of C. Baden-Fuller and M. Pitt, *Strategic Innovation* (Routledge, 1996).

Discussion

1. Which can have the greater impact on businesses: product or process innovations?
2. Examine the ways through which the state can subsidize, encourage and protect innovation in private firms. Why should the state get involved, and what difficulties arise with such involvement?
3. Assess the relationship between innovation and economic growth. Which criteria would you use to show such a relationship?
4. Select a range of consumer domestic products that illustrate the relationship between technology-push and demand-pull. Which of these two is the more significant?

5. What contribution can the size of the firm make to innovative activity?

6. Identify the major problems associated with the existence of a special function responsible for the initiation of new business ideas, such as an R&D department. What structural devices would you employ to reduce these problems?

7. Assess the innovation strategy alternatives for a manufacturer of consumer electrical goods, a major computer firm, a package holiday company, and a university.

8. To what extent is innovation the key to Glaxo Wellcome's success (Case 5.1)? What do you see as the main opportunities and threats currently facing the company?

9. What can we learn from the INMOS case about state intervention in innovation? How could INMOS have been more effective?

10. What does Case 5.5 tell us about the role of the state in innovation and the relationship between innovation and aspects of organization?

CHAPTER 6

Operations

The operations function is concerned with the creation of the goods and services offered to consumers. We clearly associate operations with manufacturing industry, but we can also see an operations function in department stores, restaurants, banks, local government, schools and hospitals. In recent years the concept has been applied to the non-manufacturing sector and there has been an exchange of ideas and techniques with manufacturing. In this edition we have chosen to use the term operations rather than production to denote a broader approach. To reinforce this broad view of operations, we will, where appropriate, cite illustrations from the non-manufacturing sector.

We begin by examining the central role played by operations in all types of organization and examine two specific aspects of that role: the design of operations systems and how those systems work. We deal with the important function of purchasing within the broader context of supply chain management. The operations function is sometimes portrayed as the function that is most isolated from the environment in which it operates. We refute that idea and examine the relationship of operations with its environment by looking at the influences of a changing economy and government policy towards manufacturing industry, factors pertaining to the labour force, the impact of technological developments and cultural differences in the way societies view and organize production. A particular reference will be made here to Japanese manufacturing industry. Our analysis of organizational aspects also explores cultural differences and their interaction with the other variables of the Business in Context model, especially the role of organization size and structure. We close the chapter by exploring strategic aspects of operations.

A central function

The operations function has a central role in most types of organization. According to some estimates it accounts for some 70 to 80 per cent of a firm's assets, expenditure and people (Hill, 1991). In addition, it is central to the firm's success by providing what the customer requires either at a profit in a private company, or within budget in a non-profit organization. It is therefore concerned with issues that are crucial to the consumer, issues of quantity, quality, availability and price; and issues that are crucial to the management of an enterprise, issues of productivity and cost.

The growth of the non-manufacturing sector has encouraged our rethinking of the operations concept. We can see clearly that significant operations issues exist in managing an airport as busy as Heathrow. Planes must take off and land safely and on time. In order for this to occur, key operations must

---

KEY CONCEPT 6.1
Operations

Operations is concerned with the transformation of a variety of inputs such as information, people, materials, finance and methods into a variety of outputs such as goods, services, profit, customer and employee satisfaction. Traditionally associated with manufacturing production, it is now generally recognized that operations is a key function in all organizations, irrespective of their primary objective. The centrality of the function means that operations has a significant influence on costs and revenue as well as organization structure.

---

be coordinated, including air traffic control, ground crews, baggage-handling, passport and customs, aircraft cleaning, refuelling and catering. In busy regional hospitals surgical operations must be carefully timed and scheduled, patients transferred to and from wards, equipment prepared and the various support systems from nursing to catering properly briefed. Techniques originally developed in manufacturing are now commonplace in non-manufacturing contexts, and senior staff in these organizations assume the role of coordinating operations. It is the importance of the operations function in solving this type of problem that led Drucker to define production (as he called it) as 'the application of logic to work' (Drucker, 1968, p. 122).

In the past 30 years, operations management has enjoyed renewed attention. A number of factors are responsible for this. Increased concerns for improved efficiency and effectiveness in operations management have stemmed from the two oil crises of the 1970s and the associated rises in the cost of fuel and raw materials, as well as the rising cost of labour. The rapidly developing globalization of business has created interest in the development of systems to coordinate operations across the globe. We noted in Chapter 2 that it is now commonplace for manufacturing firms to make products comprising of parts from around the world, or even locate labour-intensive operations in low-cost countries. The development of the operating systems to enable this to happen has itself contributed to the accelerating pace of globalization. This coordination has led to the exchange of ideas and techniques. The success of Japan as a manufacturing nation has led many firms in the West to adopt methods of just-in-time manufacture, a concept originally developed in Japan. Such developments have elevated operations management to a key role in many organizations and the primary source of competitive advantage. That competitive advantage is derived from the key objectives of the operations system. It is generally acknowledged (for example Slack *et al.*, 1998) that these are:

- quality
- dependability
- speed
- flexibility
- cost efficiency and effectiveness.

These objectives recur in our discussions throughout this chapter and a more detailed discussion of their role in operations strategy can be found in the final section.

Despite the application of similar techniques to manufacturing and non-manufacturing firms alike, some differences can be found. We examine these briefly before looking at the various elements that make up the operations function.

KEY CONCEPT 6.2
Key objectives of operations management

These are acknowledged by many to be quality, dependability, speed, flexibility, cost efficiency and effectiveness and that focus on these issues will result in competitive advantage. It has been suggested that real competitive advantage will come from a primary focus on quality, followed by dependability, speed, flexibility and finally cost. The belief is that attention to the other factors will lead to both a reduction in cost and a customer who is willing to pay more for a high-quality, reliable product. In reality operations strategies vary in the way these items are mixed.

Some differences between manufacturing and non-manufacturing industries

Both these sectors are concerned with the production of goods and services, but differences do exist between different types of organization operating in the same sector. A volume car manufacturer like Toyota has little in common with a small business making hand-crafted furniture, yet both are lumped together as manufacturing concerns. By the same token, an organization like Barclays Bank would be classed together with a small hairdressing business, as non-manufacturing concerns. We can see that the differences within each of these sectors can be as significant as those existing between them. When we examine the organizational aspects of operations later in this chapter, we make an attempt to classify different types of operation system in each sector. At this stage, however, it is worth pointing to the major differences between manufacturing and non-manufacturing:

- Manufactured goods tend to be more tangible, storable and transportable.
- A major difference concerns the part played by the customer. In a non-manufacturing concern the customer is generally more of an active participant in the process. This is especially true in education and hospitals and those organizations offering a personal service, such as hairdressers, solicitors, financial advisors, and counsellors. The interaction of the customer means that the process is often less predictable, and operation systems correspondingly more complex.
- This unpredictability means that operations are more difficult to control in the non-manufacturing sector. The degree of contact with the customer

can affect the efficiency of the operation. For example, doctors may not be able to plan their work as effectively as they would like owing to the variability in the consulting needs of patients. Productivity therefore becomes more difficult to measure and quality becomes much more a matter of subjective assessment.

● The quality of a service tends to be assessed on the basis of not only output but also the way it is delivered. Aspects of delivery can be important for perceptions of quality in manufactured goods, but less so than for services.

We examine the implications of these differences when we look at the various elements of the operations process in the next two sections.

Identifying the operations function

We have seen that an operations system exists to provide goods and services, which it does by transforming inputs into different kinds of output. We can view this as a system comprising inputs, process and outputs, which we illustrate in Figure 6.1. (See also the section on the systems approach in Chapter 1.)

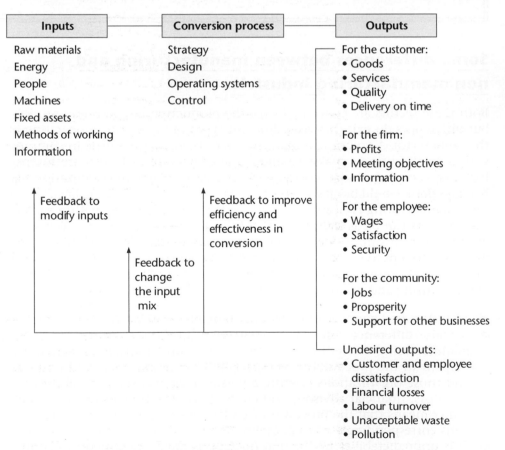

Figure **6.1** Operations as a system.

We can see clearly from Figure 6.1 that the operations function transforms the various resource inputs into the required goods and services. Three aspects of the model need further explanation.

- Not all the outputs of the system are necessarily desired outcomes. Waste, in the form of either substandard products or unused raw materials, can be a costly item in manufacturing and waste in the form of polluting chemicals can constitute an environmental hazard. Customer dissatisfaction can be an unintended output. The consequence of diners at a restaurant receiving bad service may well mean they decide never to return.
- The concept of environmental pollution introduces the notion that outputs of one system are invariably inputs to other systems. The manufactured outputs of a car components factory are clearly inputs to other firms. The increasing use of systems of global sourcing and global subcontracting by manufacturers had led to new developments in operations strategies and placed increasing emphasis on supply chain management. Wages paid to workers will invariably be passed on to shops and supermarkets, and also to such as building societies in the form of mortgage payments, which are then used to fund further investments.
- Outputs may also be considered as inputs to the same system. In this way, information gained during the production process can be used to improve the operation of the system, such as changing the supplier to improve the quality of parts and reduce the number of rejects. A large number of dissatisfied customers at a restaurant or a hairdressing salon is an indication that some element of the process needs attention. This is known as feedback. Another type of relationship can be built up between output and input when materials are recycled. In the manufacture of float glass at the Pilkington plant in St Helens, the smoothing of edges, the cutting of glass to size, and the generally fragile nature of the product mean that there are always quantities of broken glass. While measures are taken to keep this waste to an acceptable minimum, it is broken up to form 'cullet', a vital raw material in glass production.

We can see from the systems model that production is a transformation process resulting in the creation of goods and services. This provides us with a means of classifying different types of production system. Wild has identified four types, each based predominantly on a different kind of transformation (Wild, 1985):

- A transformation in the form of raw materials or components is typified by manufacturing firms, but also by such as builders and landscape gardeners.
- A change in the nature of ownership is primarily the concern of suppliers, wholesalers and retailers.
- A change of place is the focus for transport systems such as airlines and road hauliers, postal services and courier firms.
- Service industries, in particular, aim to transform the state of the customer. For example, insurance firms aim to make people feel more secure, building societies lend money for people to improve the quality of their lives

and make investments for the future, and osteopaths aim to improve the physical well-being of their patients. However, the attraction of some manufactured goods is that they also induce a change of state. The sales campaigns of certain quality cars or designer clothes stress image and the increased desirability of the driver or the wearer to members of their peer group.

Many organizations operate all four types of transformation process. A typical manufacturing firm will not only make goods, but sell and transport them direct to the consumer or to an intermediary such as a wholesaler or retailer and, in some cases, aim to make the purhaser feel good. We tend to think of restaurants as operating predominantly in the service sector, yet all restaurants have a manufacturing operation that transforms raw material foodstuffs into dishes for consumption. Retailers are not just concerned with ownership change but involved in place transformation too.

Slack *et al.* (1998) have identified three types of transformation:

- materials processing;
- information processing;
- customer processing.

Materials processing is similar to Wild's first category, but the second two offer us a slightly different perspective. Information processing occurs amongst such as accountants, librarians and people engaged in the telecommunications industry. Customer processing covers at least two of Wild's categories and can involve physical processing in the case of hospitals or hairdressers, accommodating or feeding them, in the case of hotels, transporting them, in the case of airlines, or changing their psychological state by making them feel good.

Whichever categories are used, the major link between viewing operations as a system and as a transformation process is that the transformation process is designed to add value to the various systems inputs, beyond their original cost.

A good illustration of the interrelated nature of both operations systems and the various types of transformation process can be found in the retail chain Marks & Spencer, whose primary product ranges are clothes and food and drink.

Marks & Spencer, one of the most successful retail chains in Britain, and with branches worldwide, has vigorously pursued a policy of offering high-quality products at an acceptable price to a mass market. It relies on a high turnover of goods. An important output is therefore a high level of customer satisfaction, both with the product and the service. Three kinds of feedback are important to this process. First, there is the customer's willingness to make return visits to the store. Second, there is the careful research of customer needs. Finally, there is the shop policy of accepting returned goods, which may then be repackaged and resold. The pursuit of quality is reflected in store layout and staff selection and training, but most significantly in the choice of supplier. Marks & Spencer expects a high level of quality in the goods it buys to sell on. In the 1980s this had a remarkable effect on the British textile industry. For many years the company policy was to buy British. The result was that 90 per cent of Marks & Spencer stock was British, and the company took 20 per cent of the total British output. The demands for quality standards, good design and reliable delivery led to improvements in the textile industry itself and enabled it to increase its competitiveness on a world scale, especially through the introduction of new technology. By the mid-1990s the policy had changed. A strong pound and the rising cost of British goods forced the company to diversify its sources and less than 50 per cent were bought from UK suppliers. In the clothing area many of its product lines were sourced from lower-cost suppliers in other countries, with a corresponding impact on the UK textile industry. The decision of Marks & Spencer in late 1999 not to renew the contract of its main UK supplier for underwear placed around 4000 jobs at risk in the supply industry. Many other UK textile firms had closed operations in the UK to manufacture in lower-cost labour markets. This was made possible by technological innovations, which enabled quality goods to be produced in most locations. The relationship between Marks & Spencer and its suppliers, not only in clothing but in food and drink, becomes even more complex in that many of the products are sold under the store's own label, yet manufactured by independent producers.

This is a good illustration of the complexity of inputs and outputs as well as demonstrating the fluidity of system boundaries and the involvement of Marks & Spencer in globalized manufacturing. However, its major concern, retailing, is a good illustration of transformations taking place in ownership, place, information and the state of the consumer.

Conflicting objectives and changing solutions

Any operations system is concerned with the production of a certain number and type of goods and services at a designated level of quality. Completion and delivery must be within certain time limits and within acceptable financial and social costs. The price charged must be acceptable to the consumer and must ensure sufficient quantity of sales to secure an acceptable return on investment. The entire system should have sufficient flexibility to be able to adjust to changing demands.

Consumers want goods and services to their specific requirements of quantity and quality and perhaps to be tempted by a selection of offerings. The

> ### KEY CONCEPT 6.3
> *Potential conflicts in an operations system*
>
> In most operations systems, there is inevitable tension between the needs of management to construct an efficient operation and the needs of customers. The needs of the former tend to focus on costs, while those of the latter focus on design, quality, price and delivery. Many of the techniques in the design, scheduling and control functions aim to resolve such potential conflicts.

goods and services should be easy to obtain at the time they are needed and should be sold at a price the consumers deem reasonable. If we select an unframed painting at an art shop, we know that a hand-crafted frame in a special material will cost more than framing it ourselves using a ready-made frame, and that we may have to wait some time for the job to be done by an expert. Many consumers are willing to make trade-offs, to pay more for quality, to wait for made-to-measure items. Many are not and managers are left with the task of balancing a number of potentially conflicting objectives to achieve both **customer satisfaction and the efficient utilization of resources**. This is illustrated in Figure 6.2. Such conflicts exist in all types of operations systems. We may wish to travel by air from London to Singapore, but cannot travel on the day we wish because all seats are booked. We travel two days later, but, when we arrive, we must wait two hours to get into our hotel room, because the room-cleaning schedule means our room is not ready. In both cases solutions may have been found by upgrading our flight to business class or upgrading the standard of our room to an available suite. However, such options may be at an unacceptable price. We could have re-routed our journey via another European city, but this would have added to the length of journey, or required us to fly with a less desirable airline. We could have changed hotel, but our original choice was made on the basis of convenient location and good price. A local authority cleansing department schedules its refuse collection on the basis of a once-weekly collection in each area. The inhabitants of a large apartment find this insufficient for their needs since it leads to an unpleasant build-up of rubbish. In this case an extra collection can be made, but at an additional cost to the residents.

The main reason for conflict goes back to the interrelated nature of the operations system, as the following illustration shows. In an attempt to reduce costs, managers have a number of different options. They can cut back on raw material or staff, which may result in goods of lower quality and a generally poorer service. They can expect the workforce to increase productivity for the same reward or they can gear up for higher productivity by ensuring

Customer satisfaction	V	Efficient utilization of resources
Availability of goods and services in the quantity required		Low levels of stock
		Scheduling which meets all demands
Best quality for price		Best price for quality
Good selection of innovative goods and services		Limited range creating long runs and repeat offerings. Low-cost design
Fast, reliable delivery		Scheduling to fit resources and constraints. Efficient use of raw material and labour
Flexible delivery on demand and easy access		Low-cost location. Restricted hours of working and opening

Figure **6.2** The conflicting objectives of operations management.

long production runs in the case of manufacturing or reducing the time spent with clients in the case of the service industry. All these options give rise to potential conflicts. Goods of lower quality may not be acceptable to the consumer, unless the price is cut, thus negating the original cost-cutting exercise. The workers may resist attempts by management to increase the tempo of work. In manufacturing, the introduction of long production runs has a trade-off in the form of reduced flexibility and lack of choice for the consumer.

The operations manager needs to balance the opposing forces which are the cause of such conflicts. The development of operational research during the Second World War resulted in the post-war emphasis on the 'numerate manager', a concept which found a ready application in a range of operations management techniques. These included value analysis, developments in work study, linear programming, network analysis, statistical quality control, and the emphasis on specific measures of efficiency such as machine utilization, work in progress, labour utilization and so on. Such techniques are used in the non-manufacturing sector as well, as the concepts of staff–student ratios and optimum class sizes in education will testify.

Many of the techniques mentioned above are primarily concerned with efficiency. While efficiency is important, it can distort the system. In manufacturing, the achievement of long runs may be the most efficient use of materials, machines and labour, but it can frustrate some customers who may require a quick response to their order, and valuable customers may go elsewhere. A doctor faced with a waiting room full of patients may be more efficient by limiting consultation time, but with the attendant danger that a potentially serious problem could be overlooked. Efficiency is often the goal, when greater attention needs to be paid to effectiveness in the form of adaptation and flexibility.

As a result, the application of more complex quantitative techniques can produce a limited focus. In recent years attention has shifted to a greater emphasis on the management of the whole system and its relationship with other systems. Operations managers emerge as mediators, coping with different demands both within the operations system itself and between that and other systems. This role is sometimes termed boundary management. We develop these themes in more detail in our discussion of operations strategies at the end of the chapter. In the meantime, we look a little more closely at the relationship between production and the other activities.

The relationship between operations and other functional areas

The centrality of the operations function and the boundary role of the operations manager bring into focus the relationship between the operations function and the other functional areas. Examples of such relationships include the following.

Innovation

As we saw in the previous chapter, innovation is at the heart of new product development, with obvious implications for the operations function. In manufacturing, production capabilities and capacities must be important considerations at the design and development stage. An innovative product design is little value if it cannot be made by the workforce within certain cost parameters. Similarly, a new design for a business studies degree course must take into account the skills of the teachers and the capabilities of the students.

Supply chain management

We will deal with this activity in more detail later in this chapter. As the procurer of raw materials and the guardian of the quality of those incoming materials, purchasing has a key role in the production process for manufacturing, and as we saw in the example of Marks & Spencer, for retailing as well. Purchasing also makes an important contribution to overall costing. Globalization has extended the concept of the supply chain for many organizations and its management has a significant impact on the efficiency and effectiveness of operations systems.

Marketing

Information about consumer requirements is essential to those in operations. Operations managers need to know the total demand for their product and services and when that demand is required. This forms the basis of planning. Feedback from consumers on the utility of the product or service or its value for money can assist both the R&D and operations functions in the design and creation of future products. Holiday companies frequently ask clients to complete a questionnaire about every aspect of their holiday, not only as a public relations exercise, but to improve the product and the way it is delivered.

Finance and accounting

The accounting function clearly interfaces with operations in the development of budgets and targets. In return, operations information is essential to such decisions as pricing and wage determination. The accounting function will also play a major role in decisions to replace major items of capital equipment.

Human resource management

This will assist in the recruitment, selection and training of operations staff. Other key activities include industrial relations, the design of payment systems, including incentives, and the control of the safety, health and welfare of the workforce. Traditionally, industrial relations and wage incentives assume a significant role in manufacturing industry, but the role of staff selection and training are crucial to the success of those service industries with high levels of customer contact.

Case 6.1: Eberspächer and Mercedes Benz

Eberspächer is a German manufacturer of exhaust pipes that has formed a close alliance with Mercedes Benz in Sindelfingen near Stuttgart for the supply of exhaust systems for the complete range of Mercedes cars. In recent years Mercedes Benz has formed close alliances with a number of suppliers, including the tyre manufacturer, Continental. The suppliers are all linked by a just-in-time system and many benefit by their close proximity to the main manufacturing plant at Sindelfingen. The location is a deliberate strategy by Mercedes and relocation, where necessary, is often part of a joint venture between Mercedes and its supplier. As well has having a close relationship in terms of supply, Mercedes and Eberspächer also cooperate on labour issues. Some of the jobs carried out in the Eberspächer plant are done by workers on temporary transfer from Mercedes, as an alternative to laying them off. This adds to the built-in flexibility in the integrated supply system.

The concept for an integrated supplier for exhaust pipe systems emerged after a period of planning by a multi-functional team from Mercedes Benz, involving staff from assembly, purchasing, materials planning, logistics and product engineering. The planning team developed a modular exhaust system, using interchangeable parts to make 16 different exhaust pipe types for different model variations. Four manufacturers were invited to tender for the supply contract and Eberspächer emerged as the company best able to deliver the concept as well as being the lowest-cost producer. Mercedes then entered into detailed planning with Eberspächer to develop the production system that would supply exhaust pipes, not only to the main plant at Sindelfingen, but also to a smaller plant at Rastatt and to the spare parts depot.

The production system was built around a number of core concepts. Just-in-time principles would dominate, based on optimized delivery from component manufacturers to Eberspächer, optimized production and assembly at Eberspächer and optimized delivery to the final assembly stations on the line in Mercedes Benz. The system had to have built-in flexibility, not just for changes in production volume, but also to cater for the planned expansion of production by Mercedes over time. Both just-in-time and flexibility were assisted by the close location of the main Eberspächer production facility to the Mercedes final assembly plant. In fact, Eberspächer was part of an industrial park that had grown up around Mercedes, the largest manufacturing plant in the region.

The production system that was developed was more effective and efficient than any previous system in terms of cost, speed, quality, flexibility and dependability. There was a reduction in the number of types of exhaust pipe from 32 to 16. Production time was reduced by the use of welding robots. The Eberspächer production system is built around nine welding groups. Each welding operation is the same irrespective of the type of pipe, which are differentiated by a barcode. The manufacture of the exhaust pipes is activated by a computer control system, which sends an order to the line as soon as the safety stock level reaches an agreed level. The stock level is set by Mercedes and may vary according to the needs of the vehicle manufacturer. Once made, the exhaust pipes are stored by type and transported as required either to the assembly line or to the spare parts operation.

Transport is controlled by a separate distribution company acting as a sub-contractor to Eberspächer. The transport drivers are each responsible for loading the exhaust pipes on the trucks themselves.

Flexibility is built into the system in that there is spare capacity at Eberspächer in terms of both physical welding capacity and a spare assembly team. Such flexibility is essential in a just-in-time system to cope with variations in product, volume, technical specification and in case of machine breakdown. Each assembly line in the main plant at Mercedes keeps a spare exhaust system of each type in case of damage during assembly, but given the proximity of the supply operation, an emergency supply can reach the line in 10 minutes. This backup is supported by a Mercedes requirement that each of the trucks belonging to the transport subcontractor be fitted with a hand-phone.

Considerable attention was given at the operations planning stage to design quality into the production system. In addition each employee of Eberspächer has responsibility for quality in his or her area of work. There are clear rules for quality operating between Eberspächer and its suppliers and quality is coordinated by a member of the management team who liaises regularly with a counterpart in Mercedes Benz. ■

(*Sources*: Mercedes Benz and Eberspächer KG, 1996)

The key activities of operations managment

In Figure 6.3 we offer a classification of the main activities of operations managers. We draw a distinction between the design of the operations system and the operation of that system. In this section we include a review of supply chain management.

System design
>   Product design
>   Forecasting demand
>   Capacity planning
>   Equipment design
>   Work design
>   Location

System operation
>   Operations planning
>   Scheduling
>   Quantity control
>   Quality control
>   Technology control
>   Cost control

Supply chain management
>   Purchasing and supply
>   Inventory control
>   Logistics
>   Distribution

Figure **6.3** The activities of operations management.

The design of operations systems

This involves the design of products and services people need and want and the design of processes to supply those products and services efficiently and effectively. As we saw in the last section, this invariably involves operations managers with other functional areas of the organization. We deal in turn with product design, forecasting and capacity planning, equipment design, work design, issues relating to location and, finally, the design of operations networks.

Product design

The two major decisions in product design concern first, the styling and function of the product, sometimes known as the product specification, and second, the range of products or degree of standardization to be offered. In manufacturing, decisions will also be made on the type of materials to be used. Design issues clearly interface with innovation (Chapter 5) and marketing (Chapter 7) and issues relating to these aspects of product design are discussed more fully in those chapters. Decisions about both the product specification and the product range involve the kind of conflicts discussed previously. Customers want goods and services that conform to their expectations of function, quality, reliability and cost. For the operations manager those same goods and services must be both easy and cost-effective to produce and deliver. For this reason, issues of product design also involve issues of process design.

The product design process invariably involves the development of product concepts, which are then screened to produce an end result that aims to satisfy the needs of both the consumer and the firm. Concepts can originate from an R&D department or a more informal design team within the organization. Important sources of product ideas also lie outside the organization. They can originate from market research information, through discussion with customers about their needs or from examining what the competition is doing. In the previous chapter we talked about technology-push and demand-pull. In this case we can also talk of 'competitor-push'. Information about competitors' products is important in the design stage. Many firms buy the products of their main rivals to see what they comprise and how they have been put together. Academics involved in teaching an MBA at one university might obtain the course outlines and syllabuses from another university to gain ideas about new course development. In manufacturing industry this can involve the more complex process of reverse engineering, where products are systematically taken apart to see how they were made.

The decision on which product design to follow involves considerations of acceptability, feasibility and viability for both the firm and its customers. Will it be acceptable to the market and will it be reliable enough or safe enough for customers to use? Can it be produced at a price that meets company cost and profit requirements and is attractive to the consumer? A variety of methods are available to operations managers to assist in answering these questions. **Value engineering** is a process that involves the rigorous analysis of the various elements of the product to investigate where cost savings can be made in the design or manufacture or perhaps where the element can be substituted by one of lower cost. The **Taguchi method** (named after its Japanese originator) sets out to test the robustness of the design in extreme conditions. A famous example of the Taguchi method at work was involved in the early testing of the Mercedes 'A' Class car on Swedish roads. An infrequent but not uncommon driving hazard in parts of Sweden is an elk straying across the road, at best forcing drivers to swerve and at worst causing an accident. Mercedes set up an experiment, performed in front of the motoring press, whereby its 'A' Class car would have to swerve violently to avoid a model representing an elk. On performing the test the car overturned, forcing the company to cease production and amend its original design to produce a more stable vehicle.

KEY CONCEPT 6.4
Value engineering

Value engineering is an important technique used in the design of products and services. Essentially it involves the rigorous analysis of the various elements of the product and/or service, with a view to establishing where cost savings can be made in the design or manufacture. The technique also examines where a particular element in the product or service can be substituted by one of lower cost.

In recent years in manufacturing, two systems have developed which focus upon the interface between design and production. These are CAD (computer-aided design) and CAM (computer-aided manufacture). Operating together these are known as CADCAM systems. CAD enables the designer through the use of computer graphics and computer memory to evaluate the consequences of various design alternatives. This has assisted in both the speed and the accuracy of the design stage. A linked CADCAM system has a memory bank of standard designs, and the appropriate machines and tools required for manufacture. In many industries this has assisted greatly in the development of modular production methods. A modular system exists where products are built up by the different combination of a family of standard items. In the car industry, for example, a great number of different models can be offered, yet all are based around different combinations of the same body shells, engines, gear boxes and so on. The development of such systems has had a significant impact on the ability of firms to set up global manufacturing systems with a global network of components suppliers and sub-assembly plants.

Developments in modular systems can simplify the operations process and represent a form of standardization. A lunchtime sandwich bar may appear to have a very large range of products, when in fact all are based on different combinations of a limited range of ingredients and all are made using similar production techniques. This is a case of increased standardization giving the

---

KEY CONCEPT 6.5
CADCAM

CADCAM is a linked system comprising computer-aided design and computer-aided manufacture and has revolutionized the design process in manufacturing industry. Through the use of a computer software package containing a memory bank of a variety of designs, a design engineer is able to test the feasibility of design prior to manufacture. The same software will also provide options of manufacturing methods for particular types of design. Although such systems are expensive to buy, a CADCAM system can speed up the design process considerably and offer a much wider range of design options for consideration.

---

impression of increased variety. Many companies see standardization as an important means of cost reduction. A college offering a wide variety of evening courses, some of which are poorly subscribed, may decide to rationalize its operations around the most popular courses, reducing both staffing costs and overheads. For the manufacturer, standardization often means a better utilization of resources, such as longer production runs and the opportunity to obtain discounts on the purchasing of raw materials and components in bulk. For the consumer, however, it may mean less choice, which may be acceptable if prices are reduced. One of the advantages of the modular system lies in the attempt to maximize both standardization and choice. This is the rationale behind the decision of many British universities to offer modular degree schemes. An important operations decision is the extent of standardization that is both desirable and feasible.

Forecasting demand and capacity planning

These two tasks form the basis of a series of decisions central to operations management, since it is here that the direction for the entire operation is set and resources are acquired and deployed. There is a particular need for market information and accurate predictions of demand. This is obviously much easier where goods are made to order, less so when goods are made to stock. In this case historical data is important, but even this may prove inadequate in a highly volatile market of changing demand, high levels of competition and variations in supply.

Even where demand can be forecast with some accuracy, capacity planning may not be straightforward. It can be especially sensitive to product and process innovation, and will be affected by decisions on the type of technology used, organization size and structure, the extent of subcontracting and policies concerning the intensity of labour, the size of the labour force and the hours of operation. Organizing the capacity to meet demand in some kind of sequence is known as scheduling, which we deal with under operations planning.

Capacity planning is especially difficult in service industries. In most instances, the product on offer cannot be stored when the capacity is not fully utilized, as with airline seats and perishable foods. The concern for unused capacity in the hotel industry has led some hoteliers in popular resorts to overbook rooms. This works well given the predicted number of cancellations, but can lead to holiday-makers not being accommodated in the hotel of their choice and their subsequent dissatisfaction. In some types of industry there are well-established peaks and troughs.

A number of strategies are used by service industries to reduce the difficulties imposed by capacity planning by attempting to control demand. This can be done by channelling demand or delaying demand to match available resources. A bus company or an airline will dictate demand and capacity by operating a fixed schedule, and in some cases insisting that passengers buy tickets beforehand. Extra capacity can be laid on in times of known high demand. Some services can operate a delayed delivery system to control demand and plan capacity. A garage will attempt to match the cars it accepts

training, as well as forming the basis for most types of output-related incentive schemes. The technique is applied to both manufacturing and non-manufacturing concerns. The standard method for administering drugs to hospital patients was changed as a result of work study. The old system involved drugs being kept in a locked drugs cupboard, and, for each patient, the nurse had to return to the cupboard, unlock it, and retrieve the appropriate drug. This involved most of the nurse's time in walking to and from the cupboard, and a safety risk if ever the cupboard were left unlocked. A new system was devised, which is now standard practice in most hospitals. The drugs are kept in a mobile trolley, which is moved from patient to patient. On a more esoteric level, the change from overarm to underarm pitching in baseball to achieve greater speed and accuracy is attributed to the application of work study by Frederick Winslow Taylor!

Locational decisions

The location of the operations system is generally a combination of a variety of factors. The availability and the cost of labour are important issues in determining location. The creation of science parks in close proximity to major universities enables firms to have easy access to key research skills. The decision of Hoover to relocate its operations from France to Scotland was made on the basis of lower labour costs in the latter. Wage costs form only part of this equation. The high non-wage costs of labour in Scandanavian countries makes them less than attractive for the location of labour-intensive industries, and was one reason why the employees of Volvo and their trade unions feared job losses in Sweden following the proposed merger with Renault (Case 4.4). The availability of raw materials and proximity to energy supplies and transport systems are often key decisions in the location of manufacturing plants. Ford UK and Ford Germany make use of the Thames and the Rhine respectively for the location of major manufacturing plants for the easy transport of raw materials and finished goods and as a source of water. The cost of land and property rentals is important for both manufacturing and non-manufacturing organizations alike. Specific local issues also play a part. These can include the cost of local taxes, the degree of financial assistance available, the ease or difficulty associated with planning procedures and local amenities in general.

Many of the above factors are illustrated in Case 2.5. The Singapore government deliberately set out to sell Singapore as a location for high-tech manufacturing industry. The Singapore Economic Development Board established sales offices in New York and California to market Singapore as an attractive location. The attraction was based on generous tax advantages, the provision of factory shells, excellent infrastructure, an educated, English-speaking labour force, weak trade unions and a safe location for ex-pats with good local amenities. Globalization has offered many firms potential competitive advantage through location. Cheap labour can be accessed in the emerging markets of Eastern Europe, Asia and Latin America, while know-how and specialist skills can be obtained in the USA and Western Europe.

Location is an important consideration in the service industry, especially where customers are expected to travel to receive the service. The location of a hospital on the outskirts of a town may solve the land constraint problems of a central site, but the new site must be easily accessible by patients and visitors, otherwise it is failing in its service function. Similarly, large supermarkets located on the edge of towns must make the effort of travel worthwhile in terms of a wider range of produce at cheaper prices. An important consideration here is usually the availability of ample car-parking space. Another incentive is offered in the form of cheaper petrol prices at the supermarket's own petrol stations, with even further discounts tied to the amount of purchases bought in the main store. A professional practice such as a major accounting or law firm may need to balance the advantages of operating from a Central London site, especially for client consultation and prestige purposes, against the rising costs. A prestigious location, even at considerable cost, can be seen as important for marketing purposes. A number of car showrooms are located along Park Lane despite the prohibitive rents and difficulties with traffic and parking. The advantages of prestige and presence on a busy thoroughfare are seen as effective marketing investments for the brand in general even though actual margins on that operation are low or even run at a loss.

The above factors link location decisions with the proximity of customers, their ease of access and their expectations. Proximity to customers is not a factor in the growing industry of call centres and the growth of e-commerce, discussed in Chapter 2. However, cheap rent, good telecommunications facilities and the availability of labour are important. As well as customers, the proximity to competitors may also be important. In retailing, proximity to other shops means a larger potential population of customers. The same logic also applies to the location of restaurants, and cities such as New York and Hong Kong have streets dubbed 'restaurant row'. In most major cities, areas have developed that are famous for specific activities such as the legal district, the financial district and so on. Close proximity to rivals is seen as an important source of competitive information and while such firms compete, they also collaborate to assist clients. Usually an entire support industry grows up around the firms, including specialist recruitment agencies, specialist book shops and office equipment suppliers.

The design of operations networks

This has become an area of growing importance. The influences at work here include globalization, the need for cost reduction in the transformation process, the management of the supply chain and the influence of Japanese models. Operations are viewed and designed as a network linking suppliers and customers through the transformation process. The traditional view of network design is in the form of vertical integration. Backward or downstream integration involves the incorporation of all or part of the supply chain through some form of joint venture, which may or may not involve acquisition. Forward or upstream integration involves a similar incorporation of the distribution chain.

The claimed advantages for both types of integration are:

- improved quality and dependability through a close association with suppliers and customers, involving an exchange of information and occasionally staff, and a better mutual understanding of requirements;
- an increased potential for both product and volume flexibility as well as speed of operation through the ability to synchronize the activities of all participants in the network;
- costs can be reduced through a sharing of facilities such as R&D or banking, and through the increased speed of the transformation process.

Such advantages are built into the Japanese manufacturing system, which is led by the major firms. Each major firm has several tiers of inter-linked suppliers with considerable cross-ownership between them. Raw materials suppliers are linked to components suppliers who feed into final assembly. The system is supported by a number of shared facilities, which can include technology transfer, transport and energy supply. This close relationship between a manufacturing firm and its suppliers is illustrated in Case 6.1. In this example, Eberspächer, a supplier of exhaust pipes to Mercedes Benz, is a first-tier supplier. The suppliers of components to Eberspächer are second-tier suppliers. In 1997 Ford created a company within a company in Visteon Automative Products. This was made up of four existing component supply divisions, each concerned with a different group of components. Historically there had been little coordination between them. The aim of the new company was to develop an integrated system involving all four groups in information sharing and joint design projects, producing a system solution for all vehicle component needs. Moreover, while Visteon was established under the ownership and protection of Ford as a tier-one supplier, its immediate goal was to establish itself as a supplier to any vehicle manufacturer in the world and earn at least 20 per cent of its revenue from manufacturers other than Ford.

There are questions of how far such integration can be taken and there may be problems of adequate control through acquisition strategies (see Chapter 4 for a further discussion).

Managing the operating system

We deal with two main aspects of operations management: operations planning and operations control.

Operations planning

The aim of operations planning is to ensure that sufficient goods or services are produced to meet demand. The activity involves issues of quantity, quality, timing and cost. Operations planning determines what the organization can achieve in terms of the quantity of goods and services it produces, the quality of those goods and services, the timing of their delivery, the cost of production and the degree of flexibility the organization has at its disposal. The key influences are the extent to which management can control the supply side and the demand side of the equation. In manufacturing, known customer demand over time and a dedicated just-in-time supply system can result in an effective low-cost operation. However, where there are large fluctuations in both demand and supply, inefficiencies are bound to occur, with a corresponding increase in the cost of operations. Even where planning is based on accurate information, things can go wrong. A university is able to plan its schedule of lectures for the term, semester or year based on the known numbers of students registered to take certain subjects, the availability of rooms and the constraints of staff and student timetables. However, the sudden illness of a lecturer may mean the lecture cannot take place, rooms can be double-booked and, in the case of open courses, there may be more students than space available.

A basic consideration in manufacturing is whether goods are made to stock or to order. Ford Motor Company has a policy that all cars are ordered before manufacture. On the other hand Chrysler in the USA historically made various models, which were then sold from stock. The fast-food chain McDonald's produces hamburgers to stock based on carefully prepared demand forecasts. Hamburgers that are not then sold within a certain length of time are discarded. McDonald's claim that this system provides greater operating efficiency, and they still have the flexibility to produce goods to order when stocks are inadequate. Making items to stock can mean that goods are always available when needed, but it can be costly in terms of having stock lying around. Making goods to order is more efficient but can mean that the customer has to wait.

Operations planning overlaps with issues of capacity planning which we discussed earlier. In the service industry problems of manufacturing to stock or order reveal themselves in the provision of standardized or customized items. A hairdresser will offer a standardized service to all customers, such as haircut and wash, and a customized service in the form of styling. Restaurants often attempt to offer the best of both worlds. An 'à la carte' menu offers the consumer flexibility of choice, but within a limited range of dishes. In general terms, the greater the choice, the greater the problems for the operations planner. The more dishes the chef must make to order, the longer the potential delay for the customer and the greater the difficulty in serving a group of customers at the same time. This is the reason that many restaurants will insist that large groups take a set menu.

The above examples illustrate the problems of loading, sequencing and scheduling.

Loading refers to the amount of work that can be allocated to a particular work centre, be it a department, unit or person. Effective planning usually aims to even the load through a process known as load levelling, both over time and across employees and groups. Where demand is known in advance, as in the allocation of lecturing duties in a university, loading should be a relatively straightforward operation, provided there are agreed rules as to what constitutes a fair load. In certain areas, such as the health service, where resources are tight and demand may be high, demand can be controlled by an appointments system. However, such a system must have the capacity to deal with emergencies, which often requires those with scheduled appointments to wait or have their appointments cancelled.

Sequencing relates to the order in which work is done. The basis of this can vary from firm to firm. A simple method of sequencing is on the basis of first come, first served. In certain departments of large food stores, where demand can build up periodically, this problem is tackled by having a customer numbering system, which ensures that customers are dealt with in order. In some manufacturing firms it may be more appropriate to batch work irrespective of the order date, since this is a more efficient utilization of resources. Some firms may prioritize work by customer.

The aim of **scheduling** is to balance the costs of production against demands for goods and services; to ensure that demand is met in the most efficient way possible. This, of course, gives rise to the classic dilemma of operations management, as we saw in Figure 6.2. A whole series of theories and techniques have been developed to deal with such problems. These include Gantt charts, queuing theory, linear programming and the more complex models of operational research.

The problem with all such techniques is that, while they can offer optimal solutions to the problems of production planning and scheduling, they cannot allow for all the constraints operating in a given situation, many of which cannot be measured and many of which are highly subjective. Coping with variations in supply and demand and hence the capacity of the operations system depends upon having some measure of capacity. Manufacturing firms use measures of machine and labour utilization, both hospitals and hotels use beds, universities use staff–student ratios and room size and so on. Where variations occur between capacity and demand, there are three generic coping strategies.

- Variations in demand are simply ignored and activities are constant. This results in stable employment and, in times of high demand, high utilization of resources. When demand falls, however, costs will rise through problems of over-staffing or too much stock being created. In the case of a specialist art or antiques dealer, where margins are high, long periods without customers may be acceptable. In the case of the public sector, where resources are tight, stable levels of staffing mean that customers must queue and wait for the service they require.

- Capacity can be adjusted to meet demand. This is done in manufacturing firms by overtime or hiring temporary labour when demand is high and laying off workers when demand is low. The flexible firm, discussed in Chapter 3, is a prime example of the use of labour flexibility to adjust to changes in demand. However, overtime can be expensive and hiring extra staff is only possible if there is spare capacity in the other resources, particularly machinery and equipment. Reducing the workforce carries social costs as well as financial costs where redundancy is involved. In the service industry, customer contact often makes scheduling difficult owing to the variations in time demanded by each client. In some banks this kind of problem has been tackled by the introduction of 'automatic teller machines', and a division of labour into those staff dealing with standard transactions and those dealing with more complex enquiries. The gains of adjusting capacity to meet demand are in the form of increased revenue, although where resources are stretched there may be costs associated with reduced quality.

● Demand can be adjusted to fit capacity. Demand can be increased to make use of spare capacity through price reductions, advertising and promotional campaigns and even the development of new products. Airlines often cut the price of their fares and hotels the price of their rooms to encourage more travellers in low season. A university may use spare capacity during vacations by hiring out rooms and residential accommodation for conferences. Where there is excess demand this too can be controlled. Most doctor's surgeries now operate appointment systems and football clubs can ensure that demand does not exceed capacity by making certain games all-ticket affairs. Alternative strategies here might include persuading the customer to accept a delay in delivery or subcontracting the work to another company.

Scheduling decisions can be highly sensitive and illustrate the relationship between the firm and the environment in which it operates; this is especially true of the public sector. The provision and scheduling of the railways in this country was examined in the 1960s by a committee under the leadership of Lord Beeching. The resulting Beeching Plan meant that several lines were closed and certain towns were left with no railway provision whatsoever. This created widespread political and community opposition. The debate centred around the argument as to whether some public services should continue to operate at a considerable loss or be closed, thus saving the taxpayer money, but depriving some of them of a service they may need. Similar problems face bus companies in planning their routes, especially in less populated rural areas. Planning and scheduling problems are also highly contentious in the health services. Hospitals must schedule operations according to their available resources, which means that only a specific number of non-emergency operations can be budgeted in any one year, resulting in a build-up of waiting lists.

All these illustrations take production planning and scheduling out of the domain of programmed decisions and simplistic techniques and involve social, political and ethical considerations.

Operations control

There are various types of control used in any production system. We identify these various forms of control and the mechanisms through which they are achieved below. As with all forms of control, those managing the system must determine the standards that are to operate. In some types of system such standards may be difficult to measure, for example the quality of education or social work. In other situations there may be conflict concerning the appropriateness of certain standards, for example between the firm and its customers over service standards, between marketing and production about delivery times, or between management and unions over levels of productivity.

● **Quantity control**. This is sometimes known as production control and sometimes as progress chasing. It ensures that the throughput of goods and services goes according to the planned schedule.

- **Quality control**. This ensures that the quality of the finished product or service meets the standards set in the design stage and also meets with the approval of the customer. In manufacturing it involves quality considerations about components and raw materials. It can be especially difficult in services, where standards are both variable and highly subjective. We deal with issues of quality in more detail in the next section.

- **Technology control.** This refers to the maintenance of plant or equipment. While issues of maintenance are invariably linked with manufacturing industry, the use of computers and other types of office equipment places technology control on the agenda of all organizations. The key issue is the determination of when a piece of equipment is in need of service. Many firms solve this problem by instituting a system of planned preventive maintenance. Developments in IT have meant that, in some instances, visual warnings can be installed when maintenance is required. These operate as a function of the number of times the equipment is switched on, its running time, how intensely it is used and so on. Such systems have been installed in some cars to indicate when a service is due. In some firms technology management is subcontracted through service agreements with suppliers, as in the case of photocopying machines. In many such cases equipment is leased rather than bought outright and in the case of problems, replacement is automatic. Where equipment is bought, management must make decisions about when to replace.

- **Labour control**. Issues at stake here include the extent and style of supervision and the nature and use of incentives.

- **Cost control**. There is a strong link with cost accounting and budgeting. This form of control involves the collection and analysis of accounting information about all aspects of the business and the use of comparisons, which are either historical and/or based on benchmarking against another organization.

We can see from the five types of control that there is considerable overlap. Labour control has a close relationship to quantity, quality and cost control; productivity is a function of quantity, labour and cost control. A key concern in most organizations today is quality. Many organizations have become so preoccupied with quality and a number of related techniques that we examine this phenomenon more closely in the next section.

With all types of control someone must decide upon the appropriate form of action when deviations from the standard occur. Various options are available, as the following illustrations reveal. In the case of a bottling plant, the decision is fairly straightforward. Empty bottles are washed and then closely inspected prior to being filled; bottles that are cracked or chipped are broken up, bottles that are still dirty are sent through the washing process again. A clothing manufacturer making garments for a quality-conscious retail chain, like Marks & Spencer, has other options. It may be possible to sell elsewhere items that are not acceptable to the original client. Some manufacturers sell slightly imperfect goods to their own staff or to the public as 'seconds'. Such decisions get more complex in businesses such as a restaurant, where overall quality may not be judged until the meal has been eaten, and the only redress is in the form of compensation. Assessments, especially of quality, can be highly subjective and a potential source of conflict between producer and customer.

Case 6.2: First Sound and Vision Group

The First Sound and Vision Group Ltd (FSV), formerly known as Orlake Records, makes vinyl gramophone records and represents a classic case of survival in a declining market. From 1979 to 1986, the annual trade delivery of vinyl singles in the United Kingdom fell from 89.1 million to 67.4 million, and LPs from 74.5 to 52.3 million. Over the same period the sales of cassettes increased threefold to reach 69.6 million in 1986. In the 1990s the sales of vinyl declined still further and CDs eclipsed both vinyl and cassettes in the market place. By the end of 1998, this trend had continued apace, as the following table illustrates. Competition in manufacture had become intense, not just in this country but internationally as well. Only six manufacturers of vinyl discs remain in the UK, and FSV has the capacity to fulfil UK market needs in its entirety. In spite of this dramatic decline in the market, FSV has not only maintained its output levels, but has seen a dramatic increase in market share. In 1999 there are plans to increase production, following a substantial order from the major record company, Polygram.

The market has changed since 1993. A mixed market of 7" singles, 12" LPs, and variations in the form of shape discs, picture discs and colour discs has shifted to a focus on the production of 12" singles aimed exclusively at the dance market. Much of this growth is accounted for by independent record producers and record brokers. The latter represent a one-stop shop for cutting, sleeve and label design. In this respect the BPI figures presented in Table 6.1 under-represent the sales of 12" singles. Official statistics focus on selected official outlet stores, while the 12" market also includes sales from small specialist shops, in clubs and pubs, as well as exports. These do not feature in the UK statistics. Nonetheless, the table still reveals the overwhelming dominance of the CD market.

The actual manufacture is the following stage from the recording studio. There the final tape is converted to a series of vibrations, which cut grooves into a master disc, known as the lacquer master. FSV has a plating shop, which takes this master and through an electro-forming process, makes its own moulds to form the basis of record

Table **6.1** Recorded music sales by type as a proportion of the total

	1996		1997		1998	
	NOS	£	NOS	£	NOS	£
Singles						
7"	0.8	0.2	0.7	0.2	0.5	0.1
12"	2.8	1.4	2.5	1.3	2.2	1.2
Cassette	7.1	1.9	6.9	1.7	7.1	1.9
CD	15.9	7.5	19.1	8.6	19.2	9.4
Total	26.6	11.0	29.2	11.9	29.0	12.5
Albums						
LPs	1.0	1.0	0.8	0.9	0.8	0.8
Cassette	17.8	16.1	14.2	13.2	12.2	10.8
CD	54.6	71.9	55.7	74.1	57.9	75.9
Total	73.4	89.0	70.8	88.1	71.0	87.5

▶

Continued

production. Several moulds may be required depending on the number of presses to be used, the length of the run and the uncertain working life of each mould. The actual record is made in the production department by compression moulding which presses extruded plastic on to the mould on a specially designed machine. This takes around 25 seconds for the average disc. Operations at FSV is based in two buildings. The smaller building houses the plating shop, the library of production moulds, and acts as storage for labels and sleeves. The larger building houses the production presses, the offices and offers some storage space for the finished product. However, there is not a great requirement for storage, given the fast-moving nature of the business.

Record companies may use a number of manufacturers, particularly on high-selling items. FSV manufactures for a range of different companies and as a competitive strategy attempts to meet customer needs at high quality, low cost, and in as short a time as possible. The variety of the work means that there are no standard production runs. Very large production runs associated with a vibrant 7" singles market are now a thing of the past. The largest run in 1998 was 8000 units, but production runs of 500–750 are not uncommon. The firm uses two types of presses, fully automatic and manually operated. The company has increased its number of fully automatic presses to 12, retaining seven manual machines. Certain products such as 'picture' discs and 'shape' discs can only be produced using manual machines. However, the demand for such products has declined as they were associated largely with the 'heavy metal' boom of the late 1980s. Nonetheless, management sees it as important to retain the capacity to produce special discs on manual machines, and FSV is the only company offering such a variety of products. It is felt that this offers FSV both a competitive edge and a means of gaining access to higher-volume business with some companies. Production planning and scheduling is carried out on a continuous basis at the point of order and is the responsibility of the sales order clerk and the production controller. Schedules are drawn up on the basis of 'first come, first served'.

Quality control is the responsibility of the supervisor in the plating shop, the area where master moulds are made that determine the quality of the entire operation. Quality control throughout the company relies heavily on visual checks. At the pressing stage, one finished record in every 20 is checked visually. Ninety per cent of all faults can be spotted visually by a trained operator. In addition a particular pressing is checked audibly every hour. Before storage, a further one record in 40 is checked visually, a process that is repeated after nine hours have elapsed to allow the plastic to cool down. Faults found with the moulds can sometimes be rectified manually. At the pressing stage, if repetitive faults are found in a particular run, the whole batch is destroyed. More recently, management have moved towards a system whereby quality is the responsibility of all employees and is reflected in the bonus scheme.

FSV operates with a core staff of 50 employees. As part of a cost reduction exercise the company moved from a two-shift to a day-shift system. Thirty are employed on a 40-hour week basis and 20 form two five-hour shifts. A redundancy programme was introduced to shed the required levels of labour. A side benefit of the move to a day-shift system has been improved levels of quality with increased levels of management supervision. In the past FSV employed large numbers of part-time and temporary workers. This is no longer the case and overtime is used to meet fluctuations in demand. No job descriptions are used and all staff are expected to work flexibly across a range of tasks. Operators become packers and vice versa and both supervisors and management help out in the production and packing process. As with other industries operating in areas of declining demand, some skills are difficult to find, more especially those in compression moulding. In 1999 FSV has made plans to revert to a two-shift system to meet increased demand from a major new contract with Polygram Records. FSV had been rewarded with a major contract after several years of working with the company and achieving high levels of satisfaction by fulfilling small orders to quality specifications, flexibly and on time. FSV is located in the same geographical area as Polygram, an advantage in a product market where speed of delivery is essential. The return to a major shift system will mean the inevitable rise in costs and the company could be exposed if production were to fall.

FSV has done well in such a declining market, not only in terms of survival but to plan expansion as the market contracts still further. FSV's survival and success are a feature of several interrelated factors:

- Management have targeted quality and service as key elements in gaining competitive advantage.
- Prices have generally been maintained, despite pressure from customers. FSV has not chased volume through price discounts and has maintained a niche market with several customers. Ten years ago the company saw price competition as an important strategic tool. However, whereas price discussions are held with customers once a year, discussions about quality are held for every order.
- Considerable emphasis is placed on cost efficiency. In recent years much of this has been achieved through staffing cuts, the consolidation of activity in one shift, improvements in quality, continued staff flexibility and in increased use of automation coupled with a production focus on the 12″

disc. FSV's gross margins have continued to rise despite increased materials costs and an emphasis on a lower-priced, lower-margin product in the 12″ single.
- Speed of response and dependability of delivery times is seen as vital in a business where the life span of the product may be relatively short. The firm has a strategy of fulfilling customer orders for any type of gramophone record in as short a time as possible and a reputation has been built up for low lead-times and prompt delivery.
- While special items such as shape discs, hologram discs and picture discs are much less significant in terms of volume, the company retains the flexibility to produce such items as and when required. Such flexibility has enhanced the company's reputation in the market place. ■

(*Sources*: First Sound and Vision, Dagenham, Essex; *BPI Year Book*, 1987, 1997, 1998)

Quality planning, control and assurance

From an analysis of management literature and the mission statements and internal publications of organizations, we might well conclude that organizational life in the 1990s has been dominated by thoughts of quality. Notions of quality pervade all types of organizations. Universities, under new forms of government control, have fallen upon the concept of quality like converts to a new religion. In this section we will attempt to define quality, examine its importance and review both traditional and more modern approaches to quality. The latter will take us through benchmarking, business process re-engineering (BPR) and total quality management (TQM).

Garvin (1988) and Slack *et al.* (1998) have attempted to classify what we mean by quality under a number of headings, representing different approaches. These are as follows:

- The **transcendant** approach to quality is the best possible and the best available. In their mission statements, many firms strive to be the best but such a goal is subjective, difficult to attain, usually comes at a high cost and is accompanied by high prices. Cars such as Ferrari and Rolls Royce take this approach, as do certain expensive and highly rated restaurants and hotels.
- The **manufacturing** approach takes the view that quality is conformance to design specification. This approach to quality is from the perspective of the manufacturer and may not be the view of the consumer.
- The **user-based** approach takes a utilitarian view from the perspective of the consumer and is based on the concept of 'fit for purpose'.
- The **product-based** approach sees quality in terms of both 'fit for

purpose' and 'conformance to specification' and attempts to combine the user-based and manufacturing approaches. As we have seen, there can be conflict between the two perspectives and as with any concept based on the perception of the consumer, different consumers have different expectations.

● The **value-based** approach sees quality in relative terms and as a function of cost and price. As we see later in this chapter, the differences in cost between travelling on the same plane from London to New York by Concorde as opposed to the cheapest economy ticket available can be £6,000. In both cases flight experiences will be judged in terms of the value of the service experienced by the passengers.

● As an extension of the above approach, Slack *et al.* (1998) view quality in terms of **customer expectations vs. customer perception.** Where expectations are met, quality is acceptable. Where expectations are exceeded, quality is deemed to be high, but where expectations are not met quality is seen as poor.

The traditional view of a quality product is that it conforms to specification. This is a somewhat narrow approach to quality that has been superseded by a view that focuses much more on the perspective of the customer. This does mean that quality is ultimately subjective. Nonetheless, both manufacturing and service organizations must plan to achieve standards of quality based on their operating experience. Deming (1986) argues that improved quality is a virtuous circle of lower costs, lower prices, increased market share and the provision of more jobs. The importance of quality is thus seen in terms of enhanced reputation, increased sales revenue and a better deal for customers, employees, shareholders and the society at large. In Chapter 5 we pointed to studies that suggested that consumers are willing to pay more for goods of higher quality.

The cost of quality failure can be significant. There are the famous examples of Chernobyl and the *Exxon Valdes*. At a more mundane level, an electrical fault in a new dishwasher, a battery that does not work or an airline meal that is not the one ordered by the passenger are the kind of quality problems experienced by consumers on a daily basis. In such cases the costs are those incurred by the company in scrap or replacement. However, other costs may be less easy to define, such as the customer buying another brand of dishwasher or battery the next time or changing airline for subsequent flights. Furthermore, stories of poor quality are passed around and reputations can be damaged.

Methods of quality control, assurance and improvement

In this section we compare more traditional approaches to quality, based on the notion of measurement against a performance standard, with alternative approaches, such as benchmarking, business process re-engineering and total quality management. Historically methods associated with quality have moved from control to assurance to, more recently, a focus on quality improvement.

The traditional approach to quality control involves **measurement against a performance standard**, which is sometimes referred to as 'conformance to specification'. A number of steps are involved.

- First, the performance standard or quality characteristics must be defined and specific measures applied. These can relate to such factors as dimensions, appearance, reliability, durability, speed of service, behaviour of staff, after-sales service and so on. Specifications for the paintwork on a car can include the number of coats, the evenness of the finish, the appearance of the finish and how long it will last. For hotel rooms the specification will include the number of towels and toiletries to be provided for each bathroom and the frequency with which they are changed. McDonald's use a number of specifications relating to the customer ordering process. This involves attempts to define specific measures for customer greeting, taking the order, assembling the order, presenting the order, obtaining payment and thanking the customer. Thirty-five separate steps are identified, each with its own associated measure.
- Once a measurable standard has been set, the next step is to assess goods and service against that standard to determine what is acceptable and what is not acceptable. In most processes, this can be done at different stages. In manufacturing industry it is common to find quality checks on incoming materials and components, regular checks at each stage of production and then a final examination of the finished product. This kind of process can be vital in ensuring that problems are dealt with as soon as they arise and are not passed on to the next stage in the process. The boundary between acceptable and unacceptable can vary depending on the type of product or service. In certain types of precision engineering there may be no allowable deviation from the standard. In the accident and emergency department of a busy hospital a standard may be set that each patient is seen by a nurse within 15 minutes of arrival. At exceptionally busy times or in the event of a major emergency, the standard will have to be revised. In most cases standards will have a tolerance factor built in. A number of methods are used for measuring performance against the standard. The record company in Case 6.2 uses a mixture of visual and audial checks. A decision must be made whether to check every product or service item or operate a sampling method. Where sampling is concerned, techniques of statistical quality control and statistical process control have been developed to assist the manager.
- The final decision involves the corrective action needed to close or reduce the gap between performance and the standard. This can take a variety of forms. In manufacturing, faulty items can be reworked or scrapped. In retailing, faulty or damaged goods can be replaced or a refund made to the customer. In some service industries it may be difficult to recover the situation and the only remedy may be a refund. Where flights have been delayed by some time, particularly where mechanical problems are concerned, some airlines will offer further free flights as compensation. For many service industries, recovering a problem situation to the total satisfaction of the customer can be a useful way of reinforcing customer loyalty.

● Once corrective action is taken, the process should not end. The information obtained in the quality control process should be fed back to other parts of the operating system, so that quality improvements can be made.

There are a number of problems associated with more traditional methods involving measuring performance against a standard. The approach tends to be inward-looking and emphasizes organizational criteria rather than customer criteria. The approach tends to be historical, in that faults are rectified after they occur. These problems have led managers to seek alternative approaches. We will examine two of them, benchmarking and business process re-engineering, briefly and a third, total quality management, in more detail.

Benchmarking is the comparison of performance in one organization or part of an organization against that in another, with a view to finding ways of improving performance. This is a common technique used by the major car manufacturers. Interest in the success of the Toyota production system led managers from most Western car manufacturers to benchmark their company's performance along several dimensions with that of Toyota and make visits to Japan to see such systems first-hand. Comparisons were made of the hours taken to build a car, the amount of work in progress, stock levels and vehicles made per employee. Much of the interest in these kinds of comparisons gave rise to the focus on 'lean production', discussed later in the chapter. In practice, benchmarking can be done in a variety of ways. Comparisons can be made with other departments in the same organization, with other organizations in the same business, or even in a different kind of business. Quality improvements in some public sector service industries have come from benchmarking against manufacturing firms. Benchmarking can focus on specific measures of performance, as with Toyota above, or on practices that achieve those performance levels. In many cases the focus is on both.

Benchmarking does not replace traditional methods of quality control and can operate alongside them. What benchmarking offers is a focus on the market place and on performance improvement. However, transferring the lessons learned from benchmarking exercises is not always straightforward, particularly where cross-cultural comparisons are involved. We must be careful that we are comparing like with like and that differences in performance are attributable to factors other than culture. We explore these arguments in

---

KEY CONCEPT 6.7
Benchmarking

Benchmarking is the process of improving quality through comparison with another organization or a different part of the same organization. Quality improvement is achieved through learning from the practices and methods of others and adopting them for use in your organization. There can be limitations in the transfer of such practices, especially where different cultures are involved.

KEY CONCEPT 6.8
Business process re-engineering

This is a radical approach to quality improvement with the aim of integrating all activities of the organization to focus on the customer. Invariably it involves the radical rethink of all aspects of operations in terms of cost, quality, speed, and service standard. The results often include a radical restructuring of the organization.

Chapter 2, when we discuss culture and business, and later this chapter in our discussion of lean production.

Business process re-engineering or **BPR** owes much to the work of Porter (1985) and Hammer and Champy (1994). The aim is to add value for the customer at each stage of the value chain. However, BPR sets out to be deliberately radical and aims at nothing short of dramatic improvements. This inevitably involves a fundamental rethinking of the organization and its operations. In BPR the key performance indicators are cost, quality, speed and service standards. It is an approach that aims to integrate the activities of the organization to focus them more sharply on the customer. BPR recommendations generally incorporate radical restructuring, involving reducing the number of departments, especially those dealing with customers, and reducing the numbers employed. For this reason it is not always popular with employees at any level. It has been criticized for focusing not so much on quality as cost, and its most ardent critics see it solely as a means of reducing the workforce and as a passing fad.

Total quality management

Total quality management (TQM) is a strategic approach to quality that permeates the entire organization. It goes beyond control and assurance in that it incorporates a number of different techniques and approaches and is linked to culture change in the organization.

While many see TQM as a relatively recent phenomenon, the concept emerged from the work in statistical quality control at the Western Electric Hawthorne plant in the 1930s and was primarily associated with the work of W. Edwards Deming and Joseph Juran, although the concept of 'total quality' is attributed to Armand Feigenbaum. The key ideas were introduced to Japan by the Americans as the occupying force in the immediate post-war era and found its greatest expression in Japanese manufacturing industry. Japanese techniques associated with TQM can be found in the work of such as Ishikawa and Taguchi. The basic concepts and ideas in the development of TQM can be found in Feigenbaum (1961), Deming (1986) and Juran (1988).

The essence of TQM incorporates the following:

● It is a top-down management philosophy that focuses on the needs of the customer.

KEY CONCEPT 6.9
Total quality management

TQM is a strategic approach to quality that embraces all members of the organization. The aim is to create a corporate culture that focuses on the needs of the customer by building quality into every aspect of the operation. The claimed advantages are a cost saving for the organization and an added value for the customer. It is a method of long-term continuous improvement and is linked to national standards such as BS5750 and international standards such as ISO9000. Common criticisms include its association with the introduction of a cumbersome bureaucracy and the problems of introducing such systems in low-trust cultures.

- Key values tend to include 'customer awareness', 'getting it right first time', 'continuous improvement' and 'teamworking'.
- It comprises a quality plan, which offers a structured, disciplined approach to quality and incorporates a number of systems, tools and techniques. Particular emphasis is given to the collection and analysis of information and to employee training.
- It covers all parts of the organization and often involves those organizations in the supply chain as well. Relationships between departments in the same organization, as well as those between firms in the supply chain, are governed by detailed service level agreements.
- As we can see from the key values, TQM is culturally based. Involvement of all staff is central to its philosophy. TQM statements abound with references to teamwork and creative thinking and often contain slogans about empowerment as a means of adding value.
- TQM focuses on the elimination of costs associated with control and failure. These are seen as signs of poor quality. Instead the emphasis is on prevention through the involvement of all staff. In this way all costs are reduced.
- Through its focus on continuous improvement, TQM is essentially a long-term approach.

Such elements are incorporated in the mission statement of Akzo Chemicals, a multinational employing two thousand people in the UK:

> The supply of quality products and services to meet both internal and external customer expectations and to promote the participation and development of all employees in the pursuit of continuous quality improvement.

> (Tayles and Woods, 1993, p. 3)

The classic approach to TQM is the kind associated with worldwide quality standards such as ISO 9000. The specific UK equivalent of ISO 9000 is BS

5750, established by the government through the British Standards Institute (BSI). Under BS 5750 quality is defined as an all-embracing concept involving all stages and all people in the production process.

In order to obtain British Standard 5750, firms must prepare a 'quality manual' which sets out policy and procedures on quality assurance. A key element of the policy is that companies must identify their own quality standards. There then follows an assessment process to review policy and procedures and to ensure that they are being carried out. Successful firms are awarded a certificate, which gives them the right to incorporate the standard in their marketing literature. Maintenance of the award is dependent upon follow-up inspections, usually at annual intervals. Many TQM systems go beyond the policy and procedures manual to incorporate a set of instructions associated with each job.

As Hill (1991) noted, there is a widespread belief amongst managers that they derive benefits from the introduction of a TQM system. These benefits can include a rethink and improvement of existing procedures, a 'badge' such as ISO 9000 and BS 5750, which can be used as a marketing feature, and, of course, an improvement in quality itself. The attraction of TQM to management is also seen by Hill to incorporate political factors. TQM has increased the participation of middle management in particular in the decision-making process and given them more power to get things done.

There are also a number of criticisms associated with TQM as expressed in the studies of Hill (1991) and Wilkinson *et al.* (1992). A summary is offered below.

- Despite the culture of involvement and the slogan of empowerment, the focus is on management control, leading, in some cases, to management by stress.
- TQM systems are bureaucratic, time-consuming and expensive to install and run. When associated with the demands of ISO 9000 and BS 5750, TQM has been dubbed 'quality management by manual'. Furthermore, the notion of a firm setting its own standards has been attacked as subjective and misleading for the public.
- The gains from introducing TQM are often less than those anticipated. This leads to demotivation and lack of interest in systems and procedures. The result is that the impact of the introduction of TQM fades over time.
- Despite claims for the inclusive nature of TQM, its failure is often through a lack of integration. A new set of procedures are bolted on to existing quality control and assurance systems, which leads to lack of understanding and is seen as yet another set of bureaucratic compliances.
- As we saw in our treatment of corporate culture, there is a paradox between a top-down system, which inevitably involves control, and the same system, which urges involvement and empowerment.
- TQM require high levels trust across the entire organization. It is therefore difficult to introduce TQM effectively in low-trust situations. For this reason TQM is incompatible with the job losses often associated with BPR.

Supply chain management

Supply chain management is a relatively new concept and involves a number of activities previously managed by different departments within the same organization. Purchasing and supply managers were concerned with the interface with suppliers. Inventory or stock control managers were involved with the management of stock once it had reached the organization. Distribution managers were concerned with the interface with customers. Those involved in logistics were concerned with the planning and management of materials flows in the organization, particularly at the downstream end of operations, and an interface with distribution. The concept of materials management was an early attempt at integration and defined by the Institute of Purchasing and Supply as,

> the concept requiring an organizational structure which unifies into one functional responsibility the systematic planning and control of all materials from identification of the need through to delivery to the consumer. Materials management embraces planning, purchasing, production and inventory control, storage, materials handling and physical distribution. The objectives of materials management are to optimize performance in meeting agreed customer service requirements at the same time adding to the profitability by minimizing costs and making the best use of available resources.

While this could also stand as a definition of supply chain management, the reality of materials management in many manufacturing organizations was a focus on purchasing and internal flows (Slack *et al.*, 1998).

KEY CONCEPT 6.10
Supply chain management

Supply chain management brings together a number of related activities, including purchasing and supply, inventory management, logistics, materials management and distribution. These are combined as part of an integrated strategy which aims to reduce costs for the organization and enhance satisfaction for the customer. Like many approaches in operations management, it aims to resolve the classic dilemma of both satisfying customer needs and ensuring the efficient utilization of resources (articulated in Key Concept 6.3 and Figure 6.2). Such an approach can involve suppliers and distributors in joint ventures with the organization.

Supply chain management attempts to integrate purchasing and supply, inventory management, logistics, materials management and distribution across the entire organization. In doing so supply chain management:

● takes a holistic view of the movement of materials, components and information within a single organization and in its relationship with suppliers and customers;

● extends the boundaries of a single organization to incorporate those organizations involved in upstream activities (suppliers) and those involved in downstream activities (distributors, retailers, customers), a key feature of any effective supply chain being the close relationship with suppliers on one hand and customers on the other;

● takes a strategic view of the supply chain and manages the process to reduce costs for the organization and to create added value for the customer.

A representation of supply chain management can be seen in Figure 6.4.

In any one organization there are likely to be a number of supply chains, which vary in length. A major decision, which must be made in manufacturing in particular, is the extent to which control of a supply chain extends into ownership through various forms of vertical integration. We deal with this concept elsewhere in the chapter as well as in Chapter 4. The supply chain concept can be applied to non-manufacturing organizations as well. In universities, students are part of a supply chain. Full-time students are 'supplied'

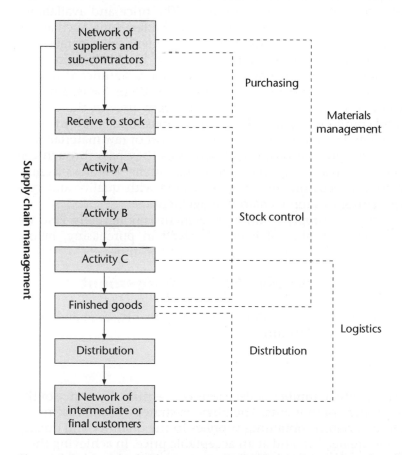

Figure **6.4** A supply chain management system: an integration of traditional functions.

by schools and colleges and part-time students by local employers. The students must fulfil certain quality requirements in the form of qualifications to gain entry. Once they have entered the university they are processed through a number of teaching, learning and assessment stages to emerge with a degree and enhanced career opportunities. While all too few universities take a holistic and strategic view of this process, elements of supply chain management are emerging. Many universities make great efforts to build up close relations with certain schools and colleges to ensure a consistent supply of known quality. In the case of the recruitment of students from overseas, universities establish joint ventures with agents in a number of countries to manage the flow more effectively. At the downstream end of the chain most universities have an established careers service to assist in employment. The creation of closer relationships between universities and employers has emerged as a key feature in the Labour government's strategy on employability through education. As students pass through the system there is attention paid to completion rates and the reduction of wastage as a measure of the quality of provision.

The importance of the supply chain concept is twofold. First, from the perspective of this book, it illustrates, more than most activities, the interaction of operations management with its environment. The price and availability of goods are influenced by various environmental considerations, such as the economics of supply and demand. However, management will operate purchasing strategies in order to control supply and demand and hence the environment. Second, supply chain management can have a significant impact on a firm's costs and hence its profitability. While the 1960s focused on rising labour costs, the oil crisis of 1973, and subsequent rises in the cost of many materials and components, brought the precarious state of raw material supply into sharp relief. Even modest savings on the cost of raw materials and greater care in the management of those materials as they pass through the organization can have a greater impact on profit than increased sales revenue. The 1990s have seen a focus on the costs associated with quality and customer care, issues central to supply chain management.

Given that the scope of supply chain management is potentially vast, we will focus on a selected number of issues involved in purchasing, before examining some associated techniques, especially just-in-time.

Purchasing issues in supply chain management

The key variables of purchasing are source, quantity, quality, time and price. We will examine each of these in turn.

Source

Management is faced with a number of decisions concerning the source of the firm's raw materials and components. The obvious strategy is one that maximizes the other four variables, obtaining supplies in the quantity and quality required, when they are needed, and at an acceptable price. In achieving these aims, managements must decide whether to produce their own materials and components or buy them from other manufacturers; and if the latter, whether to opt for a single supplier or buy from a number of different suppliers.

The 'make or buy' decision involves consideration of vertical integration, either through acquiring the raw material supplier or manufacturing your own components. This will give management greater control over the reliability of supplies, and may well add a new dimension to the firm as a supplier to others. There are considerable cost implications to such a strategy, which are not only financial. Consider the case of a firm that sets up its own foundry to manufacture its requirements for cast metal products. The foundry has to operate as a profit centre and, since it operates in an area of declining demand, contracts to do work for other firms. The foundry may be placed in a position of supplying major competitors as well as having a conflict of priorities over the respective demands of its own and other organizations. In more general terms we noted in Chapter 4 that acquisition through vertical integration may not be very successful owing to the different nature of the industries involved. The trend in manufacturing is that firms make less of the total product and rely much more on suppliers and subcontractors. We return to this theme later.

There are a number of advantages in using a single supplier. A good relationship can be built up over time, which leads to mutual commitment and dependability. Frequent communication enables problems to be solved as they arise and leads to improvements in the quality of supply. A greengrocer supplying a top restaurant will know through discussion and experience that the chef will only accept first-class produce and pre-selects accordingly. The greengrocer will also be able to advise the chef when certain types of produce are particularly good, which may affect the quantity of the order. A single supplier offers potential economies of scale and opportunities for joint development as in collaborative R&D. However, where a single supplier fails to deliver as required or where variety may be limited, there may be greater security and flexibility in using a variety of sources. Multiple suppliers can offer volume flexibility and a range of experience through dealing with different customers. Where a number of suppliers are competing for the same order, the purchaser may be able to reduce costs through price competition. The relationship between Mercedes Benz and Eberspächer in Case 6.1 is a good example of the advantages of a close relationship between manufacturer and supplier.

The relationship between supplier and purchaser is often a question of relative power. We discuss this at length in Chapter 4 and you are referred specifically to Figure 4.3. If the purchaser is in a strong position compared to the suppliers then they may have to bid for the contract, enabling the buyer to obtain the most favourable deal. Such bidding and dealing introduce a highly sensitive variable to the purchasing function, so much so that it has been defined as 'a maelstrom of human relations' (Starr, 1972, p. 271)

The personal relationships between buyers and sellers are an important ingredient in purchasing. A purchasing manager with a supply problem may well be able to solve it by using his or her personal relationship with one of the suppliers. Time, effort and expenditure are regularly involved in building up such relationships. There are also cases where personal relationships have resulted in contracts being unfairly secured and even bribery used, as some legal cases over local authority building contracts will testify.

Quantity

The major purchasing decision here is how much to order at any one time. This is a function of cost, storage capacity, and the nature of the operations system. The decision can be difficult. For example, a firm operating complex machinery on a continuous process basis may need to stock expensive replacement parts, even though they be needed only infrequently. A decision model has been developed, the 'Economic Order Quantity Model', which establishes a trade-off between the cost of acquisition and the cost of holding stock. Some firms have very precise stock and delivery requirements in an attempt to minimize material costs. This is illustrated by the 'just-in-time' method, ascribed to the Japanese and examined in the next section.

The greater the purchasing requirements, the greater the possibility of obtaining discounts. Some highly diverse organizations operate a central purchasing function to maximize such discounts. The needs of several London boroughs for certain goods is met by a central purchasing function.

Quality

The quality of incoming raw materials and components is a vital ingredient in the quality control function. The purchasing department or the materials manager is usually responsible for the acceptance sampling and inspection of incoming materials.

Time and price

The timing of a purchase is, like order quantity, a function of the needs of the operations system, storage capacity and price. Certain commodities are particularly price sensitive and there can be significant speculation. In the 1970s the price of silver rose dramatically. This was particularly significant for the film developing industry, which used silver as a major ingredient. Some companies refused to buy in a rising market, preferring to wait for what they saw as the inevitable fall. Some of those companies went out of business as their stocks ran out long before prices fell. Some firms, to offset the costs involved in stockholding, engage in hedging, a process of buying materials and stock at the current price for delivery at some future date. Other purchasing managers get involved with the futures market and options trading, although the speculative nature of some markets increases the risk in decision-making.

Two trends are particularly noticeable in manufacturing industry. These are the extension of the manufacturing process down the supply chain and the globalization of the supply industry. The nature of manufacturing industry has changed. A factory that makes the majority of its own components is now a rarity. The large manufacturing plants concentrate increasingly on the final assembly of components made elsewhere. We have already noted this in our discussion of Japanese management in Chapter 2. The advantages of getting suppliers to do the manufacturing are that wages are generally lower in the components industry and firms operating in that industry are able to specialize, often on the basis of more advanced R&D. There is also the advantage that suppliers can also bring experience gained from working with different manufacturers. In our discussion of globalization in Chapter 2, we noted that global supply chains were now common, taking advantage of lower costs in some cases and specialist know-how in others. In some industries, the twin forces of globalization and increasing subcontracting has resulted in the emergence of very large supply firms. We saw this in Chapter 1, when we examined the car industry. Two American firms, Lear and Johnson, supply 50 per cent of the total world market in car seats.

Supply chain management techniques

Traditionally techniques associated with supply chain management have focused on stock or inventory control based on the notion that too little stock causes hold-ups and too much stock at any stage in the process is costly. There is also a need to counter supplier and seasonal variations and, where possible, take advantages of economies of scale in purchasing. Techniques such as EOQ, mentioned in the last section, have been developed to balance these seemingly conflicting demands. However, such techniques focus on a limited range of variables in a highly complex area.

Two computer-based systems have been developed to deal with the more complex issues of supply chain management. These are MRP1 (Materials Requirements Planning) and MRP2 (Manufacturing Resource Planning).

Materials requirements planning (MRP1) enables managers to determine the requirements for the quantity of materials needed and the timing of that need, where there is a high degree of complexity. Manufacturing resource planning (MRP2) offers solutions at the level of the operations system and, as well as dealing with materials requirements, deals with capacity planning and scheduling. Both techniques focus on costs.

Just-in-time is a technique that has grown significantly in popularity throughout manufacturing industry. This technique lies at the heart of achieving greater efficiency through the management of the supply chain.

Just-in-time

The origins of this system are ascribed to the Toyota car plant, although similar systems operate throughout Japanese manufacturing industry. The effectiveness of the system drew the attention of Western managers and its use quickly spread by adoption and by the expansion of Japanese multinationals into other countries. 'Just-in-time' (JIT) aims to obtain the highest volume output at the lowest unit costs. The system is based on the simple principle of producing goods and services only when they are needed. Because of this, JIT is described as a 'pull-through' system, as is shown in Figure 6.5. Exact quantities are produced and specific requirements are placed on materials and parts suppliers, as well as each stage in the production process, to deliver just

KEY CONCEPT 6.11
Just-in-time

JIT aims for the highest volume of output at the lowest unit costs, based on producing goods and services only when they are needed. Starting with the customer demand for the product or service, the JIT system works backwards. Goods and services are produced for each stage of the operation only as required. For this reason JIT is sometimes referred to as a pull-through system. JIT eliminates the need for maintaining costly inventory and utilizes specific techniques such as Kanban.

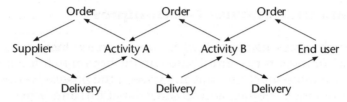

The essence of this system is that:
• Delivery follows order
• Pull-through system starts with end user
• Reduces inventory and hence costs
• Exposes problems immediately

Figure **6.5** An illustration of just-in-time.

in time for the next stage of operations. Materials intake, work-in-progress and finished stock are therefore kept at minimum levels.

Key elements of the system are customer demand, implicit notions of quality and continuous improvement, the elimination of waste, cost-effective operations, employee involvement, teamwork, close links with suppliers and customers and the need to balance supplier and user flexibility. JIT is more than a system of inventory control and involves activities across the whole organization. In the more traditional approaches, buffer inventories are built up at the start of the whole process, between each activity and at the end. The traditional system protects supply to each part of the organization and to the customer, but does lead to cash being tied up as stocks and increases the numbers employed in inventory management. Moreover, a system that relies on buffer stocks will hide inefficiencies in any part of that system. An effective JIT system removes a large proportion of those buffer stocks thereby reducing costs through excessive stock and exposing inefficiencies in the operations system. Problems are immediately brought to light and must be dealt with. For the system to work effectively:

● the operation must exist as an integrated and interdependent whole;

- a high quality of materials and components must be available at every stage;
- materials and components must flow quickly through the system;
- the system must be flexible enough to cope with variations in supply and demand.

The claimed advantages for the system are that it smooths out the production flow and reduces all types of inventory levels and hence costs. By preventing production delays it enhances planning and enables the firm to meet its delivery deadlines. At the same time, it eliminates time wasted in waiting for components, as well as over-production. Through the involvement and inter-dependence of staff it creates improved teamwork throughout the organiza-tion. JIT encourages a much closer relationship with suppliers and those able to meet the demands of the system are often offered high-volume contracts, sometimes as the sole supplier. This is a marked contrast to the kind of strate-gies used by some firms to guarantee consistent suppliers by using a number of competing components manufacturers. To obtain the maximum flexibility from JIT, it is often introduced with new multi-purpose machinery, enabling the firm to manufacture a wider range of product types in shorter runs. Most significantly, JIT demands cooperation from all stages of the production process and usually requires mechanisms for labour flexibility and teamwork, with implications for the organization structure. An illustration of JIT in oper-ation can be seen in Case 6.1.

At the Toyota factory, the system is controlled by an information system known as 'Kanban'. This is a system of cards or signals, which inform how much is to be produced by each process and the precise quantity each process should withdraw from the previous stage, which may be either another process, a materials store, or even a supplier. In Toyota, the 'Kanban' system is extended to its subcontractors, who must conform to the precise delivery requirements of the parent factory. The Kanban system is the most commonly used JIT technique and it lies at the centre of the entire system. Nothing hap-pens unless the Kanban is received.

While JIT and Kanban can strengthen the ties between company and supplier, as we saw in our earlier discussion, the system can place consider-able pressure on subcontractors who are expected to be at the call of the par-ent company. The system can only work given the willingness of suppliers to participate. This situation has frustrated some Japanese companies operating in Britain and led to protracted negotiations with British supply companies, some of which find the demands placed upon them too great for the rewards involved. JIT also means that disruptions in supply, for whatever reason, can have a dramatic impact on the entire system. A major earthquake in the Kobe region of Japan severely disrupted road and rail links. Although many manu-facturing plants were undamaged by the earthquake, supplies could not reach them and they were unable to operate because they carried insufficient stock.

Operations and the environment

The job of operations management is to produce goods and services for the customer through the most efficient utilization of resources. The achievement of these goals requires a certain amount of predictability in the supply of materials, labour, finance and so on. This may be difficult in a turbulent environment and explains why managers set up buffer systems to protect operations from unexpected changes in the environment. In practice this is achieved by having certain levels of buffer stock and groups of workers who are available when needed. This can be expensive and more effective operations systems are generally those that can respond to environmental change rather than being isolated from it.

In the past 20 years the changes that have had most impact upon operations management have been globalization, new technology and Japanese manufacturing methods such as JIT. The globalization of business has added to the complexity of operations management. We have noted elsewhere in this book how all business activities are now part of a global network. A single manufacturing firm can be involved in the assembly of components from several countries in several countries. A Hollywood film can be made in the UK using technical expertise from the UK film industry at the same time that a UK film is made only because of US financial backing. At the same time there are forces for localization, pushing operations managers into alliance with local firms as part of a JIT system.

All the environmental aspects of our model relate in some way to the operations function. In this section we will explore the more significant aspects of that relationship. We deal first with the interaction of operations, the economy and the state, with a focus on manufacturing industry. The theme of manufacturing also emerges in the examination of operations and technology, where the emphasis is on techniques based on computerization and automation. We look at the interaction of operations and labour and close the section with an examination of operating systems in different societies, with a focus on Japan.

Production, the economy and the state

Given that the operations function is central to any organization, it can be deduced that the value added is central to GDP growth. Until the 1980s, successive British governments recognized the economic importance of manufacturing through policies to encourage its growth, and through its attempts to regenerate flagging industries and firms. Since then, advocates of continued support of manufacturing industry have lost out to those who favour the operation of the free market. The decline of UK manufacturing industry is examined in more detail in Chapter 2, along with reasons why manufacturing industry is important in a healthy economy.

The state is involved in the operations function in a number of other ways. We saw in Chapter 5 how firms can be affected by regulatory laws such as those relating to the purification of waste water or the emission of toxic waste as by-products of the manufacturing process. The UK government has established measures in recognition of the role played by quality in international competition in both the manufacturing and service industries by the establishment of British Standard 5750. The government has stated its intention of giving contracts only to those firms who possess British Standard 5750 and the Department of Trade and Industry has published a register listing those companies that have been quality assessed. There are increasing signs that some industries will only buy goods and components from firms that have been quality assessed, and it is predicted that the future purchasing habits of the general consumer will be influenced by British Standard 5750. At an international level the same applies to ISO9000. As part of its regional policy, successive governments have attempted to influence the location of both manufacturing and non-manufacturing industry. This has generally focused on measures to encourage firms to locate in areas of high unemployment by giving them generous grants and tax allowances.

Operations and technology

In Chapter 2 we discussed also the influence of technology on the labour force and upon the way work is organized. We also argued that technological change has an impact not only on the operation of a particular function but also on the entire organization structure. These themes are explored in Case 5.5. The impact of technological change on operations can be seen in terms of cost, speed, flexibility, quality and dependability. Slack *et al.* (1998) also argue that a significant impact of technological change is that it forces managers to rethink their entire operations strategy.

When we think of technological change and operations, we tend to think of its application in manufacturing through computerized numerical control (CNC), robotics and other forms of automation. However, developments in computerized management information systems have affected all types of organization. In the service industry, developments in customer processing technology has changed the way we access information or obtain services, such as the booking of tickets for a rock concert. In banking the introduction of automatic teller machines and the growth of telephone and computer banking has changed the way we access banking services. This has led to significant changes in the banking industry. The number of jobs has been reduced and many banks have closed operations. Given that many banks occupied prime corner sites in many UK cities, they have been transformed into pubs and restaurants.

However, in this section we do focus on manufacturing and examine changes brought about by robotics and flexible manufacturing systems.

Robotics

The nearest analogy to an industrial robot is the human arm, to which a variety of tools can be attached to perform a variety of jobs from metalwork to painting. The majority of industrial robots operate from a fixed position with the restricted movements defined by a computer program. However, in some industries, considerable use is made of automatic guided vehicles. These are used extensively in the newspaper industry to move large paper rolls from store to the printing presses as required.

Robots offer possibilities of fast, continuous operation, improved quality and the liberation of human labour from repetitive, unhealthy and unpleasant tasks, as with paint spraying. They can reduce the need for direct labour and can be programmed to operate flexibly. Very few robots, however, possess tactile or visual capabilities and while their potential impact on manufacturing systems will be considerable, for many firms the supposed flexibility they offer a production system has been exaggerated.

> Robots cannot be reprogrammed for new models by pressing a few buttons. That is a myth.
>
> (Williams *et al.*, 1987, p. 39)

The main handicap to the more extensive use of robotics in industry is cost, involving not just the cost of the actual robot, but the high costs of developing specific software and machine tools. This problem is heightened in times of economic recession or in cheap labour economies when a plentiful supply of cheap labour may lower the motivation for such an expensive investment.

Flexible manufacturing systems

A flexible manufacturing system (FMS) brings together the various elements of advanced manufacturing engineering to solve the problem of offering consumer choice and a quick response to market changes using a minimum of working capital. Potentially it offers manufacturing industry a solution to the kind of dilemmas outlined in Figure 6.2. An FMS usually embraces computer-controlled machines, robots and an automatic transport system for moving tools and workpieces, as well as parts and raw materials. The system is supported by a computerized system for scheduling, tool selection, part selection, fault finding, machine breakdown detection and so on.

In car manufacture an FMS would enable a range of different models to be built on the same production line, with the necessary tool changes being

---

KEY CONCEPT 6.12
Flexible manufacturing systems

Flexible manufacturing systems enable a range of different models to be built using the same assembly line and pieces of equipment. The claimed advantages of FMSs are in terms of speed, flexibility, improved quality and lower costs. Most FMSs comprise a number of linked computer-controlled machines, robots and computerized transport systems. The programmed FMS selects the right tools and components for a particular job and usually has built-in mechanisms for automatic fault finding in the job and the equipment. FMS can be linked to CADCAM (Key Concept 6.5) to create computer-integrated manufacture (CIM).

automatic, and the required parts being delivered automatically to work stations in the quantity and at the time they were required. A typical FMS would incorporate a multiple tool system, a CNC machine with the capability of performing a number of different machine-tool operations. For example, the drilling of a variety of different-sized holes in a single machine part could be achieved in a single sequence of operations. Prior to such multiple tool systems such jobs would require a number of different machines, and the consequent moving of workpieces, or time-consuming changeover of machine tools. FMS is taken a stage further by computer integrated manufacturing (CIM), which links FMS to CADCAM and computer-controlled order and distribution systems.

The claimed advantages of such systems as FMS and CIM include speed, flexibility, lower costs and higher quality as below:

- higher productivity would be achieved through the better utilization of plant, materials and labour;
- a greater number of product variants would be possible in smaller batches, offering the consumer greater choice and potential satisfaction;
- reduced set-up times and consequently, shorter manufacturing lead times and a more flexible response to change;
- the need for less inventory at all stages of the production process;
- improved operations control and improved quality.

A study of eight cases of FMS in Britain revealed that at constant sales level, a fourfold increase in plant investment resulted in higher productivity, a threefold reduction in inventory and a threefold increase in profit. Further investment in plant together with an increase in sales had an even greater impact on profits (National Economic Development Office, 1985).

Despite this potential for variety, the reality for many companies is that the pay-back on such substantial investments as CNC machines, industrial robots and FMS is only feasible on long runs. Automation paid off handsomely for Volkswagen because of the high-volume production, whereas the relatively low volume of Austin-Rover's output meant that its automation turned out a poor investment (Williams *et al.*, 1987). Furthermore, as we found with robotics, only a limited range of product variety is feasible before costly programming and tooling changes are required. In any case the quest for product variety may well be a marketing myth. The continued manufacture of washing machines to the same basic design and the purchase of second cars and television sets would indicate that the consumer's need for repeat or supplementary purchases is sometimes greater than the need for variety.

Innovations in production technology undoubtedly carry the potential for a more effective and efficient production system. We have seen, however, that such enthusiasm must be tempered by the high cost and a recognition of the limitations of the new technology. Investment is no guarantee of business success and a focus on increasing market share may pay better dividends for many companies.

Further complications are caused by the impact of such developments on the labour force. The same technology that has the potential of eliminating the need for people to do noisy, dirty, dangerous work, that can improve working conditions, that offers interesting opportunities for restructuring the organization, also carries the very real threat of job displacement. It is to such issues that we now turn.

Operations and labour

The impact of the operations system on the labour force and vice versa is such a complex and well-documented area that we can only hope to introduce some of the main issues here. Some of those issues have been dealt with elsewhere in the book, notably supply and demand, labour costs, flexibility and the impact of location. We have seen how labour costs were a central issue in the proposed Renault–Volvo merger (Case 4.4). We have also examined the impact of globalization and the relocation of labour-intensive operations to lower-wage economies. In this section we deal with issues relating to deskilling and pay.

Taylorism and deskilling

The organization of labour in most operations systems is dominated by the work of F. W. Taylor and his treatise on 'scientific management' (Taylor, 1947). The thoughts attributed to the scientific management school represent an attempt to solve the problems of management incompetence. This was essentially a problem of control owing to the growing size and complexity of organizations and the growth of trade unions. The main principle of scientific management draws a distinction between planning and doing, with management, as the planners, controlling every aspect of the work process. This involves the design of tasks and work measurement, the careful selection and training of the workforce, target setting and the design of payment systems. The application and in some cases misapplication of Taylor's ideas resulted in

---

KEY CONCEPT 6.13
Taylorism

Taylorism is a system of work associated with the writings of Frederick Winslow Taylor, more especially his book *Scientific Management*. The system emerged in the early part of the twentieth century to solve the problems of management control in manufacturing organizations growing in size and complexity and to improve both the efficiency and effectiveness of manufacturing systems. The key elements of Taylorism are the distinction between planning and doing, the scientific analysis of work and the application of scientific methods to work itself and to the selection and training of people.

Taylor's work is associated with the development of work study (Key Concept 6.6). Taylor's ideas became as influential as those of any management thinker and the principles of Taylorism can be observed in most types of organization both in and outside manufacturing. His ideas have attracted much criticism, particularly for the impact of his methods on deskilling.

---

a tendency towards an extensive division of labour, work simplification and tight managerial control. Much of manufacturing industry and many of the larger production systems in non-manufacturing throughout the world exhibit elements of Taylorism, and the ideas of F.W. Taylor were popular not only among American capitalists but with Lenin and Mussolini.

Despite its widespread popularity, the scientific management approach has met with considerable criticism. Taylor's views have been labelled as authoritarian, subjective, unscientific and ultimately unfair. The main thrust of the attack is focused around the deskilling hypothesis encapsulated in the work of Braverman (1974). The extensive division of labour means that work becomes fragmented, the machine becomes more important than the worker, and control shifts from the skilled worker firmly into the hands of management, whose position is strengthened by their virtual monopoly of knowledge of the work process. Braverman saw scientific management as the essential control of labour in the production process. Deskilling occurs not only in manufacturing industry but in many service industries too, such as large banks and insurance companies. In such establishments work has been fragmented in much the same way as in manufacturing industry, and both the discretion of individual employees and their contact with the public has been reduced by the operation of programmed decisions and standard letters using computer systems.

Criticisms of Taylor's approach tend to focus on managerial control, the reduction of man to the level of a machine, its crude economic approach and even the eccentricity of Taylor himself. More than most management writers, Taylor has been subjected to much hostile criticism which has tended to mask some of the more enlightened aspects of his thinking; his views on training and participation, for example. Ultimately the widespread application of scientific management suggests that it offered solutions acceptable to many, even trade unions. Nevertheless attempts have been made to humanize the work environment, as a response either to Taylorism, his critics, or arising from other motivations. These attempts have focused on the problems brought about by deskilling.

Solutions to the problems of deskilling

Several theories and techniques have been put forward to counteract the negative impact of deskilling on the individual worker, such as a lack of job satisfaction and alienation. These attempts include human relations management, job rotation, job enlargement, job enrichment, autonomous work groups, participation schemes and the current catch-all for many of these and similar approaches, the 'Quality of Working Life' movement. We will deal with just two of these, job enrichment and autonomous work groups.

Job enrichment owes much to the motivation theories of Herzberg (1968). It focuses on the content of jobs and attempts, by redesigning the work, to give workers more responsibility, more control, a greater sense of achievement and ultimately more satisfaction. Applications tend to be more successful among white-collar jobs (where there is more scope for change) and

---

KEY CONCEPT 6.14
Quality circles

Quality circles or, as they are sometimes known, quality control circles were developed in Japan in the early 1960s as a result of the influences of US 'quality gurus' such as Deming and Juran. They work through a small group of employees from the same department or area of work. These employees meet regularly with their supervisor after work has finished to seek ways of improving the job. In Japan such groups have the authority to implement change. Such an idea was attractive to Western managers, but there were cultural barriers associated with the effective transfer of the process in many instances.

By way of contrast the concept of quality circles, while attributed to the Japanese, has a pedigree that can be traced to production committees in First World War Britain and participative management in the USA. Nonetheless it was in Japan where they spread in popularity from their inauguration in 1963. They comprise small groups of employees who work together and who volunteer to meet regularly to solve job-related problems, especially to discuss ways of improving the production process and product quality. They are supervisor-led and have the authority to implement change.

Attempts to introduce them in other countries have met with mixed results (Bradley and Hill, 1983). Those that fail generally do so because of underlying distrust between management and worker and scepticism on the part of management. In Japan they thrive on more cooperative workplace relations, but more particularly, as in Germany, on an underlying ethos that stresses product quality.

Organizational aspects of operations

The centrality of the operations function to an organization means that more often than not, the nature of the organization is significantly influenced by the nature of the operations system. In this section we will explore the interaction between the operations function and the organizational elements of our model. After a brief review of organization size, we will devote this chapter to the interrelated elements of structure, goals and organizational culture.

Operations and organization size

The size of the firm, expressed in terms of both numbers employed and capital invested, has a close relationship with the operations function. A firm dedicated to mass production is invariably large, in terms of both the number of employees and capital investment. A mass producer of motor cars, such as Ford or General Motors, will employ many thousands of workers at any one of their assembly plants throughout the world. As with most elements of the

'Business in Context' model, the influence is two-way. The sheer size and complexity of the operating system in a volume producer of automobiles will influence the size of the workforce and the capital employed. By the same token the size of the firm and its output requirements will determine the precise nature of the production system and in particular the technology employed. For example, only the largest of firms with high outputs are able to invest in highly automated production systems at profit.

The relationship persists in other types of business too. The multinational hamburger chain, McDonald's, which specializes in the mass production of a limited range of hamburgers, employs thousands in a variety of outlets throughout the world. While McDonald's investment in production technology may not be as high as a car manufacturer's, the cost of leasing prime sites in urban areas represents a considerable investment. The production technology employed in an oil refinery requires only a small proportion of labour to that employed in mass production technologies, yet the emphasis on sophisticated process technology means that capital investment is generally much higher. A very large insurance firm will almost certainly use a factory-style flow-line for the processing of the very large numbers of policies it has to handle.

The relationship between size and the operations system reveals itself most clearly through the way the operations process is organized and its impact upon organization structure.

Operations and organization structure

In Chapter 3, we introduced the popular claim that production technology and size have probably a greater influence on organization structure than any other variable. We argued then that the relationship also involved a number of other variables such as strategy, culture and the behaviour of interest groups. Nevertheless, since the operations function represents the firm's central activity it would be somewhat surprising if the structure did not reflect both the technology and the strategies associated with producing the goods and services of the organization. There are clear overlaps with our discussion of structure in Chapter 3, and you are advised to refer to the relevant parts of that chapter.

We base our analysis in this section around the classification offered by Joan Woodward, to which we have referred in Chapters 2 and 3. She and her research team studied a large number of manufacturing firms in South-east Essex and identified three main types of production technology: unit and small batch, large batch and mass, and process production. The three types accounted for key variations in organization structure. Variations occurred in the number of levels in the hierarchy, the span of control of each manager, the nature of job descriptions, the degree of written communication and the extent of functional specialization (Woodward, 1965). For example, a small batch system is depicted by a more flexible structure than a mass production plant. The most important thing to Woodward was not simply the nature of these variances but that structural design should be matched to the nature of the prevailing technology. Woodward was thus one of the earliest exponents of contingency theory (explained in Chapter 1). For instance, a small batch producer could only be successful if it adopted a flexible structure, and business failure could be attributed to a firm adopting a structure that was inappropriate to its production technology.

We will use a slightly expanded version of Woodward's classification to illustrate the relationship between the operations system and organization structure. As we have mentioned, Woodward based her work on manufacturing industry, but the classification may be used to examine structural differences in other types of business as well.

- **Project production** is a very specific kind of operations system in which the entire process is committed to the completion of a single task to customer requirements, as in the case of building a ship, fulfilling a major construction contract, developing a computer database, or carrying out an extensive management consultancy exercise. The organization structure usually comprises a project team, specifically created for the project in question. Many large construction companies use this arrangement within a broader matrix framework (Chapter 3 has a fuller discussion of matrix systems).

- **Unit and small batch production** Both project and small batch production can be classified as 'jobbing' operations. Whereas most projects are carried out on the customer's own site, small batch production is not. It may, like a project, comprise the production of a single item to customer specification. More often it represents the production of a small number of items. In manufacturing, the organization tends to be focused around a number of processes on general-purpose machines, operated by skilled labour. The organization hierarchy tends to assume a somewhat flat shape. Examples of this type of organization would include an engineering company manufacturing precision parts for aeroplane engines, or a high-class restaurant serving a limited number of customers each night.

- **Large batch and mass production** In manufacturing, the move from small to large batch production usually involves a shift to assembly line methods. In most types of large batch production, equipment is specifically designed around a particular product or range of products and involves considerable machinery in the movement of goods and materials. At its most extreme, as in a car plant, this represents mass production on a grand scale, but most mass-market domestic products are made in this way. The typical mass-production organization is labour intensive, utilizing semi-skilled labour in repetitive jobs offering little discretion to individual workers. The system is highly bureaucratized with a correspondingly larger number of management levels, inspectors, progress chasers and the like than in small batch production. Firms that come into this category usually have a combination of production types. Components tend to be manufactured in large batches in a scaling-up of typical jobbing arrangements, whereas assembly tends to be carried out using a flow-line method. Similar organization structures can be found in those service organizations catering for mass markets, such as a high street bank, a bus company or a major airline.

- **Process production** At its most extreme, large batch production represents an almost continuous flow of materials through the process. With such industries as the manufacture of chemicals or the refining of oil, true process production emerges, comprising equipment specifically designed to handle large volumes. In such organizations, the workforce generally operates in small teams dealing with a particular aspect of the process, using cognitive rather than manual skills and having much more discretion than in assembly-line work. Consequently there tends to be less management engaged in quantity and quality control, and in most cases these functions are automated. Such organizations are typified by rather tall hierarchies, but this reflects complex grading systems more often than management control.

The changes that are typified by a shift from jobbing to process operations are summarized in Figure 6.6.

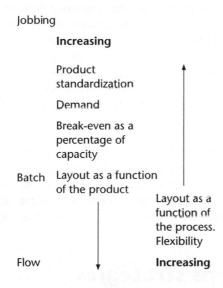

Figure **6.6** Variations in operating systems in manufacturing.

Organizational goals and culture

Given that operations is the central activity in most organizations, it is hardly surprising that there is a clear connection between the organization of operations, its associated strategies and culture at the level of the firm. The success of approaches such as TQM and JIT depends, not just on a set of techniques, but on the acceptance of a culture change by employees and those in the supply chain. Firms such as Hewlett-Packard use the layout of their operations to reinforce the prevailing corporate culture. In the case of Hewlett-Packard, an emphasis on open plan and facilities for regular meetings strengthen the culture of communication and involvement.

The notion of an organization culture based around operations is the major theme in Hayes and Wheelwright's 1984 analysis of American manufacturing industry. They support the view that a strong manufacturing base is essential to a healthy economy and that a major handicap is often the attitude of management towards the production function. They see the prevailing culture of the typical American manufacturing firm being dominated by accounting and in particular the need for a quick return on investment. Managers are highly mobile and have little interest in developing the technical know-how essential for new product development and improving the manufacturing system before they move on to better their careers. Short-term profit is seen as a measure of success and there is inadequate investment in R&D and plant improvement. Portfolio management through the buying of other companies becomes the substitute for development. Instead of operations, the emphasis is placed on marketing as the key function to stimulate existing markets through advertising and repackaged products.

For Hayes and Wheelwright the solution lies in a greater investment in innovation and, for manufacturing firms, a development of their own machine-tool industry. The development of dedicated machine tools is held to be essential to gain a competitive advantage in the product market. For many firms, this will require a change in the corporate culture, which stresses technical competence as its key criterion. This is achieved by the selection and development of technically qualified managers, a much greater investment in technical training, and a much greater focus on quality by all employees.

The Hayes and Wheelwright hypothesis draws heavily upon comparisons with Germany and Japan. While the analysis is appealing, their views of both Germany and Japan are subjective and often idealized. Furthermore, we have already seen in the previous chapter that the relationship between innovation and economic growth is speculative.

Operations strategies

We have already established in this chapter that operations is the central function in all organizations. We have also noted that there is often a conflict between the two objectives of operating efficiency and achieving customer satisfaction. We can now restate those objectives in terms of a number of key strategic elements presented in Key Concept 6.2. These are the achievement of:

- quality
- dependability
- speed
- flexibility
- cost.

These strategic objectives have formed an underlying theme to most of this chapter. They also form the link between operations and other functional areas. All the factors are involved with and dependent upon product design and development, which we dealt with in Chapter 5, and we shall see in the next chapter how such factors form the basis of marketing strategy. Achieving operations objectives would be impossible without the necessary finance and accounting control mechanisms (Chapter 9), and without recruiting, training and organizing a workforce with the necessary skills (Chapter 8).

Below we attempt to demonstrate the specific contribution to competitive advantage made by each of the five strategic objectives.

The **quality** of goods and services offers competitive advantage in terms of the dependability and attractiveness to the consumer. From the firm's perspective an emphasis on quality reduces costs and increases value added. We have seen in Chapter 5 and earlier in this chapter that goods and services of higher quality can often be offered at a higher price. While the introduction of TQM has been shown to reduce overall operating costs, some costs associated with higher-quality goods and services, such as those associated with raw materials, presentation and staffing, can be high and this is normally reflected in the price. For some firms, like Bang and Olufsen, this can be a successful strategy. For Grundig, however, the advantages of a reputation for high-quality goods was eliminated by poor control over production operations (Case 6.3).

Dependability refers to the capability of the firm to deliver its goods or services to the customer's satisfaction, not just to meet consumer expectations of quality, price and durability, but most importantly on time. This can be achieved by carrying large stocks, but this can be costly, as once again illustrated in the Grundig case. Inevitably, it involves investment in operating systems such as JIT and TQM. Both applications can reduce time and cost and reduce the need for rescheduling.

Speed of operation involves two aspects. First, there is the speed associated with the time between the product idea and its appearance on the market. Considerable advantage can be gained through the delivery of innovative products ahead of the competition. Second, there is the speed associated with the time it takes between order and delivery to the customer. This minimizes customer's waiting time, reduces inventory and can improve forecasting. The second approach is implicit in JIT and lean production.

The **flexibility** to alter products and meet volume demands with minimum lead-time are often strategies for survival in highly competitive or, in the case of First Sound and Vision (Case 6.2), declining markets. Flexibility in terms of product range and volume can offer considerable advantages in terms of the attractiveness of a wide selection of goods and services, the ability to deal effectively with fluctuations in demand and the ability to deliver on demand at the convenience of the customer. This approach does require a flexible and often multi-skilled labour force, as well as good relations with suppliers. While flexibility can be a distinct advantage, there may be just as great an advantage in going for high-volume production in a single product market. This allows the firm to take advantage of the 'experience curve', which can result in a virtuous circle of expansion. An increased market share leads to greater experience in operating the production system, resulting in lower costs. When these are passed on in the form of lower prices, the result is even greater market penetration. Such a virtuous circle can be enhanced by investment in production technology to reduce operating costs still further. This kind of strategy, while potentially successful in a expanding market, has severe limitations when the market is declining.

Cost advantage results from taking costs out of the operations process. These costs are involved in product development, the product itself and in the operating system and involve costs associated with materials, facilities and staffing. The cost advantage of Eberspächer in Case 6.1 was a major reason for Mercedes setting up a joint venture with them as a major supplier. As we see in Case 6.3, one of Grundig's major strategies for improving its poor position in the 1980s was a focus on operating costs. In some organizations there can be a trade-off with quality. A restaurant that attempts to reduce costs by buying cheaper raw materials may find that it loses reputation and trade. A problem faced by managers is that cost-cutting is an easy option. However, on its own it may not give competitive advantage unless it is integrated with improved quality, dependability and speed.

Case 6.3: Grundig

Grundig is a German company with its main manufacturing operations in Nürnberg. It is a producer of high-quality televisions, video cassette recorders, electronic office equipment and computer controls for CNC machines. It has a reputation for quality and precision which it uses as a marketing theme. It is currently owned by the Grundig family, the Dutch multinational, Philips, and by Swiss banking interests. No one group has overall control, the family still retaining 49 per cent of shares.

The company is the market leader for television sets in Germany. However, by 1984 Grundig was operating at an annual loss of DM 290 million. The reasons for the company's decline were several:

● In 1983 there were 500 different TV models in stock, some of which had not been made for five years. Stocks of all goods were operating at 28 per cent of sales.
● Grundig had invested heavily in the Philips V2000 system of video recording, which proved a marketing failure. As a consequence there is still a large stockholding of such recorders.
● The company had suffered badly in the video market at the hands of low-price Japanese competition.
● The family control of the company had been highly centralized, traditionally autocratic and somewhat idiosyncratic. Decisions were made that reflected the values of the chairman rather

than reflected good business practice in those product markets. Consequently good advice from members of Grundig staff was ignored.

In 1984, faced with these problems and high operating losses, a new chief executive was installed, who came from Philips. The goals of the company under the new regime were to maintain product quality, but to reduce operating costs, to streamline production, and to establish greater control over supplies and stocks. This was achieved through a number of measures:

● The model range was reduced quite considerably.
● The company invested in a new automated production line for the manufacture of video cassette recorders, to produce high-volume output at relatively low operating cost.
● The stocks were reduced to 19 per cent of sales.
● Stocks of raw materials and work-in-progress were cut by 14 per cent.
● Grundig attempted to rationalize its operations through a joint venture with Blaupunkt. Grundig would make televisions for Blaupunkt who would reciprocate by making car radios for Grundig.
● A much greater attention was paid to production planning, cost control and budgeting, as well as a more comprehensive effort to define market sectors.

The new strategies improved turnover per employee by 50 per cent, although the revenue per product was relatively low owing to price competition within the industry. The overall impact was measured by the transformation of an operating loss into a profit of DM 50 million by 1986.

Since 1986, the company has faced increasing competition. In 1994, it formed a joint venture with Gooding Consumer Electronics and in the same year moved into the satellite receiver and decoder market, led by a former Amstrad marketing chief. The company launched its first advertising campaign for six years.

In 1995 Grundig announced plans to shed 3000 jobs and move its operations from Germany to South Wales to take advantage of lower costs. ■

(*Source*: A. Fisher, 'The pain of recreating a culture', *Financial Times*, 1986, 1994, 1995)

Managements need to decide the most appropriate strategy for their organization. It is possible for firms operating in the same industry to have significantly different strategies. Texas Instruments has traditionally opted for high-volume production, reasonable prices and high market share of calculators and measuring equipment. Hewlett-Packard on the other hand, operating in the same markets, has concentrated on low-volume, high-quality, innovative products. Different strategies can even exist within the same organization. The Roux restaurant chain in London operates at the most expensive end of the market in its restaurant 'Le Gavroche', producing highly individual meals at high prices in luxury surroundings. At other restaurants they serve set meals at a fixed price and aim at value for money. They also provide a catering service involving a high volume of pre-prepared vacuum packed meals. These different strategies mix all the elements we have identified above. In the case of the Roux organization there is a link in terms of staff development. The different strategies enable staff to be trained and developed in less exacting situations before the management has confidence in them operating at the highest level. Most airline companies operate a variety of services on the same route, first class, business class, economy, excursion, stand-by and so on. These are all priced according to the quality of service and the dependability and flexibility offered the customer. Table 6.2 shows the cost of return fare from London to New York in February 1999 using British Airways as the carrier.

Table 6.2 demonstrates that two passengers travelling on the same plane to the same destination, one with a first-class ticket and one with an advanced purchase ticket can pay £5434 and £198 respectively. From an operations

Table 6.2 British Airways return fare structures London to New York, February 1999

	£
Concorde	6158
First Class	5434
Club Class (Business)	3208
World Traveller (Economy) – Open ticket	928
World Traveller (Economy) – APEX	198

perspective, the first-class ticket offers more flexibility, in that it can be used on any flight, while the APEX ticket can be used on a specified flight only. The first-class passenger uses much more of the aircraft's resources in terms of space and staffing levels and receives a much higher quality of service. Greater speed is offered in the check-in process and with the destination baggage handling. There are other less tangible benefits such as exclusivity and privacy. These factors increase the cost of the product and this is reflected in the price. There are, however, other factors at work, including a price based partly on what the market will bear and partly on that many first-class seats are paid for not by individuals, but as part of business travel. Such issues of pricing strategy illustrate the overlap between operations and marketing, which is discussed further in the next chapter. The variations in airline ticket prices are compounded by seasonal factors, although these tend not to affect the higher-priced tickets. In addition we have a number of market outlets all offering exactly the same product at different prices, which in turn reflect their own costs and profit goals. It is for this reason that airlines such as British Airways seldom discount their fares to travel agents.

There are a number of different views on the most effective operations strategy:

● One approach is to group the strategies around a dominant theme, using one of quality, dependability, speed, flexibility and cost. However, it is difficult to view such strategies in isolation. A strategy that focuses on quality will inevitably improve dependability and reduce certain operating costs. There are cases of firms that have pursued cost advantage to the neglect of others, with damaging effects on quality, dependability and flexibility.

● For the above reason, it is suggested that operations strategy should be internally consistent, as well as being consistent with the overall corporate strategy and the strategies of the other functional areas, notably innovation and marketing. This idea of consistency is central to the notion of the 'focused factory' (Skinner, 1974).

● However, such a focused strategy will need to be flexible to respond to the different needs of customers and, if necessary, to match the competition.

● The reality of operations strategies in many organizations is that compromises do have to be made. There may be trade-offs between quality and cost/price, quality and speed, dependability and flexibility, cost and flexibility and so on.

One approach in manufacturing that is based on an integrated strategy is the notion of 'lean production' and it is to this we now turn before a brief examination of the evaluation of operations strategies.

Lean production

Lean production is a totally integrated manufacturing strategy based on a set of ideas that emerged from the Toyota production system (Ohno, 1988). The essence of Ohno's ideas at Toyota was the elimination of all waste in the production process from the time the order is taken to the time that cash is received for the product. In this way the elimination of waste will speed up the production process, maintain a flow of work, reduce costs and result in high value added. Ohno's work at Toyota and similar methods used by firms in the Toyota supply chain, as well as elsewhere in Japan, were elevated to celebrity status through the work of the International Motor Vehicle Program at MIT. This was a detailed study 1986–90 of Japanese techniques focused on the decline of such American producers as General Motors relative to their Japanese competitors. In the best-selling book which emerged from the study, *The Machine that Changed the World*, Womack *et al.* (1990) claimed that the productivity in Japanese car plants was twice that of their American counterparts and set the standard for the rest of the world to follow. Their view was that lean production, while owing its origins to mass production, was a discretely different and superior system, and if adopted would result in the US automobile industry closing the gap on Japan.

KEY CONCEPT 6.15
Lean production

Lean production is a totally integrated strategy for manufacturing that came out of the Toyota factory in Japan and quickly found favour amongst managers in manufacturing industry across the globe. It integrates a number of key features. These include value engineering in design (Key Concept 6.4), FMS (Key Concept 6.12), an integrated supply chain with a close relationship with suppliers and distributors (Key Concept 6.10), JIT (Key Concept 6.9) and TQM (Key Concept 6.11). Lean production also represents a cultural shift for all employees, with an emphasis on flexibility and teamwork. Massive improvements in operating efficiency are associated with lean production, but these are questioned by some writers, who feel they may be limited to specific contexts. Nonetheless the impact of lean production methods in all types of manufacturing has been significant.

Lean production represents a holistic approach to manufacture and integrates a range of methods and philosophies, including JIT and TQM, discussed elsewhere in this chapter. The following represents the key features of lean production:

- just-in-time manufacture;
- total quality management;
- close contact and joint activities with a limited number of dedicated suppliers, including design and costing, leading to a mutual understanding of expectations;
- close contact with all aspects of the distribution chain;
- focus on costs at all stages of the process, including the use of value engineering in design;
- continuous improvement (which the Japanese call 'kaizen');
- state-of-the art flexible technology enabling fast set-up and changeover times;
- small batch manufacture with the ability to offer considerable variety;
- total preventative maintenance;

- teamwork is stressed throughout the process and no demarcation of duties within teams;
- employees are flexible and multi-skilled, with an absence of indirect labour;
- a delayering of management and a dramatic increase in delegation throughout the organization.

Womack *et al.* (1990) argued that the integration of the above represented a fundamental change in manufacturing strategy and covered product design, the organization of operations and relationships across the entire supply chain.

> (Lean production) ... uses less of everything compared to mass production – half the human effort in the factory, half the manufacturing space, half the investment in tools, half the engineering hours to develop a new product in half the time.
>
> (Womack *et al.*, 1990, p. 13)

Womack *et al.* argue that these advantages were found in plants with similar investment in automation and that the least automated plants in Japan were more efficient than automated plants in the USA. They further argue that the products that emerged from such systems carried half the average defects and used one-tenth of the inventory and one-fifth of the number of suppliers.

Given such evidence, it is hardly surprising that *The Machine that Changed the World* became a best-selling business book, and findings such as those of the research team at MIT led to the senior managers of the top US car firms making study tours of Japanese car plants. Undoubtedly the interest generated led to a change in the way leading Western firms such as General Motors and Ford attempted to change their operations processes and accelerated the take-up rate of JIT amongst Western manufacturers.

However, lean production is not without its critics. The claims made by the MIT research team and in Womack *et al.* have been vigorously challenged by Williams *et al.* (1992a). They argue that:

- The difference that is claimed to exist between mass and lean production methods is not empirically sustainable. Their claim is supported by Wickens (1993), a senior manager at Nissan's UK plant and advocate of Japanese methods. He argues that the Toyota-inspired system is, in fact, lean mass production, with elements of both Taylorism and Fordism.
- The 2:1 advantage claimed by lean production cannot be supported by the evidence. They produce data which show that, Toyota apart, the margin of superiority of Japanese car manufacturers is small and, in some cases, bettered by European and US car manufacturers.
- The MIT study fails to explain how the Japanese take labour out of the system. Williams *et al.* argue that the labour figures of Japanese firms cannot be compared to those of the West, because of the greater reliance of the Japanese on the subcontracting system. The headcount is in effect pushed down the supply chain, giving the impression of the 'lean organization'. Furthermore, they argue that the amount of hours worked by the Japanese worker in comparison to the West, particularly levels of overtime,

is evidence of the greater intensification of work in the Japanese firm. Trade unions around the world have been interested in this latter phenomenon. Japanese unions have been critical of a system that leads to exhausted workers and low profits, while Canadian unions have been concerned that the elimination of buffer stocks in lean production leaves workers with little control of their immediate work process (both reported in Wickens, 1993).

In many instances Williams *et al.* (1992a) argue that the MIT data is flawed or that it is not comparing like with like. A similar concern has been expressed by Ford Motor Company about the annual publication of statistics on productivity in the European car industry by the Economist Intelligence Unit. Their refusal to participate in the survey is based on the fact that plants differ in terms of age and equipment. The relevance of this to a discussion on lean production is the difficulty of separating out the relative impacts of lean production and plant modernizations.

The above debate offers two polarized positions presenting, respectively, the good and bad sides of lean production. The adoption of lean production methods in whole or part by many manufacturing firms is some indication that their management see the investment as worthwhile. Nissan in the UK (see Case 2.6) claim that lean production, as a transplanted operations system from Japan, has contributed to its status as the leading producer of cars in Europe as measured in terms of number of cars built per employee per year. In 1998 that figure was 103, with the next best performance coming from VW at Navarra in Spain and GM at Eisenbach in Germany, each with 76 cars per employee (Economist Intelligence Unit, 1999). However, an aggressive lean production system can threaten the security of many employees and it is understandable that the system has been examined closely by trade unions in many countries, including Japan itself. Wickens of Nissan sees a middle way, which harnesses the efficiency gains of lean production alongside improved working conditions, a distribution of the gains and offers stable and secure employment.

> Lean production of a type is the way forward, but it must be lean production managed by people who care about people.
>
> (Wickens, 1993, p. 89)

Evaluating operations strategies

Hayes and Wheelwright (1984) have developed a model for the evaluation of an operations strategy, based on four stages of strategic development. The original model focused on manufacturing industry and was adapted to the service sector by Chase and Hayes (1991).

● At Stage 1 the firm is reactive and the operations function is low status in the organization and has less influence than marketing and certainly finance. They term this stage **'internal neutrality'**.

● At Stage 2 the firm is more outward-looking in that it attempts to benchmark against the competition. The strategy is still reactive in that the firm is a follower rather than an innovator. They refer to this stage as **'external neutrality'**.

- At Stage 3 the firm introduces the notion of systems improvement to improve its performance across a range of activities. A clear strategy emerges and operations strategy is one of a number of linked functional strategies. This stage is referred to as **'internally supportive'**.
- At Stage 4 the operations function becomes the driving force behind the organization and its key to gaining real competitive advantage as the firm becomes a product and a process leader. They term this stage **'externally supportive'**.

We have already touched upon the Hayes and Wheelwright philosophy elsewhere in this book, notably in our discussion of an operations culture earlier in the chapter. Although adapted to apply to the service sector, this evaluation model owes much to Hayes and Wheelwright's criticisms of US manufacturing industry in the 1980s, where they argued that US firms were falling behind the competition owing to a lack of process and product innovation and a distorted focus on financial controls and short-termism. Their thesis that operations should be the key strategy fits in with its central role in most organizations. However, many organizations may operate best at Stage 3, where strategies are integrated, yet responsive to external opportunities and threats.

Summary

The operations function is a transformation process, which takes a variety of inputs such as materials and labour and turns them into goods and services. Viewed in this way the function operates in a variety of industries and settings and is not limited to manufacturing. The main activities of operations management involve the design of a system to process inputs and setting up control devices to ensure effective operation. In more recent years it is acknowledged that the operating system has expanded to incorporate all the elements of the supply chain from components to customers. The key objectives of any operations system are quality, dependability, speed, flexibility and cost.

A central problem in operations management is the reconciliation of customer satisfaction with the efficient utilization of resources. Traditionally techniques of operations management have emphasized efficiency. However, there is a growing awareness of other elements, such as the flexibility to respond to changing market demand and a need to focus on quality.

It is, however, misleading to see operations solely in terms of responding to external forces. The function has a central position in nearly all types of organization. Effective operating systems and operations management have a significant impact on the economy. Globalization has had a significant impact on operations through the geographical extension of the supply chain and the growth of global, interactive operating systems. The centrality of the function means that it exerts considerable influence on organization structure.

Changes in technology have particular relevance for operations systems, in terms of both product and process innovation. In manufacturing and the service sector alike there have been significant changes in the way goods and services are both produced and accessed by the customer. Japanese methods, especially in manufacturing industry, have been very influential and include JIT, TQM and lean production. For the labour force, operations has considerable influence over employment patterns, wage levels, health and safety, and job satisfaction.

Operations strategies are a core element of a firm's overall corporate strategy. The most successful strategies would appear to be integrate all elements of the operations system, display a clear focus and are consistent with the strategies of the other functional areas.

Further reading

Probably the most comprehensive text, in terms of coverage and examples, currently available is N. Slack *et al.*, *Operations Management*, 2nd edn (Pitman Publishing, 1998). Other good sources are S. M. Davis, *Production and Operations Management*, 6th edn (McGraw-Hill, 1998) and W. Stevenson, *Production and Operations Management*, 6th edn (McGraw-Hill, 1998). Some good cases from both manufacturing and the service sector can be found in the companion volume to the Slack *et al.*'s main text, R. Johnston *et al.*, *Cases in operations Management*, 2nd edn (Pitman Publishing, 1997). Although a little dated, an interesting and personal view, looking at strategic, cultural, and comparative issues, can be found in R H. Hayes and S.C. Wheelwright, *Restoring Our Competitive Edge* (John Wiley, 1984).

Discussion

1. Examine the similarities and differences to be found in the operations systems of manufacturing and non-manufacturing organizations. How do the operations priorities differ in a firm producing television sets for a mass market compared to those of a large regional hospital?
2. Design a systems model for a manufacturing firm, a retail organization and a university. Show both the types of transformations that are taking place and the other systems with which the firm interacts. What are the key activities and key relationships? Define the objectives of each in terms of quality, dependability, speed, flexibility and cost.
3. What strategies can be employed to solve the conflicting objectives of operating efficiency and customer satisfaction?
4. What types of impact can product design have on the operations process? How does it affect the key objectives of quality, dependability, speed, flexibility and cost?

5. Assess the impact of globalization on operations management.
6. Identify the operational aspects that influence scheduling in a restaurant, at an airport, and for a major national daily newspaper. What strategies and techniques would you employ to solve scheduling problems in these three situations?
7. Why is supply chain management an important aspect of manufacturing industry? To what extent have techniques imported from Japan assisted this process?
8. To what extent can the techniques associated with JIT and lean production be applied to a department store, a hospital and a university or college?
9. Examine the links between total quality management (TQM) and corporate culture.
10. Examine the operations strategies employed by the firms in Cases 6.1, 6.2 and 6.3. What are the major influences that have shaped those strategies and what other strategies could the management have employed in the same situation? What do the cases tell us about the relationship between operations and the other functional areas?

CHAPTER 7

Marketing

In this chapter we will examine the nature of marketing as it applies to different types of organization. We will attempt to define marketing and chart the development of marketing as a concept. The various elements of marketing, research, product, price, promotion, distribution and buyer behaviour will be analysed in turn, as will the key concepts of branding, the product life cycle, and market segmentation. As in our treatment of all functional activities we will use the Business in Context model to look at the environmental, organizational and strategic aspects of marketing. In the two previous chapters we stressed the interface between innovation, operations and marketing. This theme will be taken up in this chapter, particularly in the discussion of product development, the relationship of marketing with operations technology, the place of marketing in the organization structure, and most significantly when we examine the design of marketing strategies.

Decisions in marketing generally focus on the nature of the markets and on the products and services to serve those markets. In terms of products and services marketing is concerned with design, prices, promotion, and the means through which they are distributed. In most advanced industrial societies individuals are faced with a vast choice of such products and services, which can be acquired in a variety of ways, often at a range of prices. Advertising is a pervasive feature of modern life, often so glamorized by the media that the management decision to change its advertising agency is, for a brand like Guinness, a matter of high drama to be played out in the national press. For such reasons marketing, probably more than any other business activity, attracts strong positive and negative feelings. Many members of the public as well as many business studies students associate careers in marketing with the glamour and fictional lifestyles of the people portrayed in advertisements. Such a view is misleading, for marketing is much more than advertising and the tasks can involve the much less glamorous work of collecting detailed market information and the problems of getting metal containers made in Mansfield to a customer's factory in Bromsgrove.

It is this high-profile nature of marketing that attracts its critics. Marketing is variously accused of creating (amongst other things) an excessively materialistic society, planned product obsolescence, the high-pressure selling of poor quality products and the excessive political power of the multinational. Borrowing themes from Vance Packard, marketers are seen as 'The Hidden Persuaders' or 'The Waste Makers' or both. The marketers would counter this, listing their credits as the development and supply of products and services demanded by consumers, the provision of essential information for the shopper, and the use of marketing to create public awareness for such socially acceptable goals as improving a nation's health. Given the increasing use of marketing in political elections, it might also claim to be an important part of the democratic process.

Definitions and orientations

Marketing is human activity directed at satisfying needs and wants through exchange processes. (Kotler, 1983, p. 6)

Marketing consists of individual and organizational activities that facilitate and expedite satisfying exchange relationships in a dynamic environment through the creation, distribution, promotion and pricing of goods, services and ideas.

(Dibb *et al.*, 1997, p. 5)

The achievement of corporate goals through meeting and exceeding customer needs better than competition.

(Jobber, 1995, p. 5)

Marketing is not a specialized activity at all. It encompasses the whole business. It is the whole business seen from the point of view of its final result, that is from the customer's point of view. Concern and responsibility for marketing must therefore permeate all areas of the enterprise. (Drucker, 1968, p. 54)

The above definitions introduce a number of different aspects. Marketing is seen as:

- an interactive process,
- that is aimed at satisfying (or exceeding) customer needs,
- that operates in a competitive and dynamic environment,
- that concerns goods, services and ideas (and therefore exists in all types of organization),
- that involves activities of design, pricing, promotion and distribution,
- that is the responsibility of all members of the organization.

The following approaches to marketing have been identified. They present a generalized view of the historical development of marketing ideas.

KEY CONCEPT 7.1
Marketing

Marketing is an interactive process aimed at satisfying or even exceeding customer needs. It is concerned with the design, pricing, promotion and accessibility to the customer of goods, services and ideas. It exists in all types of organization and is the responsibility of all members of the organization.

- **The production orientation** assumes that consumers will buy what-ever is available and the emphasis should be on production and distribu-tion. This approach to marketing works best when demand is greater than supply and goods and services are relatively easy to sell. Its origins lie in the expanding populations of Europe and the USA at the end of the nine-teenth century.

- **The product orientation** assumes that goods and services will sell themselves, usually because of inherent quality and performance charac-teristics, and that sales promotion is largely unnecessary. This approach also assumes that consumers are generally well informed.

- **The selling orientation** assumes that consumers will not buy sufficient goods and services unless they are persuaded to do so by advertising, sales promotion and incentives to the sales force. This approach is often neces-sary when supply outstrips demand, or in the case of what Kotler (1983) defines as 'unsought' goods, such as encyclopaedias, or with the promo-tion of political candidates. The concept emerged with the development of the techniques of mass production and its origin is particularly associ-ated with the depression of the 1920s and 30s, more especially in the USA.

- The true **marketing orientation** shifts the attention to the consumer whereas the production and selling orientations concern themselves with the needs of the organization. The true marketing approach involves the determination of consumer needs and values and the design and supply of goods and services to satisfy them. The assumption here is that the con-sumer is sovereign and the survival of any organization depends upon the satisfaction of its customers. In this context, customers include organiza-tions as purchasers of components for manufacture or office equipment; individuals when they buy a car, go to the supermarket or eat in a restau-rant; visitors to a holiday resort; supporters of a particular political party; and even students of a university. Such an approach underpins most mod-ern definitions of marketing, as we can see above. The development of the marketing orientation is linked to increased competition, the deregulation of markets and advances in information technology. It is also linked to rational approaches to management that are based on investigation and analysis as the basis of strategy. This in turn is linked to the emergence of market research as an important activity. Piercy (1997), while rejecting the effective contribution of much market research and much of traditional marketing theory, strengthens the case of the marketing orientation. He argues most vociferously that there can be no other legitimate approach to going to market (a phrase he uses rather than marketing) than by satisfy-ing customer needs.

- **Societal marketing** takes the previous orientation a stage further. The attention is still focused on the consumer's needs, but the assumption here is that those needs are satisfied in such a way as to enhance the well-being of the consumer and society as a whole; goods and services should be socially acceptable, non-harmful and non-polluting. This approach arises from the enhanced consumer awareness of environmental issues. In many major supermarkets, shelves are dedicated to the presentation of organic foods and new product lines have been developed, such as toilet rolls and kitchen towels made from recycled paper or coffee filters using unbleached paper. Washing powder and certain foodstuffs are packaged in refillable containers and recycling bins have sprung up at supermarkets, colleges, parks and car parks. Supermarkets such as Tesco, Sainsbury and Safeway have made considerable investment in the design of new stores to present attractive buildings constructed using environment-friendly materials. In many organizations, distribution logistics, which has always been concerned with fuel efficiency, now deals with traffic reduction as a major goal.

While they do approximate to the historical development of marketing, we can see these different approaches to marketing working side by side today. Precision engineering tools tend to sell on the reputation of the product and because they are engineered to meet the exact requirements of the customer, while certain double-glazing and kitchen installation firms produce made-to-measure items that tend to be marketed using aggressive promotion and selling techniques.

If textbooks and professional journals are a reliable guide, the most popular view of marketing today as held by its practitioners is one that focuses on consumers and the determination and satisfaction of their needs. This view is not without its sceptics. J.K. Galbraith (1972) challenges the consumer-oriented marketing concept, which he calls the 'accepted sequence'. The growth of big business, the complexity of modern technologies and the correspondingly massive investments in product development have disenfranchised the consumer. 'The revised sequence' has taken over, in which complex products, beyond the understanding of the average consumer, are developed at great cost. The emphasis shifts from the satisfaction to the creation of consumer demand through investment in promotion to safeguard investments in product development.

A discussion that focuses entirely on individual consumers and manufactured products presents a somewhat restricted view of marketing. In the next section we examine the extent to which the marketing is applied in other contexts.

Marketing in different contexts

Marketing as an activity is carried out in a variety of contexts. The most obvious context is of course the sale of goods and services to individual consumers as end-users. Marketing also occurs when a firm manufacturing petrol tanks deals with vehicle and lawnmower manufacturers and the like who use petrol tanks in their products; this is sometimes referred to as industrial or organizational marketing. Equally it is not only manufactured products that may be marketed, but services such as banking and management consultancy. Holiday resorts such as Disneyland Paris (Case 7.1) have always marketed themselves to attract tourists, but in recent years other places such as Milton Keynes and Telford have engaged in marketing to attract business development. In the 1980s, the London Docklands Development Corporation used fairly aggressive marketing techniques to attract businesses, property developers and other forms of investment to a hitherto derelict site of the former London Docks. In 1965, Singapore needed inward investment to offset the loss of British bases. The government established the Economic Development Board (EDB) and set up marketing offices in the USA and other countries. The EDB represented a one-stop shop for would-be investors, offering a fast response and eliminating the need for investors to negotiate with a range of government agencies. (See Case 2.5 for more details.) In addition to the marketing of products and services, some firms actively promote themselves by presenting a corporate image to the public. Marketing is far from being the sole prerogative of profit-making organizations, as governments, political parties and charities have discovered. We will deal with each of these aspects of marketing in turn.

Organizational marketing

The concept of industrial marketing can be misleading since it implies the marketing of industrial components for the use in further manufacturing processes, as in the case of our petrol tank. Organizational marketing is a more useful term since it can accurately embrace any marketing exchange between two or more organizations. Retail organizations like Marks & Spencer engage in marketing when they buy finished goods from a variety of different sources. In modern times the state has become a very powerful consumer and a very large market in its own right. The state can use this power for social and political ends, by awarding contracts to firms in economically depressed areas or by withdrawing contracts from those firms who do not adhere to government policy on something like wage levels. In general, organizational marketing differs from consumer marketing in a number of ways. Whereas consumers buy goods and services for a variety of reasons, which may include less tangible considerations of status, organizational buyers tend to be more concerned with the utility of the product or service, as well as its contribution to their costs. Organizational buying is institutionalized and is often carried out by professionals using formalized procedures involving quotations and contracts and often as part of a close ongoing relationship between buyer and seller. In the case of a firm such as Marks & Spencer, buyers will specify in detail quality levels and often how the product must be made. We saw this illustrated in Chapter 2 by the demands made by Japanese manufacturers on their components suppliers. The concept of organizational marketing has become very important to UK local authorities. The deregulation and privatization of the 1980s and 1990s meant that many local authority services were outsourced, involving processes of competitive tendering from would-be suppliers. In the late 1990s many authorities use a principle known as 'best value', in which organizations marketing their goods and services to them must conform to fairly stringent criteria.

The marketing of services

It is only fairly recently that many service organizations have fully acknowledged the need to consider marketing in any serious way. The historical reluctance of the service industry to engage in marketing may be due to the relatively small size of many service operations, the intangible nature of many of their products, and, in the case of the professions, the constraints imposed by their own professional bodies. Significant changes have taken place. The service industry has grown and become fiercely competitive. The major banks facing competition from building societies and other financial institutions have invested heavily in advertising and other kinds of sales promotion. Many consumers are now deluged by direct mail shots from various credit card organizations. A student opening a bank account for the first time is wooed by a variety of offers such as free overdrafts and gifts. In addition the banks have been careful to target markets such as students, small businesses, and more recently those needing pensions, as well as extending their distribution network by reintroducing Saturday opening and installing automatic cash machines in a variety of locations. Airline companies have decided to package their products in a much more tangible way; business travellers are now invited to buy British Airway's 'Club Class' or Singapore Airline's 'Raffles Class' and enjoy a number of distinctive product advantages. On some airlines, economy travel has been repackaged to convey an attractive image. Thus British Airways economy class becomes 'World Traveller'. The lifting of advertising restrictions on the legal profession in Britain has led in some cases to vigorous promotion of price differentials on services such as conveyancing.

The marketing of images

Organizations such as the Post Office, British Petroleum and ICI have spent heavily to convey a specific corporate image, which may well stress efficiency, experience, breadth of operations, company size, social responsibility or all of these characteristics. Theatrical agents have always existed to promote their clients, but the concept of marketing people has been extended to present any celebrity figure who may be 'packaged' to enhance his or her earning capacity through paid public appearances. The marketing of ideas has also grown in popularity. In 1987 the British government launched a major campaign to inform the population about AIDS, and anti-smoking campaigns by a number of different organizations are now commonplace.

The case of the Post Office represents another broadening of the marketing concept to incorporate the public sector and non profit-making organizations such as charities. Political elections in Britain are now fought out by parties who invest heavily in marketing an image as well as an ideology. The Labour Party, conscious of a need to widen its appeal after three successive election defeats, targeted the young professional middle classes as future voters and tailored its appeal accordingly. Even this was not enough to win the 1992 election. This defeat led to the Party repackaging itself as 'New Labour' and aiming its appeal at non-traditional middle-class voters. The repackaging and subsequent promotional campaign, particularly the use of high-quality image advertising, was seen as a key factor in their election victory of 1997. The marketing of political parties presents an interesting combination of the marketing of organizational image, of ideas and of people.

Governments themselves use marketing. Between the financial years 1986–7 and 1987–8 there was an increase of 90 per cent in government expenditure on marketing of all types and a 287 per cent increase in advertising alone. In all, £88 million was spent on press and television advertising. For the 'European Single Market 1992' campaign, the government allocated £6.7 million for television advertising and almost £4 million for other forms of advertising and promotion (*Independent*, 12 August 1988; *The Sunday Times*, 4 September 1988). Most government departments have large press and public relations offices.

The use of marketing by governments raises ethical issues. it invariably supports the particular ideology of the party in power, and may be abused by some individuals to promote their own political careers.

Export marketing

This is often considered as a separate marketing context requiring adaptations of the product, its price and the way it is promoted to account for differences in cultural expectations or constraints imposed by the governments of nation states. Such differences have led many firms to appoint local agents in different countries to market their products or else engage in a joint venture with a local firm. The Danish brewery Carlsberg engages in such joint production ventures throughout the world either to ease the problems of distribution, to overcome government restrictions on the operation of foreign firms or both. Export marketing can be seen as part of a continuum which can involve selling goods and services overseas from a home base, through various forms of equity joint venture, to wholly owned subsidiaries in different countries.

Export marketing involves issues such as global versus local products (see Chapter 2 for a more detailed discussion of globalization). Even where global products exist they tend to be marketed in different ways to account for variations in culture and government policies.

The elements of marketing

We have already seen that the marketing concept focuses on the consumer and his or her needs. Marketing strategy is enshrined in the concept of the marketing mix, popularly referred to as the Four Ps – product, price, promotion and place. Consumers constitute an implicit rather than explicit element of the marketing mix, but we shall include them under the heading of buyer behaviour. In addition to these considerations an effective strategy requires information, usually through the process of market research. We are therefore able to identify six key elements of marketing: market research, product, price, promotion, place and buyer behaviour. The six elements will be treated as separate entities although in practice there is considerable overlap. The price of a product, especially when higher than comparable offerings, can be used as a product feature and even a method of promotion stressing the exclusivity of the offering; this in turn depends upon the consumer perceiving and acknowledging a relationship between price and quality. Packaging is a means of protecting the product, an important form of promotion, and a means of facilitating the distribution of the product. The concept of place is concerned with the way the product or service reaches the consumer; in some cases free delivery is presented as a feature of the product to mark it out from competitors. We reinforce these six elements by examining the important concepts of brands and branding, segmentation and the product life cycle in the next section.

KEY CONCEPT 7.2
The marketing mix

The marketing mix generally refers to overall marketing strategy which involves the manipulation of four key elements. These are decisions concerning the nature of the product and its design; decisions about price; decisions about sales promotion, advertising and customer awareness; and decisions concerning distribution. These four factors are popularly referred to as the four Ps; product, price, promotion and place. Two important aspects of this are not made explicit. These are market research and buyer behaviour. Decisions about the marketing mix cannot be made without researching the market in all its aspects and that includes a thorough understanding of buyer behaviour.

Market research

Market research deals with the collection and analysis of information about the other five aspects of marketing. Four types of market research can be distinguished, although there is considerable overlap between them and most firms engage in all types.

● Management needs to possess accurate information about its current marketing activities. This will include the number and value of the sales of its current range of products and services, and its market share compared to its competitors. Such information can provide useful feedback on sales variations by region and also by salesperson and may well provide the basis for implementing changes.

● Management needs to be aware of developments that are occurring in the market place, which might have a direct or indirect bearing upon the business. Such information may be about new products brought out by other companies, the relative prices of goods in shops, how competitors are promoting their products, or whether changes are taking place in the way consumers buy goods. This second activity is sometimes referred to as market intelligence for it enables management to build up a picture of the market in which they operate and chart the significant changes and trends so that strategies may be initiated and changed as appropriate.

● Market research involves feasibility testing to assess the market potential of a new product or service; to assess the consumer reaction to pricing policies or price changes; to assess the reaction of consumers to a particular advertisement and so on. When a company like Nestlé launches a new chocolate bar, the product has invariably been tested on a wide range of people, and their reactions to appearance, taste, price, value for money, and sometimes the method of promotion carefully assessed. An essential element of feasibility research is an analysis of the market itself, especially its size and composition in terms of age, sex and occupation. Customer reactions to products are often tested using in-depth interviews with individual consumers or using focus groups. A focus group is a means of finding out more about a particular product through engaging a small group of consumers or potential consumers in a group discussion led by a trained facilitator. Such groups are used in the marketing of industrial as well as consumer goods and are used widely by such firms as Hewlett-Packard and British Oxygen.

● The fourth type of research is a mixture of the previous three in that it collects information to evaluate a product and the way it is priced, promoted and acquired by the consumer as an ongoing process after the initial launch. Continuous data of this type is often collected by consumer panels. These are groups of consumers, who may be representative of the population as a whole or some specific segment of the market. Such groups are then asked to monitor such things as their purchasing habits, their TV viewing, eating habits and so on. In 1991, Taylor Neilson AGB launched a Great Britain consumer panel comprising 10 000 households to collect detailed information on most aspects of consumer purchase (Frain, 1999).

Individual organizations, especially if they are large enough, can do their own market research. However, it has developed as a specialist activity over the past 25 years or so, and numerous agencies such as Mintel and Taylor Neilson AGB have arisen offering a variety of services. Many such firms operate multinationally and among their many services offered to clients provide regular television viewing figures, so enabling firms to target and evaluate television advertising campaigns. Such firms provide their clients with regular market intelligence on market share and trends, tasks often beyond the resources of an individual company. Some market research agencies specialize by product or the type of service offered and some have built up reputations for consumer interviewing.

KEY CONCEPT 7.3
Market research

Market research involves the collection and analysis of information to gain feedback on current marketing activities, including those concerned with new product launches and testing the market response to new product proposals. It is concerned with collecting and reviewing information about competitors' product, pricing, promotion and distribution policies.

The product

In our discussion of the different contexts of marketing we saw how the term 'product' has a wide connotation and may include manufactured goods, services, people, organizations, places and ideas. A product comprises a number of elements apart from its more obvious features. These can include a brand name, packaging, after-sales service, delivery, warranty and so on. Marketing needs to consider all these aspects of the product. Free delivery or extended guarantees may be seen as essential product characteristics by some consumers.

A product line is the total number of variations of the same basic product, differentiated by quality, cost or extra features. A car manufacturer will make several versions of the same basic model with variations in engine size, type of gearbox, paintwork and so on. British Airways offers product differentiation both before and during its flights through different levels of service in each class. In response to price competition from companies such as Easyjet, British Airways launched its own subsidiary offering low-cost, 'no-frills' flights to popular European destinations. The breadth of a product line is closely related to the degree of market segmentation, a concept we introduce in the next section.

A product mix is the total number of different products offered by the firm, sometimes referred to as the product portfolio. The size of a firm's product mix can have a significant impact on its profitability in that the effect of poor performers may be lessened by the income from better selling items. However, too broad a product mix can cause problems of control. In 1982 Guinness, with a large number of highly diverse activities, sold off 40 of its subsidiaries to achieve a better control of its product portfolio (Earl, 1984).

Marketing considerations are an important input in the process of developing new products. We saw in Chapter 5 that new product development was not only potentially expensive, but also that the risk of failure was high. Extensive market research is needed concerning such aspects as the utility and acceptability of a new product's design, its target market and the likely acceptable price. An estimate may be made about likely future sales, which when set alongside likely development costs is essential in assessing the business viability of a new project. While we tend to associate new product development with manufactured goods, it has become increasingly important in the services sector. A large number of new products have been launched in the financial services sector as a result of deregulation, increased competition, technical change and more knowledgeable and sophisticated consumers.

We will return to consideration of the product in our discussion of branding, segmentation and the product life cycle.

Price

If marketing strategy were based entirely on the analysis of the neo-classical economists then price would be the most significant feature of that strategy and would be based on the concept of the price elasticity of demand. A product is price elastic if changes in price influence changes in demand. All things being equal, an increase in price will lead to a fall in demand and consequently a fall in revenue and vice versa. All things rarely are equal, and consumers can behave in an unpredictable manner. Many factors influence price and pricing strategy and operate at the environmental, organizational and strategic levels of our model. We deal with some of those factors under the following headings.

Cost

A business firm wishing to make a profit must use the cost of making a product or providing a service as an important base point in setting its prices. However, the sensitivity of most pricing decisions lies less in the cost of raw materials, labour, and the like than the understanding of those factors that may determine the extent of mark-up on the basic cost price. These include most of the factors identified below. Moreover, costs can be distorted by accounting methods, particularly those associated with apportioning overheads. For example, should overheads be calculated for individual cost centres or averaged for the whole organization? An idea often propounded by neo-classical economists is that cost and therefore price are associated with the economies of scale and that volume production will lead to price reduction. While this may be true for some products, there are many exceptions which challenge both the notion of economies of scale and the necessity of tying price to volume production. We return to these arguments in our discussion of the product life cycle and marketing strategies.

Consumer behaviour

The price of a product may well be related to what a consumer can afford and to what he or she is prepared to pay. These in turn are related to income levels, the consumer's perceptions of quality and value for money, and the consumer's budget for a particular purchase. In purchasing a new camera for a special holiday or a new word-processor for the office of a small business, the consumer's own target price based on what he or she wants to pay may be the primary factor. The range of products considered will then be limited to those priced within a range around or below the target price. A firm aiming at a particular target market may be best advised to discover the budgeting behaviour of its potential consumers before setting the price. Some firms use target pricing to influence product design. For example, where costs are likely to exceed target price, value-engineering methods will be used to reduce costs. However, there can be cases where the consumer's perception of value exceeds the target price. In 1972, Jaguar launched the XJ12 model. Demand so outstripped supply that second-hand cars were being sold for 40 per cent more than the original price. Consumer perceptions can of course be influenced by promotional activity. The brewing industry in Britain has focused its attention on the lager market. Many brands are deliberately marketed as highly priced products offering the consumer 'real' quality. This strategy was successfully pursued by the brewers of Stella Artois to establish their product in a highly competitive market. Such strategies depend heavily on 'brand image' (discussed in the next section), fashion and social influences. The lager market is aimed at the young drinker and the attractiveness (particularly to the opposite sex) and the social superiority of drinking a particular brand is stressed.

Economic factors

Price is related to the economy in a number of different ways, all of which have a potential impact on an organization's pricing policy. The affluence of consumers will have an obvious influence on their level of budgeting and regional variations may produce differential demand, especially for certain luxury items. The role of the state in managing the economy may affect both demand and prices. The control of interest rates will influence the extent of consumer credit and hence the size of an individual's budget, as will levels of taxation. During periods of high inflation the government may well introduce measures to control prices. A major influence on price for exporters is the currency exchange rate which fluctuates according to the state of the economy. In early 1985 the pound and the dollar approached parity, which made many British goods highly attractive in the USA, giving firms such as Jaguar a significant boost to their profits through increased sales. As the dollar weakened against the pound British exports became less attractive and for 1987–8 Jaguar cars announced significantly reduced profit figures due in no small part to changes in the exchange rate. (Cases 2.1 and 2.4 examine further aspects of exchange rate changes.) As a changing exchange rate brings prices of products more into line with competition from domestic suppliers or other country's imports, criteria other than price become more important. The relationship is far from simple and no matter how attractive the price of imported goods may be, it can be offset by delays in delivery, an inadequate distribution network, or a poor after-sales service.

Competition

Many firms price their products by reference to an existing market, basing their price around that offered by competitors for products of similar features and quality.

Management goals

The price of goods is often related to the extent to which managements wish to optimize profit. We saw in Chapter 2 that management goals rarely conform to simple economic models and are complicated by considerations of power, politics and personal preference. The desire of a group of managers for a larger market share for their products may result in a low price strategy to build up demand. In some firms price may be deliberately used as a promotion strategy to create an image of product quality in the eyes of the consumer.

Organizational size

The size of an organization may give it market power and the ability to manipulate market prices. This is especially true of oligopolies. The Swiss pharmaceutical firm Roche controlled by the 1970s around half of the world tranquillizer market, largely through its products Librium and Valium. This brought the firm to the attention of the Monopolies Commission, who, in 1971, accused the company's British subsidiary of exploiting the market against the public interest by charging excessive prices. We saw in Case 5.1 how Glaxo-Wellcome's market dominance with Zantac and Ventolin enabled them to charge high prices. A major supermarket chain such as Sainsbury or Tesco is able, because of its purchasing power and stock turnover, to insist on large price discounts from its suppliers.

Case 7.1: Disneyland Paris

Disneyland Paris opened its doors for business as Euro Disney in April 1992. It was the fourth of the Disney theme parks and followed the successes of Disneyland in Los Angeles (opened in 1955), Disney World in Orlando, Florida (opened in 1971) and Disneyland, Tokyo (opened in 1983).

The idea of opening a Disney theme park in Europe had been around for some time. The corporation had noted that while only 5 per cent of the visitors to its US parks came from Europe, that figure represented over 2 million visitors a year. The company felt that there was a large potential European market waiting to be tapped and it had been encouraged by the considerable success of its Tokyo operation. This was a faithful copy of Disneyland in California and convinced the Disney executives that if the Disney experience could work in Japan, the concept could be transplanted to a European location with ease.

The proposals for the development began in the early 1980s. Several countries were interested, amongst them France, Italy, Germany, Spain and, for a short time, the UK. Although Spain was a strong candidate (mainly for its weather), the eventual location was the area around Marne-la Vallée, some 30 km outside Paris. The choice of location was due to a number of factors:

● France had a stable economy and low rates of inflation.
● The location was within easy reach of a large proportion of the French population and near a major road route from Germany. The Eurotunnel project linking France and the UK was due for completion in the mid-1990s. In

all, over 300 million people were less than two hours away by air and the park would be near the major airports of Roissy and Charles de Gaulle.
● Market surveys had shown that tourism in Europe was predicted to expand significantly.
● Paris was already a highly popular vacation destination and the proximity of the park meant a large number of visitors would have an extra attraction.
● The French government were highly supportive. Finance was made available for extending existing road and rail links to the park. Low interest loans with delayed repayment terms were made available to Disney and tax concessions were granted through the reduction of VAT on goods sold in the park. The enthusiasm of the French politicians was, in part, a product of rising unemployment in the 1980s and the promise that the park would create at least 15 000 new jobs.
● Market research was carried out amongst the French and the general feedback was that the park would be welcomed.

Euro Disney was launched by a share issue in 1989, at a share price of £7.07. The Walt Disney Corporation took a 49 per cent share and 51 per cent was offered in the first instance to European investors. The flotation was popular and at the time of opening the shares were worth £16.00.

All the Disney theme parks are based around well-known Disney characters. These have proven universal appeal and are reinforced in the public's

▶

Continued

imagination by the regular re-release of Disney films such as *Snow White, Pinocchio* and *Fantasia* and the more recent policy of releasing some of the films on video. Disneyland Paris is no exception and a key feature of the experience and creation of fantasy is the interaction between staff dressed up as famous Disney characters and the customers. While the Disney characters created the main theme, each of the parks is divided into a number of imaginary worlds, each stressing a particular theme. In Disneyland Paris the imaginary worlds comprise Main St USA, Frontierland, Adventureland, Fantasyland and Discoveryland. A key element of all these 'worlds' is a number of experiences and rides with an emphasis on creativity and state-of-the-art technology. The Disney Corporation has a policy of continuous technological updating. Another key goal is quality of service, which extends beyond the theme park to hotels, catering establishments and souvenir shops. To that end, staff are carefully selected and trained. Stringent selection criteria embrace appearance codes, including rules on dress, hairstyle, weight and so on. The Disney Corporation has created a distinctive corporate culture for its theme park employees. For example, employees are known as 'cast members' and their uniforms as 'costumes' to reinforce the concept of fantasy. In support of this, all events are meticulously planned. At any one time there may be several employees dressed up as the same character, but only one may be seen at any one time in the park. The characters emerge from underground tunnels responding to a centralized control using two-way radio. The fantasy is all and two Mickey Mouses in the park at the same time would never do.

When it opened, Euro Disney had 29 rides, six hotels, a campsite, a golf course and assorted restaurants, food outlets and souvenir shops. At the outset an additional 3000 acres were acquired for future expansion. By 1996 it was expected that the theme park itself would be much bigger and would be joined by a conference centre to capture off-season trade. The Disney Corporation was proud of its new European park and claimed it as technologically superior to any that had gone before it.

Despite the overwhelming support of the national government, the Disney Corporation did encounter significant initial problems in dealing with a local bureaucracy and its planning regulations. In the first few weeks of opening, the company encountered demonstrations by local villagers objecting that the park would damage the quality of their lives. However, many locals gained substantially from the sale of land and used the money to build motels, shops and restaurants in the area

Initial reactions of the paying public were mixed. There were many complaints of high prices, long queues, poor service and technical teething problems with many of the rides. In 1993 an accident on one of the new rides attracted criticism about the safety of the park. The French were especially critical of the apparent lack of intellectual content in the park's attractions and the quote by arts commentator Anane Mnouchkine that Euro Disney was a 'cultural Chernobyl' was widely reported in the world's press. The initial problems caused another commentator to refer to it as 'corporate America's Vietnam' (*Observer*, 14 November 1993). The target attendance for the first year of 11 million was almost reached, but thereafter attendance figures fell to 9.8 million in the second year and 8.9 million in the third but rising to 10.7 million in 1995. Despite the significant criticism of the world's press, in its first year of operation Euro Disney was easily France's top attraction, with several million visitors more than the Pompidou Centre, the Eiffel Tower and the Louvre.

Perspectives on the success or otherwise of the attraction were mixed. Disney CEO Michael Reisner was quick to point out that attendance patterns at other Disney theme parks were similar in the early years. The financial failings of the European operation were, however, inescapable. In the first two tears of operation the park had lost 20 billion French francs and, from its buoyant position at opening, the share price fell from £16 to £3.55. In 1994 trading was suspended on the French stock exchange when the share price fell to less than £2. In 1993, over 10 per cent of staff were made redundant. The park was becoming a drain on the highly profitable Disney Corporation and to protect US shareholders, Disney executives put pressure on French banks and the French government to support the financial restructuring of Euro Disney. The eventual restructuring of 1994 included a relaxation of loan repayments, the leasing of some attractions and a rights issue, with a Saudi Arabian prince accumulating a large number of new shares. Despite the problems in France, the Disney empire was extended in 1995 through the purchase of ABC Television in the USA to make Disney the world's largest entertainment network.

The relative failure of Euro Disney in its early years has been attributed to economic/financial and cultural causes. In the early 1990s, the French franc was stronger than some other European currencies, notably those of the UK, Italy and Spain. French interest rates had risen, placing an additional burden on loan repayments. The effective devaluation of sterling meant a fall in UK visitors to the park of around 50 per cent. It was only marginally more expensive for a UK family of four to visit Disney World in Florida, given the relatively cheap rate of the US dollar. Even for those who came, spending was down on accommodation, food and souvenirs. Most commentators agreed that both entrance and hotel prices were too high. Price cuts were made during the first year of operation, but this meant that, for the hotels, occupancy rates had to rise to levels beyond the most optimistic estimates. While park attendance targets were almost reached, levels of operating profit were well down on targets. Market research discovered that families who stayed overnight preferred cheaper accommodation in Paris where a visit to the park could be combined with other attractions. A vicious circle was created whereby a lack of revenue meant that expansion plans for Phase 2 were shelved. The park needed more attractions so that people would need to stay overnight and push up occupancy rates. As it was, the park's attractions could all be visited in a single day. The postponement of Phase 2 also delayed the construction of a conference centre, which was planned to take up hotel space in off-season periods. Not only were the hotels contributing some 30 per cent to the overall deficit, but their lack of success meant that the company was thwarted in its plans to sell them off at a handsome profit after the first few years of operation.

Many critics claim that the early disappointments were rooted in cultural differences. The Disney experience is very American and particularly alien to elements of the French market. The French accused the attractions of lacking in intellectual content and failing to build in any way upon French cultural heritage. While the American theme parks favour fast food and have a ban on the sale of alcohol and cigarettes, the French visitors have a preference for table service and alcohol with their meals. The Japanese park made little concession to Japanese culture and had proven a great success. Disney executives believed that if the concept could work in Japan it could work anywhere. However, the Japanese were attracted to the family orientation, the uniforms and regimentation and the opportunity to buy souvenirs at every turn, all of which fitted Japanese culture. The French were less enthusiastic and early concessions were made. These were the sale of cigarettes, the availability of alcohol at table service restaurants, the choice of non-US-style food, the incorporation of European themes into the attractions and the widespread use of the French language. This became even more important as the recession in Europe made the park even more dependent on the French paying public. There were early problems with some of the cast members, who had difficulty embracing their roles with the dedication required by the Disney Corporation and labour turnover rates were around 25 per cent in the first two years. Staff morale was further undermined by redundancies. Disney was also criticized for its lack of cultural awareness in its promotion activity. The same style of promotion was used across Europe and no account was taken of cultural differences.

The financial problems of Euro Disney resulted in the company rethinking other aspects of the park's operation. In 1995 the name was changed to Disneyland Paris to give the park a stronger sense of geographical identity and associate it with the image of Paris. At the same time the name change was an attempt to disassociate the park from its earlier failures and from the link some commentators had made with other failed 'euro' projects. Further price cuts were made in 1995 of up to 20 per cent from entrance fees, hotels, food and souvenirs. The company ran its own promotional packages, including special winter deals and free entry and hotel accommodation for up to two children under 12 years old when accompanied by two paying adults. Strict codes covering working practices and dress were relaxed in an attempt to reduce labour turnover and improve morale. New attractions were added, such as a convention centre and new rides, including the Space Mountain, heralded as the most technically advanced ride in the world.

From 1995 to 1999 the recovery was steady. Attendance improved and settled at around 12.5 million a year. The company moved into operating profit and there was a steady growth of revenue year on year. Guest spending in the park had also risen and by 1998 hotel occupancy rates had exceeded 80 per cent. Recovery was aided by a

▶

Continued

weaker French franc in the latter part of the 1990s. In 1999 there were plans to open a new themed restaurant in association with McDonald's and approval was given by the French government for a second theme park based on the concept of the Disney MGM studios in Florida to open in 2002. The Disney Corporation also announced plans to open a new theme park in either Hong Kong or Shanghai.

Gilles Pélisson, the chief executive of Euro Disney SA, the controlling company of Disneyland Paris, stated in his 1998 report:

> In a tourism environment largely affected by the Football World Cup, Disneyland Paris has confirmed its position as the leading European leisure destination. 1998 was characterized by a strong improvement in operating performance and the start of important developments aimed at diversifying our product offering. All these elements strengthen our confidence in the future of the Company and we look forward to the major event of 1999, the opening of our new attraction 'Honey, I Shrunk the Audience!'.

The attraction, whose name would have matched ideally the attendance trends of the early years, now represents a growing confidence in the future of the park. ∎

(*Sources*: *Financial Times*, Feb.–July 1992, Nov. 1993, March, June 1994; *Observer*, Nov. 1993, Aug. 1995; Euro Disney SA, Annual Reports, 1995–98; Mills *et al.*, 1994.)

We began our discussion of price by challenging the all-important view attributed to the price element in marketing by neo-classical economists. A much more detailed account of the relationship between price and demand and, in particular, the limitations of the neo-classical approach may be found in the companion volume, *Economics in a Business Context* (Neale *et al.*, 2000). The role of price in marketing strategy is, as we have seen, highly complex. Nonetheless it is the only element of marketing strategy that generates income, all other items incurring cost. Pricing policy is therefore a vital strand of strategy, which because of the complexities involved is often difficult for management to judge. We return to such strategic considerations at the end of this chapter.

Promotion

We can identify five types of promotion; advertising, sales promotion, direct marketing, personal selling and publicity. The significant growth of promotion as marketing activity is a function of the growth, complexity and competitiveness of markets and the developments of appropriate technology, as in the newspaper and television industries. It was not until 1896 that newspapers, following the leadership of the *Daily Mail*, recognized the value of advertising revenue to offset rising costs (Cannon, 1986).

All types of promotional activity use psychological theory and communication models of human behaviour, but the nature of the promotion used will depend on a number of factors, including the strategy of the organization, the available budget and the type of market. While television advertising may be an appropriate medium for the promotion of consumer goods such as chocolate bars, a specialist magazine may be preferred for promoting expensive camera equipment, and personal selling may be the best way to market industrial goods to other organizations. Some forms of promotion, such as television advertising, are obvious, while others, such as shop design, are less so. The Burton Group, on taking over Debenhams, invested heavily in redesigning the department store interiors to project a new image and attract different market segments.

Promotion, like distribution, often involves management working together with representatives of other organizations. Advertising, for example, may involve the marketing manager working closely with an agency as well as representatives of the media. We will return to these aspects when we discuss the organizational aspects of marketing, and turn our attention, for the time being, to the various types of promotion.

Advertising

The management of advertising involves four major considerations; the design of the message, the selection of the media, the cost of both production and exposure and the evaluation its effectiveness.

- **The design of the message** reflects the three functions of advertising. First, it operates to inform the consumer and may be useful in creating initial demand for a product or informing consumers about such things as price changes. Second, it operates to persuade the consumer to buy the advertiser's product rather than that of a rival. This form of promotion tends to focus on specific features, which distinguish a product from its competitors, and by building up a brand image. The third function serves to remind the consumer of the product and encourage repeat purchases. Such promotion is not aimed solely at consumers, but also at wholesalers and retailers to give products shelf space. In general the nature of the message will vary in all these cases. For example, an advertisement that aims to change the buying habits of consumers will often use images with which the potential consumer identifies.
- Advertisers have a wide choice of **media,** including national and local newspapers, magazines, cinema, television, radio and posters. In recent years there has been considerable increase in the use of local independent radio and local newspapers, no doubt reflecting the expansion of both types of media. The selection of appropriate media also involves questions of timing, and an advertising campaign may be carefully scheduled to use various forms of media either concurrently or consecutively to achieve maximum impact.
- **The cost of promotion** will vary with the media selected. In 1999 the daily rate for a full-page advertisement in the *Daily Telegraph* would cost £40,500 for mono and £49,500 for colour. The comparative rates for the *Guardian* would be £18,000 and £22,000 respectively. The variation in price has little to do with the cost of production and is more a reflection on the higher circulation rates of the *Telegraph*. A similar advertisement in a local paper could cost around £2,500–3,000. While rates for national advertising have increased significantly over the past 10 years, those at the local level have remained roughly the same, an undoubted reflection of increased competition in the sector. The above costs are for exposure only

and do not include the cost of producing the advertisement. Each of those prices may vary considerably with the demand for advertising, the positioning of the advertisement, and the extent to which special deals may be struck between the buyers and sellers of advertising space. The major problem with such expenditure is the degree of waste, since much advertising can be ignored by large sections of the population and the real impact is often difficult to evaluate. We will deal with the problems of evaluation in our discussion of marketing strategy.

Sales promotion

This incorporates a wide variety of different techniques, including free samples, money-back coupons, trading stamps, contests and so on. Manufacturers promoting goods through the trade often provide attractive point-of-sale displays or product expertise in the form of a specialist salesperson. A furniture manufacturer such as Grange, a bedding firm like Dunlopillo and many of the cosmetic manufacturers train and pay their own staff to operate in department stores. Exhibitions and trade fairs are popular ways of promoting goods both to the trade and to industry as a whole. Such forms of sales promotion apply to services as well as manufactured goods. New restaurants often invite a specially targeted clientele to a launch evening. British Rail has introduced several types of fare structure to attract off-peak users, in the same way that many restaurants offer reduced-price meals to attract customers outside the hours of peak demand. These examples illustrate the interaction between sales promotion and pricing strategies.

Sales promotion is sometimes referred to as 'below-the-line' advertising and is often underestimated in considerations of promotion. It is estimated that sales promotion comprises over 70 per cent of all expenditure on promotion activity and has achieved a particularly rapid growth since the 1960s. The growth has been attributed to increasing rates of inflation and changes in management thinking. Rising inflation has made the consumer more conscious of special offers, while management have apparently grown sceptical of the effectiveness of advertising and believe there to be a much clearer and direct relationship between expenditure on sales promotion and sales.

Case 7.2 offers two different illustrations of promotion campaigns. In the first, a travel offer by Hoover, the promotion was far more popular than envisaged by the company, resulting in significant financial losses and generating bad publicity. In the second, a use of cultural stereotypes by McDonald's in Singapore proved to be an outstanding financial success for the company.

Direct marketing

This is both a form of promotion and a channel of distribution. In direct marketing, organizations deal directly with the customer without using intermediaries such as retail outlets. There are many forms, which include direct mail shots, inserts in magazines, mail order catalogues, telephone sales, faxes, coupon response forms, door-to-door leaflets and the current growth of electronic commerce. (E-commerce is dealt with in more detail in Chapter 2 and

Case 7.2: Two sales promotions

Case 7.2a: Hoover

Hoover, until recently part of the US Maytag group, operates in the highly competitive domestic products market. Hoover has been under pressure for some time and sought a plan to boost sales in the recession. This was particularly important, since most people only purchase a new domestic appliance, such as a vacuum cleaner or a washing machine, when the old one breaks down.

In the summer of 1992, Hoover executives launched a sales promotion in association with a travel firm, JSI. The offer was of two free airline tickets to one of six European destinations with the purchase of a Hoover product for £119 or more, the price of a vacuum cleaner. Hoover estimated that the offer would attract 50 000 new customers and in November and December of the same year, when sales usually fall, the offer was enlarged to offer free flights to a number of US destinations as well.

The process involved in obtaining the offer was complex. Purchasers had to make an application within 14 days and were then promised a registration form within 28 days. Provided the registration form was returned within a further 14 days, customers had up to 30 days to nominate their destinations and flight dates. Should these be unavailable, the company could nominate alternatives. Clearly, Hoover believed that the complexity of the application process would restrict the number of takers.

The promotion was successful in a spectacular fashion and sales were boosted far beyond the company's estimates. Rather than 50 000 as predicted, the offer was taken up by 200 000 with half requesting transatlantic flights. The majority of customers bought the cheapest vacuum cleaner under the terms of the offer.

Shops could not get enough stock and the Hoover production plants were placed on seven days a week operation, with the necessity of overtime payments and the hiring of extra staff to cope with the increased demand. The company was unable to cope with the applications for flights, and, in any case, insufficient flights were available. There were innumerable complaints of delay and of forms that did not arrive. Cases were brought before the Trading Standards Office and Hoover received a particularly bad press. Many who received offers of flights found them wholly unacceptable, in terms of either destination and/or date of travel. Maytag, the parent company were forced to send in an investigation team and the three executives responsible for the promotion were dismissed. Hoover had to spend an extra £20 million pounds acquiring flights, and some put the additional cost at nearer £40 million. Several thousand vacuum cleaners were being sold on the second-hand markets, with a corresponding impact on the sale of new cleaners. Since the cheapest available transatlantic flight at the time of the offer was around £200 per person, the offer was viewed by most in terms of two flights for £119, with a free vacuum cleaner thrown in.

Following the bad publicity associated with the promotion, Hoover invested £7 million in a European-wide press campaign to restore its image. However, by the middle of 1995, Hoover's market share had fallen from around 50 per cent to less than 20 per cent by volume and value. This was attributed to an adverse reaction to the free flights promotion and to the introduction by a new company of a cleaner using innovative new technology. The problems caused by the flights offer brought a particularly hostile reaction in the UK, traditionally the strongest market, where an estimated 200 000 people felt they were out of pocket on the promotion. A pressure group was formed and had little trouble enlisting 10 000 angry consumers. The new competition was likely to provide a much longer-term problem. Just after the free flights promotion, James Dyson launched a new type of vacuum cleaner without a bag, an idea that initially had been turned down by Hoover. The Dyson vacuum cleaner was an instant success and became the market leader by a long way.

Maytag, who had purchased Hoover Europe for US$300 million, now sold the company to the Italian-based firm Candy for US$170 million.

(*Sources*: *Financial Times*, *Marketing*, 1 June 1995; *Marketing Week*, 23 June 1995; *Management Today*, December 1996)

Case 7.2b: McDonald's Kiasu Burger and the fourth flavour

The global fast-food restaurant chain McDonald's has built its reputation on a well-known range of products that it offers around the world. The similarity in its product range around the world is

▶

Continued

matched by a similarity in its approach to marketing. The restaurants are easily recognizable by a common approach to design and layout. In almost every location the restaurant can be spotted underneath the sign of the 'golden arch', representing the 'M' in McDonald's. Promotional campaigns everywhere tend to emphasize family values, low cost, good-value nourishing meals and use a 'Ronald McDonald' character to appeal to children.

In reality there have always been variations in the taste and appearance owing to variations in local suppliers around the world, but the core product range remained sacrosanct. In the 1990s the product policy was relaxed to allow the introduction of local products to appeal specifically to local tastes, usually accompanied by a fierce promotional campaign. Since 1993 such a policy has operated in Singapore. The first of such products was the Kiasu Burger. Kiasu is a local Chinese dialect word in Singapore, which roughly translates as a 'fear of losing out'. The positive connotation of this word is generally associated with healthy competition and the need to be first. The negative attributes are associated with aversion to risk and even selfishness and cowardice. Kiasuism is a well-known concept in Singapore, and, since 1990, has been popularized through a comic strip character, Mr Kiasu. The character was developed by four young Singaporeans and his adventures usually depict the worst elements of Kiasuism, such as gluttony and pushing to the front of queues. The comic strip developed cult status, but soon gained wider appeal and became a local craze. The comic strip character was augmented by a range of Mr Kiasu merchandise, such as T-shirts.

A decision was made to launch a new product in May 1993 using the concept of Mr Kiasu. The company developed a local product, the Kiasu Burger, described as 'an extra large chicken patty seasoned with extra spices, marinated in extra sauce, topped with fresh lettuce, all sandwiched in an extra-large sesame seed bun'. The product was sold at 2.90 Singapore dollars and was cheaper than the rest of the McDonald's hamburger range. The product was also introduced as part of a range of value-for-money meal combinations and purchasers of the Kiasu Burger were entitled to buy a Mr Kiasu figurine for 90 cents. Four types of figurine were offered, each bearing a typical Mr Kiasu slogan, such as 'Everything also I want!' and 'Everything also must grab!'. Such slogans poked

fun, not only at Singaporean attitudes, but also at 'Singlish', a local dialect version of English. The campaign was supported by television advertising featuring Mr Kiasu as a cartoon character for the first time.

Within two months of the launch, a million were sold and the Kiasu Burger itself had become a craze. Demand for the figurines was also high. At the end of July 1993, McDonald's launched a further promotion celebrating their success and congratulating their Singaporean customers for being able to laugh at themselves. For a limited period the company offered its Kiasu Burgers and figurines at half price.

The Kiasu Burger was developed as part of a series of promotions under the banner of the 'fourth flavour'. The aim of the promotion was to increase turnover by catering specifically to local taste and the use of novelty items. Any specific 'fourth flavour' was never destined to become a permanent feature of the McDonald's product range. Instead it was planned that interest would be maintained by the introduction of a new product at regular intervals, with the subsequent phasing out of the previous 'fourth flavour'. A year after the launch of the Kiasu Burger, McDonald's Singapore introduced the chicken-based Kampung Burger. This too was based on a popular cartoon character, 'Kampung Boy', and the cartoon characters were seen in animation for the first time as the product was launched by a television commercial. McDonald's saw the product as representing traditional community values associated with village life. The promotion was accompanied by a caption contest.

In 1995, McDonald's introduced another chicken product in the form of the Love Burger. They linked the product with the importance of love within the family and ran a competition to find Singapore's longest-married couple, the prize being an anniversary party at McDonald's. Another competition was launched for newly weds and prizes of McDonald's wedding receptions were offered for the most creative love messages between couples. The Love Burger was followed the following year by the McPepper Burger, a beef hamburger in a thick spicy black pepper sauce. This was the most successful promotional item to date and the company sold over half a million in the first two weeks of the launch.

Promotional items also included desserts such as McDonaldland ice cream exclusively for the Singapore market. The ice cream container was designed as the head of one of four McDonald's characters, 'Ronald McDonald', 'Hamburglar', 'Birdie' and 'Grimace'. Earlier desserts to appeal to local taste had included mango and durian milkshakes.

While the promotions varied in their popularity, the cumulative effect was an increase in turnover for McDonald's, with a knock-on effect to its main product range. During the period of these launches from 1993 to 1997, McDonald's presence in Singapore grew from 50 to over 80 outlets on a small island of around 3 million people. ■

(*Source*: McDonald's press releases; *Straits Times*)

later in this chapter.) The kind of products and services promoted and sold in this way vary greatly as the following examples reveal. A specialist holiday company will generally advertise its brochure in a magazine and consumers may obtain a copy usually by sending in a request form attached to the advertisement or by giving details to a telephone-answering service. Customers wishing to buy a holiday usually do so by completing a booking form or after a telephone discussion with a company representative. Clothes offered by mail order were once considered more down- than up-market. This is no longer the case as clothes firms catering for up-market niche market products now offer goods by mail order and some firms, such as Lands End, have built up a considerable reputation solely on the basis of a mail order business. Theatres and restaurants use faxes to send out details of special offers. In addition many restaurants will fax their menu details to potential customers. Direct marketing is used to sell to organizations as well as to individual consumers. Most firms obtain their most frequently purchased office supplies from mail order catalogues, making orders by telephone or fax.

KEY CONCEPT 7.4
Direct marketing

Direct marketing involves setting up a direct channel between the organization and its customers. It is thus a channel for both promotion and distribution, targeting specific groups and enabling them to respond without the use of an intermediary. There are a number of methods ranging from mail shots to the use of the Internet.

The advantage claimed for direct marketing over other forms of promotion is that it can be targeted at specific groups. Unlike television or other forms of advertising, the target audience is reached with minimum wastage. Critics of direct marketing attribute to it the growth of 'junk mail' and accuse it of adding to the problems of litter as consumers discard unwanted inserts from newspapers and magazines. Despite its critics, direct marketing has grown in popularity in recent years. That popularity is associated with increasing market segmentation and developments in information technology and telecommunications. A key factor has been the growth of name and address lists of all types, which form the basis of databases used by firms in direct marketing. Effective direct marketing depends on accurate data and the ability to refine the target market in response to feedback information.

Personal selling

This is a specialized form of direct marketing favoured by the sellers of industrial goods, recognizing the importance of building up good personal relations between seller and buyer. However, the cost of employing a sales force to maintain regular contact with customers means this can be a most expensive form of promotion. In recent years a much cheaper form of personal selling has developed, especially amongst the manufacturers of double-glazing and fitted kitchens, by employing part-time workers to contact potential consumers by telephone. Such unsolicited selling has attracted much criticism from irritated consumers.

Publicity

This can be an important form of promotion in that the credibility of products or services may be enhanced by linking them with news stories. Many newspapers now have specialist business features or even supplements and such stories can be an effective way of keeping a firm and its products in the public eye. Some of the larger firms institutionalize this function by employing a specialist public relations department.

An examination of promotion raises many important issues. Advertising in particular has been challenged for developing an overly materialistic society, and the ethics of advertising goods such as cigarettes and alcohol has been questioned by a number of interest groups. The high cost of promotion campaigns using television advertising sets up considerable barriers to the entry of new firms and may operate in favour of big business. This is another reason for the growth of direct marketing.

Place

Place refers to the processes by which products and services reach the consumer and involves consideration of marketing channels and physical distribution. A marketing channel represents the flow of goods and services and may comprise several stages, involving intermediaries such as transporters, agents, wholesalers and retailers.

Intermediaries play a number of different roles. They are usually able to distribute goods to customers in a more cost-effective way than the manufacturer, particularly where goods are mass-produced and items are fast moving. The most popular daily newspapers sell millions of papers between them. This would be impossible without a complex and well-organized network of transport, wholesalers and retailers to ensure that newspapers are available for readers each morning. In this case the intermediaries break down the number of newspapers into more easily managed batches and are geographically dispersed to ensure an effective delivery. Such wholesalers and retailers handle a range of daily newspapers, and so facilitate the buying process by offering consumers choice. Manufacturers and consumers are therefore linked in a cost-effective network. The cost of a single newspaper establishing its own network would push up prices to many times their current value.

An intermediary is also an important source of market research and sales promotion since it stands in closer proximity to customers than the manufacturer. For the same reason intermediaries are often better placed to offer a comprehensive after-sales service. Some intermediaries may offer limited processing facilities such as cutting glass or mixing paint to order. For the manufacturer the intermediary shares some of the risk by buying goods in bulk to sell on (some of which may not sell), and in so doing helps finance the manufacturer's operations.

Those manufacturers seeking greater control over the distribution process have tried to integrate vertically the marketing channel network. Perhaps the clearest example of this is franchising. However, we have already noted in this chapter the power that can be wielded by big supermarket chains over some manufacturers; a case of the marketing channel controlling the manufacturer.

In charting the growth of direct marketing, we noted that not all marketing channels involve intermediaries. In the case of industrial goods it is more common for the manufacturer to deal directly with the purchaser, often by building up a relationship between the sales and purchasing departments in the respective organizations. As we saw in the discussion of supply chain management in Chapter 6, there is a growing tendency for very close relationships to be built up between components suppliers and manufacturers, particularly with the introduction of 'just-in-time' production methods. This is illustrated by Case 6.1, which examines the relationship between Mercedes Benz and Eberspächer, a supplier of exhaust systems.

In all cases it is important that the marketing channel makes the goods and services accessible to those who seek them. The importance of accessibility varies with the nature of the product on offer and the needs and wants of consumers. It is important for a fast-food restaurant to be located near centres of population and to be sited so as to encourage casual callers. Accessibility becomes less important for the prestigious restaurant rated by food guides, since customers will often be willing to travel several miles. Hospitals too, especially those offering casualty services, need to be located near to and be easily reached by the populations they serve. The increase in the sale of flowers worldwide is a direct result of the widened access that telephone sales and, more recently, the use of the Internet have produced (see Case 7.3).

The concept of the marketing channel has been revolutionized by the growth of e-commerce and Internet marketing. This was featured in Chapter 2 and will be raised later in this chapter in our discussion of the relationship between technology and marketing. It is also a central feature of Case 7.3.

Buyer behaviour

An understanding of the needs, wants and behaviour of consumers is a vital element in designing a marketing strategy. Buyer behaviour involves considerations of why people buy and how they arrive at the decision to buy. Several writers have attempted to formulate theories of consumer behaviour so that marketers can predict the outcomes of various strategies (for example, Rogers,

1962; Nicosia, 1966; Howard and Sheth, 1969). As yet the predictive validity of such theories and models leaves much to be desired.

The weakness of such theories lies in the very complexity of buyer behaviour. We have seen how changes in the economy can affect consumer perceptions of their own purchasing power. This is well illustrated by consumer reaction to prices in Disneyland Paris in Case 7.1. In addition we can identify a number of psychological and sociological influences. These include perception, attitudes, patterns of learning, motivation, personality, social class, peer groups and culture. A knowledge of such factors is an important contribution to marketing strategy and may be used in the development of the marketing mix. Advertisers use these influences in a number of ways: by linking products to certain social groups with whom the consumer identifies – by using 'experts' to extol the virtues of particular brands in an attempt to influence the perceptions and attitudes of the consumer.

Predicting buyer behaviour becomes particularly important with innovations and is an important ingredient in decisions concerning new product development. Rogers (1962) attempted to differentiate people according to their response to innovative products and identified five types: innovators, early adopters, the early majority, the late majority and laggards. The innovators and early majority comprise an estimated 15 per cent of the population and are important as opinion leaders in the diffusion of innovations. The implications for the marketing specialist is to establish the characteristics of these groups and focus the marketing communication accordingly. The diffusion of new products is seen as a chain reaction of influence between pioneering consumers and the mass market. While Rogers found that early adopters tended to be younger, more affluent, more cosmopolitan than later adopters, such generalizations, like so many models, have foundered at the sheer complexity of buyer behaviour. For example, a consumer may be an early adopter of the latest in camera technology but particularly conservative where furniture, clothes or holidays are concerned. In this case we would need to identify the opinion leaders for each product group.

Consideration of buyer behaviour often focuses attention on specific target groups. These are referred to as market segments and we deal with the concept of segmentation in the next section. Not all product markets are highly differentiated. A product such as Coca Cola is bought by the widest possible range of consumers.

Whatever the product or the target market, considerable attention is paid by many managers to the attainment of **customer loyalty**, based on the assumption that the costs of retaining existing customers are less than those associated with gaining new customers and that loyal customers mean repeat purchases. In the late 1990s, the concept of customer care has achieved fashionable status. While for many consumers there is rather more rhetoric than reality, in many organizations customer care has become the focus of training and culture change programmes, as in British Airways (see Case 8.2). In the UK, supermarkets and retail chains such as Boots and W. H. Smith have attempted to increase customer loyalty through the introduction of 'loyalty cards', in which each purchase attracts points, which can then be converted into cash refunds or, in some cases, air miles.

Customer loyalty

	High	Low
High	Satisfied stayers	Happy wanderers
Low	Hostages	Dealers

Customer satisfaction

Figure **7.1** Customer satisfaction and customer loyalty. *Source*: Piercy (1997)

Piercy (1997) questions several of the assumptions that underpin traditional approaches to customer loyalty. In particular he challenges the assumption that there is an automatic link between customer satisfaction and loyalty, as illustrated in Figure 7.1.

The classic model of customer loyalty is illustrated by the 'happy stayer'. However, there are customers who gain satisfaction yet enjoy switching brands. These Piercy describes as 'happy wanderers'. 'Hostages' are customers who have no choice either because they are tied in by contract or they are dealing with a monopoly supplier, who can exploit market power by charging a high price. 'Dealers' are customers who forever seek the best deal irrespective of brand or supplier. Because the link between loyalty and satisfaction is complex, Piercy questions the value of loyalty programmes for all but the 'happy stayers' and says that in some cases loyalty cards develop 'hostages' rather than truly satisfied customers. He challenges the notion of loyalty cards as an effective strategy in that they are easy for competitors to copy and sees them as little else but a gimmick, which does little to create real customer value.

The complexities of buyer behaviour have led some to conclude that consumer marketing is inherently more complex than is the case with industrial or organizational marketing. Such a perspective ignores the complexities in organizational marketing, which may be different from those in consumer marketing, but are just as real. These complexities include the nature of management values and organizational politics, and those involved in the relationship between the buyers and sellers of industrial and organizational goods and services.

Branding, segmentation and the product life cycle

These concepts deal with issues raised under the various headings of the marketing mix. We deal with them separately here because of their importance.

Branding

Branding is the process through which the product is given a name, logo or symbol to distinguish it from the range of other products on offer.

Branding has become big business. It has been used most profitably in fashion-conscious market segments where major producers such as Calvin Klein offer a range of clothes, fashion accessories, perfumes and toiletries, each portraying the same fashionable image under a single brand. Branding has grown significantly in the entertainment industry. Three leading opera singers appear together as 'The Three Tenors'. This has become the brand and is registered as a trademark. The brand is used not only to sell concerts, but also tapes, CDs and a range of souvenirs. Would-be copyists have been pursued vigorously through the courts. Branding is a major component of soccer, with major clubs earning a considerable proportion of their revenue through the sale of branded merchandise associated with the club. Chelsea invested £2.5 million on a new mega-store built as part of a new ground development, which also included apartments, restaurants and a hotel. The Chelsea branded goods sold in the shop include, as well as football equipment, mountain bikes, home furnishings and clothes. In 1996 Manchester United sold 850 000 official team shirts worldwide and earned over £20 million from the sale of their own branded goods, which included their own brand champagne, wine and beer!

KEY CONCEPT 7.5
Branding

Branding involves giving the product a name, logo or symbol to distinguish it from the range of products offered by competitors or even by the same organization. Branding is an important source of product differentiation in a highly competitive and dynamic environment and can apply to a single product, a range of products or an entire organization. It is used to create awareness and build up customer loyalty to ensure repeat purchases. A well-known brand is seen as a financial asset that can provide firms with considerable competitive advantage.

Brands as a means of differentiation and attraction have become especially important in recent years for a number of reasons.

- The speed of technology transfer has meant that less time is available to capitalize on competitive advantage through technological change. The brand takes over from technology as the source of differentiation.
- The markets for most consumer goods in Europe, the USA and Japan have become stagnant. Brands are an attempt to give a product more prominence in the market place.
- Amongst certain market segments, such as fashion-conscious young people, particular brands have gained considerable popularity. Firms owning

such brands have capitalized on their success by extending both the product range and the product mix under the same brand.

Brand names can be given to a single product or a whole range of products. The latter tends to identify the products with a high profile, as with the aforementioned Calvin Klein or indeed Kelloggs. In other cases it may be important to differentiate individual products even though they originate from the same stable. For example, the washing powder market is dominated by two producers, Lever and Proctor and Gamble, yet each markets a range of washing powders under different brand names. In this way the brands assume an identity of their own, so much so that many believe them to be the products of a range of different companies. There may be several reasons why a firm is keen to differentiate a number of brands within the same product range:

- to appeal to different market segments;
- to capture those consumers who like to switch brands;
- to gain more exposure and shelf space in retail outlets;
- as a means of structuring the organization around brands to create healthy internal competition, as in the case of Proctor and Gamble.

Apart from the brand name, a particular logo or mark may be used. Calvin Klein and Pierre Cardin clothes and other goods are instantly recognizable by their distinctive logo. Some manufacturers feel it important to create a brand style so that any one of their products from a given range is instantly recognizable. Alfred Sloan insisted to his design teams that all General Motors cars in the USA possessed the definitive 'GM look' (Sloan, 1986). Alfa Romeo cars are differentiated from rival brands by the use of very distinctive styling.

An important development in branding has been the growth of 'generic' or 'own' brands. These can be found especially in the major retail stores such as Sainsbury, Safeway and Tesco. A generic is a product that is sold under the brand name of the retailer and applies to all kinds of products. It may in fact be identical to a nationally known brand on the same shelf, but is generally sold at a cheaper price to appeal more to the price-conscious shopper. In some cases generics have acquired a brand image that goes beyond price and value for money to indicate real product quality. Historically, Marks & Spencer have deliberately promoted this image with their own generic name 'St Michael'. However, significant falls in profits for 1998 and 1999 may indicate that consumer perceptions of 'St Michael' have changed. The company has responded by sourcing yet more goods from cheaper overseas suppliers.

Aaker (1996) identifies the following potential attributes of a brand, which offer meaning to the consumer. These are not mutually exclusive.

- The brand can represent a **product** as in the case of Cadbury's chocolate, Kodak films and Michelin tyres.
- The brand can represent the **organization**. In this case the company has as much if not more meaning to the consumer than the product. There are certain types of consumer who, for example, will only buy their food from Harrods or their shoes from Russell and Bromley. The brand as organization is especially important in Japan, to the extent where employment

consumers who respond in a similar way to a given set of marketing stimuli (Kotler, 1983, p. 40)

The concept of segmentation is the essence of the marketing concept as identified at the beginning of the chapter; the production of goods and services to meet the specific needs of consumers.

KEY CONCEPT 7.6
Segmentation

Segmentation is the process through which the total market is broken down to create distinctive consumer groups. The criteria used to form such groups varies and may include geographical location, social class, occupation, sex, lifestyle, and so on. Once market segments have been identified, products can be developed which focus upon a particular group in an attempt to maximize both the marketing effort and the needs of consumers. Some firms specialize in catering for the needs of a particular segment only, while others produce a range of products each aimed at different segments of the same market. In this case, the branding of each product becomes especially important to distinguish it from the others. The process of broadening the segments to which a product might appeal, or changing the market segment altogether, is knows as repositioning.

Market segmentation and product differentiation go hand in hand in that products are designed, developed, promoted and even priced and distributed with a particular market segment in mind. True segmentation occurs when genuinely different products are made for the different market segments. However, segmentation is not just a feature of products, but encompasses all aspects of the marketing mix. In 1971, Coca Cola offered a global product using a global promotion campaign, emphasizing a unified world with the slogan, 'I'd like to teach the world to sing in perfect harmony.' Here was a case of an undifferentiated product promoted in an undifferentiated way. In 1993 Coca Cola, in the face of increasing competition, especially from own brands, changed its approach. The company launched a promotional campaign, which varied its approach and techniques to appeal to different segments, differentiated by age, culture, social class and lifestyle. From 1993 to 1997, world sales of Coca Cola rose by 21 per cent (*Financial Times*, 5 May 1997).

Segmentation is an increasing feature of marketing, as the following illustration of the holiday industry will show. Many package tour holiday companies originally promoted all their holidays in a single brochure, leaving the consumer to select the most appropriate holiday from the entire range offered. In 1999, Thomson Holidays offered holidays under 15 different Thomson-labelled brands, each aimed at a different market. The main brochure 'Thomson Summer Sun' caters for the mass market, but the 'A la Carte' holidays aim to capture those groups with a higher disposable income and a different lifestyle. Lifestyle is also an important consideration in the 'Ski', 'Small and Friendly', 'Sports Resorts' and 'All Inclusive' brochures.

Income differentiation is a feature of 'Faraway Shores' and 'Platinum Collection', while age and family size are reflected in 'Young at Heart' for the older market and 'Superfamily' for budget-conscious families seeking activities for children. Thomson also owns other brands which are sold under different banners to attract different markets. 'Club Freestyle' is aimed at the 18–30 market and a whole range of 'Simply' holidays, based on different country locations, offer largely self-catering accommodation in more select locations to a mainly middle-class market. While few holiday companies aim to match Thomson for product differentiation, others do target specific markets. Saga has always designed its holidays and cruises for the older age groups and marketed them accordingly. While its products are aimed at a growing market, the company recognized that an increasing proportion of that market were fitter and more active than the previous generation and did not wish to be associated with 'an older generation'. In 1999 the company attempted to change its image and broaden its market position by offering products to over 50s, emphasizing attractive lifestyle holidays.

Not all such product differentiation is motivated solely by the desire to cater for consumer needs. The growth of the winter holiday market is undoubtedly related to affluence and changing lifestyles. It is also related to the hotel owner and tour operator's desire to utilize capacity all the year round. In some cases winter holidays are aggressively promoted and attractively priced to push up market demand. In this case some segments, such as the retired population, are especially singled out.

So far we have focused upon consumer goods and services, but segmentation is a feature of industrial goods as well. Many engineering companies in the components industry have successfully targeted specific groups and tailored their products accordingly. As we saw in Chapter 2, Japanese companies often forge very close relationships with their suppliers, although this is more a case of the segment defining the product rather than the manufacturer targeting a segment.

An important strategic decision in marketing is the determination of the most appropriate segments for the marketing effort. There would appear to be three broad options:

- offering a single or a small range of products or services for a single segment or limited range of segments;
- offering many products and services to many different market segments;
- offering a single product or service for an undifferentiated mass market.

The choice will depend on a range of factors, including whether the segment can be accurately identified, whether it is large enough to be profitable, whether it can be served within certain cost constraints, and of course, management goals. A truly undifferentiated product is a rarity. A fairly ordinary product such as a can of baked beans is offered in a number of variations, with various added ingredients such as sausages or with less salt and sugar, a variation aimed at health-conscious consumers. As we saw in the case of Coca Cola, an undifferentiated product can still be offered in different ways to different market segments. In addition, the same product can be offered at

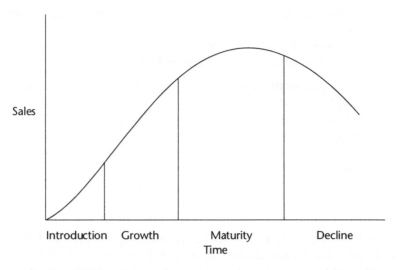

Figure **7.2** Product life cycle.

distributors become aware of the product and decide to adopt it. The costs of development and promotion are high and firms may suffer initial losses.

During the **growth** phase there is a rapid acceptance of the product and a dramatic increase in sales. This is generally sustained by improved distribution, product improvements, and even price reductions. There are normally high profits for pioneering firms but a growing market attracts competitors, leading to brand differentiation. While the production learning curve may lead to a reduction in costs, the need to satisfy an expanding market can involve costly investment in new production processes. The end of this phase is marked by a high level of competition, recognized by Wasson (1978) as a separate phase which he termed 'competitive turbulence'.

As it becomes saturated the market reaches **maturity**. Sales and profits are still high but there tends to be considerable investment in maintaining sales. This is achieved through product changes, increased promotional activity and price-cutting. Products are sometimes relaunched at this stage, usually with new features, different packaging and often an attempt to create a new image. Firms seek to maintain brand loyalty at the same time as attempting to broaden the market by repositioning. At this stage the less competitive firms drop from the product market.

The **decline** phase is marked by a falling off in sales, and while some firms do well as others leave the market, survival is often dependent upon successful product diversification.

The product life cycle can be useful as a framework for planning a marketing campaign over time and as an indication that marketing strategies need to be adjusted to match changes in the cycle. There is an implicit assumption in much of the writing that careful marketing policies can do much to slow down the cycle of decline, i.e., the cycle may be manipulated by the marketing mix. An understanding of the life cycles of a range of products may be an important factor in determining the introduction of new products and ensuring that the product mix is well represented at the introductory, growth and maturity stages. A company has significant problems if its entire product range is in the decline phase at the same time.

The utility of the product life cycle has been questioned on several counts. First, it is a gross simplification of the behaviour of markets and seems to ignore changes in the economy, the behaviour of competitors, the actions of governments and even dramatic swings in consumer fashion. Second, the cycle is highly variable for different products, in both the length of time it takes to reach the decline stage and the amount of time spent in each phase. The path for any product is extremely difficult to plot and the model is therefore a poor guide to marketing strategy. Third, even if we accept that the model is descriptive of a general process, it may be difficult to assess when a product has reached a particular stage. A temporary rise or fall in sales may be mistaken for a fundamental shift in the cycle, so that action is taken that is inappropriate at that time. Fourth, the model is criticized for ignoring the production implications of a changing market position.

Each stage of the product life cycle has implications for the design of the product, the volume and variety of production, and the nature of the process of manufacture or delivery of the service to the customer. In manufacturing the product life cycle is closely related to a process life cycle. The introductory stage of the product life cycle is marked by a highly flexible production process. As markets reach their maximum potential the capacity can only be met by relatively inflexible mass production systems. The cost of such systems necessitates a high market demand and long production runs. There is a similarity here with the 'revised sequence' (Galbraith, 1972), discussed earlier in this chapter. In this situation marketing becomes production led rather than demand led. However, in the case of manufactured goods, the relationship between the product and process life cycles has been complicated by the introduction of flexible manufacturing systems (see the discussion of this in Chapter 6).

The environmental aspects of marketing

Marketing, probably more than any other of the business functions we have dealt with, operates at the interface between the firm and its environment. We will see in this section how marketing activities are not only influenced by environmental factors, but that the management manipulation of the Four Ps represents a deliberate attempt to shape consumer behaviour and hence the market environment within which the firm operates. Marketing strategy is therefore a key element in the corporate strategy of any organization. We will view the relationship of marketing with the environment of the firm by looking in turn at the economy, the role of the state and consumer interest groups, technology, and finally cultural and social factors.

Marketing and the economy

For some, marketing as a subject has emerged as a branch of applied economics, and economic theory is used as the basis for the development of marketing strategies. Marketing activity is influenced by economic factors in a number of different ways, as the following illustrations reveal.

Major economic shifts, as in the case of manufacturing to service industry, have brought about new directions in marketing. The entry of new firms into the market place, especially in the form of overseas competition, may necessitate a change in marketing strategy for existing firms to retain their market share. In general terms, the greater the degree of competition, the greater the use of a wide range of marketing tools. In more monopolistic markets, individual firms wield considerable power in terms of the product offering, price and distribution. This is why, in some cases, as with public utilities like gas, water and electricity, regulatory bodies are established to protect consumer interest. A feature of oligopolistic competition is a tendency towards similarity of product design and price, as illustrated by car manufacturers and petrol companies.

Most societies are marked by an uneven distribution of wealth and income. Companies may therefore offer a range of goods and services reflecting such segmentation in the market place. The general level of economic activity has an impact upon marketing activity in a number of different ways. In times of prosperity where demand is high, price becomes less of a factor, particularly in the purchase of luxury goods and services. In a recession when demand falls, the emphasis usually shifts to issues of product utility and value for money. Falling demand may call for price reductions, attempts to broaden the market by appealing to new segments or diversifying into new areas of activity. In economically depressed areas, attempts by the unemployed to set up shops are often doomed to failure owing to the low levels of demand in that area. Where demand is so low, little in the way of marketing strategy can change the basic position. Changing rates of inflation together with the level of economic activity will affect savings and the availability of credit. Where price inflation rises at a faster rate than wage inflation, the demand for certain luxury goods may fall. Some firms combat this by offering favourable credit terms to customers in an attempt to boost sales.

These illustrations show how marketing strategy has often reacted to changes in the economy. However, many firms will attempt to manipulate the economy through its marketing activities. In Chapter 5 we examined the link between levels of investment in new product development and economic growth at both the level of the firm and nationally. We have seen that one of the functions of promotional activities is to persuade consumers and hence attempt to manipulate demand. We have noted several times in this book how very large companies, especially those operating globally, are able to manipulate markets to their advantage through product development, pricing and promotional strategies in such a way as to affect national economies.

While the relationship between marketing and the economy is significant, we saw in our discussion of price elasticity that economic theory has its limitations in our understanding of marketing behaviour, ignoring as it does a range of important cultural, social and psychological influences. Political and pressure group influences also play a part and it is to these we now turn.

Marketing and the role of the state

The state represents a powerful presence in the market place as a dominant employer, supplier and purchaser. We have already noted the increases in government advertising expenditure. Since the 1980s in the UK both privatization and deregulation have changed the marketing environment. The state is involved in marketing in a number of different ways:

- The state provides information on government policy.
- Advertising is often used to direct the behaviour of individuals, as in the case of health education or to encourage the unemployed to take advantage of training schemes.
- The pricing and promotional policies of state-controlled industries can be used to direct public expenditure and consumption, as was the case with energy. The potential for the government direction of markets in this way is considerable. In reality, particularly in the example of the energy industry, the actual control was often diluted through the absence of an effective coordinating policy. In terms of the present energy industry in the UK, the emphasis has shifted to the establishment of controls for now-private organizations.
- The state attempts to regulate the marketing activity of private firms in a number of different ways. Most of these measures are aimed at regulating free competition and protecting individual consumers and the environment.
  - In terms of product development, the British Standards Institute (BSI) has devised technical standards to which products should comply for ensure minimum standards of quality, and to protect both the consumer and the environment against the potentially dangerous product.
  - We have seen in Chapter 5 that the granting of patents gives inventors a monopoly to market their products in return for making their invention public. The aim of such legislation is both to reward and stimulate innovation.
  - Through its law relating to monopolies and mergers the state attempts to define and prevent unfair competition. In the UK this is controlled by the Competition Commission (formerly the Monopolies and Mergers Commission). In the USA it comes under the legal framework of the Sherman Anti-Trust Laws.
  - The abolition of resale price maintenance under The Resale Prices Act 1977 has loosened the control of major manufacturers over the market place and so protected the consumer from unfair business practices.
  - The Trade Descriptions Act 1968–72 tackled the problems of deception in advertising and sales promotion.
  - The Sale of Goods Act 1893 and The Supply of Goods (Implied Terms) Act 1972 set out the contractual rights of consumers on such issues as the return of goods and warranty.
  - Many governments attempt to limit the advertising of certain types of products such as cigarettes and alcohol.
  - Britain's membership of the EU means that firms are subject to a range

of further regulations affecting firms and consumers alike, as with the pricing of agricultural produce or the description of products when promoting them for the European market. The Consumer Protection Act of 1987 was, in part, an implementation of EU policy on product liability and price information.

Government intervention in the marketing activity of private firms is a very complex issue, no more better illustrated than in the case of cigarette advertising. In 1997 the British government attempted to place a ban on all cigarette advertising. The proposals were met by intense lobbying by a number of interested parties. For a number of years there has been a ban on the TV advertising of tobacco products. This had led to the tobacco companies seeking alternative forms of promotion, notably the use of billboard advertising and sports sponsorship. Firms controlling advertising sites and billboards naturally objected to a complete ban. In any case, the billboard advertising of tobacco was already restricted by the government to 30 per cent of the 1980 total. The biggest opposition came from sports bodies, especially those with an interest in Formula One motor racing. This is a very expensive sport that derives significant revenue from cigarette companies, with brands such as Marlboro sponsoring a successful racing team. Successful lobbying earned the ban a reprieve. Even so, several tobacco companies actively sought new ways to promote their products. There has been a switch to the direct marketing of cigarettes and a brand such as Silk Cut now has its own free magazine. Such promotion channels are much more difficult for governments to control.

The various measures outlined above are reinforced by a state bureaucracy. Many marketing issues are dealt with by The Department for Trade and Industry and government-backed offices such as The Office of Fair Trading and The Advertising Standards Authority. As we can see, many of the measures are aimed specifically at consumer protection and some of them are the direct consequence of consumer pressure groups. We now deal with such interest group activity under the heading of consumerism.

Consumerism

The concept of consumerism has developed in the past 30 years around four tenets: the right of the consumer to be informed, the right to choose, the right of redress and the right of safety. If we accept that marketing is nothing more than the effective satisfaction of consumer needs and wants, then consumerism would in fact be synonymous with marketing and the presence of organized consumer groups would be no more than an important source of information and market research. The consumer movement has, however, developed as a political interest group to represent the rights of consumers, largely because those rights are seen to be threatened by the marketing activity of many firms. It is interesting to see Baker (1991) deals with consumerism as 'marketing under attack'.

The crusades against dangerous products by people such as the American Ralph Nader and the growth and success in Britain of organizations such as The Consumers Association and The Campaign For Real Ale have raised the

---

KEY CONCEPT 7.7
Consumerism

Consumerism has developed as a social movement to inform and assist consumer choice and to act as a pressure group to represent the interests of consumers. These interests are represented to organizations in an attempt to influence product design, price and distribution. consumer interest groups also act as watchdogs to guard against unsafe products and dishonest producers. That consumers are now more aware and better informed is due largely to the activities of consumer groups and the publicity given to consumer matters over the past 30 or so years.

---

public awareness of consumer issues. At the same time magazines such as *What Car* and the popularity of consumer programmes on television and radio have fed the public need for information. Consumer information exists to satisfy a need, but like marketing promotion itself it has created an even greater need. The number of consumer magazines has proliferated. Most national newspapers now give significant editorial space to consumer matters and concern themselves with a range of consumer issues, from testing new cars and bottles of wine, to offering advice on financial matters, to highlighting sharp practice in the business world.

As well as feeding off its own publicity and success, the growth of consumerism is often related to the factors identified below:

- The public needs protection against the effects of dangerous products. A series of articles in the trade press and newspapers in the 1970s in the USA focused the public's attention on the number of accidents involving Ford Pinto cars, all the result of the location of the petrol tank. The pressure was such that Ford withdrew the model.
- The public needs protection against the dishonest behaviour of some producers. The growth of fierce competition in the home improvements market has resulted in the Office of Fair Trading receiving a number of complaints about such firms misleading the public about the true cost of credit. The Financial Services Act 1987 emerged partly to protect consumers by regulating those firms dealing with such matters as investment, insurance and pensions; several complaints had been received that investment returns were less than promised and costs were much higher than expected. Strict rules now operate for the promotion of investment and pension plans.
- The growth of pressure groups like The Campaign For Real Ale is a reaction to the monopoly power wielded by the main producers in a particular industry. The brewing industry was moving towards a market dominance by a handful of producers and the gradual elimination of beer brewed by traditional methods in favour of a product that was more easily stored and transported. The campaign not only brought pressure against the major producers to produce more 'real' ale but was successful, with the aid of

considerable media coverage, in creating a much greater public demand for that product.

● Consumers themselves are better educated, more affluent and, largely because of the growth of the consumer press, more informed. The result has been increased expectations and demand for products of a higher quality. While this is probably true for all consumers, the growth of consumerism is undoubtedly a middle-class phenomenon, closely related to the degree of affluence of particular consumer groups.

In some cases consumer pressure has been spectacularly successful. Environmental groups in Europe enlisted considerable public support to oppose Shell's dumping of its oil platform, Brent Spar, in deep water in the North Sea. The lobby caused Shell to rethink its actions. In more general terms, the consumer movement has been influential in broadening public awareness of consumer matters and bringing about a range of protective legislation. In many cases this has led to improved goods and services and more effective marketing. There are still those who feel that the consumer lobby needs to go much further to protect the rights of consumers, while others, particularly in business, may resent the influence of consumer groups on governments, fearing that excessive regulation may stifle innovation.

Marketing and technology

Marketing and technology interact in a number of different ways:

● We have seen in Chapter 5 the process of product design and development and its protection through the patent system. We also noted that marketing was an essential vehicle for the information and promotion of new products and processes.

● In our discussion of the product life cycle, we identified the clear relationship between process technology and levels of demand. It is no good management using product development, pricing and promotional strategies to increase demand if that demand cannot be met by the existing production system. The development of computerized stock systems provides greater information and access for both buyer and seller.

● Developments in technology have had significant impact upon the marketing process itself. Among the most obvious aids to marketing have been the developments that have taken place in mass distribution. A range of developments has taken place in retailing to simplify the process of purchase. The system of 'electronic funds transfer at the point of sale' (EFTPOS) may well, together with the credit card, obviate the need for cash. A wide range of goods may now be bought over the telephone using credit cards for payment, and some firms have set up computer databases of suppliers willing to offer such goods to consumers at highly competitive prices. The fax machine is used by theatres and restaurants to target potential customers. In the late 1990s we are witnessing a trading revolution through the use of the Internet (a fuller discussion of e-commerce can be found in Chapter 2 and an illustration of its use in Case 7.3).

● Developments in transport have not only improved distribution systems

Case 7.3: The growth of telemarketing in flower sales

At first glance the market for cut flowers would seem to be the province of a large number of small outlets. The reality is a highly competitive market, dominated by a small number of organizations such as Interflora in the UK and 1–800-Flowers in the USA. The business of selling and distributing cut flowers has been one of high growth and profitability. A major reason for that growth lies in the choice they offer the customer in terms of marketing channel and the widening of that choice through the increased use of telephone sales and the Internet.

The four main customer requirements would appear to be easy access, the ability of the business to meet a variety of target prices, fast delivery and the availability of expert advice. These requirements are met by three main channels. The flower shop provides expert advice and offers the customer the opportunity to choose a particular arrangement first hand. This channel is important when customers are concerned to pick the flowers themselves or when they wish to take the flowers as a gift as in the case of hospital visits or as a token when invited to someone's home. The flower shop may be preferred when buying flowers for oneself. Telesales either through a call centre or a shop still offers the opportunity to obtain expert advice, but this method may simply be more convenient, as when sending flowers as a thankyou gift or to commemorate someone's birthday or anniversary. Such a method, while saving a visit to a flower shop, does carry a handling and delivery charge. A more recent development has been the opportunity to buy and organize the delivery of flowers through the Internet. The advantage of this channel lies in its speed, easy accessibility of product and price information, and convenience. The Internet is also used by some organizations, such as Interflora, as a means of making more sales. Such organizations offer an e-mail service to remind people of key dates such as birthdays and anniversaries. The service is usually free and inevitably accompanied by an easy means of ordering flowers for immediate delivery.

In the UK, the largest operator is Interflora. This is an international organization trading as FTD in the USA, Canada and Japan and as Fleurop in parts of Europe. Interflora is a non-profit trade association owned by its members. These comprise over 58 000 florist shops across 146 countries. The members elect the company board from amongst their constituents and the board members serve for a fixed period before they are replaced. Interflora trades not only in flowers, but also chocolates and other similar gifts. The company aims to provide a seamless service to customers and prides itself on its responsiveness and innovation. The company has grown largely on the basis of telephone sales made by customers to individual shops. In the case of a delivery outside the area the florist will check the nearest Interflora member to the delivery address and pass on the order. This process used to be carried out exclusively by telephone, but the company has introduced a computerized system linking many of the member shops. There has been a recent growth in Internet business but the telephone is still the main source of orders by far.

Teleflorist is the second largest UK organization behind Interflora and operates in much the same way. However, Flowers Direct, another growing firm in the UK market, operates in a different fashion. This is a privately owned company that uses few intermediaries. Flowers Direct claims an advantage over Interflora through the operation of a 24 hours call centre. It sells and delivers not through shops but via a central warehouse and the use of couriers to deliver the flowers. Like Interflora and Teleflorist it offers an international delivery service.

1–800-Flowers is a US company and, at a consistent annual growth rate of 25 per cent maintained over the past few years, is claimed by many as one of the fastest-growing companies in any market. Initially a private company specializing in flowers, 1–800-Flowers made a private equity placement in May 1999 and began share trading on Nasdaq in August 1999. Its product range has widened to include a large range of garden products, including furniture, home décor items, speciality foods and, most recently, a range of gourmet foods. The company has its own headquarters and central staff, some of which specialize in market research to develop new product ranges and also to monitor quality and service standards. The company operates its own call centres and has its own shops branded as Bloomnet. Despite having its own shops, the majority of trading is carried out through partner florists, which number over 1500. The company started with telephone sales and direct sales

▶

399

Continued

through its own outlets. Internet sales, while only 15 per cent of the total for 1998–9, increased 85 per cent on the previous year and are viewed by the company as its major focus for the future. The company launched its website in 1995, which is not only used to promote and sell its products, but is also used to announce job vacancies and invite applications. ■

(*Sources*: Company information from Interflora and 1–800-Flowers; Friedman and Furey, 1999).

but enabled consumers to access a wider range of goods. The transnational or even transcontinental shopping trip is commonplace. Cross-channel routes are full in the weeks leading up to Christmas as UK residents travel to France to access cheaper beer, wine and spirits and other goods. Large stores in many cities around the world attempt to attract the foreign shopper. The tourist authorities in Dubai have designated a shopping month to attract even more visitors to its shops, hotels and restaurants.

The role of cultural and social influences in marketing

In our discussion of segmentation we suggested that markets were increasingly segmented and the marketing effort was correspondingly targeted at specific groups. Invariably the basis for such segmentation is social and cultural. Differences within societies and between culturally distinctive groups have resulted in different patterns of product adoption. The popularity of a product among one cultural or social group is no guarantee that it will appeal to another, totally different group. Despite the expansion of international travel, the food preferences of different cultural groups can vary widely. For example, the durian is one of the most popular fruits in South East Asia, yet its taste and smell are unpleasant to many Westerners. However, marketing does not simply react to social and cultural differences, they are actively used to promote products. Using the aspiration of one group in society to acquire the lifestyle of another group is a common theme in advertising. The growth of the teenage market is both a reflection of changing social values and a deliberate creation by producers actively seeking new business opportunities. As with other aspects of our model, the influences are invariably two-way with marketing acting as both a product and a cause of social change. Several social and cultural factors illustrate our point.

Changing demographic patterns relating to age, sex, location and naturally incomes may have a profound effect upon marketing. An ageing population in many Western industrial societies has opened up new marketing opportunities in such industries as tourism and in general focused the attention of marketers towards a sector they had previously seldom considered. Geographical shifts in population may have a considerable impact upon consumer demand and property prices. Rising property prices in London and the South East of England has had a knock-on effect on the property market of surrounding areas. This has manifested itself in changes in the types of new property being built, house prices and the way property is promoted by estate agents. Small terraced housing in areas within commuting distance of

London become desirable cottage residences to tempt the buyer with dreams of country living. Such changes also have an impact on the marketing of public transport systems.

Values and attitudes are important influences on the marketing process. Core cultural values such as family life and concern for children are constantly used in advertising, and marketing specialists take care not to transgress such social mores. An interesting variation to this is shown in Case 7.2. In 1993, McDonald's in Singapore launched a new product, the Kiasu Burger. Both the naming of the product and the accompanying promotion poked fun at a particular cultural characteristic of Singaporeans. However, the ensuing success of the product would indicate that this was taken in good part by the local population. Reference groups such as experts, peers, social classes, and those groups portraying a desired lifestyle are frequently used in marketing communication as mechanisms of attitude change. This would seem to operate across all cultures. In many countries in South East Asia a highly visible rich elite, who often favour Western and Japanese goods, are used as important trendsetters for the aspiring middle classes and play their part in cultural change. In countries such as Singapore and Malaysia the shopping mall has not only replaced small, traditional local shops. A visit to the city centre shopping malls has become an important leisure activity for the local population.

Advertising in particular uses and builds upon social attitudes, as the following examples show. Ford in the USA sold the German-built Lincoln-Mercury Scorpio as 'imported from Germany for select dealers', while for many years in the UK, Rover have promoted their cars as a product of British technology being driven by German businessmen. Both promotions used the widely held belief that the Germans develop superior technical products. The Americans use this value directly in their advertising. Rover on the other hand appear to be promoting the superiority of British technology, yet the promotion is based on the credibility of German technical know-how and the use of Germans as 'expert witnesses'. Of course, the connection between UK-built Rover cars and German technology is now stronger than ever with the purchase of Rover by BMW. Lasserre and Schütte (1999) cite the case of Club Med's attempts to sell holidays to the Japanese. The company had traditionally sold its holidays on the image of easy-going resorts and the emphasis on simple pleasure seeking. They found little interest in the Japanese market until they stressed the opportunity for holiday-makers to learn and participate in organized sporting activities. In Case 7.1 we examined several dimensions of cultural difference and the associated problems in the early days of Disneyland Paris.

Such cultural stereotyping has benefited the Germans considerably as exporters of manufactured goods and they have been especially successful with more technical products such as machine tools. Japan on the other hand had to overcome damaging negative stereotyping, which saw its exported goods in the 1920s and 1930s as cheap, imitative products (Wilkinson, 1983). The cultural stereotyping extends to the role of marketing itself and the emphasis placed on different elements of the marketing mix. The Germans are noted for their emphasis on product development and careful targeting, while the Americans are noted for their emphasis on promotional activities and selling. In Japan, spending on advertising is almost four times that in the UK (Czinkota and Ronkainen, 1995). This is undoubtedly driven by the focus in Japan, not on consumer research but on market growth and incremental product development. In Japanese consumer markets, competition is rarely based on price but on product differentiation and service.

However, as with all stereotyping we should always remember that the differences that exist within a country are often greater than those between countries. Equally the situation can change, not just culturally, but economically as well. In Japan the recession of the 1990s has led to increased price competition and in many cities there has been the growth of discount stores. The younger buyer in Japan is more attracted to Western products that reflect individualism than the more traditional older population and is more likely to buy on credit.

The organizational aspects of marketing

We have already dealt with several organizational issues elsewhere in this chapter. In examining the different orientations to marketing we saw how the marketing goals have developed over time and how much they vary between organizations. Several references have been made to the impact of organizational size on marketing. We have noted that increasing size has led to increasing specialization within the marketing function and how the costs associated with the various marketing activities have acted as barriers to entry, favouring big business in the achievement of market dominance. As we noted in Chapter 3, there is increasing recognition that so-called 'excellent' companies are built around clearly defined cultures. An important element of such organizational cultures is a close identification with the needs of the customer.

In this section we will focus on structural issues pertaining to marketing, dealing first with the way the function is organized and second with the relationships between the marketing and other functional areas.

The organization of marketing

Marketing was initially viewed as being synonymous with sales. With the growth of the firm and the development of its markets came the problems of organizing the sales force, often achieved by creating sales territories operating under a hierarchy of district and regional managers. The need for improved market research and sales promotion created research and advertising units as sub-divisions of the sales department.

The growth of increasingly complex markets, the emergence of large organizations and changing attitudes by management towards consumers all called for corresponding developments in the functional organization of business activities. Marketing emerged as a function in its own right, with the previously dominant sales department as a subsidiary activity. The marketing effort now spawned further specialisms in advertising, sales promotion and market research, and some marketing departments also assumed responsibility for new product development. In the larger organizations, marketing management became the coordination of a range of specialist marketing activities.

This functional organization of marketing mirrored functional developments occurring elsewhere in the firm, but some companies were experimenting with other forms of organizational structure. As we saw in Chapter 3 in our discussion of structure, divisionalization occurred because some firms such as General Motors found it most appropriate to organize around products or markets. The marketing efforts in many organizations went down the same route. Piercy and Morgan (1993) take up this theme of structure following strategy and see product market segmentation as the basis of organization structure and that an organization structure in harmony with the needs of the market is a source of competitive advantage.

In the 1920s Proctor and Gamble developed the concept of product management. Under this arrangement the firm is organized around its products and each brand or group of brands has its own manager. Such a structural arrangement may be necessary where product knowledge is highly technical, or where the firm is dealing in totally different product markets. The benefits that may be gained by management from such an arrangement include an increased knowledge of the product market and an ability to respond quickly to changing market demands. A healthy internal competition can be built up, leading to increased sales. Furthermore, product management has often been a good training ground for aspiring senior managers, as it interfaces with most aspects of the firm's operation. The customer gains by dealing with people who have real product knowledge. Product and brand management can be costly ways of organizing the marketing effort. Specialist activities such as advertising may be unnecessarily duplicated, or else product managers may lack expertise in the more specialized areas of marketing. In firms where every brand has its own manager there may be over-staffing of management at the lower and middle levels, with the ensuing problems of career progression.

An alternative structural arrangement would be to specialize around different markets. The markets may be differentiated geographically, by industry, or even by customer. In consumer marketing some form of geographical specialization is a fairly traditional approach. Sales forces have tended towards regional organization for ease of administration and control, and television advertising is invariably regional. The US firm Colgate-Palmolive derives the larger part of its sales revenue and profits from overseas activities and traditionally has based its organization on invidual country operations linked through a regional structure. Staff mobility within this structure has been viewed as an essential part of career development within the company. More recently, Colgate-Palmolive in its expansion into the emerging markets of Indonesia, China and Eastern Europe has established a centralized division to deal specifically with emerging markets issues alongside its traditional structures (Rosenzweig, 1995).

It is in the marketing to organizations, with the prospect of high-volume, high-value orders, that specialization by industry or by customer is regarded as a factor in increasing sales. The Xerox Information Systems Group switched from selling by product to selling by industry, and organized its marketing efforts accordingly. The advantages of this approach lie in building up a close relationship with individual customers and gaining insights into their operations. Some firms operating in the computer market, like IBM and Digital, offer a consultancy service to potential customers. This leads to improvements in the customer's own operating systems and potentially more sales for the computer company. Gaining experience of the customers' operating problems and their marketing environment is often invaluable to the process of developing new products. Such a structure would seem most appropriate where the market is becoming increasingly competitive and there are long-term advantages to be gained from building up such close relationships with customers.

As we saw in Chapter 3, organization structures rarely conform to ideal models. Many firms have marketing departments that display elements of all the structural variations identified above. A system of brand management can be backed up by a centralized research or advertising function. The marketing effort can be organized according to different industrial markets but may be further differentiated according to product. The system is further complicated in that marketing departments frequently use agencies external to the firm. The past 30 years have seen the growth of advertising agencies. Some like Saatchi and Saatchi have achieved a very high public profile as the creators of the Conservative Party's early successful election campaigns. Specialist agencies also operate in market research and sales promotion. The advantages of using agencies lie in their ability to stand back and offer an independent assessment of the firm's marketing activities, to offer specialist expertise, which the company may not possess, and to act as a source of fresh ideas.

Dealing with outside agencies can be a costly exercise and may be a potential source of conflict. In fact, any structural differentiation within the marketing function itself may set up internal conflicts. Brand differentiation and management may create competition but that same competition has the potential for unhealthy conflict. Tensions can exist between marketing management who direct operations and the sales force who must carry them out. Much wider tensions can exist in the relationship between marketing and the other functional areas and it is to this we now turn.

Marketing and other functions

The stereotype view of the relationship between marketing and operations is one of conflict. Operations staff view marketing as people who make their life difficult through promises to customers that are difficult to meet. For its part, the marketing department sees operations staff as inflexible and more concerned with the efficiency of their own systems rather than satisfying customer needs. Such myths have some basis in fact. Historically the two functions have been evaluated according to different criteria. Marketing personnel have tended to be rewarded for achieving a high sales turnover and a high market share, while the primary orientation of operations has been towards the achievement of minimum cost and a smooth operation flow. The marketing staff have been encouraged to create change by developing new opportunities, while the operations staff have tended to resist any change that increases costs. Moreover, the cultures of the two groups have traditionally differed. Marketing specialists tend to deal with vague concepts like image and customer preference and have their focus outside the organization, while operations staff tend to be internally focused and more comfortable dealing with the quantifiable.

Such conflict is not necessarily dysfunctional. Persuading customers to adopt standardized goods and services may enable the firm to offer a better service as well as reducing costs. Where conflict is disruptive it may be tackled in a number of different ways. Management might consider different reward criteria. Marketing staff could be rewarded for accurate forecasts rather than meeting some artificially contrived quota and operations staff rewarded for meeting delivery times. Conflict may also be avoided by encouraging more interaction through joint project teams and mixed career paths.

Similar tensions may occur between other functions, as with R&D over product design or with accounting over methods of payment. Nor are such conflicts the sole property of the marketing department. We have already identified the type of conflict that can emerge between the R&D and operations functions and in the next chapter we see the traditional antagonisms that occur between the HR department and line management. Such conflicts are the inevitable consequence of organizational size and managerial specialization. They may, however, be minimized by strategies focusing on coordination.

A popular current approach to integration is through culture change as illustrated by Case 8.2 in the next chapter. Organizations such as British Airways have attempted to change the behaviour of all staff and ultimately the prevailing culture to a focus on customer care. In this way, a marketing focus is being used as an integrative device for all staff in the organization irrespective of their specialism.

The strategic aspects of marketing

The process of developing a marketing strategy bears a striking resemblance to the process of developing a firm's corporate strategy, underlining the centrality of marketing to the firm's planning process. Opportunities are analysed, target markets are defined, market share objectives are set, segmentation strategy determined and the particular marketing mix is developed. The marketing mix, including issues of positioning, branding and competitive differentiation, is central to the whole process since it identifies and guides the strategic options. Strategic considerations in marketing therefore embrace all of the factors we have discussed in this chapter. We will use the four elements of the mix to examine the various strands of marketing strategy. Finally we examine how these various elements may be combined and stress the integrated nature of marketing and the other functional strategies.

at the outset. Such a strategy is used where demand is price sensitive and where economies of scale can be gained by mass production. Penetration is usually associated with competitive markets. However, the strategy can be used to discourage competition by raising the barriers of entry, since those entering the market must be certain of high sales to offset development costs. Such a strategy has been used by many firms. Texas Instruments dominated the American hand-held calculator market in this way and in 1988 Amstrad attempted to dominate the business market for personal computers by selling at 50 per cent less than its rival, Apricot. This strategy is also illustrated by the price wars amongst certain UK national newspapers in the 1990s, led by News International (see the postscript to the News International case in Chapter 1).

An alternative method is to establish what the market will bear. This usually involves getting a sample of consumers to rate products according to attribute and price and make comparisons of rival products.

We can see that the pricing decision needs to take account of a range of interconnected factors. Additional complexities can and do exist. The same product may be differentially priced for a number of reasons. It may be discounted for bulk purchase or to specific groups such as senior citizens and students. The same cinema seat may be differentially priced for different performances to even out demand and particularly to attract customers to less popular showings earlier in the week. The price may be a function of the number and type of distribution channels. Imported goods may be more expensive because they pass through more intermediaries, and products are generally more expensive in a prestigious store. Such variations can be confusing and lead to customer complaints, as some airline companies have found. The price of the same seat on the same flight may vary considerably depending upon when and where the ticket has been bought. Tickets bought well in advance and those bought on a stand-by basis are much cheaper, as are those obtained from discount agencies and 'bucket shops'.

A further complexity is that the pricing strategy generally changes over the life of a product as a function of demand, market share, and changes in the economy. Price cuts may be introduced to regenerate a product nearing the end of its life cycle or to beat off competition, and price rises may be needed to keep pace with inflation.

Promotion strategy

Earlier we identified the three main functions of a promotion strategy: to inform, to persuade, and to remind. We also suggested that effective strategy was dependent upon selecting the most appropriate message and media for the product and target market. Two important decisions remain: how much to spend and how to gauge whether a campaign has been effective or not.

It is clear to management that a promotion strategy must be affordable, yet setting an appropriate budget is far from easy. Three common methods are identified. The 'percentage-of-sales' method sets the budget according to the previous year's sales figures or is based on sales forecasts. The inherent flaw in such a strategy is that promotion is a function of sales rather than vice versa.

Nevertheless, such a method is simple and may appeal to the cautious decision-maker. The 'competitive-parity' method pegs promotional expenditure to that of the major competitors in proportion to the market share. The 'objective-and-task' method has probably the most rational appeal in that specific targets are set and the budget apportioned accordingly. Such a method enables the results of the expenditure to be assessed against the objectives.

In most organizations the marketing manager has to operate from a budget allocated as the result of some complex decision-making process involving all managers in all functional areas. Dhalla (1978) accuses many managers of short-sightedness in setting the promotional budget. He feels that promotion should be treated as a capital investment and not, as in most cases, as an operating cost. A similar approach is often taken with research and development and training.

Promotion may be evaluated on three levels. The first consideration is that the particular advertisement or sales promotion has been seen and by how many and what type of people. The second consideration is that the public and in particular the target market are aware of the product and its attributes. The final and most important consideration is that the promotion results in the desired action on the part of the target market. In the case of consumer products, the ultimate test lies in the number of sales, whereas a government campaign to reduce drinking and driving will have to be measured by the number of convictions.

The evaluation of a promotion campaign is especially difficult for two main reasons. First, a decision has to be made about the time scale for such an evaluation. Is the impact of an advertisement to be measured over a week, a month, several months or longer? Second, it may not be possible to isolate the impact of a promotional campaign from the influence of other variables such as changes in the economy, the behaviour of competitors, changes in social behaviour and so on. Accurate evaluation under such conditions may require extensive econometric models or a level of experimentation not feasible in most organizations. Few firms have done as DuPont and tested advertising expenditure in their paint market by varying the amounts in different parts of the same territory to assess the impact on sales. They discovered that the effect of the heaviest expenditure was weakest in areas where they had a high market share. Perhaps this is a pointer to the diminishing returns of advertising expenditure (case quoted in Buzzell, 1964).

Not all promotion activity has the strategic intention of increasing demand for products, as the following case illustrates. In 1987 Burroughs Wellcome had developed a drug that had been successful in trials in slowing down the effect of the AIDS virus for some people. The company was concerned that the launch would be accompanied by media exaggeration and many would be misled into thinking that a cure had been found. The product was launched simultaneously in open forums at major hotels in several American cities. In each case the launch was linked by television to a panel of medical experts and questions were encouraged. Such a promotion served to limit demand for the drug specifically to those cases who could benefit the most.

Distribution strategy

Distribution strategy is concerned with such issues as the type and number of channels, the location of those channels and how they might be controlled. A number of different channels are available, including a traditional sales force, using a partner firm to handle distribution aspects of the business, distributors, wholesalers and retailers, and more recently telemarketing and the Internet. The choice of channel depends very much on the nature of the product or service. Traditionally many organizations used sales representatives. However, the maintenance of a full-time sales force is expensive and may only be justified where transactions are complex, require face-to-face interaction, involve an element of customer training and where there is clear value added by using this form of distribution. Many organizations no longer have the need for this kind of service. Costs can be reduced significantly through the use of telephone sales, call centres and the Internet. Such forms of telemarketing and the Internet often have the advantage of operating for 24 hours a day all week. The use of a single channel may limit access to customers and a mix of channels may be required, or the use of different channels for different products.

Traditionally in manufacturing industry, distribution strategy has focused around stock policy. Incentives in the form of discounts were often given to persuade intermediaries such as warehouses to hold stock. Such strategies became less important with the increased use of just-in-time strategies. Current emphases in distribution strategy are on the range of distribution channels and the use of new technology. In this way distribution has become the key to success for many organizations. The emergence of Dell Computers from a small firm to a leading player in the personal computer market in less than five years is attributed both to its approach to customer care and to its use of direct marketing. Dell was the first computer company to focus on telesales and the Internet and its methods have been copied by competitors such as NEC. First Direct has emerged as a success in banking largely through its accessibility to customers by telephone on a 24-hour basis and, as we noted in Chapter 2, a call centre is a much cheaper way of operating a bank than a high street branch. Case 7.3 examines the growth of flower sales through telemarketing and the Internet and demonstrates how an industry has widened its customer base by focusing on specific distribution channels.

The advantages of using technology-based distribution strategies lie in lower costs, access to an expanding market and being able to focus investment and staff where they can be most effective, as in after-sales service or customer training (Friedman and Furey, 1999).

However, personal contact can still be important in some industries. Fites (1996) cites the case of Caterpillar Tractors who were successful in maintaining market share despite strong competition from the Japanese in the form of Komatsu. He argues that their success is based on their close working relationship with 186 independent dealers across the world and the support they give to customers. This is central given that the product is expensive, long-lasting and has to operate in a number of difficult environments across the globe. The company feels that the local knowledge of dealers and their close links with customers is a major feature in repeat purchases.

An integrated marketing strategy

Integration can occur along a number of different dimensions: within each component of the mix; between the various elements of the mix; between marketing and the other functional strategies; and integration of the whole company around marketing strategies focusing on enhanced customer loyalty and satisfaction. We will deal with each in turn.

- The various activities and strategies associated with each component of the mix should work together. For example, effective promotion is generally achieved through a campaign in which press and television advertising and sales promotion are carefully coordinated to achieve the maximum impact upon the consumer.
- The elements of the mix should work together. Price reductions are often accompanied by a promotion campaign and both need the reinforcement of sufficient stocks and effective distribution in anticipation of increased demand. Improvements in product quality necessitating increases in price need to be sensitively handled in promotion.
- The effective integration of marketing with the other functional strategies, especially those of innovation and production, is considered essential to the firm acquiring a competitive advantage. An effective product portfolio should be built around the skills and other resources of the organization. A business school that attempts to offer courses in international business but lacks staff with the necessary expertise may attract a poor reputation and see support for all its courses suffer as a result. Some see this integration of functional strategies as an iterative process, requiring the constant monitoring of markets, products, processes and technology, and the firm working these elements around its chosen field of distinctive competence.
- As far as marketing itself is concerned, many suggest that the strategic focus should be towards customer satisfaction and customer loyalty. To be effective this should ideally permeate across the entire organization and is therefore in itself an integrative strategy. Integrated strategies aim to enhance the reputation of the company and secure repeat purchases, but also act as an opportunity to sell additional products. Mercedes Benz at their Sindelfingen plant and headquarters on the outskirts of Stuttgart have established a visitor centre. This is linked to visits around the plant and embraces a cafeteria-style and luxury-style restaurant, a shop selling both souvenirs and more expensive extras for the car, model displays, a film theatre and a financial services department. Buyers of a new Mercedes car have the option of collecting it themselves from the factory. Those who exercise this option are met by a personal courier and are given a personalized factory tour, at the end of which they pick up their car. Not only does this generate enhanced customer satisfaction, it is often treated as a family outing, which includes a meal at the restaurant, the inevitable purchase of souvenirs and perhaps signing up for a special Mercedes credit

card at the financial services desk. Many supermarkets have attempted to enhance the customer experience by introducing a range of extra services. These include ample car parks, petrol stations and car-wash facilities, cash points, cafeterias, loyalty cards and staff employed solely to give customer information. There are dangers with such multifaceted approaches to marketing in that dissatisfaction with a peripheral element of the service can cause the customer to go elsewhere and the main sale is lost.

Summary

Marketing involves the understanding of customer needs and behaviour and the researching of markets for the effective development, pricing, promotion and distribution of goods and services. These activities operate in a number of different consumer and organizational contexts and can incorporate the marketing of people, places, company image and ideas as well as goods and services.

The product, price, promotion and distribution elements of marketing are known as the marketing mix and form the key elements of marketing strategy. There is a growing trend for firms to segment the markets in which they operate, calling for variations in the marketing mix for each target market. Another important element of the mix is the branding of products and services.

Marketing operates at the interface between the organization and its environment, and changes in the economy, state regulation, technology and social trends all call for changes in marketing strategy. Marketing managers use their knowledge of the environment, especially of those social and cultural influences that shape behaviour, in an attempt to manipulate demand for their product. In recent years marketing activities have been significantly affected by globalization, consumerism and technology-based developments such as telemarketing and Internet marketing.

The development of an effective marketing strategy depends upon an understanding of the workings of the market place, of customer needs and the appropriate mix for the market segment and prevailing environmental conditions. The implementation of that strategy depends upon the integration of marketing with the other functional specialisms, with a focus on the customer.

Further reading

There are a number of good general texts on marketing. The initial US influence and the dominance of Kotler has been challenged by a number of texts focusing on UK and European examples. Good examples of these include M. J. Baker, *Marketing*, 5th edn (Macmillan, 1991); S. Dibb *et al.*, *Marketing: Concepts and Strategies*, 3rd European edn (Houghton Miflin, 1997); and D. Jobber, *Principles and Practice of Marketing* (McGraw Hill, 1995). A good source of more academic work in marketing can be found in J. Frain, *Introduction to Marketing*, 4th edn (International Thomson Business Press, 1999). A different approach offering a highly readable account packed with interesting examples is offered by N. Piercy, *Market-led Strategic Change: Transforming the Process of Going To Market*, 2nd edn (Butterworth Heinemann, 1997).

Discussion

1. Assess Drucker's claim that marketing is not a specialized activity since it encompasses all the activities of the firm.
2. How far and in what industries do the five orientations to marketing operate today?
3. For what reasons do governments engage in marketing? Does this raise any ethical problems?
4. What type of market research information would you need in the following situations: a holiday company offering a new resort location; a manufacturer developing a new motor for domestic appliances; a restaurant owner planning a more expensive menu?
5. What factors would you consider to determine the price of the following: a new high-performance sports car; a new breakfast cereal; an MBA at an internationally known business school?
6. Why does market segmentation occur and what are its advantages and disadvantages for management and the consumer?
8. Assess the contribution of the selection of appropriate distribution channels to effective marketing strategy. What are the key issues raised in the sale of flowers as illustrated by Case 7.3?
9. To what extent can marketing activities change the environment in which the firm operates?
10. What are the essential ingredients of an effective marketing strategy for fast-moving consumer goods such as toothpaste, a luxury yacht and for a firm of professional accountants?
11. What are the key marketing issues for Disneyland Paris as illustrated by Case 7.1? Assess the cause of the problems in the early years and suggest how the company may turn current stability into profitable growth.
12. Assess the problems and opportunities presented by developments in telemarketing and Internet marketing.

CHAPTER 8

Human resource management

To use a marketing analogy, attempts were made in the 1980s to relaunch personnel management as human resource management or, as it is more commonly referred to, HRM. The process has been taking place over the past two decades to the accompaniment of 'corporate culture', 'flexibility', 'commitment', 'employee involvement' and 'TQM', all to a greater or lesser extent considered to be part of the HRM family.

Human resource management initially came to prominence in a course at the Harvard Business School, and in a seminal text is defined as,

> Human resource management (HRM) involves all management decisions and actions that affect the nature of the relationship between the organization and its employees – its human resources.
>
> (Beer *et al.*, 1984, p.1)

Most traditionally minded personnel managers would see nothing in that definition to imply that HRM has emerged as a radically different form of personnel management. Indeed, in the literature, the two terms, HRM and personnel, are used interchangeably. In this book we shall refer to personnel and personnel managers when dealing with the historical development of the function. Otherwise the term HR will be used to describe the function and HR managers or HR practitioners will be used to describe those primarily engaged in the function. The term HRM will be reserved generally for that specific movement and related strategies that emerged in the 1980s. There is no disputing that the transition from personnel to HRM has generated a substantial debate. As David Guest explains:

> To managers it seemed to offer an attractive alternative to the jaded image of personnel management and the dated rhetoric of traditional industrial relations ... among academics, it offered new hope for those who had begun to despair of the long term potential of industrial relations and personnel management as important academic subjects.
>
> (Guest, 1990, p.377)

In this chapter we will examine the extent to which HRM has supplanted traditional personnel management by comparing more traditional approaches to the new-style HRM. The development of both personnel and HRM illustrates well the workings of the Business in Context model. The growth of personnel management as a specialist activity has been influenced by a number of key environmental variables. These include the intervention of the state through an increasingly complex system of employment law, the workings of the labour market, the strength of trade unions, the state of the economy and changes in the competitive environment. In addition to these environmental factors, the role and status of personnel/HR managers themselves have had a significant influence on the scope and effectiveness of personnel/HR strategies. These same factors are associated with the development of HRM.

KEY CONCEPT 8.1
Human resource management

In many organizations, human resource management or as it is often referred to, HRM or even HR, performs the roles and duties formerly ascribed to personnel management. Many would argue that there is more than a name change and that the function has undergone an ideological shift. Traditional personnel management was concerned with recruitment, selection, training, pay, welfare and industrial relations. HRM deals with all of these, but integrates them within the overall strategy of the enterprise and sees business values as an overriding consideration. An important element of HRM is the development of a culture that stresses commitment to organizational goals, quality and flexibility. The extent to which the values of HRM have superseded those of traditional personnel management in many organizations is open to question.

We will deal with the environmental, organizational and strategic issues after we have examined the comparison between traditional approaches to personnel and HRM.

Identifying personnel/HRM

Traditional approaches to personnel

In this section we will attempt to define more traditional approaches to personnel and the activities most commonly associated with it. This will serve as a useful comparison with the supposedly different approach taken by HRM.

There would appear to be as many definitions of personnel management as there are books on the subject. This is hardly surprising, for, as we have noted, the activities are highly dependent upon the context in which they operate. For example, a discussion of personnel management in Britain would place greater emphasis upon industrial relations than it would in the USA, where trade unions play much less of a role and collective action is rarer. Despite these variations, a useful starting point is the definition offered by the Institute of Personnel Management:

> Personnel management is a responsibility of all those who manage people as well as being a description of the work of those who are employed as specialists. It is that part of management, which is concerned with people at work and with their relationships within an enterprise. It applies not only to industry and commerce, but to all fields of employment. Personnel management aims to achieve both efficiency and justice, neither of which can be pursued successfully without the other. It seems to bring together and develop into an effective organization the men and women who make up the enterprise, enabling each to make his own best contribution to its success, both as an individual and as a member of a working group. It seeks to provide fair terms and conditions of employment and satisfying work for those employed.
>
> (IPM, 1963)

If we ignore the somewhat idealistic stance and the absence of precisely defined tasks and duties, the definition stresses the dual goals of serving the needs of employees and the organization. It also serves the useful purpose of distinguishing between a business function and a departmental presence within an organization. Many students of business conclude mistakenly that all businesses conform to textbook models, relating as they do to fairly large-scale organizations differentiated into specialist departments.

Daniel and Millward (1983) estimated that if all firms, including small businesses, were considered, then 75 per cent of companies would have no specialist personnel manager, the function being performed by a manager who deals with personnel matters alongside other duties. The position is little changed in the late 1990s. For example, in many professional partnerships, such as solicitors or accountants, one of the senior partners is usually given responsibility for personnel, but would view their main role as that of a solicitor or an accountant. Some smaller firms may operate the personnel function through a one-person-secretary-cum-records department. The absence of a personnel specialist may even be deliberate policy. Hewlett-Packard, the American multinational, did not introduce a personnel department until staffing levels had reached 1200, its founders preferring personnel matters to be the responsibility of all managers (Beer *et al.*, 1985).

In Table 8.1 we present a detailed list of the various activities traditionally associated with personnel management. These activities may be categorized as people processing and industrial relations (see Key Concepts 8.2 and 8.3). The division of the personnel function along these lines was especially prevalent in large unionized firms, such as Ford, where industrial relations plays a particularly prominent role. In the 1990s, many such firms changed their structures to reflect the more integrated approach of HRM and the fact that industrial relations was no longer viewed as a problem. Nonetheless, many of the activities are still relevant to HRM.

KEY CONCEPT 8.2
People processing

People processing relates to those activities of HRM that involve the acquisition, development, motivation and control of individuals at work. It includes the various activities associated with recruitment, selection, training, appraisal, pay administration and welfare.

KEY CONCEPT 8.3
Industrial relations

Industrial relations is concerned with the relations between employers and employees and their respective representatives. These relations focus on such matters as pay, conditions, job security and forthcoming changes. The relationship involves elements of negotiation and bargaining, which in practice are usually dealt with by management on one hand and trade union representatives on the other. The importance of industrial relations is acknowledged by the state in many countries with the development of legal frameworks for its conduct. In the UK, political and economic changes and the associated ideologies and practices of HRM have, in many organizations, changed the nature of industrial relations. Such changes include a focus more on the individuals, rather than groups of employees represented by unions, although trade union activity and membership levels are still high in traditional manufacturing industry.

All firms will have a need for some of these activities identified in Table 8.1, in that management, for example, must conform to the prevailing employment laws and operate some system for paying employees. At some stage all firms will have need for the recruitment and selection of new staff or the reallocation of existing staff. The extent and formalization of these activities depends very much on the size of the labour force, the extent of trade union membership, and whether or not the firm has a specialist personnel department, as well as other influences raised in the next two sections.

Such activities may be performed in a variety of ways:

● They may be performed by a personnel specialist or a general manager with responsibility for personnel matters, or by individual managers themselves acting alone.
● In some cases, personnel specialists operate only in an advisory capacity to other managers. Members of the personnel department will advise on the setting up of personnel systems, which will be operated by other managers. Examples of this could include the establishment of a job evaluation and grading system of criteria for promotion.
● In many cases, the personnel specialists act in conjunction with other managers, as for example in interviewing candidates for a vacancy, or designing and implementing a training programme for a sales department.

Table **8.1** The traditional activities of personnel management

Activity	What it involves
Manpower planning and control	The analysis of a company's manpower needs in light of its current manpower resources and the nature of the labour market. Such planning lays the foundation for policies related to recruitment, selection, training, pay and so on.
Recruitment	The first stage usually involves a detailed job analysis followed by the selection of the most appropriate method of recruitment, be it the use of government job centres, using specialist recruitment consultants or placing advertisments in newspapers. Decisions made here aim to attract a field of suitable candidates.
Selection	The use of one or more of a variety of techniques including application forms, interviewing and tests to select the most appropriate person from a field of candidates. The interview tends to be the most favoured method of selection. Decisions are usually made against some general or specific criteria relating to the type of candidate required.
Training and management development	This involves the analysis of the type of traning required and the people to be trained, followed by the selection of the most appropriate method. This can range from simple on-the-job instruction to sending people on specific courses. In many firms the training and development of managers is seen as a special case involving long-term planning and consideration for individual career development.
Appraisal	This is a contentious issue in personnel and sometimes resisted by trade unions. It involves the setting up of formal systems to assess the contribution of individuals to the organization. The system is often designed by personnel specialists but administered by all managers.
Pay administration	This Is a complex area involving decisions about the rate of pay (often involving negotiation with trade unions), about the way pay is differentially distributed (using some form of job evaluation or individual merit rating), and about the viability of one of a variety of payment schemes such as flat rate payment, payment by results, profit-sharing and so on. Decisions made in this area have broadened to include the number and range of fringe benefits such as pensions, company cars, cheap, mortgages and the like.
Job and organizational design	In some cases personnel managers contribute to decisions about how jobs are to be carried out and how the organization is to be structured. This may involve the design and administration of programmes such as job enrichment, organizational development or the quality of working life.
Collective bargaining	Personnel management are invariably involved in the preparation of the employer's case and usually in the negotiations with employee representatives. Once collective agreements have been made, it is usually the job of the personnel manager to apply such agreements and deal with the outcomes.
Grievance and disputes handling	Related to the above, the personnel manager is usually in the front line in dealing with situations arising from individual or collective grievances. In larger firms specific procedures are laid down, but in all cases there is an expectation of the personnel to solve disputes as and when they arise.
Legal advice	With developments in employment law (outlined in the next section) many personnel managers are seen as the resident expert in legal matters pertaining to employment and act as a guide to other managers.
Employee communications and counselling	The personnel specialist is oftern given responsibility for communicating general information to the workforce as well as administering specific programmes for employee participation such as suggestion schemes. Some firms go further and involve the personnel manager in employee advice and counselling.
Personnel information and records	The need for personnel records has increased as firms have grown in size. Such records, kept by the personnel department, are often an important source of information upon which personnel decisions are based.

● In all kinds of organizations there is increasing use made of personnel consultants, particularly in the fields of recruitment and training. In this case the personnel specialist operates as a hirer, coordinator and manager of the consultant's activities.

As we have seen, in smaller firms, the activities tend to be carried out by all managers, and no specialist operates. In larger firms with formalized procedures a mixture of all four methods occurs. A personnel manager may advise the sales manager on the type of person he or she is seeking to fill a vacancy and may assist in the drafting of the job advertisement. The personnel manager may interview a number of candidates and then draw up a short-list for a second interview at which the sales manager will take a leading role. The use of consultants is appropriate for small firms where specialist personnel inputs are an intermittent requirement. In larger firms consultants are seen as a more cost-effective method of delivering certain personnel services than bearing the cost of maintaining a large internal personnel department. This is particularly the case in training and some recruitment and payroll activities.

Human resource management

The broad definition of HRM offered at the beginning of this chapter gives little hint of what activities comprise and what makes it particularly different from our traditional view of personnel management. Over the past 10 or so years the HRM concept has spawned a vast literature offering a range of varying perspectives. However, there is some measure of agreement that HRM involves a focus on:

● treating employees as individuals, but, at the same time, developing mechanisms to integrate individuals into teams;
● the careful selection, training and development of core staff;
● reward systems that stress individual performance and commitment and which are linked to employee appraisal and development;
● communication networks and the involvement of employees, preferably as individuals, but allowing for trade union involvement as well;
● emphasizing a culture which stresses commitment to organizational goals, quality and flexibility; in many cases it is recognized that this will involve a culture change, more especially in those organizations typified by confrontational industrial relations;
● the integration not only of all personnel-related policies as a meaningful whole, but also of these policies within the overall strategy of the enterprise;
● business values as an overriding consideration.

The analysis of such core characteristics of HRM has led some writers, notably Storey (1989), to see two strands emerging. One is defined as 'hard' HRM with a focus on business values and management strategy. The other is defined as 'soft' HRM, focusing as it does upon the selection, development and reward of people.

Many of the core characteristics of HRM are incorporated in Figure 8.1.

KEY CONCEPT 8.4
Hard and soft HRM

The distinction between hard and soft HRM is attributed to Storey (1989). Hard HRM focuses on business values and management strategy, whereas soft HRM focuses upon the selection, development, involvement and the reward of people.

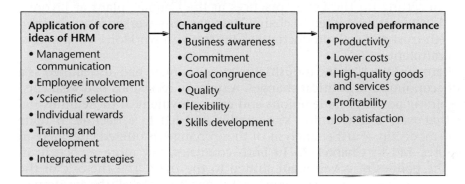

Figure **8.1** The human resource management process.

We have commented already on the relevance of the strategic, organizational and environmental contexts in shaping personnel/HRM activities. It is to a convergence of recent changes in those contexts that we must look to explain the emergence of HRM as a concept in its own right.

Significant changes in the competitive environment of most companies have placed greater emphasis on the need to innovate, the need to improve the quality of their goods and services and, above all the need to be more cost-effective in their use of labour. This in turn has resulted in many of those companies re-examining the way they select, train, use and reward employees. A significant aspect of this new competition was its global nature. Some managers looked at these global competitors for alternative models. Management practices in Japan, as we saw in Chapter 2, were used as an explanation of economic success and have been envied by managers in the West. Some of the features can be likened to Japanese employment relations practices in larger firms. In addition to these influences, changes in technology have added to the demand to use employees more flexibly than hitherto.

It is not just Japan that offers suitable HRM models. Guest (1990, 1998) consistently maintains that HRM is a distinctively American (as opposed to Japanese) phenomenon, which in some ways reflected the post-Vietnam confidence of the USA. In Chapter 3 we examined the influential movement that emerged from the USA built around the concept of corporate culture and the notion that 'excellent' companies serve as models for others to follow. Many of the companies defined by Peters and Waterman (1982) as 'excellent' operate HRM policies. IBM is such a company and aspects of its HRM policy may be found in Case 8.1. The coming together of an increasingly competitive environment and the availability of such corporate models led a group of academics at the Harvard Business School to establish HRM as a core subject on the MBA programme, based on the premise that human resources are a key area in the search for competitive advantage (Beer *et al.*, 1984, 1985). They gained inspiration not only from non-union companies such as IBM, but observed changes in more traditional unionized environments. In General Motors, for example, management worked closely with the Union of Auto Workers in setting up HRM-style practices at the Cadillac plant at Livonia, and in all its plants attempted to change management–worker relations from low to high trust and seek productivity gains through workforce cooperation and commitment.

In Britain and the USA the industrial relations climate had also altered as a result of economic and political changes. A series of recessions had weakened the bargaining power of trade unions and unemployment in those industrial sectors that were former union strongholds had led to a decline in trade union membership. (Further analysis of these changes is offered elsewhere in this chapter and in Chapter 2.) In both countries, but more especially in Britain, the politics of government shifted to the right. The rhetoric of the 'New Right' revolved around concepts such as the free market, the freedom of the individual, and the enterprise culture. The climate was therefore suitable for those managements seeking alternative models of employment relations.

Another reason for the growth of interest in HRM lies in the relationship between personnel specialists and other managers in the organization. This is a theme that re-emerges when we examine the organizational environment of HRM later in the chapter. The lack of access to strategic decision-making and low status felt by many personnel practitioners may well have created a receptive environment for HRM to flourish, with its promise of a high-level strategic approach. To other managers who saw the policies of traditional personnel management as inadequate and inappropriate for entry into the 1990s, HRM may have offered a favourable alternative.

We will now examine the extent to which these changes have resulted in HRM emerging as something distinctively different from personnel management and the extent to which the practice of HRM matches its rhetoric.

The differences between HRM and traditional personnel management

In examining whether there has been a shift away from traditional personnel practices to a more strategically oriented HRM, three positions emerge.

● There are those who see HRM as a radical departure, offering personnel managers a new strategic role and de-emphasizing industrial relations as a major activity.
● Others see little more than a title change and feel that HRM is really personnel management in a new guise, embodying as it does what is viewed as 'good' personnel practice.

Case 8.1: IBM's HR Policies

IBM is the world's largest and most successful computer manufacturer. It has been established in Britain since 1951 and is a market leader in most of its product ranges. There are no unions at IBM, the company has never experienced a strike and until 1991 had not had to lay people off. Paradoxically, many of its current employment and personnel practices were developed during the depression in the USA and many were ahead of their time. The company scrapped payment-by-results methods for its manufacturing employees in 1936, treating all employees as salaried staff and in effect offering them lifetime employment. Around the same time the company introduced job enlargement and flexible working and embarked on a programme of involving all employees in the design of new products. Employee training has always been a major feature of the company. IBM is often cited as a model for human resource management practice and one that others would do well to emulate.

In Britain the company expanded rapidly in the 1960s and continued to expand until the early 1990s. Only 27 per cent of employees work in manufacturing, the majority operating in marketing and technical services. Pay has always been high compared to other firms and labour turnover has traditionally been exceptionally low, operating for many years at around 2 per cent. The company is non-unionized. Management have always claimed that the employees have no need for a union, nor do they want one. This was supported by an ACAS survey in 1977, which discovered that only 4.9 per cent of employees wanted a union, and 91 per cent claimed they would refuse to join if one were introduced.

The lack of interest in trade union membership is almost certainly a function of IBM's corporate commitment to individualism and of terms and conditions in excess of those usually demanded by trade unions. The key features of the traditional employment practices at IBM may be summed up as follows:

- A fairly sophisticated system of manpower planning, employee recruitment and training.
- Lifetime employment for all employees with the expectation that employees will change jobs as and when required.
- Single status for all employees in terms of canteens, facilities, and fringe benefits. The only exceptions are overtime payment for manufacturing workers and company cars for some senior management and some sales staff.
- Salaries are determined centrally, usually by making a favourable comparison with other firms. The exercise is carried out annually to ensure pay rates keep ahead of those in other companies. Once established, increases are always based on merit and determined through a management-by-objectives type of appraisal scheme.
- Training is emphasized, with management receiving an average of 40 days training a year (40 times the national average). Much of the training focuses upon human resource management.
- An opinion survey of all staff is held every two years, to ascertain attitudes towards such factors as working practices, pay and conditions, and personnel practices. The response rates are very high.
- Emphasis is placed upon managers sorting out their own problems. A centralized personnel function operates a 'hands off' policy. The company prefers to leave personnel matters to individual managers, especially grievance handling.
- The company operates two formalized communication procedures. A 'Speak Up' system encourages employees to raise business-related problems, while an 'Open Door' system allows employees to appeal against decisions taken by their own managers.

For many years such policies have been well liked by employees. The company has always expected a great deal of its employees, but offers them secure jobs at relatively high rates of pay. While the firm operates a philosophy which stresses individuality as part of its commitment to entrepreneurship, individuals are nevertheless expected to conform to IBM norms of behaviour, even to participating in out-of-work company social events and activities. The company has also been accused of operating a recruitment policy that ensures that only those committed to the IBM way will be selected. In general, sceptics have attempted to label IBM as running an oppressive system, which is only possible in the rarefied environment of a successful hi-tech company. However, any firm that has developed such a strong corporate culture leaves itself open to attack by those who see it as too good to be true.

▶

Continued

By 1991 IBM faced a different kind of attack. The computer market had become even more competitive, both in terms of the number of firms competing and in terms of customers expecting much more for their money. Faced with an unprecedented fall in profits IBM confronted its own lifetime employment policies by embarking on a strategy of cutting labour costs. This needed to be done quickly as the impact of the recession accelerated, not only in the UK but in IBM worldwide. Given the low labour turnover and the absence of opportunity to transfer employees to other IBM operations, the company introduced a programme of voluntary redundancy. It offered an attractive package, amounting to an average two years' salary per employee with support mechanisms such as advice on job seeking and personal finance as well as general counselling. In addition, time off was freely given for job interviews and those employees with company cars were allowed to buy them at favourable terms.

From the company's point of view, it was important to ensure that they did not lose key employees and management constructed manpower planning models to determine target groups and target areas of operation. IBM's internal communication system was used to explain the need for the strategy, to encourage volunteers and to prepare those the company considered ineligible. Use was made of briefing groups, information releases, information packs and one-day briefing sessions. In addition employees had access to individual advice. The result of the exercise was a reduction in headcount of 15 per cent of which only 2.3 per cent represented 'normal' turnover. The reduction exceeded the company's expectations. A positive outcome was that some employees used the opportunity to establish their own business out of their IBM activities. The company actively encouraged this and gave assistance reflected in a reduced redundancy package. The companies that were established in this way initially sold back their services to IBM. However, there were cases of dissatisfaction where some employees were prevented from taking advantage of the offer.

In 1993, a further 25 000 jobs were shed globally and altogether IBM had reduced its global workforce by 110 000 in a six year period. Most of the redundancies continued to be voluntary. Although non-unionized, in countries like Germany and Sweden IBM was forced to consult with works councils, bodies that can and do wield considerable power. Even here, the high trust built up over the years ensured a smooth execution of policy.

Some would advocate that the IBM HR policies made it possible to carry out a relatively trouble-free programme of voluntary redundancy, not just in the UK, but across the globe. However, the extent to which it offers other companies a model to follow may well be limited by the ability of their management to carry such policies through effectively in non-IBM settings. For IBM itself, the redundancy programme struck at the heart of one of its key human resource policies. The resilience of those policies lay in the continued commitment of retained employees in an increasingly competitive environment, and in particular the management of those employees aggrieved by the redundancy policy itself. In 1998, as part of its continued commitment to both globalization and HRM, IBM set up a multi-country HR centre to address global strategic issues. ∎

(*Sources:* Drucker, 1968; Bassett, 1986; Peach, 1992; *Business Europe*, 1993; *Financial Times*, 1998–9)

● Those subscribing to a middle if somewhat cautious position recognize that changes have taken place in such areas as labour flexibility, employee involvement, appraisal and training. Furthermore they see some attempts by British firms to blend HRM with traditional industrial relations. However, they view the changes as yet as neither significant nor widespread (Storey, 1992).

Legge (1989), while arguing considerable similarity between what both personnel management and HRM set out to achieve, sees in HRM some important differences. First, she views HRM as being much more about management. Personnel is no longer about the treatment of the shop floor, but there has been a switch of emphasis to focus on issues of management development and management teambuilding. Furthermore, HRM is the prerogative of senior management whereas personnel management was viewed as an activity to be carried out by more junior managers. Second, she argues that HRM has elevated human resource issues to a position of key strategic importance. Third, she sees that HRM is about organizational culture and culture change in a way that traditional personnel management never was. Finally, she and others sense a major difference in the language of HRM, which borrows heavily from the rhetoric of the 'New Right'. Storey (1992) identifies 27 points of difference between HRM and traditional personnel, in terms of beliefs and assumptions, strategic aspects, relationship with line managers and key leavers. For example, in personnel, conflict was institutionalized, whereas in HRM it is de-emphasized. In personnel pay was based on job evaluation, but under HRM it moves to a system of individual performance-related pay.

The different positions and perspectives offered above have presented researchers with a number of hypotheses to test and there has been no shortage of research activity into the changing role of personnel/HR managers. Major studies have been established at the London School of Economics, Warwick University and at Cranfield, the latter examining HRM practices across Europe. (Good summaries of this and other research can be found in Guest, 1990, 1991; Brewster and Bournois, 1991; and Storey, 1992.)

Clearly there are companies that conform to the classic characteristics of HRM. In this league are firms such as IBM, Hewlett-Packard and British firms such as Marks & Spencer and British Airways. For example, we see in Case 8.2 how British Airways invested heavily in a massive training programme to change the culture of its organization towards a greater emphasis on customer care. However, most of these classic companies were known for their sophisticated approaches to personnel long before HRM emerged. Indeed we might argue that HRM is a product of such companies and hence they cannot be offered as evidence of an HRM revolution. Furthermore, there is some evidence to suggest that, in firms such as IBM, commitment of employees has waned in the face of successive job cuts (Guest, 1998).

Many of the techniques associated with HRM such as employee involvement, quality circles, increased flexibility, psychological selection testing, appraisal, new forms of individualized payment systems and various methods of culture change have been introduced in a number of companies. However, there is little evidence of any grand design and in many instances the techniques have been introduced in a piecemeal fashion or even in isolation. This position may have emerged as a result of the lack of consensus about what HRM entails; for many practitioners it remains a woolly concept. Sparrow and Marchington (1998) put its lack of popularity amongst line managers down to its lack of a 'wow' factor in offering them instant solutions. Some firms have experienced mixed results. Ford UK achieved a measure of flexibility in its assembly-line operations through the reduction in demarcation and by redefining jobs to the extent of reducing 500 differently defined assembly jobs to just 50 (McKinlay and Starkey, 1992). The same company, however, failed in its attempt to persuade the unions to accept both quality circles and a formalized system of employee involvement, the latter having enjoyed a measure of success in Ford USA.

For the United Kingdom, at least, the research is sanguine about there being a significant shift from personnel to HRM. The focus has been on the extent to which HRM practices occur and has hardly begun to explore the extent to which such practices result in the kinds of favourable outcomes envisaged for the firm and its employees. The evidence does point to differences in application and this will be discussed in the next section when we explore environmental influences. A major obstacle to a strategic approach to HRM in the UK is the traditional short-termism of much management thinking, often the result of shareholder pressure. (Further details of this debate may be found in Chapters 2 and 9.) In addition to this is the traditional low status of HR managers and their inability to influence strategy. (Further details of this debate can be found in the discussion of organizational issues later in the chapter.) This reinforces the view of personnel/HRM as a product of its environmental and organizational contexts. The position is not always so negative. Fenwick and Murton (2000) cite Bosch, AEG, Honda, Nestlé and the Virgin Group as examples of firms where effective HRM policies have been possible:

> However, where pressures for short-term results are less immediate, skilled workers at a premium and employee development a key factor in competitveness, HRM policies may be more in evidence.
>
> (Fenwick and Murton, 2000, p.138)

Despite the lack of hard evidence, the language of HRM has clearly infiltrated personnel practice. Examination of job advertisements in the then IPM journal for March 1993 reveals that of the 77 positions advertised, only 26 per cent have HRM in their job title. Of the other advertisements 36 per cent have personnel management in their job title and the remaining 38 per cent refer to a specialism within personnel, the large majority being training and development. However, closer examination of the non-HRM-titled jobs reveals that a good proportion make some reference to HRM. For example, an advertisement for the job of personnel manager is subtitled 'managing the change from personnel to HRM' and several of the training vacancies emphasize development and culture change. An interesting fact to emerge is that the title HRM tends to be reserved for the higher-status and more highly paid positions. We will return to this issue when discussing the organizational context of HRM.

In 1994, some 10 years after HRM first came to prominence, the professional body for practitioners still called itself 'The Institute of Personnel Managers' (IPM), although it dubbed its journal 'Personnel Management' with the added subtitle of 'the magazine for human resource professionals.' During that year, the IPM changed its name to the Institute of Personnel and Development (IPD), while its journal became known as 'People Management', described as 'the magazine for professionals in personnel, training and development'.

The review of job advertisements carried out in March 1993 was repeated in May 1999. There were two significant differences; the magazine was now published twice monthly and it now incorporated a greater concern for training and development. The number of jobs advertised had risen considerably to 187. Nevertheless, since the review is far from scientific, little should be assumed from this. Nevertheless, the review is indicative of how the language of HRM has further infiltrated job titles. The emphasis of advertised jobs has swung even more towards the use of the terms HR or HRM, with 44 per cent of all jobs advertised so called. This applies even in the lower-graded and lower-paid posts. Twenty per cent of jobs advertised still refer to personnel management, with a large number of these in the public sector. While, as before, the more senior of these positions refer to HRM in the sub-text, it is interesting to note that senior positions at both Oxford and Cambridge Universities retain a somewhat traditional view of personnel management. Thirty-six per cent of posts refer to specialist roles, particularly in training. As before, many of these are described in HR terms with frequent reference to culture change in organizations.

While retaining the name 'personnel', there was evidence that the IPD had begun to embrace the language and rhetoric of HRM.

> Personnel is an important part of the management process and not an exclusive function. It is an enabling activity with responsibilities for core organizational values in relation to people.

> (Personnel Standards Lead Body, 1993, p.1)

The core strategies identified in the same document clearly owe considerable allegiance to developments in HRM. In its position statement to launch the renamed institute, the IPD (1995) views people as central to a firm's ability to respond to a rapidly changing competitive position. They stress the importance of commitment to training and development, continuous improvement, self-management and customer focus, all as part of a long-term strategy.

There are those who see the need for coherent HRM strategies as greater than ever (Beardwell and Holden, 1997; Sparrow and Marchington, 1998). Such analyses cite the radical changes that have taken place in work and organizations over the past 15 years, especially volatile labour markets, the simultaneous strengthening of senior and weakening of junior management roles and job losses in the face of almost continual restructuring. The HR systems in most firms remain dated and are based around jobs and cost minimization.

> The majority of firms, after a period of denial, perceive that there is low morale, a trust gap and a desire for a new set of HRM tools, practices and priorities at the millennium.

> (Sparrow and Marchington, 1998, p. 16)

Most, however, remain sceptical of the ability of HRM to deliver. As we have seen above, there is little evidence to suggest its application by practitioners. There is little evidence of increased commitment, culture change and links between HRM and improved performance. It is difficult to persuade employees of the benefits of a 'soft' HRM when they are more concerned with keeping their jobs. Paradoxically this threat of unemployment makes employee compliance easier and, for many managers, removes the need for complex HRM strategies. For Guest,

> It seems that HRM has always been a minority activity, therefore the surprise in its limited application is only a surprise to those who have swallowed the rhetoric of its more enthusiastic advocates.

> (Guest, 1998, p. 51)

In fact much of the literature focuses on the language and rhetoric of HRM almost as much as its application. To some it is language that legitimizes management action, while to others the language can actually shape ideas and hence initiate change. However, Fenwick and Murton (2000) conclude that ultimately the whole HRM debate is manufactured by academics. This echoes sentiments expressed by Guest on the first page of this chapter, and probably explains why many students find the personnel/HRM debate so baffling.

In the section on HRM strategy at the end of this chapter we return to the theme of HRM as strategic innovation or the product of management opportunism in the light of environmental changes. We now turn our attention to the examination of the environmental context of personnel/HRM.

The environmental aspects of HRM

In the previous section we examined the emergence of HRM and associated this with certain environmental changes, such as increasing competition and the weakened position of trade unions. In fact, the development of personnel management as a specialist function in organizations owes much to the influence of external events. The growth of markets and the creation of the joint stock company led to increases in the size of the firm with a corresponding demand for recruitment, training and some centralized payment administration system. The growth of trade unions, especially in Britain, created the need for industrial relations specialists among management. The impact of two world wars created problems for the labour supply and a corresponding attention being paid to training methods and employee consultation. Full employment in the 1960s once again focused the attention on labour shortages and methods used to tackle them, such as the retraining of existing staff and active recruitment from other companies. In the 1970s the focus turned to state intervention and the problems created by new technology, while the 1980s brought us HRM, legislation to change the nature of industrial relations and the transplantation of practices from other countries. We can see that all five environmental aspects of our model interact in some significant way with the personnel/HRM function. We deal with each one in turn.

The role of the state

The state operating through government policies and the legal system has had considerable influence on the personnel function in three major areas: through legislation, through manpower policies concerned with the supply of labour and education and training, and through third-party intervention.

Employment legislation

Employment legislation is concerned with the rights and obligations of employers and employees and the conduct of industrial relations. The growth in employment law in the 1960s and 1970s and the 1980s laws governing the conduct of industrial relations have had a significant impact on the work of

Table **8.2** Major employment law since 1960

Factories Act 1961
Contract of Employment Act 1963,1972
The Industrial Training Act 1965
Race Relations Act 1968,1976
Equal Pay Act 1970
Industrial Relations Act 1971
Employment and Training Act 1973
Health and Safety at Work Act 1974
Trade Union and Labour Relations Act 1974,1976
Sex Discrimination Act 1975, 1986
Employment Protection Act 1975
Employment Protection (Consolidation) Act 1978
Employment Act 1980
Employment Act 1982
Trade Union Act 1984
Wages Act 1986
Employment Act 1988
Employment Act 1989
Employment Act 1990
Trade Union and Labour Relations (Consolidation) Act 1992
Trade Union Reform and Employment Rights Act 1993
Employment Rights Act 1996
Employment Rights (Disputes Resolution) Act 1998
National Minimum Wage Regulations 1999

the HR specialist. In Table 8.2 we show the growth of employment legislation since 1960 by listing the major Acts of Parliament.

Many of the laws have had a direct impact upon the day-to-day work of personnel/HR managers. The Industrial Training Act 1964, with its introduction of the levy-grant system for approved training, resulted in the expansion of training programmes and, correspondingly, training departments and training managers. Recruitment advertisements must be carefully drafted so as not to contravene race and sex discrimination legislation. The Arbitration, Conciliation and Advisory Service (ACAS) set up by the Employment Protection Act 1975 had, for a time, a significant impact on the conduct of industrial relations. Several of the laws have set up a judicial system of Industrial Tribunals (Employment Tribunals since 1993), as in the case of redundancy and unfair dismissal cases. Such cases are often prepared by the personnel/HRM specialist. Despite the growth in the tribunal and the number of cases petitioned, only a small percentage reach the final stages, although there are signs in the late 1990s that more cases are being heard. Most cases are dealt with through a variety of conciliation procedures, sometimes involving ACAS (described later in this section), but almost inevitably involving the HR specialist. The expansion of employment law has been an important causal factor in the increased number of HR specialists.

Some commentators see the expansion of labour law as a vehicle for the increased status of personnel/HR managers (for example Legge, 1978). This has been reinforced by studies of the role of the HR manager following the introduction of industrial relations legislation of the 1980s (Millward and Stevens, 1986; Millward *et al.*, 1992). Managers faced with a complex array of new legal provisions seek expert advice and often turn to the HR specialist as their source. However, not all such legislation had had the impact predicted. The Industrial Relations Act 1971 attracted much media attention and was elevated to the status of a political *cause célèbre*. In reality its provisions were dismissed by some managers as much as they were by the trade union movement, its measures were largely ignored and its impact lessened long before its repeal in 1974.

In the 1980s industrial relations entered a new phase and legislation came to the forefront. There is clear indication that this aspect of HRM has been politicized as never before. Historically, the Labour Party, with its traditional allegiances to the trade union movement, has introduced legislation which has tended to establish and further the rights of individual workers. The Conservative Party on the other hand has been more concerned with establishing laws that control the internal affairs of trade unions and attempt to regulate collective bargaining. As new laws have been introduced and repealed by successive governments, personnel managers have had to respond and amend policies accordingly. The politicization of personnel management is seen most clearly in the public sector. In the 1980s and the 1990s, trade unions in coal mining and the health service took stands against government policy on such issues as pit and hospital closures, on pay restraints and attempts to reduce public spending in general. This has clearly placed HR management in those industries in a political arena where consultation and collective bargaining with trade unions have considerable political implications.

The legislation of the 1980s was based on the assumption that trade union power needed to be curbed, that individuals should be free to choose whether they join a union and that the general public needed protection against the damaging affects of strikes and other forms of industrial action. The series of five Employment Acts from 1980 to 1990 represent a cumulative strengthening of the law relating to industrial relations and deregulation at the workplace. These five Acts were consolidated under the Trade Union and Labour Relations Act of 1992. Together with the Trade Union Act of 1984 and the Trade Union Reform and Employment Rights Act of 1993 they have built up a collection of laws that changed the nature of industrial relations in the UK and form the basis of collective employment law today. The major changes included the following:

- Trade unions as organizations became legally responsible for the actions of their members.
- The occasions when strikes could be called were limited and had to be subject to a ballot.
- Senior trade union officials had to re-present themselves for re-election every five years by secret ballot.
- The closed shop was effectively outlawed.
- Union members had to check-off and effectively renew their membership at regular intervals.
- Contribution to political funds became subject to a ballot.

The 1980s and 1990s legislation represented a major shift in the government's attitude towards industrial relations. The impact of the legislation has been difficult to assess. From 1979 to 1989 there was a 50 per cent reduction in registered closed shops, although this may be as much a factor of the loss of employment in manufacturing as a direct result of the legislation (Edwards *et al.*, 1992). Certainly the anticipated conflict over union electoral and political fund issues did not materialize and nearly all unions appear to be operating this aspect of the legislation willingly. The check-off has resulted in union members failing to renew their membership, although there is great variation between unions.

Much media attention has been directed towards the impact of the legislation on strikes. Mercury, the communications company, successfully took legal action against the Post Office Engineering Union when they refused to join up the British Telecom network to the Mercury system. Mercury had acquired the right to operate an independent telephone service under the government's liberalization and privatization policy. The union claimed that its refusal to work and eventual strike action were to protect jobs in British Telecom. The court ruled that the action was primarily an opposition to government policy, hence political and therefore illegal.

Many of the court actions have involved smaller employers who have probably most to lose from a dispute. It was Mercury and not British Telecom that took action against British Telecom's workers. Many larger companies are still reluctant to use the courts for fear of alienating their workforce. Contrary to the image of industrial relations portrayed in the popular press, management and workforce, indeed management and unions, in most firms, have reasonably good relations, which recourse to law may damage. Nonetheless the legislation of the 1980s has changed significantly the nature of collective bargaining and consequently the work of personnel specialists. There has been a marked reduction in the number of recorded disputes in British industry. This could be related to changes in the law. It could also be related to economic conditions, which we will discuss later. In some cases it is clear that changes in legislation have been accompanied by deliberate attempts on the part of management to change the employment relations culture of the enterprise. In part this is an attempt to replace traditional adversarial bargaining with a more cooperative approach. This theme recurs in our discussion of labour matters later in this section and when we discuss personnel strategies at the end of the chapter.

While there has always been a reluctance for UK employers to use the courts, there is evidence of a greater willingness on the part of individuals to use the legislative process. ACAS has reported that in 1998 there were record numbers of cases brought by individuals against employers in Employment Tribunals. During 1998 all cases increased by 6 per cent, the majority relating to unfair dismissal. Cases relating to discrimination on grounds of disability doubled (reported in *People Management*, May 1999).

With hindsight, the legislation of the 1980s and 1990s has been part of a range of influences that have altered the map of industrial relations in the UK. Other factors have also been significant. These include economic recession, particularly affecting the manufacturing industry, privatization and restructuring in the face of global competition. The combination of these factors has led to a reduction in the workforce and a reduction in union membership to its lowest level for 60 years. The nature of collective bargaining has changed and management have been able to push through changes unopposed. Chapter 2 offers a further analysis.

The election of a Labour government in the UK in 1997 was viewed by some, not least trade unions themselves, as the start of a new legislative era, in which individual and collective rights of employees were to be strengthened. The early signs are that the government has accepted the existing legislative framework of its Conservative predecessors. However, the 1999 White Paper, 'Fairness at Work', and the subsequent Employment Relations Bill promise some reform. The Bill aims at providing 'fair treatment' for employees, by such proposals as reducing the qualifying time for unfair dismissal cases and raising the award limit. It proposes giving employees the legal right to be recognized to conduct collective bargaining and, generally, easing provisions for union recognition. Its proposals have also been dubbed 'family friendly' through the extension of maternity rights and the enabling of time off for family emergencies. The proposals are seen as being based on the 'culture of partnership'. While for some this is an attempt to rebalance the legislation more in favour of employees, it is done within the rhetoric of HRM. Both the White Paper and the Bill speak of 'building on the commitment of the work force'; measures for the fair treatment of employees are motivated by the need to underpin more flexible practices; and new proposals for collective bargaining are to achieve 'business objectives'.

Manpower policies

There have been attempts by successive governments to achieve a stable balance between supply and demand in the labour market through a series of manpower policies. For 20 years after the end of the Second World War unemployment remained below 2 per cent and the major concern was the development of mechanisms to improve the supply of skilled labour. Certainly since 1852 governments have been consistent in their criticism of the quantity and quality of training in British industry. A government White Paper in 1962 linked the inadequacy of training in British industry to the nation's economic problems and the result was the Industrial Training Act 1964 referred to earlier. Its impact was immediate, with a dramatic increase in levels of training. Training Boards were set up for each industry and several innovations were introduced. The Engineering Industry Training Board radically restructured its apprenticeship scheme to produce trainees with more flexible skills in a shorter time. Skills shortages, however, have persisted to dog British industry. A fuller analysis of training and the role of the state can be found in Chapter 2.

Despite the continuing skills shortages in some areas the focus shifted to introducing measures to combat the problem of rising unemployment. Such measures have tended to fall into two categories: those aiming to increase the demand for labour and those aimed at reducing the total supply. Schemes to increase the demand for labour have included wages subsidies, job creation, community enterprise programmes and the youth training scheme. Measures to reduce the labour supply have included early retirement, job release, temporary short-time working and job splitting. None of these were especially successful.

Government training programmes have been introduced to tackle both the problems of skills shortages and unemployment. Youth Training (YT) and its predecessors, the Youth Training Scheme (YTS) and the Youth Opportunities Programme (YOP), have been in operation since 1982 and in 1987 the Job Training Scheme was introduced for long-term unemployed adults. Since the mid-1980s the government have also attempted to influence both the content and values of school education, based on comparative information which shows British workers to be less educated, less qualified, and receive less training than those in countries with whom we are in direct economic competition. This has resulted in the Training and Vocational Education Initiative (TVEI) and the attempt to secure a series of national standards and certification in education and skills development through the National Council for Vocational Qualifications (NCVQ). In more general terms the government has attempted to foster not only vocational skills but also a business culture amongst the population through the introduction of a National Curriculum for primary schoolchildren.

The extent to which such initiatives have been successful in raising levels of training is debatable. Some firms use schemes such as YT and YTS as sources of cheap labour and relatively few trainees obtain permanent employment. If the government saw the Youth Training Scheme as an attempt to introduce to Britain a German-style apprenticeship training programme, then it has largely failed. The unions were sceptical, fearing such schemes will disrupt traditional patterns of recruitment and dilute skills. A big obstacle to the government's attempts to raise the profile of training lies with business itself. Many firms tend to see training as a cost rather than an investment, and a cost that can easily be cut in the pursuit of short-term goals.

Third-party intervention

Governments have always been willing to intervene in those industrial disputes they see as damaging to the nation's economy. The government currently funds the Arbitration, Conciliation and Advisory Service (ACAS), set up in 1974 and given statutory rights under the Employment Protection Act 1975. ACAS consists of a full-time chairman and nine part-time members made up of equal parts of TUC nominees, CBI nominees and academics. It is staffed by civil servants. ACAS is therefore a state mechanism, which attempts to influence the conduct of industrial relations without either party having recourse to the use of law.

Given the reduction in the number of disputes, the role of ACAS as a mediator is less significant today. Indeed, the 1993 legislation removed its responsibility for the promotion of collective bargaining. As we enter the new millennium, ACAS retains its role of advising on policy and practice, dealing with such current issues as flexibility. A major change, however has been an increased involvement with employees as individuals. ACAS figures in 1999 show that requests for individual advice and individual conciliation are rising at around 15 per cent a year.

The role of the economy

In the 1960s and 1970s there was an unprecedented increase in those involved in personnel work. Membership of the Institute of Personnel Management increased from 4308 members in 1959 to over 10 000 in 1969. It then doubled its membership to 20 194 by 1979. As a rough guide, it is estimated that members of the Institute represent half those involved in personnel HRM.

While we have attributed part of the growth to developments in legislation, there is a clear correlation between personnel management and the state of the economy. In the two decades of full employment prior to the early 1970s considerable emphasis was placed on recruitment, selection, training and payment systems, to overcome labour shortages and to assist in the substitution and retention of skilled labour. During the same period the increased bargaining power of the trade union movement, especially at workplace level, resulted in increases in shopfloor collective bargaining and hence an increased workload for the personnel manager.

Traditional activities of personnel management such as recruitment and training are clearly related to full employment economies. The continued growth of personnel throughout the 1970s is harder to reconcile with the economic expansion argument since it was a period of slowdown and considerable economic problems. However, if we see the growth of the personnel function as a reactive process where organizational responses lag behind the real stimulus, then the growth of the 1970s may be seen as a response to problems first recognized in the late 1950s and early 1960s. Its impact upon personnel management organization extended well into the 1970s.

Given the hypothesis that economic growth and full employment lead to a thriving and active personnel function, then the reverse hypothesis might also be true: that an economic recession will not only reduce the need for recruitment selection and training, but that the negotiating power of trade unions will be impaired, resulting in a reduction of the extent and frequency of collective bargaining negotiations.

The evidence, however, paints a different picture. A study of personnel during a particularly severe recession 1980–2 reported that personnel managers had survived better than most other management groups. New opportunities to demonstrate competence had been created in redundancy management and in achieving lower wage settlements in a generally peaceful industrial relations climate (Guest, 1982). While the economy picked up in the latter part of the 1980s, a further recession occurred at the beginning of the 1990s. Despite these fluctuations, HRM, as a function of Institute membership, appeared to flourish. By 1993, membership had risen to just over 30 000 with a further 20 000 registered as student members. By mid-1999 membership stood at 86 000 with a further 12 000 student members. Much of this large increase in membership is associated with a merger in 1994 between the Institute of Personnel Management and the Institute of Training and Development to form the Institute of Personnel and Development.

There could be several explanations for the durability of personnel/HR. As we saw in Chapter 2, structural changes in the economy were especially severe upon traditional manufacturing. HR managers clearly suffered job losses in manufacturing, but there has been a growth of opportunities in other sectors, notably the service sector and newer high-tech industries. There has also been an influx of foreign multinationals, many of whom display more sophisticated human resource strategies than their British counterparts. In addition to such changes, new types of employment have emerged with an emphasis on flexibility, bringing with it a demand for training and the management of part-time and contract workers.

In one area, industrial relations, there has been reduction in the traditional activities of collective bargaining and dispute management. Unions are weaker, disputes fewer and settlements tend to be speedier. Nevertheless, where bargaining is still the norm, there has been a decentralization of activities placing more and not less emphasis on the role of workplace industrial relations managers. We have already seen how HRM offers the personnel function new strategic directions and that the British experience is one where HRM is not incompatible with trade union negotiation. This is amply illustrated at Perkins Diesels (Case 8.3) with the negotiation of new work practices. The Perkins case is also a good example of the work of personnel specialists during a recession.

An illustration of HR policies changing over time may be found also in a longitudinal study over a decade in a retail bank (Holden and Wilkinson, 1999). The researchers found that with the 1980s banking boom, a number of 'soft' HRM measures were introduced. These were linked to the introduction of TQM and 'customer care' initiatives and included an emphasis on commitment, teambuilding and involvement. The bank unions were incorporated in this process. A watershed was reached in 1991 when the bank experienced operating losses. The following years saw the introduction of a number of 'hard' HRM policies, such as direct communication with the workforce rather than involving the union, and a series of downsizing and restructuring measures. The union resisted initially, but were eventually sidelined. Management became much more directive as survival became the major issue.

Economic factors have clearly shaped HR strategies and these will be examined in the final section in this chapter. In all cases, however, economic influences must be seen in conjunction with the role of the state, the power of trade unions, management ideology and the organization structure. This reinforces the idea that the elements of our model cannot be viewed in isolation.

HRM and the labour force

From our brief review of traditional personnel activities in Figure 8.1 we can see that the personnel function interacts with the labour force in two ways. It deals with individuals in the labour market through the activities of manpower planning, recruitment, selection, training and by administering payment and other reward and control systems. Second, it deals with the organized labour force through the mechanisms of joint consultation, collective bargaining and conflict management. We have already referred to these two activities in terms of people processing and industrial relations management. Even with the coming of HRM we may still regard these as the core work of the HRM function. As we noted in the first section of this chapter, the difference between traditional personnel and HRM is largely one of emphasis. We examine the interaction between the HRM function and the labour force by examining these two aspects of HR work.

People processing

Operating within a given labour market, the HR manager will attempt to fulfil the organization's demand for labour. This will be achieved mainly through the processes of recruitment, selection and training, often within the framework of a manpower plan. In some cases the labour market will act as a total constraint to the extent that severe labour shortages in a given area may cause management to rethink its plans. In other cases the labour market operates as a partial constraint, and attempts will be made to entice workers away from existing jobs by offering them attractive pay packages and opportunities for career development. This can cause high levels of mobility among certain groups with scarce skills in an otherwise depressed labour market. A good example of this in the late 1990s can be found in the IT consulting industry, where scarce skills and an abundance of work have resulted in high levels of mobility and spiralling salaries. In other cases the firm attempts to change the composition of the labour market, meeting labour shortages by training substitute labour or by attracting certain groups back to work, such as married women with children, by providing working conditions compatible with school hours. The increased use of flexible employment practices has been one of the reasons for the proportion of women in the workforce rising from 33 per cent in 1951 to 48 per cent in 1990 (Edwards *et al.*, 1992).

The student relying on textbooks may be forgiven for the assumption that HRM is an exercise in scientific management. This exercise is a matching process between the labour market and the needs of the organization employing a variety of scientifically based techniques of selection, training and employee motivation and retention. The student is confronted by a vast literature expounding such theories and offering a variety of such techniques. However, part of this literature has concentrated upon a critique of these same theories, analyses and techniques, often labelling them as intuitive and subjective. A good illustration of this is to be found in the process of employee selection.

HRM textbooks see selection in terms of a matching process between the candidate and the job description. The decision to employ or reject a candidate is ultimately the prerogative of line management, but the administration of the process tends to be carried out by HR specialists applying scientific principles of structured interviewing and psychological testing.

In most cases there will be a job description resulting from a job analysis. The process of creating a job description will generate criteria against which job candidates will be judged. Managers will use such information to build up stereotypes of 'ideal' candidates. However, the job description could well be dated and in any case, the manager is just as likely to establish criteria based upon his or her own prejudices.

The most popular form of selection method is the interview. Management literature abounds with advice for the would-be interviewer, but such advice owes more to general experience and deductive reasoning than it does to empirical research. There is considerable evidence that the interview is a relatively poor selection device and is particularly poor in terms of cost-effectiveness to the company. However, it is retained because no better method has yet been devised and because it allows management to exercise judgement in the selection process.

If we view other areas of personnel processing we will find much the same story. Attempts by HR managers to use 'scientific techniques' often adapted from the behaviourial sciences have met with mixed results. This is true of a range of techniques incorporating the use of psychological tests, in selection and placement, appraisal schemes, approaches to training and devising methods of payment to increase worker motivation.

The major problems with using such techniques in people processing are reliability and validity. Reliability refers to the extent to which a measure of consistency can be achieved, as, for example, in getting interviewers to behave in a similar fashion and ask candidates similar questions. Validity refers to the extent to which a technique used in personnel has some practical value for the organization. Does a selection interview actually discriminate between suitable and unsuitable candidates? Will a training programme lead to improved worker performance?

Because of such problems, HR managers have difficulty in proving that the work they do contributes in a measurable way to the effectiveness of the organization. For example, the results of a management development programme may not be apparent for a number of years, if at all, and many of the managers may have left the organization by that time. The difficulty of HRM proving its worth is a theme developed when we examine the relationship between HRM and an organization's goals later in this chapter. It is not surprising that many HR managers feel safer dealing with the day-to-day firefighting of industrial relations problems than devising policies and procedures where the outcome is uncertain. It is to industrial relations that we next turn our attention.

Industrial relations management

We can identify four major activities associated with industrial relations management.

The recognition of trade unions

This involves both the recognition of the employee right to organize and the recognition of the union right to represent employees in such matters as wage negotiation. In some industries recognition has been slow. The recognition of the National Union of Bank Employees by the major clearing banks was only achieved in 1967 after considerable disruption and strike action. In other cases management will positively encourage their employees to join trade unions since they view a healthy union membership as contributing to the stability of workplace relations. This acceptance and encouragement has been a major factor in trade union growth and consequently the development of the personnel function. In recent years there have been new variations on the theme of recognition.

A key approach in companies such as IBM (as illustrated in Case 8.1), Hewlett-Packard and Marks & Spencer is the development of employment relations strategies that do not involve trade unions. The growth of Japanese firms in Britain and their preference for company unions has led to the establishment of single union agreements being made in companies such as Nissan (Case 2.6) and Sanyo. Under such agreements management will allow only

---

KEY CONCEPT 8.5
Trade union recognition

This involves the recognition by employers of the rights of employees to join and be represented by a trade union. Until the late 1990s such recognition had always been voluntary and the subject of intense conflict where such recognition was denied. However, recognition is now a legal right provided it is supported by the majority of employees. Nonetheless, the weakening of trade unions in the 1980s and 1990s in the UK, as a result of changing politics, economics and workplace cultures, has led to de-recognition becoming a more significant activity.

one trade union to represent all employees in the workforce. The News International case (see Chapter 1) is an interesting one. A single union deal was originally agreed between the management and the EETPU (the electricians' union). Subsequently the union has been de-recognized for bargaining purposes. Such de-recognition has been widely predicted in the face of weakened unions and alternative HRM strategies. This is largely supported by recent evidence. Over 50 per cent of workplaces in the UK have no recognized trade union and the workplaces with no union members at all rose from 36 per cent in 1990 to 47 per cent in 1998. Furthermore, there is evidence that firms set up in the 1980s are less likely to accept unions (Cully *et al.*, 1998).

Collective bargaining

We can see in Table 8.1 that collective bargaining involves management and unions in the negotiation of wages and conditions. The growth of localized bargaining in the 1950s and 1960s widened the role of both personnel managers and shop stewards as actual negotiators. The 1980s and 1990s were noted, initially, for a move to increased decentralization of bargaining and more recently to an absence of bargaining altogether as management de-recognize trade unions and favour alternative schemes of pay negotiation and employee involvement. There is clear evidence of an increase in the use of performance-related pay (PRP), usually on an individual basis (Millward *et al.*, 1992). Where collective bargaining is still the norm, the HR manager usually assists in policy formulation, research and the actual negotiating process itself. The frequency of collective bargaining has been reduced with the move to two- and, in some cases, three-year agreements (Millward *et al.*, 1992).

KEY CONCEPT 8.6
Collective bargaining

Collective bargaining is a process in which the representatives of employers and the representatives of employees negotiate wages, conditions and other related aspects.

Disputes and grievance procedure

In most organizations conflict is inevitable either as part of the collective bargaining process or between staff in the operation of their roles. Many firms operate a disputes and grievance procedure to resolve such conflicts. HR managers are normally involved in the development and operation of such procedures. In most cases the formalization and complexity of the procedure is directly related to the size of the firm. In the 1990s there has been a clear growth in the number of *individual* disputes and grievances taken against employing organizations and the willingness of individuals to take civil action in the courts on issues of perceived unfair dismissal and discrimination.

Administering procedures relating to employee participation

These can involve a sophisticated arrangement of works councils and employee committees, as employed by the John Lewis partnership. For many firms, however, it involves no more than the administration of an employee suggestion scheme. As we saw in the first section of this chapter, HRM favours employee involvement over collective bargaining. This has led to a renewed interest in forms of participation such as works councils and briefing groups.

In 1980 a survey of personnel management in manufacturing industry and the health service found that those working in personnel regarded industrial relations as their most important activity (Guest and Horwood, 1980). Since then of course, as we have noted, industrial relations management has undergone considerable shifts in emphasis. This is especially true for industrial relations, although we should be cautious about the speed and extent of that change. There may be a number of possible models of operating industrial relations at the level of the firm. We will view these when we discuss HR strategies at the end of this chapter. Nonetheless these changes have led some commentators to speak of the 'New Industrial Relations'.

The concept of 'New Industrial Relations' would appear to have had at least three incarnations. In the 1980s it was associated with practices brought in with Japanese transplants in firms such as Nissan. Such 'new' approaches usually embraced a legally binding contract between the firm and the unions, a peace clause where employees agree not to strike while the contract is in force and an agreement on pendulum arbitration to settle any dispute. Pendulum arbitration is a system whereby an independent arbitrator must opt wholly for the position of one side or the other. Around the same time, the term 'employee relations' came to be used in many firms instead of 'industrial relations'. Supposedly the latter term is associated with trade unions, adversarial negotiations and conflict, while the former conjures images of a more cooperative approach involving the entire workforce. Currently the main features of 'New Industrial Relations' would appear to have much in common with 'soft' HRM. Union involvement is accepted, but pay rises are linked to productivity and the acceptance of more flexible working practices. Exemplars of this 'New IR' include Rover, Shell, ICI and Mobil. Such changes have even been accepted by the TUC, labelled as the 'Partnership'. For John Monks, its General Secretary, 'Partnership' means, for the employee, job security, an extension of involvement, fair financial rewards and an investment in training. In return the organization gets increased flexibility, commitment, an acceptance of the need to change and cooperation with management (Monks, 1998). This may, of course, be the only pragmatic approach available in the face of a weakened trade union movement and, in some cases, management using this to increase pressure on the workforce.

HRM and technology

In Chapter 2 we examined the impact of technology and in particular technical change on jobs. We deal with two areas of significance to HRM: training and industrial relations, although the type of technology and changes in technology have implications for recruitment, selection and payment systems as well.

Technical change invariably results in a mismatch between the needs of the firm and the skills of the workforce. For example, there are more jobs in Scotland in micro-electronics than in coal and iron and steel, its more traditional industrial base. Some firms tackle the mismatch by the use of outside contractors, but longer-term cost-effectiveness will probably lie in developing training programmes. Such training focuses not only on the development of 'high-tech' skills but upon general workforce orientation towards using new technology, as in using computer terminals to input data, and upon more general management training. The creation of a more flexible workforce has been identified as a training priority for many organizations.

The commonly accepted view of the impact of technical change on industrial relations, doubtless fuelled by media coverage of events at places such as Wapping (Chapter 1), is that it created problems, largely because trade unions resist change. This resistance is inevitably linked to fears over job losses, deskilling and increased management control. It was such issues that concerned the Fleet Street print workers for several years in their opposition to photocomposition.

However, certain factors may temper this perspective. The TUC has, for many years, adopted a stated policy of influencing the direction of new technology to maximize its benefits and minimize its costs. A survey by Daniel (1987) concluded that the reaction of most workers to technical change has been favourable. He found that technical change was equated with investment and optimism, and was often seen as a route to better jobs and higher wages.

There is, however, general agreement that in many companies the level of consultation over technical change issues is low. This was a major cause of the failure of the TUC's attempt to introduce 'New Technology Agreements' in the 1980s and a major cause of problems in general.

The nature of the technology offers some groups of workers more bargaining power than others because they operate and control key technologies. This power has an impact on the negotiating process. A number of disputes in the 1970s in British Leyland were centred on the toolroom, where stoppages involving relatively small numbers of the total workforce caused the entire operation to cease since those who manufacture the tools for a particular industry are central to the entire operation. Mineworkers have traditionally used their position as the providers of an essential fuel supply as strong bargaining weapon. In their disputes of 1972 and 1974 the National Union of Mineworkers used an overtime ban as a tactical weapon to reduce coal stocks in the power stations before calling for an 'all out' strike. The resulting power cuts and their impact on the rest of industry was a significant influence in the collective bargaining process. Not all workers enjoy bargaining power as a result of controlling key technologies. The postal workers in their dispute of 1971 had their case weakened by firms using alternative courier services for mail and by making greater use of alternative technology in the form of the telephone service.

With the decline in the coverage and frequency of collective bargaining the incidences of strategic groups using their collective power is rare. Instead we see groups with scarce skills, such as IT consultants, using their labour market position to gain high rewards.

Changes in technology have had an impact on HRM itself. Computerized record-keeping has long been a feature of many HR departments. More recently those same departments have taken advantage of specialist software packages, such as Peoplesoft. These not only offer a framework for HR records and planning, but provide links with the firm's accounting systems as well.

Cultural influences

We have noted the considerable influences exerted by the state and the level of economic activity upon HRM activities. It is therefore not surprising that differences in practice can also be traced to cultural variations. Differences may be observed between the operation of HRM in different countries, as the following illustrations will show.

In Britain the function clearly reflects the growth of trade union activity and a general preference for localized collective bargaining. In the USA the activities of personnel are shaped by prevailing social attitudes which favour the use of law and which tend to be distrustful of trade unions. As a consequence much greater use is made of the law in such matters as the employment contract, equal opportunities and trade union collective bargaining. In addition there is much lower trade union membership than in Britain and therefore much less evidence of traditional industrial relations activity by HR managers. In fact some companies in the USA have developed HR strategies which actively discourage trade union organizations and focus on keeping the unions out by offering attractive welfare provisions and pay packages. In Germany, with its highly centralized system of collective bargaining, industrial relations is not a major concern of the HR manager. Specialist management functions such as HR play a much smaller role in Germany than elsewhere, a correspondingly higher status being accorded to line management. There would appear to be little interest in the more traditional techniques of personnel/HR management such as the use of job analysis and job descriptions. In major companies in Japan, HR policies reflect the operation of a dual-labour market bestowing considerable advantages on a privileged group of employees, including lifetime employment, seniority payments and a whole range of company welfare provisions. (The section on Japanese management in Chapter 2 has a fuller account.)

Despite these differences there is some evidence of practices converging. We have already noted the influence of Japanese companies in Britain and the interest in single union, 'no-strike' agreements. Many American companies operating in Britain tend to be non-unionized and the type of strategies employed by firms like Hewlett-Packard and IBM (Cases 3.6 and 8.1) have gained currency amongst personnel practitioners in Britain. There is an increased use of law in employment in the UK, and in Japan lifetime employment and seniority principles are exchanged for more 'Western' practices.

Developments in HRM are central to this theme of convergence. The assumption that economic and structural change will push firms towards a common HRM model was investigated as part of a study of HRM practices across Europe (Brewster and Bournois, 1991; Brewster et al., 1991). The study found considerable variation in HRM practice, particularly between Britain and the rest of Europe. The idea of a common model was challenged by different national institutional and legal frameworks. Guest (1990) goes further and puts forward a case that HRM is probably culturally specific to the USA. He likens the core characteristics of HRM to those of the 'American Dream' with its emphasis on individualism, hard work, reward, and fighting the frontier, which in this case is represented both by inefficient practices and by Japanese competition. Nonetheless we have seen instances where HRM strategies do work in a non-US and indeed a British setting. For an explanation of this we must return to the discussion in Chapter 2 concerning comparative management. In most national settings management practices are derived from a number of influences, some of which will be cultural, while others will relate to more common themes of technology, markets and organizational size.

On a different level altogether, one similarity would appear to exist. Wherever HR management is practised it has been traditionally dogged by a low-status image. In the following section we will explore reasons for this and in our discussion of personnel strategies suggest why this may be changing.

Organizational aspects of HRM

In this section we will view the relationship between organization size and HR activities and focus on the relationship between HRM and other management activities in the organization structure. A major theme to emerge in the dealings with management from other functional areas is that of goal conflict. Attempts to resolve such conflict are currently focused upon organizational culture and strategic HRM. We will deal with this aspect at the end of the section.

HRM and organization size

The relationship between the growth of the firm and the development of formalization, differentiation and specialization has already been discussed in Chapter 3. The development of personnel management departments in firms during the early part of the twentieth century can be clearly attributed to the increasing size of the organization. A control mechanism was needed, particularly in the areas of recruitment and payment systems, giving rise to specialist positions of 'wages officer' and 'labour officer'. Such positions concerned themselves with recruitment, discipline, timekeeping and general administration of the payment system, including the control of bonus payments. This growth of the size of firms was also a major factor in the changes in collective bargaining, placing more emphasis on bargaining within individual firms rather than at industry level. We have already noted how this resulted in the creation of industrial relations specialists.

A comprehensive survey of UK practices noted that whereas only 7 per cent of firms employing fewer than 50 people had personnel HR specialists, the proportion rose to 93 per cent for firms employing over 2000 people (Daniel and Millward, 1983). Furthermore, we can see that the increasing size of the firm has led to increasing specialization within personnel/HRM itself, although current practice may be reversing that trend.

HRM, organization structure and goals

There is growing evidence, not only in Britain but also throughout Europe, that HRM has become decentralized. This relates in part to the increasing adoption of new approaches with an emphasis on a greater involvement of line managers. However, in Britain, decentralization has also occurred in those firms that retain traditional collective bargaining. A major reason offered for this change is the decreasing role that is played by employers' associations. They play much less of a role in all aspects of business in Britain than elsewhere. For example, major car companies such as Ford, Vauxhall and Peugeot-Talbot have opted out of membership of their employers' association in Britain, but they have retained membership of associations in other European countries where they operate (Edwards *et al.*, 1992). Despite the trend towards decentralization, several large organizations such as Marks & Spencer retain a large centralized presence.

The spread of HRM practices has been cited for the increase in power and influence amongst HR practitioners. Torrington (1989) tends to support that view, but remains somewhat sceptical.

> Most of those in the personnel function who espouse Human Resource Management are doing so in search of enhanced status and power. With the obsession about innovation that currently pervades management thinking, a change of label is a useful indication of innovation, even if you are not too sure there is anything different in the package.
>
> (Torrington, 1989, p. 64)

While there is considerable disagreement as to whether power and influence have increased, there is no disagreement that traditionally the personnel function did not enjoy high status within many organizations. The same is also claimed for HRM. We can identify three problem areas:

● conflict between HR and other functional managers (these are sometimes referred to generically as line managers);
● difficulties encountered by HR managers in proving their worth to the organization either because of the suspicion of line management towards new techniques or because of the way HR managers organize their work;
● conflict within HRM itself between professional and organizational goals.

In general the research has focused on case studies where problems have been identified in the relationship between personnel/HRM and other departments. Little is known about how successful HR departments operate and how they successfully integrate with other functional areas. This may well give a somewhat stereotyped view of the HRM function and ignore a wide range of situations where HR managers are happy with their role and are seen to be effective. The various cases should be viewed within the limitation.

Much of what follows in this section is derived from earlier work by Karen Legge, in which she refers exclusively to the personnel function and personnel managers. So as not to cause confusion, these terms are retained. Although now over 20 years old, her perspectives offer considerable insights into intra-organizational conflict and status issues, and, more significantly, the problems and issues are recognizable by today's HR practitioners.

Much of Legge's analysis is based on the line and staff model. This has often been used to analyse the personnel function, depicting personnel operating in an advisory capacity only.

> The personnel department here is as it should be, as service to the line. For example, if we want more labour they get it, train it, and arrange for it to be paid. They provide information for negotiating too, but I do the real negotiating.
>
> (General Works Manager quoted in Legge, 1978, p. 51)

Legge sees this relationship between personnel and line management as a basis for conflict in that line have a 'confused, hazy and/or stereotyped perception of the potential nature and scope of a personnel department's activities' and 'tend to consider that personnel departments are "out of touch" with the kind of problems and constraints which face them' (Legge, 1978, p. 52). In particular, other managers feel that personnel do not identify as closely as they do with the profit goals of the organization.

In her case studies Legge saw a vicious circle operating, as illustrated in Figure 8.2. Personnel are not involved in planning and decision-making,

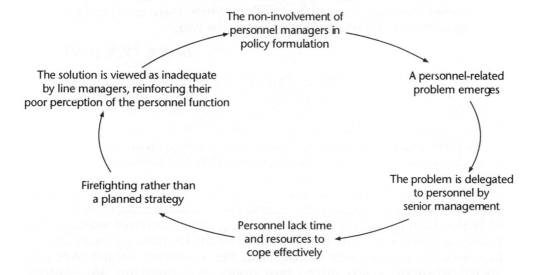

Figure **8.2** A vicious circle depicting the relationship between personnel and line management. Source: after Legge (1978).

resulting in human resource problems that are left to personnel to sort out; pressure of time and lack of resources lead to crisis management resulting in line management having a poor perception of the personnel function and hence its non-involvement in decision-making. The circle is reinforced by the failure on the part of some line managers to recognize the need for a specialist role for personnel since many personnel activities are carried out by all managers, as in the case of selection and training. Attempts to break free of the circle by personnel specialists adopting specialized techniques based on the behaviourial sciences are often rebuffed by a suspicious line management. In this way, carefully constructed appraisal schemes flounder in the face of line management opposition. As a result, Legge sees many personnel mangers 'opt for an easy life' and concentrate on a more acceptable welfare role.

In a study of personnel management in manufacturing and the health service, personnel themselves contributed to the kind of problems Karen Legge outlined. Personnel managers enjoyed crisis management and took on a variety of different activities to boost their credibility in the eyes of the rest of management. This resulted in too broad and too heavy a workload with the consequence of ineffectiveness and incompetence. Personnel management were thus unable to contribute effectively to the goals of the organization as identified by line management and reinforced the vicious circle (Guest and Horwood, 1980).

The question of effectiveness and personnel proving their worth was also raised by Legge.

> Personnel management by definition, is chiefly concerned with the acquisition, maintenance and development of one of the resources (ie, the human resource) through which the organisational ends are achieved rather than with the ends themselves. They are concerned with means rather than ends and inputs rather than outputs, and in situations where there is difficulty in determining the relationship between the two.
>
> (Legge, 1978, p. 60)

The two consequences of this are first that the credit for a successful personnel policy is taken to line management who actually perform the policy, but personnel carry the blame for an ineffective policy. Second, it is extremely difficult to quantify the outcome of personnel activity or even isolate its effect. As we have already mentioned, the success of a management development programme may be so diffuse and long-term that any financial assessment is impossible.

The following example illustrates the difficulty personnel/HR managers have in proving their value to the organization. A bus company in the north of England was concerned about the growing labour turnover among its bus drivers and used exit interviews conducted by the HR manager in an attempt to reduce the number who actually left. The interviews, which were conducted whenever a bus driver gave notice of terminating his contract, appeared to have very little impact for the first six months, but then the numbers leaving began to fall. Closer examination of this particular situation revealed that during the period when turnover was highest, a bus company in a neighbouring area was recruiting at a higher basic wage, while the time of falling turnover coincided with a downturn in the economy when all job opportunities were much scarcer. In other words, HR practitioners often deal with external forces outside their control.

We can now see that the first two problem areas are linked. The conflict between HR managers and other managers is a function of HR managers' seeming inability to prove their worth.

Our third problem area concerns the potential conflict between organizational and professional goals. HR managers are popularly portrayed as a group in the middle, owing allegiance to both the needs of the workforce and the needs of the organization they serve. As we saw from the IPM's definition of personnel management at the beginning of this chapter, there is no conflict in that the good professional is concerned 'to achieve efficiency and justice, neither of which can be achieved without the other'. It is clear that professional high ideals can conflict with the daily pressures of getting the job done. In practice, however, practitioners rarely feel such conflict. They generally see themselves as part of the management group and as such subscribe to management goals, even though they do not always operate as line management would like.

The kind of problems identified above can be tackled through the creation of an organization culture that stresses cooperation and consensus. It is to this we now turn.

The role of organizational culture

We have seen how HR managers reflect the culture of a particular enterprise. In general terms, the activities of HRM, especially those concerned with recruitment, selection and training, ensure that employees fit the prevailing culture of the firm. This takes on a more fundamental aspect in those firms that have identified a mission and build their organization culture around that mission. We dealt with such aspects more fully when we dealt with organizational cultures in Chapter 3. In such firms HRM assumes a role of major importance.

In the 1980s it was common for many local authorities to attempt to change the culture of their organizations in accordance with (usually) a guiding political ideology. The focus is usually on the criteria used in the recruitment and selection of new staff, with a special concern for equal opportunities, as the following job advertisement reveals:

> As part of Lambeth's Equal Opportunities Policy, applications are welcome from people regardless of race, creed, nationality, age, sex, sexual orientation or responsibility for children or dependents.
>
> (from the *Guardian*, 20 November 1985)

In the late 1990s such affirmative action tended to be replaced by more general and less positive statements, such as 'striving to achieve equal opportunities'.

Case 8.2: British Airways

British Airways was formed in 1972 through a merger between BEA and BOAC. It possessed a very extensive route network, an exceptionally good safety record, and, in Heathrow, an enviable operating base within easy reach of London. Its first decade of operation was typified by a number of problems and in 1982 the company reported losses of £100 million. The problems were over-staffing, a lack of operating efficiency compared to its major competitors, a series of industrial disputes and a particularly bad image with the travelling public. Part of the problem was attributed to a highly bureaucratic organization structure and decision-making process, typical of many nationalized industries. In British Airway's case the problem was compounded by a hierarchical structure that reflected the armed forces rather than a business operating in a fast-changing environment. By the 1980s the airline business was more competitive than ever and new entrants such as Virgin had quickly developed favourable reputations based upon low price and quality service. By 1983 the government had announced its intentions to de-nationalize the airline and the recently appointed chairman and chief executive were given a clear message that the company had to be made commercially viable.

The workforce was cut by some 20 000 and certain routes were withdrawn. A much greater attention was paid to marketing and organizational changes were made, including a reduction in hierarchical levels and a de-emphasis of status differences and job titles. In 1983 the company launched its major culture change initiative which used as its focus customer care. This was based upon research carried out on effective behaviour in the caring professions and the experience of SAS (Scandinavian Airlines) in implementing a similar programme. British Airways enlisted the help of the same consultants as those involved in the SAS project.

Two major training initiatives were launched. The 'Putting People First' campaign was aimed, initially, at those employees in direct contact with the general public, such as check-in staff and cabin crew, although it was extended to other groups as well. The 'Managing People First' campaign was aimed primarily at middle and senior management. Both campaigns were based on customer perceptions that portrayed British Airways as bureaucratic and saw its staff, while competent, as aloof and uncaring. The assumptions upon which the campaigns were

launched were that people perform best when given the maximum support by their peers and, most importantly, by their supervisors, and when given maximum discretion in solving problems. Human resources staff were given training in organization change by the consultants and much of the responsibility for personnel issues was passed to line management.

'Putting People First' training confronted staff in groups with the negative image of British Airways held by its customers and encouraged employees to suggest ways of changing it. Role playing was also used through which staff were encouraged to use their own initiatives to resolve customer problems such as flight delays and lost luggage. Presentations were given of what various people and groups in the organization did on a daily basis in an attempt to break down barriers and build a greater sense of identity. An important part of the process was the involvement of the chief executive, Colin Marshall, who was present for at least part of the training sessions. An important outcome of the sessions was the creation of 'Customer First Teams', a variation of the quality circle concept.

'Managing People First' was a five-day residential programme for managers. The programme comprised three elements: the encouragement of managers to adopt a more visible, open and dynamic style; the coaching, training and supporting of subordinates; and an attempt to get managers to link the goals of their part of the operations with overall corporate objectives. As part of the latter process managers were encouraged to develop their ideal of the company's mission. At the same time a management appraisal scheme was launched and tied in to an individual reward system with both performance-related pay and share options.

In 1988 profits of £320 million were reported by British Airways. Customer feedback was favourable and the airline received several awards for its customer service in the business press. The feedback from employees on their perception of the company was equally encouraging. Measured in terms of profitability and customer and employee satisfaction, the change appears to have worked. As with all major changes there were conflicts, notably between maintaining customer care and cutting costs at the same time, a clear case of 'soft' vs. 'hard' HRM. Some commentators see that problems still exist in the form of an insecure middle management, too much functional specialization and an overemphasis at the top on acquisitions and takeovers. Others believe these to be relatively understandable but minor issues in a major culture change, successfully tested by a further series of job losses as a result of the recession and the Gulf War in the 1990s.

However, the airline hit financial problems by the mid-1990s and embarked on a series of cost-cutting exercises in the light of falling demand, especially for business class seats. The exercises also incorporated the use of the lower-cost 777 aircraft on long-haul flights instead of the traditional 747 and the launch of 'Go', a cut-price airline, as a wholly owned subsidiary.

Further problems befell BA from 1997 to 1999. In 1997 there was a damaging three-day strike by cabin crew, largely as a protest over cost cuts. In 1998 the company faced considerable criticism when it replaced its traditional Union Jack tailfin with ethnic designs from across the globe, a policy that it reversed in 1999. In the same year, attempts to form the world's largest airline alliance with American Airlines and other carriers were contested by competitors such as Virgin and questioned by US regulatory bodies and consumer groups. The following year a much looser alliance was formed with Quantas, Cathay Pacific, Canadian Airlines, Iberia and Finn Air. In 1999 the company was fined £4.4 million by the European Commission for abusing its dominant market position, which included offering travel agents financial incentives for favouring BA.

The net result of such problems was a dramatic fall in share price and a worsening of relations with staff. Although a new agreement was reached with pilots in 1999, the company decided to re-strengthen its message of earlier years in an attempt to win the hearts and minds, not only of its employees, but of its customers as well. The new initiative was called, not surprisingly, 'Putting People First Again'. ■

(*Sources*: Bruce, 1987; Hampden-Turner, 1990; Höpfl *et al.*, 1992; Kay, 1993; *Financial Times*, 1998–9)

We can see from Case 8.1 that IBM lays great store by selecting the right type of individual, investigating heavily in management training and establishing excellent conditions of employment. In cases 2.6 and 3.6 in Nissan and Hewlett-Packard respectively, the importance of selection again emerges. In Hewlett-Packard the culture is sustained by paying attention to management styles, as in their technique of 'management by wandering around'. In all these cases the senior management see employment relations as a major route to establishing the kind of company they want.

We have seen already that the development of organizational culture, which stresses commitment, quality and flexibility, is a central device of HRM. For many organizations this implies a strategic change. It is to the notion of HRM strategy that we now turn.

Human resource management strategies

We have already noted that HRM not only places great emphasis upon a strategic approach to human resource issues, but also that such strategies aim for total integration within the corporate objectives of the enterprise. Such a strategic approach is a relatively recent phenomenon. Just over two decades ago an examination of a variety of companies revealed that specific personnel and industrial relations policies were notable by their absence. From her case studies Legge concluded:

> In company decision-making, the personnel management considerations involved in production, marketing and finance

decisions were not so much overruled (although this also occurred ...) as went by default.

(Legge, 1978, p. 37)

She noted that where policy did exist it was fragmented, short-term and largely reactive. Traditionally, where HR strategies have existed they have been based around manpower planning. We shall examine this first before attempting to map out some alternative models.

Manpower planning

This process is concerned with matching future manpower requirements with future manpower availability and involves consideration of both the quantity and the quality of the labour force, including the analysis of such factors as the age profile of the staff. A variety of techniques have been used, from simple demand–supply models to more sophisticated statistical models of the type traditionally used by the Civil Service to plan its own manpower requirements. The output of a manpower planning exercise should set the guidelines for HR strategies in recruitment, selection, training, retirement and so on. The resulting strategies will vary depending on the relationship of the predicted future demand to predicted future supply.

For example, a firm whose demand for labour exceeds the predicted supply may have to consider changes in its payment strategies with a view to attract more recruits or investigate the possibilities of introducing new technology to replace labour. Where the existing labour supply exceeds the predicted future demands then plans may have to be formulated for early retirement, redundancy or perhaps looking to marketing strategies to increase the demand for the firm's goods and services. Even where demand and supply are evenly matched, a manpower planning exercise may well give management useful insights into the nature of labour utilization and suggest where improvements can be made.

The reality, of course, is much more complex than the kind of model illustrated above. Such complexities are often the result of long lead-times and the impact of other variables over which management have little control. The planning of the supply of future medical doctors is an exercise that must incorporate projected birth rates and death rates, take account of the age profile of the nation and examine trends in disease and illness. Given that the training time of future doctors is at least seven years, allowance must be made for drop-out rates along the way as well. Even if these complexities are overcome, the exercise can be jeopardized by national cut-backs in healthcare spending or changes in EU law which extend the pool of available labour.

In the late 1980s management were fed considerable information about 'the demographic time-bomb', a forecast of a declining birth rate and its likely impact on the recruitment of school leavers in the 1990s. Some firms such as Ford Motor Company set up programmes to counteract a shortfall in the future supply of labour by building closer relationships with local schools and by projecting an improved image to the local community. In practice, any likely impact of a declining birth rate was mitigated by a recession and an increasing trend towards smaller workforces. Rather than scratching around for new recruits, most companies were more active in making employees redundant.

Links to corporate strategy

As a result of interest in HRM, there has been renewed discussion of the relationship between HR strategy and the corporate objectives of the enterprise. There are obvious examples where a change in business strategy leads to a corresponding change in the HR strategy. Survival in a recession may depend on either cutting back on operations or developing new areas of operation. In a recession clear policies may need to emerge on redundancy, as we saw with IBM in Case 8.1, or more flexible ways of working are introduced to cut costs. The development of new products and markets calls for new skills, which may necessitate recruiting new staff or retraining existing employees. Whenever the 'rules' of the business change there is generally an implication for HR policy. In higher education, new arrangements for funding have placed emphasis upon the research and publications record of the academic staff. Many of the newer universities, created from the old polytechnic sector, are attempting to build up their research and publications record through the recruitment of staff who can offer them those skills and who can bring with them a healthy publications record. The emphasis is therefore shifting away from teaching to research. This has implications not only for recruitment and selection, but the promotion and development policies for existing staff.

Different product markets call for variations in HR strategy. A simple way of illustrating this is to use the Boston Consulting Group matrix that we introduced in Chapter 4. This seems to have found renewed favour amongst HR academics (see for example Purcell, 1989).

In a 'cash cow' product market the emphasis is upon stable, low-cost production to 'milk' the profits. HR policies associated with 'cash cows' are those that ensure stability and continuity and include formalized procedures for job evaluation, a focus on welfare provision to retain staff, and, where unions are involved, highly structured collective bargaining. 'Cash cows' may be associated with a need to keep costs to a minimum and may be associated with the use of a flexible labour force and high numbers of part-timers. However, as Purcell points out, the very profitability of 'cash cows' may lead to complacency such as over-manning.

Where 'stars' and 'question marks' are concerned the emphasis shifts to operating a more flexible approach. HR priorities become the selection and development of innovative staff and the creation of teams across different functional specialisms. The long-term uncertainty associated with both 'stars' and 'question marks' places emphasis upon the management of change.

For 'dogs' the focus turns to cutting losses. This may mean redundancy programmes and it may involve retraining, transfer and even relocation.

Case 8.3: The Perkins Engine Group

In the 1990s, the Perkins Engine Group was owned by the Canadian firm Varity, a company that also controlled Massey Ferguson. Perkins makes diesel engines of all types ranging from seven to 1500 brake horsepower. Its main manufacturing operation, Peterborough Engines, is based in the town of the same name and currently employs nearly three-quarters of the total workforce. Despite the acquisition of Rolls Royce Diesel Engines in 1984 and Lesley Gardner Diesels in 1986, the overall size of the company was reduced from over 10 000 in the 1970s to 4900 in 1989. Such a change was not been possible without a significant change in HR strategies and in the work of the HR function.

In the late 1970s the company appeared to be in a healthy position. The demand for its products was high and the concern was to operate at full capacity. The plant was working seven days a week and the 10 000 employees were working an average of 10 per cent overtime per person. The company was turning out 1000 diesel engines a day with 86 per cent of these destined for the export market. The company adopted fairly typical personnel and industrial relations strategies for the engineering industry. Payment-by-results was the norm, training tended to focus on an engineering apprenticeship programme, and industrial relations negotiation was highly centralized. The main trade union at Perkins (the AUEW) was strong, with a high membership amongst shop-floor employees. There were a high number of short unofficial disputes that were highly localized. The high demand for the company's product meant that stoppages had to be avoided at all costs. The strategy adopted by the company was for a central personnel department to handle all industrial relations matters, including the negotiation for local disputes, in a bid to formalize procedures and take grievances away from their immediate location. As a consequence, local line management were seldom involved in industrial relations and related personnel issues.

In 1980 the demand for diesel engines fell sharply. In response the management opted for a strict control of all overtime working, introduced short-time working, changed working practices to enhance the competitiveness of the firm and embarked on a series of voluntary and compulsory redundancies.

The urgency of change was all the greater because of the company's heavy reliance on export markets and hence competition from diesel engine manufacturers all over the world, competing for a declining market share. The management recognized that such changes could not be made without consultation with the trade unions and the workforce, so that communication became the key to the implementation of the strategic changes. The changes were brought about through a variety of methods:

● All changes were negotiated with the trade union and the AUEW participated fully in the exercise. The union recognized that survival of the firm was the issue, but found the dilemma of protecting jobs for some while sanctioning the redundancy of others difficult to reconcile with traditional trade union practices. The redundancy issue was particularly difficult in that management could not afford to let go all those who wanted to under a generous voluntary scheme. The financial burden would be too high and such programmes might leave the company under-staffed in certain key areas. Compulsory redundancy was therefore inevitable with the subsequent difficult negotiations and disputes.

● The union had also to agree to new work practices. These generally involved the broadening of jobs and the introduction of more flexible work methods through the ending of demarcation agreements. Discussion and negotiation on this issue was specific to individual departments and sections, effectively decentralizing industrial relations. Line management became much more involved in personnel matters as the emphasis on the introduction of new work practices was shifted to man-management at the local level.

● There was a concern that all employees received a clear picture of the threats facing the company and fear that information could easily be distorted. The director took it upon himself to brief personally all senior management and trade union leaders. Team briefings were held throughout the organization. A company video was produced which examined the current position and explained the need for change. A training school programme was set up which gave sessions on the firm's position and encouraged feedback.

● A 'Fair Days Work Charter' was produced which stressed the need for all employees, both staff and hourly paid, to work for the whole day; to achieve output and quality targets set by management; to suggest ways of improving work methods and equipment; and to work cooperatively.

By 1982 employment levels had been reduced to 6000, but it was decided that the strategy had to continue throughout the 1980s despite the acquisition of new plants such as Rolls Royce. Redundancy became an annual exercise with the usual mix of voluntary and compulsory to preserve key skills. Three new strategies emerged.

First, a major reorganization took place. The company was restructured around autonomous strategic business units operating as independent profit centres. Senior management were given considerable responsibility and scope to enhance the competitiveness of their business unit. Entrepreneurship was encouraged and a fair proportion of senior management salary was tied to performance. There were plans to extend this scheme to all employees at some future date.

Second, considerable emphasis was placed on the training of employees to widen their range of skills to enhance flexibility and to increase the general level of skill throughout the organization. The company's programme was considered successful enough for them to win a National Training Award in 1987.

Third, new investments were made in automation to improve quality and reduce staffing costs. Assistance with modernization was obtained by the company participating in an EEC-funded project for the furtherance of technology transfer by the dissemination of operating experience and best practice.

As a result of the various changes the company has become much leaner, focusing on the employment of skilled, flexible employees. Consequently the company's workforce remained stable for a number of years.

In 1996, Perkins became part of the LucasVarity automotive and aerospace consortium. In 1997 Perkins was sold to the Caterpillar Engineering Group. A proposed alliance with Volkswagen for the provision of electronic diesel injection engines fell through, as this would have required too much investment to move into what would have been a new type of business for Perkins. By 1999 Perkins still employed over 4000 workers and had played a major part in making up in part for falling profits elsewhere in the Caterpillar Group. ■

(*Sources*: Jackson, 1983; Company information, 1988; *Financial Times*, 1995–9)

New approaches to strategy?

The pressure on human resource managers to be strategic is almost as intense now as the campaign to persuade us to eat healthily. We all believe it is a good thing to be strategic – career progressive for ourselves, prestigious for our profession and it might even do our organizations good as well.

(Herriot and Pinder, 1992, p. 36)

The emergence of HRM was viewed by some as a strategic lifeline to a group of practitioners without a clear strategy. However, we have seen that the classic HRM approach is perhaps more talked about than practised and that there are significant variations. We will attempt to identify some of those variations by constructing a model of HRM practice in a British context.

We present a model in Figure 8.3, which is based upon the work of Fox (1974a), Purcell and Sisson (1983) and Guest (1989, 1990).

The model identifies two broad categories, unitarist and pluralist. The unitarist approach emphasizes shared goals while the pluralist approach acknowledges that different groups within the organization may have different goals. We have identified several variations.

Unitarist

    Traditional unitarist

    Sophisticated unitarist

Pluralist

    New industrial relations pluralist

    Opportunistic pluralist

    Sophisticated pluralist

    Traditional pluralist

Figure **8.3** Approaches to HRM

KEY CONCEPT 8.7
Unitary and pluralist frames of reference

The unitarist frame of reference emphasizes shared goals amongst all members of the organization. Those managers who hold such a perspective find it difficult to acknowledge that trade unions have a legitimate role in their organization. A pluralist frame of reference acknowledges that different groups within the organization may have different goals. Within such a perspective, trade unions are seen as legitimate representatives of the wishes of employees.

The *traditional unitarists* represent management whose predominant view is the opposition to all kinds of trade union groups. Such a strategy can result in direct confrontation, as was seen in the much-publicized Grunwick dispute of 1976 when the managing director of a film processing plant in Southall denied union recognition to a group of Asian workers. The ensuing dispute had racial as well as industrial relations implications. The 1980s and 1990s has seen traditional unitarists engage more readily in redundancy programmes and be more willing to use contract labour (Millward *et al.*, 1992). It was predicted that the political and economic changes of the 1980s would encourage the traditional unitarists to emerge from their closets embodied in 'macho-management' stereotypes, with Michael Edwardes (ex of British Leyland) and Ian McGregor (ex of British Steel and the Coal Board) as the hero figures. However, such stereotypes perhaps owe more to media distortion than accurate analysis.

The *sophisticated unitarists* are those companies like IBM and Hewlett-Packard that are the role models for HRM practice. In such companies considerable time and effort is taken to ensure workforce commitment to overall company objectives. Such companies are typified by fairly sophisticated personnel policies in selection, training, reward systems and employee involvement. The majority also happen to be non-union.

New industrial relations pluralists are to be found in those firms that espouse the 'single union, no strike philosophy' that we have encountered earlier in the chapter. The models for such companies are the Japanese transplants such as Nissan and Toyota. Many such companies attempt to involve their employees through a works council or similar institution. Probably many managers in this category are aspiring unitarists.

The *opportunistic pluralists* represent those managers in unionized firms who have used the economic and political climate as an opportunity to roll back the influence of the trade unions. They have found no need to adopt the aggressive anti-union stance of the traditional unitarists and are still prepared to work within a pluralist framework. As Kessler and Bayliss write,

> most managers took the line that since they could get what they wanted through negotiations or by acting unilaterally, there was no need to attack the unions.
>
> (Kessler and Bayliss, 1992b, p. 35)

The idea of opportunism occurs frequently in any discussion of HRM in a UK context, particularly with reference to the application of 'hard' HRM and its association with job cuts. Such opportunism is also associated with an absence of long-term strategy.

The *sophisticated pluralists* on the other hand see consultation and negotiation with trade unions as the keystone of their HR policies. Such firms have well-established procedures for determining pay and conditions and often have mechanisms for employee participation. Managers in this category see that change is necessary but prefer it to be agreed with employees rather than imposed upon them. Ferner and Hyman (1992a) found such an approach more common in European countries other than Britain, but it can be found here as well. Most of the major oil companies, British Airways and some local governments exhibit such strategies. Perkins Diesels (Case 8.3) also see negotiation as an important part of organization change. The sophisticated pluralist approach suggests that HRM is not incompatible with trade unionism.

Traditional pluralists tend not to be strategically oriented, preferring instead to adopt the standard reactive response to problems. They manage by 'fire-fighting', and as such fit in well with our illustrations of personnel management when we discussed the influence of organizational structure and goals upon the HR function.

As we have mentioned throughout this chapter, there is much discussion of firms shifting towards an HRM approach. The above classification implies that managers have not one, but several models from which to choose. However, as we saw in our discussion of organizational culture in Chapter 3, culture change is particularly difficult. The adoption of HRM policies is not only costly, but may well meet with resistance from the shop-floor as well as management. It is not by chance that HRM strategies are often associated with greenfield sites. Nonetheless there is enough evidence to suggest that HR practitioners are reacting to changing circumstances. The relative weakness of trade unions has reduced the need for extensive exercises in collective bargaining and conflict management. We have seen how some managers have used this as an opportunity to reduce manning levels and increase labour flexibility. In declining industries there is a reduction in recruitment and training and a focus on redundancy and early retirement. In growth areas there is an increased concern for the selection, development and retention of a core group of employees.

We can see from these models that there is considerable variation in HR strategy and that the explanation for the variation is a function of a number of key variables. These are the variables that form the basis of the Business in Context model, namely the state, the economy, culture, technology, the labour force, organization size, structure, goals and ownership.

Summary

The role and activities of human resource management would appear to be reactive, particularly to some problem or crisis. The development of the function is clearly related to economic growth, the increasing size of organizations, government legislation and policy, the growth of the labour movement and developments in collective bargaining. Expectations of the decline of the function in the face of an economy in recession and the decline in numbers and influence of the trade union movement are, as yet, premature. A new role has emerged which gives the former personnel management a new name, HRM, and a new focus, which stresses strategic management. At present, evidence as to the widespread existence and influence of the new role is mixed.

Focus on the activity of HRM in the UK reveals an historic preoccupation with industrial relations, while an analysis of other types of activity reveals a largely intuitive and subjective approach behind a scientific facade. The weakening of the trade union movement throughout the 1980s and 1990s has tended to play down the significance of industrial relations. However, such issues are still at the forefront in more traditional manufacturing, as in the car industry.

Traditionally personnel managers have had low status as a result of their historic association with a welfare role and the fact that most of their activities can be carried out by all managers.

Such analyses at the level of the firm may well explain a lack of personnel strategy beyond the basic manpower planning, although initiatives in the direction of HRM may alter this state of affairs. However, perhaps too much emphasis has been placed upon the problems of the role and more evidence is needed of effective operation and, in particular, the effectiveness of newly styled HRM policies. Indeed, many firms are displaying a greater concern for productivity and cost-effectiveness and are de-emphasizing traditional industrial relations. Traditional approaches can still be found, however, in many firms.

Further reading

I. Beardwell and L. Holden, eds, *Human Resource Management: A Contemporary Perspective*, 2nd edn (Pitman Publishing, 1997) offers a wide coverage of most of the key areas of HRM, including some interesting international comparisons. Such comparative illustrations are also a feature of A. Price, *Human Resource Management in a Business Context* (International Thomson, 1997), a companion volume in this series. A good source of information, offering a variety of perspectives, is P.R. Sparrow and M. Marchington, *Human Resource Management: The New Agenda* (Financial Times/Pitman Publishing, 1998). An interesting analysis of the role of the personnel specialist that is still relevant today is offered by K. Legge, *Power, Innovation and Problem-solving in Personnel Management* (McGraw-Hill, 1978). A readable approach to industrial relations, including all the more recent developments, is offered by S. Kessler and F. Bayliss, *Contemporary British Industrial Relations*, 3rd edn (Macmillan, 1998) and a good source of current information on industrial relations based on survey data is offered in M. Cully *et al.*, *The 1998 Workplace Employee Relations Survey: First Findings* (DTI, 1998).

Discussion

1. Is there a case for the elimination of human resource specialists, so that the function can be performed by all managers?
2. Assess the role of the state in the development of the personnel and HRM function. How has that role changed and what has been the impact since 1980?
3. In what way have economic changes affected what personnel/HRM managers do, and the way they go about their activities?
4. How significant is industrial relations today? What changes do you foresee in the main activities?
5. What are the main sources of tension between personnel/HRM and other management groups? What strategies are available to reduce such tensions?
6. To what extent is HRM a separate activity from personnel management?
7. How would you establish a manpower plan for a) a small, expanding computer software firm, b) a medium-sized firm manufacturing electrical components for the car industry and c) a new university? What key issues emerge in each case?
8. Examine the key environmental, organizational and strategic issues in each of the three cases offered in this chapter. What lessons are to be learnt by other firms from the situations faced by these three companies?
9. Do HRM policies need to vary for the public as opposed to the private sector?

CHAPTER 9

Finance and accounting

In this chapter we examine the role played by the finance and accounting function in the operation of a business. We identify three main functions. First, we discuss the raising of funds or financial management. Second, we examine the contribution of accounting to management control and decision-making, often referred to as management accounting. Third, we look at the function of financial reporting. We show these three elements in Figure 9.1, and deliberately portray them as overlapping activities. For example, a manager who decides on a strategy of business expansion into new markets and new process technologies (a decision based on management accounting calculations) will need to present accounting information to a bank or another potential investor (financial reporting) to persuade them to back the expansion with the necessary capital (financial management).

Figure **9.1** Finance and accounting activities.

Accounting procedures and processes are very much a product of the organizational and wider environments in which they operate. We will examine the various economic, legal and social influences on the finance and accounting function, and look at variations resulting from the size of the organization, ownership patterns and organization structure. We shall also look at the accounting practices of large multi-divisional companies by examining the procedures for cost allocation and transfer pricing. We end the chapter by giving a broad overview on the contribution of finance and accounting strategies to overall management strategy.

Throughout this chapter it is the intention to present accounting not as a series of technical calculations but as a management function that is influenced significantly by those who prepare and use accounting information. For example, the determination and disclosure of profit levels will be guided by regulations governing accounting practice. It may also be influenced by the wish to minimize liability for tax and the relationship with a variety of stakeholders, including employees and shareholders. It may also be influenced by a desire for merger or by the forthcoming wage negotiations with trade unions. Budgets are determined by management to guide future activities in accordance with plans. The process of budget setting and resource allocation is, in many organizations, a product of organizational politics, power and influence.

It is not our intention to give an introduction to bookkeeping and various accounting techniques. There are a range of suitable introductory books that students may consult and we recommend some at the end of this chapter. Those seeking a much broader coverage of the finance and accounting issues in organizations should refer to the accompanying accounting text in this series by Berry and Jarvis (1997). Many of the issues are also dealt with in more depth in the series economics text by Neale *et al.* (2000).

Finance and accounting in business

Accountants form the largest professional group in Britain, and, numerically at least, are much more significant here than elsewhere. A survey carried out in the 1980s established the presence of 120 000 qualified accountants in Britain, compared with 20 000 in France, and only 6000 in Japan and 4000 in the former West Germany (Handy, 1987). Many of those accountants in Britain operate in business either as finance and accounting specialists or as general managers. Professional accountancy is often regarded as a training route for senior management in this country.

As we shall see later, such statistics reflect a difference in the nature of businesses in the various countries and may even be misleading. For example, the management accounting function exists in many German firms, but is performed by business economists. The variations in the number of accountants in different countries are, however, thought by some to reflect significant cultural differences in the way businesses operate. It has often been claimed that the traditional accountant's attitude to risk aversion can hold back entrepreneurial decision-making and, as we have seen elsewhere in this book, a preoccupation with short-term accounting calculations and financial returns may have damaged the long-term competitiveness of manufacturing industry. This is a theme that has been explored in the USA by Hayes and Wheelwright (1984) and in Chapters 5 and 6 of this book.

As stated in our introduction, we shall examine the function in terms of the three activities of financial management, management accounting and financial reporting, depicted in Figure 9.1.

Financial management

Financial management is concerned with the raising of capital to finance the organization's operations and with ensuring that the company can generate sufficient revenue to cover the cost of raising this finance. That cost may be in the form of interest rates payable to banks or dividend paid out to shareholders. There is a clear overlap with management accounting in that the funds must be managed by putting them to the most effective use. For example, investments must be carefully appraised. We may identify four sources of finance, share capital, loan capital, internal funding, and the state. We return to some of the themes outlined in this section in our discussion of cultural differences in finance and accounting later in the chapter.

Share capital

The issue of shares is a means whereby capital can be raised by devolving ownership of a company to a number of shareholders. In return for their investment, shareholders become part-owners of the company and are entitled to a payment each year in proportion to the number of shares held, and, usually, in proportion to the firm's profit levels. Such payments are known as dividend. We have already noted in Chapter 3 that this process, resulting from legal changes in most industrial countries in the nineteenth century, enabled firms to grow dramatically in size. The creation of the limited liability company not only raised finance in this way but reduced the risk for individuals, who could not be held personally responsible for financial losses incurred by the firm.

There are different types of share capital:

- **Preference shares** attract a fixed rate of dividend, usually payable twice yearly. Such agreed dividend must be paid irrespective of the financial performance of the company, but in times of hardship, payment may be deferred until such time as it can be afforded by the company. In this case the shares are known as cumulative preference shares, since the dividend accumulates until it is paid. Preference shareholders have a preference over other shareholders when assets are sold in cases of liquidation.
- **Ordinary shares** form the majority of all share capital. Owners of ordinary shares do not receive a guaranteed dividend, but they are normally entitled to a share of the profits after deductions for tax and payment to preference shareholders. Traditionally there are two types of ordinary share, those with voting rights and those without. However, non-voting shares are becoming increasingly rare and several companies have changed the status of their non-voting shares to give the owners voting rights. Ordinary shareholders can vote to elect the directors of the company.
- **Deferred shares** are fairly rare, but the owners of such shares only receive a dividend payment when the dividend for ordinary shareholders reaches an agreed level.
- **Golden shares** refer to those shares retained by governments in the case of privatization issue. The retention is to prevent hostile takeover. In some cases the government may limit the size of shareholding as a condition of the share issue. For example, no one individual may own more than 15 per cent of the British Airports Authority.

The major source of finance from shares comes in the form of new share issues. Despite the recent publicity given to this through the popular share issues when such as British Telecom and British Gas were privatized, probably less than 10 per cent of all finance comes from share issue (Wilson, 1980). In recent years the emergence of venture capital has had significant impact on the financing of small firms. Overall, however, shares still play a minor role in the raising of funds and evidence suggests that where new share issues do play a part, the money is spent not on investing in current activities, but to fund acquisitions (Mayer, 1988).

The stock market was created to encourage potential investors to finance businesses over which they had no direct control, yet for the majority it is simply a secondary market in which shares are bought and sold by investors, with no funding activity involved. A great deal of stock market activity revolves around the dealings of financial intermediaries. We have discussed their role alongside more general issues relating to the separation of ownership and control in Chapter 3. While funding and share trading are two separate activities, those holding large numbers of shares can influence management decision-making in that, if sufficient numbers of shares are traded, then the company itself is traded. Managements tend to be aware that new owners may have different agendas from those of their predecessors.

Loan capital

This represents a riskier form of financing than share capital. With share capital, dividend payment can be deferred and the capital itself does not have to be paid back except when the company is liquidated. With nearly all forms of loan capital, interest must be paid on due dates and some interest charges can be high. The usefulness of loan capital depends on the rate of interest, the time required for repayment and the security that needs to be offered. There are many types of loan financing and we examine a selection below.

KEY CONCEPT 9.3
Loan capital

Loan capital is raised by borrowing money from a third party and can take many forms. The major forms of loan capital are loans from banks or other financial institutions, debentures, overdrafts, factoring, leasing and trade credit. Loan capital carries more risks than other forms of financing in that interest must be paid and, with most types of loan credit, the capital must be paid back within a stated period of time.

Debentures are negotiable instruments that can be bought and sold on the stock market. They are issued in return for loans secured on the fixed assets of a company. The main advantage of debentures over shares is that interest paid can be offset against tax, whereas this is not the case for share dividend.

Bank borrowing is more common than raising finance through share issues, but on the whole UK banks are less willing to lend and less willing to take an active role in the management of business activities than their counterparts in other countries. Banks play a much more significant and much more integrated role in France, Japan and Germany. In countries such as Germany, lending terms are also more favourable to industrial borrowers as far as both interest rates and the length of the pay-back period are concerned. Not only are UK banks somewhat conservative in their lending policies, they are also, when acting as institutional investors, quite likely to sell their shares when things go wrong. Inadvertently, through their activities on the stock market, banks may weaken the financial position of a company, which can encourage a takeover bid. The reluctance of UK banks to finance business was argued by the Wilson Report to be a function of the poor performance of UK industrial firms, which did not merit investment (Wilson, 1980). There is more recent evidence that the banks are conscious of their poor image as far as investment is concerned and all the major high street banks have engaged in costly advertising and publicity campaigns to attract the business borrower. Managers will always view high interest rates as the major obstacle to bank borrowing. The high interest rates operating in the UK for much of the 1980s and early 1990s as part of the government's attack on inflation acted as such an obstacle. Loans may also be obtained from other types of financial institution, although in the UK, banks predominate.

Overdrafts are used by many businesses as a source of loan capital and many firms have permanent or semi-permanent overdraft arrangements with the bank. While this is perceived as usual by many managers, many banks feel less comfortable with such arrangements.

Leasing is a form of loan capital in that the firm will acquire assets that it has not bought, but leased from another firm. Many company cars, security systems and photocopiers are acquired in this way. Leasing agreements usually provide other benefits such as service agreements or replacement after so many years or in the case of a breakdown. Leasing has become very popular for many items over the past 25 years, although the tax advantages associated with leasing have recently been reduced.

Factoring is a means of raising capital. A factoring company will buy debts owing to a firm at some 70–80 per cent of their real invoice value. While money is lost on the value of the invoice, this can be a useful way of improving cash flow quickly.

Trade credit is a form of loan capital in that payment is delayed for an agreed period, thus assisting cash flow.

Other forms of financing

Internal funding has been shown by many studies to be a major source of funding for most private companies in Britain. Studies in the 1980s suggested that many firms obtain as much as 70 per cent of funds this way (Wilson, 1980; Mayer, 1988). The position would appear to be little different at the end of the 1990s. The finance will come mainly from the redistribution of profits, although funding can be raised through the sale of assets. There are several reasons why management prefer to finance their businesses internally. The major factor is the fear that the involvement of banks and shareholders will weaken their control of the company. This is certainly the case as far as bank borrowing is concerned, but less so for shareholders. However, as we saw in Chapter 3, institutional investors can have considerable influence on management decisions. The shareholding route may be especially resisted by small business owners fearing a diminution of their control over the business. As we suggested above, there is a major reluctance on the part of UK managers to borrow from banks when interest rates are high and when the banks impose short pay-back periods.

State funding plays a relatively minor role in the funding of UK business. Apart from the investment in prestige projects such as Concorde and microchips, the activities of the state in Britain have generally been restricted to supporting declining industries and firms and preventing mass unemployment in economically deprived regions. This would seem to be the logic behind the government's regional policy and its investment in British Steel and British Leyland. Since 1979, the UK governments have generally espoused a free market economy and such funding activity has been limited. We refer you to Chapters 2 and 5 for a further discussion of such issues. Although many governments like the UK have reduced or even stopped the direct funding of business, indirect funding still plays a significant role. Japanese firms such as Nissan have benefited from government assistance in their establishment of UK bases. In Singapore, the government has pursued a deliberate policy of providing certain infrastructures and offering tax advantages to attract leading high-tech companies to the country (see Case 2.5) There are a number of other factors which influence the source of finance. The attitude of management to risk may be an important factor. A cautious manager may wish to limit the extent of bank borrowing at all costs. The extent to which internal funds can be made available depends on the ability of management to satisfy its shareholders through dividend pay-out. There are also significant differences in the funding of activities between large and small firms, a point we shall return to later in the chapter.

Management accounting

Management accounting is the application of accounting techniques to provide management with the information to assist in the processes of planning and control. There is a clear overlap with financial management in that management accounting is concerned with the use of funds, and with financial reporting in that management accounting uses the data collected as a basis for its calculations.

KEY CONCEPT 9.4
Management Accounting

Management accounting is concerned with the planning, coordination and control of funds. It involves such activities as budgeting, costing, investment appraisal and the management of cash flows. Through such activities, management is provided with necessary information to assist in decision-making.

In terms of planning, management accounting assists in the formulation of plans for other functional areas. For example, an assessment of future labour costs will assist the process of manpower planning. Predictions of the future cost of raw materials will help in devising appropriate purchasing strategies and, where predicted costs are high, may even stimulate the development of new products using alternative materials. An important contribution to the planning process is the assistance offered by management accounting techniques of investment appraisal in selecting the most appropriate course of action from a range of alternatives. Such techniques are more valuable as environments become increasingly complex.

Management accounting plays a very important role in the wider process of management control. It enables clear parameters to be set in the form of budgets and represents a method by which many problems can be sensed and measured. It is especially useful as a control tool for three reasons. First, the data produced offer management one of the few methods of quantifying the effect of their decisions and of the organization's operations. Second, management accounting integrates the information from all the activities of the business and enables management to view operations as a whole. Third, it deals with the control of funds that are essential to an organization's survival.

We deal with five aspects of management accounting. These are budgeting, cost accounting, investment appraisal, the management of cash flows, and the contribution of the management accountant to management decisions. There is considerable overlap between these categories. For example, the control of assets would inevitably involve budgetary control, and the contribution to general management decisions would include all the other four categories. Management accounting is central to strategic planning and many of the issues reappear when we discuss strategy at the end of this chapter. For the moment we examine each of the categories in turn.

Budgeting and budgetary control

A budget is a quantitative statement of expectations concerning the allocation of resources and performance. The two aspects of budgeting are the establishment of standards and the setting up of mechanisms to measure and control performance. As a result, budgeting has a central position in the design of most management and accounting information systems.

KEY CONCEPT 9.5
Budgeting

Budgets are devices for planning and control. They establish standards to be attained, including those for income and expenditure and mechanisms through which activities can be measured against the standards. Budgeting is a means of allocating funds and resources, of delegating authority and of motivating employees and is above all a vital control of all activities.

Budgets are used in many different ways: to allocate funds and supplies, as a means of delegating management authority, as targets to motivate employees, and as a means of control of both spending and performance. For example, the University of East London allocates funds to each department designated as a cost centre. The allocation varies according to the size of the department and the nature of its work, so that science and engineering may get a large capital expenditure budget to purchase essential equipment. Budgets are allocated under a number of headings, including equipment, office supplies, library purchases, the funding of conferences for staff and so on. Such a mechanism serves two main purposes. First, it attempts to ensure that expenditure keeps within clearly defined limits. Second, it spreads the complex task of managing this expenditure by delegating to department heads.

Budgets are normally based on historic information, usually last year's budget. In a highly bureaucratic organization, resistant to change, this can cause difficulties when the needs of organization members change, or in highly dynamic environments. In such cases changes may not be represented in budget allocation, which is based on out-of-date information.

In all organizations there are often significant difficulties in changing the budget allocations. This is because budgeting is a bargaining process dealing with the allocation of scarce resources and those with most to lose have a vested interest in maintaining the status quo. It is for this reason that increasing attention has been given to the behavioural aspects of budgeting. The bargaining process can be useful in that it can force management to confront long-held assumptions and face up to underlying tensions which affect decision-making. However, there is a danger that conflict will be dysfunctional. This is especially true where budgeting in the form of targets is used as a control device, and more so where it forms the basis of the organization's reward system. In this case and also where scarce resources are at stake there may be a temptation for managers to distort information to place both them and their departments in the most favourable light.

Budgeting is therefore inseparable from the process of organizational politics and the way the organization is structured. In some cases this process has been acknowledged and attempts have been made to introduce some form of participation in the budget planning process.

Cost accounting

Cost accounting involves the analysis and allocation of costs. In large organizations this can be a complex process involving paper transactions between different units, especially in multi-divisional firms. We return to this aspect when we discuss the influence of organization structure on accounting procedures. The nature of costs varies considerably. Some costs such as rents are relatively fixed, while others such as the amount of raw materials used by a manufacturing firm will vary with the intensity of production. Some costs, such as wages, are highly detailed, while others such as expenditure on hospitality can be relatively vague. A variety of terms are used to describe various types of costing. **Direct costs** are those that can be directly ascribed to a specific product, while **indirect costs** relate to more general overheads such as labour, heating, lighting and so on and are more difficult to trace to a particular product. The traditional method for sharing out indirect costs across the organization is known as **absorption costing**. In some organizations, absorption costing has been replaced by **activity-based costing**. This method focuses on those activities that drive the costs in a particular product and is reckoned to be a more realistic method for apportioning costs, especially in more advanced technological systems, where indirect costs are much more significant than direct costs.

Activity-based costing is one of a range of relatively new costing techniques which challenge traditional cost accounting methods. In many manufacturing organizations, technological and competitive changes are taking place, which are challenging the basis of historical costs, and management is having to devise new methods. These changes include the introduction of new manufacturing technology to reduce the cost of production and a renewed

KEY CONCEPT 9.6
Costing

Costing is the means by which the costs of producing goods and services are calculated. It is therefore an important ingredient of pricing. Some costs, such as those associated with bought-in raw materials and components, are relatively easy to ascribe to particular goods and services. Others such as rent, labour or the costs of providing a prestigious corporate HQ are more difficult to relate to specific items. A range of costing techniques such as absorption costing and activity-based costing have been developed to apportion such indirect costs.

emphasis placed upon improving quality, increasing operating efficiency and reducing the uncertainty of materials and components supply. We have referred to these changes elsewhere in this book, as with our discussion of target costing in Chapter 7.

Investment appraisal

Capital investment involves the commitment of funds now with the expectation of acceptable earnings in the future. Such decisions are made about the purchase or renting of new or additional premises, investment in new equipment, the development of a new product, or even the acquisition of another business. A careful appraisal of such investments is necessary owing to the usually large amounts involved and the key impact such investments might have on the future viability of the company. A variety of investment appraisal methods have been devised, including pay-back, rate of return, net present value (NPV) and yield.

KEY CONCEPT 9.7
Investment appraisal

Investment appraisal is the process of calculating whether an investment is cost-effective in the short, medium or long term. Such appraisals can relate to the acquisition of another firm, the development of a new product or the purchase of a new piece of equipment. A commonly used technique is net present value.

NPV is a popular method since it estimates future returns on investment, but assesses them on current values. Management is therefore able to make more informed judgements. Despite the popularity and frequency of their use, NPV calculations are not without problems. They are difficult to use for long-term investments without management making some rather big assumptions about such as the future behaviour of markets and the future costs of raw materials. The more assumptions that have to be made, the less accurate the forecasts are likely to be. A problem associated with this is that strong management commitment to a particular investment project may result in a self-fulfilling NPV calculation. The figures are simply made to work to justify the decision. A study of the coal, steel and car industry in Britain in the 1970s concluded that large investments were justified on the basis of highly dubious input data; investment decisions that were subsequently proved unwise (Williams *et al.*, 1986).

The management of cash flows

The management of cash flows is concerned with the movement of cash into and out of the organization. This is an important activity since the firm needs to ensure that it has sufficient cash to cover its current expenditure. Many small firms find their severest problems occur with the management of cash flows. A business start-up has a considerable cash outflow to begin with and it may be some time before sufficient revenue is established to cover these initial costs. Several businesses have ceased trading with full order books, simply because they have insufficient incoming cash to pay bank interest charges and so are unable to stay in business and capitalize on their orders.

KEY CONCEPT 9.8
Cash flows

Cash which flows in and out of a firm is vital to its survival. Without adequate cash flows a firm may have insufficient funds to pay its bills and may cease to trade, even though it may possess a high-quality product and a healthy order book.

Cash-flow management can be particularly difficult in times of high inflation, when there is a danger that profits become absorbed by escalating costs. Some firms also experience cash-flow difficulties in expanding economies. In such situations there is a temptation to turn profit, not into cash, but into new investments by budgeting against future profits. Such a situation led Laker Airways to overreach itself by investing in expensive new passenger aircraft at a time when its markets were limited by the restrictive practices of other airlines. The company was forced into liquidation.

A current concern of cash-flow management is the management of stocks. Many manufacturing firms are attempting to reduce their outgoings through a better control of inventory. Strategies employed include the development of close links with a limited number of suppliers and operating such production control methods as 'Just-in-time' (Chapter 6 has a fuller discussion of such strategies).

General contribution to management decision-making

Any discussion of the various elements of management activity can give the misleading impression that such activities are discrete. In reality the work of the management accountant does not focus on any one of these activities singly but uses them all in conjunction to assist in the general process of management decision-making on an ongoing basis. The accountant would be expected to contribute to most types of management decision, and certainly would have an input in major decisions such as plant closure and decisions to make or buy.

Financial reporting

Financial reporting involves the collection and presentation of data for use in financial management and management accounting. In most countries there are minimum legal requirements governing the kind of statement that must be produced. In the UK, the requirement is for a profit and loss account, a balance sheet, a director's report and an auditor's report. For those firms listed on the stock exchange there is an additional requirement of an interim, usually half-yearly, report. Within the legal requirements, some variation is allowed. For example, some companies, such as British Airways, now report in euros. Others, such as the Natwest Group, produce an annual review and a summary statement as an alternative to the full annual report and accounts, believing the former to be more accessible than the latter (Holmes and Sugden, 1999). In recent years the Internet has become significant as a reporting channel and it is a requirement in the USA for some companies to post results on the Internet.

The two major forms of financial statement for companies are the balance sheet and the profit and loss account. Examples of these two statements from the J. Sainsbury Group are presented in Figures 9.2 and 9.3. Both these statements and accompanying information are available on the Internet.

KEY CONCEPT 9.9
Financial reporting

Financial reporting is the presentation of financial information in a form that is useful to interested parties. In most countries the form of such information is prescribed by law. In addition, in the UK, firms are expected to conform to the requirements of the Statements of Standard Accounting Practice (SSAPs), which are being superseded by Financial Reporting Standards (FRSs). Such information is useful in management decision-making, for potential investors and for a firm's competitors. Since the financial information is available to such a wide audience, management must decide on the extent of disclosure beyond the minimum required by law.

The **profit and loss account** provides detail of a firm's income and expenditure throughout a stated period of time, known as the accounting period. The profit and loss account must include the figures from two accounting periods. In almost all cases this involves presenting a comparison of the current figures with those from the previous year.

Group profit and loss account
for the 52 weeks to 7 March 1998

	1998 £m	1997 £m
Group sales including VAT and sales taxes	**15,496**	14,312
VAT and sales taxes	**996**	917
Group sales excluding VAT and sales taxes	**14,500**	13,395
Cost of sales	**13,289**	12,363
Exceptional cost of sales – Texas Homecare integration costs	–	50
Gross profit	**1,211**	982
Adminitrative expenses	**357**	287
Year 2000 costs	**20**	–
Group operating profit before profit sharing	**834**	695
Profit sharing	**44**	37
Group operating profit	**790**	658
Associated Undertakings – share of profit	**16**	19
Profit on sale of properties	**3**	8
Loss on disposal of a subsidiary	**–12**	–
Profit on ordinary activities before interest	**797**	685
Net interest payable	**78**	76
Profit on ordinary activities before tax	**719**	609
Tax on profit on ordinary activities	**236**	208
Profit on ordinary activities after tax	**483**	401
Minority equity interest	**4**	2
Profit for the financial year	**487**	403
Equity dividends	**264**	226
Retained profit	**223**	177
Earnings per share	**26.1p**	22.0p
Exceptional cost of sales	–	1.8p
Loss(profit) on sale of properties and disposal of a subsidiary	0.5p	–0.4p
Earnings per share before exceptional costs of sales and loss/profit on sale of properties and disposal of a subsidiary	**26.6p**	23.4p
Fully diluted earnings per share	**25.7p**	21.8p
Fully diluted earnings per share before exceptional costs of sales and loss/profit on sales of properties and disposal of a subsidiary	**26.2p**	23.1p

Figure **9.2** Profit and loss account for J. Sainsbury Group, 1998

Group balance sheet

for the 52 weeks to 7 March 1998

	Group	
	1998 **£m**	1997 £m
Fixed assets		
Tangible assets	**6,133**	5,893
Investments	**151**	148
	6,284	6,041
Current assets		
Stocks	**743**	744
Debtors	**229**	236
Investments	**14**	7
Sainsbury's Bank	**1,584**	17
	2,840	1,245
Creditors: due within one year		
Sainsbury's Bank	**–1,502**	–7
Other	**–2499**	–2,797
	–4,001	–2,804
Net current liabilities	**–1,161**	–1,559
Total assets less current liabilities	**5,123**	4,482
Creditors: due after one year		
Convertible Capital Bonds	**–**	–156
Other	**–949**	–595
Provisions for liabilities and charges	**–24**	–55
Total net assets	**4,150**	3,676
Capital and reserves		
Called up share captital	**476**	460
Share premium account	**1,295**	1,097
Revaluation reserve	**38**	33
Profit and loss account	**2,303**	2,081
Equity shareholders' funds	**4,112**	3,671
Minority equity interests	**38**	5
Total capital employed	**4,150**	3,676

Figure **9.3** Balance sheet for J. Sainsbury Group, 1998

The **balance sheet** represents the summary of a firm's financial position at a fixed point in time. The balance sheet is a statement of a firm's assets and liabilities at the end of the last day of the accounting period. A balance sheet will differentiate between **fixed assets**, such as land, buildings and machinery, and **current assets**, such as cash and stock. Assets can also include such intangible aspects such as goodwill.

KEY CONCEPT 9.10
Types of financial report

There are two main types of financial report. The **profit and loss account** is a statement of profit and loss in a defined accounting period. The report presents a summary of revenues and shows the expenses incurred in earning the revenues. The difference between the two is the profit or loss. The **balance sheet** is a statement of assets and liabilities at the close of business on the last day of the accounting year. In addition to these two reports, some firms prepare a **statement of cash flows**, which is a measure of the solvency of an enterprise.

A third form of statement is produced by some companies. This is the **cash-flow statement**. This details the movement of cash during an accounting period and is very useful for planning and control purposes. The cash-flow statement has replaced the statement of source and application of funds. While the profit and loss account and the balance sheet are measures of the profitability of a firm, the balance sheet is a measure of its solvency.

The form and content of such statements in the UK are determined partly by law and partly by requirements of professional bodies and other interested parties, such as the government and the Bank of England. The legal framework for financial statements was drawn up in various Companies Acts 1948–85, with the 1985 Companies Act providing the current requirements. A further set of regulations was provided by the Accounting Standards Committee (ASC), made up of representatives from the various accounting professions, which issued Statements of Standard Accounting Practice (SSAPs). Criticisms of the SSAPs from both the professions and managers led to a rethink and from 1990, the SSAPs are being gradually replaced by Financial Reporting Standards (FRS), which were the recommendations of the Dearing Report. Fifteen such FRSs have been issued to 1999. The Dearing Report also set up a new structure as outlined in Figure 9.4.

The Financial Reporting Council is appointed by the government and the Bank of England. The Financial Reporting Review Panel examines those statements that are in potential breach of the requirements of the 1985 Companies Act, specifically those that may contravene the requirement for a 'true and fair view'. As well as issuing the Financial Reporting Standards, the Accounting Standards Board has also established an 'urgent issues task force' to make recommendations, which reflect the highly dynamic state of modern global business.

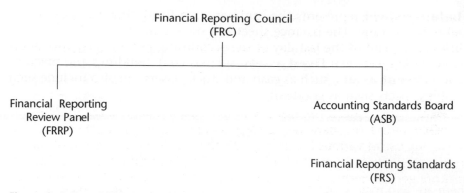

Figure **9.4** Post-1990 structure governing financial reporting established by Dearing.

The legislation, the SSAPs and the FRSs combine to form Generally Accepted Accounting Practice (GAAP). There is a UK GAAP and a US GAAP, which are sets of practically based accounting rules. There are of course significant differences between the UK and the US regulations, although some companies, notably Shell and BT, report under both systems. There is a divergence of accounting practices across the world. For example, whereas the UK and USA operate to more practically based rules such as FRSs in the case of the UK, Germany and France are more strictly controlled by legislation. Such divergence has led to the creation of a supranational body, the International Accounting Standards Committee, which has a goal of harmonization.

The various financial reports are particularly useful to management in the planning, organizing and controlling of resources. It is not only management who are interested in the financial information of individual businesses; the following also have need of such information:

● The **state** requires public companies to be accountable and present their accounting information in a standardized form according to the requirements of the various Companies Acts 1948–85. All public companies must present to Companies House a balance sheet, a profit and loss account, a directors' report, an auditor's report and notes on the accounts where necessary. As we shall see later, there is some relaxation of these requirements for smaller businesses, but only relating to the extent of information provided. However, these relaxations have had little real impact since small firms must still produce detailed information for the tax authorities and usually banks. As well as stipulating the various accounts to be presented the law also determines what must be disclosed. The broad content of a balance sheet and a profit and loss account is presented in Figures 9.2 and 9.3 respectively. Apart from the law, the state in the UK now plays a more interventionist role in the development of Financial Reporting Standards through the involvement of the government and the Bank of England. The state also requires financial information to levy appropriate taxes on businesses. The nature of the tax laws certainly affects how firms report, and most use reporting conventions that minimize their liability for tax. The accounting information provided by firms under the requirements of the Companies Acts and tax law is used by the state for the purposes of economic planning and forecasting.

- **Investors** need the information to make informed judgements about future investments, as well as needing to protect their existing investments. The accountability of public companies to their investors was the major factor in the development of rules governing disclosure.
- **Employees** may need the information, especially if they are involved in a profit-sharing or share ownership scheme. There is evidence of the increasing use of various forms of profit sharing. Published accounts are of course particularly useful to trade unions in planning wage negotiations. In more general terms, a company concerned to involve its employees in the running of the enterprise may see the disclosure of financial information as an important element of the participation process.
- **Creditors** such as banks and suppliers are naturally concerned with the firm's liquidity and need to assess the risk involved in offering credit and of course to safeguard against fraud.
- **Competitors** usually find the financial information particularly useful as a yardstick against which their own performance may be measured, and may derive useful insights into what other firms are doing.
- **Customers** will use the information to ascertain the risk of placing expensive or long-term contracts and perhaps to assess the fairness of a company's pricing policy.

The major issue in financial reporting is the extent of disclosure. The wide availability of the accounts of public companies certainly influences their content and the way information is presented. Managements have a fair amount of discretion since much of the content of accounts is subject to interpretation, such as allowances for depreciation and the valuation of assets. As a result, firms are often accused of manipulating their financial information to minimize tax liability or to present a strong position to shareholders. In addition firms are also conscious that financial information will be available to competitors and may wish to hide certain facts from them. We have already seen in our discussion of management accounting that financial information can be presented in such a way as to legitimize certain courses of action in preference to others. All this reinforces the notion that accounting is a behavioural and political rather than a technical exercise. Clarke *et al.* (1999) go further in an Australian study of the corporate collapse of certain Australian firms, such as the Bond Corporation, the Adelaide Steamship Company and the Parry Corporation. They show how accounts for such companies were not only produced under existing regulations, but were subject to the legal requirements of external audit. Despite this the firms concerned managed to keep hidden their real financial positions and eventually collapsed. Similar cases can be found in the UK, notably Polly Peck, BCCI and Maxwell Communications. Cases like these have focused attention of both the professions and academics on both the content and format of financial reports and the role of the auditor.

The environmental aspects of finance and accounting

In the last section we saw that financial reporting was greatly influenced by state regulations concerning the disclosure of information for public account-ability and for reasons of collecting taxes. In this section we focus on two fur-ther environmental influences on the accounting and finance function: the economy and cultural differences.

In keeping with our Business in Context model, influences are two-way. The finance and accounting practices of firms have an impact upon the envi-ronment in which they operate. Economic resources in society are often allo-cated on the basis of accounting information. We have noted elsewhere in this book the growing tendency for firms to engage in the buying and selling of other companies. Financial information is vital to this activity. The closure of the Cortonwood colliery in South Yorkshire was based on accounting infor-mation provided for the management of the National Coal Board. The impact of such closures on the local community is considerable. The impact in this case precipitated a bitter coal-mining strike, which lasted over a year. (A dis-cussion of the kind of accounting procedures which resulted in the closure of Cortonwood can be found in Berry *et al.*, 1985. We return to this case at the end of the chapter.)

The role of the economy

In general, accounting practices will vary according to the nature of the econ-omy in which they operate. For example, in many Third World countries there is little need for sophisticated accounting techniques and systems of basic cash accounting predominate. The raising of finance that we discussed in the previous section is a function of the state of the market and the way this influences profit levels, share prices and bank interest rates. Two specific economic features have held particular interest for accountants: inflation and currency exchange.

The relatively high rates of inflation experienced by the British economy in the 1970s led accountants to rethink the basis for their calculations, made popular the concept of inflation accounting and resulted in a government report (The Sandilands Committee on Inflation Accounting). A major prob-lem in times of high inflation is that profits can be overstated by basing costs on historic data made largely irrelevant by inflation. In such situations sys-tems of adjusting balance sheets to account for fluctuating prices were devel-oped. While these have less relevance today, inflation accounting techniques are widely used in such countries as Brazil.

Like inflation, fluctuations in currency exchange rates make historic cost accounting difficult. The effect is particularly significant for those firms reliant on export markets, as with Swiss firms Nestlé and Ciba Geigy with over 90 per cent of their business outside Switzerland.

Cultural differences

Two main issues are discussed here. We look first at differences in financial systems and then at variations in financial reporting.

There are some fundamental differences between major countries in the way businesses are financed. Prevezer (1994) has looked at comparisons between the UK, Germany and Japan and Owen (1996) has focused on differences between the UK and Germany. What follows in the first part of this section is largely a summary of their work.

In the UK shareholders play a key role. Seventy-five per cent of all shares are owned by institutional shareholders, who tend to possess diversified share portfolios and have little if any connection with the firm. The share market in the UK is highly volatile with a much higher proportion of shares being traded than in any other country. As a result of such share trading activity, the UK experiences a higher proportion of takeovers, many of them hostile. Banks own shares in UK companies but tend to operate like other institutional shareholders. Under such a system, the primary objective of institutional investors is to make money for their own shareholders. They therefore have a preference for selling shares when events are not going to their liking, rather than attempting to influence policy. In response, managers tend to be very aware of the need to maintain share price and to keep such investors happy with high rates of dividend. Indeed, the average amounts of dividend paid by UK companies is 1.5 to 2 times higher than in the USA, 2.5 to 3 times higher than in Germany and 3 to 4 times higher than in Japan.

In Germany the ownership patterns are much more stable. There are fewer stock market quoted firms. Those with shareholders tend to be dominated by one or two major shareholders owning around 25 per cent of the company and having a seat on the Supervisory Board. Takeovers are strictly controlled by law and hostile takeovers are very rare. Banks tend to have a much closer relationship with firms and bank representatives regularly take a place on the board. Employees in Germany also play a role as board members, enshrined in the laws relating to co-determination.

In Japan as in the UK 75 per cent of shares are owned by institutions. However, unlike the UK, the trading of such shares occurs very little. Most of the share trading is amongst those householders owning shares. This is a complete reversal of the situation in the UK. The institutional shareholders have a close relationship with the firms and takeovers are rare. Banks play a major role and, in some cases, are members of large corporate groupings or have a substantial ownership interest in companies. In manufacturing, suppliers also play a major role in that they are often part-owned by the major firms they supply. The Japanese system is one where there is a very close relationship between firms, banks and suppliers.

Such differences as those existing between the UK, Germany and Japan have led many to hold the UK financial system as being responsible for the spread of short-termism, lack of investment and long-term strategy and hence the comparative industrial decline of the UK. While Owen (1996) agrees in part with such an analysis he raises a number of questions. He argues that in the period 1950–80 the UK was indeed outperformed by Germany, but it was also outperformed by France and Italy. All three countries possessed different financial systems, thereby making links between industrial performance and specific financial systems difficult. He further argues that if long-termism was such an advantage to Germany then it would show up most in those industries where long-term investment would be an advantage. He examines pharmaceuticals and electronics. In the former, both the UK and Germany have performed well, whereas in the latter, both lag some way behind the Japanese. He suggests there are other more significant factors at work in these cases. While he acknowledges that the instability of the UK system creates damaging takeovers, citing the British Motor Corporation and its merger with Leyland, he believes it gives the UK economy a certain flexibility and dynamism. Nonetheless there are advantages associated with the more stable patterns of ownership and control of German firms. However, by the end of the 1990s there are signs that the systems of Britain and Germany are slowly moving towards one another.

Many differences can be observed in the accounting practices of different countries. These differences reflect a variety of factors such as the nature of the legal system, the pattern of ownership and control, the system of taxation, the strength of the accountancy profession, and the general social climate. We have already noted such variations in our section on financial reporting.

In France and Germany, financial reporting systems are highly prescribed by law, yet there tends to be less emphasis on financial reporting in France largely because of the dominance of family ownership, and hence the private nature of many companies. In the UK and the USA reporting requirements are less prescriptive but the information needs of shareholders are much greater, especially in the USA where share ownership is more diffuse. Patterns of ownership are themselves related to the influence of the accounting profession. Public ownership requires accountability and hence accountants play a major role in the auditing of company accounts. Much less auditing is required in France, which may account for their relatively low numbers of accountants. In general, a social climate that encourages openness, social responsibility and consumerism, as in the USA, results in significantly different patterns in the disclosure of financial information than those found in a much more closed society such as Switzerland.

There has been considerable pressure for the standardization of accounting practices across countries. This is one of the tasks of the International Accounting Standards Committee. Some harmonization has taken place within the EU and this was reflected by certain changes in the financial reporting requirements of British firms. The pressure for standardization comes from a variety of quarters. Financial reports prepared in one country are used by financial analysts and investors in another as part of the growing internationalization of capital. In manufacturing, global operations and sourcing of components have hastened the need for internationally usable financial information. Standardization would greatly assist multinational companies to consolidate their accounts, assess potential acquisitions more effectively and even enable them to transfer accounting staff from one country to another more easily. This is just part of the vast changes that have accompanied the globalization of the economy. It should not be forgotten that many of the major accounting firms operate multinationally too and harmonization would greatly assist their operations.

The organizational aspects of finance and accounting

The nature of any organization impinges significantly upon accounting procedures. This is inevitably shown when changes occur in ownership or in the goals of the enterprise, bringing about changes in the organizational culture. For example, the takeover of one firm by another may well result in the consolidation of accounts and perhaps a change in the accounting practices. The privatization of a number of companies in Britain since the 1980s has changed the nature of many of those organizations from a service centre to a profit centre with a corresponding impact upon accounting practices. In the public sector, significant changes are taking place as well. In Case 4.3 we presented the changes that were occurring in the new universities as a result of incorporation in 1989. One major change has been the withdrawal of local authority accounting controls and the subsequent elevation of the management accounting function within universities themselves. Another change affecting all public sector organizations has been the greater emphasis placed on income generation beyond that normally provided. This places an extra burden upon public bodies but may also give them greater flexibility to pursue their own goals. We may conclude that the nature of the accounting practices is a function of the goals of the organization.

For the remainder of this section we focus on two organizational issues; the accounting implications of the size of the firm, and the influence of structure on accounting procedures. The two issues are linked as we shall see when we examine the problems of cost allocation and transfer pricing in large multidivisional firms.

The accounting requirements of large and small firms

Differences in the size of businesses affects their ability to raise capital, the complexity of their accounting procedures and controls, and the extent of their financial reporting. Differences are therefore to be found in all the three functions of finance and accounting that we identified in Figure 9.1.

Larger firms, not suprisingly, have much more complex accounting procedures and generally employ a number of professional accountants in a specialized functional department. In smaller firms the accounting function is often external to the firm with a subsequent reliance on the advice of an outsider, who may not have the detailed knowledge of an internal management accountant. Larger firms may have the problems of satisfying large numbers of shareholders, but their very size often gives them an advantage in raising funds from external sources. In any event, large and complex organizations can often finance themselves internally through their ability to switch funds from one unit to another. Small firms have much more problems raising finance and tend to be more concerned with the management of cash flows.

As with the proposals to harmonize accounting procedures between nation states, there is a lobby to standardize practices across all types of firms irrespective of their size. However, the cost of preparing complex financial statements can be daunting for a small business and the benefits of such information much less than for larger firms. Paradoxically in the light of its general views on harmonization, the EU champions different accounting practices for large and small firms. This was reflected in Britain in the 1981 Companies Act which removed the requirement of smaller firms to produce profit and loss accounts and directors' reports and introduced less onerous requirements for balance sheet information. In reality, however, this does not appear to meet the information needs of banks on which small companies are so heavily dependent for finance. To satisfy their lending requirements, banks are insisting on stringent financial control mechanisms in small firms and much more detailed financial reporting than is required by law (Berry *et al.*, 1987). As a result, the pressure for standardization may well come from the banking community.

Organization structure, cost allocation and transfer pricing

We have already seen how organization structure and accounting procedures tend to reinforce one another, in that a large organization may delegate responsibility and control costs through the creation of individual budget centres. In very large organizations, the structure generally matches the finance and accounting responsibilities of the firm. A centralized headquarters will act as an investment centre determining new initiatives, as well as allocating profit targets for each division. In turn the divisions will determine targets for each operating unit and designate each one as a cost centre in control of a budget. There are occasions when mismatches can occur, as in the case of a department manager who has no effective budget, and hence limited powers of operation.

The operation of budgetary control can produce a more efficient and effective management control system. It also carries the potential problem of encouraging functional insularity to the detriment of the firm as a whole. Units can become so preoccupied with achieving their own targets and keeping within their own budgets that they may refuse calls for assistance from other units through the fear that this will erode their own performance levels. In some manufacturing firms this has resulted in a total lack of continuity between departments and between production shifts. This has led some firms to examine team-building techniques developed by social psychologists to enhance greater cooperation.

Such problems increase with the size of the firm and with the necessity for funds to flow across many different units of the same organization. The problems come to a head in large multi-divisional firms where each unit operates as a profit centre and is accountable to top management for the achievement of predetermined profit targets. We examine two aspects of this problem: cost allocation and transfer pricing.

The problems of **cost allocation** occur when central services such as headquarters administration, research and development, and perhaps maintenance must be paid for by those units in the organization with the responsibility for generating income and profit. A decision needs to be made on the basis of the apportionment of such costs (see the reference to absorption costing in the section on management accounting). Some firms vary cost allocation according to the size of the profit centre, as a proportion of their costs, or the extent to which use is made of the central services. The final criteria is often difficult to measure accurately, but any method is open to challenge by those managers who see their profits eroded by costs which lie outside their control. Some managers are resentful that their efforts are diluted by sections of the firm that do not generate income but merely incur costs. In some cases this has resulted in the marginality of service departments such as HRM and R&D. Once again accounting becomes the focus for political debate at the level of the firm. While accounting is itself a largely advisory function, the importance to decision-making of financial information, which is largely controlled by accountants, often enables the accountant in the organization to wield considerable power and influence.

Transfer pricing is the process through which goods and services produced in one section of the organization are sold internally for use by another. The need for transfer pricing mechanisms is a function of the development of the multi-divisional firm and associated profit centres. An effectively operated transfer pricing mechanism can contribute to the optimum allocation of a firm's resources and to the motivation of division managers towards efficient operation and hence to the overall prosperity of the organization.

Such mechanisms occur wherever there is a need in one unit of the organization for the services of another. A form of transfer pricing occurs in higher education as the following illustration reveals. Universities and other colleges tend to be organized around specialist subject departments. A department that offers a business studies course may have the need for specialist law inputs which reside outside that department. In many colleges a transfer pricing system has been devised whereby those departments servicing another are allocated points based on the number of hours and students they service. These points with those generated from their own departments form the basis for staffing allocations. A major problem with such a mechanism is that it may encourage departments only to service those areas where they can ensure high rates of return.

This is a similar problem to the one we outlined when we discussed organization structure in Chapter 3. A foundry operating as a profit centre in a manufacturing firm may find that the pressure to meet targets conflicts with the demands placed upon it for goods from other units in the same organization. Management may be faced with the dilemma of having to meet internal demand when higher returns may be obtained through meeting the requirements of customers external to the firm. The issue of transfer pricing is particularly pertinent to the operation of global firms and it is to this aspect we now turn.

Transfer pricing and the global firm

A great deal of transfer pricing activity occurs between member organizations of large multinational corporations. Such activity has increased dramatically in recent years with developments in the global economy. While this can cause the kind of organizational political problems outlined above, there are three main reasons for the extensiveness of such activity. These relate to issues of taxation, competition and issues relating to the need of the multinational to protect itself against social, economic and political changes occurring in the host country. These issues should be viewed in conjunction with the discussion on globalization and multinationals in Chapter 2.

- **Tax reasons**. Through its activities worldwide, a multinational company can move profits from high to low tax areas using the transfer pricing mechanism. Firms operating in high tax areas are charged inflated prices for goods and services produced in low tax areas. While this represents only a paper exchange of funds within the same organization it can result in some firms showing a much greater profit than others. In normal circumstances pressure is brought to bear on poorly performing profit centres. Such problems may be avoided by the use of dual reporting systems, one for external consumption and the other for internal use only.
- **Competition reasons.** Some multinationals subsidize member firms through the transfer price mechanism. In order that a new company may develop itself in an established market the other firms could supply goods and services at low prices, buying back the finished products at a high price.
- **Protection against change**. A multinational will wish to protect itself against those economic and political changes that threaten its prosperity and ultimate existence. Problems caused by high inflation, currency exchange and devaluation in a particular country can be tackled by charging high prices for goods supplied to the subsidiary in that country, and buying goods back at low prices. By operating in this way the multinational keeps finance in the family and prevents it being siphoned off by individual nation states.

In Chapter 1 we introduced the case of News International, now part of News Corporation, a global company controlled by Rupert Murdoch. The company makes very good use of its global presence by accessing the various advantages accorded by the tax laws and accounting regulations in the many countries in which it operates. Indeed the attractiveness of some of those countries is their status as a tax haven. News Corporation has a highly complex financial structure with a large number of subsidiary companies. In 1996, 49 of those subsidiaries were registered in the British Virgin Islands where corporation tax is 1 per cent per annum and 29 were in the Cayman Islands under a similar tax regime. As a general rule the company will pay loans in countries with high levels of corporation tax and collect profits in countries where tax levels are low. As a result News Corporation in 1995 declared profits of £793 million, yet paid less than 10 per cent in taxes, when the usual rate for a UK,

US or Australian company is between 20 and 40 per cent. News Corporation also makes large capital investments and is renowned for setting up new businesses. This it does with maximum tax benefit, particularly where it can obtain tax relief in high tax countries. All this has been achieved within the laws and accounting regulations of the various countries within which News Corporation operates.

Some multinationals do come into direct conflict with the governments of those countries in which they operate. Such a conflict was between the Swiss pharmaceutical firm Roche and the UK Monopolies and Mergers Committee in 1971. The company stood accused of operating an unfair monopoly on its tranquilizer products, Librium and Valium, and thus making excessive profits. The UK representatives were unable to present a fully detailed case, since, as a company operating under Swiss law, there was certain financial information it did not have to disclose.

Strategic aspects of finance and accounting

The three functions of finance and accounting represent strategies of financing and controlling operations, of distributing resources and power through budget allocation, and of information disclosure. Additionally, financial tools and information are invariably used in the making of strategic decisions in other functional areas, such as the decision to invest in new products or equipment, or to take on extra staff. Financial analyses form the basis of most acquisition attempts.

We can therefore see that the finance and accounting function assists management decision-making on a number of key issues that are central to the viability of the firm. These issues include the sources of funds, investment decisions, acceptable levels of debt, the minimization of tax liability and the extent of the pay-out to shareholders.

As with all the functional areas we have discussed in this book there is a growing recognition that the strategies associated with the different activities are linked in some kind of synergistic way. In manufacturing industry evidence is emerging that cost and quality are not necessarily trade-offs but essential ingredients of the same strategy. A greater attention focused on improving product quality can also be successful in lowering costs. This can become a virtuous circle in that extra funds are released for further investment in quality improvement.

Throughout this chapter we have been careful to point out the inexact nature of accounting methods. We can summarize the various limitations on the use of accounting information in strategy formulation:

● Because of the problems of measuring many aspects of business activities, accounting information can be highly subjective.
● Financial statements are summaries. Information is therefore selected and interpreted according to the needs of the compiler and user of financial statements.
● As a result of the above, financial information is often used deliberately to

achieve political ends such as the justification of an investment decision or a pay offer.

- There is an added danger in all this in that many assume the data to be scientific and objective, and use it accordingly.
- Because of the bias in accounting to what can effectively be measured, management may place undue emphasis on short-term results and neglect the longer-term implications of strategic decisions, or base too many decisions on historic data which is made redundant by changing circumstances.

A good illustration of the interpretative problems associated with accounting information is offered by the NCB decision to close Cortonwood Colliery as part of its rationalization strategy. A Monopoly and Mergers Commission Report calculated the revenue of the colliery at £44.3 per tonne, while its costs were calculated at £50.5 per tonne. On these figures the mine was clearly unprofitable and losing the Coal Board in excess of £1.7 million a year. A study of the accounting methods used by the NCB questioned the basis for many of the costs used, but more significantly suggested that many of the costs such as surface damage and essential services would not be avoided by closing the colliery. If these unavoidable costs are eliminated from the equation as constants, then Cortonwood could be shown to be making a net contribution of £5.45 per tonne of coal mined (Berry *et al.*, 1985).

Summary

The finance and accounting function in business comprises financial management, management accounting, and financial reporting.

Financial management is concerned with the funding of the business and ensuring such funds can be met by the organization. The major sources of finance are share capital, various forms of loan capital, state finance and internally generated funds, usually through the reinvestment of profit. It is this last source that would appear to be most significant for firms in Britain.

Management accounting is concerned with assisting management in planning and control. It involves the preparation and control of budgets, the analysis and allocation of costs, the appraisal of capital investments, the management of cash flows and general contribution to strategic decision-making.

Financial reporting involves the preparation of financial statements such as the balance sheet, profit and loss account and cash flow statements. Financial reporting must conform to a legal and regulatory framework and must take account of the needs of the various groups who are to use this information. Major issues are whether the accounts represent a true and fair picture and the extent of disclosure.

The finance and accounting function is greatly influenced by the environment in which it operates. Financial reporting is subject to strict state controls and accounting practices have developed to cope with economic changes such as inflation and fluctuations in the value of currency. Despite pressures to harmonize accounting practices there are considerable differences between countries, reflecting a number of cultural influences.

Accounting practices vary also with the size of the organization, with large and small companies having their own special problems. As organizations increase in size and develop appropriate structures, decisions will have to be made on the allocation of costs and transfer pricing. The latter becomes a particularly useful mechanism in the hands of the multinational corporation.

Accounting information forms the basis for most strategic decisions within the organization. Its value should be placed alongside a number of limitations, not least of which are the subjective nature of accounts and the role played by accounting information to justify organizational political decisions.

Further reading

A good start is the companion volume in this series, A. Berry and R. Jarvis, *Accounting in a Business Context*, 3rd. edn (International Thomson, 1997). As well as covering the fundamentals of finance and accounting it offers a discussion on the key organizational and environmental influences. Two other basic texts are useful. These are J. R. Dyson, *Accounting for Non-Accounting Students*, 4th edn (Financial Times Management, 1997) and R. Dodge, *Foundations of Business Accounting*, 2nd edn (International Thomson, 1997). An excellent guide to financial reporting and the interpretation of company reports and accounts is G. Holmes and A. Sugden, *Interpreting Company Reports and Accounts*, 7th edn (Pearson Education, 1999). A series of useful discussions on mangement accounting and related issues can be found in C. Emmanuel and D. Otley, *Readings in Accounting for Management Control* (International Thomson, 1995).

Discussion

1. What is the value of the professional accountant to business? Why do professional accountants proliferate in the UK?
2. Why is the internal funding of business so popular in the UK?
3. What would be the most appropriate methods the following organizations could use to raise revenue to fund new activities: a very small firm just making a mark in the office supplies market; a university; a multinational car manufacturer?
4. What specific contributions can the management accountant make to strategic decision-making? What limitations can be placed on the value of this contribution?
5. Identify the different needs of the users of accounting information. Can current methods of financial reporting hope to satisfy them all?
6. What are the specific finance and accounting problems and priorities for small as opposed to large companies?
7. What are the advantages and disadvantages to various interested parties associated with cost allocation and transfer pricing activities in global firms?

8. Identify the behavioural and political nature of management accounting. What problems does this cause and how might they be minimized?
9. What changes do you predict for finance and accounting as a result of developments in IT and the Internet?

References

Aaker, D. A. (1996) *Building Strong Brands*, Free Press, New York.

Abernathy, W. J. and Utterback, J. M. (1978) Patterns of industrial innovation, in R. R. Rothberg (ed.), *Corporate Strategy and Product Innovation*, 2nd edn., Free Press, New York.

Adam, G. (1975) Multinational corporations and world-wide sourcing, in H. Radice (ed.), *International Firms and Modern Imperialism*, Penguin, Harmondsworth.

Adcroft, A., Cutler, T., Haslam, C., Williams, K. and Williams, J. (1991) Hanson and ICI: the consequences of financial engineering, *University of East London, Occasional Papers in Business, Economy and Society*, No. 2.

Aiello, P. (1991) Building a joint venture in China: the case of Chrysler and the Beijing Jeep Corporation, *Journal of General Management*, **17**, 2, pp. 47–64.

Ansoff, H. I. (1968) *Corporate Strategy*, Penguin, Harmondsworth.

Ansoff, H. I. and Stewart, J. M. (1967) Strategies for a technology-based business, *Harvard Business Review*, **45**, Nov.–Dec., pp. 71–83.

Armstrong, P., Glyn, A. and Harrison, J. (1991) *Capitalism Since 1945*, Basil Blackwell, Oxford.

Atkinson, J. (1984) Manpower strategies for flexible organizations, *Personnel Management*, Aug., pp. 28–31.

Baden-Fuller, C. and Pitt, M. (1996) *Strategic Innovation*, Routledge, London.

Baker, M. J. (1991) *Marketing*, 5th edn, Macmillan, London.

Bannock, G. (1981) *The Economics of Small Firms: Return from the Wilderness*, Basil Blackwell, Oxford.

Barrell, R. and Pain, N. (1997) *The Growth of Foreign Direct Investment in Europe*, NIESR, London.

Barry, J., Chandler, J., Clark, H., Johnston, R. and Needle, D. (2000) *Organization and Management: A Critical Text*, International Thomson Business Press, London.

Bart, C. K. and Baetz, M. C. (1999) The relationship between mission statements and firm performance: an exploratory study, *Journal of Management Studies*, **35**, 6, pp. 823–53.

Bartlett, C. A. and Ghoshal, S. (1995) *Transnational Management: Texts, Cases and Readings in Cross-border Management*, 2nd edn, Irwin, Chicago, Ill.

Bassett, P. (1986) *Strike Free*, Macmillan, London.

Beardwell, I. (1997) Human resource management and Japan, in I. Beardwell and L. Holden (eds), *Human Resource Management: A Contemporary Perspective*, 2nd edn, Pitman Publishing, London.

Beardwell, I. and Holden, L. (eds). (1997) *Human Resource Management: A Contemporary Perspective*, 2nd edn, Pitman Publishing, London.

Beasley, J. E. (1985) Strategies for corporate and business success – a survey, *OMEGA*, **13**, 1, pp. 51–8.

Beatson, M. (1995) *Labour Market Flexibility*, Employment Department Research Series No. 44, DfEE, Sheffield.

Beer, M., Spector, B., Lawrence, P., Quinn Mills, D. and Walton, R.E. (1984) *Managing Human Assets*, Free Press, New York.

Beer, M., Spector, B., Lawrence, P., Quinn Mills, D. and Walton, R.E. (1985) *Human Resource Management, The General Managers Perspective: Text and Cases*, Free Press, New York.

Bell, D. (1973) *The Coming of the Post-industrial Society*, Basic Books, New York.

Berle, A. A. (1954) *The Twentieth Century Capitalist Revolution*, Harcourt Brace, New York.

Berle, A. A. and Means, G. C. (1932) *The Modern Corporation and Private Property*, Macmillan, New York.

Berry, A. and Jarvis, R. (1997) *Accounting in a Business Context*, 3rd edn, International Thomson Business Press, London.

Berry, A., Citron, D. and Jarvis, R. (1987) *The Information Needs of Bankers Dealing with Large and Small Companies: with Particular Reference to Proposed Changes in Legislation*, Certified Research Report 7, Certified Accountant Publications, London.

Berry, T., Capps, T., Cooper, D., Hooper, T. and Lowe, T. (1985) NCB accounts – a mine of misinformation, *Accountancy*, Jan., pp.10–12.

Bhaskar, K. (1980) *The Future of the World Motor Industry*, Kogan Page, London.

Binks, M. and Jennings, A. (1986) New firms as a source of industrial re-generation, in M. Scott (ed.), *Small Firms Growth and Development*, Gower, Aldershot.

Bird, D., Beatson, M. and Butcher, S. (1993) Membership of trade unions, *Employment Gazette*, May, pp. 189–96.

Blauner, R. (1964) *Alienation and Freedom*, University of Chicago Press, Chicago.

Bloomfield, B. P., Coombs, R., Knights, D. and Littler, D. (1997) *Information Technology and Organizations: Strategies, Networks and Integration*, Oxford University Press, Oxford.

Bolton, J. (1971) *Small Firms: the Report of the Committee of Inquiry into Small Firms*, HMSO, Cmd. 4811, London.

Bowen, A., Buxton, T. and Ricketts, M. (1992) The economics of innovation: setting the scene, in A. Bowen and M. Ricketts (eds), *Stimulating Innovation in Industry: The Challenge for the United Kingdom*, Kogan Page/NEDO, London.

Bowen, D. (1992) Bigger is better in Britain's battered industry, *Independent on Sunday*, 26th July.

Bradley, K. and Hill, S. (1983) After Japan: the Quality Circle transplant and productive efficiency, *British Journal of Industrial Relations*, **21**, 3, pp. 291–311.

Braverman, H. (1974) *Labor and Monopoly Capital*, Monthly Review Press, New York.

Brewster, C. and Bournois, F. (1991) Human resource management: a European perspective, *Personnel Review*, **20**, 6, pp 4–13.

Brewster, C., Hegewisch, A. and Lockhart, J.T. (1991) Researching human resource management: methodology of the Price Waterhouse Cranfield Project on European Trends, *Personnel Review*, **20**, 6, pp 36–40.

Bright, G., Colvin, M., Loveridge, J., Page, R. and Thompson, C. (1983) *Moving Forward: Small Businesses and the Economy*, Conservative Political Centre, London.

Brittan, S. (1983) The myth of the Kondratieff, *Financial Times*, 7 April.

Brossard, M. and Maurice, M. (1976) Is there a universal model of organizational structure?, *International Studies of Management and Organization*, **6**, pp. 11–45.

Brouthers, K. D., Brouthers, L. E. and Harris, P. C. (1997) The five stages of the co-operative venture strategy process, *Journal of General Management*, **23**, 1, pp. 39–52.

Brown, A. (1998) *Organizational Culture*, 2nd edn, Financial Times Pitman, London.

Bruce, M. (1987) Managing people first – bringing the service concept into British Airways, *Independent and Commercial Training*, March–April.

Buchan, J. (1993) Withdrawal symptoms, *Independent on Sunday Review*, 23 April, pp. 2–5.

Burnham, J. (1941) *The Managerial Revolution*, Day, New York.

Burns, T. and Stalker, G. M. (1966) *The Management of Innovation*, Tavistock, London.

Burrell, G. and Morgan, G. (1979) *Sociological Paradigms and Organizational Analysis*, Heinemann, London.

Burrows, G. (1986) *No-strike Agreements and Pendulum Arbitration*, Institute of Personnel Management, London.

Buzzell, R. D. (1964) Mathematical Models and Marketing Management, *Harvard University*, Boston, Mass.

Callon, S. (1995) *Divided Sun: MITI and the Breakdown of Japanese High-Tech Policy 1975–1993*, Stanford University Press, Stanford, Calif.

Cannon, T. (1986) *Basic Marketing*, 2nd edn, Holt Rinehart & Winston, Eastbourne.

Carr, A. Z. (1968) Is business bluffing ethical?, *Harvard Business Review*, **46**, Jan.–Feb., pp. 143–53.

Carroll, D.T. (1983) A disappointing search for excellence, *Harvard Business Review*, **63**, Nov.–Dec., pp. 78–88.

Casey, B. (1986) The dual apprenticeship system, *British Journal of Industrial Relations*, **14**, 1, pp. 63–82.

Cecchini, P. (1988) *The European Challenge 1992: The Benefits of a Single Market*, Wildwood House, Aldershot.

Chaharbaghi, K. and Newman, V. (1996) Innovating: towards an integrated learning model, *Management Decision*, **34**, 4.

Chandler, A. D. (1962) *Strategy and Structure: Chapters in the History of American Capitalism*, MIT Press, Cambridge, Mass.

Chandler, A. D. (1977) *The Visible Hand: the Managerial Revolution in American Business*, Harvard University Press, Cambridge, Mass.

Channon, D. F. (1973) *The Strategy and Structure of British Enterprise*, Macmillan, London.

Chase, R. and Hayes, R. H. (1991) Beefing up operations in service firms, *Sloan Management Review*, Fall, pp. 15–26.

Child, J. (1969) *The Business Enterprise in Modern Industrial Society*, Collier-Macmillan, London.

Child, J. (1972) Organizational structure, environment and performance: the role of strategic choice, *Sociology*, **6**, pp. 1–21.

Child, J. (1984) New technology and developments in management organization, *OMEGA*, **12**, 3, pp. 211–23.

Child, J. and Kieser, A. (1979) Organization and managerial roles in British and West German companies: an examination of the culture-free hypothesis, in C. J. Lammers and D. J. Hickson (eds), *Organizations Alike and Unlike*, Routledge and Kegan Paul, London.

Child, J., Fores, M., Glover, I. and Lawrence, P. (1983) A price to pay? Professionalism and work organization in Britain and West Germany, *Sociology*, 17, 1, pp. 63–77.

Chong Li Choy (1990) Business in the development of Singapore, in Chong Li Choy *et al.* (eds), *Business, Society and Development in Singapore*, Times Academic Press, Singapore.

Clarke, F. I., Dean, G. W. and Oliver, K.G. (1999) *Corporate Collapse: Regulatory Accounting and Ethical Failure*, Cambridge University Press, Cambridge.

Coleman, T. (1988) Travels with a Rover, *Guardian*, 13 Aug.

Collin, A. and Holden, L. (1997) The national framework for vocational education and training, in I. Beardwell and L. Holden (eds), *Human Resource Management: A Contemporary Perspective*, 2nd edn, Pitman Publishing, London.

Connon, H. (1992) Glaxo invests £1bn. Hot-house to foster discovery, *Independent*, 9 June.

Cooper, R. and Chew, W. B. (1996) Control tomorrow's costs through today's designs, *Harvard Business Review*, Jan.–Feb., pp. 88–97.

Crouch, C. J. (1978) The changing role of the state in industrial relations in Western Europe, in C. J. Crouch and A. Pizzorno (eds), *The Resurgence of Class Conflict in Western Europe Since 1968*, Vol. 1, Macmillan, London.

Cully, M., Woodland, S., O'Reilly, A., Dix, G., Millward, N., Bryson, A. and Forth, J. (1998) *The 1998 Workplace Employee Relations Survey: First Findings*, DTI, London.

Curran, J. (1986) *Bolton Fifteen Years On: A Review and Analysis of Small Business Research in Britain 1971–86*, Small Business Trust, London.

Cyert, R. M. and March, J. G. (1963) *A Behavioural Theory of the Firm*, Prentice Hall, Englewood Cliffs, NJ.

Czinkota, M. R. and Ronkainen, I. A. (1995) *International Marketing*, Dryden Press, New York.

Daft, R. L. (1982) Bureaucratic v non-bureaucratic structures and the process of innovation and change, in S. B. Bachovach (ed.), *Research in the Sociology of Organizations*, JAI Press, Greenwich.

Dale, B. G. (1994) *Managing Quality*, 2nd edn, Prentice Hall, London.

Daly, M. (1987) Lifespan of businesses registered for VAT, *British Business*, 3 April, pp. 28–9.

Daly, M. (1991) VAT registrations and de-registrations in 1990, *Employment Gazette*, Nov., pp. 579–88.

Damanpour, F., Szabat, K. A. and Evan, W. M. (1989) The relationship between types of innovation and organization performance, *Journal of Management Studies*, **26**, 6, pp. 587–601.

Daniel, W.W. (1987) *Workplace Industrial Relations and Technical Change*, Policy Studies Institute, London.

Daniel, W.W., and Millward, N. (1983) *Workplace Industrial Relations in Britain*, Heineman, London.

Daniels, C. (1991) *The Management Challenge of Information Technology*, Economist Intelligence Unit and Business International, London.

Datta, D. K. (1988) International joint ventures: a framework for analysis, *Journal of General Management*, **14**, 2, pp. 78–91.

Davis, C. (1999) Smoother operators, *People Management*, **5**, 9, pp. 56–7.

Davis, S. M. and Lawrence, P.R. (eds) (1977) *Matrix*, Addison-Wesley, Reading, Mass.

Davis, S. M., Aquilano, N. and Chase, R. (1998) *Fundamentals of Operations Management*, 3rd edn, McGraw-Hill, London.

Dawson, S. (1986) *Analysing Organizations,* Macmillan, London.

De Wit, B. and Meyer, R. (1998) *Strategy: Process, Content, Context: An International Perspective*, International Thomson Business Press, London.

Deal, T.E. and Kennedy, A.A., (1982) *Corporate Cultures*, Penguin, Harmondsworth.

Deming, W. E. (1986) *Out of Crisis: Quality, Productivity and Competitive Position*, Cambridge University Press, Cambridge.

Dhalla, N. K. (1978) Assessing the long-term value of advertising, *Harvard Business Review*, Jan.–Feb., pp. 87–95.

Dibb, S., Simpkin, L., Pride, W. M. and Ferrell, O. C. (1997) *Marketing: Concepts and Strategies*, 3rd European edn, Houghton Miflin, Boston, Ma.

Dore, R. (1973) *British Factory – Japanese Factory*, University of Berkeley Press, Berkeley, Calif.

Dore, R. (1997) Good jobs, no jobs and bad jobs, *Industrial relations Journal*, **28**, 4, pp. 262–8.

Drucker, P. E. (1964) *Managing for Results*, Harper & Row, New York.

Drucker, P. E. (1968) *The Practice of Management*, Pan Books, London.

Drucker, P. E. (1985) *Innovation and Entrpreneurship*, Heinemann, London.

Duke, O. (1994) The Triumph over adversity, *The Guardian*, 24 Dec.

Dyson, J. R. (1997) *Accounting for Non-Accounting Students*, 4th edn, Financial Times Management, London.

Earl, M. J. (1989) *Management Strategies for Information Technology*, Prentice Hall International, Hemel Hempstead.

Earl, P. E. (1984) *The Corporate Imagination: How Big Companies Make Mistakes*, Wheatsheaf Books, Brighton.

Economist Intelligence Unit (1999) *The World in 1999*, London.

Edwards, P., Hall, M., Hyman, R., Marginson, P., Sisson, K., Waddington, J. and Winchester, D. (1992) Great Britain: still muddling through, in A. Ferner and R. Hyman (eds), *Industrial Relations in the New Europe*, Basil Blackwell, Oxford.

Eilon, S. (1985) Recasting the die, *OMEGA*, **13**, 3, pp. 135–42.

Ekvall, G. (1991) The organizational culture of idea-management: a creative climate for the management of ideas, in J. Henry and D. Walker (eds), *Managing Innovation*, Sage/OU, London.

El-Namiki, M. (1993) *Contemporary Dynamics of Entrepreneurship*, Netherlands International Institute for Management, Netherlands.

Elger, T. and Smith, C. (1994) *Global Japanization? The Transnational Transformation of the Labour Process*, Routledge, London

Emmanuel, C. and Otley, D. (1995) *Readings in Accounting for Management Control*, International Thomson, London.

Emery, F. and Thorsrud, E. (1976) *Democracy at Work*, Nijhoff, Leiden, Netherlands.

Evans, H. (1983) *Good Times Bad Times*, Weidenfeld and Nicholson, London.

Fagan, M. (1991) Is it right that the scientists should take the decisions?, *Independent*, 10 June.

Feigenbaum, A. V. (1961) *Total Quality Control*, McGraw Hill, London.

Fenwick, P. and Murton, A. (2000), Human resource management and industrial relations, in J. Barry *et al.*, *Organization and Management: A Critical Text*, International Thomson Business Press, London.

Ferner, A. and Hyman, R. (1992a) Industrial relations on the Continent: a model of co-operation?, *Personnel Management*, Aug., **24**, 8, pp. 32–4.

Ferner, A. and Hyman, R. (1992b) *Industrial Relations in the New Europe*, Basil Blackwell, Oxford.

Feurer, R., Chaharbaghi, K. and Wargin, J. (1995) Analysis of strategy formulation and implementation at Hewlett-Packard, *Management Decision*, 33, 10, pp. 4–16.

Fites, D. V. (1996) Make your dealers your partners, *Harvard Business Review*, March–April, pp. 84–95.

Fox, A. (1974a) *Beyond Contract: Work, Trust and Power Relations*, Faber & Faber, London.

Fox, A. (1974b) *Man Mismanagement*, Faber & Faber, London.

Foy, N. (1983) The public productivity poser, *Management Today*, July, pp. 67–71.

Frain, J. (1999) *Introduction to Marketing*, 4th edn, International Thomson Business Press, London.

Freeman, C. (1989) R&D, technical change and investment in the UK, in F. Green (ed.), *Restructuring the UK Economy*, Harvester Wheatsheaf, London.

Friedman, L. G. and Furey, T. R. (1999) The Channel Advantage, Butterworth-Heinemann, Oxford.

Friedman, M. (1970) The social responsibility of business is to increase profits, *New York Times Magazine*, 13 Sept., New York.

Galbraith, J. K. (1972) *The New Industrial State*, 2nd edn, Penguin, Harmondsworth.

Galbraith, J. R. (1971) Matrix organization designs, *Business Horizons*, **14**, pp. 29–40.

Galbraith, J. R. and Nathanson, D. A. (1978) *Strategy Implementation: The Role of Structure and Process*, West Publishing Co., St. Paul, Minnesota.

Gamble, A. (1985) *Britain in Decline*, Macmillan, London.

Ganguly, P. and Bannock, G. (1985) *UK Small Business Statistics and International Comparisons*, Harper & Row, London.

Garvin, D. A. (1988) *Managing Quality*, The Free Press, New York.

Giddens, A. (1998) *The Third Way: The Renewal of Social Democracy*, Polity Press, Cambridge.

Gill, C., Krieger, H. and Froehlich, D. (1992) The employment impact of new technology: recent European evidence, *Journal of General Management*, **18**, 2, pp. 1–13.

Goldthorpe, J. (1977) Industrial relations in Great Britain: a critique of reformism, in T. Clarke and L. Clements (eds), *Trade Unions under Capitalism*, Fontana, Glasgow.

Goodstein, L.D. and Burke, W.W. (1991) Creating successful organization change, *Organizational Dynamics*, **19**, 4, pp. 5–19.

Gordan, G.G. and Ditomaso, N. (1992) Predicting corporate performance from organizational culture, *Journal of Management Studies*, **29**, 6, pp. 783–98.

Gould, A. and Keeble, D. (1984) New firms and rural industrialization in East Anglia, *Regional Studies*, **18**, 3, pp. 189–201.

Grant, W. and Marsh, D. (1977) *The CBI*, Hodder & Stroughton, London.

Greater London Council (1983) *Small Firms and the London Industrial Strategy*, Economic Policy Group Strategy Document, No. 4, GLC, London.

Greenly, D. (1999) Journey of joint discovery, *Paper presented at the Ford Global Dean's Conference*, Cologne, Germany, May.

Greenley, G. E. (1990) Does strategic planning improve company performance?, in D. Asch and C. Bowman (eds), *Readings in Strategic Management*, Macmillan, London.

Guest, D.E. (1982) Has the recession really hit personnel management?, *Personnel Management*, Oct., pp. 36–9.

Guest, D.E. (1989) Human resource management: its implications for industrial relations and trade unions, in J. Storey (ed.), *New Perspectives in Human Resource Management*, Routledge, London.

Guest, D.E. (1990) Human resource management and the American dream, *Journal of Management Studies*, **27**, 4, pp. 377–97.

Guest, D.E. (1991) Personnel management: the end of orthodoxy?, *British Journal of Industrial Relations*, **29**, 2, pp. 149–75.

Guest, D.E. (1998) Beyond HRM: commitment and the contract culture, in P.R. Sparrow and M. Marchington (eds), *Human Resource Management: The New Agenda*, Financial Times/Pitman Publishing, London.

Guest D.E. and Horwood, R. (1980) *The Role and Effectiveness of Personnel Managers: A Preliminary Report*, The Nancy Seear Fellowship Personnel Management Research Programme, Research Report No. 1, LSE, London.

Hahn, C. (1993) The importance of manufacturing in a robust economy, *RSA Journal*, June, pp. 540–9.

Hakim, C. (1996) *Key Issues in Women's Work*, Athlone Press, London.

Hall, S. (1998) The great moving nowhere show, *Marxism Today*, Nov.–Dec., pp. 9–14.

Hamel, G. and Prahalad, C. K. (1990) The core competence of the corporation, *Harvard Business Review*, **68**, 3, pp. 79–91.

Hamel, G. and Prahalad, C. K. (1994) *Competing for the Future*, Harvard Business School Press, Boston, Mass.

Hammer, M. and Champy, J. (1994) *Re-engineering the Corporation: a Manifesto for Business Revolution*, Nicholas Brealey, London.

Hampden-Turner, C. (1990) *Corporate Culture Management: From Vicious to Virtuous Circles*, Economist Books, Hutchinson, London.

Hampden-Turner, C. and Trompenaars, A. (1993) *The Seven Cultures of Capitalism*, Currency Doubleday, New York.

Hampden-Turner, C. and Trompenaars, F. (1997) *Mastering the Infinite Game: How East Asian Values are Transforming Business Practices*, Capstone, Oxford.

Handy, C. (1993) *Understanding Organizations*, 4th edn, Penguin, Harmondsworth.

Handy, C. (1987) *The Making of Managers: A Report on Management Education, Training and Development in the USA, West Germany, France, Japan and the United Kingdom*, MSC, NEDC and BIM, London.

Harbison, F. and Myers, C.A. (1959) *Management in the Industrial World: An International Analysis*, McGraw Hill, New York.

Harris, N. (1999) *European Business*, 2nd edn, Macmillan, London.

Harrison, C. R. (1972) Understanding your organization's character, *Harvard Business Review*, **50**, 3, pp. 119–128,

Harrison, P. (1981) *Inside the Third World*, 2nd edn, Penguin, Harmondsworth.

Hayek, F. A. (1984) *1980s Unemployment and the Unions*, Institute for Economic Affairs, London.

Hayes, R. H. and Wheelwright, S. C. (1984) *Restoring Our Competitive Edge: Competing Through Manufacturing*, John Wiley, New York.

Heald, D. (1985) Will privatization of public enterprizes solve the problems of control?, *Public Administration,* 16, Spring, pp. 7–22.

Held, D. (1998) The timid tendency, *Marxism Today*, Nov.–Dec., pp 24–7.

Henderson, C. (1998) *Asia Falling?*, McGraw Hill, Singapore.

Herriot, P. and Pinder, B. (1992) Human resource strategy in a changing world, *Personnel Management*, Aug., **24**, 8, pp. 36–9.

Herzberg, F. (1968) One more time: how do you motivate employees?, *Harvard Business Review*, **46**, pp. 53–62.

Hetherington, P. (1986) Perfection in the land of rising productivity, *Guardian*, 5 Mar., p. 23.

Hickson, D. J., Pugh, D. S. and Pheysey, D. (1969) Operation technology and organization structure: an empirical appraisal, *Administrative Science Quarterly*, **14**, pp. 378–97.

Hill, S. (1991) Why quality circles failed but total quality management succeeded, *British Journal of Industrial Relations*, **29**, 4, pp. 541–68.

Hill, T. (1991) *Production and Operations Management: Text and Cases*, Prentice Hall, London.

Hitt, M. and Ireland, D. (1987) Peters and Waterman revisited: the unending quest for excellence, *Academy of Management Executive*, **1**, 2, pp. 91–8.

Hobsbawm, E.J. (1968) *Industry and Empire*, Weidenfeld and Nicholson, London.

Hofer, C. W. and Schendel, D. (1978) *Strategy Formulation: Analytical Concepts*, West Publishing, St. Paul, Minnesota.

Hofstede, G. H. (1980a) *Culture's Consequences: International Differences in Work-related Values*, Sage, London.

Hofstede, G. H. (1980b) Motivation, leadership and organization: do American theories apply abroad?, *Organizational Dynamics*, Summer, pp. 42–63.

Hofstede, G. H. and Bond, M. H. (1988) The Confucius connection: from cultural roots to economic growth, *Organizational Dynamics*, **16**, 4, pp. 4–21.

Hofstede, G. H. (1994) *Cultures and Organizations: Intercultural Cooperation and its Importance for Survival*, McGraw Hill International, London.

Holden, L. and Wilkinson, A. (1999) Long-term patterns in strategic HRM: case study evidence, *Occasional Paper 51*, Leicester Business School, Leicester.

Holmes, G. and Sugden, A. (1999) *Interpreting Company Reports and Accounts*, 7th edn, Pearson Education, Harlow.

Höpfl, H., Smith, S. and Spencer, S. (1992) Values and Valuations: The Conflict Between Culture Change and Job Cuts, *Personnel Review*, **21**, 1, pp. 24–37.

Howard, J. A. and Sheth, J. N. (1969) *The Theory of Buyer Behaviour*, John Wiley, New York.

Hutton, W. (1994) *The State We're In*, Jonathan Cape, London.

Hyman, R. (1972) *Disputes Procedure in Action*, Heinemann, London.

Institute of Personnel and Development (1995) *People Make the Difference*, IPD, London.

Institute of Personnel Management (1963) Statement on personnel management and personnel policies, *Personnel Management*, March.

Jackson, P. (1983) How Perkins positively tackled the recession, *Personnel Management*, Nov., pp. 24–7.

Jessop, R. (1980) The transformation of the state in Post-war Britain, in R. Scase (ed.), *The State in Western Europe*, Croom-Helm, London.

Jewkes, J., Sawers, D. and Stillerman, R. (1970) *The Sources of Innovation*, W. W. Norton, New York.

Jobber, D. (1995) *Principles and Practice of Marketing*, McGraw Hill, Maidenhead.

Johnson, G. and Scholes, K. (1997) *Exploring Corporate Strategy: Text and Cases*, 4th edn, Prentice Hall, London.

Jomo, K.S. (1998) *Tigers in Trouble: Financial Governance, Liberalisation and Crises in East Asia*, Zed Books, London.

Jones, G. (1996) *The Evolution of International Business: An Introduction*, Routledge, London.

Juran, J. M., (1988) *Quality Control Handbook*, McGraw Hill, New York.

Kamata, S. (1983) *Japan in the Passing Lane*, Allen & Unwin, London.

Kaplinsky, R. (1983) Firm size and technical change in a dynamic context, *The Journal of Industrial Economics*, **32**, 1, pp. 39–59.

Kay, J. (1992) Innovations in corporate strategy, in A. Bowen and M. Ricketts (eds), *Stimulating Innovation in Industry: The Challenge for the United Kingdom*, Kogan Page/NEDO, London.

Kay, J. (1993) *Foundations of Corporate Success: How Business Strategies Add Value*, Oxford University Press, Oxford.

Kennedy, C. (1988) Global strategies for 3M, *Long Range Planning*, **21**, 1, pp. 9–17.

Kerr, C., Dunlop, J.T., Harbison, F. and Myers, C.A. (1973) *Industrialism and Industrial Man*, Penguin, Harmondsworth.

Kessler, S. and Bayliss, F. (1992a) The changing face of industrial relations, *Personnel Management*, May, **24**, 5, pp. 34–7.

Kessler, S. and Bayliss, F. (1992b) *Contemporary British Industrial Relations*, Macmillan, London.

Kessler, S. and Bayliss, F. (1998) *Contemporary British Industrial Relations*, 3rd edn, Macmillan, London.

Kondratieff, N. D. (1935) The long waves in economic life, *Review of Economic Statistics*, **17**, pp. 105–115.

Kotler, P. (1983) *Principles of Marketing*, 2nd edn, Prentice Hall, Englewood Cliffs, NJ.

Kumar, K. (1978) *Prophecy and Progress*, Penguin, Harmondsworth.

Lane, K. A. (1985) The UK machine tool industry, *OMEGA*, **13**, 4, pp. 247–9.

Lasserre, P. and Schütte, H. (1999) *Strategy and Management in Asia Pacific*, McGraw-Hill, London.

Lawrence, P. (1980) *Managers and Management in West Germany* Croom Helm, London.

Lawrence, P. R. and Lorsch, J. (1967) *Organization and Environment*, Harvard University Press, Cambridge, Mass.

Lei, D. (1989) Strategies for global competition, *Long Range Planning*, **22**, 1, pp. 102–9.

Legge, K. (1978) *Power, Innovation and Problem-solving in Personnel Management*, Mcgraw Hill, London.

Legge, K. (1989) Human resource management: a critical analysis, in J. Storey (ed.) *New Perspectives in Human Resource Management*, Routledge, London.

Legge, K. (1998) Flexibility: the gift wrapping of employment degradation?, in P.R. Sparrow and M. Marchington (eds), *Human Resource Management: The New Agenda*, Financial Times/Pitman Publishing, London.

Levitt, T. (1960) Marketing myopia, *Harvard Business Review*, **38**, July-Aug., pp. 24–47.

Levitt, T (1975) Marketing myopia: retrospective commentary, *Harvard Business Review*, **53**, Sept.–Oct., pp. 177–81.

Lewis, M., Fitzgerald, R. and Harvey, C. (1996) *The Growth of Nations: Culture, Competitiveness and the Problem of Globalization*, Bristol Academic Press, Bristol.

Lindblom, C. E. (1959) The science of muddling through, *Public Administration Review*, **19**, 2, pp. 79–88.

Lorenz, C. (1994) Ford's global matrix gamble, *Financial Times,* 16 Dec.

Lynch, R. E. (1997) *Corporate Strategy*, Pitman Publishing, London.

Lyons, M. P. (1991) Joint ventures as strategic choice – a literature review, *Long Range Planning*, **24**, 4, pp. 130–44.

McClean, M. and Rowlands, T. (1985) *The INMOS Saga: a Triumph of National Enterprise*, Frances Pinter, London.

McClelland, D. (1961) *The Achieving Society*, Van Nostrand, Princeton.

McIntosh, M. (1998) Introduction, in Financial Times Management, *Visions of Ethical Business*, Financial Times Management, London.

McKinlay, A. and Starkey, K. (1992) Strategy and human resource management, *The International Journal of Human Resource Management*, **3**, 3, pp. 435–50.

Mansfield, E. (1963) Size of firm, market structure and innovation, *Journal of Political Economy*, 71, 6, pp. 556–76

Marris, R. L. (1964) *The Economic Theory of Managerial Capitalism*, Macmillan, London.

Mayer, C. (1988) New issues in corporate finance, *European Economic Review,* June.

Medcof, J. W. (1997) Why too many alliances end in divorce, *Long Range Planning*, **30**, 5, pp. 718–32.

Mensch, G. (1979) *Stalemate in Technology*, Ballinger, Cambridge, Mass.

Miles, R.E. and Snow, C.C. (1978) *Organizational Strategy, Structure and Process,* McGraw Hill, London.

Miliband, R. (1969) *The State in Capitalist Society*, Quartet, London.

Miller, A. and Dess, G. G. (1996) *Strategic Management*, 2nd edn, McGraw Hill, New York.

Mills, R., Dimech Debeno, J.and Dimech Debeno, V. (1994) Euro Disney: A Mickey Mouse Project?, *The European Management Journal*, **12**, 3, pp. 306–314.

Millward, N. and Stevens, S. (1986) *British Workplace Industrial Relations 1980–84*, Gower, Aldershot.

Millward, N., Stevens, S., Smart, D. and Hawes, W.R. (1992) *Workplace Industrial Relations in Transition: the ED/ESRC/PSI/ACAS Surveys*, Dartmouth, Aldershot.

Mintzberg, H. (1973) Strategy making in 3 modes, *California Management Review*, **16**, Winter, pp. 44–53.

Mintzberg, H. (1990) The Design School: reconsidering the basic premises of strategic management, *Strategic Management Journal*, **11**, pp. 176–95.

Mintzberg, H. and Quinn, J. B. (1991) *The Strategy Process*, 2nd edn, Prentice Hall, London.

Monks, J. (1998) Trade unions: enterprise and the future, in P.R. Sparrow and M. Marchington (eds), *Human Resource Management: The New Agenda*, Financial Times/Pitman Publishing, London.

Mowery, D. C. and Rosenberg N. (1989) *Technology and the Pursuit of Economic Growth*, Cambridge University Press, Cambridge.

Murton, A. (2000) Labour markets and flexibility: current debates and the European dimension, in J. Barry *et al.*, (eds) *Organization and Management: A Critical Text*, International Thomson Business Press, London.

Naisbitt, J. (1996) *Mega-trends Asia*, Nicholas Brealey Publishing, London.

Narin, F. (1993) Patent citation analysis: the strategic application of technology indicators, *Patent World*, **51**, April, pp. 25–30.

Neale, A., Haslam, C. and Johal, S. (2000) *Economics in a Business Context*, 3rd edn, International Thomson Business Press, London.

Needle, D. J. (1984) The selection process in Britain and West Germany: a cross-national study, unpublished MSc thesis, London School of Economics.

Needle, D. J. and Needle, J. (1991) The value of patents, *Patent World*, 35, Sept., pp. 20–36.

Needle, D. J. (2000) Culture at the level of the firm: organizational and corporate perspectives, in J. Barry *et al.* (eds), *Organization and Management: A Critical Text*, International Thomson Business Press, London.

Nicosia, F. M. (1966) *Consumer Decision Processes: Marketing and Advertising Implications*, Prentice Hall, Englewood Cliffs, NJ.

Ohno, T. (1988) *Toyota Production System: Beyond Large Scale Production*, Productivity Press, Cambridge, Mass.

Owen, G (1996) The impact of financial systems on British and German industrial performance, presented at *PERC Conference on Stakeholder Capitalism*, 29 March.

Parker, R. C. (1982) *The Management of Innovation*, John Wiley & Sons, Chichester.

Pascale, R.and Rohlen, T. P. (1983) The Mazda turnaround, *Journal of Japanese Studies*, **9**, 2, pp. 219–63.

Paul, W. and Robertson, K. (1970) *Job Enrichment and Employee Motivation*, Gower Press, London.

Pavitt, K. (1983) Characteristics of innovative activity in British industry, *OMEGA*, **11**, 2, pp. 113–30.

Peach, L. (1992) Parting by mutual agreement: IBM's transition to manpower cuts, *Personnel Management*, **24**, 3, pp. 40–3.

Peck, M. J. and Goto, A. (1982) Technology and economic growth: the case of Japan, in M. L. Tushman and W. L. Moore (eds), *Readings in the Management of Innovation*, Pitman Books, London.

Peltu, M. and Land, F. (1987) *Thomson Travel: TOP Travel Agents Reservation System*, London Business School, London.

Perrow, C. (1961) The analysis of goals in complex organizations, *American Sociological Review*, 26, pp. 854–66.

Personnel Standards Lead Body (1993) *A Perspective on Personnel*, Personnel Standards Lead Body, London.

Peters, T. J. (1987) *Thriving on Chaos*, Macmillan, London.

Peters, T. J. and Waterman, R. H., (1982) *In Search of Excellence: Lessons from America's Best Run Companies*, Harper & Row, London.

Pettigrew, A. M. (1973) *The Politics of Organizational Decision-making*, Tavistock, London.

Piercy, N. E. and Morgan N. A. (1993) Strategic and operational market segmentation: a management analysis, *Journal of Strategic Marketing*, **1**, pp. 123–40.

Piercy, N. (1997) *Market-led Strategic Change: Transforming the Process of Going To Market*, 2nd edn, Butterworth Heinemann, Oxford.

Pirie, I. (2000) The social politics of business ethics, in J. Barry *et al.* (eds), *Organization and Management: A Critical Text*, International Thomson Business Press.

Pollert, A. (1987) The flexible firm: a model in search of reality (or a policy in search of a practice)?, *Warwick Papers in Industrial Relations*, No. 19.

Porter, M. E. (1980) *Competitive Strategy: Techniques for Analyzing Industries and Competitors*, Free Press, New York.

Porter, M.E. (1985) *Competitive Advantage: Creating and Sustaining Superior Performance*, Free Press, New York.

Porter, M. E. (1990) *The Competitive Advantage of Nations*, Macmillan, London.

Porter, M. E. (1996) *On Competition*, Harvard Business School Press, Boston, Mass.

Preece, D. (1995) *Organizations and Technical Change: Strategy, Objectives and Involvement*, Routledge, London.

Prevezer, M. (1994) Overview: capital and control, in T. Buxton, P. Chapman and P. Temple (eds), *Britain's Economic Performance*, Routledge, London.

Price, R. and Bain, G. S. (1983) Union growth in Britain: retrospect and prospect, *British Journal of Industrial Relations*, 21, pp. 339–55.

Pricewaterhouse Coopers (1999) *Privacy…a Weak Link in the Cyber-chain: Privacy Risk Management in the Information Economy*, Pricewaterhouse Coopers, London.

Pugh, D. S. (1969) The context of organization structures, *Administrative Science Quarterly*, **14**, pp. 570 81.

Purcell, J. and Sisson, K. (1983) Strategies and practice in the management of industrial relations, in G.S. Bain (ed.), *Industrial Relations in Britain*, Blackwell, Oxford.

Purcell, J. (1989) The impact of corporate strategy on human resource management, in J. Storey (ed.) *New Perspectives in Human Resource Management*, Routledge, London.

Rainnie, A. (1985) Small firms, big problems: the political economy of small business, *Capital and Class*, **25**, Spring, pp. 140–68.

Randlesome, C. (1993) *Business Cultures in Europe*, 2nd edn, Butterworth-Heinemann, London.

Ray, C. A. (1986) Corporate Culture: The Last Frontier of Control, *Journal of Management Studies*, **23**, 3, pp. 287–97.

Reich, R. (1993) *The Work of Nations: Preparing Ourselves for 21st Century Capitalism*, Vintage Books, New York.

Rice, A. K. (1958) *Productivity and Social Organization*, Tavistock, London.

Richards, M. D. (1978) *Organizational Goal Structures*, West Publishing, St. Paul, Minnesota.

Rifkin, J. (1995) The end of work, *New Statesman and Society*, 9 June, pp. 18–25.

Rogers, E. M. (1962) *Diffusion of Innovations*, Free Press, New York.

Rohwer, J. (1995) *Asia Rising*, Butterworth Heinemann Asia, Singapore.

Rosenzweig, P. M. (1995) Colgate Palmolive: managing international careers, in C. A. Bartlett and S. Ghoshal (eds), *Transnational Management: Texts, Cases and Readings in Cross-border Management*, 2nd edn, Irwin, Chicago, Ill.

Rothwell, R. and Zegveld, W. (1981) *Industrial Innovation and Public Policy*, Frances Pinter, London.

Rumelt, R. (1974) *Strategy, Structure and Economic Performance*, Harvard University Press, Cambridge, Mass.

Sandberg, W. R. (1984) Norton Villiers Triumph and the Meridien Cooperative, in W.F. Glueck and L.R. Jauch (eds) *Business Policy and Strategic Management*, 4th edn, McGraw Hill, Singapore.

Scase, R. and Goffee, R. (1980) *The Real World of the Small Business Owner*, Croom Helm, London.

Schein, E.H. (1990) Organizational Culture, *American Psychologist*, **45**, 2, pp. 109–19.

Schein, E.H. (1996) *Strategic Pragmatism: The Culture of Singapore's Economic Development Board*, Toppan, Singapore.

Schmookler, J. (1966) *Invention and Economic Growth*, Harvard University Press, Cambridge, Mass.

Scholz, C. (1987) Corporate culture, *Long Range Planning*, **20**, 4, pp. 78–87.

Schumpeter, J. A. (1939) *Business Cycles*, McGraw-Hill, London.

Schumpeter, J. A. (1961) *The Theory of Economic Development*, Oxford University Press, Oxford.

Scott, J. P. (1979) *Corporations, Classes and Capitalism*, Hutchinson, London.

Selznick, P. (1949) *TVA and the Grass Roots*, University of California Press, Berkley, Calif.

Sethi, S., Namiki, N. and Swanson, C. (1984) *The False Promise of the Japanese Miracle*, Pitman, London.

Sharp, M. and Walker, W. (1994) Thatcherism and technological advance, in T. Buxton, P. Chapman, and P. Temple (eds), *Britain's Economic Performance*, Routledge, London.

Sheehan, R. (1967) Proprietors in the world of big business, *Fortune,* 15 June.

Skinner, W. (1974) The focused factory, *Harvard Business Review*, May–June, pp. 113–21.

Silver, J. (1987) The ideology of excellence: management and neo-conservatism, *Studies in Political Economy*, **24**, pp. 5–29.

Slack, N., Chambers, S., Harland, C., Harrison, A. and Johnston, R. (1998) *Operations Management*, 2nd edn, Pitman Publishing, London.

Sloan, A. P. (1986) *My Years with General Motors*, Harmondsworth, Penguin.

Smircich, L. (1983) Concepts of culture and organizational analysis, *Administrative Science Quarterly*, **28**, pp. 339–58.

Solow, R. W. (1957) Technical change and the aggregate production function, *Review of Economics and Statistics*, **1**, 3, pp. 312–20.

Sorge, A. and Warner, M. (1980) Manpower training, manufacturing organization and workplace relations in Great Britain and West Germany, *British Journal of Industrial Relations*, Nov., pp. 318–33.

Souder, W. and Sherman, J. (1994) *Managing New Technology Development*, McGraw Hill, New York.

Sparrow, P. and Marchington, M. (1998) Introduction: is HRM in Crisis?, in P.R. Sparrow and M. Marchington, *Human Resource Management: The New Agenda*, Financial Times/Pitman Publishing, London.

Stanworth, C. (1998) Telework and the information age, *New Technology, Work and Employment*, **13**, 1, pp. 51–62.

Starr, M. K. (1972) *Production Management: Systems and Synthesis*, Prentice Hall Inc., Englewood Cliffs, NJ.

Steedman, H. and Wagner, K. (1987) A second look at productivity, machinery and skills in Britain and Germany, *National Institute Economic Review*, Nov., pp. 84–94.

Stevenson, W. (1998) *Production and Operations Management*, 6th edn, McGraw-Hill, London.

Stewart, H. and Gallagher, C. C. (1985) Business death and firm size in the UK, *International Small Business Journal*, **4**, 1.

Stopford, J. M., Channon, D. F. and Constable, J. (1980) *Cases in Strategic Management*, John Wiley and Sons, Chichester.

Storey, J. (ed.) (1989) *New Perspectives in Human Resource Management*, Routledge, London.

Storey, J. (1992) *Developments in the Management of Human Resources: An Analytical Review*, Basil Blackwell, Oxford.

Storey, J. (1994) *Understanding the Small Business Sector*, Routledge, London.

Storey, J., Okasaki-Ward, L., Edwards, P. K., Gow, I. and Sisson, K. (1991) Managerial careers and management development: a comparative analysis of Britain and Japan, *HRM Journal*, **1**, 3, pp. 33–58.

Tayles, M. and Woods, M. (1993) Total quality management at Akzo, *Research Update*, **3**, 1, CIMA Research Foundation.

Taylor, F. W. (1947) *Scientific Management*, Harper & Row, New York.

Thomas, T. and Eyres, B. (1998) Why an ethical business is not an altruistic business, in Financial Times Management, *Visions of Ethical Business*, Financial Times Management, London.

Thompson, P. and McHugh, D. (1990) *Work Organizations: A Critical Perspective*, Macmillan, London.

Tidd, J., Bessant, J. and Pavitt, K. (1997) *Managing Innovation: Integrating Technological, Market and Organizational Change*, John Wiley & Sons, London.

Tighe, C. (1986) Behind the lines at Nissan, *Sunday Times*, 13 April, p. 67.

Torrington, D. (1989) Human resource management and the personnel function, in J. Storey (ed.), *New Perspectives in Human Resource Management*, Routledge, London.

Trist, E. L. and Bamforth, K. W. (1951) Some social and psychological consequences of the Long-wall method of coal getting, *Human Relations*, **4**, pp. 3–38.

Trompenaars, F. (1993) *Riding the Waves of Culture: Understanding Cultural Diversity in Business*, The Economist Books, London.

Walters, M. (1995) *Globalization*, Routledge, London.

Walton, R. E. (1987) *Innovating to Compete*, Jossey Bass, San Francisco, Calif.

Wasson, C. R. (1978) *Dynamic Competitive Strategy and Product Life Cycles*, Austin Press, Austin, Texas.

Watson, T. J. (1994) *In Search of Management: Culture, Chaos and Control in Management Work*, Routledge, London.

Wells, J. (1989) Uneven development and deindustrialization in the UK since 1979, in F. Green (ed.), *The Restructuring of the UK Economy*, Harvester Wheatsheaf, London.

Whipp, R., Rosenfeld, R. and Pettigrew, A. (1989) Culture and competitiveness: evidence from two mature UK industries, *Journal of Management Studies*, **26**, 6, pp. 561–85.

White, M. and Trevor, M. (1983) *Under Japanese Management – The Experience of British Workers*, Heinemann, London.

Whittington, R. (1993) *What Is Strategy – And Does It Matter?*, Routledge, London.

Wickens, P. D. (1993) Lean production and beyond: the system, its critics and the future, *Human Resource Management Journal*, **3**, 4, pp. 75–90.

Wiener, M. J. (1981) *English Culture and the Decline of the Industrial Spirit 1850–1980*, Cambridge University Press, Cambridge.

Wild, R. (1985) *The Essentials of Production and Operations Management*, Holt Rinehart & Winston, London.

Wilkinson, A., Marchington, M., Goodman, J. and Ackers, P. (1992) Total quality management and employee involvement, *Human Resource Management Journal*, **2**, 4, pp. 1–20.

Wilkinson, B. (1986) *The Shopfloor Politics of New Technology*, Gower, Aldershot.

Wilkinson, E. (1983) *Japan Versus Europe*, Penguin, Harmondsworth.

Williams, A., Dobson, P. and Walters, M. (1989) *Changing Culture: New Organizational Approaches*, Institute of Personnel Management, London.

Williams, K., Haslam, C., Wardlow, A. and Williams, J. (1986) Accounting for the failure in nationalized industries – coal, steel and cars since 1970, *Economy and Society*, **15**, 2, pp. 167–219.

Williams, K., Cutler, T., Wardlow, A. and Williams, J. (1987) The end of mass production?, *Economy and Society*, **16**, 3, pp. 405–39.

Williams, K., Haslam, C., Williams, J. and Cutler, T. (1992a) Against lean production, *Economy and Society*, **21**, 3, pp. 321–54.

Williams, K., Haslam, C., Williams, J., Adcroft, A. and Johal, S. (1992b) Factories or warehouses: Japanese manufacturing foreign direct investment in Britain and the United States, *University of East London Occasional Papers in Business, Economy and Society, No. 6.*

Williams, K., Haslam, C., Johal, S, Williams, J and Adcroft, A. (1994) *Cars: Analysis, History, Cases*, Bergbahn, London.

Williams, V. (1984) Employment implications of new technology, *Employment Gazette*, **92** ,5, pp. 210–15.

Williamson, O. E. (1991) Strategizing, economizing and economic organization, *Strategic Management Journal*, **12**, pp. 75–94.

Willmott, H. (1993) Strength is Ignorance; Slavery is Freedom: Managing Culture in Modern Organizations, *Journal of Management Studies*, 30,(4), 515–552.

Wilson (1980) *Report of the Committee to Review the Functioning of Financial Institutions*, HMSO, London.

Winkler, J. T. (1977) The coming corporatism, in R. Skidelsky (ed.), *The End of the Keynesian Era*, Macmillan, London.

Womack, J., Jones, D. T. and Roos, D. (1990) *The Machine that Changed the World: the Story of Lean Production*, Rawson Associates, New York.

Wong Kwei Chong (1991) The style of managing in a multicultural society, in J.M.Putti (ed.), *Management: Asian Context*, McGraw Hill, Singapore.

Woodall, P. (1996) The end of work?, *The Economist*, 28 Sept., pp. S19–23.

Woodward, J. (1965) *Industrial Organization: Theory and Practice*, Oxford University Press, Oxford.

World Bank (1997) *The State in a Changing World,* World Development Report, Oxford University Press, Oxford.

Author index

Subject index